WONDROUS CURIOSITIES

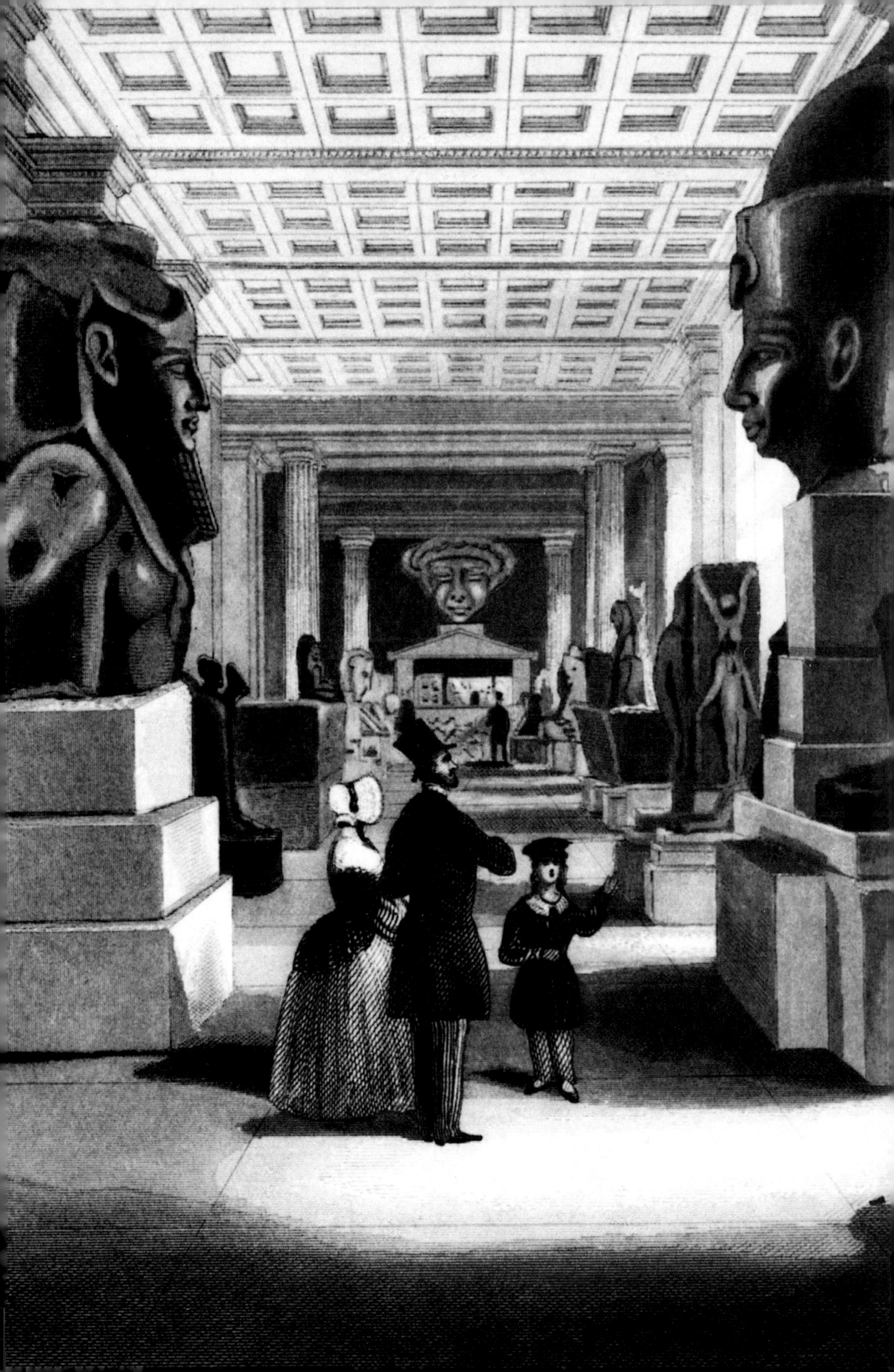

Wondrous Curiosities

ANCIENT EGYPT AT THE BRITISH MUSEUM

Stephanie Moser

The University of Chicago Press

CHICAGO & LONDON

The University of Chicago Press, Chicago 60637
The University of Chicago Press, Ltd., London

Paperback edition 2012
Printed in China

21 20 19 18 17 16 15 14 13 12 2 3 4 5 6

ISBN-13: 978-0-226-54209-6 (cloth)
ISBN-13: 978-0-226-54210-2 (paper)
ISBN-10: 0-226-54209-2 (cloth)
ISBN-10: 0-226-54210-6 (paper)

Published with the assistance of the Getty Foundation.

Library of Congress Cataloging-in-Publication Data

Moser, Stephanie.
Wondrous curiosities : ancient Egypt at the British Museum/Stephanie Moser.
p. cm.
Includes bibliographical references and index.
ISBN 0-226-54209-2 (cloth: alk. paper)
1. Egypt—Antiques—Exhibitions. 2. British Museum—Exhibitions. I. Title.
DT59.L65M67 2006
932.0074'42132—dc22

2005038001

∞ This paper meets the requirements of ANSI/NISO Z39.48-1992 (Permanence of Paper).

FOR ELWYN

Contents

List of Illustrations

PLATES *(following p. 160)*

FIGURES

Acknowledgments

This research could not have been carried out without the invaluable help and encouragement provided by the Department of Ancient Egypt and Sudan at the British Museum. For early access to the department's material (when an archives section did not exist), and discussion on the feasibility of the project, I would like to acknowledge Richard Parkinson. Throughout the duration of research, I benefited enormously from the advice of Patricia Usick, Harry James (now retired), John Taylor, Nigel Strudwick, and again, Richard Parkinson. Jeffrey Spencer and Tania Watkins were also very helpful regarding picture research and permissions. In addition to the museum's Egyptology staff, I am greatly indebted to those working in the Central Archives, particularly Christopher Date and Gary Thorn. While the expertise of Christopher Date was invaluable in seeking to determine the appropriate materials for investigating my subject, Gary Thorn's enthusiasm and assistance with my seemingly endless queries will never be forgotten. Members of other departments in the museum also offered useful insights on the history of the institution, notably Marjorie Caygill from the Directorate, and Margaret Hall from the Design Department. Finally, Sarah Collins kindly provided access to archival material held in the Department of the Ancient Near East; and Ian Jenkins, from the Department of Greek and Roman Antiquities, offered information on various aspects of the museum's sculpture collections.

Many colleagues from a range of research specialities shared ideas and offered comments on various parts of the book. On the history of collecting and museums, I am particularly grateful to Arthur MacGregor, Nick Merriman, and Lorraine Daston. On the representation of Egypt, I would like to acknowledge Lynn Meskell, Dominic Montserrat, Richard Parkinson, and Sally Macdonald. On the history of Egyptology and Britain's role in the emergence of the field, I am very grateful to Stephen Quirke. I would especially like to acknowledge the generosity of Stephen in sharing his encyclopedic knowledge of Egyptology with me. On Egyptian history, I am grateful to Donald Reid, Timothy Mitchell, and Lila Abu-Lugod. On the role of art history in defining ancient cultures, I am indebted to Sam Smiles and Fredrick Bohrer, both of whom offered fascinating perspectives on the visual culture of the nineteenth century. Todd Porterfield was also very helpful, providing useful comparative insights on the Louvre, as was Brian Curran, who shared knowledge on early Renaissance representations of Egypt. Finally, Robin Wade offered reflections upon the issues faced in attempting to redisplay the museum's Egyptian collection in the 1980s, a task which saw the last major installation I studied finally dismantled.

Beyond Europe, my colleagues and friends in Egypt have been a constant support, expressing much enthusiasm for my interest in Egyptian museums and the dispersal of Egyptian antiquities to distant realms. Here I would particularly like to thank Farid Mansour, Adel Aiesh, Lamya Nasser el Nemr, and Ali Soloman. Returning to England, colleagues and doctoral researchers in my department at Southampton have also been very supportive and helpful. While David Peacock and Simon Keay provided much intellectual inspiration, I thank Darren Glazier, David Hinton, Alistair Jones, Karol Kulik, James Phillips, and Monique Scott for reading through various versions of chapters. Particular gratitude is also expressed to David Peacock for dragging me away from the British Museum archives to encounter the "real" Egypt that is Quseir. Other colleagues who read the manuscript and offered useful suggestions include Hannah Sackett, Michael Seymour, and Lowri Jones. From Southampton I would also like to thank the library staff who provided assistance, particularly Pam Wake and Allison Godridge, who helped track down elusive material. Sandra Plumb and Jim Wood, of the Archaeology office, were similarly helpful, offering their support throughout. Finally, staff from the University of Chicago Press have been most helpful in seeing this book through the various production stages. I thank Susan Bielstein, Anthony Burton, and Carol Saller.

Beyond the world of academe and libraries, it was my family, and especially my husband, Alex, who ensured that writing this book was an immensely enjoyable experience. I thank them for all their love and support.

Introduction

MUSEUM DISPLAY, REPRESENTATION, AND ANCIENT EGYPT

On a cold winter's day in January 1759, a group of individuals assembled in the courtyard of Montagu House in Bloomsbury, London. They had come to view the contents of the newly created British Museum, rumored to contain a vast collection of wonders and rarities. For these initial visitors and the many that followed, the museum provided an exciting glimpse into distant and little-known terrains. Of particular significance was the opportunity to see the ancient relics from the great civilizations of Greece, Rome, and Egypt first-hand. Indeed, one of the first exhibits visitors would have encountered was a decorated mummy case from ancient Egypt alongside its long deceased inhabitant. Few would have seen anything like this before, and in those early days, the representation of ancient Egypt at the museum captivated visitors in a way that it still does today.

The idea that museum displays have a unique power in engaging visitors and in offering them profound connections with the past is certainly not new. In 1784 the historian William Hutton (1723–1815) visited the internationally renowned British Museum and reflected upon the potential of the many "wonders" exhibited there to excite an interest in the past:

> If a man pass two minutes in a room, in which are a thousand things to demand his attention, he cannot find time to bestow on them a glance each. . . . If I see wonders which I do not understand, they are no wonders to me. Should a piece of withered paper lie on the floor, I should, without regard, shuffle it from under my feet. But if am told it is a letter written by Edward the Sixth, that information sets a value upon the piece, it becomes a choice morsel of antiquity, and I seize it with rapture.[1]

Despite his frustration at being bombarded with a plethora of unexplained objects, Hutton's reaction to the early displays of the British Museum reveals how at this early stage in the history of public museums, exhibitions of objects were recognized as providing an opportunity to understand the past in a manner that could not be achieved by other modes of discourse. More significantly perhaps, it suggests that museums could achieve this only by providing a context in which the objects were to be understood. This book is about the creation of such contexts, and its central thesis is that museum displays should be recognized as a distinctive genre of communication because they do not simply transmit knowledge, but rather, create it.

In exploring the role museum displays have played in the construction of knowledge, this study looks at how exhibitions have shaped our understanding of ancient cultures. More specifically, it looks at the presentation of ancient Egyptian material in the British Museum from 1759 to 1880, demonstrating how a series of distinct identities were created for ancient Egypt through five major installations. With an outstanding collection of Egyptian antiquities and several purpose-built galleries to house it, the museum played an instrumental role in constructing images of ancient Egypt that were to prevail in subsequent understandings of this remarkable culture.

MUSEUM DISPLAY AND KNOWLEDGE CONSTRUCTION

Recent research in museum studies and other disciplines has begun to explore how exhibitions are central to the shaping of knowledge.[2] The question of how meaning is produced in exhibitions has centered on demonstrating how certain arrangements or styles of presenting objects have constructed a particular view of a subject. This not only requires an investigation of what kinds of objects are present or absent in a display, but demands a more comprehensive investigation of the representational system that has been created for the depiction of a subject. It is here that we see how a new "life" emerges for objects once they are placed in an exhibitionary setting. For instance, new stories are told when certain objects become associated with others and when they are placed in a framework designed for viewing or visual consumption. In this sense, museum displays are an important genre of representation because they construct narratives through the practice of arranging objects within a particular space. Thus, the decisions that are made about all aspects of the presentation of a set of objects serve to structure our understanding of the subject we are viewing in important ways. More specifically, the arrangement of material culture creates a "mental picture" that functions as an interpretive framework for understanding a particular theme, cultural group, or historical episode. Finally, recent work in museum studies has shown how visitors are active in attributing meaning to objects and in contributing to the stories that museum displays tell.[3] Thus, reception is an integral part of the knowledge creation enterprise: it is not just the objects and the manner of display that create meaning—the visitors themselves are also part of the process.[4]

Despite some important work by anthropologists on the subject of how museum displays create meaning, the conventions of knowledge construction in museum exhibition have rarely been explored in any detail.[5] Furthermore, while scholars have shown how museums have been fundamental to the establishment of particular disciplines, few have examined how displays have been central to the establishment of ideas and scientific theories.[6] Furthermore, although ethnographic studies of the socially constructed process through which exhibitions are created have recently been carried out, there are yet to be any major studies that establish how such exhibitions produce knowledge.[7] Thus, despite increasing awareness of the fact that museum displays impart messages and endorse various theoretical perspectives, the wider issue of how exhibitions define subjects and disciplines remains underinvestigated, and we still know very little about the *manner* in which displays contribute to the process of creating knowledge.[8] The neglect of these important questions reflects how museum displays have traditionally been dismissed as "popular representations" not thought to be authored in the same way as academic texts are, and thus they have not been recognized as interpretations in their own right. It also reflects how scholars have been reticent to embark upon such research because there is no clearly articulated methodology to guide such investigations. For instance, how does one "read" a museum display? How can an exhibition be systematically broken down so as to yield important insights on the properties according to which knowledge is constituted? One of the greatest challenges of the research presented here has been the delineation of a methodology that enables one to unravel the connection between display and knowledge making.

In order to demonstrate precisely how exhibitions "make" knowledge, this book examines how the Egyptian antiquities presented by the British Museum were acquired, displayed, and then received by museum audiences. While "acquisition" refers to the content of the displays, "arrangement" refers to the manner according to which the objects were distributed, and "reception" addresses how visitors responded to the exhibits. The idea that is subsequently developed throughout this book is that museum exhibition makes use of its own distinctive conventions to create meaning. More particularly, a set of criteria pertaining to each of the categories of acquisition, display, and reception were scrutinized. For acquisition, the kinds of collections (e.g., whether they were small and haphazard, specialized, or single objects), the methods by which they were acquired (e.g., whether they were donated, purchased, or excavated), the types of objects included in them (whether they constituted a representative sample or a selective set of objects), who made the decisions on their acquisition (e.g., museum trustees, museum staff, or outside experts), and finally, their relationship to the state of knowledge on the subject were all considered. The criteria examined in order to establish how the arrangement of the collections contributed to knowledge construction included the space allocated to the display of the collection (the size and scale of the room), the location of the collection in the museum (e.g., relative to other galleries), the way in which the collection was structured or organized (e.g., content-based or aesthetically based), how the objects were spatially distributed (e.g., symmetrical or random layout), the setting or architecture and design of the room and building in which the collection was displayed (e.g., décor, lighting, wall color), and finally, the "interpretive aids" used to present the collection (e.g., labels, guidebooks, guides). Analysis of the reception of the displays examined audience (e.g., range of visitors and their interests), conditions of access to the museum (e.g., opening times, application procedure), and scholarly context (e.g., state of Egyptology, other theoretical frameworks).

The data that were collected in order to analyze each of the areas outlined above were obtained from a wide variety of sources. Of critical importance was the range of documentation held in the Central Archive of the British Museum, which included detailed minutes of meetings (from general "board" meetings to small subcommittee meetings), reports (by departments and museum directors), official museum correspondence, museum guidebooks, illustrative materials (engravings, photographs, architectural drawings and sketches), submissions to government, parliamentary papers and select enquiries. Other departments of the museum also provided material relevant to the research project, including lists of collections obtained by the Antiquities Department, correspondence, and illustrations.[9] While these materials yielded crucial insights into acquisition and display, the primary sources on reception that were scrutinized included media reports, predominantly periodical articles and engravings, commercial guidebooks, "popular" texts on ancient Egypt, and personal accounts of visits to the museum that were recorded in diaries and travel accounts.

Theoretical resources included recent research on the history of collecting, the history of science, museum studies, art history, anthropology, and archaeology. In exploring the question of whether exhibitions of objects make a significant contribution to knowledge production, it has also been necessary to consult the diverse range of literature that considers the topic of representation. The pioneering work of historians of science on visual representation has been central here, where it has been shown how illustrations depicting scientific phenomena have been pivotal to defining these subjects.[10] Studies by historians of art and cultural historians have also exerted their influence, providing insights into how visual representations have determined unique understandings of ancient cultures.[11] The recently established field of "archaeological representation" has sought to develop this idea, demonstrating that representations such as illustrations, museum displays, media reports, and films are not merely by-products of academic research, but rather, that they have their own distinctive ways of participating in the process of making meaning.[12] Like other research in this fast-growing field, *Wondrous Curiosities* challenges the idea that the knowledge created by academics is simply "filtered down to the masses" through an illustration or museum display. The notion that researchers are solely responsible for creating meaning about the past is a false assumption that diverts our attention from the fact that representations have their own unique conventions and ways of communicating. Thus, knowledge is not simply created by researchers and then diffused into popular culture (i.e., a one-way process); it is also created by many other kinds types of discourse which in themselves shape the ideas of researchers.[13]

Finally, this study of the representation of ancient Egypt also takes into account the recent literature on material culture studies and research on the role of museums in defining cultural difference. While the former considers the myriad ways in which objects are attributed with meaning, the latter seeks to outline the significance of display in creating identities for cultural groups.[14] This research has important implications for this study because it has documented how non-Western cultures have traditionally been presented as static and without history. This characteristic of museum displays is significant because it has played a formative and clearly political role in determining the status of cultural groups in contemporary society. Related to this is the concept of visual colonialism and the process by which exhibitions sever objects from their wider cultural context.[15] While this has been explored in accounts of the historical practice of assembling ethnographic objects in museums, it has not been explicitly addressed in relation to ancient civilizations.

EXHIBITING ANTIQUITIES

The presentation of objects in museums from the Renaissance to the present day has had a profound effect on the construction of ideas about the history of humanity. From the eighteenth century, the increasing presence of items of antiquity in museums played a key role in defining ancient peoples and creating a sense of life in the distant past. With the arrangement of substantial collections of antiquities in the national museums of the nineteenth century, a major tradition in representing ancient cultures was firmly established, and museum exhibitions became a crucial means of communicating ideas about the past. It has long been recognized by historians of collecting that museums have since played a central role in the presentation of the ancient world to Western audiences.[16] However, we still know very little about how the exhibition of major national collections has contributed to our understanding of ancient cultures, such as those of Greece, Rome, and Egypt. Furthermore, there are no detailed studies of the reception of museum displays and of how the public consumption of exhibitions may have contributed to shaping ideas about ancient civilizations.[17] This neglect stems from the fact that histories of museums have tended to focus on the emergence of museums as vast repositories of great collections rather than on how the displays of the collections played a role in knowledge making. The tendency to document how collections were acquired, as opposed to reconstructing how they were arranged and received, also reflects scholars' reluctance to accord the practice of presentation a significant role in the creation of meaning about the past.

Increasingly, however, researchers in classics, anthropology, and archaeology are acknowledging how ancient material culture cannot be divorced from its own history of consumption and presentation. Objects are now recognized as having their own complex "histories," their original creation and function constituting only one chapter in a trajectory of existence that includes subsequent reuse, discovery, presentation, and interpretation.[18]

Throughout this book it is argued that ancient material remains are imbued with distinctive meanings from the museum context. By displaying items of material culture that had been donated, purchased, or unearthed from excavations, museums have played a vital role in explaining past cultures. More significantly, by exhibiting collections of antiquities in particular ways, museums have actively functioned to define cultures or societies from the past. Thus, museum displays have influenced scholarly understandings of the past because they have established interpretive frameworks that served to structure subsequent study. The British Museum and its representation of ancient Egypt were selected as an ideal focus for exploring this central theme for three main reasons. First, any analysis of how museum displays have constructed knowledge about antiquity must consider the British Museum because it has had such a fundamental historic and international role in the collection and presentation of antiquities.[19] Second, the establishment of the museum in 1753 signified the creation of a major public institution that would serve to reinforce, and indeed, create, the nation's sense of identity. Thus, collections not only were acquired in order to increase knowledge and understanding of the world, but were accumulated as part of a wider agenda that involved guiding the public in their conception of taste and informing them about Britain's central role in international affairs. Third, the British Museum acquired many substantial collections of antiquities in the late eighteenth and early nineteenth centuries, among which was included one of the most significant collections of Egyptian antiquities.[20] While modern Egyptologists have defined it as the most famous Egyptian collection outside Egypt, former directors of the museum have highlighted the role of the Egyptian displays as the greatest visitor attraction of the institution.[21] Although other collections of Egyptian antiquities were displayed in Europe in the first half of the nineteenth century (e.g., at the Vatican, the Louvre, the Museum of Turin, and the Neues Museum), it was the British Museum that assembled the first large installation on ancient Egypt in a purpose-built gallery in 1808.[22] Furthermore, what makes the study of the presentation of ancient Egypt at the British Museum so very intriguing are the circumstances of acquisition for the many significant Egyptian collections it displayed. From the turn of the century until the 1840s a flood of Egyptian objects arrived at the museum, providing a unique opportunity for Britain to lead the world in the presentation of such antiquities. Finally, even though something of the story of displaying ancient Egypt at the British Museum has been told by archaeologists and Egyptologists from the museum, there is still much to investigate in terms of how the displays created ideas of ancient Egypt that remain influential today.[23]

REPRESENTING EGYPT

The representation of ancient Egypt is one of the most pervasive and established practices in the Western consumption of the past.[24] Indeed, one of the key issues concerning the portrayal of ancient Egypt is that we have come to "know it so well" through its popular manifestations. Signs of a European interest in representing ancient Egypt began in the classical period, were revived late in the medieval period, and grew in popularity in the Renaissance, when Egyptian antiquities were featured in collections in Italy, Germany, and France.[25] Fueled by increased travel to Egypt in the seventeenth and eighteenth centuries, and inspired by the illustrated travel accounts that were subsequently published in Europe, an iconography of ancient Egypt was effectively created in which pyramids, sphinxes, and obelisks reigned supreme.[26] This iconography, or set of key visual icons, was promptly endorsed and transmitted through other visual media, particularly the decorative arts.[27] The already emerging "Egyptian Revival" was then strongly reinforced by the French expedition to Egypt under Napoleon, and by the middle of the nineteenth century Egyptian motifs had become a common and readily adaptable feature of visual culture that were appropriated in interior design schemes.[28]

One of the major themes that is explored in this book is the extent to which the British Museum's representation of ancient Egypt facilitated an understanding of this culture before the field of Egyptology was formally established. While the tradition of appropriating ancient Egyptian motifs in art, design, and architecture had already made a significant contribution to the characterization of ancient Egypt, these understandings remained essentially superficial and two-dimensional; it was the portrayal of this civilization in the galleries of the British Museum that was instrumental in defining a more concrete vision of ancient Egypt for a wider audience. Furthermore, studies on the West's "discovery" of ancient Egypt from the Renaissance to the establishment of Egyptology in the mid-nineteenth century have tended to focus on the role of travel accounts and the recording of the monuments; and despite the appearance of a number of studies examining how photographers, writers, filmmakers, and the media have portrayed ancient Egypt, the contribution of museum display to the process of "knowing" ancient Egypt remains to be documented.[29]

Finally, while most of the work on the Western consumption of ancient Egypt has shown how this ancient culture attracted a great deal of popular interest because of its mysterious and exotic implications, and also because of its biblical associations, the manner and extent to which these representations defined ancient Egypt have not yet been fully explored.[30] For instance, while the numerous studies of "Egyptomania" inform us about the ways in which the European discovery of Egypt influenced architecture, fine art, and the decorative arts, they do not attribute these manifestations of interest in ancient Egypt with a significant role in influencing scholarly knowledge about the subject. Additionally, while scholars have begun to acknowledge that the discipline of Egyptology has been shaped not just by scientific discoveries, but also by the assumptions, beliefs, and methods of researchers, the role of museum display in this process has not yet been seriously addressed.[31] It appears that like the artistic and literary representations of ancient Egypt, museological ones have been seen as separate from and inconsequential to academic discourse.[32]

THE FOCUS AND SCOPE OF THE BOOK

In presenting an analysis of the representation of ancient Egypt, this book focuses on the genre of museum display and its contribution to defining this ancient culture. Thus, this book is not about ancient Egypt, but rather, the process by which it has come to be understood. Similarly, it is not concerned with the archaeological or historical significance of the objects under discussion or the history of the discovery, recording, and excavation of monuments in Egypt, but rather, with the way in which the British Museum acquired particular sets of objects and arranged them for public consumption, and how these displays were subsequently received by visitors. While a range of Egyptian antiquities found their way into the British Museum during the eighteenth and nineteenth centuries, much of the focus here is on the main sculpture collections, as they created such a powerful impression and did so much to shape the nineteenth-century conception of ancient Egypt.[33] No less significant is the fact that it is the sculptures that are best documented with regard to how they were removed from Egypt, placed on display in the galleries, and perceived by museum audiences.

The temporal limits for this study, 1759–1880, have been determined by the fact that it was during this period that the five major installations so central in defining ancient Egypt were created. Furthermore, the period 1759–1880 can be classified as a distinctive phase in Egyptology, which was significantly different from the one that followed. For instance, it was during the latter part of the nineteenth century that the discipline of Egyptology became institutionalized and professionalized and, thus, that a completely new era in the understanding of ancient Egypt began.[34] Of prime importance in Britain was the formation of the Egypt Exploration Fund (later Society) in 1882: this important organization carried out large-scale and pioneering work on Egyptian sites and donated most of its early finds to the British Museum and later the Petrie Museum at the University College London.[35] Furthermore, besides the major European museums, American museums also started to have a significant impact on work being carried out in Egypt from the 1880s. Notable here was the Metropolitan Museum of Art in New York, the Museum of Fine Art in Boston, and the Art Institute in Chicago, all of which initiated archaeological projects in Egypt.[36] Finally, important developments in Egypt marked the institutionalization of Egyptology in this country in the second half of the nineteenth century, especially the establishment of the national Antiquities Service in 1857, and the national museum in 1863.[37]

Another chapter in the consumption of ancient Egypt also began in the latter part of the nineteenth century. That the context of consumption, or the extent to which people showed an interest in ancient Egypt, entered a completely new dimension around this time is evident in the late nineteenth-century vogue for history painting and the proliferation of artworks depicting "the exotic Orient" during this time.[38] It could also be seen in the production of much popular literature, both fiction and nonfiction, which satisfied the growing appetite for ancient Egypt. Finally, developments in the British Museum also encourage a terminal date of 1880 for this study. Until this time there was no formal collection policy pertaining to the Egyptian material, with objects and collections primarily being acquired as they were offered for sale or as a result of donation. While a more active approach to acquiring Egyptian antiquities was established after the mid-nineteenth century by Samuel Birch, collection development proper began in the late nineteenth century under Ernest A. T. Wallis Budge, who regularly traveled to Egypt to make purchases and who saw the collection swell by two thirds.

* * *

Wondrous Curiosities opens with a chapter on the early modern scientific collections of the sixteenth and seventeenth centuries. The rationale for beginning with this important period in the history of collecting is that it was during this time that strategies for presenting objects were developed with the purpose of communicating knowledge. Thus, the aim in this first chapter is to document the emergence of display techniques and conventions and to see how they were deployed for presenting the first didactic or study collections. Chapter 1 also seeks to provide an understanding of the context in which Egyptian antiquities were collected and put on display prior to the British Museum's "original" installation, as the ways in which such objects were initially featured in displays designed to communicate knowledge (as opposed to those intended to aesthetically please), were instrumental in determining how they were subsequently presented in the first public museums. Finally, it is fundamental to know something of the history of collecting and its relation to the growth of disciplines if one is to make sense of the unique contributions made by the British Museum in defining ancient Egypt. Following this "enframing" chapter, the book then presents an account of the way Egyptian antiquities were defined by the museum through detailed analyses of the five major installations they created. While chapter 2 looks at the foundational display of 1759 based on Sir Hans Sloane's collection, chapter 3 examines the 1808 exhibition designed to present the collection of sculptures seized from the French in 1801. Chapter 4 moves on to discuss the installation created to display the set of antiquities purchased from Henry Salt in 1823, and chapter 5 deals with the newly constructed Egyptian sculpture gallery of 1834 and the new Egyptian Room of 1837. Finally, chapter 6 provides an account of the last major exhibition of Egyptian antiquities, completed in 1854. The conclusion then brings together the main findings concerning acquisition, display, and reception in order to make more general arguments about the museum's profoundly significant role in the construction of knowledge about ancient Egypt.

1 To Pleasurably Serve the Mind

THE DIDACTIC STUDY COLLECTIONS OF THE EARLY MODERN PERIOD

Before examining the representation of ancient Egypt in the galleries of the British Museum, it is important to outline the history of the display of collections, as this provides the context for understanding how the presentation of objects first functioned to construct knowledge. Such a task takes us back to the late sixteenth century or the early modern period, when the Church, royal families, the aristocracy, and emerging professionals and scholars established the tradition of amassing collections of art, natural history, cultural exotica, and antiquities. Although the practice of forming collections had begun much earlier than this, it is in association with early modern collecting that objects were collected as a means of learning, and more specifically, that a set of exhibition strategies were created for presenting ideas and making arguments about the world. It was also in the context of early modern collecting that scholars and early scientists began to acknowledge the potential of display as a powerful means of advancing theories, defining subjects, and building disciplines. Thus, displays became recognized as much more than useful devices for "pleasurably serving the mind"; these were valuable tools that would quickly become indispensable to the pursuit of knowledge making.[1] This chapter focuses on the creation of a set of conventions for museum display, which were developed in association with the presentation of early scholarly or scientific collections. The emphasis on these more "professional" collections as opposed to the royal and aristocratic ones that were so distinctive of the time, stems from the fact that it is with the former that we see an explicit attempt to structure knowledge through display. More fundamentally, the early scientific collections pioneered the communication of knowledge about nature and culture through museum display, setting up strategies for exhibition that were subsequently adopted by the more specialized collectors of the eighteenth century and in the first public museums.

EARLY MODERN COLLECTING

Collecting and displaying assemblages of cultural, natural and scientific objects was a distinctive characteristic of the early modern period.[2] Indeed, such was the popularity of collecting, that by the mid-seventeenth-century "cabinets of curiosities" were an obligatory component of all good aristocratic homes. Thus, no longer was collecting solely the province of the royalty and the clergy; now the nobility and the aspiring professional classes sought to reaffirm their identity by forming collections. This passion for collecting must be understood in the context of several significant developments that converged around this time. The rediscovery of the classical world, the growth of modern science, travel to the New World, the proliferation of international trade, and the rise of an art-consuming public in Europe all contributed to the desire to possess and display objects.[3] The fashion for collecting must also be seen in the context of other representational practices of the time such as court masques and royal entries, where the public consumption of costume, theater, and visual spectacle took place.[4]

Also known as *Kunst* and *Wunderkammern*, cabinets of curiosities featured a range of natural and cultural objects, including works of art, specimens of natural history, ethnographic items from the New World and Asia, antiquities, coins and medals, geological and botanical specimens, scientific instruments, portrait busts, and books. Characteristic of this type of collecting was an interest in obtaining wondrous and bizarre objects that were rare, and the tendency to juxtapose *artificialia* (cultural objects) and *naturalia* (items of natural history) in displays. For the wealthiest collectors, particularly favored items included hybrid creations or ornamental works that combined precious metals, such as gold, with natural objects, such as corals and ostrich eggs.[5]

Initially collections were formed in the royal courts, such as those of the Medici and the Hapsburgs, but it was not long before professionals such as medics and the growing communities of scientific and humanist scholars started to collect and display objects of wonder and scientific interest. Thus, by the mid-seventeenth century two different types of "cabinets of curiosities" had emerged. On one hand there were the art-oriented collections formed by the nobility and the clergy, which were designed to offer testimony of their wealth and influence, and on the other there were the natural history type of cabinets created by scientists and scholars, which were designed to aid their studies and communicate knowledge. Sometimes referred to as encyclopedic collections, these latter cabinets were central to the rise of scholarly disciplines such as zoology, botany, and anthropology. With the proliferation of these knowledge-based collections, the eclectic cabinets of curiosities of the sixteenth century soon began to diminish in popularity, with the more specialized cabinets featuring artworks or scientific specimens becoming the accepted mode of collecting.[6] Even so, many early scientific collections of the seventeenth century retained their status as cabinets of curiosities because they contained examples of the rare and unusual, and because their creators maintained an encyclopedic approach to collecting.

The display practices that endowed objects with the power to represent knowledge first emerged in Italy, and were adopted soon after in the north of the Alps and then in the rest of Europe. That Italy played a leading role in presenting the professional or early scientific collections reflects its close connections with the humanist and scientific revival.[7] For instance, while the German collections tended to focus more on artworks, the Italian collections showed a passion for natural history. Furthermore, the differences between the collections of northern Europe and those of southern Europe can be attributed to distinctive approaches in the study of humanism. In Italy, for instance, the interest in humanism was focused on classical antiquity, which meant that personages of the Church were equated with the gods of classical antiquity. In the north of Europe, however, the focus was on humanity being at the center of the universe, and thus collectors and scholars aimed at gaining a better understanding of the universe and a closer personal relationship with God.

While the practice of collecting bizarre and wondrous objects had existed prior to the creation of the early modern collections, it did not reflect the same degree of interest in learning through objects. In medieval collections, for instance, the focus tended to be on religious relics, and little concern was expressed with how the objects in the collection might be related to each other or how they could be classified.[8] Thus, the motivation for acquiring objects was inspired by beliefs in the miraculous and the fantastic and did not reflect a wider interest in learning about the world.[9] Early modern collections also marked a significant departure from previous collecting traditions in the sense that they included specimens and objects from faraway places. Europe's mercantile exploits and travel to the New World brought opportunities to acquire all sorts of "curiosities" never seen before in Europe. Finally, what distinguished early modern collecting was the way in which the collections became so closely connected with the advancement of knowledge. The role of such resources in the rise of the experimental and observational sciences is the most important testimony to this fact, but also significant was the contribution of collections to the formation of the disciplines of art history and anthropology.[10]

An important motivation for the creation of cabinets of curiosities was the role they played in establishing status and personal worth. Collections were authored statements in the sense that they aimed to communicate something about the collector as much as they did about the meaning of the collection. As documents on self-identity, collections offered tangible evidence of the extent of one's influence, place, and connections in society. Furthermore, while for royalty and clergy collections functioned as symbols of their powerful status and vast wealth, for aspiring courtiers, scientists, and scholars, collections were symbols of their rising social rank and membership in the emerging scholarly communities.[11] In this sense, collecting became integral to asserting one's cultivation and education, where knowledge of the classics and recent scientific discoveries were seen as an important part of being an enlightened citizen.[12]

The new type of curiosities collection that emerged at the end of the sixteenth century and which differed from the royal collections is described here as the "didactic study" collection. Created by early scientists, physicians, and scholars, these collections tended to be more oriented toward natural history; however, in addition to zoological, geological, and botanical specimens, ethnographic objects and antiquities were incorporated. The eclectic quality of such collections reflected the concern of their owners to acquire examples of the diverse range of natural and cultural specimens that could be found in the world, an interest closely tied to the popularity of Pliny's famous encyclopedia of nature, *Historia naturalis*.[13] The didactic study collections were also characterized by a tendency to focus on objects thought to have medicinal and therapeutic properties, revealing a link to the work of apothecaries. That the creators of such repositories of objects were using their collections for study and scientific research is revealed by the fact that they invested serious efforts in producing catalogues which attempted to classify the range of objects they possessed. Thus, the didactic study collections were created as aids to research and the practice of medicine, differing in their aim from the royal collections, which were designed to celebrate wonder and satisfy a curiosity in the strange and marvelous.[14] Indeed, the creators of the early scientific collections expressed intolerance for the princely cabinets of curiosities, which they thought were "more intent upon stunning boys, women, and 'ignorants,' than upon educating scholars about nature."[15] That said, however, the didactic study collections still served a role in satisfying the curiosity for the bizarre.

While the production of catalogues was one way of learning from the didactic study collections, another and perhaps more powerful way of gaining knowledge from them was through the medium of display. No sooner had they started arranging their collections for presentation to an audience, than collectors began to recognize the ability of displays to impart knowledge, and before long they became interested in the effect that particular styles of arrangement could have. Beyond wanting to convey information through their arrangements, collectors sought to produce an interesting or pleasurable visual experience for their visitors and accordingly sought to emphasize the aesthetic qualities that objects and groups of objects had. Thus, it was not just the contents or the scientific value of the collections that were designed to impress, but the manner in which they were distributed. However, the didactic study collections were not simply thrown together for aesthetic effect, but rather, were treated as vehicles through which the world could be understood. More specifically, the displays functioned as a visual testament to the diversity of life in the universe, constituting a specific strategy for making sense of, and indeed controlling, the chaos that nature seemed to represent.[16] In this sense, the displays of the didactic study collections represented an attempt to convey meaning through the arrangement of objects; they were designed to facilitate an understanding of the connections and relationships between objects by making visible what was difficult to see. For instance, the display of a variety of life forms conveyed the notion of biological diversity better than a textual explanation of the idea (see below).

We now turn to the major examples of early modern didactic study collections. In seeking to delineate how a set of display conventions was created by the pioneering collector-scientists, we are primarily dependant on the illustrations of their collections that survive. While collectors listed and classified the range of objects in their collections in catalogues, rarely did they describe how these objects were distributed in their "exhibition" rooms. Despite this, a number of images of displays were incorporated within the catalogues of these early collections, which provide some idea of how objects were arranged.[17] Although they do not necessarily present an entirely accurate record of the way specific collections were laid out, they nevertheless provide an important source of information on the style and manner of display and on the general display conventions that were being adopted at the time.[18]

COORDINATING CHAOS

The first known image of a didactic study collection is that which features Ferrante Imperato's (1550–1625) collection in Naples (fig. 1.1). Imperato was a pharmacist and naturalist who created a collection for the purpose of research and teaching, and the engraving of his collection appeared in the catalogue *Dell' historia naturale* of 1599. Depicting a vast array of objects distributed in purpose-built display cabinets, shelves, and drawers, this is a highly significant document in the history of collecting because it conveys how the early study collections, although concerned with learning and the imparting of information, utilized aesthetic presentation to achieve their aims. Indeed, the picture reveals how the tension between didactic organization and aesthetic presentation, which was to become a preoccupying concern of early museums, was manifested at the earliest stages in the creation of knowledge-based collections.

The engraving of Imperato's collection suggests that a great deal of attention has been devoted to its presentation and the potential impact that this might have on its audience. On the right-hand wall of the room is an elaborate piece of furniture specifically designed to showcase parts of the collection. Several of the drawers and cupboards are featured open so as to make visible the kinds of objects that were stored within this impressive unit. While the cupboards on the ground level reveal an abundance of containers, jars, and urns, those above them incorporate ornate mini-cabinets with a series of intricate drawers in which were housed Imperato's extensive collection of gems and minerals. On the higher shelf are

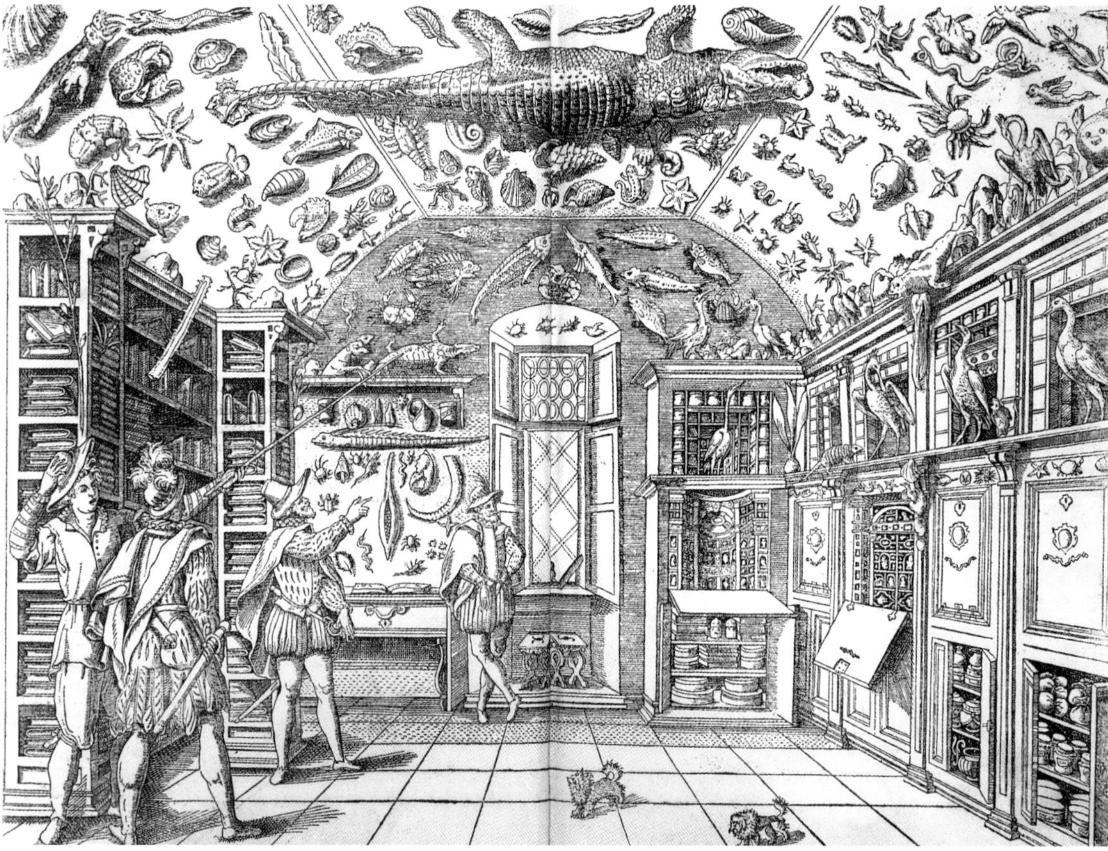

1.1. Ferrante Imperato's collection in Naples. Engraving in Imperato's *Dell' historia naturale* of 1599.

large birds in recessed sections; the skull of a pelican hanging from the top of the shelf and the carapace of an armadillo perched on the bottom of it serve to break up the repeated pattern that characterizes this section of the display. On the top of the cabinet a range of natural history specimens are featured, including birds, corals, and rocks; the mineral specimens reflect Imperato's pharmacological interests in the power of stones to cure and prevent disease.[19] Standing out among this rather crowded accumulation are a seal that appears to be suspended off the edge of the shelf and a puffer fish. Whether this arrangement on the top of the cabinet is an attempt to place the specimens in some kind of environmental context is not clear, but it looks more naturalistic than the neatly distributed range of specimens in the alcove above the window and across the ceiling.

The ceiling is clearly the focus of attention in the picture, as suggested by the gestures of the figures, including Imperato's son Francesco. Covered with an arrangement of natural history specimens that are predominantly marine in origin, the ceiling is characterized by an aesthetically structured distribution. For instance, the objects on the right and left sections of the ceiling are arranged in lines that follow the horizontal plane corresponding with the shelving units, while the items in the central sections are arranged around the centerpiece of the whole collection—the large crocodile. Not only was this crocodile of great interest because of its size and rarity, but it also had symbolic significance for Imperato, as it was the family emblem.[20] Besides the crocodile, highlights of the ceiling installation include the walrus, the large shells, and the variety of bizarre-looking fish. While some specimens appear to be more typical than others, such as the crustaceans, others are much more unusual and seem to have exaggerated features, such as the prehistoric-like lizards. On the back wall there appears to be a desk upon which an open book is placed. Together with the shelves stacked with books along the left-hand wall, this suggests that the collection is not just a source of awe and contemplation, but also a site of study and investigation.

This dynamic image can generally be seen as corresponding with the catalogue in which it appears; this being structured according to the categories of animal, vegetable, and mineral, and featuring many illustrations of maritime species, plants, corals, shells, and insects. Although it is difficult to locate the specimens featured in the display in the illustrations of individual specimens in the book, the overall arrangement can be seen as conveying the four basic classificatory elements that distinguished the collection: earth, water, air, and fire. For instance, the marine specimens on the ceiling represent water; the birds on the top shelves represent air; the minerals and gems on the middle shelves represent earth; and the *artificialia* (cultural items) on the lower shelves represent fire.[21]

A clear distinction can be seen between this image, which is designed to portray an aura of knowledge and learning, and the more painterly renderings of royal collections, which emphasized their function as sources of aesthetic delight. For instance, the room has the feel of a study or as a place where the collector and his colleagues could assemble for informed dialogue.[22] The emphasis on natural history specimens also distinguishes it from the royal cabinets.[23] However, while the picture reveals that displays such as these were designed for study, it also demonstrates how, like the royal displays, these arrangements were intended for consumption. That the objects were meant to be viewed is emphasized by the inclusion of the figures, all three of whom are engaging with the objects displayed around them. Indeed, the active gestures of these visitors reinforce the idea that a connection is being made between seeing and learning.[24] Clearly, these displays were not designed to be passively consumed by visitors; they were created as a form of dialogue between the collector and his peers.[25] Finally, the picture can be seen as visual testimony to Imperato's status as a learned individual, where his collection was a symbol of his identity as a professional or early modern scientist. Whether or not he intended to, Imperato appears to have set an important precedent with this picture, as it quickly became adapted as a model for presenting the didactic study collections of the seventeenth century.

As for a display strategy for his collection, the prevailing characteristic of Imperato's installation is the intensive use of space, where objects appear to have been crammed onto every available surface and piece of furniture. The idea of displaying objects on ceilings was not Imperato's invention, as this practice had already been employed in churches from medieval times; however, what was new was the designation of the ceiling as a distinct and primary display zone.[26] The use of all available surfaces for display appears to be intended to maximize the visual experience for the visitor. However, the effect of crowding so many objects into such a confined space is that the display appears chaotic. In this sense, the visual impact of the arrangement tends to overshadow its intellectual content or its potential as an aid to research. Indeed, the display conveys the appearance of an apothecary shop, where a dizzying abundance of unusual specimens are juxtaposed.[27] Furthermore, the ornate display furniture enhances the aesthetic appearance of the display, particularly the enticing miniature drawers in the specimen cabinets. Having noted the visual effect of the display, however, it is important to emphasize the structure that exists amid the "chaos." Imperato's collection was not simply aimed to visually impress; the objects have been organized according to a classificatory system, and in this sense the primary aim of the display is to impart a scientific message. In this way, Imperato's arrangement served to satisfy the mind as well as the eyes. Finally, Imperato has presented his collection in a *studiolo*, a distinctive room type which evolved in the Renaissance to combine display and study purposes.[28]

PATTERN AND SYMMETRY

Another important example of how early scientific collections were arranged for viewing is the engraving of Francesco Calceolari's (1521–1600) collection in Verona, which was published in 1622 in the catalogue *Musaeum Francesco Calceolari* by Benedetto Ceruto and Andrea Chiocco (fig. 1.2).[29] Calceolari was a pharmacist, and his collection, which was primarily focused on natural history, was created with the purpose of providing materials that would enable him to treat diseases.[30] The image of his collection is significant because it demonstrates how the use of symmetry and the patterned effect it created became a convention of display practice.[31] While symmetric arrangement had been adopted to create a picturesque effect in the presentation of sculptures in the great collections of Europe, it was used in the didactic study collections for an additional purpose, which was to communicate ideas about the relationships between specimens. The use of symmetry in this context was effectively achieved in Calceolari's display, where natural and cultural items were presented together in a manner that was both scientifically meaningful and aesthetically interesting. Although the same degree of pattern and symmetry is lacking in the image of Imperato's collection, both pictures still appear to be similar.[32] The question of whether one was influenced by the other is difficult to ascertain

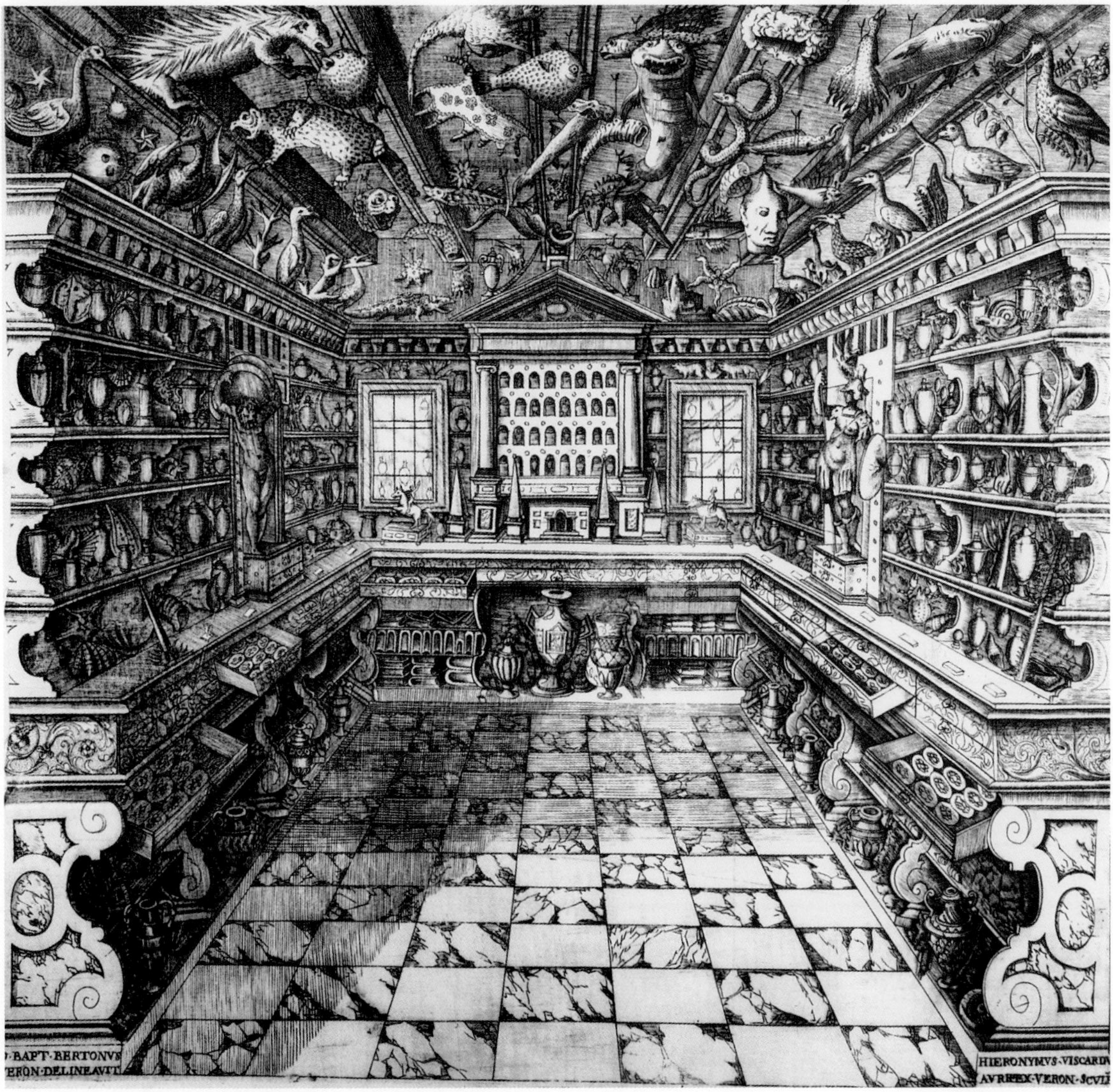

1.2. Francesco Calceolari's collection in Verona. Engraving in Benedetto Ceruto and Andrea Chiocco's *Musaeum Francesco Calceolari* of 1622.

because Calceolari's collection was known to have been in existence earlier than the publication of Imperato's image, and thus it may have influenced Imperato's arrangement rather than being based upon it.[33]

The engraving of Calceolari's "museum" shows three sides of a room fitted out with an ornate shelving system that is supported by a number of ornately decorated drawers and cupboards. On the back wall, an inbuilt cabinet framed with a tympanum and Doric columns is featured. The items of *artificialia* and *naturalia* fill every available space on each of the five levels of shelving, with shells and other marine specimens displayed alongside urns, jars, and figurines. On the bottom shelf, the statues of Atlas and Minerva serve to break up the rhythm that the smaller objects create. As in Imperato's display, birds are placed along the top of the shelving system, with a few botanical specimens and what appear to be corals situated alongside them. In front of the cabinet on the back wall are four obelisk-like sculptures and two small horse figurines that are symmetrically arranged, with an architectural model in the center. Beneath the cabinet, books are stacked neatly on either side of three large vases. The ceiling is crammed with specimens, including stuffed animals, fish, lizards, and more unusual items such as a human head or death mask, what appears to be a raccoon, and a narwhal's tusk, the latter having been sent to Calceolari in 1565 by the imperial court doctor of Austria for use as an antidote against poisons.[34]

This illustration shows some correlation to the catalogue of Calceolari's collection, which is structured according to the same basic categories Imperato employed—animal, vegetable, and mineral. The engravings of individual specimens in the catalogue also correspond with the picture, including the puffer fish, a sea urchin, a ray-like creature with a tail, geological specimens, fossils, antiquities (in the form of an Egyptian stela), and lizards.[35] It is notable that *artificialia* play more of a role here than they do in Imperato's picture, with urns, vases, and statuary placed amid the items of natural history. This is indicative of the fact that when the collection was taken over by Calceolari's heir, Francesco the Younger, more cultural and curiosity-type items were added to the display.[36] Despite this, it is clear that the display is intended to facilitate learning rather than just aesthetic stimulation. Indeed, the inscription accompanying the image reinforces this idea, stating "Viewer, insert your eyes—Contemplate the wonders of Calceolari's museum and pleasurably serve your mind."[37]

Calceolari's display is distinguished by its use of pattern and symmetry to create an aesthetic impact.[38] That different classes or types of objects were juxtaposed to create an overall effect can clearly be seen on the top of the shelves where contrasting items have been placed in between the birds. Symmetry is also emphasized with the matching of ornaments along the back shelf under the windows, and with the placement of the large sculptures on either side of the room facing each other. Two kinds of symmetric arrangement can be identified here; the first involves placing different kinds of objects in between similar objects, and the second (in which the former is incorporated), involves creating general clusters of similar objects.[39] While Imperato's display was asymmetrical with no "matching" of the displays on either side of the room, Calceolari's display is clearly designed to be visually balanced, providing visitors with a striking impression upon first entering the room. This symmetrical arrangement was accentuated by use of the horizontal line to display objects. For instance, while Imperato's shelves were more box-like and appeared in the form of a set of separate cabinets, Calceolari's shelves continued around all the walls of the room. This linear style of presentation enhanced a sense of structure and order, but more significantly perhaps, the placing of objects on the same plane allowed for continuity of vision, making it easier to see objects in relationship to each other, and facilitating comprehension of the collection as a whole. Another result of this strategy of symmetrical arrangement was that objects assumed a dual role as imparters of knowledge. For instance, it was not just the qualities of individual objects that were highlighted, but rather, their ability to "perform" alongside, or become meaningful in association with, other objects. Thus, the exhibition of such collections was not just intended to mirror the classificatory schemes outlined in the catalogues—e.g., water, earth, air—it was also intended to show how objects were part of a broader narrative. The ability of displays to situate objects in such dualistic roles, where they could be manipulated to create visual messages, ensured that they were quickly recognized as a powerful representational tool.

LABELS AND LEARNING

An idea of how the displays of the didactic study collections functioned as aids to research can be gleaned from two illustrations of notable collections in Germany and Copenhagen. First is the engraving of Basilius Besler's (1561–1629) collection in Nuremberg, which appeared in the illustrated catalogue *Fasciculus rariorum et aspectu dignorum varii generis quae collegit et suis impensis aeri ad vivum incidi curavit atque evulgavit* of 1616 (fig. 1.3), and second is the oft-reproduced engraving of Ole Worm's (1588–1654) display in Copenhagen, which originally appeared in his catalogue *Musei Wormiani Historia* of 1655 (fig. 1.4).[40] While Besler was an apothecary and botanist, and his collection was used to further his interest in the natural world, Worm was a medic, natural philosopher, and early antiquarian, and his collection was used for teaching at the University of Copenhagen. Of particular significance in both of these displays was the use of labeling, which emphasized that these collections functioned as a resource for learning. Labeling was not only an important signifier that such displays were intended to inform rather than entertain, it also suggested that efforts were being made to make the displays more readily comprehensible to visitors.

In Besler's image we can see how the collection has been displayed on low shelves lining the walls, in large recessed sections on the walls above them, and on the ceiling. The drawers that are incorporated into the shelves contain smaller objects, while the walls and ceiling are covered with much larger specimens of marine, plant, and animal life, with some cultural pieces dispersed among them. Compartmentalized storage boxes with labels designating their contents are situated on the bottom shelves, above which can be seen giant crustaceans and shells, horns, a chameleon, sawfish saw, turtle, puffer fish, statue, and a large urn. A large sign or banner advertising the display dominates the whole back wall, informing the viewer of Besler's profession as a pharmacist, chemist, and botanist.[41] Above the banner is a shelf upon which urns and large figured stones are displayed. The other wall of the room features a large ray, corals, more lizards, and a series of books placed along the top shelf. Notably, prime

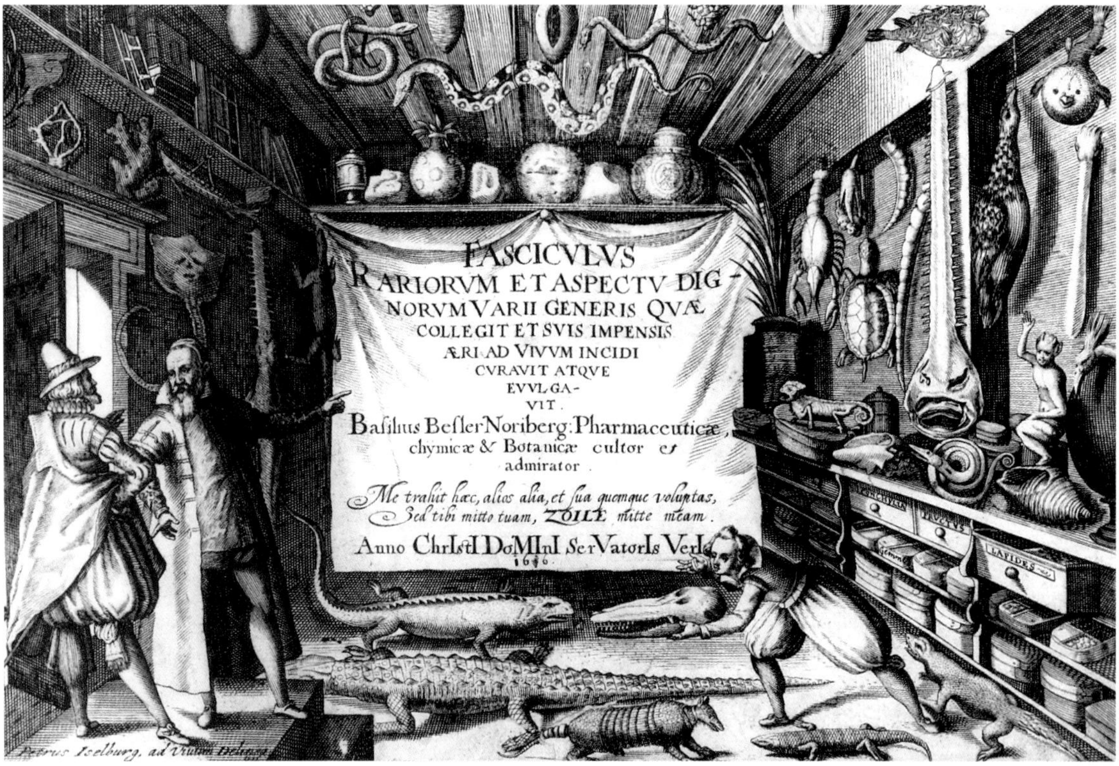
FASCICVLVS
RARIORVM ET ASPECTV DIG-
NORVM VARII GENERIS QVÆ
COLLEGIT ET SVIS IMPENSIS
ÆRI AD VIVVM INCIDI
CVRAVIT ATQVE
EVVLGA-
VIT.
Basilius Besler Noriberg: Pharmaceuticæ,
chymicæ & Botanicæ cultor et
admirator.
Me trahit hæc, alios alia, et sua quemque voluptas,
Sed tibi mitto tuam, ZOILE, mitte meam.
Anno ChrIstI DoMInI SerVatorIs VerI
1616.
LAPIDES

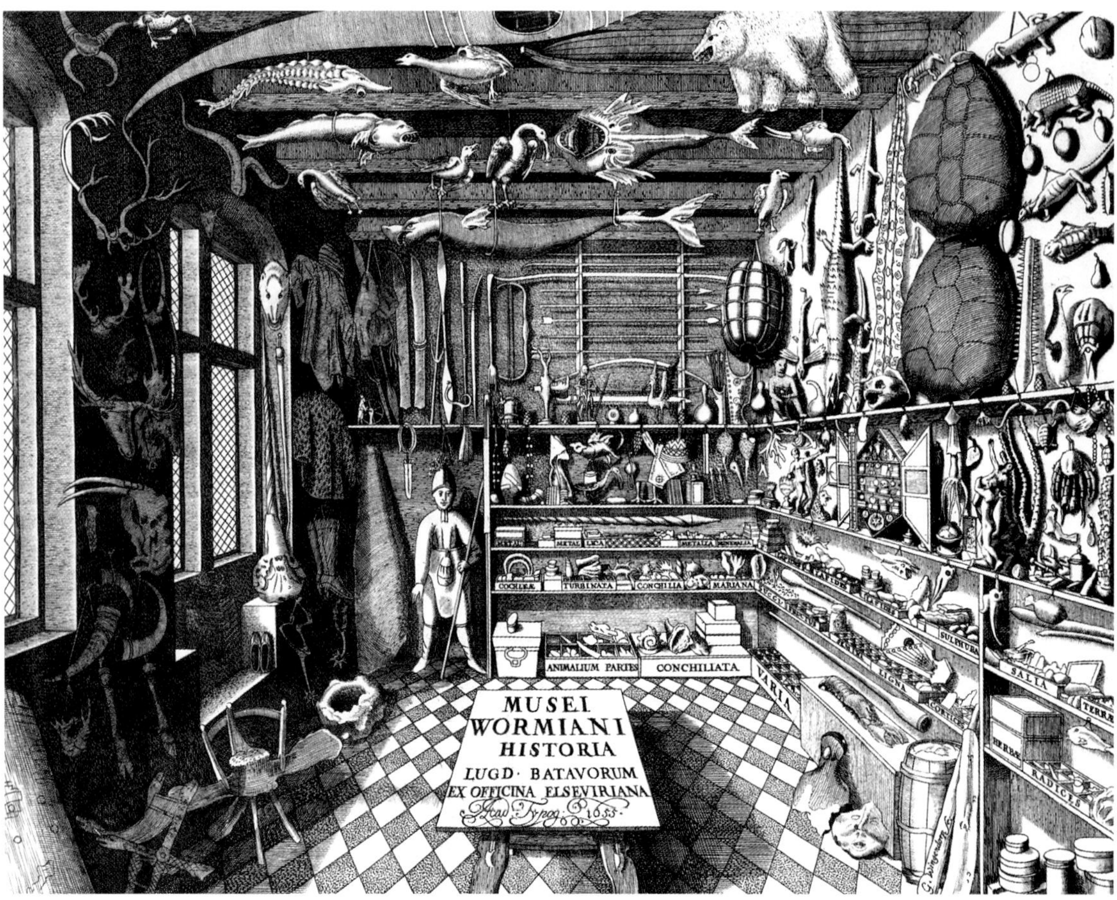
MUSEI
WORMIANI
HISTORIA
LUGD. BATAVORUM
EX OFFICINA ELSEVIRIANA
Acad. Typog. 1655.
COCHLEÆ
TURBINATA
CONCHILIA
MARIANA
ANIMALIUM PARTES
CONCHILIATA
VARIA
LIGNA
SULPHURA
SALIA
HERBÆ
RADICES

1.3. *(facing)* Basilius Besler's collection in Nuremberg. Engraving in Besler's *Fasciculus rariorum et aspectu dignorum varii generis quae collegit et suis impensis aeri ad vivum incidi curavit atque evulgavit* of 1616.

1.4. *(facing)* Ole Worm's collection in Copenhagen. Engraving in Worm's *Musei Wormiani Historia* of 1655.

position is given to the coconuts and other large seeds in the ceiling arrangement, which reflect Besler's profession as a botanist.[42] Also of interest are the large lizards, crocodile, and armadillo which dominate the floor space.[43] While the central figure, probably Besler, draws his visitor's attention to the delights of his collection, the crouching figure on the right offers a large crocodile skull for inspection.

Like Besler's display, Worm's collection is laid out in a plain room, with a simple shelving system. On the floor around all the walls are featured a variety of specimens, containers, and large objects. Of note are the large geode, the stool with terminals carved in the form of snake heads, the whale's vertebra that has been transformed into a piece of furniture, and the stone with a human-like face.[44] Neatly labeled drawers containing the smaller items sit on the shelves on the right wall, with larger shelves above them featuring a bewildering assortment of both natural and cultural objects. Highlights here include the two figurines (one a replica of Giovanni da Bologna's *Rape of the Sabine Woman*), a penguin-like bird display, the gourds, a variety of birds' feet, squid, a mini-cabinet, the now compulsory armadillo, and the sitting miniature bear, who appears to be holding an egg. The walls have the same variety of lizards, crustaceans, turtle shells, and stuffed birds that we have seen in the Imperato, Calceolari, and Besler displays. Notable here, however, are the ethnographic items from China, the Americas, and Turkey, which are dispersed among the natural objects and neatly arranged in rows along the back wall. Of particular interest among the ethnographic objects is the mannequin figure clothed in fur and skin garments from Greenland.

While the inclusion of ethnographic items provided a more cultural dimension than had been seen in the earlier images of didactic study collections, this was not a new trend in exhibiting collections, as ethnographic objects were often included in the royal collections of the time. The difference here was that rarely had they been placed in such close alliance with natural history specimens in the context of a reference or scientific collection. The presence of ethnographic objects in Worm's arrangement was thus significant because it marked the beginnings of anthropology.[45] Beyond the ethnographic objects, also significant is the narwhal's skull and tusk featured in the window recess, Worm having refuted that the tusk was a unicorn's horn in 1638. The ceiling, which is not as crowded as Imperato's or Calceolari's, continues the trend of combining ethnographic and natural history specimens, among which can be identified a polar bear, a shark, some unusual looking fish, birds, and a kayak.

The didactic role of Besler's and Worm's collections is demonstrated by the fact that there is a very close relationship between their catalogues and the specimens featured in their displays. In the case of Besler's display, each of the specimens is drawn with great accuracy, making them immediately identifiable in the illustrated catalogue.[46] Worm's image also closely corresponds with his catalogue, which is illustrated with a variety

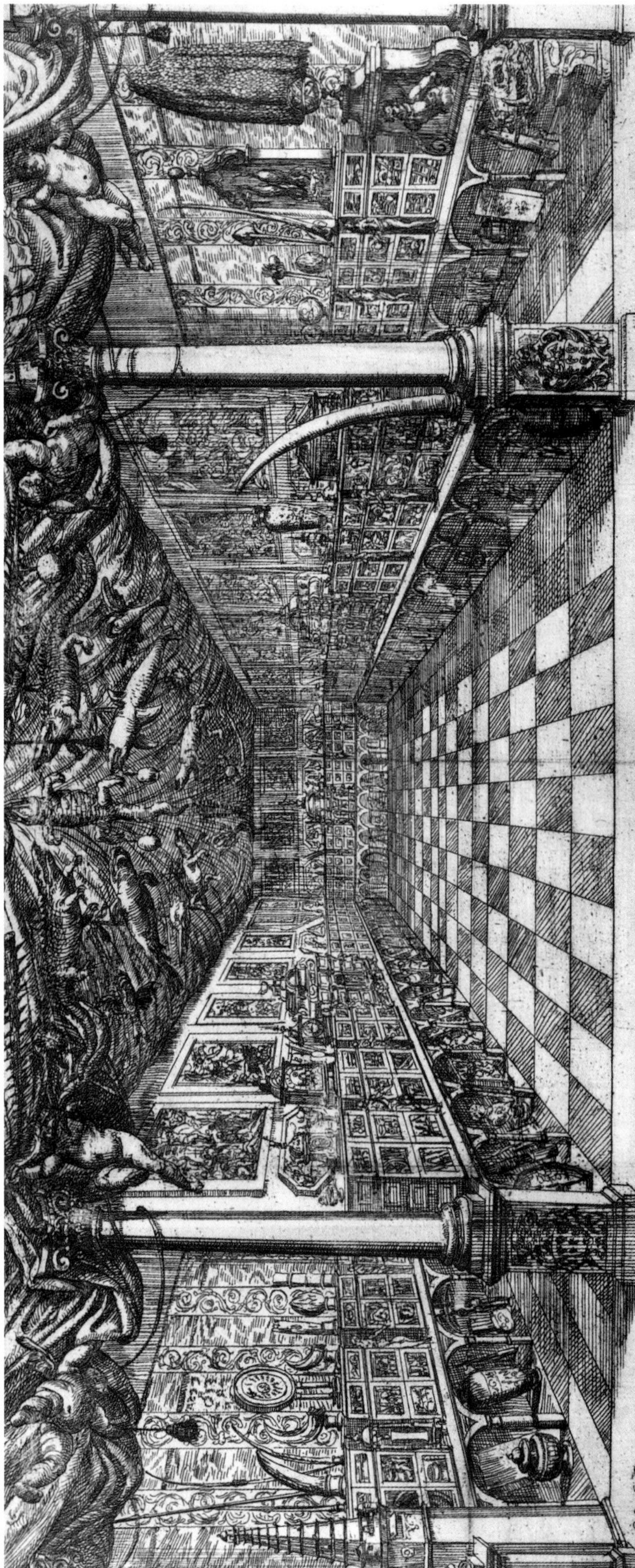

1.5. *(facing)* Manfredo Settala's collection in Milan. Engraving by Cesare Fiore in Paolo Maria Terzago and Pietro Francesco Scarabelli's *Museo ò Galeria adunata dal Sapere, e dallo Studio Del Sig. Canonico Manfredo Settala* of 1677.

of specimens, including many of those featured in the display.[47] Indeed, the illustration of Worm's collection has been described as a more faithful representation of his "museum" than the other images of European proto-museums because it had so many identifiable objects in it.[48] Also distinctive of Besler's and Worm's displays is the lack of concern for aesthetic effect so characteristic of their Italian counterparts.[49] This is evidenced by the absence of symmetrical or any other aesthetic arrangement, the minimal architectural features or embellishments, and the use of plain rather than elaborate display furniture, all of which had been emphasized in the Imperato and Calceolari images. Indeed, Besler's and Worm's displays look comparatively plain, not appearing to exhibit any concern for the striking impact that could be achieved through such exhibitionary strategies. However, these collectors may have sought to avoid such strategies, choosing to emphasize the didactic function of their collections, rather than indulging in a flair for design. This priority is suggested by the introduction of labels on the specimens, a convention which revealed the concern for developing taxonomic or classificatory systems at the time. Another convention that we see emerging in the didactic displays of collectors like Besler and Worm is the way in which particular specimens or objects assume an iconic status. For example, the puffer fish, the sawfish saw, the narwhal's tusk, the chameleon, and the armadillo were icons that signified the quality and status of the collections. Alongside crocodiles and Egyptian shabtis (funerary figurines), such items became must-haves for any collection of note. Thus, although furthering knowledge was a primary motivation for creating the displays, collectors still sought to achieve credibility through their possession of items bestowed with a desirable or highly collectible status.

ENTERTAINMENT AND LEARNING

From the mid- to late seventeenth century, the didactic study collections were increasingly presented with an audience in mind. Two illustrations of collections from Italy demonstrate how such cabinets were being opened up to appeal to visitors other than medics and scientists, including the representation of Manfredo Settala's (1600–1680) collection in Milan, which was published in 1664 by Paolo Maria Terzago in *Musaeum Septalianum* (fig. 1.5), and the image of Ferdinando Cospi's (1606–1683) display in Bologna, which was published in 1677 in Lorenzo Legati's catalogue *Museum Cospiano Annesso a quello del famoso Ulisse Aldrovandi* (fig. 1.6). While Settala inherited his collection from his father, Lodovico Settala, a physician who focused his efforts on acquiring scientific and mathematical specimens, Cospi was a Medici courtier whose collection was greatly enhanced by the acquisition of the scientist Ulisse Aldrovandi's vast collection.[50] Although the research status of these two individuals' collections has been questioned, their displays are of great importance in the history of museums because they aspired to combine an educational and entertainment function.[51]

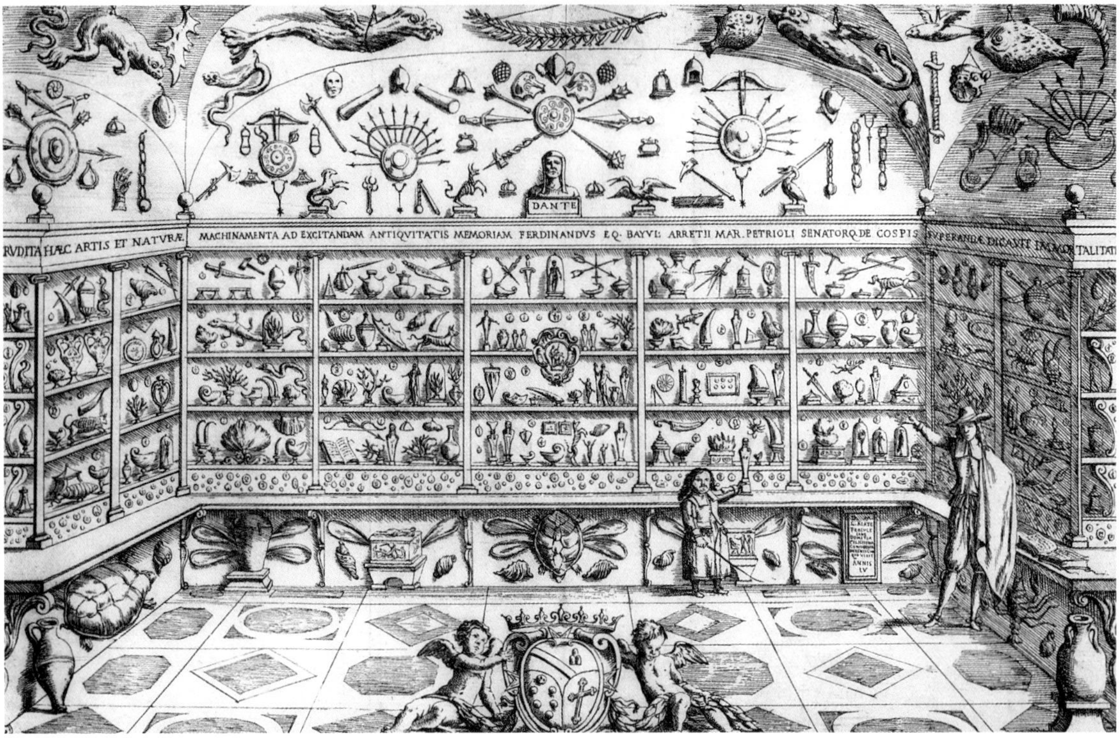

1.6. Ferdinando Cospi's collection in Bologna. Engraving by G. M. Mitelli in Lorenzo Legati's *Museum Cospiano Annesso a quello del famoso Ulisse Aldrovandi* of 1677.

With its highly decorative and patterned effect, the image of Settala's display has an immediate impact upon the viewer.[52] Here a very large display space has been broken up into three sections divided by large columns. Along the floors are small alcoves filled with larger pieces, such as busts and pots. Above them are sets of drawers filled with smaller objects, which are separated by sculptures. Sitting on top of the drawers are larger pieces, including statues, ethnographic objects, geological items, plants, zoological objects, and mechanical and musical instruments. The walls above the drawers or mini-cabinets on the outside section appear to be decorated with elaborate designs, whereas paintings line the walls of the inner section. On the far right is the large skull of a horned animal, while directly opposite it in the left corner of the room is an unusual architectural model. The ceiling has the now familiar distribution of large marine specimens, but these have been hung from billowing fabric and are accompanied by smiling cherubs. Beyond the style of presentation, what distinguishes this collection is the addition of technical and mechanical instruments, many of which Settala made himself.[53]

Like Settala's display, Cospi's display has been arranged on a shelving system that continues around the walls of the room. On the shelves are small statues, mounted corals, knives, shells, a number of Egyptian shabtis, an armadillo, and funerary urns.[54] Some specimens along the bottom shelf have been singled out and encased in miniature glass domes. The small round objects placed on the back walls of the shelves and along the bottom of the shelving unit may be coins or medals. Underneath the shelves are innovative visual arrangements of larger pieces, including turtle shells, funerary urns, and inscriptions. Above the shelves is another aesthetic arrangement featuring weapons and armor, sculptures, and what appears to be a death mask. The ceiling, which is not entirely visible, is covered with marine specimens, including the now familiar shark and puffer fish. At the bottom of the picture is the Cospi coat of arms joined by six palle of the Medici family of Tuscany. Featured in the image are Cospi himself, who invites the viewer rather than a featured guest to look at his marvels, and his dwarf custodian Sebastiano Biavati, who was included in the catalogue in the chapter on human monsters.[55]

With its neatly lined rows of cabinets and paintings in the central section and the repeated vertical lines of the decorated walls in the outer sections, Settala's installation creates a complementary symmetrical arrangement.[56] This style of display, together with the addition of draping fabric, generates a sumptuous atmosphere that has clearly been designed with visitors in mind. The fact that the illustration places more emphasis on the decorative effect of the exhibition layout than on communicating the contents of the collection suggests that the collector was as proud of the former as he was the latter. Even if the individual specimens did not delight the visitors, the overall effect of the display would certainly do so. Similarly, the layout of Cospi's collection would have had an impressive effect as a visual experience. The patterned microarrangements would have distracted the visitor from the scientific significance or informational potential of the objects on display. Additionally, the mixing up of so many different types of objects would have had a bewildering as opposed to clearly digestible didactic effect. The lack of taxonomic coherence may have reflected the fact that Settala and Cospi were not scientists themselves, even though their collections were originally created by scientists. Despite this, what is important to emphasize is that a great deal of attention has been paid to the presentation of the objects in both Settala's and Cospi's displays, and that a major investment has been made in exhibiting important scientific collections. While their exhibitionary style appears to be focused on generating an emotional rather than intellectual response, this does not mean that their collections were simply designed for aesthetic consumption. What is significant about these images is that they capture how the dual functions of learning and entertaining were being combined in early museums. Settala and Cospi intended to instruct and inform, but they also sought to widen the appeal of their collections by making them works of art in themselves.

Another convention of display that appears to have emerged by this time is the use of a guide to present the collection. The significance of using a guide was that he directed the visitor's viewing experience and was the primary "interpretive aid" for understanding the collection. In this

1.7. *(facing)* Athanasius Kircher's collection in Rome. Engraving in Kircher's *Romani Collegii Societatis Jesu Musaeum Celeberrimum* of 1678.

sense, we see how viewing a collection was a structured experience, with visitors seeing objects in accompaniment with a verbal explanation. While Imperato's and Besler's images featured guides, Cospi's custodian is particularly interesting because it suggests that this dwarf guide was part of the collection itself.

SPACE AND DESIGN

The didactic study collections reached a turning point when the spaces in which they were organized were transformed from adapted rooms in private houses into large purpose-built "public" galleries with designed interiors. In addition, display spaces were transformed by the inclusion of larger and more monumental objects, particularly antiquities. This latter point is well evidenced in the picture featuring the collection of the Jesuits in Collegio Romano, curated by Athanasius Kircher and published in 1678 in his catalogue *Romani Collegii Societatis Jesu Musaeum Celeberrimum* (fig. 1.7).[57] Kircher (1602–1680) was a scholar and Jesuit priest who was also a professor of mathematics and languages. With its impressive vaulted ceilings featuring astronomical and other designs, Kircher's museum conveys much about the changing style in which didactic study collections came to be arranged in the late seventeenth and early eighteenth centuries.

Immediately capturing our attention in the image is the series of obelisks featured on elaborate pedestals, signifying Kircher's quest to understand the meaning of the inscriptions on these monuments.[58] Not only did these objects have great physical presence when displayed in an interior setting, but they created a particular effect, whereby the eye was immediately drawn to singular objects as opposed to rows or groups of objects. Notable in this picture is the long room on the right, which is characterized by a symmetrical sequence of pedestals upon which busts have been placed. With the introduction of these pedestals, the lower display spaces have been sacrificed in order to accentuate the artworks aligned along the walls. Also sacrificed is the use of the ceiling to present specimens; instead of sea monsters and lizards, we now have a vista of the skies. On the left of the picture we can see the more familiar rows of smaller objects, or "curiosities," alongside which is a mounted human skeleton. Consistent with the display practices of the time, a large crocodile has been suspended from the ceiling.

This display differs from the ones previously discussed in that while it is still scholarly in its orientation, it lacks the focus on natural history specimens that is characteristic of the others. Nevertheless, the representation of Kircher's collection reveals how the settings in which items were displayed were opened up to create an environment that was more conducive to public viewing. As opposed to a study-like room crammed with objects, here is a space that looks as though it has been designed for the job of accommodating and displaying a collection. Furthermore, whereas in

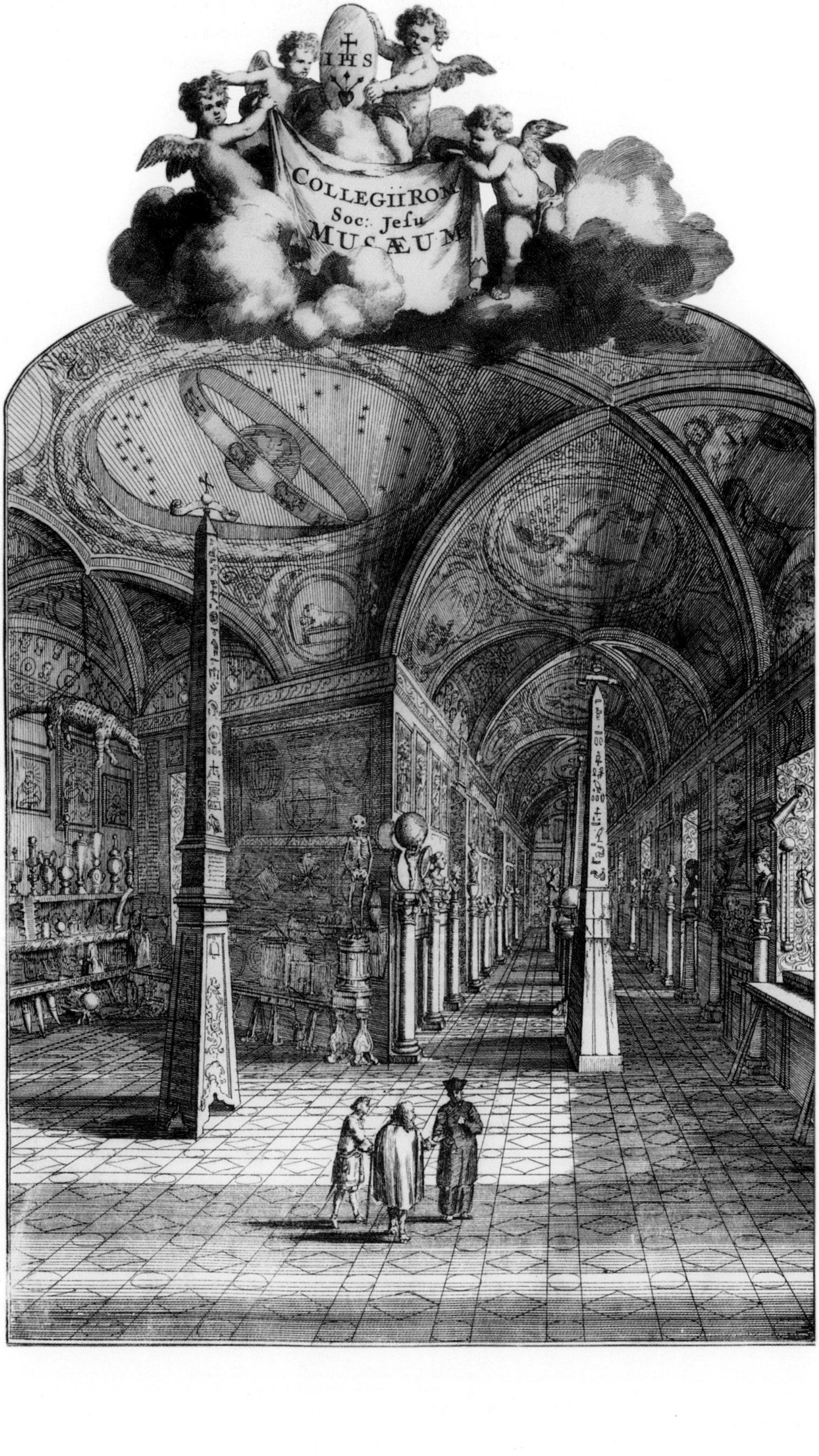
IHS
COLLEGII ROM
Soc: Jesu
MUSÆUM

the pictures of Imperato's and Calceolari's displays the arranged objects are the focus of attention, here it is not just the objects that attract our attention but the space within which they have been presented. While displays of art in the royal collections often had this quality (because of the impressive architectural spaces that were available for displaying collections in castles and stately homes), these didactic collections were typically presented in much smaller spaces that functioned as studio environments. Kircher's display represents something in between the two, where the presentation of objects in the context of a gallery setting is achieved, yet at the same time the collection is laid out for scientific appraisal. Furthermore, the vaulted ceilings, large pedestals, and monumental objects all work together in shaping the architecture of the room and giving it a distinctive sense of design. The obelisks, which have been placed in a row down the middle of the room, as opposed to being lined up along the walls, also take on a more three-dimensional quality, functioning as objects that are to be engaged with and studied as opposed to being merely observed. Thus, with Kircher's museum a major new convention has been introduced to the didactic study collections, with the space within which the objects were arranged asserting itself as a central component in the overall display strategy.

EXHIBITION STRATEGIES

In the sixteenth and seventeenth centuries little was written on the manner in which objects should be exhibited and how display techniques might communicate particular ideas. Some collectors, however, may have found guidance in the work of the Flemish physician Samuel Quiccheberg (1529–1567), who produced the first major museological treatise in 1565.[59] In his *Inscriptiones vel tituli theatri amplissimi*, Quiccheberg outlined a basic system based on materials, where he specified that objects should be arranged according to five major classes, including (1) a library incorporating histories, genealogies, topographic pictures, and architectural models; (2) *artificialia* including cultural items such as sculptures, architectural fragments, metal objects, coins, and weights; (3) *naturalia* including animal, plant, mineral, and human remains; (4) technical instruments and costumes; and (5) images, inscriptions, and paintings, including portraits. In practice, however, the basic division by which objects tended to be organized for display was whether they were works of nature (*naturalia*) or humanity (*artificialia*). If there were further divisions, they usually involved grouping objects according to their raw materials and common function. Thus, the basic organizing principle for arranging collections was classificatory, where similar types of objects or those made of the same material were placed together. These were then often presented in a sequence that corresponded with the shelves, with geological specimens typically featured on the bottom shelves, botanical specimens above them, zoological specimens on top of them, and then cultural material on the top shelves or vice versa. Size was also a determining feature, with smaller objects placed on the shelves, and the larger specimens attached to the upper wall or suspended from the ceiling. There were no strict rules, however, and presentation often reflected personal taste.

Acknowledging that the pictures discussed in this chapter may not have been entirely accurate representations of the way the didactic study collections were arranged, it is nevertheless still possible to identify a basic set of exhibition strategies that were developed for presenting such collections. It is evident from these early images that displaying collections was not just a matter of sorting objects according to type or material, and then placing them in situations that were easy to visually digest. Rather, display was a strategic practice that aimed to both impart messages and create a visual effect. So, although these collections have been characterized as conforming to a study-style of presentation, where objects "stood in closed ranks on shelves," they also increasingly became concerned with issues of arrangement, where the spatial patterns created by objects were intended to communicate particular ideas.[60] In this sense, both the individual objects and the display as a whole functioned as sources of information, collections being intended to communicate on a number of levels.

Although the didactic study displays initially seem chaotic,[61] with items crammed on shelves and hung from walls and ceilings, they were thoughtfully arranged "documents" that were designed to demonstrate the diversity of life on earth. Intended to provide a visual testimony of the vastness of God's creation, the displays of Imperato and his successors aimed to present a representative sample of a wider picture.[62] Not only was this achieved by visually demonstrating the variety of specimens that could be found on the earth, but it was emphasized by creating particular arrangements of these specimens, which drew out the similarities and differences between them. Furthermore, the arrangement of objects placed them in interpretive contexts that shaped how particular objects came to be understood. For example, the different types of natural history specimens came to be understood in relation to each other as exemplars of biological diversity.[63] Thus, the power of these early museological arrangements was that they expressed ideas and concepts that when articulated through the medium of display became more comprehensible. As visual statements, these exhibitions offered tangible testimony of the diversity of species and in this sense, seeing became equated with knowing. So while objects could be understood as independent specimens, they were accorded with far greater meaning when featured in an arrangement alongside other objects.

In these didactic study collections, we can identify at least six main display strategies. First was the maximum use of all the available spaces to display as many items as was physically possible. This created a strong visual effect, with the dense amalgamation of objects generating a sense of awe and wonder. Second was the use of symmetrical and patterned arrangements to emphasize particular aspects of the collection and to suggest affinities between objects. These arrangements also had a powerful effect, encouraging the viewer to take in the whole collection as a visual entity in its own right. Thus, as opposed to seeing objects as individual specimens, visitors were encouraged to see them as part of a wider conceptual network. A third convention was the introduction of interpretive aids such as labels and guides, who would facilitate an understanding of the collection. The practice of labeling objects was particularly significant as it revealed how the classification of objects became a primary concern of collector scientists, and it signified how displays were more explicitly designed to impart knowledge. Furthermore, the use of a guide to present the display suggests that visitors' understanding of the arrangements was not only facilitated by, but was directed by, another interpretive agent. Fourth was the use of architectural features and interior design to enhance the visual impact of the collection. Elaborate display furniture, ornate pedestals, decorated ceilings, and other such enhancements all contributed to the meaning of the collection. The investment in such edifices signified the recognition of the role of the audience in consuming the collection, where displays were "framed" as if they were works of art in themselves. Fifth was the designation of particular objects as display icons assuming an identity or symbolism that served to enhance the status of the collection and its owner. The attribution of objects with an iconic status also revealed how collectors were establishing their own visual language for communicating with each other, and suggested that objects were being valued for their display as well as scientific potential. Finally, a sixth convention was the creation of a "museum" space, or more specifically, a gallery in which the attributes of the collection could be better presented. While the layout of collections become more easily comprehensible in such spaces, the research or study function of the collections tended to be overshadowed by their potential as sources of aesthetic contemplation.

As collecting became more widespread in the late seventeenth and early eighteenth centuries, many of the displays that were initially intended to further the knowledge of scientists and professionals became transformed into popular attractions for the aspiring upper classes. This reflected the growing awareness that displays of objects and specimens had the ability to entertain as well as educate. The power of such accumulations to satisfy other agendas, particularly national and economic ones, also became apparent and was soon exploited by the pioneers of public museums in the mid-to-late eighteenth century. It was in this context that major displays of Egyptian antiquities were first presented in Europe, and more specifically, that they were featured in the first public national museum—the British Museum in London.

2 Wondrous Curiosities

THE DISPLAY OF THE SLOANE COLLECTION OF EGYPTIAN ANTIQUITIES, 1759

Just as the displays of the early modern collectors had functioned as a resource for learning and as visual testimony of the owner's social status, the exhibitions mounted in the first national museums of the eighteenth century served as vehicles for study and as symbols of their nation's standing in the world. The ways in which antiquities were exhibited in the galleries of the first public museums of Europe reveal how displays of objects were used not only to communicate ideas about past cultures, but to reflect upon the connection of ancient societies to present ones. The beginnings of such representational practices can be traced to the mid-eighteenth century, when the first national, secular, and public museum was founded in London. Established in 1753, the British Museum signified an important step in the way museums structured knowledge about the world, and of particular significance was the role this institution assumed in defining the ancient past. While not initially well represented in the museum, antiquities soon became its main highlight, a development associated with the imperialistic endeavors of Britain, where antiquities from the Mediterranean and other regions were accumulated as part of a wider project to assert Britain's wealth and influence. In addition to this political role, the museum's antiquities collections were used to interpret how Western culture had originated and evolved, and their presentation played a key role in telling the story of the "progress" of art. This story was intended to instruct society on matters of taste and how taste could be emulated. Among the ancient cultures represented in the museum's narrative of civilization and the emergence of art was that of Egypt. With its rarely seen and exotic range of antiquities, this culture quickly assumed a central role in the museum's quest to bring the achievements of the ancient world to light. Prior to this agenda, however, was the crucial part that ancient Egypt played in establishing the museum's identity as a vast repository of curiosities and wonders.

The display of the British Museum's first collection of Egyptian antiquities, which consisted of a number of objects included in the founding collection of Sir Hans Sloane (1660–1753) and several major donations from other benefactors, was of crucial importance in defining ancient

Egypt as one of the world's main sources of "wondrous curiosities." Presented as objects that were designed to surprise and entertain, as opposed to those that were intended to inform and enlighten, the Egyptian antiquities were rendered of little consequence in comparison with the many other objects that featured in the museum. Despite this, the reception of the museum's early displays reveals how visitors avidly consumed the curiosities from Egypt, finding in them an opportunity to be awestruck, delighted, shocked, and repulsed.

ACQUISITION

The first Egyptian antiquities to be displayed in the British Museum came as part of its founding collection, which was offered to the government by the physician and collector Sir Hans Sloane.[1] Upon his death in 1753, Sloane's vast collection of natural history specimens, books and manuscripts, antiquities, scientific objects, coins and medals, and ethnographic pieces was made available to the government at the cost price of £20,000. On June 7, 1753 an Act of Parliament for the establishment of the British Museum was passed, giving rise to the creation of the first national, publicly funded museum.[2] Run by a board of forty-eight trustees, including leading figures in Britain such as the Archbishop of Canterbury, the Lord Chancellor, and the Speaker of the House of Commons, the new museum was situated in Montagu House, Bloomsbury, London (fig. 2.1).[3] Opened to the public on the fifteenth of January, 1759, the museum provided access to its diverse range of collections via a system of guided visits.[4] While it initially functioned as a vast "cabinet of curiosities" that any visitor to London should not miss, the museum soon became a place for scientists to consult specimens, for antiquarians to study the documents and material remains of the past, and for aesthetes and artists to contemplate the merits of ancient art. Tensions between those who saw the museum as a research institution and those who wanted to facilitate greater public access to the collections arose early on, with the government and the media criticizing the museum's lack of concern for making the collections as accessible as possible.[5]

The new museum's collection of antiquities was not a substantive one, reflecting Sloane's major focus on natural history, books, and manuscripts. Of the 1,125 antiquities or "Things relating to the Customs of ancient Times, or Antiquities, Urns, Instruments, &c" in the collection, only 160 were Egyptian.[6] These included figures made from bronze (votive statuettes featuring gods in animal or animal-headed forms), shabtis (small funerary figurines found with the dead in their tombs), scarabs (funerary artifacts symbolizing rebirth), a mummy, a stela, and small pieces of sculpture (figs. 2.2–2.5).[7] While over a third of these items came from the collection of the Roman Cardinal Filippo Antonio Gualtieri (1660–1728), others

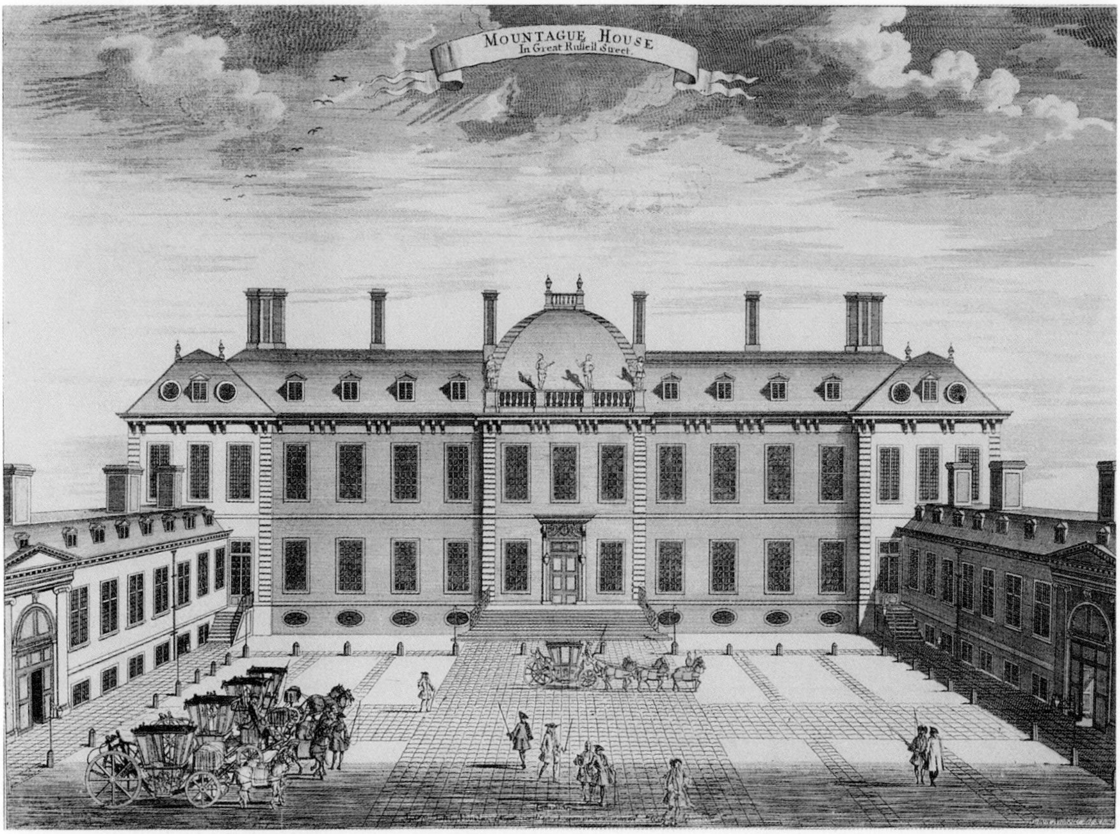

2.1. Montagu House, Bloomsbury, London, 1714. Engraving by Sutton Nicholls. Illustrations of the British Museum (CE 115/1/10), British Museum, Central Archives.

came from British travelers and collectors, notably George Sandys (1578–1644), Robert Huntington (1637–1701), John Kemp (1665–1717), and John Montagu, the fourth Earl of Sandwich (1718–1792).[8]

Before the museum was opened to the public, its collection of Egyptian antiquities was significantly enhanced by several donations, the first being a set of objects presented by Colonel William Lethieullier (1701–1756) in 1756.[9] The highlight of this collection was a complete mummy with its decorated case, which became well known as a result of being illustrated in 1724 by the engraver to the Society of Antiquaries of London, George Vertue (1684–1756; fig. 2.6), and again in 1737 by the antiquarian Alexander Gordon (c.1692–c.1754).[10] That the mummy was perceived to be of some significance is also suggested by the fact that a group of trustees went to visit Lethieullier's son to thank the family for this special gift, and that this event was subsequently reported in the *Gentleman's Magazine*.[11] Following this visit, more donations of Egyptian antiquities were made by the Lethieullier family, including those presented by Colonel William's son Pitt Lethieullier and his cousin Smart Lethieullier (fig. 2.7).[12] Unlike Sloane, both William and Pitt Lethieullier had been members of the short-lived Egyptian Society, the former having traveled to Egypt in 1721.[13]

2.2. Objects in Sloane's collection of Egyptian antiquities. Engraving in Alexander Gordon's *Twenty-five Plates of All the Egyptian Mummies, and Other Egyptian Antiquities in England*, 1737, plate iv. The stela is EA 511.

2.3. Objects in the British Museum's first Egyptian displays: "*Vas Ægyptium*, a Canopus, with Osiris'-Head, or that of a Hawk"; "An Egyptian Ring, the Figure I take to be a Sphinx"; "A *Canopus*, the Cover of a Dog's Head." Engraving in *Museum Britannicum* by J. and A. van Rymsdyk, 1778, table 13, figs. 2, 3, 4. Figure 2 is one of the canopic jars of a man named Horudja (EA 37937), Twenty-sixth Dynasty. Figure 3 is one of the canopic jars of a man named Imhotep (EA 37945), Late Period.

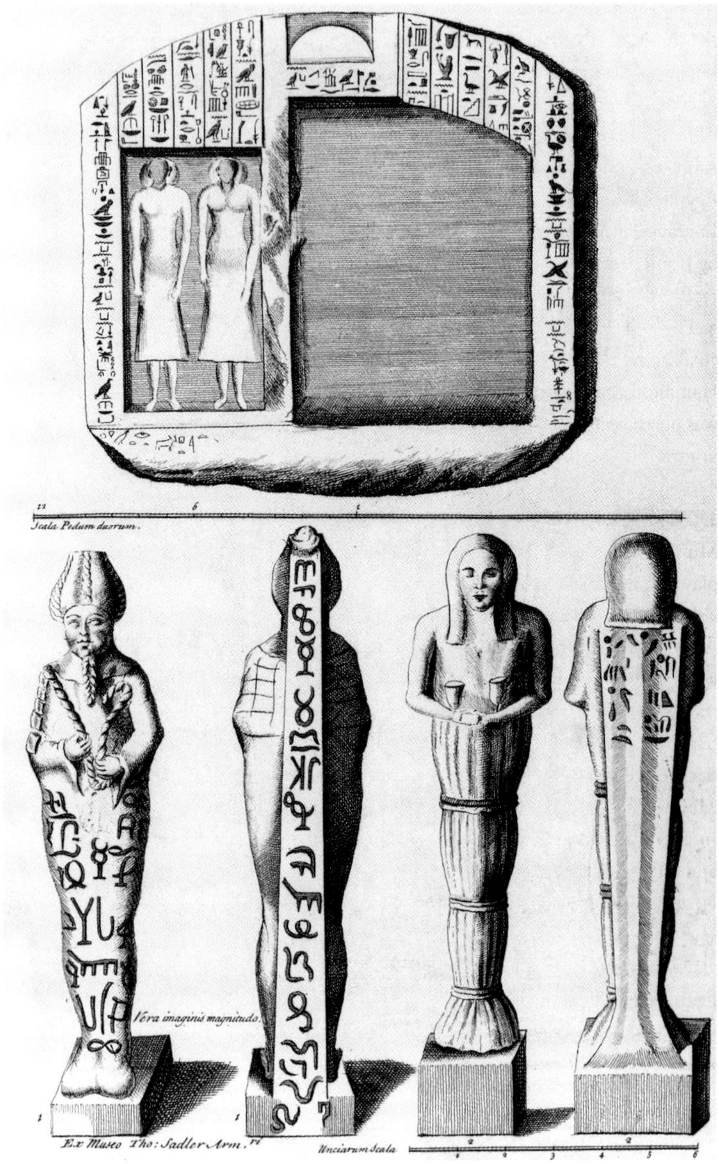

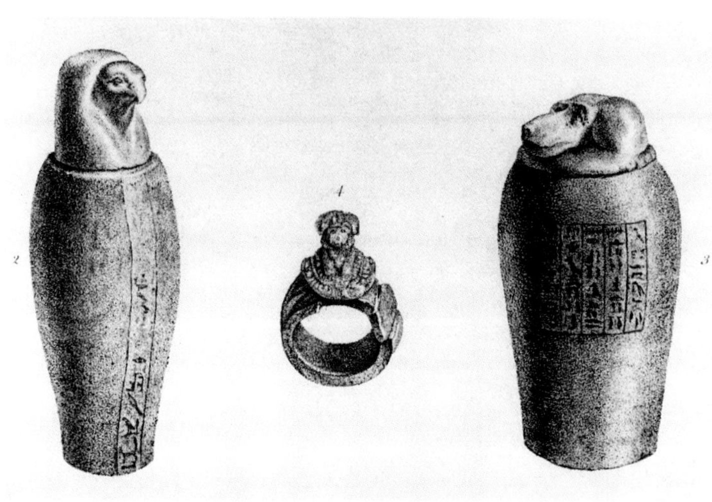

2.4. Objects in the British Museum's first Egyptian displays: "An *Egyptian Amulet*, a *Scarabæus* or *Beetle* . . ."; "The Posterior Part of this Amulet—, on which are the Egyptian *Characters*. . . ." Engraving in *Museum Britannicum* by J. and A. van Rymsdyk, 1778, table 14, figs. 2 and 3. This heart scarab (EA 7858) came from Sir William Hamiliton's collection, which was purchased by the museum in 1772.

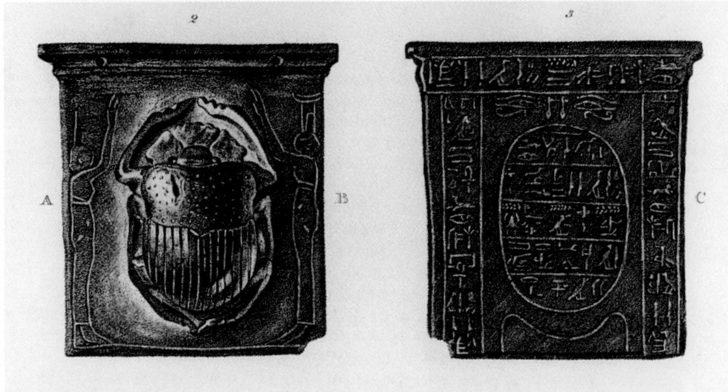

2.5. Objects in the British Museum's first Egyptian displays: "*A Sistrum,* from *Cardinal Gualtieri's* Collection, it's an Ancient Musical Instrument or rattle in the form of a Racket, traversed by four moveable bars, the ends of which are like Serpents Tails"; "*Osiris*, with a Mitre on its Head . . ."; "*Isis*, sitting, with *Orus* in her Lap, and a *Calathus* or Basket on her Head. . . ." Engraving in *Museum Britannicum* by J. and A. van Rymsdyk, 1778, table 29, figs. 1, 2, 3. The sistrum (GR 1756.1-1.541) was from Sloane's collection and is Roman, not Egyptian; the figure of Osiris is EA 60597.

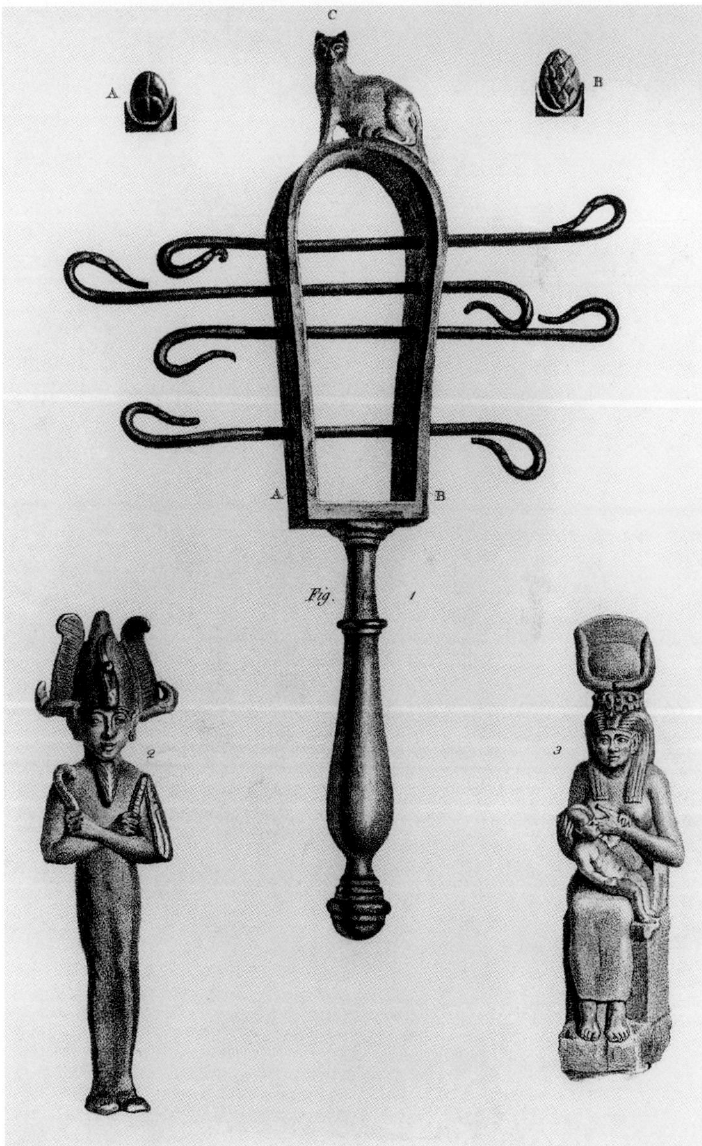

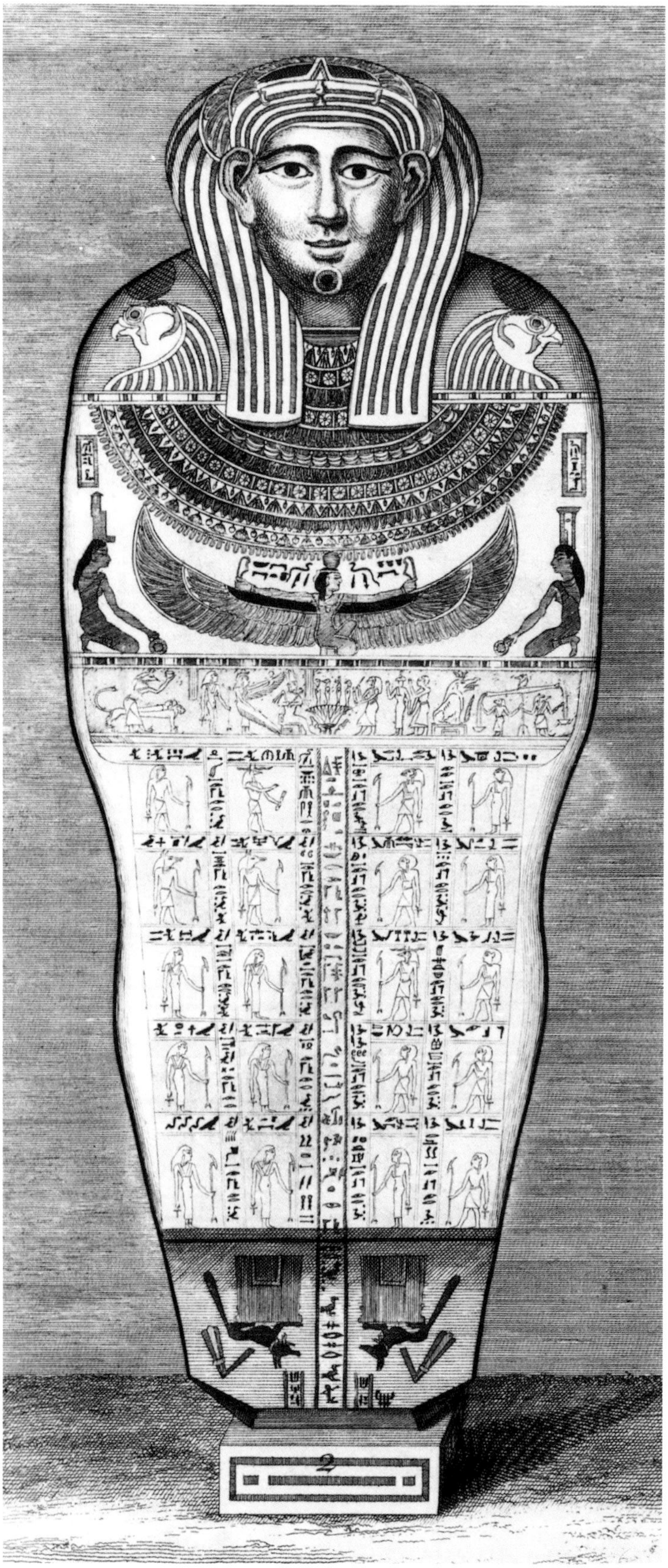

2.6. Inner coffin of Irtyru (EA 6695) from Memphis, Twenty-sixth Dynasty. Donated by Colonel William Lethieullier in 1756. Engraving by George Vertue, *Cadaver balsamo conditum: Simul cum loculo ferali* ἀνθρωποειδή . . . 1724, plates 31, 32.

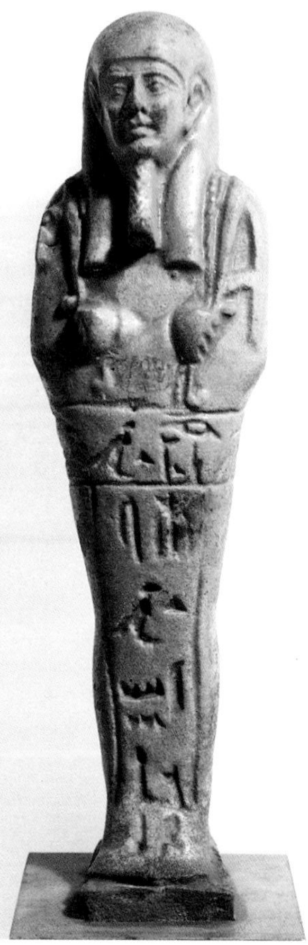

2.7. Shabti of Tarudj (EA 9183), Twenty-sixth Dynasty. Donated to the British Museum by Pitt Lethieullier in 1756.

After the museum's opening, a number of other Egyptian antiquities were added to the its display, including those presented in 1766 and 1767 by King George III and John Stuart, the third Earl of Bute (1713–1792). These had initially been sent from Egypt by Edward Wortley Montagu (1713–1776) to his brother-in-law the Earl of Bute, who in turn presented them to George III. Included among these objects were the architectural slabs of Nectanebo I and Psamtek (figs. 2.8–2.9), a limestone relief (fig. 2.10), a sphinx, a mummy and its coffin (plate 1), and a figure of Pa-sr.[14] A few years later, in 1771, one of the museum's trustees, the lawyer and collector Matthew Duane (1707–1785), donated a small sculpture,[15] and in 1772 more Egyptian antiquities came as part of the purchase of Sir William Hamilton's (1731–1803) collection of classical antiquities, including figurines, scarabs (fig. 2.4) and two small mummies.[16] In 1785, the museum made its first purchase of Egyptian antiquities, these being two small stelae sold at the auction of Duane's collection.[17] With all these additions, the Egyptian collection had started to become more substantial; however, it was completely overshadowed by the acquisition of Hamilton's vast collection of Greek vases in 1772, which constituted the museum's first major collection of antiquities and marked the beginnings of the supremacy of the classical collections.[18]

The significance of the museum's first collection of Egyptian antiquities must be understood in relation to the history of interest in acquiring objects from ancient Egypt. Such a practice can be dated to the first century BC, when Egyptian antiquities were taken back to Rome, particularly obelisks and sculptures of sphinxes and lions.[19] The "collection" of Egyptian antiquities continued throughout classical times, with objects being transported to Rome until the middle of the fourth century AD. Interest in accumulating Egyptian artifacts took a new direction in the Middle Ages, when mummies or more specifically, *mummia*, was sought for its assumed medical properties.[20] In the sixteenth century, when antiquities started to feature more prominently in collections, Egyptian objects became a popular and highly sought-after commodity. Collectors became increasingly interested in ancient Egyptian objects not only because it was becoming easier to purchase such items, but because works on Egyptian antiquities were being published.[21] While the smaller items tended to be included in the encyclopedic or didactic study collections of the seventeenth century, larger sculptures featured in some of the major art collections in Rome in the eighteenth century.[22] Such works were recognized to be symbolically interesting in that they had been appropriated for political purposes. In sixteenth-century Rome, for example, pontiffs used obelisks and lion statues to signify Rome's ancient power.[23] A sign of the desire to gain something intellectually from the Egyptian objects in early modern collections is the depiction of them in illustrated catalogues of collections, and of special note here was the work of Athanasius Kircher, which focused on interpreting the inscriptions on the obelisks in the Museum of the College

2.8. Architectural slab of Nectanebo I (EA 22) found in Alexandria, Thirtieth Dynasty. Donated to the British Museum in 1766 by King George III.

2.9. Architectural slab of Psamtek (EA 20) found in Alexandria, Twenty-sixth Dynasty. Donated to the British Museum in 1766 by King George III.

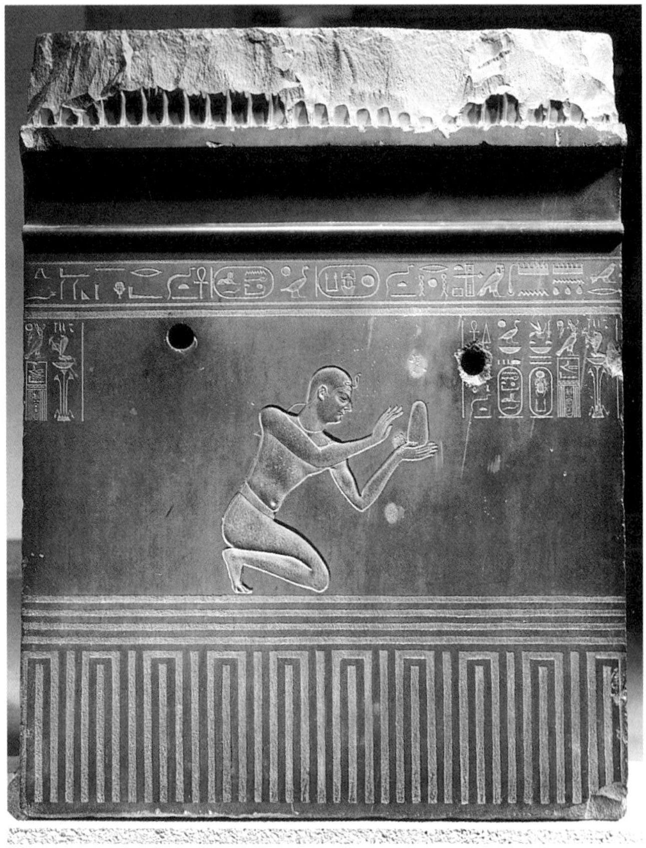

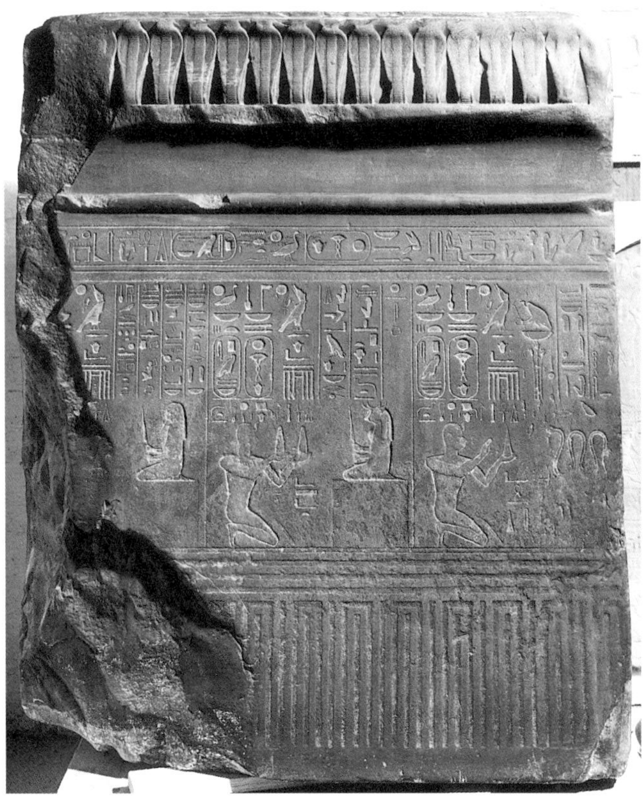

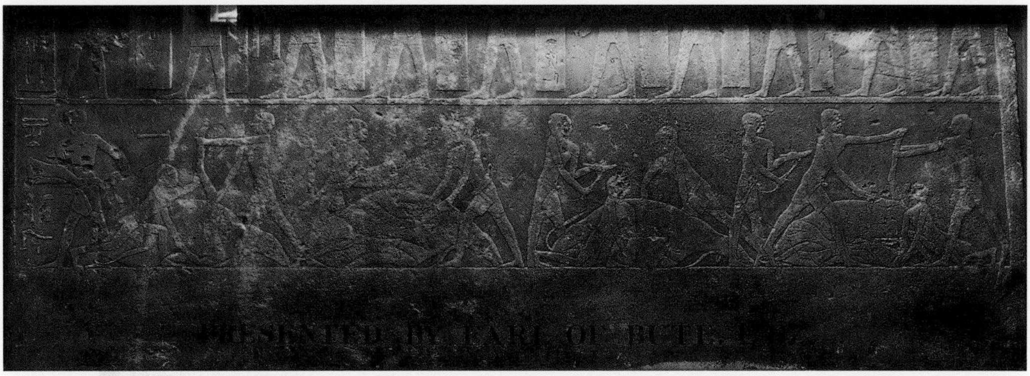

2.10. Relief depicting the slaying of oxen (EA 430), Fifth Dynasty. Donated to the British Museum in 1767 by the Earl of Bute.

of the Society of Jesus in Rome (see fig. 1.7).[24] Early European scholarly institutions were also according ancient Egypt with some significance; the University of Leiden, for example, accumulated Egyptian archaeological specimens and put them on display.[25]

Thus, by the time the British Museum was founded there was a precedent for situating Egyptian antiquities in both scientific and artistic collections. That the array of Egyptian antiquities was not particularly impressive reflects the fact that Sloane did not devote any special efforts to building up this component of his collection, and that the objects he acquired came to him more by chance than dedicated searching.[26] Like the other British collectors who had Egyptian antiquities in their possession, Sloane was conducting a practice consistent with wider collecting behavior in Europe. Described as "magpie" collectors, these individuals typically incorporated antiquities to "round off" their collections.[27] That Sloane's collection was consistent with those of other leading naturalist and antiquarian collectors is suggested by a 1737 British publication on Egyptian antiquities by Alexander Gordon, which illustrates similar types of items held in other notable collections in the country.[28] At the time such collectors were active, interest in acquiring ancient Egyptian items was still restricted to easily transportable "exotic" specimens such as shabtis, scarabs, small statues, and the occasional mummy, which were brought to England by diplomats, merchants, and travelers.[29] Collectors like Sloane were keen to include such items in their displays because they were iconic curiosities. More specifically, they were unusual and rare and had the same currency as crocodiles, armadillos, puffer fish, narwhal's tusks, and other such desirable "collectibles." That Egyptian items had such a status can be seen in the engraving of Ferdinando Cospi's display of 1677 (fig. 1.6), where the custodian holds an Egyptian figurine in his hand, offering it for view. Furthermore, Egyptian antiquities were sought after because they possessed many of the wondrous qualities that collectors were attracted by—they were culturally exotic, strange, and unusual in size.[30]

While mummies and mummy cases provided a fascinating glimpse into death, the votive figurines featuring animal gods were seen as testament to the existence of a bizarre religion long gone. Furthermore, the color and design of the mummy cases and the miniature size of many of the figurines made them appealing as display items. Like other antiquities, the Egyptian objects were often associated with natural history items because of their material or medicinal associations. For example, because mummies were valued more for their assumed pharmaceutical properties than their historical significance, they were often included in cabinets containing natural specimens thought to have remedial application. When the royal and papal art collectors joined the apothecaries and naturalists in seeking to obtain mummies for their collections, they had a different motivation for such acquisitions. Like the crocodile and armadillo, mummies quickly acquired an iconic status, becoming a sought-after addition for every worthy collection. For example, we know that mummies were included in the collections of the Grand Duke of Tuscany, Cardinal Flavio Chigi, and Peter Paul Rubens.[31] Later, in the seventeenth century, Egyptian mummies were a highlight in the famous collections of Nicolas-Claude Fabri de Peiresc and Père Claude Du Molinet, and in the cabinet of the University of Leiden.[32]

Having argued that the Egyptian antiquities in the museum's first collection were regarded as curiosities, it is important to note that they were collected as part of a much larger scientific collection, and thus to some degree, their informational value was recognized. More specifically, alongside the other antiquities these objects were considered useful for illustrating the "customs of ancient times." In this sense, the Egyptian objects, which constituted a part of the antiquities component of Sloane's encyclopedic collection, signified the emergence of antiquarianism. Like other antiquities, they were initially incorporated in early modern collections as examples of the strange and unusual; however, they were increasingly treated as objects with scientific significance in the sense that they could be used as evidence of human history.[33] At the time of the establishment of the museum, Egyptian antiquities, like Greek and Roman ones, were being collected in Europe as a means of shedding light on the past. The antiquarians Bernard de Montfauçon and the Comte de Caylus, for example, produced major studies on the antiquities held in European collections in the early to mid-eighteenth century.[34] Thus, antiquities from Egypt, Greece, and Rome were sought after not only because they were desirable curiosities, but because they were seen to have potential as historical documents. Furthermore, for some collectors antiquities were familiar due to their links with classical myths and legends, while for others they were interesting because of the materials from which they were manufactured; this latter feature rendering them of importance as evidence on the history of nature.[35] Prehistoric artifacts from Europe were also included in early modern collections, but these were usually displayed alongside the geological and natural specimens such as fossils, because their function was not known.[36] While stone implements came to be seen as examples of nature's great powers of creativity, bones were popular because they were thought to be the remains of giants from the Old Testament.[37] Sometimes prehistoric items were confused with the ethnographic objects acquired through travel to the New World. While the desire to incorporate prehistoric stone artifacts was related to the development of early geological interests, it also reflected the desire to possess examples of the rare and the mysterious. Thus, archaeological materials were classified as both *naturalia* and *artificialia*; *artificialia* typically including coins, figurines, and utensils, and *naturalia* typically including bones, fossils, and prehistoric artifacts. Like ethnographic items, they were valued as objects that provided a glimpse into the customs of different nations.[38]

Although the Egyptian antiquities that went on display at the British Museum in 1759 included a greater quantity of material than was typically featured in many other European collections, it was eclectic rather than specialized and constituted an extremely limited set of data upon which to generate an understanding of ancient Egypt. Indeed, one of the most distinctive features of the eighteenth-century collections of Egyptian antiquities, such as Sloane's, was that they represented such a selective range of the material that existed.[39] A major factor here of course, was what was actually available to purchase on the collectors' market. It appears that beyond mummies, the smaller objects such as figurines and shabtis were chosen because they possessed the features characteristic of the "ideal" curiosity and thus were seen as having good display potential. Such items were also most easily transportable by travelers and merchants. Objects valued as documents of art or as evidence of history were not sought after until much later; it was not until the 1820s that items like papyri and sculptures with inscriptions or hieroglyphs were widely demanded by collectors.[40] Thus, the museum's first collection of Egyptian antiquities was not valuable or significant in an aesthetic or archaeological sense, but rather can be described as constituting a miscellaneous assortment of curious items.

DISPLAY

Instructions for the arrangement of the Egyptian collection in the British Museum were incorporated within a general plan for the distribution of Sloane's collection in Montagu House. Presented in two documents prepared in 1756 and 1757 by the curator of Sloane's collection, James Empson, this plan reveals how seriously the issue of display was taken and that a systematic approach was promoted from the start.[41] For instance, in the introduction to the plan great emphasis was placed on making the collection comprehensible to the new audience to whom it would be directed:

> How much so ever a private Person may be at Liberty arbitrarily to dispose and place his Curiosities; We are sensible that the British Museum, being a public Institution subject to the Visits of the Judicious & Intelligent,

as well as Curious, Notice will taken, whether or no[t] the Collection has been arranged in a methodical manner. For this reason we have pitched on the following Course, being the most simple & most natural, & on that Account appearing to us the most eligible to be pursued. We immediately divide the whole Collection into two Parts, viz, the *Natural* & *Artificial* Curiosities, and arrange them accordingly.[42]

The "methodical," "simple," and "natural" approach that was deemed to be the best way to present the collection appears to have involved a basic division of the specimens of natural history and the cultural items; however, within the natural history component further subdivisions were made according to specimen type. These classifications were elucidated upon in the second document prepared by Empson, where the imparting of a didactic message is emphasized. Asserting that the "most valuable part of this collection consists of things relating to Natural History," Empson proceeds to explain the knowledge that may be conveyed through arrangement:

All the Articles that come under this head may be properly classed in the three general divisions of Fossils, Vegetables, & Animals. Of these the Fossils are the most simple; & therefore may properly be disposed in the first Rank: next to them the Vegetables: & lastly the Animal Substances. By this arrangement the spectator will be gradually conducted from the Simplest to the most compound & most perfect of Nature's Productions.[43]

Thus, the order in which these specimens appear in the rooms is intended to instruct the visitor on the hierarchy or evolution of nature. Structured according to the principles of Carl Linnaeus's taxonomic system, the display of the museum's natural history collections was laid out in a sequence; in this sense the museum sought to tell a story that would unfold as the visitor proceeded from room to room.[44]

Although instruction was the aim of the museum's exhibition plan, importance was still placed on the aesthetic qualities of the objects. For instance, an assessment of their visual appeal was used to determine where they were to be placed in relation to each other:

We intend, according to the Nature and Characteristick of each of these Matters, to subdivide them & in disposing of each Subdivision, to take particular Care, that those Matters may be brought nearest the Sight as are most pleasing to the Eye and of most Consideration; placing the Rest, in proportion as they are less so, higher & higher on the Shelves above them and those that are still inferior, in the Drawers under each Subdivision. We conceive, that such a Disposition will, afford great Ease to the Spectator and be no less convenient to the Officer in Shewing them.[45]

The concept that those objects which are more "pleasing to the eye" will occupy the central shelves and those which are "inferior" should be relegated to higher shelves and drawers below, reveals how visual appeal remained a main criterion for arranging the collections. However, it is not only their aesthetic qualities that guarantee objects the best viewing conditions; they must also be "of most consideration." Although not stated, this probably refers to the rarity of the specimens. Finally, the notion that this kind of arrangement will offer the visitor "great ease," suggests that the aim was to make the displays immediately comprehensible upon entering the room.

Beyond the general plan, more specific decisions were made about the best way to display antiquities in the new museum. Cabinets, it was suggested, were not needed for the larger antiquities, and the large stones with inscriptions were to be placed between the windows and at the sides of the rooms so as not to fill up the center of the rooms.[46] Furthermore, a decision was made to paint the insides of the shelves a light color in order to enhance the visibility of objects.[47] When Hamilton's collection of Greek vases was acquired in 1772, more detailed ideas concerning the display of antiquities were elaborated upon. Like many other collectors, Hamilton was very particular about the conditions in which his collection could be best appreciated, and he instructed museum staff on the crucial importance of light and the need for display furniture "without any carving or useless ornament.'[48]

Intimately related to the museum's general plans for exhibition were the decisions made about display furniture, room decoration, and lighting. Most of the discussion on these subjects focused on the style of cabinets that would be created to house the books and manuscripts, with decisions concerning the display of antiquities being delayed because "It is not Easy to Judge what Number or kind of Cases or Cabinets, may be fit for the most Valuable of the Natural and Artificial Curiosities of the Sloanian Collection, as the Different Subjects may want different Sorts."[49] However, the trustees did establish that the rooms for displaying the objects should be hung with green or other colored paper of a "handsome" damask pattern, and that curtains of serge and worsted damask be fitted.[50] When decisions finally had to be made about how to present the antiquities, the trustees ordered the construction of glass cases for the more valuable objects; these were to be glazed on all sides and made mobile so that they could be moved to face the light.[51] The less valuable objects were to be displayed in cases fronted with brass wire and curtains. That lighting was an important consideration in the display of the collection is reflected by the decision to house the antiquities and natural curiosities on the first floor, where they would be best lit.[52] That said, it is important to note that Montagu House was a stately mansion, not a purpose-built museum, and thus the room size and lighting were generally inappropriate for display.

Two rooms in the new museum featured displays of antiquities; the majority of rooms were laid out with natural history specimens and the vast collection of books and manuscripts (fig. 2.11). That the space dedicated to antiquities was so limited in comparison to that reserved for natural history reveals the relatively insignificant status of the antiquities collection. Despite these restrictions however, the Egyptian antiquities claimed a prime viewing position on account of being included in the select range of objects featured at the museum entrance and in the main hall, and more significantly because they were a central feature of the first exhibition room, which was reserved for donations.[53] Indeed, upon first entering the gate of the museum, visitors would have immediately seen Egyptian antiquities, as displayed under the colonnade were "two pieces of greenish marble . . . both sides covered with hieroglyphics," which were thought to have belonged to the "mausoleum of Cleopatra."[54] The next encounter they would have had with Egyptian antiquities was in the hall where Egyptian coffins were displayed.[55] Besides "some other objects of curiosity," such as blocks of stone from the Giant's Causeway in Ireland, a lump of lava from Mount Vesuvius, and a skeleton of a sea unicorn, these coffins were said to "immediately engage the attention of a stranger."[56]

After absorbing the delights of these rarities, visitors would then have met with a selection of Egyptian objects in the first exhibition room, which was situated at the top of the stairs (see fig. 2.11). It was here that the visitor would have been instantly struck by the display of four mummies, including two larger ones and two smaller ones.[57] In Edmund Powlett's guide of 1761, for instance, the exhibition room is described as containing "several very curious Articles given by Colonel Lethullier, his Brothers, and other Benefactors" and of these, Powlett states that "I shall first mention an Egyptian mummy."[58] This mummy was displayed in one corner of the room in a mahogany case with a glass lid and sides, and displayed upright so that "the whole may be exposed to view" (fig. 2.6).[59] Another early account suggests that this case could be rotated by turning a handle.[60] Placed next to the feet of the mummy were a skull and other bones from another mummy, and near its head were placed "some of those small earthen Idols which are . . . to be put by the Embalmers into the Cavities of the Body."[61] In another corner of the room was the coffin for the mummy, which had a square display case above it containing "Utensils belonging to the Deceased, and deposited near the Body," two models of mummies, an urn with the remains of an ibis, and several "Idols in Bronze."[62] Of the two smaller mummies in the display, one was probably the fake modern mummy from Sloane's collection, constituting a bundle of ibis bones wrapped in reused mummy wrappings.[63]

Other items from the Lethieullier collections that were displayed in this room were exhibited in the individual display boxes that they had been presented to the museum in. Featured alongside the Egyptian antiquities in the other cabinets were items of natural history, including corals, a large brainstone, and the petrified backbone of an elephant.[64] Zoological specimens preserved in spirits included a vulture's head, some serpents, birds, spiders, and lizards. Of particular note, we are told, were a "fine young

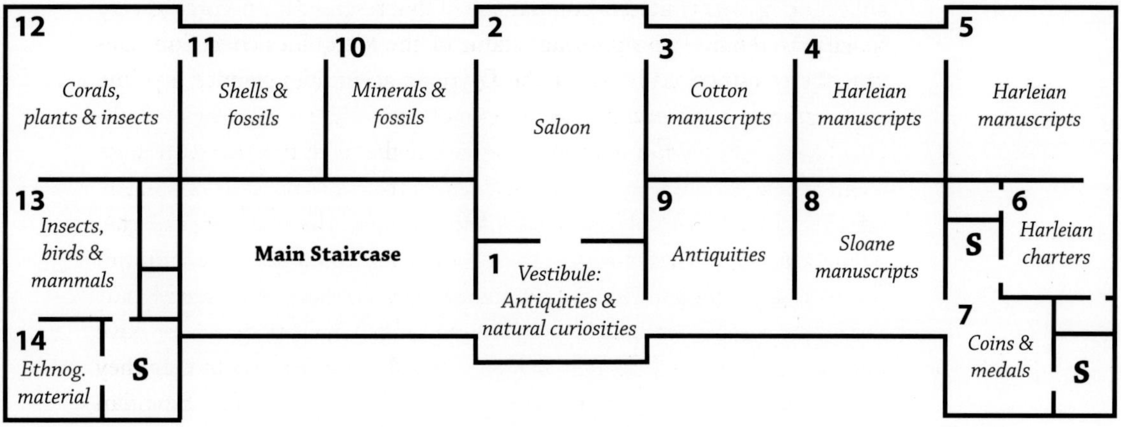

2.11. Schematic room plan of the first story of the British Museum in 1759, indicating the contents of the rooms and the order in which they were shown to visitors. S = stairs.

Flamingo stuffed," a wasp's nest "well worth observing with Attention, being a most curious specimen," "a Sea Fan, and a Sea Feather," and "a fine jay from the East Indies."[65]

In addition to the museum entrance, the main hall, and the first exhibition room, objects from the Egyptian collection were displayed in the room assigned to presenting antiquities (see fig. 2.11). This would have been viewed after proceeding through the rooms dedicated to manuscripts and coins and medals, and before seeing the natural history rooms.[66] Alongside the classical antiquities and "several Chinese and Japanese images" were featured "a great number of Egyptian antiquities," including bronze, stone, and ceramic figures representing various Egyptian deities and animals, urns or canopic jars, and other objects.[67] Highlighted among these was a sistrum (fig. 2.5), described as a musical instrument in the form of a racket with several moveable bars and used by the priests of Isis in religious ceremonies.[68] Also mentioned was an urn containing an ibis, "a bas relief in marble representing the idol of Mendes in Egypt," an alabaster urn with a hawk's head cover, "small earthen figures shaped like mummies," amulets with loops, figures of cats, a monkey sculpture, scarabs, a statue of a lion in stone, a sphinx in "white stone," and "oblong pieces of enamelled earth, notched to mark the rising and falling of the Nile."[69] Antiquities of miniature size, probably amulets featuring Egyptian gods, are also highlighted as a feature of the display; "some of them are so extremely small, that they are fixed on little cushions to avoid their being lost."[70] After leaving the antiquities room and proceeding to the natural history displays, visitors would have had another chance to see some Egyptian antiquities; one example being the pestle, mortar, and plate made of porphyry.[71]

Before these early displays were finally dismantled in 1808, several important changes occurred in their organization. Most significant perhaps, was the removal of the natural history specimens from the first exhibition room toward the end of the century, marking the end of the juxtaposition of natural and cultural objects in the same display. While this may have addressed the problem of the first exhibition room appearing like a collection of miscellaneous wonders, the Egyptian mummies continued to be displayed alongside "an amazing number of curious articles" such as Oliver Cromwell's watch and a picture painted on a cobweb.[72] Other accounts, however, suggest that by the end of the eighteenth century the displays were arranged in a more systematic manner in the first exhibition room, where smaller Egyptian items appeared in cases next to ones featuring the remains from Herculaneum and Pompeii. For example, in James Malcolm's guide *Londinium Redivivum* we are informed that a case in this room entitled "Images Deorum Egyptiacorum" contains Egyptian idols of metal, stone, and wood. Many of these, Malcolm observes, are "very small and rude," however there is a "bust of a female, which might be mistaken for a Roman work from the execution."[73] Egyptian antiquities were also included in the "South Sea Room" opened in 1778, which was devoted to ethnographic items from the South Pacific. For example, here a "breastplate from the Friendly Islands is contrasted with another from the breast of an Egyptian mummy, and exhibiting a singular coincidence."[74]

In establishing what the first displays of Egyptian antiquities communicated to visitors, or more precisely, how the museum constructed an identity for ancient Egypt through its arrangement of such objects, we must look beyond the display strategies (or lack of them) articulated by the museum to consider how much space was dedicated to presenting the collection, where it was located, how it was structured, the manner in which objects were spatially arranged, the architectural and interior settings they were featured in, and the interpretive aids that were used to present them. In terms of space, the antiquities collections occupied a very small part of the overall exhibition area, and within this, the Egyptian antiquities claimed a limited space. In the antiquities room, for example, ten display cases were devoted to classical antiquities, of which only one was assigned to the Egyptian objects. This difference in quantity communicated something about the status and importance of Egyptian antiquities. For instance, the predominance of material from Rome implied that these were objects of greater interest to collectors than were the curios from Egypt.[75] Another significant observation to make is that the museum's collections were presented in small rooms, Montagu House being a domestic as opposed to public building. This would have affected the viewing experience, emphasizing the status of the museum as a repository of curiosities.

The location of the Egyptian collection was also significant in what it revealed about the museum's attitude to ancient Egypt. For instance, the collection was not presented together as a coherent entity, but rather was dispersed in various display spaces. The distribution of the collection in this manner revealed how Egyptian antiquities were not recognized as having scientific or intellectual credibility in the same way that the natural history specimens were, the latter being grouped together in a more organized or typologically consistent way. Despite this significant difference, however, the Egyptian remains enjoyed prime viewing spaces in the museum. For instance, not only were they situated in the entrance areas of the museum, but they were a highlight of the first exhibition room. On account of featuring so prominently in what would have been the visitors' first impressions of the museum, the Egyptian antiquities were likely to have had a profound and everlasting effect. Furthermore, these areas would have effectively set the tone for the rest of the museum, providing an idea of what was to come. By using such spaces to feature the larger individual items of an unusual nature, the museum was unconsciously defining itself as a cabinet of curiosities.

As regards the organization of the Egyptian collection, although labels were used to distinguish the contents of the cabinets as Egyptian, Etruscan, or Roman, the museum's concern for systematic presentation, as expressed in their plans for distribution of the collections, was not reflected in the displays of antiquities. Indeed, the main criteria for structuring the collections appear to have been donor, object-type as curiosity, and cultural group. For example, the Egyptian objects in the first exhibition room were donated by the Lethieulliers; the isolated objects featured in the entrance were placed here alongside other curiosities; and those deposited in the antiquities room appear in the broadly defined Egyptian cabinet. In all of these contexts, the Egyptian objects were "classified" in a manner that differed very little from the eclectic combinations characteristic of cabinets of curiosities from the sixteenth and seventeenth centuries. To be fair, however, the antiquities arrangements also conveyed the encyclopedic and scientific nature of Sloane's collecting, and in this sense were presented as ethnographic documents. For instance, displayed alongside ethnographic items from North America, South America, India, China, and Japan, the Egyptian items were included in the collection to communicate a sense of what the habits and customs of people from distant times and remote places were like. It is perhaps not surprising that the antiquities were arranged in such a manner, as in the mid-eighteenth century there were no formal archaeological systems or frameworks to guide the classification of objects (beyond sorting them according to subject and type).

On the other hand, important changes were taking place in antiquarianism at the time, where attempts were being made to establish approaches to ancient material culture that were more systematic and scientific (or chronological).[76] For instance, a major system advanced for the interpretation of ancient art and antiquities was that of the German art historian, Johann Joachim Winckelmann.[77] This model saw antiquities placed in a progressivist schema leading to classical Greek sculpture, with Egyptian art representing the primitive beginnings. However, because the museum's collection of antiquities predominantly included the smaller types of objects typically found in a curiosity cabinet, as opposed to the antique sculptures typically featured in royal palaces, its arrangement was not structured according to the aesthetic principles outlined by Winckelmann. Furthermore, it appears that because the main focus of the museum's collections was the natural history and manuscript collections, no real effort was devoted to applying scholarly ideas to the presentation of antiquities. This bias is reinforced in Empson's plan, where the principles of Linnaeus were designated as the basis for structuring the natural history collections, and by the fact that no such equivalent is cited for the other collections. Thus, the antiquities displays did not reveal the same concern for arranging specimens according to the latest theoretical ideas as did the natural history displays, where specimens were distributed according to class, genus, and species so as to communicate the existence of a sense of order in nature. It was not until nearly fifty years later, when the museum's first main collections of antique sculpture were acquired, that antiquities were presented with the intention of conveying the principles of a discipline or field of study. In this case, it was the principles of art history that structured the presentation of the antiquities, where the goal was to place objects within a system that indicated the level of their "progression" in relation to each other.

From descriptions of the displays, it appears that specimens and artifacts were crowded into cabinets and shelves. It appears that very little was left freestanding or unprotected by a case, a significant factor here being the security of the collection. The abundance of objects enhanced the sense of awe and wonder visitors would experience, creating its own dizzying visual effect. Significantly, however, the ceilings, which were heavily utilized in early modern displays, were abandoned as a display zone. As for the juxtaposition or spatial relationship of objects, it appears that the smaller objects were randomly clustered together in the cabinets, and the larger ones that were situated outside or placed in the entrance hall were featured alongside other curiosities. This is with the exception of the mummies, of course, which were featured alongside shabtis, urns, and amulets in the first exhibition room. In a paradoxical way, this can be perceived as an extremely early and unconscious attempt at contextual presentation, where objects found in association with each other were displayed together. Even so, the museum's curators were far more explicit about how natural history specimens related to each other, and by contrast, the layout of the antiquities was not done in order to demonstrate a connection between the different types or classes of antiquities. It is also significant that the Egyptian antiquities were displayed alongside both the natural and artificial objects in the museum. The association of Egyptian antiquities with the natural curiosities in the first exhibition room enhanced their status as weird and wondrous objects more than as antiquities, and in this sense they were as at home with the unusual specimens of natural history as they were with other items of antiquity. The mummies, for instance, were just as connected to the petrified backbone of an elephant as they were to the ancient utensils from Pompeii. Based on the idea that objects are defined by their associations with other objects as much as they are by their original function, it is clear that the Egyptian antiquities were defined first and foremost as curiosities, and that their identity as antiquities was neglected.

As regards the architecture of the building in which the collection was housed and the interior decoration of the rooms in which it was displayed, it is clear that the Egyptian antiquities' status as curiosities was reinforced here as well. Distinguished by its highly ornate interiors, Montagu House was well known for its grand staircase and elaborately painted ceilings depicting classical mythology.[78] Like the wasp's nest, large crocodile, and other curious specimens, the Egyptian remains would have stood out as strange objects in the context of this ornately decorated mansion. Furthermore, the more notable Egyptian items, especially the mummies, would have been seen immediately after proceeding up the famous staircase and viewing the images of Greek gods on the ceilings. Such a contrast would have emphasized the exotic and foreign nature of Egyptian antiquities. With regard to the decoration of the rooms, we know that consideration was given to the fabrics, wall color, and display furniture that would be most suited to present the collections; however, these were quite modest when compared to those employed in contemporary private collections (e.g., tables "without useless ornament"). Finally, on the subject of interpretive aids, some labeling was used, but this was sparse and basic. As there was no official guidebook and commercial ones were rare, the guides (museum's officers) appear to have been the primary vehicle through which visitors gained information to the displays. Their lack of knowledge and manner (see "Reception" section below) suggests that although the general purpose of the displays was to inform and enlighten, they were ostensibly presented as curiosities.

While on a specific level, the Egyptian objects in the museum were presented in the manner of the cabinets of curiosities, on a more general level they conveyed the didactic type of presentation being developed by collectors in the eighteenth century. Thus, although they were reminiscent of the former style of display in that specimens of *artificialia* and *naturalia* were combined in an eclectic manner, they were also representative of the more scientific types of displays in that the presence of different classes of objects was intended to communicate the emergence of new fields of study. Furthermore, in collections like that of Sloane, the delineation of specialized disciplines was becoming apparent. For example, Sloane's natural history collections were recognized as comprehensive, particularly the botanic component. Thus, the Egyptian collection was associated with a well-known scientific collection and to some extent assumed a scientific status.

In summary, the arrangement of Egyptian antiquities at the British Museum played a key role in constructing an identity for such objects as "wondrous curiosities." The definition of "curiosities" warrants some attention here, since such objects were imbued with a wide variety of meanings. Presented as examples of the strange and unusual amid larger collections of cultural and natural material, curiosities were often used to signify something that was unknowable and mysterious. On the other hand, they were presented as objects that were deemed appropriate for superficial consumption rather than deeper intellectual contemplation. Another distinctive characteristic of curiosities was their independence from a meaningful developmental sequence; rather, they existed as timeless, isolated examples of the strange.[79] Even so, objects could be defined as curiosities through association. For example, an Egyptian figurine displayed as part of an art collection would have been defined by association as art, but if situated alongside a wasp nest and the skeleton of a sea unicorn, would be firmly typecast as a curiosity. In this sense, the term "curiosity" functions on both a specific and a general level. Finally, and perhaps most significant, curiosities were defined by the emotions they generated or the immediate response they elicited from viewer—these typically being awe and amazement.

The museum's displays of ancient Egypt can be seen as adopting the primary characteristics of early modern displays outlined in chapter 1. More specifically, the display of the Egyptian objects at the museum differs very little from the way in which they were displayed in the didactic study collections, where they were typically featured alongside other rarities and unusual specimens.[80] In these "proto-museums" antiquities were often incorporated into the displays as a point of contrast for the items of natural history. The same might be said for the museum's first displays of Egyptian material, where the objects were compared more often to the natural history items than the other antiquities. Furthermore, in the early modern collections, the amassing together of many different types of objects would have encouraged visitors to see the Egyptian antiquities in terms of their place in a much wider picture, which was that of the world itself. Here they were but one part of the universe, demonstrating, like the other curiosities, its capacity to produce wonders. Within this framework, antiquities spoke far more about the taste for the curious than they did about the history of ancient civilizations.

Having noted this attribution of meaning, it is important to acknowledge that by the mid-eighteenth century Egyptian antiquities were being presented according to two basic modes of exhibition. While the first and most common method was to display these objects as curiosities, as exemplified in the British Museum, the second was to present them according to the conventions of sculptural display established in the early art collections of the Renaissance, where they were defined as aesthetic objects.[81] Even when they were featured alongside other works of antique sculpture, however, the Egyptian works were presented as exotica amid the larger collections of classical art, and in this sense they were still cast as curiosities. This treatment of Egyptian antiquities in art collections and at the museum is hardly surprising, considering that so little was known about the origins and significance of such antiquities at the time. However, while the somewhat casual approach to presenting the Egyptian material may be forgiven, the fact remains that an identity was unintentionally bestowed upon this set of objects by the way they were placed in the rooms of the museum.

RECEPTION

In analyzing the reception of the Egyptian displays it is necessary to determine who the audiences of the museum were in its early days, what the conditions of access to the museum were at the time, and how knowledge of ancient Egypt and other theoretical frameworks may have had an impact on museum visitors. In considering how these factors would have conditioned the types of responses visitors had to the exhibits, it is also important to take into account the individual perspectives each visitor would have brought to his or her perception of the Egyptian collection. Knowledge of the range of visitors who would have seen the first Egyptian exhibits can be gained from the museum's regulations on access, which were very restrictive and would have immediately excluded many members of society. For instance, in seeking to gain admission to the museum, visitors had to apply in writing for a ticket beforehand, and with only ten tickets per hour available for the weekdays in which the museum was open, it was clear that only the well connected or well educated would be guaranteed entry.[82] Furthermore, the trustees themselves seemed somewhat reluctant when referring to the museum's intention to be accessible to the general public. Stating that the collections were "chiefly designed for the use of learned and studious men, both natives and foreigners," they add that the "advantages accruing from it [the museum] should be rendered as general as possible."[83]

From visitor accounts we know that the types of people who applied for tickets to the museum predominantly included scholars, artists, antiquarians, collectors, scientists, writers, and travelers. However, as indicated in Empson's plan on the arrangement of the collections, the museum anticipated visits not only from the "judicious and intelligent," but also from the "curious."[84] While this suggests that the uneducated visitor was included in the museum's audience, Empson was probably referring to those advantaged members of society seeking to have an entertaining experience. For such people, a visit to the museum would have been a fashionable pastime or social obligation; however, as there were no other institutions of this kind in London, many would have been genuinely interested in seeing such a place.[85] An illuminating perspective on the presence of the less educated in the galleries of the new museum appears in a guide to London from 1774, where we are informed of the futility of the visits made by the "ignorant" and the "idle":

> This is certainly one of the most valuable institutions for promoting literary knowledge in the universe, and the vast number of valuable manuscripts

has already thrown great light on the history of England. But when we consider the vast number of idle people, who come to view the curiosities, and who by their ignorance can never relish their beauties, we cannot help applying it to the following words of the poet:

'Tis strange the miser should his cares employ
To gain those riches he can ne'er enjoy.
Is it less strange the prodigal should waste
His wealth, to purchase what he ne'er can taste?
Not for himself he sees, or hears, or eats,
Artists must chuse him masters, music, meats.
He buys for Topham drawings and designs,
For Fountains statues, and for Curio coins.
Old monkish manuscripts for Hearne alone,
And books for Mead, and rarities for Sloane.
Think you these things are for himself? no more
than his fine wife (my lord) or fine whore.
—*Pope's Epistle to the Earl of Burlington.*

There are but few people, even at this age, who can relish all, or even any of the beauties of those curiosities in the British Museum. Idle girls, or, which is still worse, idle men and women, may go there and admire, for a few minutes, the color of a snake, or the enormous jaws of a crocodile; but they will return neither wiser nor better; the image will soon be effaced from their minds, their understandings being as much darkened as their memories are unretentive.[86]

. .

Finally, while the museum was open to women and children, these visitors were not permitted to see the "monsters" and "anatomical preparations" (skeletons and body parts) contained in the base story as these were judged to be "not proper objects for all persons, particularly women with Child."[87]

The museum's displays were created at a time of growing academic interest in the monuments of ancient Egypt. Indeed, by the time the museum had presented its first displays, European thought on ancient Egypt had developed beyond a general curiosity with its culture and heritage, to a scholarly concern with the physical remnants of its history.[88] This interest in the monuments of ancient Egypt was certainly not new, however, having grown out of a long-standing tradition of study that began in the classical period.[89] This tradition was further fueled in the medieval period by the crusaders and religious pilgrims who traveled to Egypt as part of their journeys to the Holy Land.[90] A more intense fascination with ancient Egyptian monuments began to flourish in the fifteenth and sixteenth centuries in association with their illustration in travel accounts and the reerection of obelisks in Rome.[91] Inspired by images and stories of the mysterious land of Egypt, a few adventurous scholars then set off to make more accurate recordings of the surviving monuments.[92] The publication of more detailed travelers' accounts of Egypt,[93] the recording of the monuments of Egypt,[94] the emergence of a scholarly interest in ancient Egypt in Britain,[95] and the involvement of British artists in the representation of Egypt[96] all contributed to the establishment of an antiquarian interest in ancient Egypt in the seventeenth century, which was beginning to flourish when the museum first opened its doors to the public in 1759.[97] More specifically, two important publications, namely Richard Pococke's *A Description of the East and Some Other Countries* of 1743–1745, and Frederick Norden's *Travels to Egypt and Nubia* of 1757, were contemporary with the museum's displays and may have inspired some interest in them.[98]

Finally, while a few of the more educated visitors may have had some background knowledge of the antiquities of ancient Egypt, the museum's displays were more likely to have been interpreted through a range of other lenses or frameworks. For instance, ancient Egypt was already familiar to people through classical studies, biblical history, the history of art, esoteric knowledge, and also through its representation in art, architecture, and the decorative arts,[99] and in operas, plays, and novels.[100] From these sources, a set of visual icons had already been identified with ancient Egypt, including pyramids, mummies, sphinxes, obelisks, and hieroglyphs. Thus, despite the lack of academic knowledge about Egypt, visitors were still likely to have arrived with some perceptions about this ancient culture.

Egyptologists working in the museum in the twentieth century have commented on the lack of appeal that the first exhibition of Egyptian antiquities at the museum would have had.[101] However, the reception of the displays in the early museum guidebooks, guides to London, media reviews, and visitors' accounts suggests that the Egyptian antiquities attracted a great deal of attention and were viewed as one of the major highlights of the museum. In the first guide to the museum, over four of the sixteen pages are devoted to the Egyptian material, and more description is provided for the Egyptian "curiosities" and "bronzes" than any other category of object represented.[102] Similarly, Edmund Powlett's guide to the museum of 1761 offers a lengthy description of Lethieullier's mummy and its significance, with more than four of the six pages assigned to the first exhibition room being devoted to the Egyptian items.[103] Alexander Thomson's guidebook of 1767 also discusses the mummies at length, as well as the "pieces of greenish marble" thought to belong to the "mausoleum of Cleopatra."[104] The appeal of the Egyptian antiquities is also suggested by the fact that three of the thirty plates in the first illustrated guide to the museum featured Egyptian items (figs. 2.3–2.5). Despite this, the main author of this guide, Jan van Rymsdyk, did not seem to have been entirely enamored with the Egyptian antiquities: "It is not my Intention to put myself in Perspiration concerning any of the Hieroglyphic Emblems, or Monstrosities of the Egyptians, for it is all Labour in vain, or washing a Blackamore white."[105] Furthermore, even though the illustrations of the

Egyptian antiquities were comparable in number to those featuring classical and other antiquities, suggesting that they were perceived to be of some importance, this guidebook focused on the more unusual objects in the museum and therefore reinforced the status of Egyptian antiquities as curiosities.[106] Interest in the Egyptian antiquities above other collections in the museum is also seen in London guidebooks and the media. In *London and Its Environs Described* of 1761, for example, the only specific object referred to in the museum is the mummy in the vestibule, and the *Imperial Magazine* reproduced the long section from Powlett on the mummies for its readers.[107]

Beyond the more formal accounts in the guidebooks, early visitors' comments indicate how popular the Egyptian antiquities were. Indeed, before the museum was even opened the Egyptian mummies were singled out among the collections. Catherine Talbot, for example, who visited the museum in 1756, commented that she "liked it much better now, inhabited by Valuable Mss [manuscripts], Silent Pictures, & Ancient Mummies, than I should have done when it was filled with Miserable Fine People."[108] From these early days until the end of the century, an interest in the mummies (including their coffins) was expressed in many visitors' accounts. For example, in the Reverend Weeden Butler's play of 1767 they are singled out as a highlight for the visiting party; in 1780 the boy John Coltman recalled them as the first thing he saw; in 1782 Carl Philip Moritz highlighted them; in 1786 Sophie La Roche referred to the "swathings of Egyptian mummies"; and in 1791 Gebhardt Wendeborn noted that together with the other items in hall they "immediately engaged the attention of a stranger."[109] The focus on mummies in these accounts was hardly surprising, since complete mummies were so rare in British collections.[110] However, it is significant that among the many other thousands of rarities in the museum, it is typically the mummies that are referred to by visitors.

That the Egyptian antiquities might be appreciated for their informational potential is suggested only in a very general sense. For example, when commenting on the antiquities room in 1761, Powlett stated how "Many Things deemed of small Value by a vulgar Observer, when viewed by the Learned are found to be of abundant Use to Science."[111] Thus, the notion that the seemingly unimpressive assemblage of antiquities might have some value for learning and study is presented in relation to the idea that these objects were useful for illustrating cultural progress and the history of art. Indeed, Powlett informs the visitor that in the displays of the "artificial" productions "we may here see the Progress of Art in the different Ages of the World."[112] Within this scheme, the Egyptian antiquities were destined to become defined as a primitive form of art that was more closely allied to the modern ethnographic objects than the classical antiquities.

Despite the focus on the mummies, early visitors did refer to other

Egyptian antiquities, and some even offered evaluations of these objects. For example, in 1790 the Russian traveler Nikolai Karamzin highlighted "an amazing Egyptian cup of porous clay," advising that "if you fill it with water and insert a lettuce seed into any of its external pores, it will take root and within a few days will send forth shoots."[113] More detailed, however, was the assessment of Egyptian antiquities offered in Alexander Thomson's account of 1767, which after observing that the Egyptians had "degenerated into so gros [*sic*] and amazing an idolatry," then proceeded to outline the role of ancient Egypt in the museum:

> I have now got among the antiquities of those parts of Greece and Italy, where all the polite arts were carried to the highest perfection. But the stop I made in Hetruria, has greatly weakened the contrast, which I expected would be stronger, had I passed immediately from the Nile to the Tyber. From a land where a deity was represented with the head of a dog; where a lion was the most respectable inhabitant of one city, and an ox of another; from a people immersed in mystery, to Rome and Athens, where wit and elegance resided; the cities of heroes and demi-gods.[114]

Thus, the display of Etruscan antiquities is considered to weaken the educational effect or impact that would be made if the visitor went straight from the primitive-looking Egyptian remains to the perfectly assembled Greek ones. Here we see how ancient Egypt is expected to serve as a heuristic device, its purpose being to demonstrate the extent of the achievements of the ancient Greeks. A similar view is conveyed in Weeden Butler's play on the museum, where upon being asked if he had seen a mummy, the character Index replies: "No I neither Madam. But there is the case to put one in, if you chose it. Those hieroglyphical scrawls, that awkward stiffness, their vile Daublings, and a variety of uncouth *et ceteras*, may convince you of its being a genuine Egyptian effort of art."[115] Although intended to be humorous, the lines assigned to this fictional visitor give us an idea of how the Egyptian antiquities were devalued because of their style and content. The "awkward stiffness" or lack of movement in the objects was a common response to Egyptian antiquities that was to remain a focal point for attack over the next century.

Such assessments reflect how it was primarily through biblical history and theories of the history of art that the Egyptian antiquities were understood. For instance, curiosity about how these remains could shed light on the stories of the Old Testament concerned the visitor more than a desire to learn about Egyptian culture itself. More significantly, within the context of biblical history, ancient Egypt was often described in negative terms, and this appears to have influenced visitors' perception of the remains. For example, in the well-known physician and collector John Woodward's treatise, "Of the Wisdom of the Antient Egyptians," ancient Egypt is defined as a society characterized by its vanity, boastfulness, carelessness, superstition, indulgence in adultery, theft, and the "wearing of promiscuous garments."[116] Egyptian religion is described as "sunk in idolatry" and as "undoubtedly the wildest and most fantastic that the sun ever saw." Woodward argues that by worshiping animals as gods, the ancient Egyptians "not only exposed religion to scoffs and derision, but likewise laid a foundation for the most wretched sort of superstition among the more simple and weak people."[117] What is significant in this appraisal is that it is closely aligned with a critique of the artistic productions of ancient Egyptians, with sculpture described as "not only rude, but done in a manner much different from that of Greece."[118] After denouncing their skills in architecture, Woodward proceeds to outline their lack of success in sculpting:

> There never appears one single figure that shews any thing of art or good work. Their limbs are stiff, and ill-proportioned; their bodies awkward, shapeless, and far inferior to the life. Nor were the formers of them wanting only in art and performance, for their design was bad. No people living had ever so enormous and perverse a fancy as they appear to have had. They really aimed at something that was hideous, deformed, and monstrous; a beast, or a fowl, with the head and face of a man; the head of a dog, or some other brute, of an hawk, or the like, upon an human figure. . . . They seem to have affected what was ugly and irregular, as much as the Greeks, the Romans, and others, who had something of spirit and a genteel fancy, did what was handsome, well-proportioned, beautiful, and like nature. . . . In like manner in their historical or hieroglyphical gravings, upon their obelisks, and other monuments, every thing is flat, stiff, and ill finished.[119]

Here we see the prominence of a theme that would come to characterize many subsequent assessments of Egyptian antiquities—Egyptian art was inferior because it did not imitate nature. That the objects were not judged in their own right, or in terms of what they aimed to achieve, is shown by the comparisons to Greek and Roman antiquities where they were typically found wanting.

The negative appraisals of Egyptian art also reflected contemporary ideas in scholarship on the history of art, and in philosophical debates on aesthetics, where concepts of beauty and the sublime were expounded upon. In the former, the influence of Johann Winckelmann was paramount; his classic text *The History of Ancient Art* of 1764 articulated the principles by which all ancient art came to be understood.[120] His historical scheme, in which the development of ancient art culminated with the accomplishment of the ancient Greeks, relegated Egyptian antiquities to a primitive stage in the evolution of art, where they were seen as not having attained the beauty and grace of classical Greek art. More specifically, within this framework Egyptian art became a foil to Greek art, functioning as its primitive and hopelessly inferior precursor. This negative assessment centered on the idea that Egyptian artists were deficient in representing the human figure; noting their "incorrect rendering" of bodily parts and their "feeble markings of the muscles and bones," Winckelmann described the Egyptian portrayal of figures as "stiff and constrained" and with "no action at all."[121] In this sense, Winckelmann can be seen as formalizing the view that Egyptian antiquities should be displayed separately from Greek and Roman ones because they failed to possess the same qualities of refinement, grace, and beauty. In the museum, the classical antiquities were better suited to the architectural mode of presentation that saw interior decoration and architectural features all work together to evoke a sense of grandeur and beauty.

In eighteenth-century aesthetic discourse, concepts of beauty were articulated in relation to advancing theories for moral improvement in society, and within this context Egyptian antiquities were also devalued because as curiosities they did not exhibit any traits that could be remotely connected with beauty.[122] Although Winckelmann's views and aesthetic discourse were highly influential in promoting the dismissal of Egyptian art, more optimistic evaluations could be found in the work of others. While Norden expressed a more appreciative attitude toward the style of Egyptian monuments,[123] the leading proponent of a "pro-Egyptian" approach was the architect and engraver Giovanni Battista Piranesi. Challenging Winckelmann's characterization of Egyptian sculpture, Piranesi articulated the first "modern" evaluation of Egyptian art.[124] In comparing the two Greek- and Egyptian-style sculpted lions on the Acqua Felice fountain in Rome, he asserted the cause of Egyptian art in a way that had not been done before:

> What majesty in the Egyptian ones, what gravity and wisdom, what union, and modification of parts! How artfully are those parts set off which are agreeable to architecture, while those are suppressed which are not advantageous to it! Those other lions on the contrary, which are exactly copied from nature, and to which the artist capriciously gave what attitude he pleased, what have they to do there? They only serve to diminish the great effect which the Egyptian ones gave to the architecture of that fountain.[125]

Further praise came with the observation that the sculptor of the sphinx on the Campus Martius obelisk had a "perfect knowledge of all that is good and beautiful in nature. I am certain that an understanding eye will see in it not only the grand and the majestick [*sic*], which no one denies to the Egyptians, but likewise that delicacy, that fleshiness, and that palpableness, which is supposed to have been known only to the Greeks, and never to the Egyptians."[126] Despite Piranesi's attempt to accord Egyptian sculpture with its own distinctive artistic accomplishments, it would be some time before others were able to describe it in this way.[127] Furthermore, while his bold attempts to create an Egyptian taste in design were criticized at the time, they were to become highly influential in establishing a vogue for Egyptomania.[128]

Beyond the religious, art historical, and philosophical frameworks, the reception of the Egyptian displays also revealed an awareness of the esoteric associations of ancient Egypt. Since Greek and Roman times Egyptian cults had been popular, and in the mid-eighteenth century an interest in Egyptian religion was still apparent.[129] The connection of ancient Egypt with mysticism is closely associated with the translation of a series of texts referred to as the *Corpus Hermeticum* in 1463. These were thought to have been written by an Egyptian priest and philosopher called Hermes Trismegistus, who was described as the founder of ancient pagan religion, but they are now known to have been compiled in Roman times. While ancient Egypt was already thought to be a source of great wisdom and magic, the museum's display of animal deities and other "strange" idols carved in stone would have greatly enhanced this idea.

The wider visual context in which the Egyptian antiquities were presented would also have influenced how they were perceived, and in this sense it is important to note the perception of the museum as a giant cabinet of curiosities. That the museum was seen as a repository of wonders is evidenced in accounts in the topographical books on London; John Entick, for example, commented on the "amazing number and variety of curiosities" in his *A New and Accurate History and Survey of London*.[130] A far more vivid impression of the museum written by John Coltman, a boy of twelve, gives an idea of the context in which the Egyptian antiquities would have been viewed:

> It [the British Museum] is a very grand building, consisting of a great many rooms, all filled with curiosities. First we saw Egyptians that had been dead three thousand years ago. Next we saw the skull of an elephant, and the Queen of Otaheite's hat, the crown big enough to hold you, and the brim of it not much unlike the mat that lies at the bottom of our stairs. There was a piece of the wall of Babylon, and the head-dress of a lady five thousand years ago. In another room there was all sorts of birds; birds of Paradise, and humming birds, the most beautiful colours that I could imagine. The next room was filled with all kinds of serpents and lizards once alive, and some of them with wings. There was a pair of gloves made of the beards of mussels; also some snakes and rattle-snakes, and sword fishes, etc., and a crocodile which was such a monstrous great thing, he could have eaten three or four men for a breakfast. We next saw the jaw-bone and head of a whale; the jaw-bone was such a monstrous thing, I could have stood upright in it. There were thousands of other things, which I have not time to enumerate, and, indeed, we could not stay to look at half of them.[131]

This lively account conveys how visitors encountered Egyptian objects in association with a range of curious items, all of which were assembled together in order to create an immediate impact. While children like John Coltman were delighted with the size and diversity of the collections in the museum, the more learned visitors were critical of it. Writing of his visit in 1784, the French naturalist Barthélemy Faujas de Saint-Fond expressed his disappointment at the "crowd of heterogeneous objects" added to Sloane's original collection, which were "calculated rather to distract, than to command the attention."[132] As a scientist, Faujas de Saint Fond considered the orderly presentation of specimens to be of prime importance and here again he expressed great dissatisfaction: "everything is out of its place; and this assemblage is rather an immense magazine, in which things seem to have been thrown together at random."[133] Faujas de Saint Fond would have been disappointed with Coltman's letter, as his aspirations for the museum would have seen children responding in an altogether different manner: "In a word, youth, so inquisitive, and so fond of novelty, will here find no excitement to study by the attractive lure that is so capable of cultivating his tastes when these are flattered and captivated by a collection wherein order and neatness reign throughout all its arrangement."[134] Thus, for some visitors, the arrangement of the collections was recognized to be an important factor in according objects with meaning. This role is further emphasized in relation to the education of artists: "It may be presumed, that as long as so repulsive a confusion is suffered to continue, no artists will ever be induced to go there, to acquire those branches of information which relate to the materials he uses, and the sources whence they are derived."[135]

Responses such as these emphasize the extent to which all the contents of the museum were reduced to superficial curiosities of little value in learning. The idea that the great diversity of things to see overwhelmed visitors is also conveyed by the Reverend Thomas Campbell, who said of his visit to the British Museum in 1775 that "the sight was so various that it is hard to remember anything distinctly."[136] The perception of Egyptian antiquities would also have been strongly shaped by the first encounter that visitors had with them, this first impression creating an immediate visual impact that was hard to discard or replace. The decision to place the donations to the museum in a separate room, which resulted in the mummies being separated from the rest of the Egyptian collection, was thus a very important one. Here, alongside the skull of an elephant, Egyptian antiquities were defined as wonders or curiosities. This meant that they were not seen as objects of learning, but rather, were received as a form of "light entertainment." Like the stuffed jaybird and large brainstone, Egyptian antiquities were valued for their shock value as opposed to their instructional content.

Finally, in addressing how the Egyptian antiquities were received it is also important to describe the general nature of the viewing experience that visitors would have had at the museum. With little or no background knowledge on ancient Egypt, and with little assistance in the way of labels and informed knowledge from the guides, visitors could not be expected to have had more than a superficial response to Egyptian antiquities. For instance, there were no official guidebooks; the few popular handbooks that were available were highly selective in what they chose to describe; the labeling of objects was limited and sporadic; and the guides had very little knowledge of the collections.[137] Furthermore, since the trustees recommended that smaller objects be locked in drawers with glass or wire to protect them, we do not know how much was visible upon entering a room, or indeed, was shown to visitors.[138] Most significant, however, was the fact that people were not able to walk freely among the collections and that the guided tour they were given was very short. Commenting on the speedy nature of his visit in 1784, William Hutton provides a fascinating glimpse into the museum in its early days:

> We assembled on the spot, about ten in number. . . . We began to move pretty fast, when I asked with some surprise, whether there were none to inform us what the curiosities were as we went on? A tall genteel young man *in person*, who seemed to be our conductor, replied with some warmth, "What! Would you have me tell you everything in the museum? How is it possible? Besides, are not the names written upon many of them?" I was too much humbled by this reply to utter another word. . . .
>
> If a man pass two minutes in a room, in which are a thousand things to demand his attention, he cannot find time to bestow on them a glance each. . . .
>
> If I see wonders which I do not understand, they are no wonders to me. Should a piece of withered paper lie on the floor, I should, without regard, shuffle it from under my feet. But if am told, it is a letter written by Edward the Sixth, that information sets a value upon the piece, it becomes a choice morsel of antiquity, and I seize it with rapture. . . .
>
> The history and the object must go together; if one is wanting, the other is of little value. . . .
>
> It grieved me to think how much I lost for want of a little information. In about thirty minutes we finished our silent journey through this princely mansion, which would well have taken thirty days. . . .
>
> I had laid more stress on the British Museum than on anything I should see in London. It was the only sight that disgusted me."[139]

Besides conveying how difficult it would have been to spend any considerable time appreciating the collections, this account tells us many things about the context in which objects such as the antiquities were received. For instance, it is suggested that labels were placed on some of the objects and that this was considered to be a satisfactory explanation of their significance. However, Hutton's comments imply that the labels were either so sparsely distributed or that they were not read because visitors did not get the opportunity to stop and consult them. Furthermore, it is clear that visitors could not rely on their guide to provide an explanation of the objects. Hutton's assertion that a visit to the museum is of no use unless the objects are properly described reveals how some visitors were no longer satisfied with the consumption of objects as items of awe and wonder. His poignant statement that the "history and object must go together" demonstrates that there were those who expected more than just visual spectacle.

European visitors were equally critical of the viewing conditions in which they viewed the collections. For example, in 1772 the French writer Pierre-Jean Grosely commented that "the cursory view that visiters [*sic*] are obliged to be satisfied with, through fear of encroaching upon their complaisance, makes them over look a number of objects which deserve to be attentively considered."[140] Furthermore, the German visitor Carl Philip Moritz outlined the effect of being so rushed: "The rapidly passing through this vast suite of rooms, in a space of time, little, if at all, exceeding an hour; with leisure just to cast one poor longing look of astonishment on all these stupendous treasures of natural curiosities, antiquities, and literature; in the contemplation of which you could with pleasure spend years, and a whole life might be employed in the study of them—quite confuses, stuns and overpowers one."[141] He also reflected on the subject of guidebooks, reporting that although the guidebook he had brought from Germany was a source of great interest to the other members of his group, it was met with "scornful astonishment" from the custodian.[142] Finally, the German visitor Frederick Kielmansegge reasserted these criticisms in a more general critique of museums in Britain. On the problems of the qualifications of the guides, for example, he observed, "The people who show you over such places are porters, or caretakers, who seldom know much about them, merely show visitors round, and are glad when they leave. They earn their money so easily that they show you nothing at all, or only such objects as they consider worth seeing, which are usually well-known things, and to be seen every day in any collection; so that the rarest objects often escape the eye, and remain unobserved."[143]

Kielmansegge also referred to the short time allocated for viewing museum collections, noting that "it is only a pity that so little time is allowed to strangers in such places, that they can only see everything superficially, and cannot give sufficient attention to the objects of most interest."[144] Thus, like many other visitors to the British Museum, this foreign visitor identified temporal constraints as a major obstacle in interpreting the exhibits.

In conclusion, the reception of the Egyptian displays, although generally positive, was essentially a very superficial one. This both reflected and stemmed from the fact that the displays defined Egyptian antiquities as curiosities. And in this sense, the style or manner of exhibition contributed significantly to the way they were perceived. For example, if the larger objects such as the stela and the mummies had been put with the smaller antiquities in the antiquities room, the Egyptian antiquities may have appeared more like a coherent set of antiquities as opposed to one that was randomly dispersed around the museum.

* * *

The Museum's first collection of Egyptian antiquities was acquired rather serendipitously, indicating the tendency of major collectors like Sloane to include an antiquarian component in his collection because it was accepted practice to include some exotic antiquities. The range of objects was limited to desirable items that already had associations with mystery and awe and although the first displays of Egyptian antiquities in the museum did not intend to present them as highlights of the collection, their physical situation in the museum accorded them with a significant status. This was not an intentional act on the behalf of the trustees; rather, it resulted from a simple decision to distribute recently donated items in the first exhibition room. Presented as a disparate collection of miscellaneous objects, the museum defined the Egyptian antiquities as "wondrous curiosities," encouraging visitors to perceive them as strange and unknown trinkets of little scholarly merit. The reception of the early displays suggests that although the Egyptian remains were perceived as curiosities, they nevertheless obtained a special status as being some of the most celebrated objects of the museum. It was not long, however, before the opportunity came to add new layers of meaning to this definition of ancient Egypt. With the arrival of an important set of sculptural remains in 1802, Egyptian antiquities moved out of the domain of simply being curiosities—but now they were presented with a new set of problems in asserting their distinctiveness as objects of scientific and historical worth.

3 Colossal Monstrosities

THE TOWNLEY INSTALLATION OF EGYPTIAN ANTIQUITIES, 1808

In 1808 a major installation of Egyptian antiquities was opened at the British Museum in their first purpose-built gallery—the Townley Gallery. Featuring an impressive collection of sculptures, this exhibition was one of the museum's great achievements of the nineteenth century, and it played an important role in securing Britain's status as an international leader in the presentation of ancient Egypt. Since the collection upon which this exhibition was based came into the museum's possession through a major military victory over the French in 1801, it gained much notoriety in the media and was enormously popular with visitors. Indeed, it is with the installation of 1808 that we see Egyptian antiquities acquiring a new symbolic status in Britain as celebrated trophies of war. Furthermore, with its first major display of ancient Egyptian sculptures, the museum made an important contribution to defining ancient Egypt within the framework of aesthetics. Here the presentation of Egyptian antiquities in association with recently acquired Greek and Roman sculptures saw ancient Egypt firmly established as a primitive precursor to these more "civilized" ancient cultures. More specifically, the arrangement of Egyptian antiquities was presented as a comparative aid for demonstrating the supremacy of ancient Greek art, serving a heuristic function as a the baseline that would enable scholars and artists to appreciate the achievements of the classical world. In addition, the Egyptian antiquities continued to fulfill their established role as wondrous curiosities; their unusual size, subject matter, and aesthetic style ensured their prime position as crowd-pullers that satisfied an appetite for the strange and bizarre.

ACQUISITION

When the French forces landed in Egypt in 1798 to conquer the Ottoman leaders who were ruling the country, a team of 167 scientists and technicians accompanied them with the aim of recording the monuments and natural history of Egypt.[1] Under their leader, Napoleon Bonaparte, the French aimed to challenge British control of the trade route from the Mediterranean through the Red Sea and then on to India. They also sought to provide a comprehensive illustrative record of the antiquities, people, and environment of Egypt. This scholarly expedition was a fundamental part of the military campaign itself, the rationale being that the information collected would enable the French to better conquer Egypt. Although the scientific team was primarily made up of cartographers and engineers, it also included archaeologists, architects, artists, astronomers, chemists, naturalists, musicians, and shipbuilders. Much of the focus of the expedition was on antiquities, however, which the French made a significant investment in recording and collecting during the short time they were in Egypt.[2]

After landing in Egypt in June 1798, the French seized Alexandria and then quickly went on to defeat the Mamlukes at the Battle of the Pyramids near Cairo on July 21. Their victory was short-lived, however, as the British under Nelson had come to prevent the French gaining control of Egypt, and promptly went on to defeat them in the Battle of the Nile at Aboukir Bay on the August 1, 1798. The British subsequently joined with the Turks to drive the French out, and in 1799 Napoleon fled from Egypt, leaving a much-reduced French army. On the second of September 1801, the French surrendered to the British and Turkish armies, with the treaty that was drawn up stating that all antiquities possessed by the French "shall be considered as public property and subject to the disposal of the generals of the combined army."[3] This stipulation was rejected by the scholars of the French Commission, who in a deputation to the commander in chief of the British Army, General Hutchinson, threatened to destroy all their work rather than relinquish it to the British.[4] While Hutchinson agreed that they could keep their documents and natural history collections, he demanded that the antiquities be surrendered. Thus, Colonel Turner, the commander of the Third Regiment of Guards, took possession of the collection of antiquities and presented it to King George III, who in turn gave it to the British Museum. Arriving in London in 1802, the items included in this collection were described in a list drawn up by Turner:

1. An Egyptian Sarcophagus
2. D'o [ditto]
3. D'o [ditto]
4. A Colossal fist
5. Five fragments of Statues with Lion's Heads
6. A mutilated figure kneeling
7. Two antique Statues, Roman, as large as life
8. A stone with three inscriptions
9. Four statues with Lion's Heads, as large as life
10. Two small fragments of Statues with Lion's heads
11. A small figure kneeling
12. Five fragments of Statues with Lions Heads

13. A Fragment of a Sarcophagus
14. Two Obelisks
15. A Colossal Ram's head
16. A Statue of a Woman sitting
17. A Fragment of a Statue with a Lions Head
18. A Stone with hieroglyphics
A chest of Oriental manuscripts
Three large pieces of Columns of Porphyry
One D'o [ditto] of Granite.[5]

Among this group of sculptures it was the sarcophagi (of Nectanebo II and Hapmen; see plates 2 and 3), the statues with lion's heads (of Sekhmet), the obelisks (of Nectanebo II), the colossal ram's head and colossal fist of Ramesses II, the statue of a "woman" (Roy) sitting, and the stone with three inscriptions (the Rosetta Stone) that were assigned the most importance (figs. 3.1–3.7).[6] With these acquisitions, the beginnings of the museum's Egyptian sculpture collection began, and although modern Egyptologists have stated that there were no "masterpieces" among the objects seized from the French, many of the sculptures remain favorites of the collection to this day.[7] What is most significant, however, is the fact that the acquisition of this set of objects saw the museum's Egyptian collection instantly transformed from a limited and disparate one that was primarily made up of smaller antiquities, to a substantial and more cohesive one that was characterized by larger sculptural works.

In addition to the works acquired from the French, the museum's Egyptian collection was augmented by several other objects around this time. In listing the thirty-nine objects displayed in the Egyptian sculpture gallery, the museum's first *Synopsis* or guidebook of 1808 reveals that most of the new additions in this room had come to the museum as donations, rather than as purchases.[8] For example, four objects were presented by Earl Spencer, two by Charles Townley, and one each from Dr. Nancroft and Mr. T. Philipe.[9] The *Synopsis* also mentions that the bulk of the collection in the smaller Egyptian room came to the museum via donations from Sir Hans Sloane, William Hamilton, Charles Townley, the Lethieulliers (William, Pitt, and Smart), and Thomas Hollis.[10] To this it is added that "a small number of articles likewise have been occasionally purchased by order of the trustees," but it is not clear what these items were and why they were purchased.[11] The information on acquisition provided in the *Synopsis* is significant because it reveals that the Egyptian collection was not intentionally developed, but rather, grew through donation and, in the case of the 1802 acquisition, through accident. Thus, like the Sloane collection, the 1802 set of sculptures was not acquired as a result of scholarly interest in ancient Egypt, or with the aim of advancing knowledge on this ancient culture.

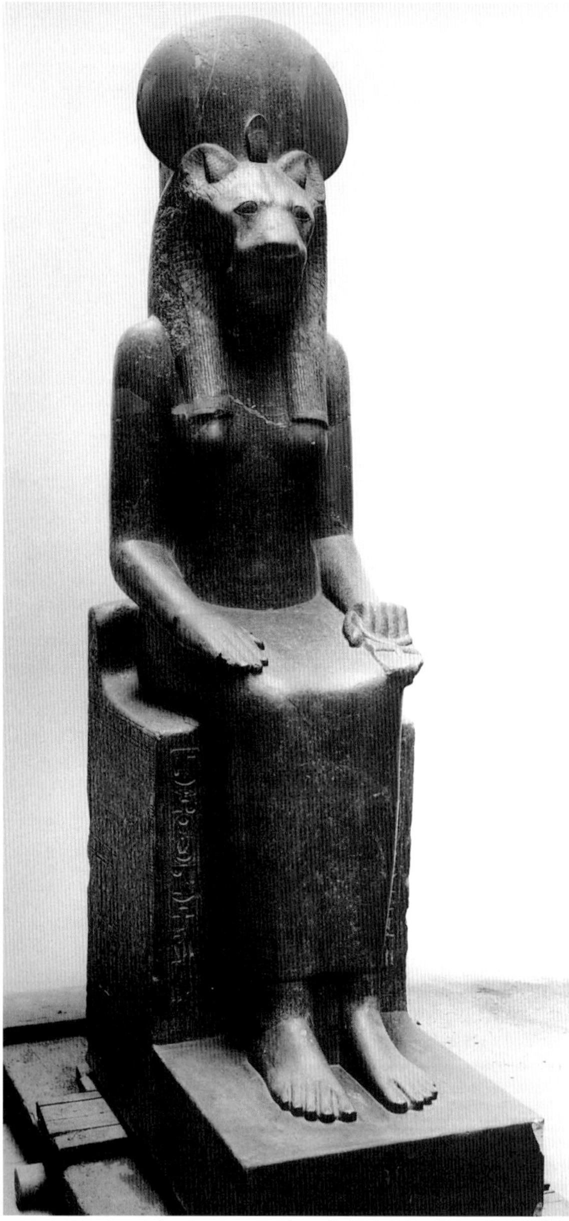

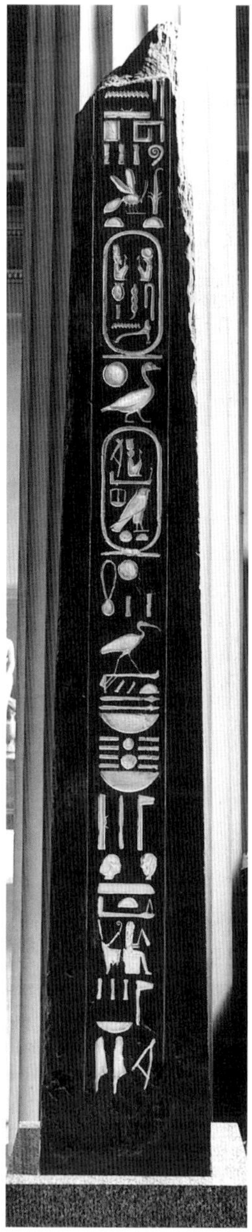

3.2a

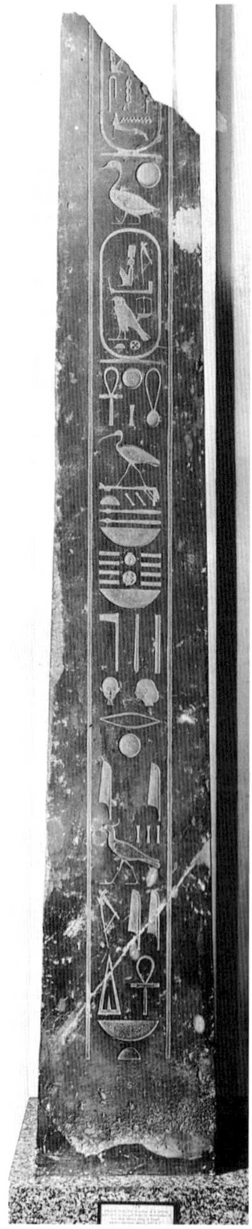

3.2b

3.1. Statue of Sekhmet (EA 88) from Karnak, Thebes, Eighteenth Dynasty. Acquired by the British Museum in 1802 as part of the British victory over the French in Egypt in 1801.

3.2a and 3.2b. Two obelisks of Nectanebo II (EA 523, 524) found in Cairo, Thirtieth Dynasty. Acquired by the British Museum in 1802 as part of the British victory over the French in Egypt in 1801.

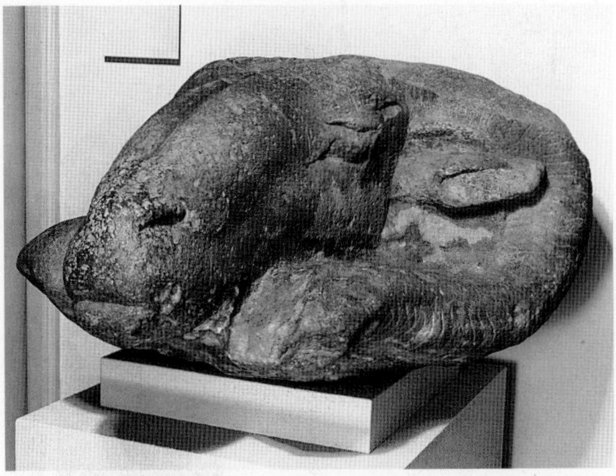

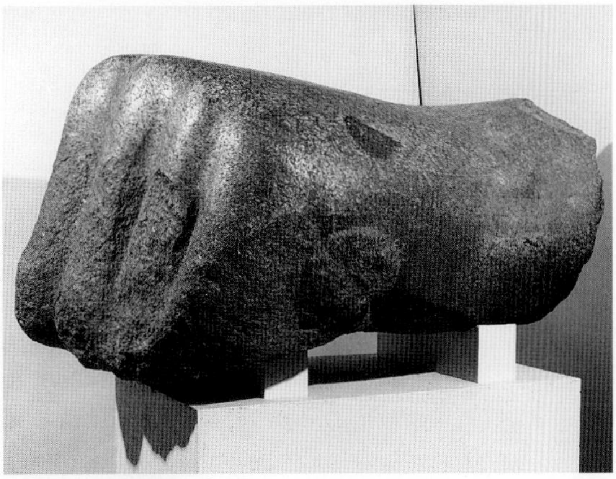

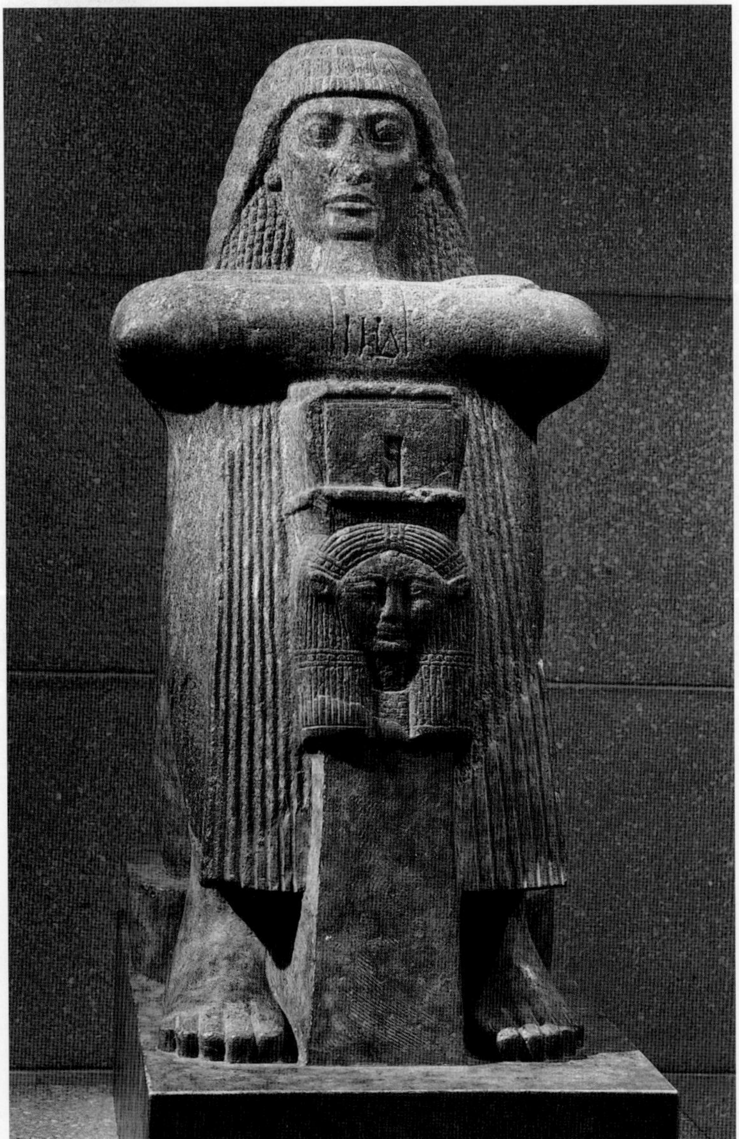

3.3. Colossal ram's head (EA 14) from Karnak, Eighteenth Dynasty. Acquired by the British Museum in 1802 as part of the British victory over the French in Egypt in 1801.

3.4. Colossal fist from a statue of Ramesses II (EA 9) from Memphis, Nineteenth Dynasty. Acquired by the British Museum in 1802 as part of the British victory over the French in Egypt in 1801.

3.5. Statue of Roy (EA 81) from Karnak, Nineteenth Dynasty. Acquired by the British Museum in 1802 as part of the British victory over the French in Egypt in 1801.

3.6. The Rosetta Stone (EA 24) from Fort St. Julien, el-Rashid (Rosetta), Ptolemaic. Acquired by the British Museum in 1802 as part of the British victory over the French in Egypt in 1801.

3.7a–c. Original sketches of the main objects seized from the French in 1801. In "An Account of Pieces of Ancient Sculptures Taken by the British Forces in Egypt . . ." British Museum, Department of Ancient Egypt and Sudan.

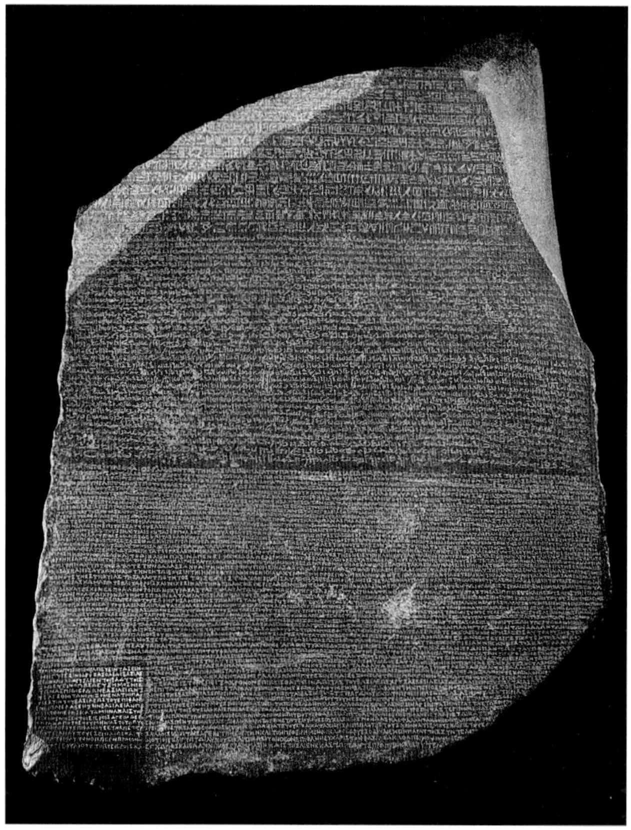

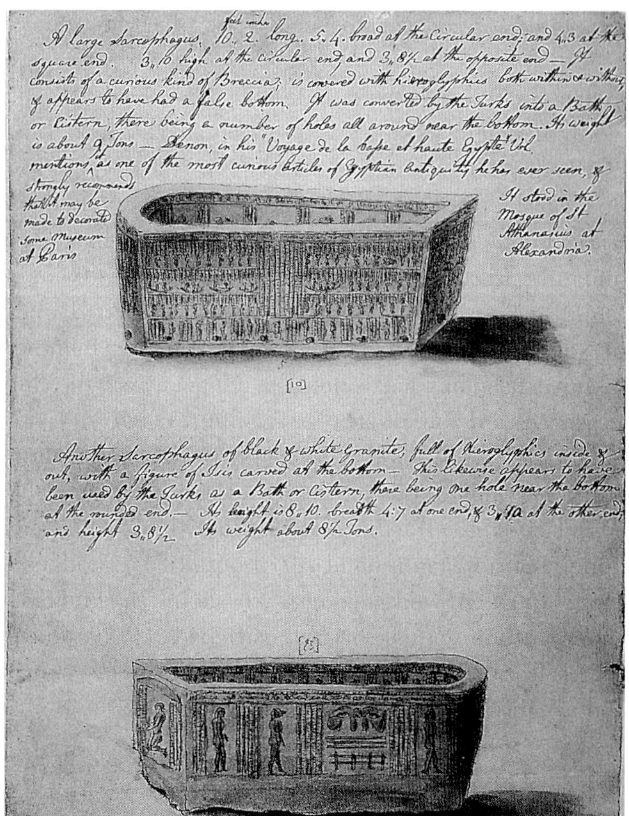

3.7a

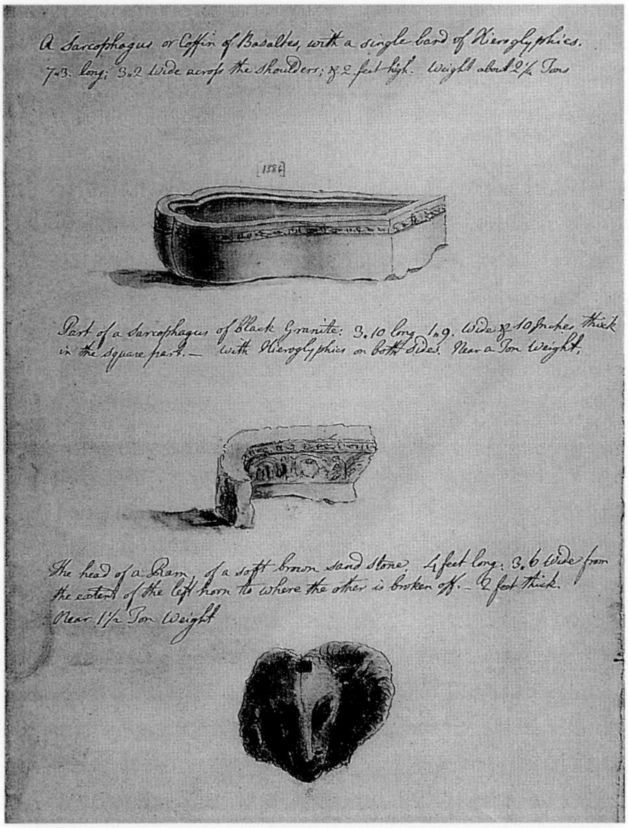
A Sarcophagus or Coffin of Basaltes, with a single band of Hieroglyphics.
7.3. long; 3.2 Wide across the Shoulders; & 2 feet high. Weight about 2½ Tons
[1887]
Part of a Sarcophagus of Black Granite: 3.10 long 1.9. Wide & 10 Inches thick
in the square part. — with Hieroglyphics on both Sides. Near a Ton Weight.
The head of a Ram, of a soft brown sand stone; 4 feet long. 3.6 Wide from
the extent of the left horn to where the other is broken off. — 2 feet thick.
Near 1½ Ton Weight

3.7b

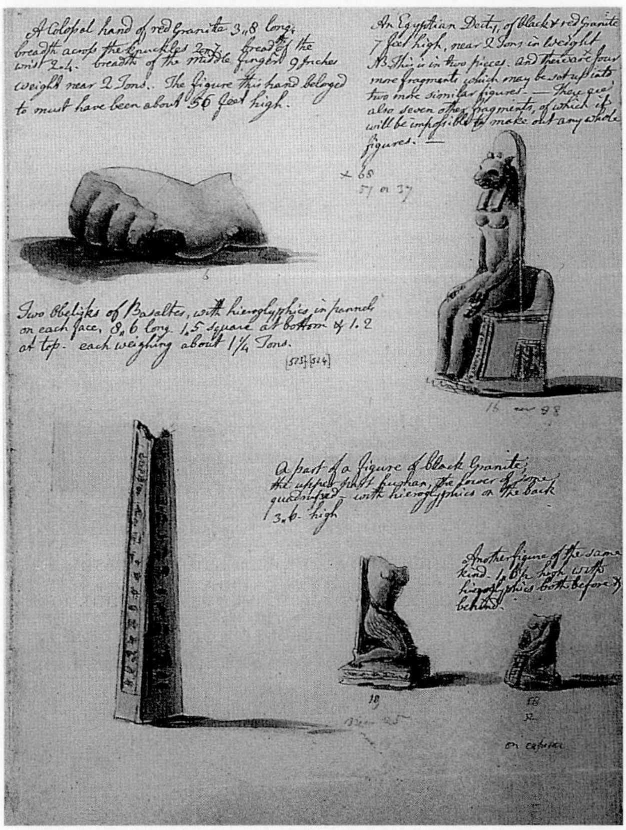
A Colossal hand of red Granite 3.8 long.
breadth across the knuckles 2.7. breadth of the
wrist 2.4. breadth of the middle finger 9 Inches
Weight near 2 Tons. The figure this hand belonged
to must have been about 56 feet high.
An Egyptian Deity, of Black & red Granite
7 feet high, near 2 Tons in Weight
NB This is in two pieces. and there are four
more fragments which may be set up into
two more similar figures. — There are
also seven other fragments, of which it
will be impossible to make out any whole
figures.
Two Obelisks of Basaltes, with hieroglyphics in pannels
on each face, 8.6 long. 1.5 square at bottom & 1.2
at top. each weighing about 1¼ Tons.
A part of a figure of black Granite;
the upper part human, the lower of some
quadruped; with hieroglyphics on the back
3.6 high
Another figure of the same
kind. 1.6 high with
hieroglyphics both before &
behind.

3.7c

Paradoxically, however, this collection was acquired as a result of the first major research expedition on Egyptian antiquities, which had expanded knowledge of the subject considerably. Indeed, the contribution of Bonaparte's scientific and artistic commission to the systematic study of Egyptian antiquities and to the subsequent establishment of Egyptology as a discipline cannot be overemphasized.[12] Most significantly, it was because of this expedition the Rosetta Stone was discovered (and thus hieroglyphs were deciphered), and two major publication projects on the monuments and antiquities of Egypt were completed.[13] The first of these to appear was Vivant Denon's three-volume work *Voyage dans la Basse et la Haute Egypte* of 1802, and the second was the *Description de l'Egypte*, which came out later in 1809–1825, and which included an impressive ten volumes of text and fourteen volumes of plates.[14] With their comprehensive and detailed accounts of the sites and monuments, these publications asserted the "scientific" potential of Egyptian antiquities like none before them; more importantly perhaps, they were extensively illustrated like no other works had been.[15]

Although Egyptian antiquities had assumed new-found importance as a result of the French expeditions, the British Museum does not appear to have been interested or influenced by these research developments. If anything, the French association with Egyptian antiquities and their positive evaluation of the distinctive artistic style of these works only served to strengthen the rejection of them by the British. Indeed, if this particular set of objects had been offered for sale to the museum, as was William Hamilton's collection of vases, it is doubtful that the trustees would have even considered purchasing it. Thus, it was more through obligation to present a collection donated by the king than through interest in ancient Egypt that the trustees accepted the objects.

Despite the museum's lack of interest in Egyptian antiquities, the much enlarged collection was accorded some importance in the museum's *Synopsis*. For instance, after thanking the king for his generous donation of the antiquities seized from the French, it is stated that "this establishment is also indebted to the munificence of the same gracious sovereign for a considerable collection of antiquities, and some natural productions, chiefly Egyptian, and among them one of the finest Mummies perhaps now in Europe, which were sent to the late Earl of Bute by Edward Wortley Montagu, Esq., and presented by the former to His Majesty, who was pleased to transfer it to the Trustees of the museum."[16] The Lethieullier family are also acknowledged for their enrichment of the Egyptian collection, "who, so early as the year 1756, began their benefactions, and continued them for several years, thereby materially increasing the collection of Egyptian Antiquities, to which they added two mummies, and a great number of idols, utensils, and other implements."[17] Clearly, the attention accorded to the Egyptian collection derived more from the circumstances in which the objects were acquired than from the aesthetic or scholarly value accorded to them. Indeed, that the king so readily transferred the mummy given to him by the Earl of Bute suggests that he was not interested in keeping it for the royal collections. Furthermore, that the mummy is highlighted as one of the "finest" perhaps now in Europe implies that this was the most significant item among the collection. The emphasis on royal donations, along with the Anglo-French rivalry so characteristic of the time, also explains why in introducing the new collection of 1802 to visitors, the *Synopsis* fails to mention how these antiquities were collected as a result of a major and unprecedented research expedition to Egypt. Egyptian antiquities may have been elevated from being perceived as wondrous curiosities, but it was as tokens of British might rather than as objects with research potential that they were valued.

Although the Egyptian collection had been significantly expanded, the range of objects remained limited in terms of providing a representative sample of Egyptian antiquities. As with the first installation of 1759, this revealed how collecting in Egypt was still fairly restrictive. The acquisition of the sculptures marked a significant departure, however, in that the transport of these objects to Europe required a far greater investment. Such objects had never before been seen in Britain; the colossal sarcophagi and figures of animal gods, for example, hardly featured in other European collections. Until this time, the Egyptian objects in collections had been easily transportable items, brought back by travelers and merchants. With the involvement of the mighty ships of empire, it was now possible to transport colossal objects of enormous weight. This profound change in the nature of the collection had major implications for the way ancient Egypt was defined in the galleries of the museum. No longer simply inconsequential items of a curious nature, the Egyptian antiquities were now featured as key participants in a dialogue on art and taste. Furthermore, the French had been selective in their approach to making this collection, focusing on pieces they considered important to be fine examples of Egyptian art. In this sense, the British had serendipitously acquired the first major collection of Egyptian antiquities that had been gathered in a somewhat systematic or focused manner.

DISPLAY

In the summer of 1802, the antiquities seized in Egypt arrived in London. As there was no place in the museum suitable for displaying them, the objects had to be temporarily housed in sheds in the courtyard.[18] The Rosetta Stone was initially deposited in the Library of the Society of Antiquaries, until later in the year when it was moved to the museum to join the other objects. In order to accommodate the new arrivals it was deemed necessary to construct a new antiquities building, and in drawing up plans for

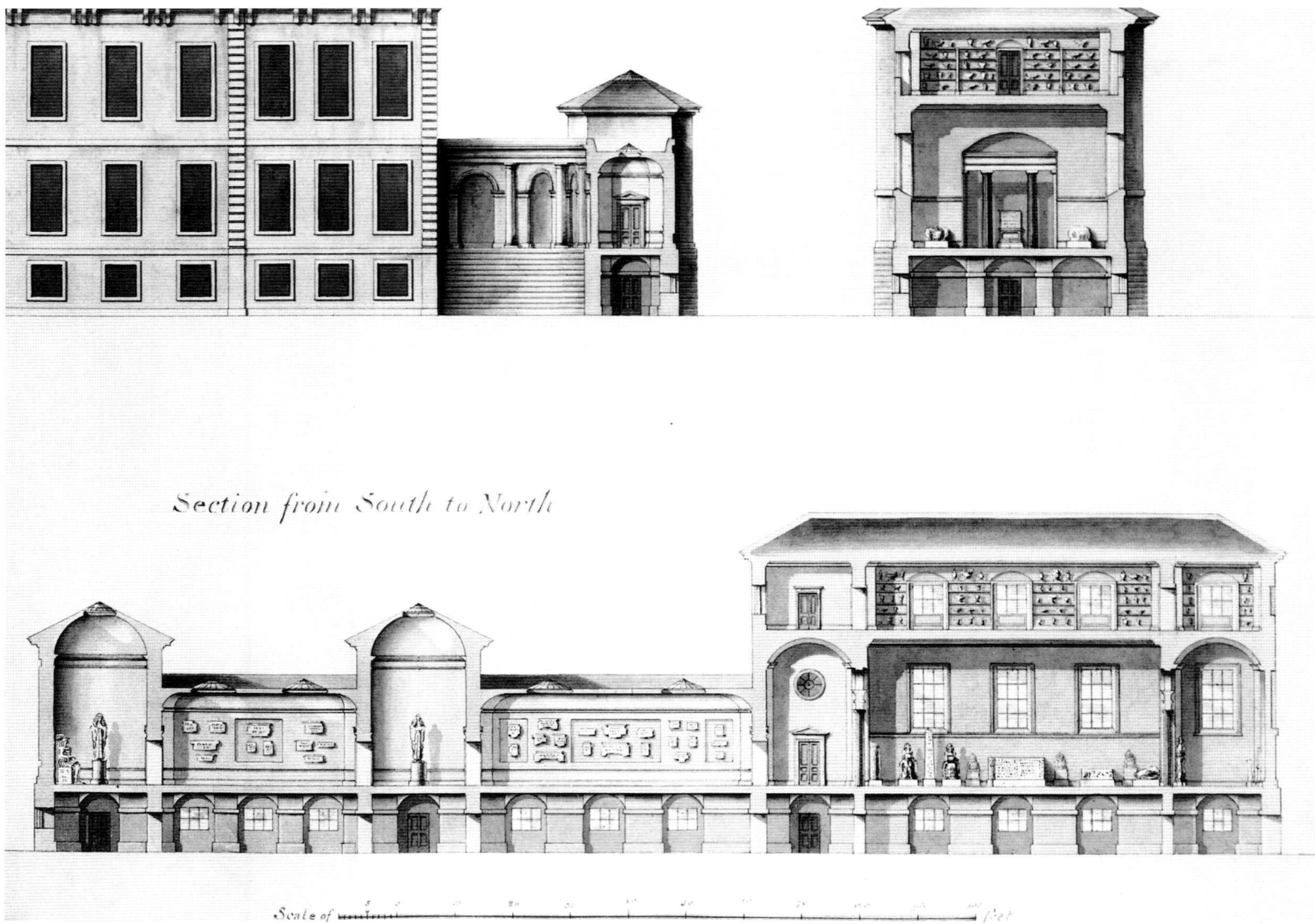
Section from South to North
Scale of 5 0 10 20 30 40 50 60 70 80 90 100 feet

3.8. (*facing*) Elevation of the new Townley building featuring Egyptian antiquities. By George Saunders 1803. Plans and Drawings of the British Museum (CE 48/4/5), British Museum, Central Archives.

such a structure, a committee of museum trustees was formed including Sir Joseph Banks, Sir William Hamilton, and Charles Townley. This committee then consulted with the architect given the responsibility for designing an appropriate extension to the museum, George Saunders.[19] In 1803 Saunders's plans were presented to the trustees by the committee, where it was proposed that a new wing be built at the northwest corner of the museum (fig. 3.8).[20] Approving Saunders's plans, the trustees petitioned Parliament in 1804 for a grant of £16,000 to enable them to proceed.[21] The House of Commons agreed to provide £8,000 to begin the work, and by the end of the year the foundations of the new building had been laid.[22] When Charles Townley died in 1805 and his well-known collection of classical sculptures was purchased by the museum, changes were made to the designs for the new building in order to accommodate this new set of antiquities.[23] With much of the exhibition space now devoted to the presentation of Townley's sculptures, the new extension thus became known as the Townley Gallery. On June 3, 1808, Queen Charlotte opened the new gallery, with the Egyptian antiquities featured in two of the thirteen rooms (plate 4). While the main Egyptian gallery contained the larger sculptures, the other Egyptian room contained the smaller antiquities previously displayed in the antiquities room and in the first exhibition room of the main museum building.[24]

When it came to determining a display strategy for the distribution of antiquities within the Townley Gallery, the building committee emphasized their qualifications for making decisions about how the sculptures would best be exhibited.[25] They claimed, for instance, to have met repeatedly at Charles Townley's house, "where they had abundant opportunities of studying the most approved methods of exhibiting works of Sculpture to advantage."[26] With clear ideas on how the sculptures should be arranged, the committee had Saunders include visual guidelines for the distribution of Egyptian sculptures in his elevations (see right-hand side of fig. 3.8).[27] Here it is possible to identify the sarcophagi, the obelisks, the porphyry column, and the ram's head, all of which appear to be placed in a basic symmetrical arrangement. More detailed decisions on the arrangement of the Egyptian sculptures were made by Henry Tresham, professor of painting at the Royal Academy, and Richard Westmacott, a sculptor and professor at the Royal Academy, both of whom were responsible for the layout of the classical sculptures in the Townley Gallery.[28] In his account of the arrangement of the collections in the new antiquities building, Westmacott only briefly referred to the distribution of the Egyptian objects, revealing that despite being the original reason for the erection of the building, they were not considered to be important in the overall scheme for arranging the antique sculptures. Indeed, the only major concern appears to have been the placement of the sarcophagus of Nectanebo II in the center of the gallery, which reflected the perception that this, along with the Rosetta Stone, was chief among the Egyptian antiquities.[29]

In terms of space, the Egyptian collection had claimed a very substantial increase in its accommodation (fig. 3.9). As the largest gallery in the Townley building, the Egyptian sculpture gallery was fifty feet long and thirty-three feet wide, the total size of the building being ninety feet long and forty-five feet wide. No longer were the Egyptian antiquities forced to compete with other objects in small, ill-suited rooms; with this new gallery-sized space they would have appeared more like a distinctive set of antiquities than an assortment of incidental curiosities. More significantly perhaps, in having their own separate gallery, the Egyptian antiquities were given the opportunity to appear as a major collection. As the first such collection available for public viewing in Britain, the display assumed an authoritative role in what it communicated about ancient Egypt. Concerning location, the two Egyptian rooms were situated between the galleries featuring Greek and Roman works, and just before the last room, which contained the finest pieces in the Townley collection. This gallery was reserved for the highlights of the museum's antiquities collection because it was at the end of the building and had the advantage of several sources of light. By placing the Egyptian collection immediately before such "treasures," a strong contrast was created whereby the artistic attainments of the classical world were made more apparent. Furthermore, by situating the Egyptian galleries in the middle of a sequence of classical galleries, the museum rendered them as something of an interruption to a theme. Finally, although it was a sizable gallery, the main Egyptian room was greatly outnumbered by all the classical galleries and in this sense would have come across as an "aside" rather than a speciality or central focus of the museum.

Although aesthetic principles guided the arrangement of the classical antiquities in the Townley Gallery, there was still some concern with structuring the collection according to subject matter. For instance, while some objects were clustered together because they were similar in size, other objects—like portraits—were grouped by theme.[30] A structured approach to the organization of the collection was called for prior to the completion of the gallery. In 1806, for example, the trustees insisted that more labeling of the items be introduced to structure the collections more clearly. However, such concerns for structure were not extended to the Egyptian collection, which lacked any thematic or contextual presentation. While it may be argued that this was because there was little knowledge upon which to guide the ordering of the Egyptian antiquities, there were precedents in thematically arranging Egyptian works. For example, at the villa of Cardinal Alessandro Albani in Rome, a display featuring Egyptian sculptures that was created around 1750–1760 situated them in a recreated Egyptian salon.[31] Other key examples include the Museo Pio-Clementino in Rome, opened at the Vatican in 1771, where Pope Clement XIV Ganganelli presented the collection of ancient papyri in a room with Egyptian décor. Similarly, at the Villa Borghese in Rome, completed in 1772, Egyptian antiquities were

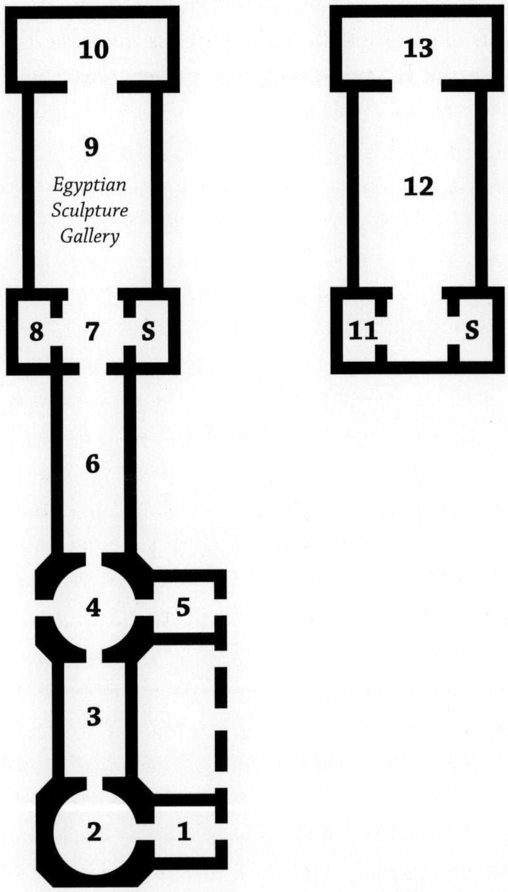

3.9. Schematic diagram of the two floors of the Townley Gallery, 1808. The Egyptian objects were displayed in rooms 8 and 9. (Rooms 1–7, 10, and 12 = Greek and Roman antiquities; room 11 = coins and medals; room 13 = print room; S = stairs. Rooms 1 and 5 adjoined the main museum building). Adapted from Cook (1977: fig. 42).

displayed in a room sumptuously decorated in the Egyptian style. Thus, while organization of the collections according to subject may have been difficult, the trustees and their appointed gallery designers might have considered adopting such trends in "contextual" presentation.

In addition, the trustees do not appear to have been affected by recent developments in Europe concerning the organization of art and antiquities in museums. Here, challenges were made to the aesthetic mode of exhibition, calling for a more systematic and chronological arrangement of art.[32] This development reflected the redefining of the great art museums as didactic institutions, where the public could be educated about the history of art. The founders of the Musée du Louvre played a critical role here, debating at length the classification of objects and the manner of their distribution.[33] Despite the decision to present the collections in an orderly chronological manner, the Louvre's first installations followed the traditional mode of presenting objects according to their stylistic qualities.[34] However, this inconsistency was soon corrected with a revised installation based on a more chronological mode of arrangement.[35] Thus, while the British Museum was working on the presentation of its first major collections of antique sculpture, a battle between two major modes of display was being waged. And despite the Louvre's experimentation with both modes, the British Museum expressed a firm allegiance to the picturesque model.

Some idea of the arrangement of the Egyptian antiquities in the Townley Gallery can be seen in the image published in *The Repository of Arts, Literature, Commerce, Manufactures, Fashions, and Politics* in 1810 (plate 4). The two large sarcophagi are the more clearly visible of the collection; with the obelisks and architectural slabs also recognizable.[36] Clearly, the size and general shape of the objects were the main criteria that determined their position, the aim being to create a sense of balance in the room through pairings of similar objects and the use of vertical and horizontal contrasts. Thus, in correspondence with the display of the sculptures in the other galleries, use of pattern and symmetry was the main display principle.[37] Furthermore, the aligning of the Egyptian objects along the walls ensured that visitors could peruse the remnants of this ancient culture in an uninterrupted fashion, taking everything in at a glance from one end of the gallery. With this kind of arrangement, where there were no objects in the center of the room to detain or engage one, visitors were effectively encouraged to pass through the room quite quickly, getting the sense that this was a thoroughfare to a more important destination. More specifically, this style of display allowed the visitor to get a glimpse of the more valued objects lying ahead, and in this case we can see how the focal or end point of the Egyptian gallery was not an Egyptian piece, but rather the classical sculpture of Discobolus placed just beyond the doorway in a central position.[38] This object, which would have constantly been in the line of vision of the visitor, would have functioned as an enticement to proceed through the Egyptian gallery into the classical one beyond it. Finally, the Discobolus sculpture would have marked a sharp contrast to the contents of the Egyptian gallery, emphasizing how different these works of art were. While the Egyptian objects appeared static, massive in scale and stylistically unusual, the classical masterpiece was full of movement, well proportioned in relation to the size of the building, and aesthetically familiar.

A major disparity between the Egyptian galleries and the classical ones can be seen in the use of display furniture and other such props. When original plans for the Townley Gallery were being made in 1803, the building committee informed the trustees that in addition to housing the Egyptian works there would also be space available for displaying "fine statues and other valuable works of art, which require sky lights and recesses of particular shapes to show them properly."[39] A clear distinction between the Egyptian and classical antiquities was made here, where the former were not deemed important enough to warrant unnecessary embellishments and the latter were described as needing particular display conditions. That such enhancements were not advocated for the Egyptian antiquities can be seen in Saunders's figure (fig. 3.8), where the classical galleries could make full use of the walls, where isolated Greek and Roman statues are featured on elaborate pedestals and in large recesses, and where reliefs are arranged in picturesque combinations on the walls. In comparison to this, the display furniture for the Egyptian display looks rather limited. Furthermore, the other Townley galleries also had more impressive entrances and exits, demarcated by terminal statues raised to eye level.[40] In contrast, the Egyptian gallery was framed with the two low-lying architectural slabs of Nectanebo I and Psamtek. A far more impressive way to introduce the collection would have been to mark the entrance with the pair of Nectanebo II obelisks.

That the staff from the Department of Antiquities were not involved in the layout of the collections reveals how the task of arrangement was assigned to experts in fine arts as opposed to scholars of antiquities.[41] This is significant because it reveals how the objects were primarily treated as aesthetic documents, as opposed to sources of historical information. This idea is further evidenced in the words of Westmacott, who stated that the objects were placed "in the situations which appear to those gentleman the most proper," essentially meaning that the objects were arranged aesthetically, or in a picturesque manner.[42] This style of arrangement, where the aim was to create a visually harmonious composition, was based on the mode of sculptural display established in the major art museums of Europe. Adopting this mode of presenting antique sculpture meant that the museum was guided by a set of conventions that had evolved for exhibiting sculpture since the sixteenth and seventeenth centuries. The central concern here was to place sculptures in arrangements that were harmonious with their architectural setting. Indeed, by the late eighteenth century, sculptures were often treated as an integral part of the architectural scheme, and the display of ancient sculpture had become a major feature of architectural decoration in the fine country homes of Europe.[43] Here grand entrance halls and saloons were decorated with collections of marble figures to make an impact. As opposed to being designed to impart knowledge, the style of this presentation revealed that aesthetic concerns were of foremost importance. The conventions for exhibiting sculptures in this context included elevating the objects on impressive stone pedestals (that were designed to enhance their scale and place them in commanding positions at eye level); spacing the sculptures evenly (to give an orderly appearance and create a sense of repeated patterning); aligning the works in rows parallel with the walls of the room (so that visitors could view the collection as a whole with ease); creating wall niches in which single objects were housed (so as to make them a highlight of the display); and placing them in symmetrical arrangements (in order to emphasize their compatibility with one another).[44] In addition to these basic display "rules," the sculptures were placed in rooms that were elaborately decorated with features such a wall paintings, sumptuous drapery, and ceiling ornaments.

With regard to the architectural style and interior design of the galleries in which the Egyptian collections were accommodated, the museum was reluctant to adopt the more flamboyant mode of presenting sculptures that was evident in the major private collections of Britain.[45] Significantly, however, the trustees did adopt some of these traits in their display of the classical antiquities in the other rooms of the Townley Gallery. For instance, the Egyptian gallery lacked decorative features such as wall niches, which were distinctive of the classical galleries. This disparity, where the Egyptian antiquities were presented according to a more much basic display style, would have communicated something about the value and significance of the collections being presented. More generally, the architectural setting and interior decoration of the museum were an important part of the presentation frame within which the Egyptian antiquities were defined. Designed in the Palladian style, the Townley building had classical elements that were compatible with the Roman and Greek antiquities displayed within. Thus, while the Greek columns at the end of the Egyptian gallery would have been complimentary with the classical statues, they would have appeared at odds with the Egyptian ones. Furthermore, although the architecture of the Townley Gallery was distinguished by modest decorative elements, the interiors of the main museum building retained their exuberant style. For instance, we can see from Augustus Pugin and Thomas Rowlandson's etching of the hall and staircase of the museum from 1808 that this was a building conveying "a magnificence becoming the residence of a nobleman" (fig. 3.10).[46] The sense of atmosphere in the museum was thus still shaped by the impressive entrance, where the staircase adorned with elaborate ironwork and the sumptuous paintings created a sense of opulence.[47] As the gestures of the visitors suggest, the interiors were obviously a key part of the museum's attraction. This decorative ambience would have contrasted with the sparsely decorated and somber gallery in which the Egyptian antiquities were accommodated, defining them as different and as not fitting in.

A critical factor in providing good viewing conditions for antique sculpture was lighting, and in this area it appears that the Egyptian remains were not accorded equal treatment to those of the classical ones.[48] We can see from Saunders's elevation of 1803 (fig. 3.8), that large side windows would have provided the major source of light for the Egyptian antiquities, in contrast to the other galleries in the building. Although the museum was pioneering in its adoption of a system of top-lighting for the antiquities galleries, it did not provide these ideal lighting conditions for the Egyptian gallery because the trustees thought the characteristics of the Egyptian pieces did not possess the "finer" qualities of classical sculpture.[49] Sidelighting had important implications for the presentation of the Egyptian sculpture, as not only would it have left the room quite dark at certain times of the day, but more significantly, it would have cast an uneven light on the objects, leaving many of their features in shadow. Despite these negative points, the poor lighting conditions also worked in the

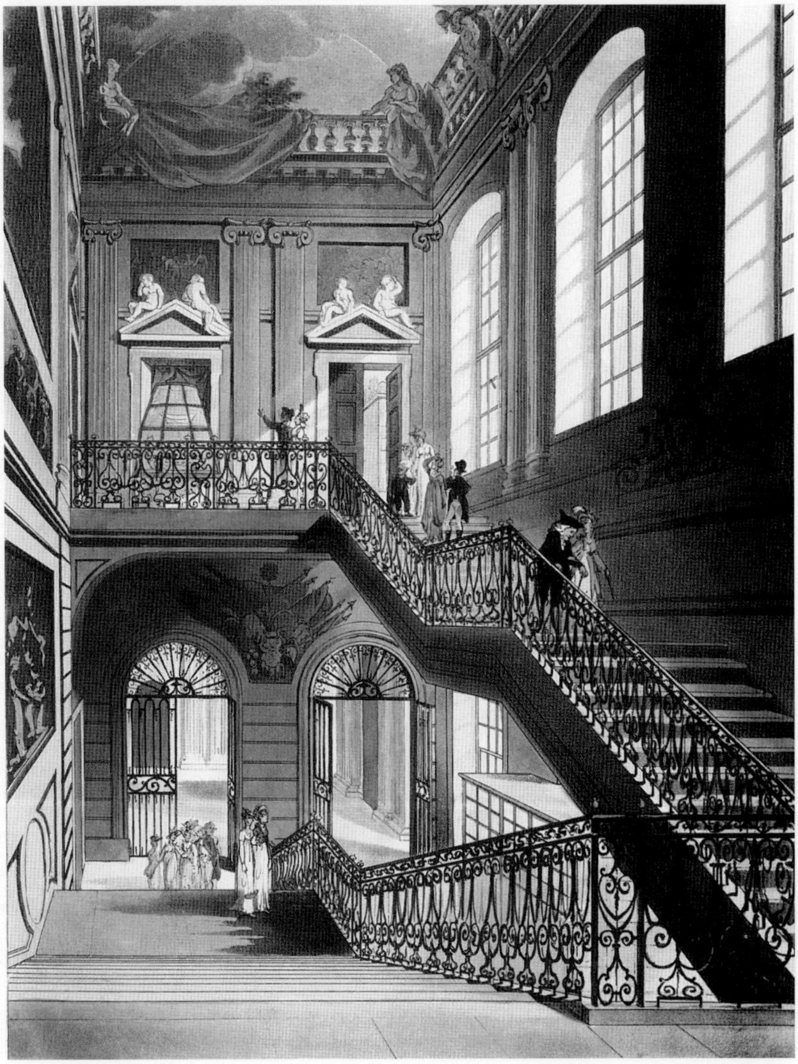

3.10. The hall and staircase of the British Museum. Etching by Augustus Pugin and Thomas Rowlandson. Published in Rudolph Ackermann's *The Microcosm of London* (1808), vol. 1, plate 14.

favor of the Egyptian antiquities in that they enhanced the dark and mysterious qualities of the pieces.

The color of the walls in the Egyptian gallery also contributed to the definition of the works exhibited within. Initially the trustees had intended that the walls in the Townley Gallery would be papered in imitation of green granite, but for economic reasons they agreed to the walls being painted in distemper, which resulted in a "plain stone color."[50] Distemper and the use of a stone color were not unusual for the time, neutral shades such as this being advocated by architects and designers in the early nineteenth century.[51] Furthermore, this was a public museum, not a private gallery, and it was probably considered wise to adopt a more neutral color than the rich color schemes common in private galleries.[52] Nevertheless, the light gray granite color would have enhanced the stony and somewhat stark and foreboding qualities of the Egyptian sculptures.[53] Additionally, the stony color would have made a strong contrast to the brighter color schemes used for presenting Egyptian antiquities in Europe and more particularly, in Britain at the time. For instance, in the Egyptian room of Thomas Hope's house in London, the walls were painted in "pale yellow" and "bluish green" as inspired by Egyptian wall paintings.[54]

Finally, as regards the museum's provision of aids to facilitate interpretation of the exhibits, it appears that some attention was paid to the issue of labeling. This derived from an inspection report carried out by the trustees in 1805, where the lack of labels was highlighted, as was the need to provide concise explanations of the contents of the rooms for the guides.[55] Stating that "it is obvious that strangers will view the museum with more satisfaction in proportion as they are more readily and correctly informed of the nature of the Collection which they are inspecting," the trustees urged the placement of descriptive labels on the cases and recommended "putting into the hands of the Exhibition Officer some concise explanation of the Contents of each Room."[56] More conscientious efforts were made to ensure that the antiquities collections were more accessible for visitors when a separate Department of Antiquities, Coins, and Medals was created in 1807, with Taylor Combe as its head.[57] Making a statement of the activities to be undertaken under its aegis, the new department emphasized the need to produce a guide for visitors.[58] The publication of a guidebook to explain the objects was particularly important for the reception of the museum's collections as there were so few aids to understanding the little-known objects on display. Conscious of the urgency of having such a resource available for the opening of the new building, the trustees repeated their call for a "hand catalogue" for visitors early in 1808.[59] Providing a brief introduction to the collections, this handbook of *Synopsis* offered little more than lists of objects.[60] Furthermore, the introduction to the Egyptian collection focused more on identifying the donators of the objects than on conveying the significance of Egyptian antiquities themselves. Thus, although the *Synopsis* presented basic descriptions of the items on display, the museum still relied on its guides to provide visitors with information on the collections. The guides, who were under pressure to explain all aspects of the antiquities collections, may have had little to add to the limited information provided.

In its display of Egyptian antiquities in the new Townley Gallery, the museum, albeit unconsciously, made a clear statement that these objects were alien and strange. More specifically, the manner in which the collection was presented served to define Egyptian works as "colossal monstrosities." While "colossal" connoted something that was oversized and not refined, "monstrous" referred to the juxtaposition of animal features with the human form, which offended religious sensibilities. It was the combination of these two designations that resulted in a negative image of ancient Egypt, and although not intentionally put forward as an interpretation by the trustees, this was the image that prevailed. Furthermore, this identity was reinforced by the museum's vision of ancient Egypt as significantly different from the presentation of Egyptian sculptures in other European collections of antique sculpture. For instance, when Egyptian sculptures had started to become a feature of major art collections in the sixteenth and seventeenth centuries, they were situated alongside classical works in sumptuous architectural settings.[61] Although they were presented here as exotic specimens of art rather than as examples of great artistic beauty, their status was elevated as a result of being blended in with the classical works. For example, when the first display that was devoted exclusively to Egyptian and Egyptianizing sculptures was created within the Palazzo Nuovo in the Capitoline Museum in Rome in 1748, the objects were presented in the same kind of sumptuous surroundings that the classical works had been featured in.[62] The British Museum nonetheless made a clear distinction between classical and Egyptian sculpture, with the latter clearly denied the same investment in display. Nor were the trustees and display designers influenced by the trend of situating Egyptian antiquities in rooms decorated with Egyptian-inspired design, which served to provide them with a more contextualized or meaningful status. In this sense, the museum's installation broke with the Italian and French tradition of presenting Egyptian antiquities in more picturesque settings.[63]

In comparison to the classical antiquities, the museum's Egyptian sculptures sat uncomfortably as objects of art. Previously, Egyptian sculptures had been incorporated within larger displays predominantly featuring classical works, and within this context they offered an interesting addition to the display rather than an alternative to the classical works. With the museum's major installation, Egyptian antiquities were presented as a discrete body of objects that effectively competed with the other sets of antiquities. And in comparison to the classical works, the Egyptian antiquities came off badly. In addition to the different display conditions, there were fundamental differences in the nature of the Egyptian and classical antiquities. For example, the monumentality of the Egyptian objects meant that they were not proportionally compatible with the room size; they appeared bulky and oversized compared with the Greek and Roman sculptures. Furthermore, whereas the classical antiquities appeared to be in compatible architectural surroundings, the Egyptian sculptures were clearly in an alien architectural environment. Finally, situated in close physical proximity to the galleries of classical sculptures, the Egyptian antiquities inevitably became a source of comparison, quickly assuming the status of a vehicle through which the qualities of the "more evolved" objects from Greece and Rome could be appreciated. More specifically, the Egyptian antiquities were used to illustrate Winckelmann's framework evaluating antiquities, where objects were situated within a sequence of development and improvement, and where Greek works were considered the climax of perfection. Within this progressivist schema a very clear statement on how ancient Egypt should be viewed was being made.

Despite this differential treatment of the classical and Egyptian antiquities, the arrangement of the Egyptian collection in the Townley Gallery provided an exciting and tangible alternative to the glimpses of things Egyptian in Europe at the time. A public gallery specially designed to feature only Egyptian objects was a major development in the presentation of ancient Egypt. When the Musée des Antiquités opened at the Louvre in 1800, for instance, only a few Egyptian objects were included, and even these were of dubious origin.[64] By providing a unique opportunity to see a substantial number of sculptural works assembled in one room, the museum offered a picture of ancient Egypt that was substantially different from the visions featured in the publications of the French expedition and the decorative designs being executed in neoclassical art. In addition to this, the museum's Egyptian galleries gave people a chance to see at firsthand evidence of ancient mortuary practices that were profoundly different from their own.

RECEPTION

Although audiences of the museum had not significantly changed since the late eighteenth century, other important developments had taken place which may have affected the makeup of the visitor population. For instance, in 1807 new rules for visitors wishing to view and study the antiquities were introduced, making it possible to view the antiquities galleries separately from the rest of the museum.[65] This development was important because it meant that people could spend more time inspecting the various collections and treat them more as a resource for learning than a source of wonder. It was also important because it signified the wider recognition that a community of scholars with a specialist interest in antiquities existed in Britain.

As for scholarly developments which may have had an impact on the reception of the 1808 display, the impact of Denon's *Voyage dans la Basse et la Haute Egypte* was fundamental.[66] Translated into English in 1803, this book would have provided the more learned of museum-visiting audiences with some insight into the impressive archaeological record of Egypt.[67] Beyond this, other major European works on ancient Egypt had been published just prior to the display, including Jörgen Zoëga's study of obelisks and hieroglyphs, Quatremère de Quincy's book on Egyptian architecture, and William Richard Hamilton's (1777–1859) major work on the antiquities of Egypt, *Aegyptiaca*, which was instrumental in establishing a scholarly approach to ancient Egypt in England.[68] For antiquarians, objects like the Nectanebo II sarcophagus and the Rosetta Stone would have attracted attention because of their historical significance; the sarcophagus being thought to be the tomb of Alexander the Great, and the Rosetta Stone being recognized as a document of immense linguistic importance.[69]

For those visitors with more of an aesthetic orientation, some appreciation of Egyptian antiquities may have been inspired by Denon's work, which in addition to having great scholarly significance, is credited with initiating a popular craze for ancient Egypt that quickly spread over Europe.[70] Coinciding with the flourishing neoclassical movement in European art, the publication of Denon's book provided a vast source of ancient pictorial motifs that could be appropriated by artists, architects, and designers.[71] In Britain, a leading advocate of the Egyptian style was Thomas Hope, who created an Egyptian room in his London house. Here, Egyptian antiquities, including a mummy, were displayed among sumptuous Egyptian designs.[72] The wider dissemination of Egyptian designs was pioneered by the china makers Josiah Wedgwood and his son Josiah Wedgwood II, who featured a range of Egyptian-inspired objects in their product range. Finally, for those visitors with more of an interest in spectacle and entertainment, an appetite for ancient Egypt may have developed in association with its representation in festivals, magic lantern shows, theater performances, and novels around this time.[73]

The museum's new Egyptian display was likely to have attracted a great deal of public interest simply because nothing like it had been seen in London before. The objects were fascinating not only because they were covered with strange "picture-writing" that nobody understood, but because they were testimony to the private and intimate contexts of important figures no longer living. Furthermore, in addition to being unusual as types of objects, the sculptures could not have failed to attract visitors' attention because of their monumental size.[74] As we saw in the discussion of early modern collections in chapter 1, size, whether minute or massive, was a key attribute in determining an object's status as a curiosity, and in this sense, we can envisage the impact that the enormous sarcophagus of Nectanebo II must have had.[75] Above all of these factors, however, was the fact that this new collection of sculptures was won from the French during recent hostilities, and thus had enormous currency for Britain's national pride. A review of Hamilton's *Aegyptiaca* articulates the new connection that Britain had assumed with Egypt:

> It would be difficult, we think, for any person who loves the cause of humanity, or who feels for the honour and character of the British nation, to read without emotion the account which Mr. Hamilton gives of the state of Egypt in 1801 and 1802. The brilliant achievements of the English, both by sea and land, had filled the inhabitants of the country with admiration of our skill and of our valour in the field; and the high reputations which we bore for good faith, as well as our real or pretended zeal in the cause of justice and liberty, attracted toward us the greater portion of the mixed and persecuted population of Egypt. Our gallant soldiers

were hailed, not only as heroes who had vanquished the warlike and veteran legions of France, but as the restorers of their rights to an oppressed and divided people.[76]

The newly arrived Egyptian antiquities thus offered tangible testimony of the bravery and successes of the British. These were not "impassive" objects like those acquired in 1753—these were laden with meaning because they signified victory over the French.

Prior to the new installation of 1808, Egyptian antiquities had not been highly valued in Britain. That they were not seriously recognized as antiquities is suggested in the following review of the museum from 1802: "The rooms containing Egyptian, Etruscan, and Roman antiquities, as well as the American idols, deserve particular attention. All the articles from Pompeii and Herculaneum, will be viewed with reverence, by the lovers of antiquities. The utensils, instruments, and clothing of distant nations, convey a clearer conception of the people who make and use them, that can never be obtained from descriptions."[77] Here we can see how Egyptian antiquities were excluded from those objects deemed to be of interest to "lovers of antiquities"; a situation that was to drastically change with the exhibition of 1808, where visitors could now see that impressive sculptures, not just trinkets and mummies, were manufactured by the ancient Egyptians. However, since the museum had also acquired the impressive Townley collection of classical sculptures during this period, the Egyptian objects were not able to take the center stage. Thus, no sooner had the opportunity arrived for the Egyptian objects to be recognized as important antiquities than it was promptly taken away.

When the collection seized by the British in Egypt arrived in England, the event was reported with excitement in the press. On August 10, 1802, the *Times* announced: "About a fortnight since, a vessel arrived in the River from Egypt, which contained a great number of Egyptian antiquities, collected by the French army, and become the property of the Conquerors. A few days since a number of them were conveyed to the British Museum; they were so extremely massif [*sic*] many of them, that wooden frames were obliged to be made for them, or it would have been impossible to have moved them."[78] In describing the antiquities that had been acquired by the "Conquerors," the writer continues to focus on their massive size as opposed to their ability to shed new light on world history. For example, the sarcophagus of Nectanebo II is described as an "immense stone-bath," the fist as a "prodigious hand," and we are informed that the sarcophagus of Hapmen took eleven horses to transport. Also interesting is the description of the statues of Sekhmet as "monsters," signaling how the word "monster" would now commonly be used when referring to these anthropomorphic figures. The only object mentioned in terms of its historical significance is the Rosetta Stone, this being described as a "very curious stone" that "proves to be an Edict of their Priest for deifying one of the Ptolemies for his great and good deeds done for his country."[79] This recognition reflected the fact that the Rosetta Stone was the only object in the collection that was legible and thus identifiable because of its Greek text.

The authors of London guidebooks were also quick in responding to the arrival of the Egyptian objects at the museum. In his *Londinium Redivivum*, James Malcolm noted that "the ponderous spoils of our Egyptian campaign are at present under two temporary sheds, in the quadrangle. Of those the huge baths and coffins covered with hieroglyphicks are the most interesting. To which may be added, the deities, the enormous clenched hand, and excellent ram's head, in friable stone; together with coffins, fragments of grand columns, and two Romans in statuary marble."[80] In *Tegg and Castleman's New Picture of London*, H. J. Sarrett also reported on the "valuable curiosities" lately arrived from Egypt, highlighting how "two most beautiful Sarcophagi adorned with Hieroglyphicks, are the admiration of every lover of antiquities."[81] Finally, in *The Picture of London for 1808*, John Feltham referred to the museum's acquisition of the spoils of the Egyptian campaign, observing that among these the most curious is the large sarcophagus—a "beautiful remain."[82] It is significant that all three of these accounts highlight the sarcophagi, with their size, hieroglyphic inscriptions, and function designating them as highly unusual objects.

Once opened in 1808, the new displays on Egypt were mentioned in most of the accounts of the museum's new purpose-built antiquities gallery. While many of these highlighted particular objects from the Egyptian gallery, they were also distinguished by a subtext in which the Egyptian collection was denigrated and belittled. For example, in an anonymous account in *The Repository of Arts, Literature, Commerce, Manufactures, Fashions, and Politics*, the reception of the display is suggested not so much by what it said about the objects, but rather what is not said.[83] For instance, although the two sarcophagi and the Rosetta Stone are singled out, there is a lengthy and glowing description of the Greek and Roman antiquities exhibited in the new galleries, whereas the Egyptian rooms are mentioned only briefly and without any of the flattering terminology used to present the former. It appears that the Egyptian displays are overlooked because, unlike the classical antiquities, they are not thought to have any role in the present: "On the advantages likely to accrue to the arts of our own country from the preservation of these classical monuments, or the benefits derived by artists from the study of the antique, we shall not stop to make a single remark; these are considerations which cannot fail to strike every person possessing the smallest degree of taste and intelligence."[84]

Thus, while the classical antiquities are perceived to be instrumental in guiding the contemporary production of arts and in training future artists, Egyptian antiquities are deemed to have no such value. Because they did not possess the same ability to bring about the "revolution" in national taste that had apparently resulted from the acquisition of the Hamilton collection of vases, they were relegated to being of little use to society. It seems somewhat surprising then, that the illustration accompanying this article features the main Egyptian galleries (plate 4). This suggests perhaps, that the editors were using the popular or exotic appeal of ancient Egypt as a way of attracting their readers' attention to the article.

That the new Egyptian display of 1808 was perceived in a negative light is even more evident in a review from the *Gentleman's Magazine*:

> Were an obscure individual like myself allowed to offer any strictures, I would venture to observe, that the Egyptian Collections, consisting chiefly of large stone coffins, and massive uncouth figures, ought never to have been placed on an upper story, and among the elegant Greek and Roman sculptures. Besides, that their weight and huge bulk renders them only fit for a ground floor: their nature being chiefly sepulchral, it would be much more in character to see them in the solemn recess of a Catacomb, which, in this instance, should be fitted up in the Egyptian style.[85]

Written by Joseph Planta, the principal librarian of the museum, this article reveals something of the disdain felt toward the Egyptian antiquities among the learned members of society. The idea that the Egyptian sculptures be relegated to a lower floor away from the "elegant" Greek and Roman sculptures suggests that their presence was thought to taint the classical works. Furthermore, because of the association of the objects with funerary practice, it is recommended that they be displayed differently from the classical works, which have a more obvious artistic and decorative function. An article in the *Edinburgh Review* reinforced this perspective:

> The characters of the Egyptian architecture have long been known to the inquisitive. Gigantic in all its proportions, it seems rather to have aimed at overwhelming the imagination by vastness, than at enchanting it by elegance; and while ideas of grandeur and power are irresistibly excited by the enormous masses that are piled into regularity by human labour, we are oppressed by a certain cumbrous and severe uniformity of execution, that banishes every idea of inventive freedom, and indicates the designs of an insulated and monastic corporation.[86]

The notion that the monuments were designed to impress simply because they were colossal, and that artistic creativity was suppressed by a rigid mode of production, was a judgment that failed to appreciate the unique style of Egyptian art. Furthermore, the description of the style of Egyptian architecture as "oppressive" and the argument that it was created by an "insulated" population indicate a highly judgmental and condescending attitude toward ancient Egyptian society.

Although the above comments suggest that Egyptian antiquities were not considered legitimate contenders in terms of art, it is important to acknowledge that positive appraisals of their aesthetic qualities were also articulated around this time. A leading proponent of this somewhat kinder view of Egyptian monuments was Thomas Hope, the designer who had dedicated a whole room to ancient Egypt in his famous London house: "Real Egyptian monuments, built out of the hardest materials, cut out of the most prodigious blocks, even where they please not the eye, through the elegance of the shapes, still amaze the intellect, through the immensity of their size, and the indestructibility of their nature."[87] Even though he reiterated the notion that Egyptian sculpture was characterized by a lack of elegance and grace, Hope looked for other features that might be celebrated—particularly the monumentality and permanence of Egyptian art. Such perspectives were reminiscent of the positive evaluation that been articulated earlier by Giovanni Battista Piranesi; his perspective being distinguished by its recognition of the unique architectural context of Egyptian antiquities.[88]

Also characteristic of the reception of the museum's Egyptian displays was the contradictory way in which the objects were described. The French visitor Louis Simond, for example, recognized the significance of the Rosetta Stone, but described the other Egyptian antiquities as "monstrous."[89] This perspective corresponded with wider attitudes to Egyptian antiquities articulated in the press at the time. In a review of Hamilton's *Aegyptiaca* in the *Edinburgh Review*, for example, what initially seems like positive evaluation soon changes its tone:

> Since the age of Herodotus to the present time, no country seems to have attracted the attention of strangers so powerfully as Egypt. It is not only the grandeur, the number, the variety, and the antiquity of Egyptian monuments, but in their peculiarity, that the traveller finds matter for curious and interesting speculation. . . .
>
> When we consider the stupendous monuments of their labours, we can scarcely doubt, that they felt and aspired to the Sublime; but of the Beautiful, they seem to have had scarcely an idea. In Painting and in Sculpture, their taste seems at all times to have been very low and imperfect. The forms which they represented are often deficient, rude and unfinished. There is, indeed, almost universally, a kind of stiffness by which we recognise the productions of the Egyptian artists, who appear never to have remarked the beauty of the waving outline, nor the graces of its elegant and endless varieties.[90]

With any appreciation of artistic merit ruled out, "awe and curiosity" are identified as the only reactions one can be expected to have in relation to Egyptian antiquities.[91]

Beyond the negative, positive, and contradictory appraisals, another feature of the reception of the 1808 installation was the way in which the exhibit was appropriated for reflection on contemporary political issues. The sarcophagus of Nectanebo II, for example, provided a perfect opportunity to comment unfavorably on the French:

> This sarcophagus was forcibly taken from the mosque of St. Athanasius in Alexandria by the French, in spite of the howlings and lamentations of the inhabitants, to whom it was the object of superstitious veneration; and on the capitulation of Alexandria to the British, it fell into the hands of the conquerors. It had then been long removed from the sight and adoration of the people of Alexandria; it was already destined for Europe. However it might have been obtained by the French, it was to us the prize of war. Lastly, it was a most tempting article: and, on all these accounts, we seized it, brought it to England, and placed it in the British Museum, where it now lies, a wonder to the ignorant and a riddle to the wise. Seriously, although we are of the opinion that the acquisition of this treasure by our victorious army, stands on very different ground from the lawless seizure of it by the pretended deliverers of Egypt, yet it seems a nice inquiry, whether conquest strictly conferred on us the right of converting it to our own use, and whether the feelings of those, to whom it had previously belonged, were sufficiently consulted in this transaction.[92]

Aside from the characterization of the French as savage plunderers, this article offers a thoughtful reflection upon the moral issue of whether it is right that the great sarcophagus be "converted" for the use of the British without the permission of its owners. Such considerations were rarely, if ever, discussed when the museum negotiated for successive collections and objects.

The conditions and interpretive aids available for viewing antiquities in the museum at this time also give us an idea of the context in which visitors received the 1808 installation. Although the museum had by that time been open for fifty years, there was still a lack of accessible explanatory materials for the visitor. For those who could not afford, or who did not wish to purchase, the *Synopsis*, the labels on the objects and the commentary of the guide would have provided insight into the collections, and here it appears that both were still wanting. Grave concerns were still expressed about the nature of the tours offered by the museum. A writer for the *Times*, for example, remarked, "It cannot but disgust every visitor of true taste to be hurried through a suite of apartments, crowded with curious objects, by a person, who is himself frequently at a loss to answer properly the questions put to him, and who discharges the duties of his office with such expedition, that at the end of an hour and a half he informs you that you have seen everything."[93]

That the guides lacked sufficient knowledge to present the collections was also emphasized by the visitor Louis Simond: "We had not time allowed to examine anything; our conductor pushed on without minding questions, or unable to answer them, but treating the company with double *entendres* and witticisms on various subjects of natural history, in a style of vulgarity and impudence which I should not have expected to have met in this place, and in this country."[94]

In order to solve these problems, the author of the *Times* critique suggests that visitors be allowed to stay as long as they please and that catalogues for the temporary use of the visitors be deposited in each room. Both of these measures, it is ventured, would render the museum "honourable and useful to the country at large."[95] As it would be some time before accessibility to the collections operated on such a basis, there is little doubt that only the most superficial views of the antiquities could be gained. This would have been exacerbated by the fact that most visitors had little or no background knowledge upon which to make their viewing of the collections more comprehensible.

Finally, the way in which the visitors are depicted interacting with the Egyptian display provides another source of information on the way the collections were received. In plate 4, for instance, two men are shown standing up on the pedestals that support the sarcophagi and peering into their depths, while a woman (on the right) and a child (on the left) also appear to be touching them. This contrasts with the images of the Greek and Roman galleries, where visitors are shown at a respectable distance from the objects, and indicates that while the classical sculptures were revered as cultural objects of high esteem, the Egyptian pieces were perceived as curiosities to be engaged with on a more familiar level. Furthermore, one of the main rules of the museum was not to touch the objects, and it is significant that this regulation appears to have been broken when it came to the Egyptian remains. While breaking this fundamental rule suggested a lack of respect for the Egyptian antiquities, it also implied that visitors were not intimidated by them in the way they might have been by classical works.

* * *

Like the 1759 displays, the 1808 installation of Egyptian antiquities reveals how the circumstances in which Egyptian antiquities were collected, acquired, and displayed were critical in determining their reception. Although numerous traditions for representing ancient Egypt existed before the museum's Townley installation was opened, the arrangement of ancient Egyptian sculptures in London at this early stage in the nineteenth century constituted a significant development in the construction of knowledge about ancient Egypt. Although the trustees and designers of the display did not make any explicit attempt to communicate particular ideas about Egypt through the 1808 installation, this did not mean that the displays did not impart certain messages. Thought not to share the same aesthetic qualities as the classical works, the Egyptian sculptures were defined and perceived as "colossal monstrosities." This is demonstrated by the simple fact that they were denied the same display conditions as the other antiquities collections and that less effort was invested in the specifics of their arrangement. Presented with a spirit of obligation rather than choice, the museum saw in Egyptian antiquities a heuristic potential, where such objects could be used as part of a comparative approach to understanding style and thus make visible the attainments of classical art. Despite this, the Egyptian antiquities served a key role in bolstering national pride, and their status as symbols of British military power ensured that they were celebrated rather than ignored. Furthermore, with so little known about the history and chronology of ancient Egypt, these were antiquities that did not require background knowledge in order to appreciate, and thus they maintained their attraction as wondrous curiosities that were less intellectually demanding than the classical works. Considering the lack of knowledge about Egyptian history at this time, the displays can also be seen as reflecting ignorance as much as prejudice.

4 Monumental Masterpieces

THE EXHIBITION OF THE COLLECTION OF HENRY SALT, 1823

The acquisition of the French collection of Egyptian antiquities in 1802 and the Townley collection of classical sculptures in 1805 was soon followed by the arrival of two more major collections of antique sculpture at the British Museum. With the purchase of the Phigaleian marbles in 1815 and the Elgin collection of Greek marbles in 1816, the museum firmly established its identity as an internationally famous repository of antiquities.[1] This development had occurred in association with Britain's military activities overseas and its increasing consular presence in foreign cities. Indeed, it was in this context that a new breed of government official emerged: more permanently stationed in cities in the Mediterranean and Africa, such individuals started to accumulate collections of antiquities, which they offered for sale or donated to their nation.[2] This practice led to the initiation of archaeological excavations in order to obtain more significant sculptural works that could be sold as part of more substantial collections to the major museums of Europe.

Exemplifying this trend was the British Museum's acquisition of an impressive collection of Egyptian monumental sculptures from the consul Henry Salt (1780–1827) in 1823. Salt had relied on the heroic efforts of his agent, Giovanni Battista Belzoni (1778–1823), to form this astonishing collection, and as a consequence of acquiring this set of objects the museum secured its status as the world leader in the presentation of Egyptian antiquity. Once again, the decision to purchase this set of objects was not the result of the museum's concern to develop the Egyptian collection, but rather, represented a reluctant acceptance of an offer too good to refuse. The protracted negotiations between Salt and the trustees over the price of the collection reveal much about the perception of Egyptian antiquities and their value, and like the installations before it, the display of the Salt sculptures played a critical role in creating new visions of ancient Egypt in Britain. When this particular set of objects was exhibited, for instance, the identity of Egyptian antiquities as artworks was asserted, with some "masterpieces" finally being acknowledged to exist among the collection. Despite this newfound recognition, however, the identity of

Egyptian antiquities as "wondrous curiosities" and "colossal monstrosities" remained as strong as ever; the museum's new definition of Egyptian antiquities simply added another layer of meaning to these objects. Maintaining their appeal to a range of audiences visiting the museum, the Egyptian displays demonstrated a unique ability to simultaneously please and offend. Thus, while the new displays of 1823 encouraged an aesthetic appreciation of the Egyptian antiquities, they retained their focus on the superficial emotional reaction that such objects engendered.

ACQUISITION

Of the European countries involved in consular collecting activity in Egypt in the early nineteenth century, France and Britain were the main contenders.[3] And between these two nations, it was the French who initially dominated the scene, with their consul, Bernardino Drovetti (1775–1852), initiating a major campaign of amassing collections for sale in Europe.[4] The British, however, wasted no time in adopting a similar project of excavating for collections, with the consul Henry Salt and his agent Giovanni Belzoni becoming strong competitors for Drovetti.[5] Indeed, Salt had only just become the British consul general in Egypt in March 1816 and by June he had already arranged for Belzoni to begin a highly productive campaign of removing colossal sculptures. The creation of such collections reflected how Egypt had become more accessible to Europeans after Muhammad Ali took power in 1805. More specifically, when Egypt was handed back to the Turks and Muhammad Ali became ruler of Egypt, Europeans were encouraged to visit and participate in the modernization of the country. As a related gesture, Muhammad Ali provided consuls with permits to excavate ancient sites, which facilitated the removal of colossal sculptures from Egypt. The European consuls residing in Egypt quickly took advantage of this opportunity, establishing themselves as collectors and traders of antiquities. Furthermore, the major national museums of Europe soon started to benefit from the programs of excavation undertaken by these zealous consuls, resulting in the formation of several important collections of colossal sculptures.

When Salt began collecting antiquities for the British Museum in 1816, he was far behind Drovetti, who he noted was "buying up everything to complete a collection upon which he has been engaged for some years."[6] Salt claimed to have encouraged Drovetti to offer this substantial collection for sale to the museum, stating that he did "not know whether it is rich enough to buy it" as it "will not be sold for less than three or four thousand pounds."[7] Perhaps it was learning of Drovetti's collection and its value that encouraged Salt to start making his own, as he soon declared similar interests—"I am so bit with the prospect of what may still be done in Upper Egypt, as to feel unable to abstain from forming a collection myself."[8] Most significantly perhaps, Salt claimed to have been encouraged by the influential trustee Sir Joseph Banks (1743–1820) to collect for the museum.[9] Indeed, the extent of the investment that Salt subsequently made in excavating for antiquities, suggested that he anticipated a good return for the sale of such items to the museum. This confidence, however, appears to have been unfounded, as Salt soon found that he could not rely on his home country to purchase his collections for the price he envisaged.

Salt's involvement with the museum began with the arrival of one of the most famous and iconic Egyptian objects ever to reach Britain—the "Younger Memnon" or colossal bust of Ramesses II from Thebes, which was acquired by the museum in November 1818 (plate 5).[10] Although others had attempted to remove this massive sculpture, the project had been abandoned due to its difficult nature.[11] Unperturbed by previous failures, Salt's agent Belzoni took up the challenge after the explorer Johann Ludwig Burckhardt (1784–1817) suggested the great bust be presented to the British Museum. With Salt's backing, an impressive transportation project was begun, but Belzoni encountered numerous obstacles, such as troubles with the local workmen and attempts by Drovetti to halt the proceedings.[12] Beyond his colorful recounting of the dramas entailed, Belzoni's comments on the state in which he found the statue are significant because they reveal how the removal of antiquities from their homeland to countries such as Britain was seen as a positive and almost liberating act: "I found it near the remains of its body and chair, with its face upwards, and apparently smiling on me, at the thought of being taken to England."[13] Also significant is Belzoni's description of the process by which the great bust was finally placed on the Nile, as it reflects the divergence of opinion among scholars as to the value of this sculpture: "I had to consider, that if this piece of antiquity should fall into the Nile, my return to Europe would not be very welcome, particularly to the antiquaries; though I have reason to believe, that some among the great body of its scientific men would rather have seen it sunk in the Nile, than where it is now deposited."[14] Despite such fears, Belzoni successfully accomplished the task of transporting the sculpture to England, where it was presented as a gift to the museum by Salt and Burckhardt. Significantly, the trustees do not appear to have appreciated this substantial donation, as they failed to thank or acknowledge Salt or Burckhardt for it.[15] Indeed, the keeper of antiquities, Taylor Combe, expressed nothing but disdain for the new arrival.[16]

After removing the great bust of Ramesses II in 1816, Belzoni remained busy excavating a substantial number of monumental sculptures in Egypt, particularly in the temple of Mut at Karnak, Thebes. Engaging accounts of these exploits appeared in Belzoni's *Narrative of the Operations and Recent Discoveries within the Pyramids, Temples, Tombs, and Excavations in Egypt and Nubia* of 1820, and in Charles Irby and James Mangles's *Travels in Egypt and Nubia, Syria and Asia Minor* of 1823, where the many turmoils experienced

4.1. Upper part of a colossal statue of Amenhotep III (EA 3) from Thebes, Eighteenth Dynasty. Acquired by the British Museum in 1823 as part of the Henry Salt collection.

4.2a and 4.2b. Two seated statues of Amenhotep III (EA 4, 5) from Thebes, Eighteenth Dynasty. Acquired by the British Museum in 1823 as part of the Henry Salt collection.

4.3a and 4.3b. Two heads of Amenhotep III (EA 6, 7) from Thebes, Eighteenth Dynasty. Acquired by the British Museum in 1823 as part of the Henry Salt collection.

during Belzoni's collecting campaign are described.[17] Belzoni's persistence in dealing with such obstacles led to the acquisition of a large number of major sculptures, including the colossal head of Amenhotep III (plate 6) and its detached arm,[18] the colossal limestone bust of Amenhotep III (fig. 4.1), two seated statues of Amenhotep III (fig. 4.2), two heads of Amenhotep III (fig. 4.3), the seated figure of Seti II (fig. 4.4), the sculpture with figures of Thutmose III, Montu-Re, and Hathor (fig. 4.5),[19] the statue of King Thutmose III (fig. 4.6),[20] six seated statues of the goddess of Sekhmet (fig. 4.7),[21] the statue of a priest Itu, wife Henutweret and son Neferhebef (fig. 4.8), two hawk-headed sphinxes (fig. 4.9), the upper part of a sculpture of Queen Ahmose-Merytamun (fig. 4.10), a papyrus-shaped column (fig. 4.11), and the statue of Osorkon I as the Nile god Hapy (fig. 4.12). In addition to the larger sculptures, many other objects were included in Salt's collection, such as stelae (plate 7), wall paintings, papyri, and funerary figurines (plate 8).[22] Of these, the series of wall-painting fragments from the tomb of the scribe Nebamun in Thebes were particularly significant because they provided an intimate glimpse into aspects of daily life (plate 9).[23] Finally, key objects that were excavated by Belzoni, but which never made it to the museum, included the sarcophagus of Ramesses III and the unique calcite or Egyptian alabaster sarcophagus of Seti I.[24]

Not long after the arrival of the colossal bust of Ramesses II in England, Salt offered his collection of Egyptian antiquities for sale to the trustees, emphasizing how the specimens were testimony to the artistic abilities of the ancient Egyptians and that they demonstrated how the Greeks "borrowed the rudiments, if not more, from this extraordinary people."[25] Capitalizing on the British rivalry with France, he warned the trustees that the French had expressed an interest in purchasing his collection at a good price; however he reassured them with patriotic claims that he did not want to see the objects leave England.[26] Salt's offer, which came with a list of the items and an estimate of their price, caused great offence to Sir Joseph Banks because it was sent as a personal letter to William Richard Hamilton, rather than as a public document to the trustees. Salt was subsequently accused of being a "dealer, a Jew, a second Lord Elgin," because he privately stated a calculation of the value of the collection.[27] Trying to clear up what he thought was a misunderstanding on behalf of Banks, Salt stated that "I feel most exceedingly hurt and distressed at my meaning, expressed in a letter to Mr. Hamilton, having been so completely misunderstood."[28] He then admitted that it was his fault to have enclosed a list of the objects with his private estimation of their value, and emphasized that in doing so he was not seeking to set up a standard for the government to follow.

Not giving up, Salt repeated his offer to Banks, enclosing a letter from Belzoni that offered his services in excavating and collecting in Egypt to the museum.[29] The trustees promptly rejected both offers; with Banks revealing his true estimation of Egyptian antiquities:

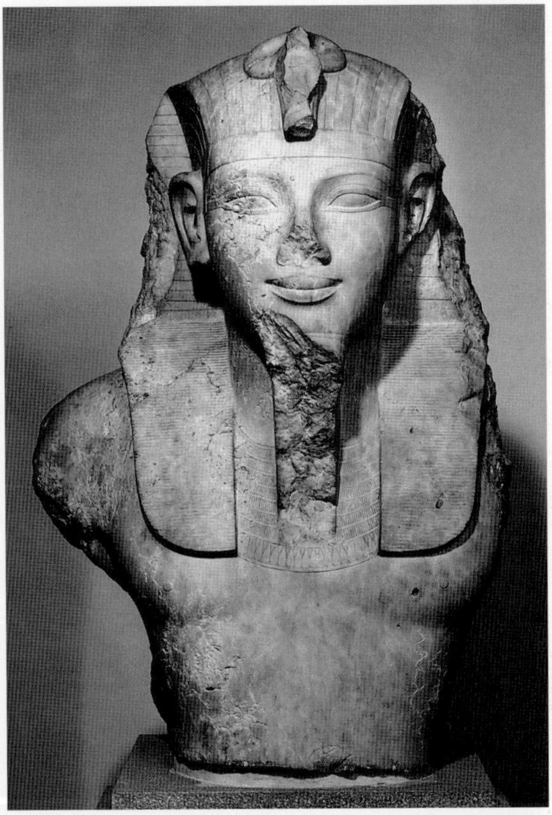
4.1

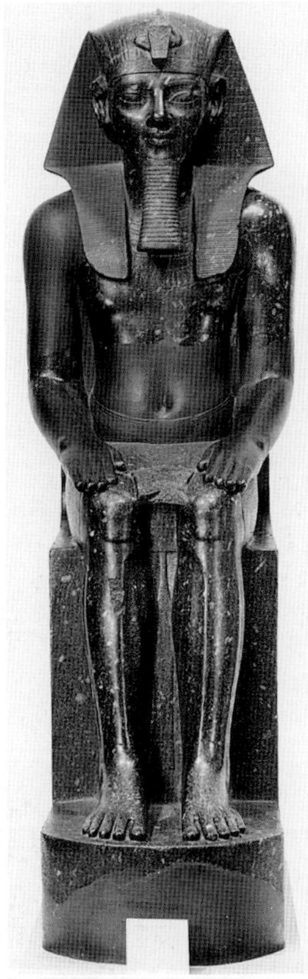
4.2a

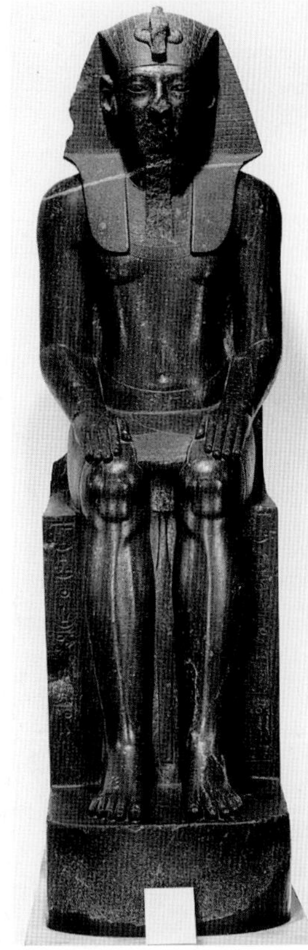
4.2b

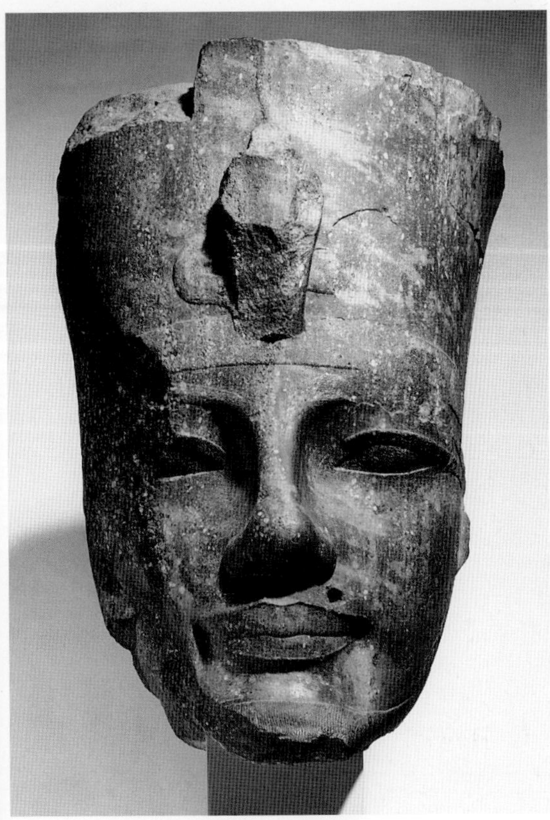
4.3a

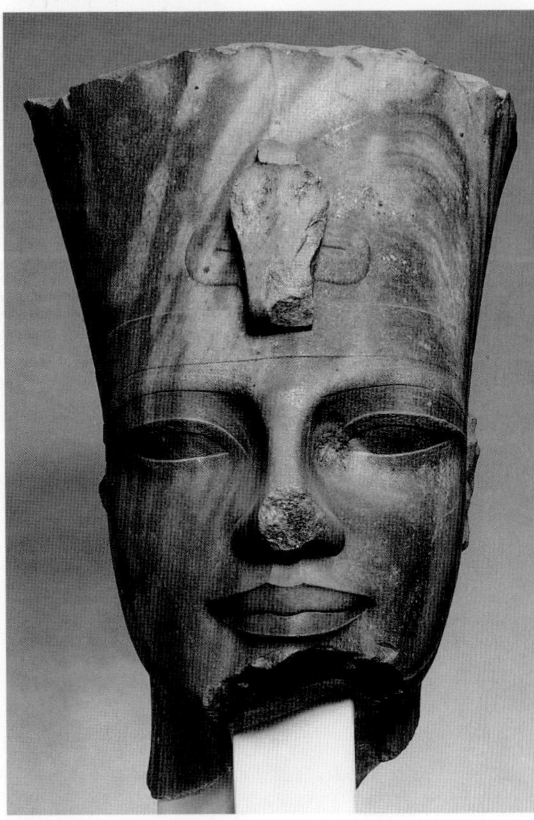
4.3b

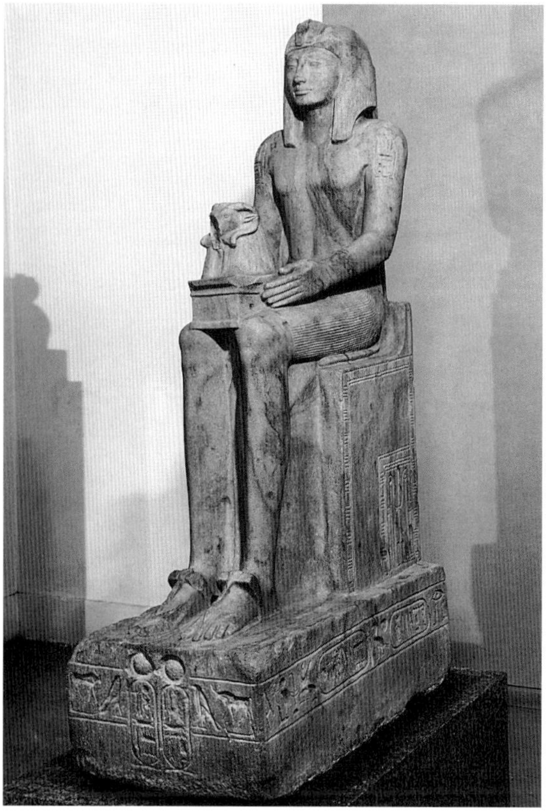

4.4

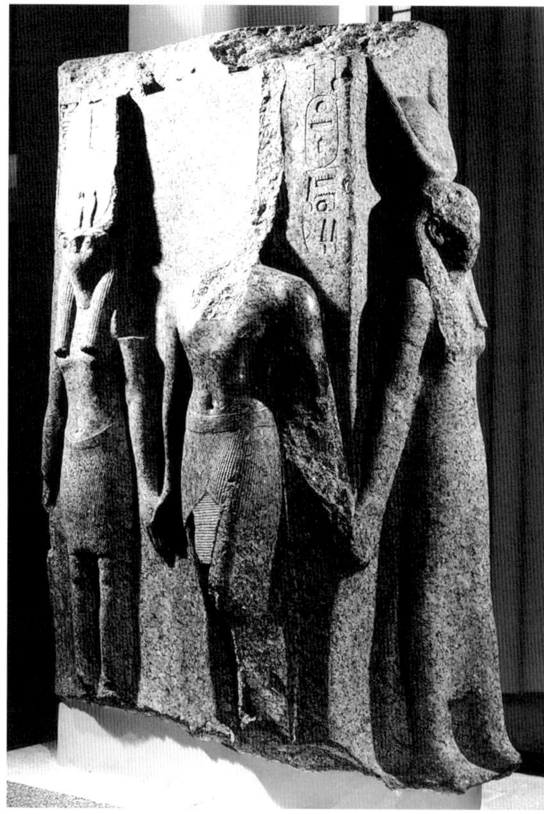

4.5

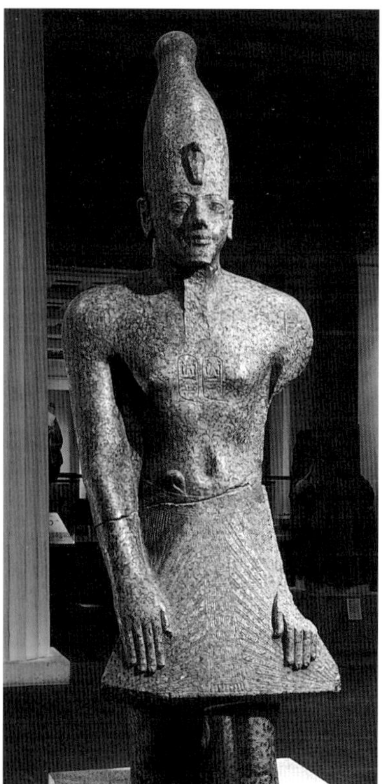

4.6

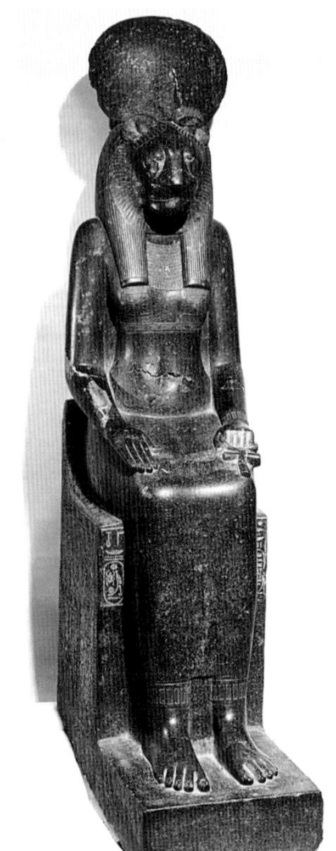

4.7a

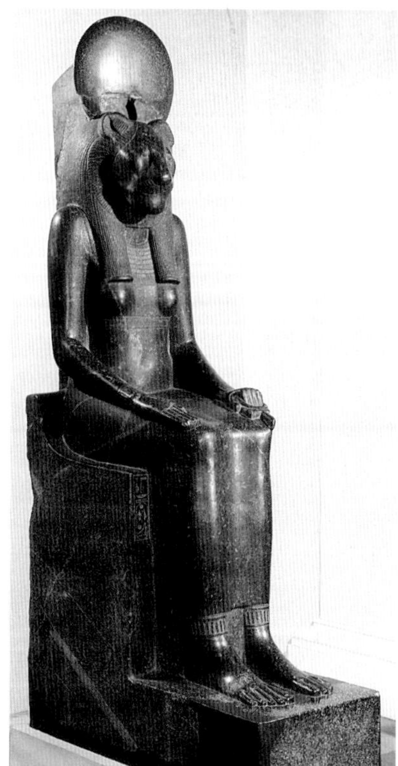

4.7b

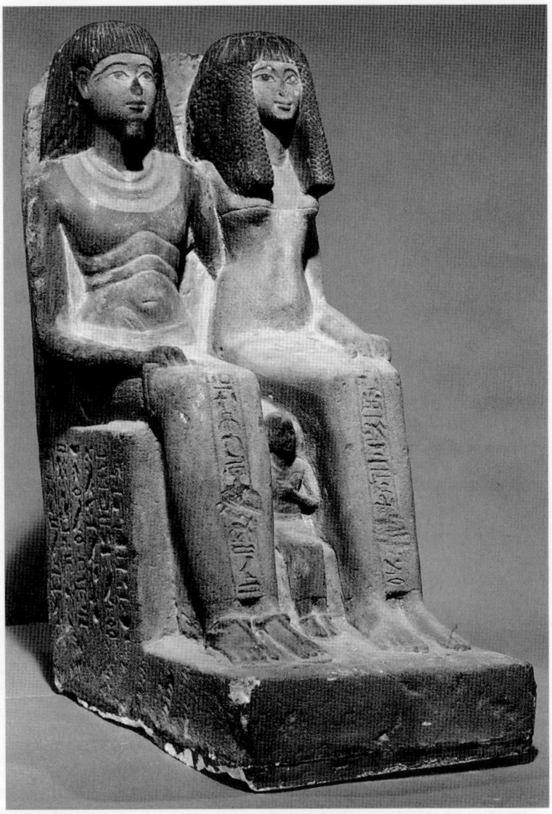

4.8

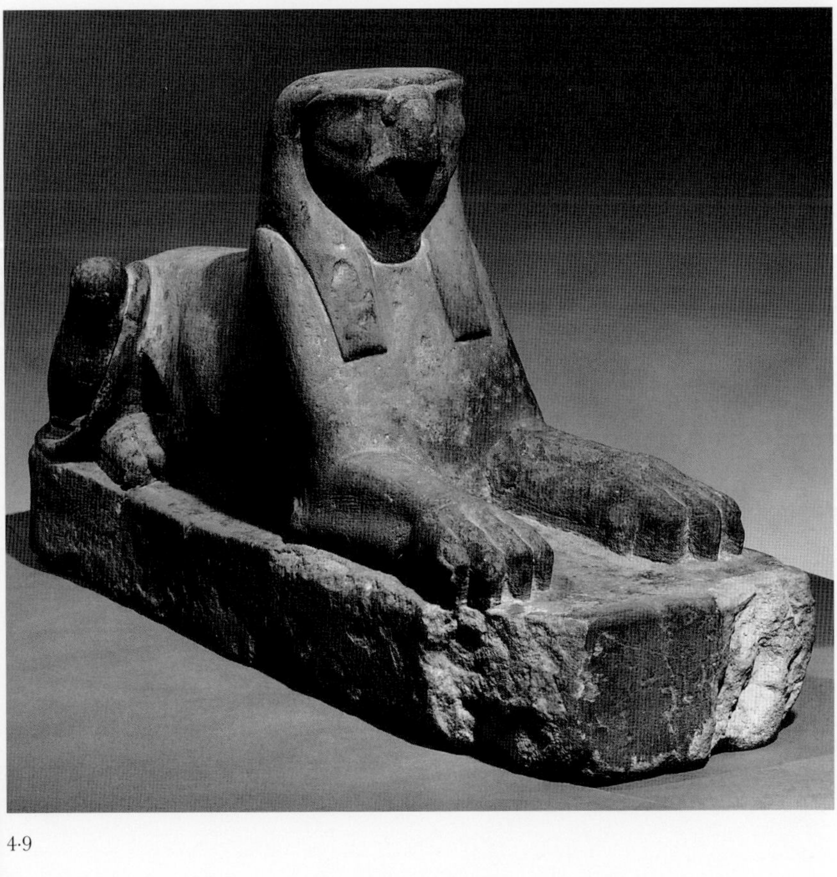

4.9

4.4. Statue of Seti II (EA 26) from Karnak, Thebes, Nineteenth Dynasty. Acquired by the British Museum in 1823 as part of the Henry Salt collection.

4.5. Sculpture with Thutmose III and deities (EA 12) from Karnak, Thebes, Eighteenth Dynasty. Acquired by the British Museum in 1823 as part of the Henry Salt collection.

4.6. Statue of a king, probably Thutmose III (EA 61) from Karnak, Thebes, Eighteenth Dynasty. Acquired in by the British Museum 1823 as part of the Henry Salt collection.

4.7a and 4.7b. Two statues of Sekhmet (EA 63, 517) from Thebes, Eighteenth Dynasty. Acquired in by the British Museum 1823 as part of the Henry Salt collection.

4.8. Statue of priest Itu, wife Henutweret, and son Neferhebef (EA 31), probably from Thebes, Eighteenth Dynasty. Acquired by the British Museum in 1823 as part of the Henry Salt collection.

4.9. One of a pair of hawk-headed sphinxes (EA 13) from Abu Simbel, Nineteenth Dynasty. Acquired by the British Museum in 1823 as part of the Henry Salt collection.

4.10. Upper part of a statue of a queen with the names Sitamun and Ahmose-Merytamun inscribed on the base (EA 93) from Karnak, Thebes, Eighteenth Dynasty. Acquired by the British Museum in 1823 as part of the Henry Salt collection.

4.11. Column in the form of a papyrus bundle (EA 64) from Cairo, Middle Kingdom. Acquired by the British Museum in 1823 as part of the Henry Salt collection.

4.12. Statue of the Nile god Hapy (EA 8) from Karnak, Twenty-second Dynasty. Acquired by the British Museum in 1823 as part of the Henry Salt collection.

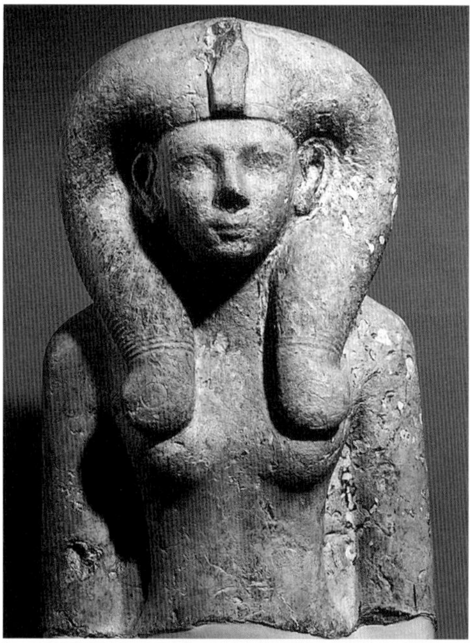

4.10

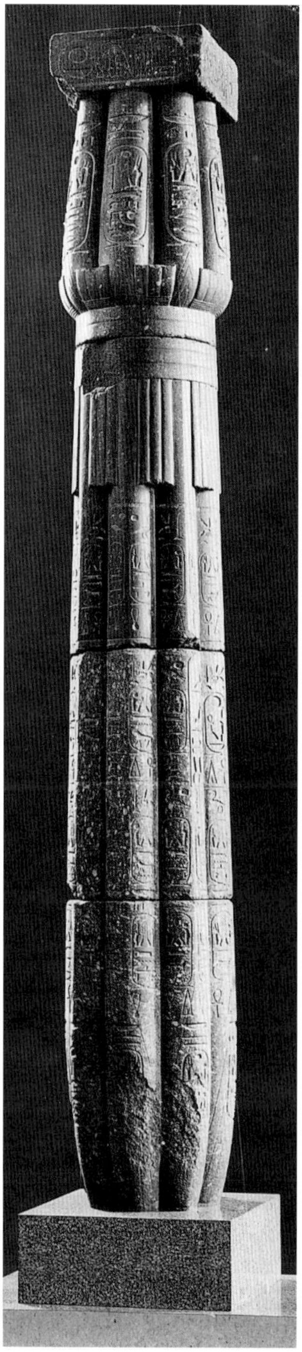

4.11

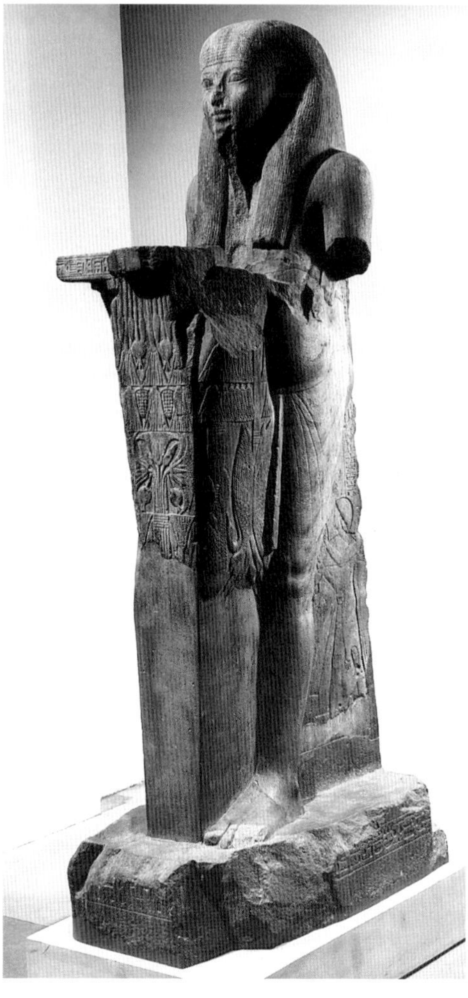

4.12

> Though in truth we are here much satisfied with the Memnon [Ramesses II], and consider it as a *chef-d'oeuvre* of Egyptian sculpture; yet we have not placed that statue among the works of *Fine Art*. It stands in the Egyptian Rooms. Whether any statue that has been found in Egypt can be brought into competition with the grand works of the Townley Gallery remains to be proved; unless however they really are so, the prices you have set upon your acquisitions are very unlikely to be realized in Europe. I cannot help being sorry that you have abandoned your original intention of placing yourself *in the hands of the public*.[30]

Banks's lack of enthusiasm about Salt's collection not only reflected the fact that he was a natural historian as opposed to an antiquarian, but reveals how he subscribed to the general attitude expressed toward ancient Egyptian art at the time. More specifically, Banks's response demonstrated that one primary set of criteria existed for evaluating all antiquities and this was their aesthetic worth. Indeed, Banks reminds Salt that even though the bust of Ramesses II is acknowledged to be important, it is still not comparable with the classical sculpture and thus has been relegated to the Egyptian rooms. This suggests that it was definable as "art" only when in the company of the other Egyptian antiquities.

While resistance to the purchase of Salt's collection indicated disinterest, even hostility, toward Egyptian antiquities, other factors must also be taken into account when considering the trustees' response. Primary among these were economic concerns, which Hamilton himself explained to Salt when attempting to account for Banks's rejection: "I can only unite with Sir Joseph in recommending to you not to dip too deep in search of the hidden treasures of Egyptian sculpture, for in these economical times, John Bull may be easily induced to withhold his purse-strings, even at the risk of losing the unique monuments which you have discovered."[31]

Thus, to put the purchase of Salt's Egyptian antiquities into perspective, this collection was being offered at a time when large sums of money had just been spent procuring other antiquities collections. The Elgin and Phigaleian marbles, for instance, had been recently purchased for £35,000 and £19,000, respectively.[32] The trustees were thus wary of making more pleas to the Treasury for collections they had no room to house. That the general economic climate of Europe was also an influencing factor is suggested by the fact that other European governments were also resistant to purchasing large collections of Egyptian antiquities, a good example being France's rejection of the collection offered by Giuseppe Passalacqua (1797–1865).[33]

Despite Banks's negative assessment of Egyptian antiquities, some trustees championed their merits and expressed concern that the collection offered by Salt was being rejected without more consideration. In a letter to Banks, the naval officer Charles Yorke (1799–1873) emphasized the risk of losing the Egyptian sculptures to another country:

> It is impossible for any man, I think, who has any pretensions to scholarship or classical taste not to feel *highly* interested in the discoveries which have lately been made in the line of Egyptian antiquities, especially since the arrival of our friend Salt at his destined station; and, although "a *rigid economy* is so much *the order of the day*," I cannot help hoping that the House of Commons may be induced to supply the museum with adequate funds (not necessarily extravagant) to enable the Trustees to secure for the British nation the most important and curious of the antiquities which have been obtained by Mr. Salt, and those who have acted with him with so much credit and glory to themselves. I particularly allude to the sarcophagus from the "regal tombs," the "sycamore statues" found in them, the "bust from Thebes" which is spoken of, and the "papyri." It would be an indelible disgrace if such articles as these were either permitted to find their way to any foreign museum, or were to become a *ruinous charge* and a *subject* of *regret* and mortification to those who have had the spirit, the intelligence, and the perseverance to obtain them. Surely this can never be; and, even should the House of Commons prove so tasteless and supine, I trust the Prince Regent will never suffer so great a blemish to fall on the national honour.[34]

Hamilton also reinforced the value of Salt's collection, emphasizing the "expediency of taking some public measure for ensuring to the museum this valuable Collection of Egyptian antiquities."[35] He then suggested to the trustees that they make an application to the government for a ship to be sent to Alexandria to retrieve Salt's collection. Hamilton's letters appear to have influenced Banks, who subsequently agreed to support Salt's proposal at the next trustees' meeting.[36] Banks also followed up Hamilton's suggestion regarding transportation of the collection, requesting from the Admiralty that the next ship sent to Alexandria would be directed to transport Salt's antiquities. Despite this request, however, two years later in 1821, Salt's antiquities had still not arrived in Britain. A repeated plea to Admiralty for a vessel to transport the antiquities finally saw the Salt collection arrive in November 1821.[37]

With the arrival of Salt's impressive collection of monumental sculptures in the museum, one would have assumed that the issue of payment would have soon been resolved. However, the trustees appeared to have been reluctant to pay for this acquisition, and in 1822 Salt wrote to remind them that the sale of his collection had still not been settled.[38] Included in this letter was an explanation of the great expense Salt had incurred in making the collection and an estimation of its value at over £3,000. Not happy with Salt's estimate, the trustees resolved that Salt appoint a representative to make a valuation of his collection, and over the course of the next year the agent Bingham Richards negotiated with the trustees over the price.[39] Salt encouraged Richards to try to get £4,000 for the collection, stating that "otherwise I shall feel myself aggrieved."[40] Thus, Richards started negotiations by pushing for a higher payment of £5,000, reminding the trustees that it was Salt's wish for the whole collection to stay in the museum, and that Sir Joseph Banks, now deceased, had encouraged the formation of the collection.[41] Richards hoped to secure the sale by citing how the museum's main competitors, the French and the Prussians, had already made offers of £2,000 for the alabaster sarcophagus.[42] In case the threat of losing such objects to other nations was not enough to clinch the sale, Richards adopted the strategy of appealing to the trustees' humanity and sense of honor: "Mr. Salt has dedicated his time and property to this object even to the extent of neglecting his private interest, leaving it to others to amuse and instruct the public, whilst he quietly and unostentatiously persevered in the object he has in view—viz: to put his native country in possession of the most interesting and valuable objects of antient [*sic*] art which Egypt could produce."[43]

Emphasizing Salt's national loyalty and sacrifices in forming the collection appears to have worked, as Richards was soon informed that the trustees would purchase the collection, with the exception of the sarcophagus, for £2,000.[44] The reason for this low offer, as expressed by the principal trustee, was unavailability of funds and lack of interest in Egyptian antiquities.[45] Richards did not hide his disappointment with the offer when communicating it to Salt: "*Better* may be done for you, worse cannot. So much has been said of *economy*, and so little in *approbation* of Egyptian antiquities, that I was almost afraid you would be left in *the lurch* entirely. . . . There was no question, nor even a hint, as to a separate valuation of your Collection. . . . I do not think that, considering all things, the Trustees have evinced any disposition to be liberal toward you, and I do not expect that either yourself, or your friends, will be satisfied."[46]

Salt was bitterly upset to hear this news, responding, "If I am to have less than four thousand for the *whole*, I shall think myself *very ill-used*, for it must be remembered that Sir Joseph Banks *pressed me into the service*."[47] Despite his protestations, the trustees would not budge, and in June 1823 a draft of £2,000 was reluctantly accepted by Salt.[48]

Negotiations between Salt and the trustees were not yet over, however, as there was still some confusion over whether the highly unique alabaster sarcophagus of Seti I was available for sale. Belzoni had tried to negotiate with the trustees over its purchase in 1821, reminding them of an arrangement he had made with Salt whereby he was entitled to half the amount received over £2,000.[49] Belzoni offered to wave his share of the profit if he was given permission to exhibit the sarcophagus in the exhibition he had created in the Egyptian Hall in London; however, the trustees did not agree to this suggestion and rejected the purchase.[50] Three years later, in 1824, the issue of the sarcophagus was raised again when the architect and collector John Soane expressed an interest in purchasing it, but was informed by Richards that the trustees had not confirmed their refusal of it.[51] Confusing matters, the trustees reopened negotiations on the sarcophagus with Richards, asking him to name a "sum which would satisfy Mr. Salt as a reimbursement for his expenses."[52] Richards initially named a price of £5,000 and then dropped it to £3,000 when the trustees said they would offer only £2,000. Although advised by the traveler and collector William Bankes to negotiate with the Bavarian or any other government for the sale of the sarcophagus at £4,000, Richards resolved to give the trustees the option of purchasing the sarcophagus for £2,000.[53] It was too late, however, as the trustees once again rejected the offer and the sarcophagus ended up going to Soane.[54]

The dealings over the acquisition of Salt's collection reveal that this set of objects was not thought to be a desirable addition to the museum. The trustees' sense of indifference toward Egyptian antiquities is suggested by the fact that they let the whole affair take six years to resolve. More significant perhaps, was the price they negotiated for the collection, which was paltry compared with that paid for other antiquities collections of similar size and significance.[55] While it appears that the personal views of the powerful trustee Banks may have been influential in hindering the purchase of the collection, the lack of aesthetic appreciation of Egyptian antiquities at the time rendered them an undesirable acquisition for the museum. Furthermore, there was little research interest in Egyptian antiquities in Britain, and despite the recent publication of the important series of volumes on Egyptian antiquities resulting from the French expedition, together with Jean-François Champollion's (1790–1832) *L'Egypte sous les pharaons* of 1814, the British remained skeptical about the scholarly potential of Egyptian antiquities. The fact that the main proponents of an academic approach to Egyptian antiquities were the French may of course account for this attitude. However, it is significant that the king of France had also rejected the collection offered by their own Consul Drovetti around this time. So although respected individuals like Yorke and George Annesley the Earl of Mountnorris (1870–1844) vouched for the merits of the collection, the trustees remained uninspired by Egyptian antiquities and justified their offer of a low price on the basis that there was a lack of interest in Egypt.[56] Indeed, the main reasons for purchasing the collection appear to have been to prevent the French from getting it and because it was cheap. The French did not lose out, however, as Salt offered his second and far more substantive collection of Egyptian antiquities to the king of France (for the Louvre) for £10,000.[57] Deeply embittered by his experience with the British Museum, Salt appears to have swallowed his national pride and chosen the French as more willing customers.

The misunderstanding that arose when Salt tried to settle on a price for his collection reflected the fact that so little was known about the significance of Egyptian antiquities. For instance, the trustees appear to have resented Salt's volunteering prices for items when he was not a scholar or connoisseur of antiquities. Furthermore, Salt seems to have been perceived by the trustees as a money-hungry collector who was taking advantage of his post as consul. Both of these failings were unfairly leveled at Salt, as not only was it well known that the office of consul was poorly paid and that collecting was a way of securing funds for retirement, but Salt did have a sound knowledge and genuine interest in the antiquities he recovered.[58] Indeed, Salt was very proud of the quality of his collection, a fact which he reminded Richards of in 1824: "You know I had made up my mind to make *great* sacrifices:—the object being attained in having enriched the museum with a Collection which must be estimated hereafter as the finest one in Europe, as far as regards statuary. The Trustees cannot, at least, deprive me of this honour."[59]

Finally, unlike the previous collections of Egyptian antiquities acquired by the museum, Salt's collection was far from a random assortment of objects or merely part of a larger collection of antiquities. It represented a genuine attempt to create a comprehensive Egyptian collection, and in its entirety would have constituted a scientifically significant collection. However, although the objects that were acquired from Salt significantly enlarged the museum's Egyptian collection, these were not representative of the diverse range of antiquities from Egypt. While a greater number of object categories were included in his collection, Salt, like the other collectors in Egypt, tended to focus on acquiring major sculptural works as opposed to systematically sampling all that was available. This collecting strategy was no doubt guided by the fact that Salt intended to sell his collection, and thus in order to make it appealing to potential buyers he dedicated his efforts to recovering large, visually impressive pieces. Salt's focus was also driven by political factors in Egypt, where there was a sense of urgency to recover colossal sculptures before other consular representatives scooped them up. Aware that there was a finite resource of monumental works of this nature, Salt was keen to target them above other, more common, objects. As striking as they might be in a museum gallery, however, colossal busts of kings and statues of animal gods constituted only a small sample of the types of antiquities upon which an assessment of ancient Egyptian culture could be based.

DISPLAY

The inclusion of the colossal bust of Ramesses II in the Egyptian Room of the Townley Gallery in 1819 completely transformed the installation of 1808. While people had thought the sarcophagi acquired in 1802 were colossal, these objects were dwarfed by the monumental bust from Thebes. Considered a feat of technical engineering in itself, the installation of the sculpture in the gallery was accorded much ceremony and documented

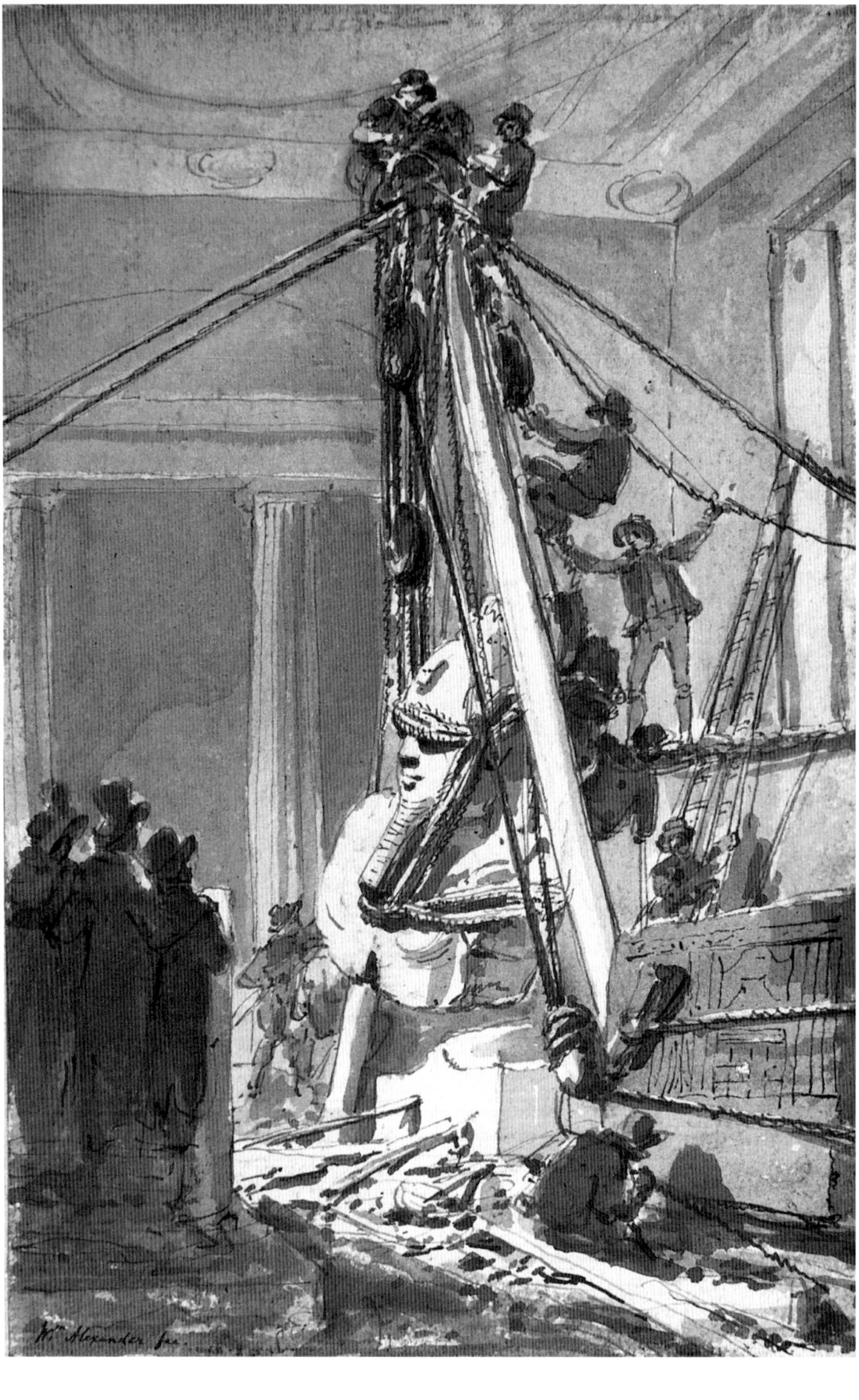
Wm Alexander fec.

4.13. *(facing)* Installation of the colossal head of Ramesses II in the Townley Gallery in 1819. Illustrations of the British Museum (CE 115/1/199). British Museum, Central Archives.

in an illustration (fig. 4.13). The decision as to where this statue would be placed was made by a subcommittee that was appointed to consult with the museum's newly appointed architect, Robert Smirke (1780–1867), on the matter.[60] Positioned at the end of the gallery, with its face turned into the center of the room and facing the light that came in from the side windows, the bust of Ramesses II completely disrupted the symmetric arrangement that had characterized the gallery since 1808. Having nothing comparable to the great bust, the trustees chose the comparatively small sculpture of a falcon to sit opposite it.[61] Placed on a larger pedestal than the others in the room, the colossal sculpture was greatly enhanced, and although in the company of sculptures rendered in a similar artistic style, it appeared somewhat out of proportion in comparison with them. Furthermore, the lighter color of the top half of the sculpture provided a contrast with the darker stone of which most of the other objects in the room were constructed.

Another view of how the spatial distribution of the objects in the Egyptian gallery was transformed by the addition of Ramesses II reinforces how the central organizational principle according to which the objects were arranged was one of symmetry (plate 10). More apparent here, however, is the strategic placement of the obelisks to break up the line of vision one would encounter upon entering the gallery. This image also gives us some idea of the stark and cold atmosphere of the gallery, where we can see the assemblage of dark and bulky sculptures towering above two Arab visitors. Whether these represented genuine visitors to the museum or were an imaginative addition designed to give the room an exotic or "Oriental" feel is difficult to tell. What is more interesting, however, is the fact that they are shown to be avidly contemplating the Discobolus, with their backs turned on the Egyptian works. Thus, like the engraving from 1810 (plate 4), this image makes the major point of interest in the Egyptian gallery the classical sculpture in the adjoining gallery. Another view of the display emphasizes the scale and sense of presence that the colossal bust of Ramesses II had in the gallery (fig. 4.14).[62] It also provides an idea of the problems that would have been experienced with viewing distance, wherein visitors would have not been able to stand sufficiently apart from the colossal sculpture in order to view it properly. The original context of such large works would have allowed them to be seen from a distance, and thus the new architectural setting for the sculpture was wholly inadequate for its proper appreciation. Furthermore, this engraving enhances the stony and cold feel of the room, with its diminished source of light from the windows and the stone slabs on the floor.

In 1823, the unbalanced appearance of the Egyptian gallery was soon transformed by the inclusion of the colossal sculptures purchased from Salt (fig. 4.15). With the installation of the head of Amenhotep III opposite the bust of Ramesses II, symmetrical order was restored, but many more sculptures were added at the same time, and one can but imagine how

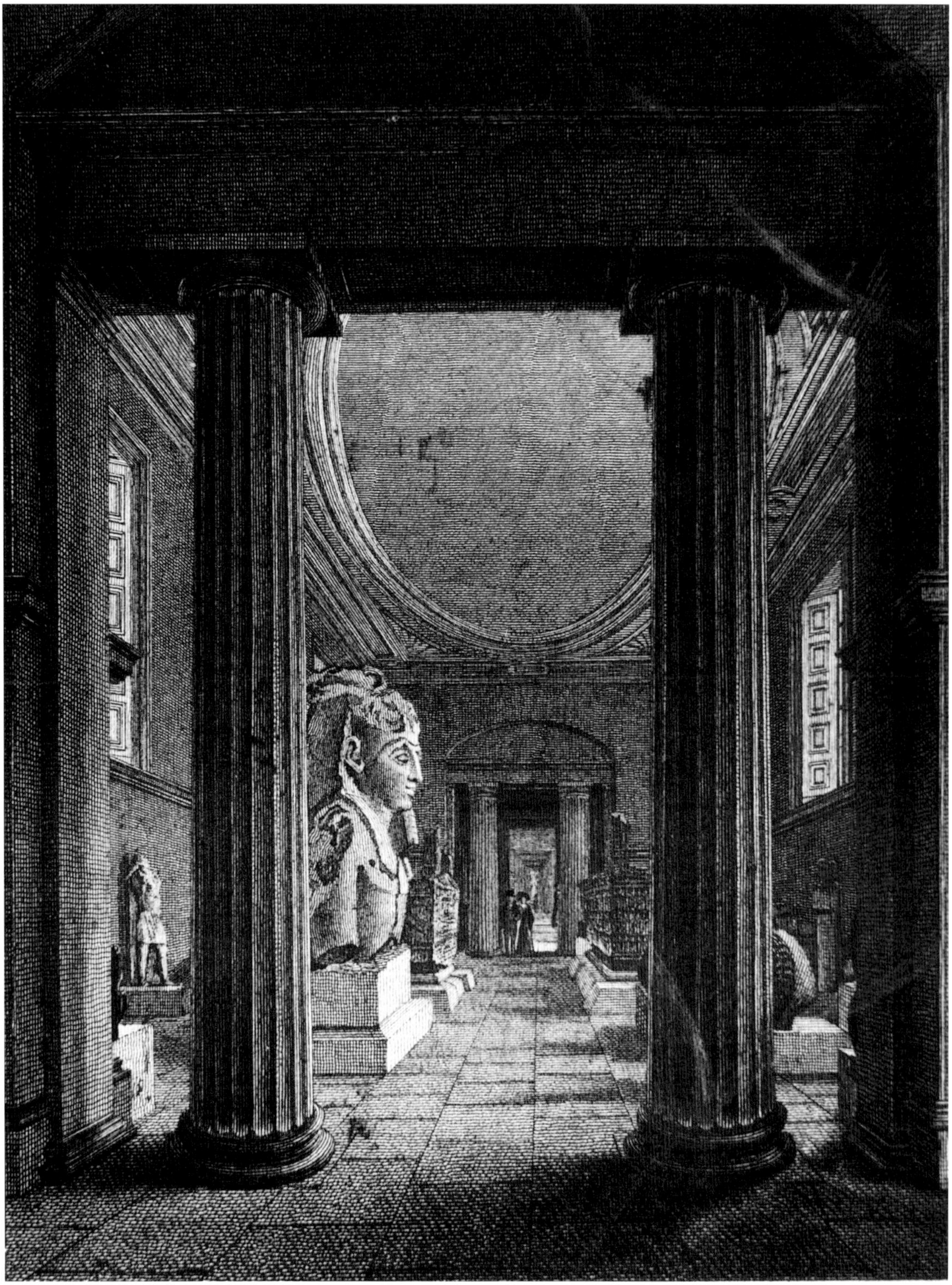

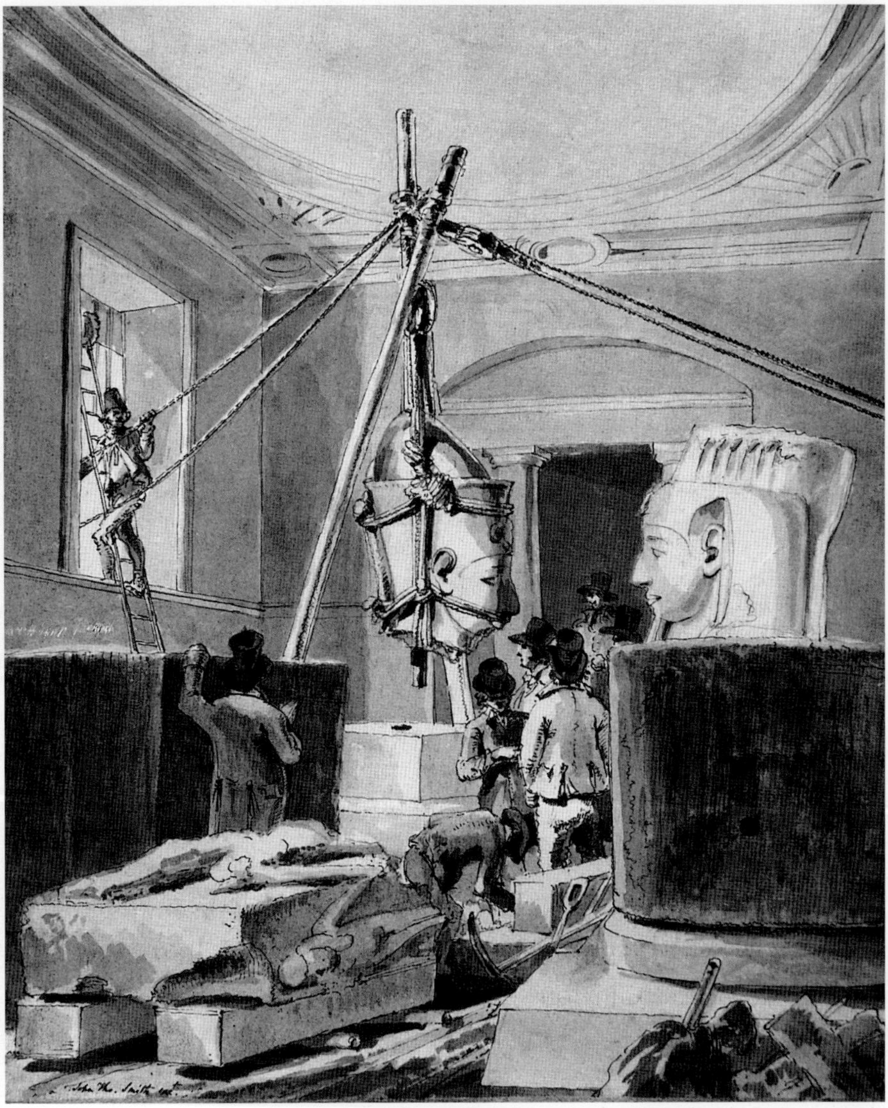

4.14. *(facing)* View of the Townley Gallery. Engraving by Charles Heath after Frederick Mackenzie, c.1825. Illustrations of the British Museum (CE 115/1/23). British Museum, Central Archives.

4.15. Installation of the colossal bust of Amenhotep III in the Townley Gallery. Drawing by John Thomas Smith, c.1824. Illustrations of the British Museum (CE 115/1/200). British Museum, Central Archives.

overcrowded the room must have become. It is not possible to tell whether the installation of 1808 was dismantled and redistributed in order to highlight different objects. In the 1808 display, for example, the sarcophagi were clearly the focus of attention, having been strategically placed in the center of the row of objects that lined the walls of the room. One can assume, however, that the efforts involved in moving such heavy pieces would have prevented a complete rearrangement of the gallery, and that the sculptures purchased from Salt were slotted in wherever possible. It is also not possible to establish whether the smaller antiquities acquired as part of this collection, such as the papyri, wall paintings, and domestic items, were dispersed among the larger sculptures or placed in the room immediately preceding the Egyptian gallery, where the mummies were located.

It seems likely, however, that these items were crammed in with the latter, a precedent that had been set with the separation of objects according to size. Indeed, the 1823 installation appears to have maintained the same display conventions that were established for the 1808 exhibition, constituting an adaptation of the "rules" that had been created to best showcase the classical sculptures.

While much remained the same in terms of the museum's approach to object layout, important changes had taken place in the provision of interpretive aids for viewing the antiquities collections. The most significant among these was the ability of visitors to view the collections without being supervised, as guides were no longer used after 1810. This meant that people could be more self-directed in their visits to the Egyptian gallery, which may have encouraged closer scrutiny of the individual objects on display. It also would have resulted in visitors becoming more dependant on the museum's provision of guidebooks; and to this end the museum regularly updated *Synopsis*.

The relation of the Egyptian display to other galleries remained a key factor in the museum's definition of ancient Egypt, and here images of the other antiquities galleries in the museum provide a useful point of comparison. George Scharf's picture of one of the classical sculpture galleries from 1827, for example, gives us a sense of how different the rooms accommodating the Greek and Roman works were from the Egyptian galleries (fig. 4.16). Here we notice how the Greek and Roman statues are elevated on ornately carved pedestals and bathed in light. Characterized by their relaxed poses and flowing robes, the classical sculptures are in proportion with the architecture of the building and compatible with the decorative scheme. The picture is also important because it reminds us what visitors would have seen immediately before arriving in the Egyptian gallery. For instance, after appreciating these pleasurable pieces, the visitor would suddenly be faced with a darker room where chunky objects cut out of colossal blocks of stone had been accumulated. One can thus imagine how the Egyptian antiquities would have appeared a little strange and out of context. In a later picture featuring the principal staircase of the museum we are reminded of the prevalence of classical imagery in the overall decorative scheme of the museum (fig. 4.17). Enhancing this sense of magnificence and the overall classic feel of the grand staircase are the architectural details framing the murals. After seeing these gentle images of reclining nudes in picturesque landscapes and then the classical works that inspired them, it would have been somewhat confronting to take in the scale, form, and style of the Egyptian sculptures.

Although the Egyptian sculpture collection was sufficiently substantial to demand serious attention toward its presentation, the trustees did not consider exhibiting Egyptian antiquities in a manner that was distinctive to them. Indeed, there appears to have been no interest in determining a mode of display that was appropriate for the Egyptian works; they had

4.16. View of the classical sculpture galleries in the Townley extension. Sketch by George Scharf the Elder, 1827. British Museum, Department of Prints and Drawings, no. 1862-6-14-632.

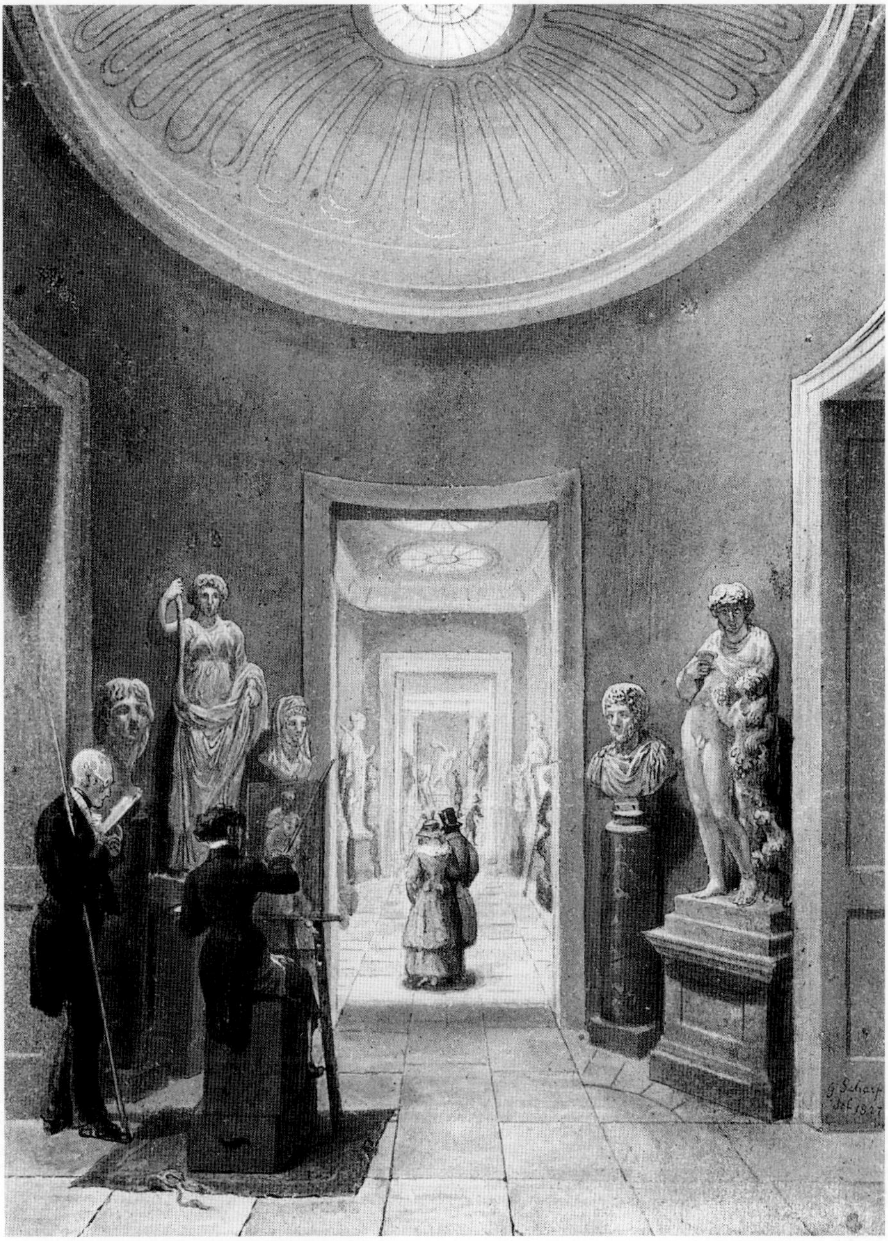

to fit into the existing scheme, not matter how unsuited it was. That the trustees did not adopt the recent trends established for presenting Egyptian antiquities in Europe further reflects their indifference to them. For instance, the new Egyptian gallery that opened at the Louvre in 1818 featured the lavishly decorated Salle d'Isis, which housed a smaller collection of Egyptian antiquities than the British Museum possessed, but which was augmented with Egyptianizing works from later periods.[63] Decorated in an Egyptian style, the Louvre's new gallery demonstrated a concern for presenting antiquities in an interior setting that was compatible with their

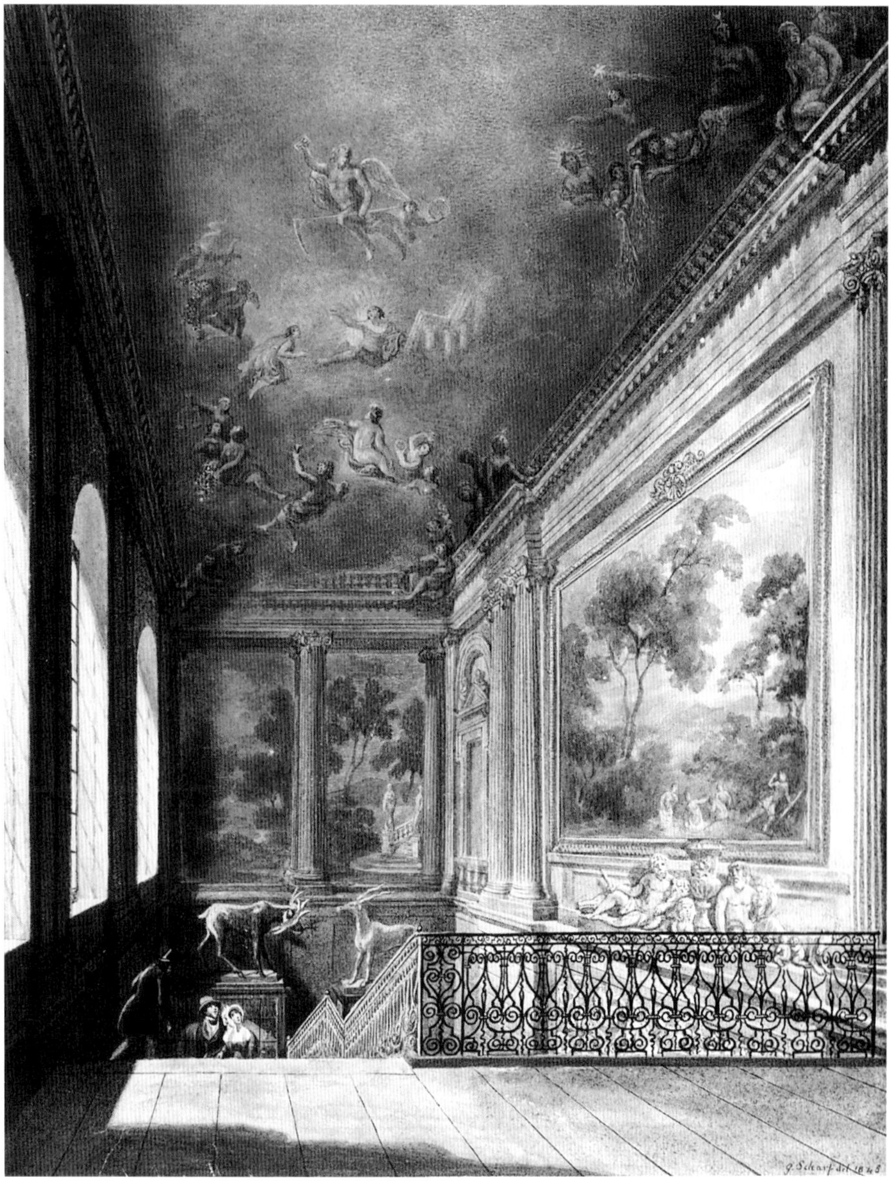

4.17. The staircase of the British Museum. Watercolor by George Scharf the Elder, 1845. British Museum, Department of Prints and Drawings, no. 1862–6-14–629.

artistic traits. The British resistance to matching the décor of the room to its contents in this way reveals the different attitudes of the French and the British toward ancient Egypt, where France's special treatment of the Egyptian antiquities reflected their national attachment to this ancient civilization.

While it is comprehensible that the trustees did not wish to follow the Louvre example, it is perhaps more significant that they were not influenced by the pioneering exhibition of Egyptian antiquities held at the Egyptian Hall in London in 1821.[64] Created by Belzoni and featuring his own Egyptian antiquities, this exhibition was characterized by its life-size reconstruction of two chambers from Seti I's tomb.[65] While the Egyptian Hall was already known for this kind of interpretative presentation, where specimens were situated in reconstructions of their original context or habitat, Belzoni's exhibition went a step further in creating a truly atmospheric visiting experience.[66] With its low ceilings and candlelit chambers, the tomb display provided the visitor with a real sense of the cramped environment of such ancient sites. And if the tomb experience was not stimulating enough, visitors could sit in a large room decorated with full-scale reconstructions of the wall paintings from the tomb, laboriously copied by the Italian explorer Alessandro Ricci under Belzoni. Other aids further enhanced the understanding of this exhibition, such as the architectural models that presented three-dimensional representations of major monuments of Egypt.[67] The success of such strategies in facilitating an understanding of ancient Egypt was such that some commentators urged the museum to follow suit. The *New Monthly Magazine*, for example, stated that "it would, we think, be well worthy of the trustees of the British Museum, to have such a work modelled and attached to their collection of Egyptian Antiquities; where the man of learning might have access to it, for the purposes of consulting the antiquities of ancient Egypt, and the curious might at once be instructed and delighted."[68] Despite the fact that Belzoni's innovative developments in the presentation of ancient Egypt were very favorably received in the press and periodicals of the day, the trustees were reluctant to adopt such theatrical modes of presentation.

Unlike the Louvre and Belzoni installations, which were distinguished by their use of reconstructions and decoration to enliven the subject, the museum's new display presented a restrained and conservative vision of ancient Egypt. While part of the explanation for this was that the museum did not see itself as a source of entertainment, and thus tended to be understated in its mode of presentation, much of the explanation lies in the fact that it did not even cross the trustees' minds to treat Egyptian antiquities differently. Having noted this lack of investment in accommodating the Egyptian antiquities, however, it is fundamental to note the power of Egyptian antiquities in asserting their own sense of authority. The mere presence of the monumental bust of Ramesses II in the Townley Gallery saw a new identity instantly bestowed upon the Egyptian collection. Towering above all of the other objects in the museum, this sculpture asserted its own unique power; with a majesty and sense of assuredness, this single object defied any attempts to belittle it. This was a "monumental masterpiece" and no matter how it was displayed, the aura it commanded was transferred to many of the other objects in its company.

The installation of 1823 had several important implications for the way ancient Egypt was defined by the museum. In particular, the inclusion of the Salt collection of sculptures made the gigantic nature of Egyptian antiquities even more pronounced. Furthermore, the addition of more portraits, or figurative pieces, such as the sculptures of Ramesses II, of

Amenhotep III, of Seti II, of King Thutmose III and of Queen Ahmose-Merytamun, gave a sense that ancient Egypt was ruled by powerful historic figures and not just by strange animal gods. Thus, a glimpse of history was introduced and the emphasis on death, which had been conveyed by the sarcophagi in the 1808 installation and the mummies in the 1759 one, was now complemented with another image of ancient Egypt. Indeed, the idea that ancient Egypt was a land of mighty rulers rendered it less monstrous and mysterious and more familiar (or Western) in a historical sense.

RECEPTION

Responses to the new display of Egyptian antiquities at the museum were likely to have been shaped by a number of important developments, both inside and outside the museum, which had taken place prior to its opening. Within the museum, the most important change to take place was that after 1810 visitors were no longer hindered by the necessity of applying for a ticket to enter. This would have had a significant impact on the types of visitors who went to the museum, and although it was not until the 1830s that a much wider spectrum of people began to enter its doors, the beginnings of this trend were occurring around the time the 1823 installation was completed. Of prime importance outside the museum was the success of Belzoni's exhibition, which had attracted vast visitor numbers and which in conjunction with Belzoni's immensely popular *Narrative of the Operations and Recent Discoveries within the Pyramids, Temples, Tombs, and Excavations in Egypt and Nubia* had generated a wider popular interest in ancient Egypt.[69] In addition to appealing to a wider audience than the more scholarly tomes on ancient Egypt, Belzoni's book provided much new detail on the antiquities of Egypt, particularly the lesser known monuments of Upper Egypt, and in this sense it was of as much interest to antiquarians as it was to those keen on a ripping good yarn. Furthermore, for those educated visitors who read the learned journals of the day, interest in the museum's exhibition of the Salt collection was likely to have been stimulated by the colorful stories of Belzoni's heroic efforts in transporting the antiquities to England.[70] Such reports generated a fascination for the exploits of Belzoni and imbued the subject of ancient Egypt with an exciting flavor of adventure. Other visitors may have been encouraged to visit the museum by expressions of admiration on the part of poets such as Byron, Keats, and Shelley and artists such as Haydon, who had responded very favorably to the sculpture of Ramesses II.[71]

As soon as they arrived in the country, Salt's sculptures attracted interest from the media. The *Gentleman's Magazine*, for example, informed its readers of this important addition to the museum: "They are at present dispersed in the museum, till a receptacle is formed, for their classification and better disposition, worthy of their merit, and adequate to the taste displayed in their selection."[72] Rarely, if ever, had the word "taste" been used in a sentence discussing Egyptian antiquities. Furthermore, in listing the main sculptures in Salt's collection, this article used terms typically reserved for classical antiquities such as "beautiful workmanship," "beautiful countenance," "delicately beautiful," and "of singular beauty."[73] Such responses not only reflect how learned visitors were seeing Egyptian antiquities through the lens of aesthetic theories articulated at the time, particularly in regard to the concept of beauty, but also convey a general shift in attitude toward ancient Egypt, where positive responses to antiquities were no longer perceived to be the sole preserve of classical works. The explanation for this shift lay in the effect of one object upon all those whose eyes gazed upon it. Ramesses II was received with much acclaim by scholars, writers, connoisseurs of art, and the media. Indeed, prior to the arrival of this object in England, Hamilton had declared it to be "certainly the most beautiful and perfect piece of Egyptian sculpture that can be seen throughout the whole country," and Burckhardt had described it as a "beautiful specimen of Egyptian workmanship" which deserves to be "an object of general admiration."[74] The significance of this single sculpture for the reception of Egyptian antiquity cannot be overemphasized, for once it was installed in the Townley Gallery, the aesthetic qualities of Egyptian antiquities finally became more widely recognized.[75] Particularly important was the approval of this work by the art and literary establishment; the *Annals of the Fine Arts*, for example, commented on the beauty of the face, and the writer Thomas de Quincy highlighted its beautiful smile.[76] Here we can see how it was the facial expression of the sculpture, more than its monumental size or exotic attributes, that was appreciated. Furthermore, while the media's interest in the sculpture tended to focus on the dramatic story of its removal and transportation to England, they still recognized its aesthetic worth.[77] The *Quarterly Review*, for example, described it as "without doubt the finest specimen of an ancient Egyptian sculpture which has yet been discovered."[78] This appreciation of the aesthetic qualities of the sculpture of Ramesses II signifies how Egyptian antiquities came to be recognized as more than curiosities or monstrosities—now they were entitled to be considered works of art. Testimony to this were the positive responses to Egyptian works other than the sculpture of Ramesses II appearing in other publications. For example, in Irby and Mangles's *Travels in Egypt and Nubia, Syria and Asia Minor* of 1823, a far more appreciative view of Egyptian monuments was offered. On one of the colossal sculptures at the Temple of Abu Simbel, for instance, they remarked, it "exhibits one of the most perfect specimens of beauty imaginable."[79]

Despite the newfound recognition of Egyptian antiquities as "monumental masterpieces," the tendency to denigrate the achievements of ancient Egyptian artists remained. Readers of the *New Monthly Magazine*, for example, were informed that the Egyptian or "Eastern style, . . . contrary to the Western, depended upon bulk rather than beauty; upon strength and uniformity, and upon massiveness of light and shade, rather than upon elegance of individual parts and the graceful proportions of a whole, for its magnificence."[80] The idea that these qualities of Egyptian monuments indicated inferiority in artistic achievement was further elaborated on in an article from the *Annals of the Fine Arts*: "They bear the character of the infancy of art, rude in their design, yet imposing in their massiveness and extraordinary size; they attest more to the vast power and perseverance of the bodily powers, than great exertions of a cultivated mind. The spectator views them with but a mournful satisfaction, and they appear to bear the epitaph of departed centuries, which have been laid prostrate before them."[81] With these failings, the style of Egyptian art could be appreciated only in limited terms. Yet again, the size of the works remained the major source of attraction, but since this was not considered to provide testimony of a "cultivated mind," it could not but fail when compared with the qualities of classical antiquities.

A more specific response to the displays at the museum reveals how a new paradox characterized the appreciation and reception of Egyptian antiquities in guidebooks of the time. In his detailed assessment of the 1823 installation, which appeared in his *Guide to the Beauties of the British Museum* of 1826, Peter Patmore sought to instruct visitors on a new way of appreciating Egyptian art.[82] While on one hand, the objects were seen as evidence of a great civilization worthy of awe and respect, on the other, they were seen to be lacking in true or pure artistry. For instance, in introducing the Egyptian collection Patmore notes its significance and uniqueness: "In admitting, however, its [the British Museum's] general inferiority to some others, and in particular to that of the Louvre, it must be understood that we exclude its collection of Egyptian antiquities. In *those* it is greatly richer than any other gallery in the world: and as objects of rarity, no less than of real and deep historical interest, they are of the first importance."[83]

Having asserted the value of the collection in terms of its rarity and historical importance, Patmore then elaborates on the response such antiquities engender: "The wonders which modern discovery has placed before us, in connection with the Arts of Egypt, exercise an almost painful and oppressive effect on the imagination, when we permit it to be directed fully and exclusively toward them. They aggrandize, to a vast extent, our notions of the physical power of the race of beings to which we belong."[84] Thus, the colossal sculptures are seen to create a profound reaction of awe, demonstrating the capacity of humans to build such monumental works. Moving beyond these initial responses, Patmore seeks to qualify the distinctiveness of Egyptian art, challenging the comparative mode of evaluation that had prevailed in its assessment. For instance, while admitting that the Egyptian objects appear to be "rude" when compared with the Greek and Roman sculptures, he argues that this "epithet is assuredly not applicable" because the sculptures achieve what they intend to do.[85] More specifically, because the aim of Egyptian sculpture is not simply to represent human and natural beings, it should not be judged with "a direct reference to the human form in its natural state."[86] Attempting to define precisely what it is that Egyptian sculpture aims to achieve, Patmore describes it as having a "shadowy" character, where the forms were imaginative and not intended to represent anything real. To make this idea comprehensible, he presents a comparison between Egyptian sculpture and the forms we "see in feverish dreams, and which haunt us in that nervous affection called the *night-mare*."[87] Thus, Egyptian sculpture is intended to produce forms that are not to be remembered as visible objects, but rather to "be felt, as we feel the impression of a dream long after we have forgotten all the detail of its form and circumstances."[88] This is highly significant because Egyptian antiquities were being described in a way that had typically been applied only to classical antiquities. For instance, the reception of classical antiquities was distinguished by the way in which the effect of the sculptures on the viewer was described. Now Egyptian antiquities were also being defined in terms of the feelings they inspired.

In order to demonstrate the "shadowy" character of Egyptian sculpture, Patmore proceeds to offer detailed descriptions of some of the Salt sculptures. Beginning with the block sculpture with figures of Thutmose III, Montu-Re, and Hathor (fig. 4.5), we are informed that

> though there is an absolute want of *expression* in these figures a uniform smoothness of surface, which precludes all appearance of life or action—yet the workmanship cannot be called rude. In fact, the figures lie upon the surface, not like imitations of anything real, but like shadows. There is nothing distinct about them—nothing made out. There is no detail. They are all like each other too, and like nothing else. "There is no speculation in them." In a word, the huge block of stone before us is scarcely at all changed in its character by the sculptures that are upon it. It is not a piece of sculpture, but a piece of stone.[89]

While this attempt at articulating the distinctiveness of Egyptian art reveals a genuine attempt to understand Egyptian antiquities, it also reflects the difficulties people had in making sense of them. Clearly, they were now being valued more as objects worthy of study, but they were still not seen as objects of art in the same way as were the Greek and Roman sculptures. Even the bust of Ramesses II, which had qualified as an aesthetic piece in the minds of many aesthetes, was thought to be lacking: "Nothing can be more beautifully executed, in point of mere workmanship, than this noble fragment; but there is no life in it—no character—no expression. It is like a beautiful mask . . . We do not feel the least degree of human sympathy with this face because there is nothing individualised about it; the impression is therefore merely shadowy—like that of an outline."[90]

Thus, Egyptian art fails not because of its quality of production or execution, but because it does not convey likeness in a way that we can easily engage with. The different qualities of Egyptian sculpture, or its more abstract nature, are not valued as aesthetic achievements because they do not allow the viewer to relate to the work in a conventional way. This notion is also evident in Patmore's description of the colossal head of Amenhotep III (plate 6): "It also possesses the same characteristic want of character. . . . [It is] without any individual expression . . . without any sexual expression. . . . It has a *national* character, but nothing more. Perhaps nothing that has been seen in this country, or even in Egypt itself, is calculated to convey a more true, and at the same time favourable impression of Egyptian art, than this beautiful fragment; for the workmanship of it is exquisite."[91]

Although described as "beautiful," it is primarily the workmanship of such objects that deems them worthy of the visitors' attention. And while the evaluation of the Egyptian objects in the museum's collection appears to end here, the full force of Patmore's comments can be seen even more clearly in the description of the Elgin and Phigaleian marbles, which are presented with an entirely different vocabulary. Words such as "excellence," "perfect," "spirit," "vitality," "superior," "beautiful," "grandeur," and "magnificent" abound in connection with the discussion of these objects, emphasizing Patmore's view that it is only with Greek and Roman art that we can see "absolute vitality communicated to dead stone."[92] Within this evaluative framework it appears that the Egyptians were considered to have not yet learned how to use stone sculpture as a means of capturing the spirit and essence of life.

An idea of how the Egyptian installation of 1823 was received can also be gained from contemporary images of visitors in the galleries of the museum. In Scharf's picture of the classical galleries from 1827 (fig. 4.16), the figures inform us that artists and aesthetes would go to the classical sculpture galleries to study the works on display. There are no equivalent images of visitors for the Egyptian galleries, thus accentuating how the Greek and Roman works were received as role models that should be emulated, whereas the Egyptian works were received as oddities or rather, as examples of what should be overcome. Indeed, as noted earlier, the visitors in the 1820 illustration (plate 10) are looking toward the Discobolus rather than reflecting upon the statues in their midst. Furthermore, in an image of visitors in the entrance of the museum (fig. 4.17), we are drawn to the gestures of the well-dressed couple in the picture, who like the figures in Pugin and Rowlandson's illustration of 1808 (fig. 3.10), are shown to be actively absorbing the decorative delights surrounding them. This reaction is altogether different from that of the visitors climbing on the sarcophagi (plate 4), suggesting that a differential level of respect existed for the Egyptian antiquities.

Important insights into how the museum's new installation would have been received can also be gleaned from the reviews of Belzoni's exhibition of 1821. Visitors to the museum's Egyptian gallery were likely to have seen this highly popular exhibition, which offered a far more contextual and colorful idea of ancient Egypt than the museum's interpretation.[93] With its combination of life-size reconstructions of the chambers of Seti

I's tomb, decorated walls, and scale models, Belzoni's exhibition provided a range of visual media through which ancient Egypt could be understood. Indeed, the impact of the reconstructions was so great that visitors talked of "experiencing" ancient Egypt in a way that they had no other ancient civilization:

> The translations of Mr. Denon's work, by Mr. Holt and Mr. Aikin, have familiarized the English reader with the nature of Egyptian antiquities, as far as verbal accounts can effect that object; while accompanying prints, copied from some of those in the French works, have communicated a visual, and therefore a more satisfactory knowledge of part of those relics. But the most gratifying consequence of exploring the remains of ancient Egypt, in its supply of amusement with information, is the representation of the Egyptian Tomb, Temples, and Pyramid, recently visited by Mr. Belzoni, together with some curiosities brought with him from Egypt. Not only are the former presented to the eye in models which contain, to a fraction, the forms and hue of the originals, but two of the imitated chambers of the tomb are of their exact size; so that to the eye, and, in no partial degree, to fancy's eye, you sit in them as in the realities themselves, and are in the presence of objects that fill the mind with pleasing wonder, conscious as it is, at the time, of its own transient existence in its rapidly wasting tenement, the body.[94]

Such reactions indicate how Belzoni's exhibition saw interest in ancient Egypt taking on a new dimension. One can understand how the visitors who enjoyed being immersed in a reconstructed ancient world may have felt disappointed with the comparatively unimaginative representation of ancient Egypt they encountered at the museum.

At Belzoni's exhibition, visitors also acknowledge the emotional impact of ancient Egypt:

> In viewing these models of galleries and halls, through which, he [Belzoni] says, he wandered "with astonishment at every step" at their number, the vivid colours and extraordinary figures on the walls and ceilings, the mummies scattered in various places, the statues of fine earth, &c. we may well conceive the deep emotions with which he must have been impressed, not only from their antiquity, but from the historical, religious, and sepulchral character of the object. The emotion must indeed, on these occasions, be of grand and poetical nature; fed as the imagination is by the strangeness and stillness of the scene, and the partly ascertained, and partly unknown nature of the objects.[95]

This account reveals how the antiquities of Egypt possessed numerous qualities or associations that rendered them interesting and appealing to a wide range of audiences. For those with religious, antiquarian, or historical interests, there was something to engage with; those seeking entertainment, a sense of excitement, and mystery were also catered for. In addition, there were the continued feelings of nationalism stirred by the objects and the opportunities they offered to insult the French.[96]

More generally, it appears that some visitors still found the displays at the museum reminiscent of a curiosity cabinet. Despite the new freedom in viewing the collections and particularly the lack of restrictions on time, which previous visitors had highlighted as a key problem, it appears that they still found it difficult to take in the contents of the museum because of the "strange mishmash of objets d'art, natural exhibits, curiosities, books and models. . . . There are undoubtedly many interesting things in the various rooms; however, I must to my shame confess that from seeing too many similar remarkable things, I am in the mood to feel a kind of indigestion at the sight of them."[97]

Supporting this view of the German writer Price Pückler-Muskau, the American visitor Nathaniel Wheaton observed: "The result of a *first* visit to such an institution must always be unsatisfactory; it being impossible to carry away distinct impressions, where so many objects, and those so rare and curious, solicit attention. . . . Having wearied my attention among minerals and manuscripts, and sarcophagi from Egypt and pottery from Herculaneum, and the spoils of the Parthenon, and statuary in every stage of mutilation and decay, I returned to my lodgings."[98] Despite the fact that he was wearied by the sheer volume of things to see, it is noteworthy that among the things Wheaton did remember were the objects from Egypt. Thus, while it may have been difficult to obtain any "distinct impressions" from a first visit, the Egyptian objects still made an impact.

Finally, a most useful source of information on how visitors were likely to have responded to the museum's new installation on ancient Egypt is the detailed account of visitor types at Belzoni's exhibition provided by the writer Marguerite Gardiner, Countess of Blessington.[99] Although it does not describe how visitors received the museum's installation, this account provides a unique and very important insight into how people responded to representations of ancient Egypt at the time. For instance, in reporting on her visit to the exhibition, the countess described a wide spectrum of people who were present:

> A party of school-boys were amusing themselves by discovering likenesses to each other, in the monstrous deities displayed on the wall; and a governess was answering the enquiries of her young pupils, "If there ever existed men with lions', apes', and foxes' heads?" by sententiously reading extracts from Belzoni's Description, not a word of which the little innocents could understand. One old lady remarked, that "The Tomb was not at all alarming when people got used to it"; and another said, "it made her melancholy, by reminding her of the death of her dear first husband, the worthy Alderman, to whose memory she had erected a very genteel one." Two vulgar looking old men declared their conviction that "It was all a hum, for had there been such a place, Lord Nelson would have said

> *summat* about it, in his dispatches"; and another person of the same class, said that, "For his part, he did not like foreigners; and why did no Englishman never find this *here* place? he should not wonder if, in the end, Mr. Belzoni, or whatever his name is, was found to be like that Baron who wrote so many fibs." The first speaker observed that, "Any man, who would go for to say, as *how* men had apes' faces (though his own bore a striking likeness to one) would say anything.[100]

Here we have a range of visitors including schoolchildren, a teacher, elderly ladies, "vulgar looking" elderly men, "another person of the same class," and the writer herself, who was representing the informed "society lady." This listing of the wide spectrum of visitor types is invaluable because it informs us about the different meanings people both gained and contributed to the perception of ancient Egypt. Besides inspiring visitors to confront death as a personal issue, the Egyptian antiquities provided a source of amusement for children, served as a symbol of British military might, and presented an opportunity to express xenophobic ideas about foreigners (i.e., the reaction to Belzoni's being Italian). It appears that few actually responded to the significance of the antiquities as historical or archaeological evidence, such as the "poor teacher," who had to quote from Belzoni's account, as she knew nothing of the subject herself.

Added to the rich mix already described by the countess is a "party of fashionables" including two ladies who were accompanied by two "*Dandies* of the first class." In expressing their disdain for the exhibition with gasps of "What an odd place!" and "O dear, how disagreeable the smell is!" this group sum up their disappointment as follows:

> "Do pray let us leave this tiresome stupid place, where there is not a single thing to be seen worth looking at, and where the company is so intolerably vulgar. I really fancied it was a fashionable morning lounge, where one would meet every soul worth meeting in town, for, as to looking at a set of Egyptian frights it never entered my head; I have not heard of Egypt since my governess used to bore me about it when I was learning geography; and as to tombs and pyramids, I have a perfect horror of them." Another of the ladies observed, that she "hated every thing Egyptian ever since she had heard of the plagues." And the third begged, that "in decrying Egypt and its productions, they would except Egyptian pebbles, which were beautiful, and took an exquisite polish."
>
> "Oh! Pray do look at the female ornaments (exclaimed one of the ladies); did you ever see such horrid things? Only fancy any woman of taste wearing them: well, I declare those same Egyptians must have been dreadfully vulgar, and the women must have looked hideously when adorned in such finery. How surprised they would have been at seeing Wirgman's beautiful trinkets, or the sweet tasteful jewellery at Howel and James's."[101]

Whether it is the bad company or the frightful subject of the exhibition that most offends is difficult to establish. What this condemnation does reveal, however, is that it was acceptable to speak about Egyptian antiquities in such derogatory terms. One can assume that these "fashionables" would have been far more respectful if talking about classical antiquities, whereas expressions of horror when referring to Egyptian objects would not have been out of the ordinary.

Although written to amuse, Lady Blessington's account tells us much that is important when considering how displays of ancient Egypt were consumed. While it may be true that the museum did not attract the many different types of visitors that Belzoni's exhibition did, it would be wrong to assume that it catered only to the learned aesthete or scholar. Above all, Lady Blessington's account reveals how there was "something for everyone" when it came to Egyptian antiquities. By this ancient culture it was possible to be horrified, amused, informed, repulsed, mystified, shocked, fascinated, awestruck, insulted or entertained. Indeed, Lady Blessington appears to make this point herself when she observes,

> "The tomb levels all distinctions," though a trite observation, is one, the truth of which has never been doubted; and, if it were, a visit to the tomb of Psammis would convince the most incredulous: for here persons of all ranks meet, and justle each other with impunity. The fine lady, who holds her *vinaigrette* to her nostrils, and remarks to her attending beau, "What a dreadfully shocking place it is"; and that "there is not a single person of fashion there," is elbowed by a fat red faced woman, who looks like the mistress of a gin shop, and who declares to her spouse that, "She would give a shilling for a glass of aniseed; for looking at *them there* mummies has made her feel so queerish."[102]

In addition to these contrasting types are added an old lady and her two grand-daughters, a simple-looking country girl and her companion, and a "very showy dressed woman" and her children. Lady Blessington's survey of all these visitors concludes with a sense of despair as to their ignorance "on historical, geographical, and chronological points" and even more so, their apathy:

> It was plain that they came to the Tomb merely to pass away an hour, or in the expectation of meeting their acquaintances; but as to feeling any interest in the scene before them, or drawing any moral inference from it, they seemed as little inclined, as if they had been in the round room of the Opera House on a crowded night. Wrapt up in their own self-satisfied ignorance, the works or monuments of antiquity boast no attraction for them; and strange to say, the metropolis of a country that professes to surpass all others in civilisation and morals, presents, in some of its inhabitants, examples of ignorance and want of reflection, scarcely equalled in any other part of the civilised world.[103]

Here we see the intimate connection between viewing antiquities and moral improvement affirmed; however, learning and instruction were equally emphasized. For instance, despite her pessimism about the lack of reflection on works of antiquity, Lady Blessington does manage to identify some visitors of a more decent caliber amid the ignorant throng: "A gentleman, who appeared to be tutor, and two young lads, were attentively examining the model, and comparing it with Belzoni's Narrative; and the questions they asked, and the observations which they made, shewed a spirit of enquiry and intelligence pleasing to witness; while his answers, full of good sense and information, marked how well qualified he was to convey instruction."

Deemed to be behaving as they should, these visitors are using relevant texts to make sense of the exhibits and, unlike the other people, have clearly come with the intention of gaining some knowledge. However, despite her endorsement of this approach to viewing the exhibition, Lady Blessington reveals that she, too, is not immune from making biased assessments of the displays before her: "Two or three fine young women, simply but elegantly attired, with their graceful attitudes, and undulating draperies, formed an agreeable contrast to the stiff and disproportioned forms of the grotesque Egyptian female figures."[104]

Not only does this comment reveal that the judgments of the educated are little different to the reactions of the "vulgar" visitor, it also helps to explain why there was so much disdain for the qualities of Egyptian design as manifested in the ancient sculptures exhibited in the museum. For instance, the sculptures of Egyptian figures were criticized not only because they contrasted so sharply with the highly esteemed ancient Greek works, but because they conflicted so strongly with the fashions of the day.

* * *

The museum's acquisition of the Salt sculptures greatly enhanced the 1808 installation of Egyptian antiquities in the Townley Gallery. No longer just "wondrous curiosities" and "colossal monstrosities," Egyptian antiquities had then also attained the status of "monumental masterpieces." Egyptian antiquities were at last gaining recognition as products of a nation capable of constructing works of an extraordinary and accomplished nature. Despite this newfound respect, however, the museum's behavior over the acquisition of Salt's collection suggests that for the majority of trustees, the Egyptian sculptures were still a tolerated oddity rather than a respected art form. This attitude is further evidenced in the installation of 1823, which revealed a continued lack of interest in determining the appropriate modes for presenting Egyptian objects in a museum setting. While the trustees may have neglected improving the exhibitionary environment for the new collection of sculptures, however, the Egyptian gallery demonstrated a unique ability to offer different things to different audiences.

While those with an interest in religion, antiquities, or universal history would have found something of interest, those fascinated by mysteries or who had an appetite for the exotic would have also been catered to. Beyond these, of course, there was the never-ending appeal to those with an interest in the strange and bizarre.

5 Accessible Oddities

THE NEW SMIRKE GALLERY AND EGYPTIAN ROOM, 1834 AND 1837

By the 1830s the European consuls had expanded their excavation programs in Egypt, and more national museums began to acquire large collections of ancient Egyptian material. Notable collections of Egyptian antiquities that went on display around this time included those in Florence, Turin, Paris (the Louvre), and Rome (the Vatican).[1] While the French and British consuls still dominated the antiquities scene in Egypt, independent collectors soon joined them, forming their own extensive collections. Despite developments within Egypt that sought to thwart the increasing exodus of antiquities, objects destined for the great museums of Europe were excavated at an alarming rate.[2] Furthermore, many more substantial collections were created in association with the scholarly and artistic expeditions to Egypt undertaken in the 1830s. It was as a result of these changes that the British Museum's collection of Egyptian antiquities was greatly expanded and diversified, and more significantly, that the opportunity came to provide yet another vision of ancient Egypt. The major acquisitions during this period included the collections of the British bookseller Joseph Sams (1784–1860), that of Henry Salt (his third collection), and that of the Greek collector Giovanni Anastasi (1780–1860), all of which represented a greater range of archaeological material from Egypt than previous collections. While the purchase of these collections revealed that attitudes to ancient Egypt were changing and that a more purposeful approach to acquiring Egyptian antiquities was emerging, the circumstances in which they came to the museum reveal how the nature of acquisition during this time was still essentially serendipitous. Despite this, the many hundreds of new objects that were acquired from the three collections of Sams, Salt, and Anastasi conveyed a far more comprehensive view of ancient Egypt than had previously been presented.

Accommodated in a new sculpture gallery opened in 1834 and a new Egyptian Room opened in 1837, the museum's latest installment of Egyptian antiquities was presented in a display style similar to the installations of 1808 and 1823. However, the new architectural setting assigned to these objects a more impressive status than they had had previously. The displays of the smaller antiquities, which had been overshadowed by the arrangements of the sculptural works in the Townley Gallery, now commanded their own attention. Constituting a very substantial and important component of the Egyptian collection, the everyday objects acquired through Sams, Salt, and Anastasi were arranged in a newly built room that was situated on the upper story of the museum. This "Egyptian Room" provided the opportunity to introduce new ways of presenting the diverse range of Egyptian material now possessed by the museum, and it is here that we see yet another identity created for Egyptian antiquities. In addition to the "wondrous curiosities" of 1759, the "colossal monstrosities" of 1808, and the "monumental masterpieces" of 1823, ancient Egypt was now defined as the ultimate source of "accessible oddities." This identity referred to the way in which ancient Egypt was presented as a familiar civilization with objects and cultural practices "just like ours." At the same time, however, the antiquities remained just that little bit different and thus appeared as oddities. Finally, the reception of the new ancient Egyptian displays demonstrates that visitors responded extremely favorably to the museum's new installations and its revised interpretation of ancient Egypt. Despite this, audiences were still hungry for the previous incarnations so successfully constructed by the museum and their expectations of an exotic ancient Egypt continued to influence their reception of the displays.

ACQUISITION

An understanding of the acquisition of Egyptian antiquities in the museum at this time must take into account the significant developments that took place within the museum during the 1830s. Of crucial importance was the 1835 parliamentary inquiry into the management of the museum, as this provides key insights into how the Egyptian collection was assessed and valued by museum staff and the government. Furthermore, stemming from concern about how government money was being spent by the museum, this inquiry elicited important information on the museum's acquisition policies and on the development of the Egyptian collection.[3] On the subject of acquisition, for example, the inquiry questioned the purchase of the Salt collection, with the principal librarian, Henry Ellis, being asked to explain why the collection was initially declined.[4] When Ellis informed the chair, Sotheron Estcourt, that the decision was based on an assessment of the collection by Julius Millingen, he was then asked, "Should you consider Mr. Millingen a person capable of valuing such a collection of antiquities as that of Mr. Salt?"[5] To this Ellis admitted that he did not "know what Mr. Millingen's knowledge of Egyptian antiquities may be, but for the Greek and Roman antiquities I believe he has been long consulted by those who purchase them."[6] This line of questioning reflected how the government was not satisfied with the museum's procedure of making assessments on collections and suggested that they were concerned with the credentials of those "authorities" used to testify to the value of antiquities. When it came to Egyptian antiquities, the trustees had been satisfied with the assessments of classical scholars instead of seeking experts on Egypt. While this may have reflected the fact that there was a dearth of Egyptian specialists in the country, it also suggested that the trustees valued the views of classical experts above those with other specialties, no matter how relevant. That the inquiry raised the issue of how more qualified people could be drawn upon to evaluate the Egyptian collections indicates that the government was aware that there were far better individuals to do the job.

Persisting with the acquisition of Egyptian antiquities, the inquiry then turned to the controversial topic of the alabaster sarcophagus, which had been offered for sale by Salt and Belzoni in 1821. Refused by the trustees, this highly significant object was subsequently bought by John Soane. In an almost incredulous manner, Estcourt asked for confirmation that "a private individual paid 2,000£ for that sarcophagus, one of the most extraordinary specimens of Egyptian antiquity in this country, which the trustees allowed to go out of their custody without having even communicated an answer to Mr. Salt as to the sum they were willing to give for that and his other antiquities?"[7] Estcourt then challenged Ellis on the museum's conduct toward Salt, asking him, "Do you conceive that the negotiation was conducted upon those generous and liberal principles which ought to mark the purchase of objects of antiquities possessing national interest between the trustees of the National Museum and a private individual?" to which Ellis replied, "To the best of my recollection they [Soane] gave the price which Mr. Richards offered them at: at all events Mr. Richards accepted the price proposed."[8] The report then records how Salt was so dissatisfied with the price the museum gave him for his collection that he offered his second collection of Egyptian antiquities to the French government.[9] It was fortunate for the trustees that their purchase of the collection of Joseph Sams (see below), which was finalized just before the inquiry, was not also raised at this juncture, as there were striking parallels with the way this collector was treated.

It appears that the select committee did not realize that the conduct by the trustees regarding the Salt collection stemmed as much from the attitude toward Egyptian antiquities as it did the lack of a formal procedure on acquisition. However, the inquiry did reveal failings in the museum's conduct regarding the acquisition of Egyptian antiquities that needed to be addressed. To this end, recommendations were made to ensure that the purchase of collections was done in a less ad hoc manner than it had been in the past. It was suggested, for instance, that a regulation should be introduced whereby a written report on the "character, value, and desirableness" of collections was presented by the heads of departments to the trustees, which would then be presented to Parliament for a grant in

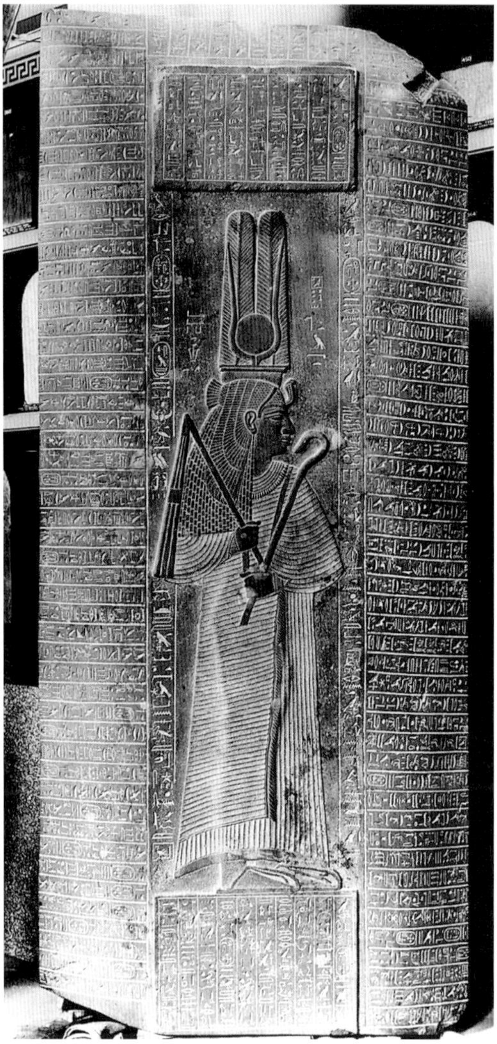

5.1

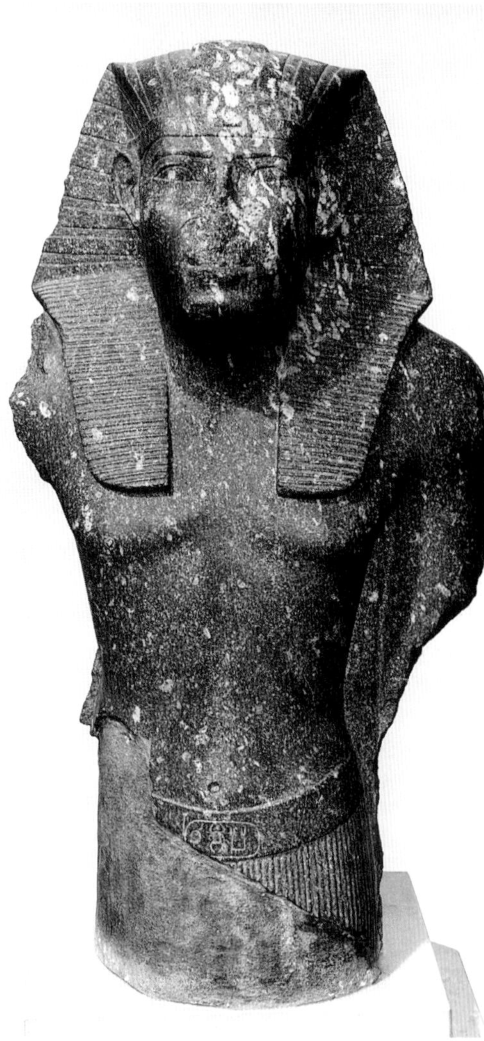

5.3

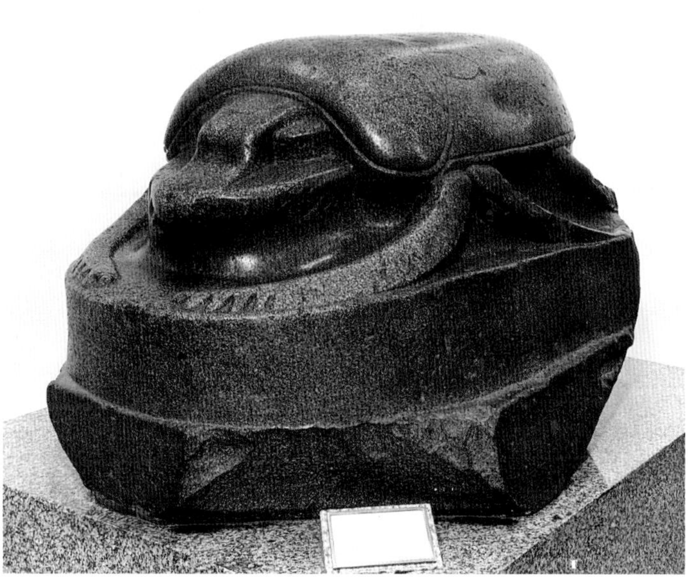

5.2

5.1. Sarcophagus of Ankhnesneferibra, daughter of Psamtek II (EA 32) from Thebes, Twenty-sixth Dynasty. Purchased by the British Museum in 1836.

5.2. Monumental sculpture of a scarab beetle (EA 74), found in Istanbul, possibly Ptolemaic. Donated to the British Museum in 1838 by Lord Elgin.

5.3. Statue of Senwosret I (EA 44), thought to be from Karnak, Twelfth Dynasty. Donated to the British Museum in 1838 by Richard Howard Vyse.

aid of the purchase of any collection.[10] Furthermore, the government put forward three proposals that they thought might improve the current procedures of acquisition. First was the idea that "travelling naturalists and others" be employed to collect for the museum in foreign countries; second was the suggestion that naturalists and "persons versed in antiquities" could accompany "expeditions of discovery, sent out under the directions of the Admiralty"; and third was the proposition that consuls, British ministers, and other government agents abroad be used to acquire collections.[11] The trustees supported the last option, stating that they wished to enlarge the collections through the efforts of the officers of the navy and army and other government officials who were serving abroad.[12] This approach to collection development had actually been articulated earlier by the trustees themselves. In 1818, for instance, it was stated that English representatives abroad should "avail themselves of any opportunities that may offer of obtaining, at moderate prices, such articles as to the best of their information are likely to prove useful acquisitions."[13] While this attempt to form a collection policy affected the growth of the Egyptian collection to some extent, the collection continued to be enriched by purchases made from enterprising individuals.

Despite the select committee's recommendation that a more formal and aggressive system be set up for purchasing collections, the trustees of the museum had little need to initiate an acquisition program when it came to Egyptian antiquities. Barely a month passed in the 1830s when the trustees were not approached with an offer to purchase a collection or significant object, resulting in thousands of antiquities being transported from Egypt to the museum in this decade alone.[14] Particularly notable was the addition of vast numbers of smaller objects, stelae, and papyri, which were obtained from the purchase of the extensive collections of Joseph Sams, Henry Salt, and Giovanni Anastasi.[15] Many more such items were acquired through the purchase of smaller collections from John Barker (1771–1849), James Burton (1788–1862) and Giovanni d'Athanasi, and from donations made by John Gardner Wilkinson (1797–1875).[16] In addition to these collections, several objects of significance were acquired by the museum during this period. Of particular note was the Abydos King List bought in 1837, the two lion statues from Soleb donated by Lord Prudhoe in 1835 (plate 11), the sarcophagus of Ankhnesneferibra purchased in 1836 (fig. 5.1), the colossal beetle donated by Lord Elgin in 1835 (fig. 5.2), the statue of Senwosret I and the sarcophagus of Nesisut donated by Richard Howard Vyse in 1838 and 1839 respectively (figs. 5.3–5.4), and the baboon sculpture purchased from John Barker in 1833 (fig. 5.5).[17] Many other sculptures that were accepted by the trustees never made it to the museum because they were destroyed en route or because negotiations to purchase them fell through. While an important example of the former was the statue of a sphinx from Alexandria, important examples of the latter

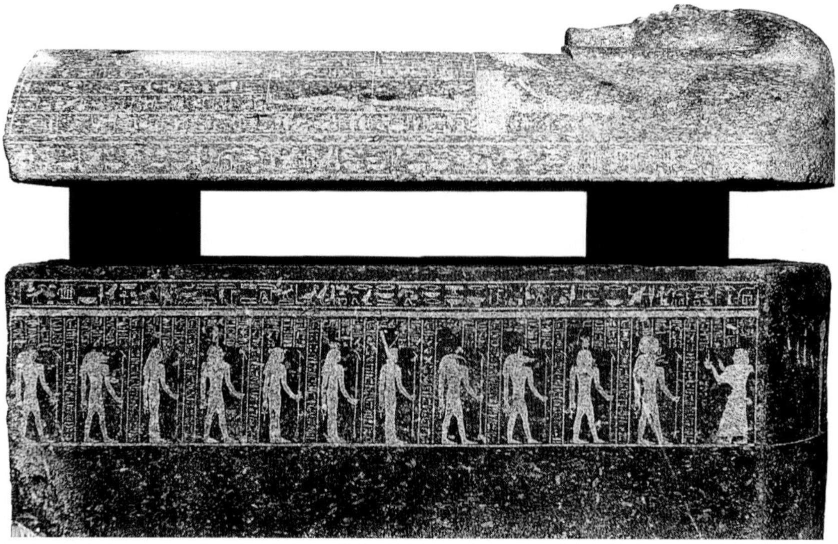

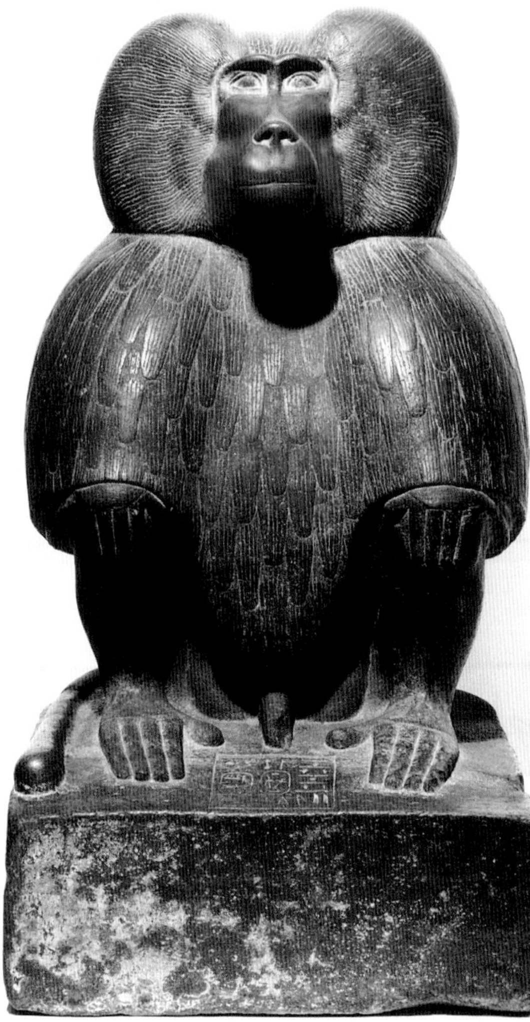

5.4. *(facing, above)* Sarcophagus of Nesisut (EA 30), from Giza, Twenty-seventh Dynasty. Donated to the British Museum in 1839 by Richard Howard Vyse.

5.5. *(facing, below)* Statue of a baboon (EA 38), Eighteenth Dynasty. Purchased by the British Museum in 1833 from the sale of John Barker's collection.

were the colossal statue of Ramesses II from Memphis (see below), and the statue of Sarapis.[18] Another great loss from around this time was the four highly significant literary papyri that were offered to the trustees by d'Athanasi in 1841, but which went to the Berlin Museum.[19]

Although collectors did obtain smaller antiquities (including written and inscribed material) in the 1820s, they still tended to focus on obtaining pieces that they considered visually impressive and thus suitable for display, particularly larger sculptures. During the 1830s, however, the significance of everyday objects was increasingly recognized, and although statues were still sought after, collectors broadened their interests to include the range of domestic and industrial antiquities that were now more readily available on the collectors' market.[20] The appointment of Samuel Birch (1813–1885) as assistant in the Department of Antiquities at the museum in 1836 played an important role here, as he was the first curator dedicated to the subject of Egyptology and as such took a very active role in broadening out the collection and ensuring that it became more representative.[21] Indeed, the appointment of Birch can be seen as signifying the beginnings of Egyptology at the museum, as prior to this no member of staff had been capable of assessing the significance of the Egyptian antiquities or had been active in developing the collection. It was also during this time that the keeper of antiquities, Edward Hawkins (1780–1867), assumed a far more assertive role in identifying and assessing items that he thought should be added to the Egyptian collection.[22] Furthermore, Hawkins became responsible for investigating the significance of the major objects being considered by the trustees, and was given the authority to make decisions on the purchase of smaller collections.[23]

Other significant developments concerning the acquisition of Egyptian antiquities included the trustees' increasing interest in purchasing objects from auctions, and their agreement to purchase objects from Europe.[24] Of greater significance, however, was the fact that there was now a body of recognized Egyptologists whom the trustees were willing to call upon to assess the value of collections. Beyond responding to requests from the museum to make such assessments, this growing community of specialists also encouraged the trustees to make particular acquisitions. Key examples here include Wilkinson's involvement in the acquisition of the colossal statue of Ramesses II from Memphis and the sarcophagus of Ankhnesneferibra, and Edward Lane's (1801–1876) involvement in the dealings over the statue of Sarapis.[25] Also worth noting was the fact that individual trustees began to actively promote major Egyptian purchases, a major example being the sarcophagus of Ankhnesneferibra, which the Duke of Hamilton positively appraised and encouraged the trustees to buy (fig. 5.1).[26] Despite these signs of a more serious interest in developing the Egyptian collection, the trustees remained somewhat reluctant to invest in ancient Egypt; hence, their rejection of an offer by the collector Giovanni d'Athanasi to procure another major Egyptian collection for the museum.[27]

In 1833 negotiations began for the acquisition of a major collection of Egyptian antiquities offered by the bookseller and collector Joseph Sams. Offered to the trustees for £4,000, Sams's collection included over two thousand objects, which he obtained from his own travels in Egypt and from purchases he made from other individuals who worked in Egypt.[28] Although not rich in larger sculptures, the collection included a wealth and diversity of other items such as stelae, scarabs, furniture, foodstuffs, and papyri (fig. 5.6 and plate 12). Sams's collection was significant because it was relatively comprehensive considering the nature of collecting at the time.[29] Furthermore, although Sams had sold some of his most significant items to other collectors, he was keen to dispose of his collection in its entirety and thus considered the museum to be the most appropriate home for it. Reminiscent of Salt's dealings with the museum, a lengthy correspondence between Sams and the trustees took place over the purchase, revealing that despite the wider appreciation of Egyptian antiquities in Britain, the trustees' attitude toward them essentially remained one of indifference.

It is clear from the many testimonials that Sams presented in association with his offer that this was a highly significant accumulation of objects. The numismatist William Martin Leake (1777–1860), for example, emphasized the importance of the scarabs, "some of which are curious for their inscriptions, others for their workmanship, and all for the materials in which they are wrought."[30] The Earl of Mountnorris also attested to the value and reasonable price of the collection, expressing "surprise that so many new and interesting articles could have been collected by an individual who was not a permanent resident in Egypt for many years."[31] He also drew attention to the set of mummies included in the collection, which he stated were not to be "equalled in any other collection."[32] Hoping to stir feelings of national pride as motivation for purchasing the collection, the earl reminded the trustees that Salt's second collection had been lost to the museum because it had been offered to the French:

> Most sincerely do I hope that the wretched economy which is now the order of the day, will not deprive the nation of this interesting collection—a collection all the more valuable to the British Museum as it contains so many small articles in which line your present collection is so very deficient. I think that if this is purchased you will be able to boast of having the finest Egyptian Museum in Europe although unfortunately Mr. Salt's second collection was permitted to go to Paris. If this present opportunity is lost I am fearful that there is very little chance of another occurring.[33]

In addition to these private testimonials, a public appraisal of the collection appeared in the *Gentleman's Magazine* in 1833.[34] This report highlighted several features of the collection, including a marble sarcophagus

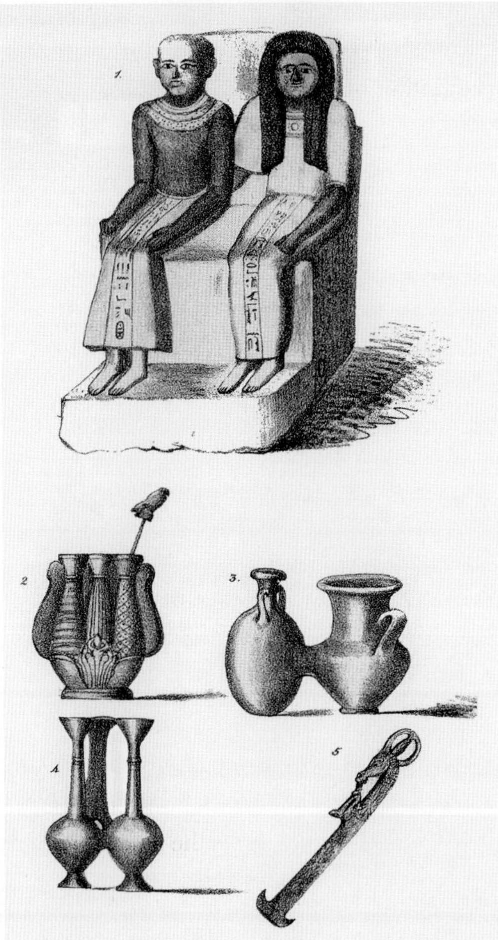

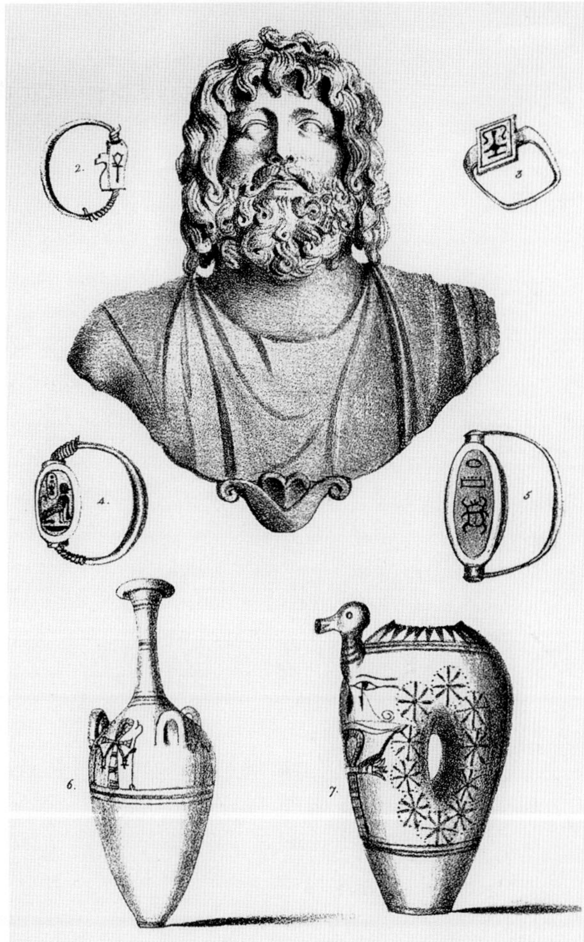

5.6a and 5.6b. Sketches of some of the antiquities in Joseph Sams's collection. *Gentleman's Magazine* 1833: 312–313.

with a mummy inside, the stelae (fifty-four in total), the mummies (six in total), the scarabs, a basket of preserved fruit, boxes of ancient grains, alabaster tables, vases, and ancient manuscripts. Emphasizing the uniqueness of the collection, the author of this report concluded that "the nation is deeply indebted to the gentleman—a private individual—who has thus expended his property, devoted his time and talents, and even risked his life and health in the acquisition of objects which so much enrich our native country."[35] The fact that Sams was offering his collection to the museum at a very moderate sum was also mentioned, and it was asserted that it would be a "national disgrace" if the collection were "permitted to pass to another country."[36] Despite these positive appraisals, the trustees were reluctant to take the collection and postponed making a decision on Sams's offer. Following the submission of a report on the value of the collection by Hawkins, the trustees declined to purchase it at the price asked.[37] However, recognizing that it was "very desirable the collection should be obtained for the benefit of the country," the museum suggested that the price for it be reduced.[38]

Sams responded to the trustees in much the same way as Salt had done ten years before, asserting that his motivation for selling his collection to the museum centered on his loyalty to the nation and that he truly desired the collection to remain in the country:

> I immediately replied, that as he [the visitor bearing the museum's reply], and many knew, I had from the first, particularly wished these valuable collections should become the property of the country, to be attached to our noble National Repository—and that therefore, tho' they were thought by good judges quite worth the first sum*[see below], I would yet rather lose, or take less, than that they should ever pass to another kingdom, or be dispersed. After the toil, expense, and danger, I incurred in amassing, and obtaining them, it would cause me great regret to see them leave our native country. Under this feeling, and to promote the object in view, I said, and requested the gentleman to inform you, that I would then put them at 500£ less, viz at 3500—also, as I had obtained by purchase lately, several rare articles sent recently to England by our consul in Egypt, which I had added to my collections, anxious as I was, to increase their interest and riches by any really important objects—these I would likewise add at the reduced sum—being very desirous to make the offer acceptable to you . . .
>
> *permit me to hint that if you knew the time, expense, and labour that have been bestowed for them (to say nothing of risks and dangers) you would I believe, think even this remuneration small.[39]

In addition to stressing his desire to see the collection retained in Britain, Sams was at pains to inform the trustees of the great lengths he had gone to in assembling it. Over the next few months he repeatedly wrote to the trustees stating these points again and again. He also commented on the fact that most of the trustees had not seen his collection, with an aside that those who had come to see it did so "only in a slight and hurried manner."[40] Drawing their attention to the article on his collection in the *Gentleman's Magazine*, Sams reminded them that three "distinct, eminent and learned persons" had emphasized its value.[41] However, his offer of a reduced price, of the inclusion of more objects, and of the presentation of further testimonials was still rejected, and the trustees offered £3,000 instead.[42] Anxious that his collection "should remain in this country, and become the property of the nation," Sams accepted this price.[43] The trustees then resolved to ask Treasury for the funds, asking Charles Yorke, William Martin Leake, William Bankes, and the Earl of Mountnorris for letters on the value of the collection, which they would submit with their application.[44]

While he was happy to verify the merits of Sams's collection, Yorke expressed some discomfort with being asked to judge its monetary value: "Tho' I am an admirer of Egyptian antiquities, and have to a certain degree studied the subject, yet I am no collector and do not present to be a positive judge of the value of such articles."[45] Leake's response to a request to prepare a written testimony on Sams's collection is also interesting, as it suggests that access to the antiquities was considered necessary for the discipline of Egyptology to develop, and that this was being prevented by the distribution of such objects in private rather than public collections:

> According to the best of my recollection, the three points to which the inquiries of the Trustees were directed, were the utility of making a large collection of monuments in illustration of Egyptian archaeology, the degree of merit of Mr. Sams's collection, and its pecuniary value. In regard to the first, there can hardly be a difference of opinion. It is obvious that the little progress made, until of late, in Egyptian archaeology, and in the explanation of the existing monuments of ancient Egypt, which from their quantity, variety and general good preservation, offer the most extensive of all fields of research in ancient literature, has been mainly owing to the want of a sufficient number of good examples easily accessible to persons desirous of devoting themselves to this study, the monuments which have been brought to Europe having generally been dispersed in private collections, and the drawings of those which remain in Egypt being too frequently deficient in that degree of accuracy which experience shews to be absolutely required, to enable us to arrive at any well founded conclusions in this pursuit. It would be a subject of just regret, therefore, should such a collection as Mr. Sams's, which has required considerable time, care and exertion to bring together, and which is interesting from its great variety of objects, be dispersed by an auction.[46]

Here Sams's collection is not being promoted because of the unique and spectacular objects it contains—objects that would offer great popular appeal and further establish the museum's reputation as a repository of great discoveries—rather, the justification offered for the purchase of the collection is that it will serve scientific purposes, allowing those wishing to study such objects the opportunity to do so. Beyond emphasizing the value of material culture in the study of the past, Leake's testimony reinforces the notion that it was the role of the museum to contribute to the establishment of scholarly disciplines.

Just as the trustees had been lukewarm in their response to Sams's collection, so was the Treasury. Not only did they request a "more full and particular examination of collection," but they stated that they were prepared to pay only £2,500 if the collection was still considered "desirable."[47] Furthermore, the Treasury picked up on the fact that the evaluators of the collection may not have been the most appropriate individuals to undertake such a task and suggested that two or three people who were "practically acquainted with the pecuniary value of objects of antiquity" were sought.[48] This request reveals that while the trustees may not have recognized it, the government saw the scholarly evaluation of antiquities as a matter completely different from the assessment of their pecuniary value.

The document that was compiled by the trustees for the Treasury went far beyond providing testimonials of two or three individuals. Entitled "Testimonials to the Character of Mr. Sams's Egyptian Antiquities," this letter included the signatures of no fewer than fourteen individuals:

> The extensive Egyptian Collections obtained, and brought to England by Mr. J. Sams, consist of above Two Thousand, two hundred articles, many of which are considered to be unique, some of which relate to eminent Pharaohs. Specimens of the Arts, and Manufactures of Ancient Egypt, in great variety. Twenty one exceedingly curious Manuscripts on Papyrus. Several Statues, in marble, basalt, and stone, bearing the names of ancient Pharaohs. Necklaces, Gems and Signets, set in gold, likewise possessing Pharaonic names. Several remarkable Sarcophagi in wood, and perhaps the most ancient Quadro, or moveable Painting, in the world. Six different specimens of Mummies, with cases finely decorated; and an extraordinary Sarcophagus of polished marble, the top beautifully sculptured, partly as a human figure. This fine monument, may be compared in interest and value, to the one for which alone, Sir John Soane gave £2000. It is not so large but has its cover, and a mummy within it, in fine preservation, neither of which the other possesses. The collections together, which would take a volume to describe, we think highly worthy, and important, to be placed in our National Repository; and we judge the whole to be moderate in price, at the sum of £4000, which the proprietor considers, at least, they *ought* to bring him. He has however, agreed to accept £3000, for the collections, from the Trustees of the British Museum, rather than they should pass to another country, or be disposed of to any Foreign Court. We the undersigned having examined them consider these collections very valuable, and highly interesting; particularly desirable to be rendered beneficial to the public by being deposited in the British Museum, and at the above sum, very cheap.[49]

Included among the signatories on the document were those of S. Sotheby and Son, the leading antiques and fine arts dealers of London.[50] These names alone satisfied the request that more qualified people be called upon to vouch for the collection.

While the Treasury considered the trustees' document, Sams wrote expressing his dismay at their reduced offer, listing several grounds upon which the museum should reconsider paying the originally reduced price of £3,000. The main things he emphasized were the scientific and comprehensive nature of the collection, its reasonable price, and the threat of losing the collection to another nation. His appeals to the latter were aimed, once again, to stir feelings of national pride among the trustees.[51] He also referred to another offer of purchase "from a liberal and highly respectable quarter," which he had refused due to "a principle of honour and integrity." In reinforcing the scientific value of his collection, Sams drew the trustees' attention to the fact that leading authorities had vouched for its uniqueness and the presence of many rare objects, and he spent some time listing the credentials of the individuals who had signed the testimonial of the collection.[52] Concluding his appeal with an assertion of the moderate price of the collection, Sams reiterated that many had estimated it to be worth double what he asked for and that he was only asking for small compensation—"You may indeed give even Ten thousand, for a collection, should one turn up, and it may not be worth, nor have the many rare and unique objects in it, these collections have. I well know, some wd [would] ask Ten thousand for these, and blamed me for not so doing." Sams then signed off, refusing to reduce the price of £3,000 and adding a final comment about the role the collection would play in enriching the national museum—which was "so deficient in objects of this kind, even compared to various of the *petty* continental states."[53]

Many more letters between Sams and the trustees were exchanged over the following months, giving the impression that Sams made it part of his daily routine to remind the museum of the merits of his collection.[54] One cannot help but admire the tenacity of Sams and appreciate the sense of frustration that he felt in waiting for a decision to be made. Hoping to bring the deal to a close, Sams compared his collection to the antiquities in Sotheby's stores, informing the trustees that the largest of the Sotheby collections amounted to only about a quarter of his collection.[55] This last-ditched attempt failed to secure the price he expected, and when he was finally informed that Treasury was not prepared to pay more than £2,500, he reluctantly accepted the offer, "anxious as he always has been, and is, that the rare and extensive collections should be deposited in the National Museum."[56] Like Salt, Sams could not help informing the trustees how unhappy he was with the way the whole matter had been dealt with; not only had it taken two years to resolve, but he was "much injured thro' the honorable part he has acted to the museum, in this long period of time that he has with anxiety, been waiting: not to mention the great trouble he has cheerfully taken to show the collection to many parties and individuals when desired from anyone of the museum, in consequence of the intended purchase; each inspection costing mostly above a day's diligent labour."[57] He then presented the museum with a summary of the whole affair, including some negative comments about Hawkins, who he claimed had assured him the collection would be purchased. No apology or explanation appears to have been sent in reply to this letter, the only action documented being an advisory note to Richard Westmacott that he should revise his planned arrangement of the Egyptian antiquities in the new gallery to accommodate Sams's collection.[58]

The acquisition of the Sams collection made a major impact on the museum's Egyptian collection. Greatly expanding the range and number of smaller antiquities, it provided a wealth of objects that could be used to shed light on aspects of ancient Egyptian life previously not studied. Like the two other major Egyptian collections purchased during this period, Sams's collection played a key part in the recognition of Egyptian archaeology as a worthy subject of study and played a significant role in changing the public's attitude to ancient Egypt.

The Third Collection of Henry Salt

Barely a year had passed since the acquisition of Sams's collection, when the third major collection of Henry Salt (now deceased) went up for sale at Sotheby's in London.[59] Most of this collection of over 1,270 items was formed from 1824 to 1827, and it was expected to bring in more than £7,000. Although there were some sculptural pieces, including the statue of the Viceroy Paser (fig. 5.7), a statue of Ankhwa (fig. 5.8), and a kneeling figure of Ramesses II,[60] the highlight of the collection were the many hundreds of smaller items, including ornaments, jewelry, wooden objects, furniture, tools, and papyri (figs. 5.9–5.12 and plate 13). This collection was celebrated in the art and collecting world. In his *Works of Art and Artists in England*, for example, Gustav Waagen spoke very highly of the ornaments, jewelry and engraved stones.[61]

On hearing that Salt's collection would be auctioned, the trustees arranged to view it, summoning a meeting of the antiquities subcommittee and instructing Hawkins to investigate the objects on offer.[62] A week later, the subcommittee reported that the collector Lord Ashburton had gone through the collection in detail and "though unable to judge accurately of its merits, he was of opinion that it could not from the amplitude and choiceness of its objects, be otherwise than worthy of the attention of the Trustees."[63] Not wishing to make a decision based on this assessment alone, the trustees requested that Hawkins obtain "fuller testimonies to the value of the collections," a task that was swiftly fulfilled by Wilkinson, John Davidson, George Tomlinson, and William Martin Leake, all of whom testified to the merits of the collection and to the importance of purchasing much of it for the museum.[64] To these assessments, Hawkins added his own testimony, emphasizing how collections such as this were unlikely to form again within any short period, "that there were very numerous objects differing entirely from those already in the museum," and that the "lots which were really important to the museum might probably be acquired for a sum not exceeding six thousand pounds."[65] Satisfied with this information, the trustees wrote to the Treasury requesting £6,000 to acquire Salt's collection. The case they made for the purchase was presented as follows:

> The objects now offered for sale, derive a peculiar value from the circumstance that the localities in which they were respectively found are well authenticated, that many of them illustrate in which degree the scientific

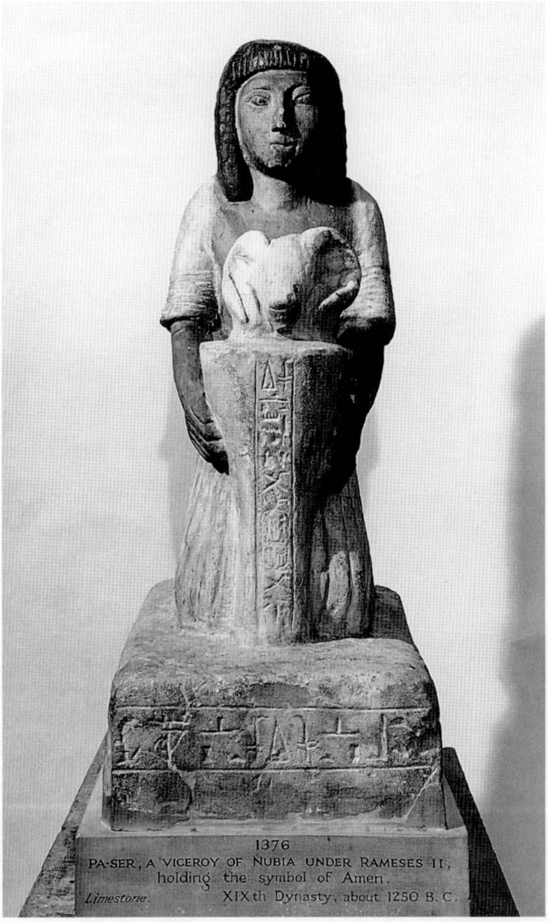

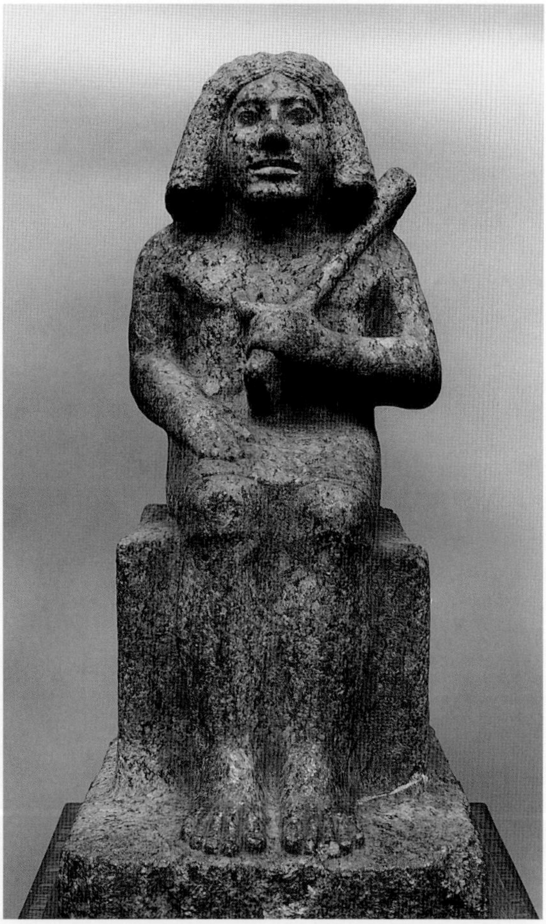

5.7. Statue of the Viceroy Paser (EA 1376) from Abu Simbel, Nineteenth Dynasty. Purchased by the British Museum in 1835 at the sale of Henry Salt's third collection.

5.8. Statue of Ankhwa (EA 171), possibly from Saqqara, Third Dynasty. Purchased by the British Museum in 1835 at the sale of Henry Salt's third collection.

> pursuits of the ancient Egyptians, and the practice of the liberal as well as of the mechanical arts among that remarkable people; and lastly that an opportunity of enriching the national collections such as the present can hardly be expected to occur again within a short period, if at all since we are not likely to have any countryman of our own resident in Egypt, whose means of acquisition and zeal in acquiring will equal those of the late Mr. Salt, and even if we had, the prohibition to excavate now strictly enforced by Ibrahim Pasha, would prevent his success.[66]

It is somewhat ironic that after being so reluctant to purchase Salt's first collection for its true value, the trustees were now enthusiastic about acquiring much of his third one for the asking price. Beyond the emphasis on the scientific significance of the collection, this appeal is important in that it refers to the changing climate in which the excavation and recovery of antiquities from Egypt was taking place. Not only did the trustees refer to the fact that it was unlikely that the British would see another collection like that of Salt formed by their consular representative in Egypt,

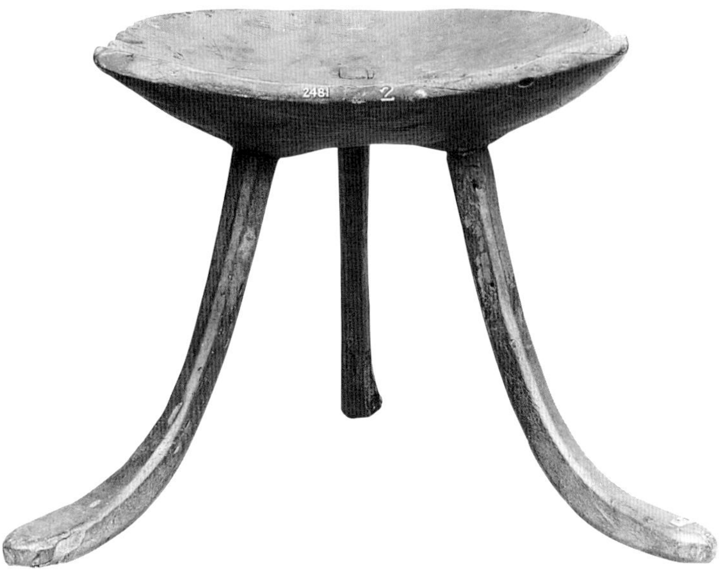

5.9

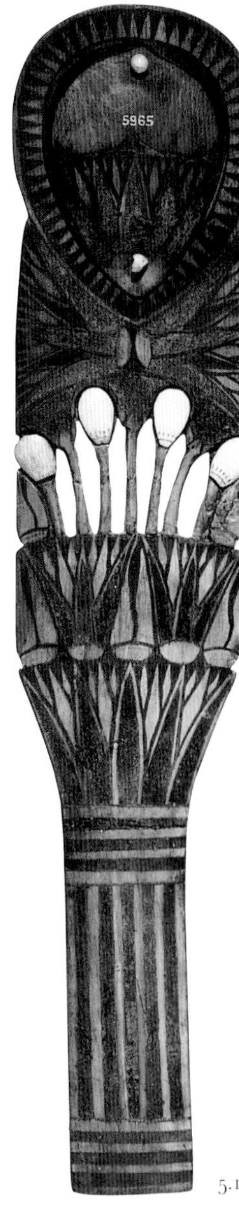

5.10

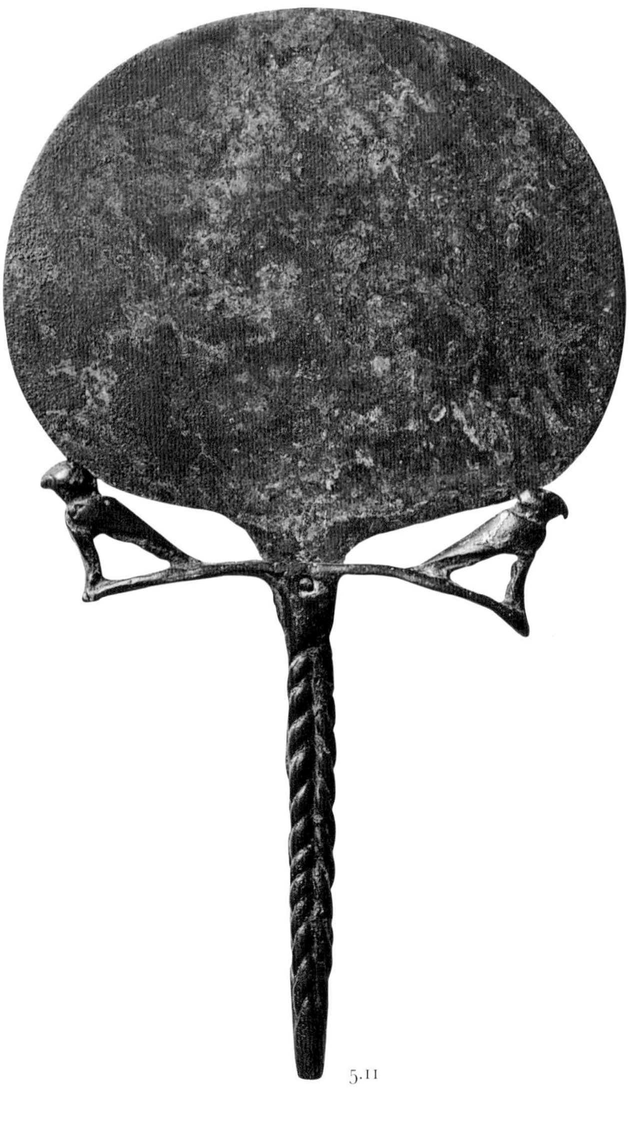

5.11

5.9. Wooden stool (EA 2481) from Thebes, Eighteenth Dynasty. Purchased by the British Museum in 1835 at the sale of Henry Salt's third collection.

5.10. Spoon in the shape of a bouquet (EA 5965) thought to be from Memphis, Eighteenth Dynasty. Purchased by the British Museum in 1835 at the sale of Henry Salt's third collection.

5.11. Bronze mirror (EA 2731), Middle Kingdom. Purchased by the British Museum in 1835 at the sale of Henry Salt's third collection.

5.12. Hieratic papyrus recording complaint by Amennakht (EA 10055), Ramesside. Purchased by the British Museum in 1835 at the sale of Henry Salt's third collection.

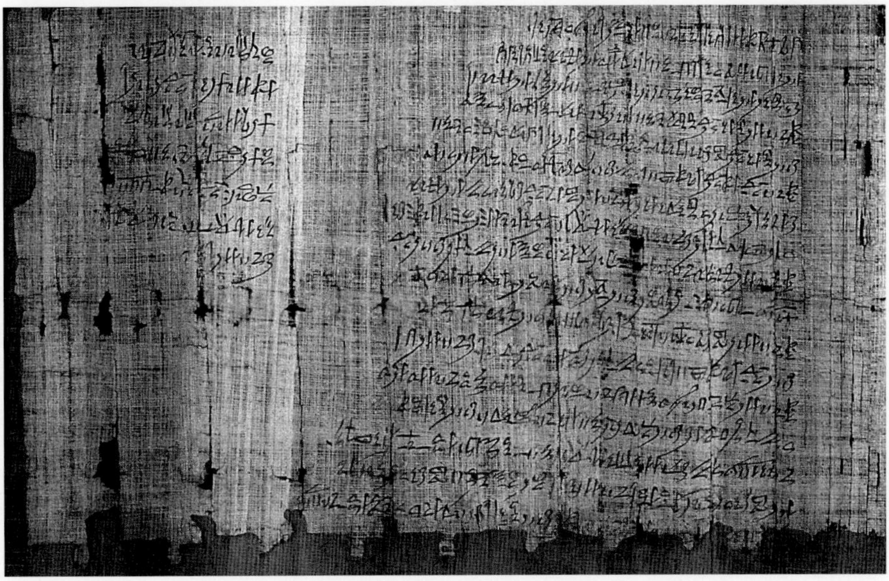

they also noted the new restrictions on excavation that had been introduced that year (1835) by the Egyptian pasha. Furthermore, that the objects are deemed valuable because they are well provenanced is also significant because it indicates that archaeological context was beginning to be recognized as an important factor in the status of the antiquities. Although a real appreciation for documenting where objects were found in Egyptian stratigraphic contexts is attributed to Flinders Petrie much later in the nineteenth century, it is still noteworthy that at this early stage some people were aware that knowing precise locations of objects enhanced their scientific value.[67]

Two days before the auction of Salt's collection was to take place, Parliament agreed to the trustees' request and Hawkins was able to buy much of it for a total of £4,805.16.[68] Like Sams's collection, this acquisition constituted a significant boost to the smaller-objects component of the Egyptian collection. While it appears that the museum purchased it for fear of never having such an opportunity again, it is also the case that they recognized the potential of the collection as a resource for study. This apparently sudden change in attitude reflected how the trustees were finally acknowledging the existence of Egyptology.

The Collection of Giovanni Anastasi

Soon after the purchase of Salt's collection, the trustees began negotiating for yet another major collection of Egyptian antiquities. The Greek merchant Giovanni Anastasi was an avid collector who had amassed over a hundred stelae, fifty papyri, sculptures, and other objects, which he offered to the trustees for £6,000 in 1836.[69] While the collection included some

5.13. (*facing, left*) Sarcophagus of Sasobek (EA 17), possibly from Sais, Twenty-sixth Dynasty. Purchased by the British Museum in 1839 as part of the collection of Giovanni Anastasi.

5.14. (*facing, right*) Sarcophagus of Pahemnetjer (EA 18) from Saqqara, Nineteenth Dynasty. Purchased by the British Museum in 1839 as part of the collection of Giovanni Anastasi.

larger sculptural pieces (in particular two sarcophagi, figs. 5.13–5.14; and the limestone sculpture of a couple, fig. 5.15),[70] the stelae and papyri were of great significance for understanding Egyptian history. Accompanying Anastasi's offer was a testimonial by Wilkinson, who informed the trustees that not only was the collection very extensive, but that it "contained many very valuable objects," and was "not dear" at the price of £6,000.[71] As had become customary by now, Hawkins was asked to inspect the catalogues of the collection and provide a report on its value.[72] Two years later and with no action taken, Wilkinson reminded the trustees of the offer of Anastasi's collection, to which he was informed that "under existing circumstances" they were "not able to treat for the acquisition of the Signor's collection."[73]

Despite the refusal of Anastasi's collection, in 1839 the Treasury informed the trustees that they would give £1,600 for the purchase of the collection, dependant on them providing "more precise information with respect to the contents and value of the manuscripts contained in it than had hitherto been obtained."[74] At their next meeting the trustees heard verbal testimonials from the Prussian scholar Christian Bunsen (1791–1860) and the German Egyptologist Karl Richard Lepsius (1810–1884), who were acting as Anastasi's representatives.[75] Lepsius presented a highly detailed and scholarly account of the papyri in the collection, asserting their "high historical importance."[76] Together with Bunsen, he also recommended the purchase of the papyri offered for sale by the French collector François Sallier (1764–1831), which he argued would be of use in understanding Anastasi's collection.[77] The trustees offered 40,000 francs for Anastasi's collection, noting that they were "unwilling to incur the risqué of the collection being lost to the country by any dilatory negociations [*sic*]."[78] However, they postponed making a decision on Sallier's collection until the negotiations for Anastasi's were resolved; once this took place they agreed to its purchase and by the end of the year both Anastasi's and Sallier's collections arrived at the museum.[79]

Although the trustees initially appeared uninterested in Anastasi's collection, once Treasury agreed to support the purchase, the trustees did not delay the acquisition. The arrival of Anastasi's collection not only signified a breakthrough in the museum's attitude to Egyptian antiquities, but was critical to the establishment of the scholarly status of the Egyptian collection. Together with Sams's and Salt's collections, this addition saw the establishment of a formidable Egyptian study collection in Britain.

Significant Objects

In addition to negotiations for the major collections of Sams, Salt, and Anastasi, lengthy negotiations over the purchase of several large sculptures were carried out in the 1830s. Although it never made it to the museum, the statue of Ramesses II at Met Rahina, or ancient Memphis,

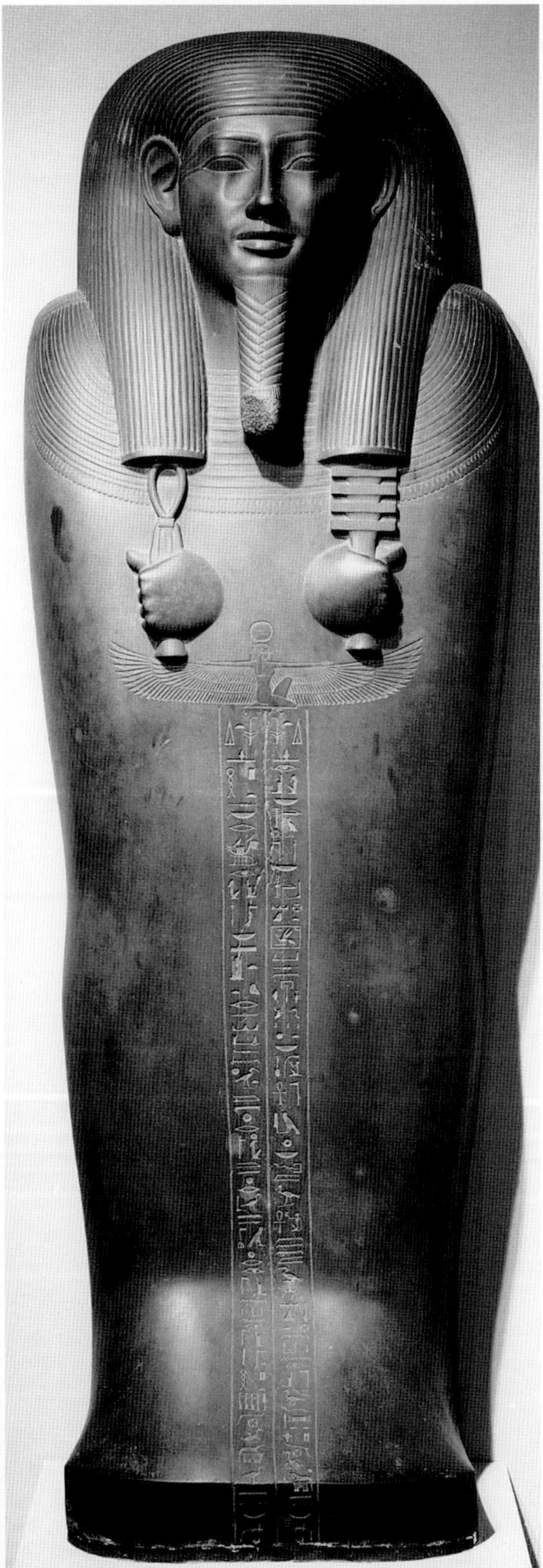

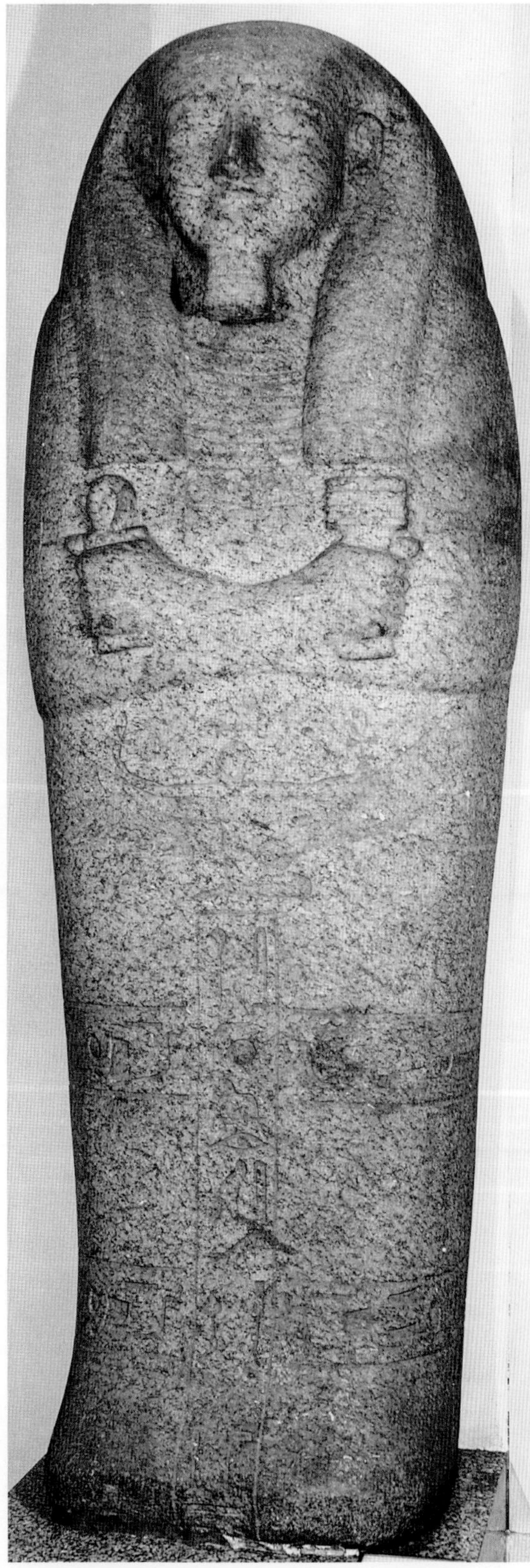

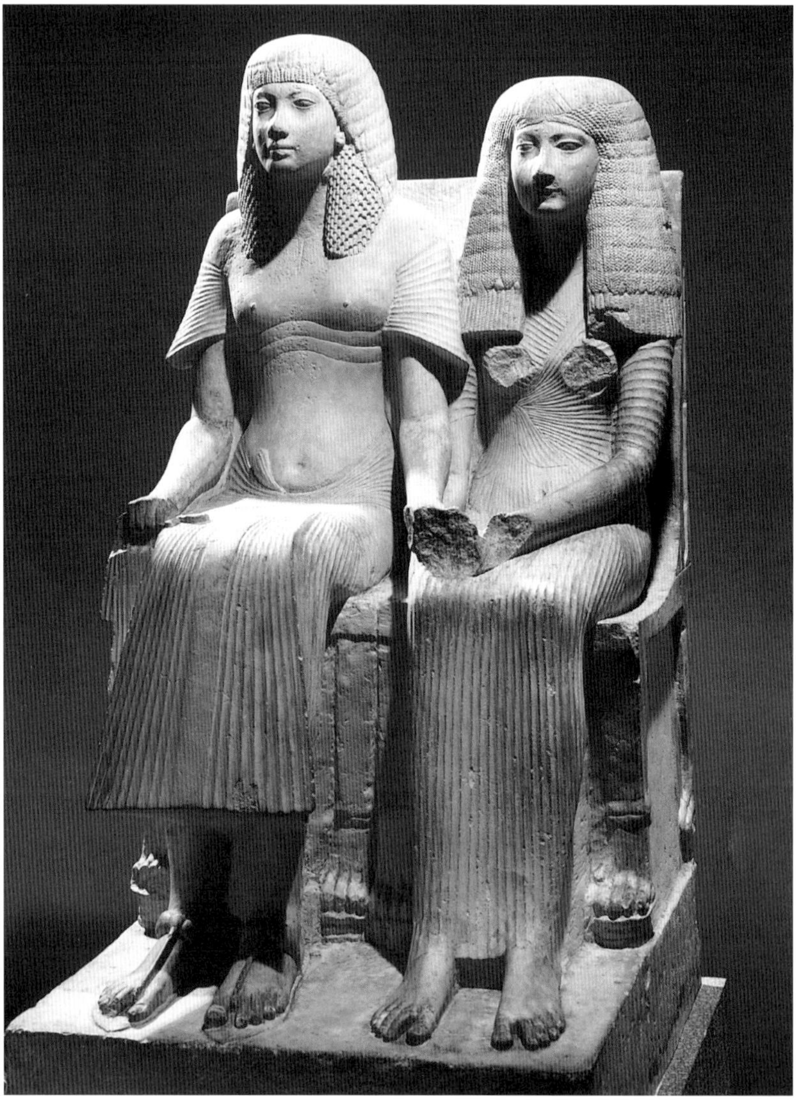

5.15. Statue of an unnamed man and woman (EA 36), Eighteenth or Nineteenth Dynasty. Purchased by the British Museum in 1839 as part of the collection of Giovanni Anastasi.

was a key example, and the story of its loss offers important insights into what the museum sought to gain by extending its collection of colossal sculptures. In 1835 the trustees received a communication from Wilkinson offering this statue as a gift from the chancellor of the British consulate in Egypt, Charles Sloane.[80] The trustees subsequently requested that Wilkinson provide an estimate of the transportation costs for removing the statue from Memphis to Alexandria.[81] The price of £5,000 that Wilkinson accordingly quoted did not appeal, so they asked the secretary of state for foreign affairs, Lord Palmerston, for permission to ask the British consul at Alexandria, Colonel Campbell, to provide another estimate.[82] In the meantime, the trustees had accepted Sloane's offer of the statue, contingent on the Treasury funding its transport to England. However, no further action was taken on the matter until Wilkinson urged that something be done before the waters of the Nile rose.[83] Explaining the delay, Colonel Campbell reported to the trustees that neither he nor Sloane had been able to "find any person who would venture to give any detailed or professional opinion either as to the means of removing the statue or the expense attending such an operation."[84] The matter was then referred to Hawkins, who was instructed to establish the value of the statue and cost of its transportation to England.[85] Hawkins subsequently reported that although the back of the statue was "corroded and somewhat defaced," the front was in good preservation, and of "very good workmanship"; concerning its removal, Hawkins reported that he had discussed the matter with Giovanni d'Athanasi, who offered to transport it to Alexandria for the sum of £1,500.[86]

Based on these enquiries, the trustees decided that they could not afford removal of the statue, and suggested that the most economical way of transporting the statue to England would be to cut it up into several portions.[87] Agreeing with this course of action, Hawkins then proceeded to investigate how much this alternative solution would cost.[88] After consultation with Joseph Bonomi (1796–1878), the British artist working in Egypt, Hawkins reported that sawing up the statue would be a considerable task as it weighed about sixty tons; furthermore, a stonemason advised that the cheapest way of sawing so hard a material would be to erect a steam engine, and that the expenses for this would amount to £20,000.[89] With the prospect of acquiring the statue becoming increasingly complicated, the trustees resolved that Hawkins report more fully on the "value of this statue in its bearing upon history, archaeology or art, as to the total probable expense of bringing it to England, and as to the means which the museum affords of exhibiting and preserving the statue if it were brought here."[90] This response signified that the museum was including the historical and archaeological value of Egyptian sculptures as an important criterion in their acquisition. The request was also significant as this was the first time the conditions for displaying and conserving antiquities appear to have been of consideration in their acquisition.

Hawkins's further investigations on the great statue of Ramesses II revealed that removal of it in its entirety would be extremely expensive, as the cost of moving it to Alexandria for £1,500 would be supplemented with the considerable cost of putting it on board a vessel and getting it to England and then to the museum. On the issue of exhibition, Hawkins stated that the museum buildings were not high enough to display it, and more funds would be needed to erect a "suitable place for its exhibition." Finally Hawkins argued that since the magnitude of the statue was an "important point in its estimation, and that the feelings excited by its magnitude would be much abated by its division into parts," he did not recommend its transport to England. Despite this verdict, Hawkins ventured that "all which is really valuable about the monument is the head, which is of excellent workmanship and probably a portrait: and that if the proprietor would consent to such a mutilation it would be very desirable to bring so much of the statue to England."[91] One could hardly imagine such a suggestion being made about classical sculptures, and perhaps it was an awareness of the controversial nature of this idea that led the trustees to reject the project of transporting the statue to England. Also noteworthy in Hawkins's assessment was the comment about the magnitude of the statue, reflecting how monumentality was an important feature in the reception of Egyptian antiquities.

In 1838, over a year after the trustees had refused the statue, Wilkinson informed the trustees that he had an offer from a railway engineer to move the statue to Alexandria for £600.[92] Hawkins supported this offer, reminding the trustees of his view that much of the statue was not of interest and that they could facilitate its removal by cutting off the legs. That this would reduce the height of the statue and make it more suited for display was mentioned as an added bonus.[93] Wilkinson also reaffirmed his appraisal of the statue, noting that the "face was well preserved as well as the body and that part of the legs which remains: and that it was a fine monument of Egyptian art."[94] The trustees then revised their position, resolving to pay for the transport costs in bringing the statue to England, and with the proviso that the statue was conveyed "from Alexandria to England on board one of Her Majesty's ships of war, or otherwise, at a moderate charge."[95] The quote of £1,300 for transport on a merchant vessel, which was received by the trustees, prompted them to ask Admiralty whether a ship of war would be willing to transport the statue.[96] The Admiralty were lukewarm in their response, stating that they felt it unlikely that the "Lords Commissioners would consent to cut up the decks of one of Her Majesty's vessels in order to receive the colossal statue."[97] Although further investigations had been made of the cost for transport on a merchant vessel and a cheaper quote of £600 had been given, the trustees decided that the statue should not be removed until a "fit place for its reception and exhibition could be found," and that they would make an application to the Treasury for funds to erect a new building to receive the statue.[98]

The matter of transporting the statue was not raised again until 1846 when Bonomi suggested several methods by which it might be brought to England.[99] Hawkins expressed his doubts as to whether it was worth returning to this subject, commenting that "as there was little new to be learned from the statue it was doubtful whether its acquisition, in its mutilated state would be worth the cost, even if the most economical means of removal were adopted."[100] The trustees adjourned making a decision, and were not prompted again on the matter until 1852 when Hawkins reported that "the mutilated parts below the hands and the remains of the upper part of the head dress, might be removed without damage to the sculpture," but despite this, the statue was still very large and the cost of removal would exceed its value.[101] The situation became further complicated when the trustees were informed of the pasha of Egypt's increasing reluctance to let antiquities be taken from the country.[102] Nothing more was heard until 1887, when the trustees wrote to the prime minister recommending the removal of the statue to England, a suggestion that was rejected.[103] Final mention of the statue "supposed to belong to the British Museum, but now in the mud at Sakkara," was made when it was suggested that the shrine at Philae be exchanged for it.[104] Thus ends the British story of the colossal statue of Ramesses II from Memphis, which although "acquired" by the museum fifty years previously, never made it to the gallery. The museum never completely abandoned the sculpture, however, as a cast of the head was exhibited in the new installation of 1854 (see fig. 6.9 below).

This important object, which would have made a very impressive addition to the Egyptian sculpture collection, appears to have been accepted as an acquisition primarily because it was offered for free. Despite Hawkins's evaluation that it was not of great historical or archaeological merit, it appears that the trustees continued to negotiate over its acquisition because it would have enhanced their existing strengths in presenting colossal monuments, and because it would not have incurred any great financial burden.

In summary, in the 1830s there was a veritable explosion in the accumulation of Egyptian antiquities by the museum. Still not actively sought by the trustees, the Egyptian objects that came to the museum were acquired more by chance. If they could have predicted the phenomenal success of these new Egyptian collections with visitors, the trustees might have altered their stance, which by that time was becoming rapidly outmoded. More specifically, the trustees appear to have ignored the growth in academic research on ancient Egypt carried out by individual scholars and research teams in the 1820s. Primary here was the contribution that Wilkinson had made to establishing Egyptology in Britain.[105] Wilkinson went to Egypt in 1821 and stayed twelve years to survey the main sites, and his publications did much to further knowledge of the range of antiquities from ancient Egypt, particularly his *Topography of Thebes and General Survey of Egypt* of 1835 and *The Manners and Customs of the Ancient Egyptians* of 1837.[106] Beyond Wilkinson, there were several other British travelers and artists who contributed to the development of Egyptology in the country, notably James Burton, who traveled with Wilkinson to the Eastern Desert and Red Sea in 1824, Frederick Catherwood (1799–1855), who traveled to Egypt in 1823, Robert Hay (1799–1863) and Joseph Bonomi (1796–1878), who traveled together in Egypt from 1824 to 1828, and Edward Lane, who went to Egypt in 1825 and joined James Burton.[107] A growing appreciation of Egyptian antiquities in Britain also resulted from the major surveying projects undertaken by other Europeans. Of particular note here was the two-year expedition of Champollion and Ippolito Rosellini (1800–1843) to survey the monuments of Egypt in 1828.[108] Above all of this research activity, however, was the formal recognition of Egyptology as a discipline as a result of the breakthrough in the decipherment of hieroglyphs.[109] Despite the weight and impact of the recent work on ancient Egypt, the trustees remained disinterested in the subject and their attitude to the major acquisitions of the 1830s reflects this. It was in spite of this that the museum's Egyptian collection was very considerably enhanced by innumerable important antiquities—significant more as part of a whole than as individually unique specimens.

DISPLAY

The arrival of the new Egyptian collections in the 1830s coincided with the construction of some major new museum buildings, in which a new gallery for the Egyptian antiquities was included.[110] Specifically intended to house the museum's antiquities collections, the new neoclassical west wing designed by Robert Smirke provided yet another opportunity to create a purpose-built gallery for the Egyptian antiquities. This new accommodation was desperately needed, as overcrowding had already become a major problem in the Egyptian galleries prior to the arrival of the new collections.[111] From an early stage in construction, there was controversy over the new architectural features proposed for the antiquities galleries, which were to have important implications for the definition of the Egyptian works. For instance, in 1828, two years after work had begun on the west wing, concerns were raised over how the architecture of the new building would affect the arrangement of antiquities. Of prime concern to the members of the museum's subcommittee for antiquities was the inclusion of a line of pilasters projecting from the walls inside the main galleries, which they thought would "interfere with the disposition of statues and other works of art, and more particularly with any long and continued frieze, or series of bas reliefs, if any such should be acquired in future."[112] By now, the practice of placing sculptures in a line along the wall, where they could all be seen together at a glance from a central vantage point, was established practice at the museum. With the proposed row of pilasters, the trustees felt that this method of viewing the collections would be disrupted. Despite their protestations and their demand that Westmacott be consulted about the problem before work continued, the pilasters remained part of the plan, and in 1833, when arrangements were being made for the installation of the Egyptian sculptures in their new gallery, the different style of gallery architecture had to be taken into account.[113]

The Sculpture Gallery, 1834

By the summer of 1834, all the Egyptian sculptures had been moved into the new Smirke Gallery and placed upon pedestals to elevate and support them.[114] While the complex maneuvers that were adopted for the removal of the colossal sculptures from the old Townley Gallery are conveyed in a series of sketches produced in 1834 (figs. 5.16–5.19),[115] a plan of 1836 conveys the size of the new gallery, revealing that it was not insubstantial

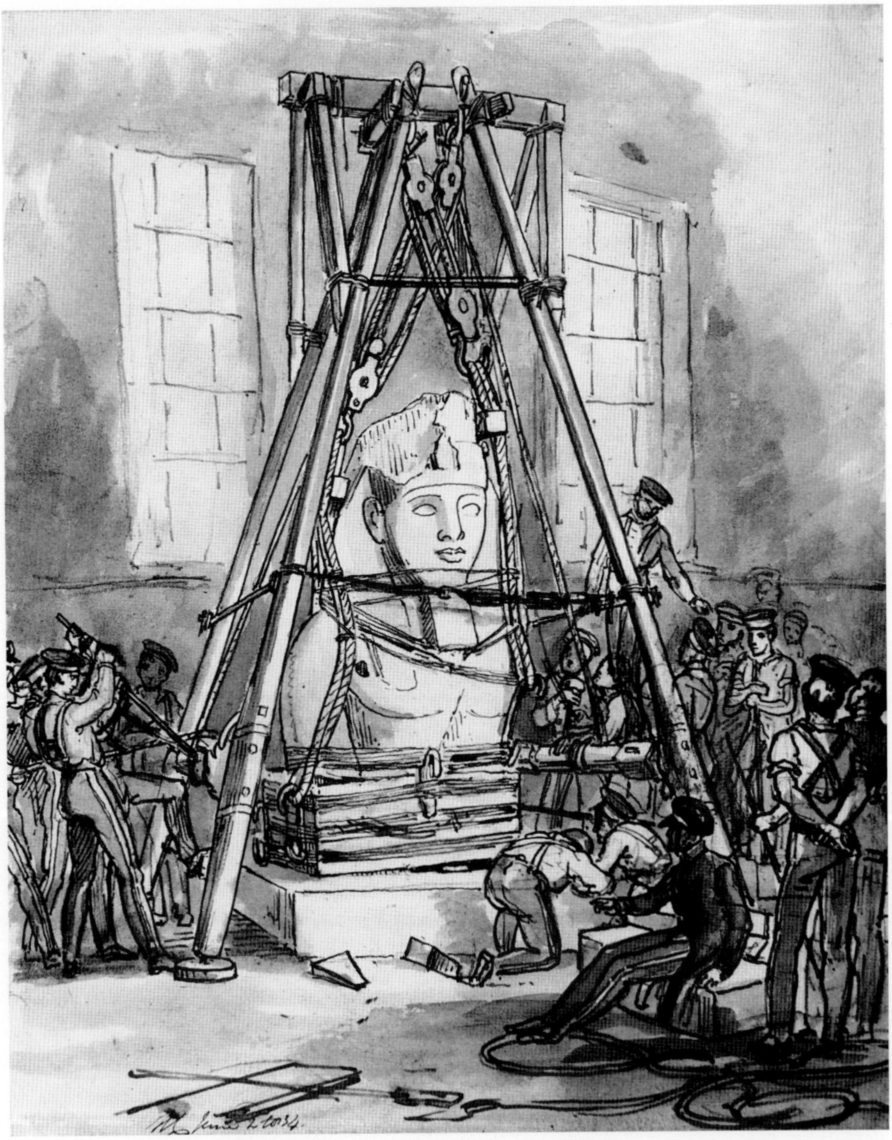

5.16. Removal of the colossal bust of Ramesses II from the Townley Gallery. Dated June 2, 1834. Illustrations of the British Museum (CE 115/1/205). British Museum, Central Archives.

when compared to the other antiquities galleries (fig. 5.20). Indeed, the new Egyptian sculpture gallery was equal in size to the gallery designated for the Elgin Marbles. In addition to conveying a sense that the Egyptian antiquities were worthy of attention, the extended space ensured that the distribution of objects was not so crowded. Furthermore, the high ceiling of the new gallery enhanced the sense of space in which the Egyptian sculptures were featured, lessening the cramped feeling of the Townley Gallery. Finally, in the northern section of the new addition, the Egyptian gallery, or "Saloon," as it was known, would have been immediately visible upon entering the main antiquities wing of the museum. By gaining such a prime "viewing space," the Egyptian collection was inevitably accorded some importance.

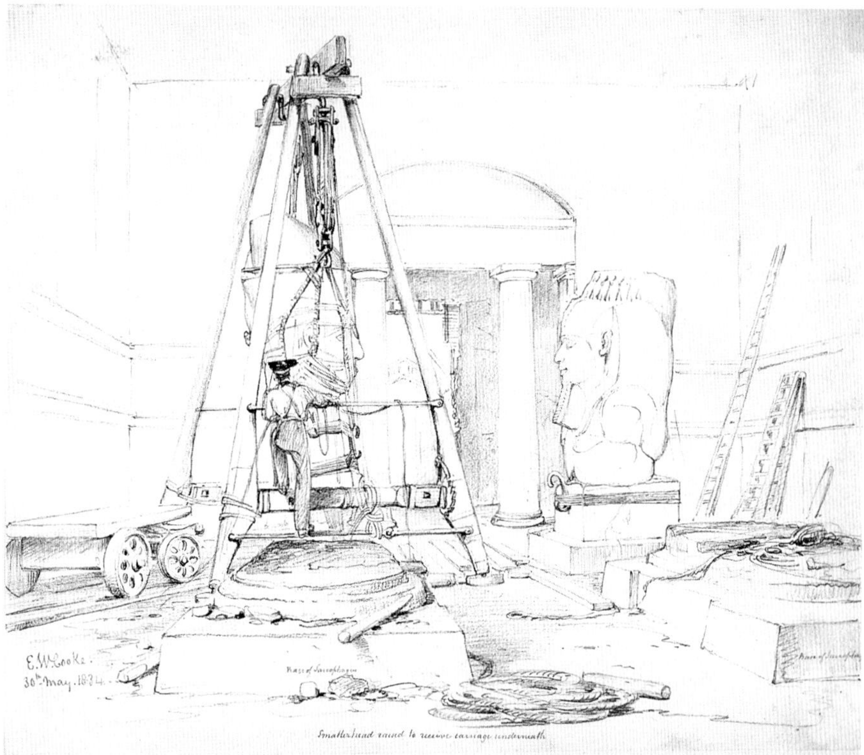
E. W. Cooke.
30th May. 1834.
Base of Sarcophagus
Smaller Head raised to receive carriage underneath

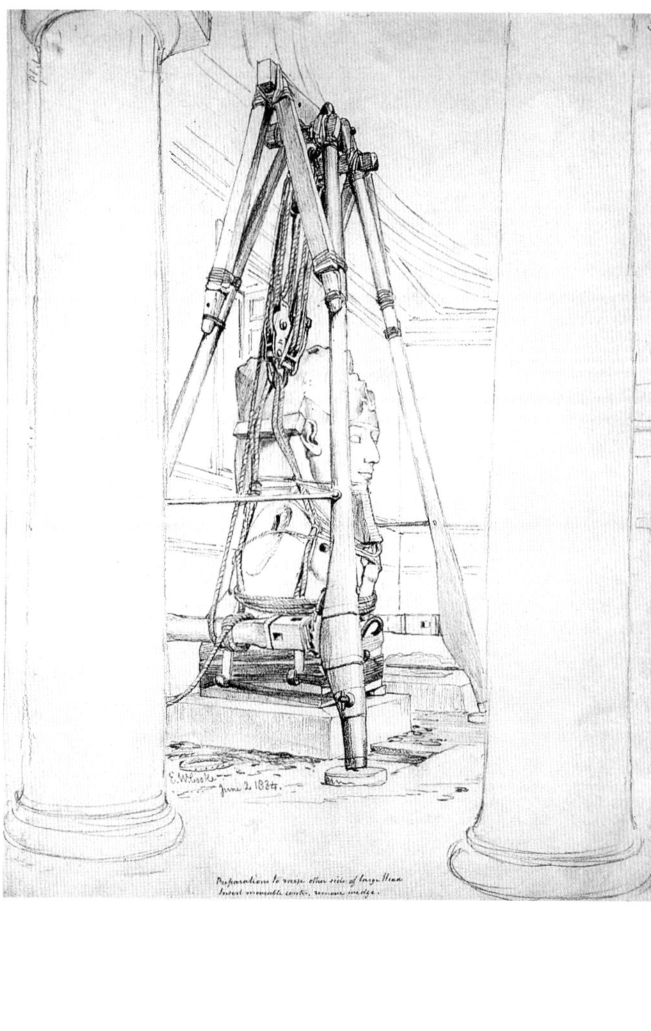
E. W. Cooke June 2 1834.
Preparations to raise other side of large Head
Insert moveable centre, remove wedge.

5.17. (*facing, above*) Removal of the colossal head of Amenhotep III from the Townley Gallery. Drawing by E. W. Cooke, May 29, 1834, entitled "Removal of smaller head." British Museum, Department of Prints and Drawings, Sketchbook of E. W. Cooke, no. 1914.2.6.2.

5.18. (*facing, below*) Removal of the colossal bust of Ramesses II from the Townley Gallery. Drawing by E. W. Cooke, June 2, 1834, and entitled "Preparation to raise other side of large Head." British Museum, Department of Prints and Drawings, Sketchbook of E. W. Cooke, no. 1914.2.6.6.

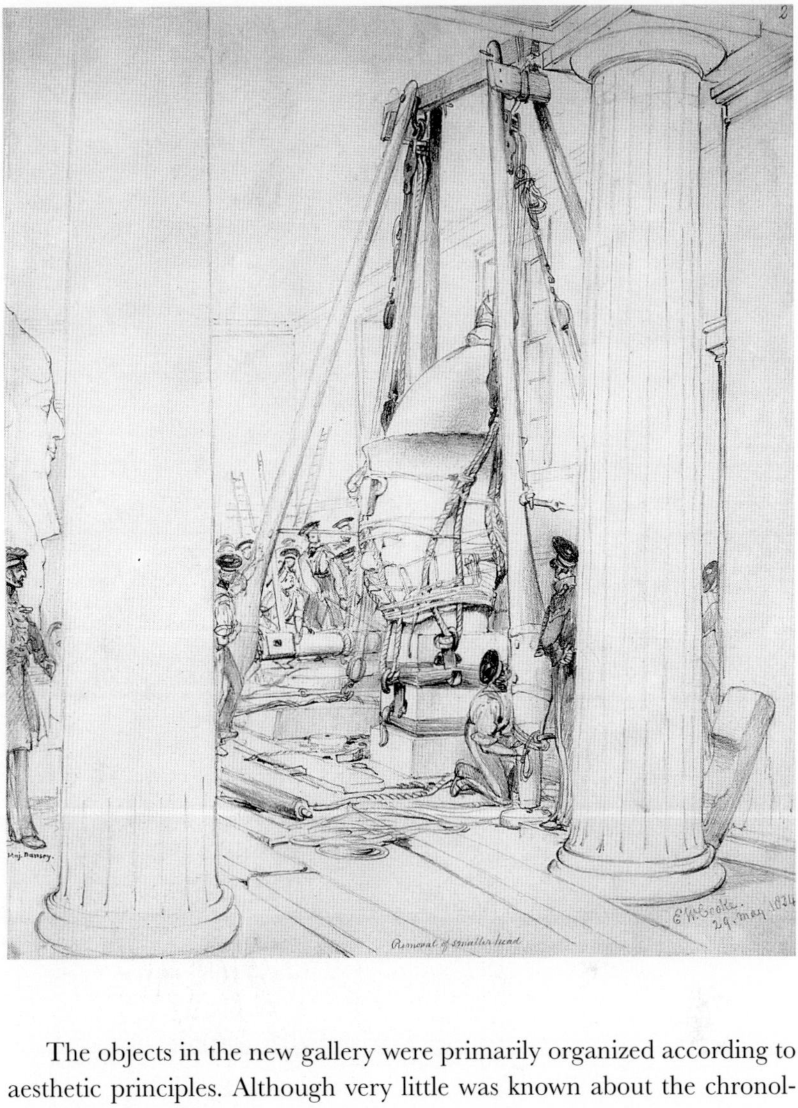

5.19. Removal of the colossal head of Amenhotep III from the Townley Gallery. Drawing by E. W. Cooke, May 30, 1834, and entitled "Smaller head raised to receive carriage underneath." British Museum, Department of Prints and Drawings, Sketchbook of E.,W. Cooke, no. 1914.2.6.5.

The objects in the new gallery were primarily organized according to aesthetic principles. Although very little was known about the chronology of ancient Egypt at the time, it appears that no investment was made in considering whether the collection might be structured according to its content or informational significance. This allegiance to the "picturesque" mode of presentation contrasted with the new methods of organizing collections that were being introduced in other European museums. Notable in this regard were the Louvre's new Egyptian galleries, set up in 1826–1827, where a historical or scientific approach was adopted for the presentation of the collection. More specifically, the objects were arranged according to themes such as religion, royal history, and daily life, and in this sense were structured according to what was known about ancient Egypt, as opposed to what merely looked good. Even more significant perhaps were the developments at the new Glyptothek museum in Munich, where a historical approach for arranging antiquities was implemented, with the rooms being laid out in a sequence that mapped chronological

GENERAL PLAN OF THE NEW BUILDINGS OF THE MUSEUM. 1.

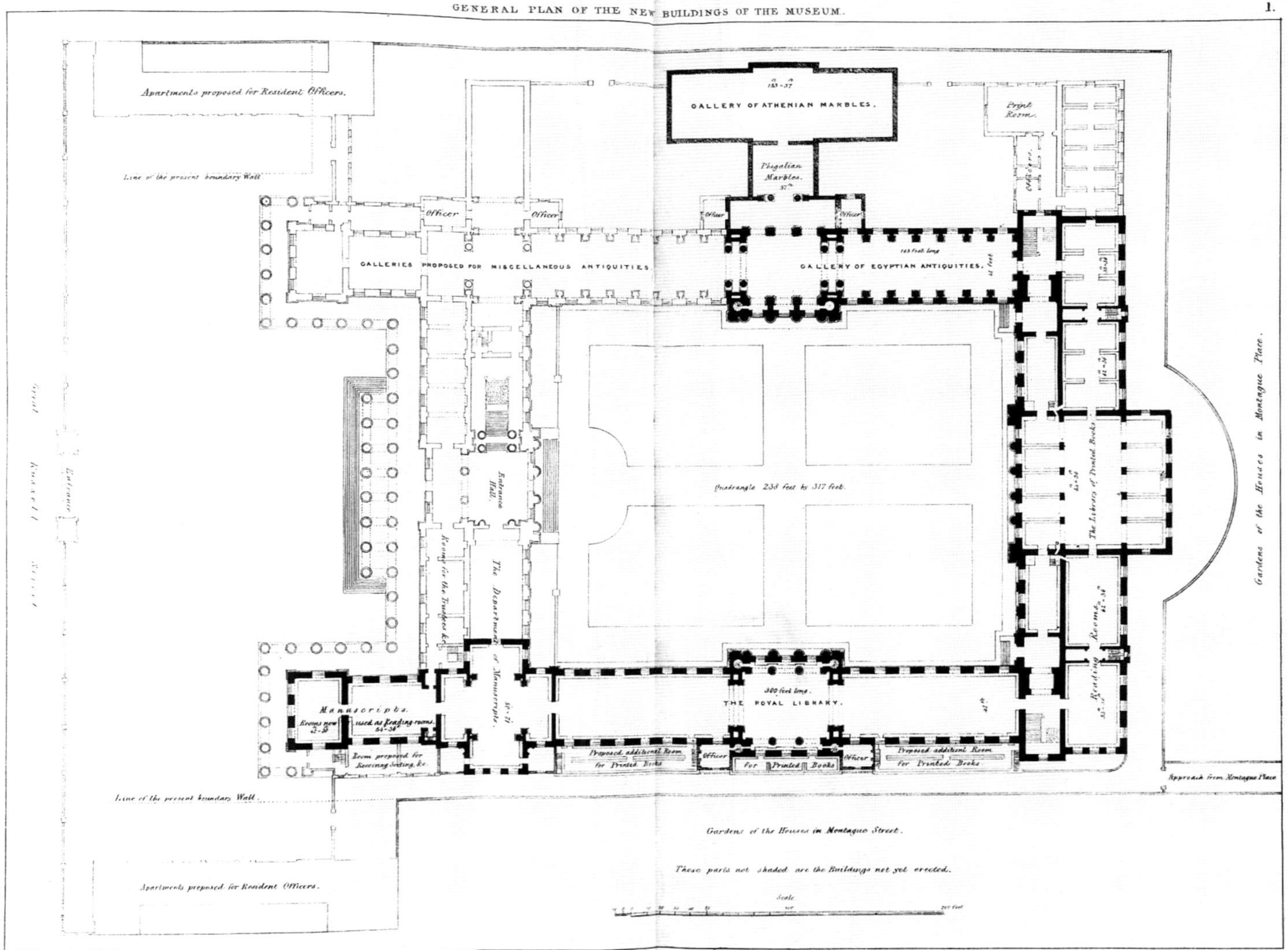

C. J. Richardson del.

Ordered by the House of Commons to be Printed, 14th July 1836.

140.

5.20. *(facing)* Plan of the new extensions to the museum, with completed work marked in bold. The new Egyptian gallery can be seen on the upper right. Lithograph by C. J. Richardson after Robert Smirke, produced by the Trustees for the Select Committee of 1835–1836. Illustrations of the British Museum, (CE 115/1/35), British Museum, Central Archives.

development.[116] This signified a marked advance in the presentation of antiquities as for the first time temporal or archaeological criteria were used to make sense of the objects.

The décor of the museum's new galleries also offered a stark contrast to other Egyptian displays created in Europe around the same time. The Louvre, for example, maintained its tradition of using Egyptianizing décor to present its new galleries in 1826. Characterized by their elaborate ceiling paintings featuring Egyptian-inspired scenes, the Louvre's displays aimed to be far more than decorative in function, with the paintings being central to the "message" of the exhibition.[117] Inspired by Champollion's decipherment of hieroglyphs, the paintings not only asserted France's role in the "discovery" of Egypt, but functioned as a powerful statement on France's scientific achievements.[118] Similarly, at the Vatican's Egyptian Museum, Egyptian architectural features and decorative motifs were incorporated within the display to provide a context for the antiquities.[119] The trustees avoided adopting either of these exhibition strategies, revealing their reluctance to interfere with the style of presentation that had been established with the first antiquities gallery in 1808. Furthermore, the different approaches to exhibiting ancient Egypt in Britain and in France reveal the contrasting attitudes to this ancient culture held by both nations. While for France ancient Egypt was critical to Egypt's expression of national identity, for Britain it was nothing more than a stepping stone on the path to ancient Greece. Thus, in the French museological representation of ancient Egypt there was an intimate connection between the display of antiquities and the accompanying history paintings.

When it came to the arrangement of objects within the gallery, the most obvious change in the British Museum's Smirke Gallery was the removal of the bust of Ramesses II and the colossal head of Amenhotep III from the end of the room, as they had been in the Townley Gallery, to the center of the room.[120] While this repositioning of the two heads created a greater sense of symmetric balance in the room, it still did not provide adequate viewing space to appreciate the individual sculptures, since the viewer could not stand back at the distance required to see each object properly. The museum determined that the rest of the sculptures would be exhibited "in two lines along the room in the same manner as at present."[121] However, because of the new pilasters, a different arrangement was needed. It is possible to get some idea of this new arrangement in an illustration showing the installation of the bust of Ramesses II in the new gallery (fig. 5.21). Here we can observe how the larger objects have been placed in a line in front of the pilasters and how a second row of objects has been introduced behind this main one, with the smaller sculptures being placed in between the pilasters. A layered effect was thus created, where one row of objects would not have been immediately visible upon entering the gallery. Furthermore, this second row of objects added another symmetrical dimension to the arrangement, with the heights of

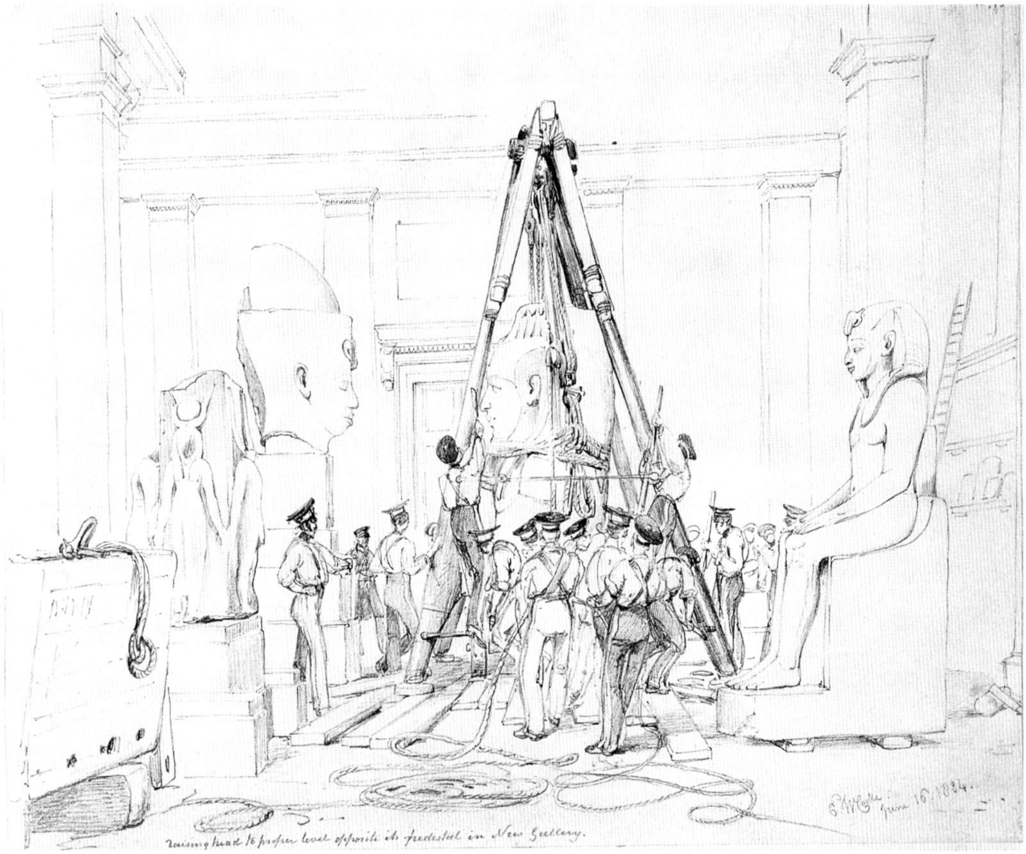

5.21. Installation of the colossal bust of Ramesses II in the new Smirke Gallery. Drawing by E. W. Cooke, June 16, 1834, and entitled "Raising head to proper level opposite its pedestal in New Gallery." British Museum, Department of Prints and Drawings, Sketchbook of E. W. Cooke, no. 1914.2.6.21.

5.22. (*facing*) The Egyptian sculpture gallery, looking south. Engraving in *Pinnock's Guide to Knowledge*, September 19, 1835, cover.

these smaller objects alternating with those of the larger objects in front of them. The sense of order that this new arrangement conveyed is evident in an image from 1835, where the objects in the front row are fully visible, while those in the second are obscured from view. (fig. 5.22).[122] Significantly, while it was the size of the objects that determined their situation either in front of the pilasters or tucked between them, visitors perceived this distribution as reflecting an object's worth. Indeed, the author of the article that accompanies the 1835 image stated that the new arrangement placed "the most interesting objects" in the row in the center of the room, while behind these, "fragments and objects of second rate value are placed."[123] Thus, the simple act of arranging a second row of sculptures set back from the larger pieces created an instant division in status.

Another significant change in the spatial distribution of the Egyptian objects was the creation of a striking entrance to the gallery a year after its opening. The two lions donated by Lord Prudhoe in 1835 were promptly incorporated as the terminal figures marking the entrance to the gallery. This can be seen in the image of 1836, where the two lion sculptures have been given a prime position alongside the large Doric columns (fig. 5.23). Appearing like guardians of the gallery, the shape and height of the lions provide a strong visual contrast with the obelisks placed immediately

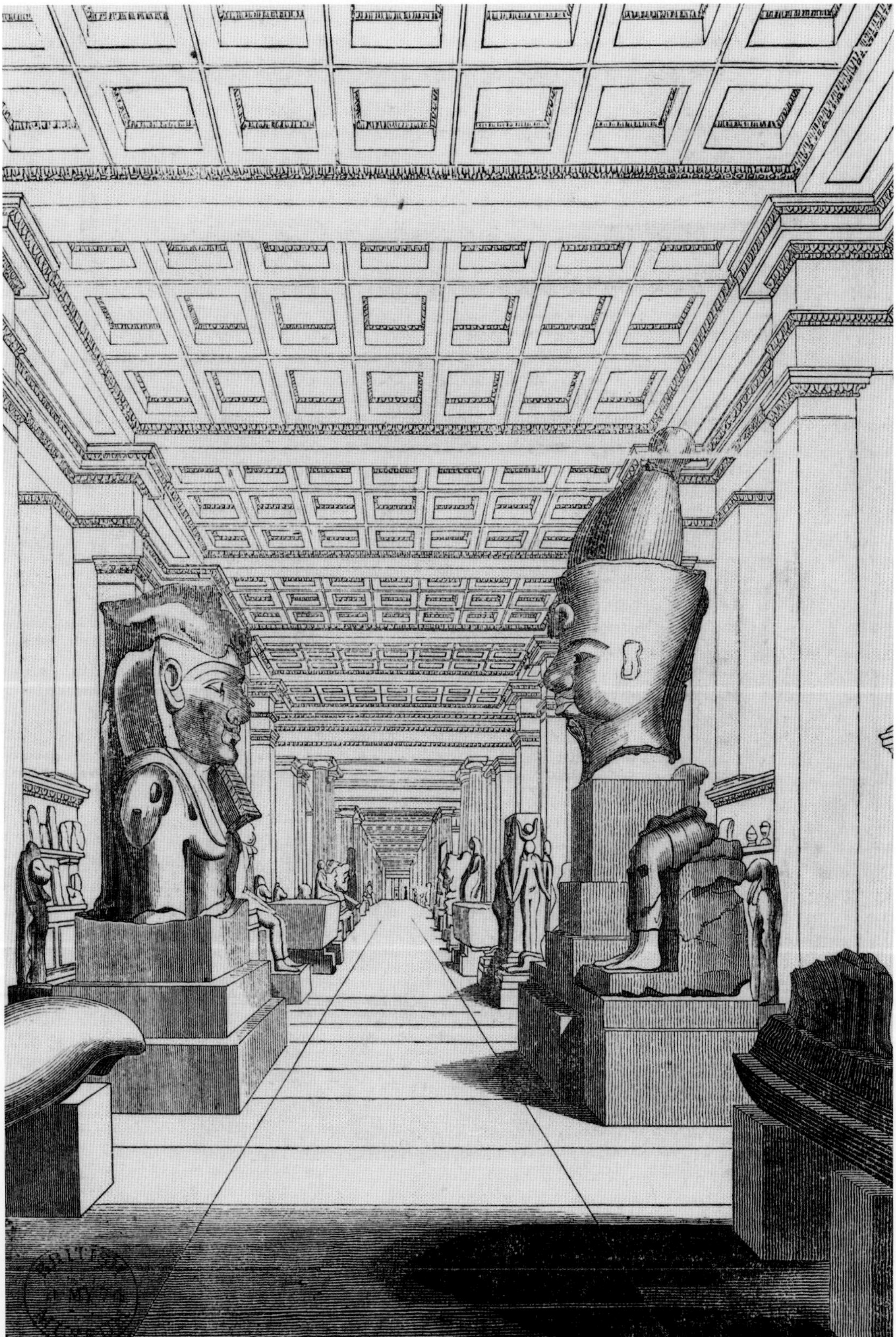

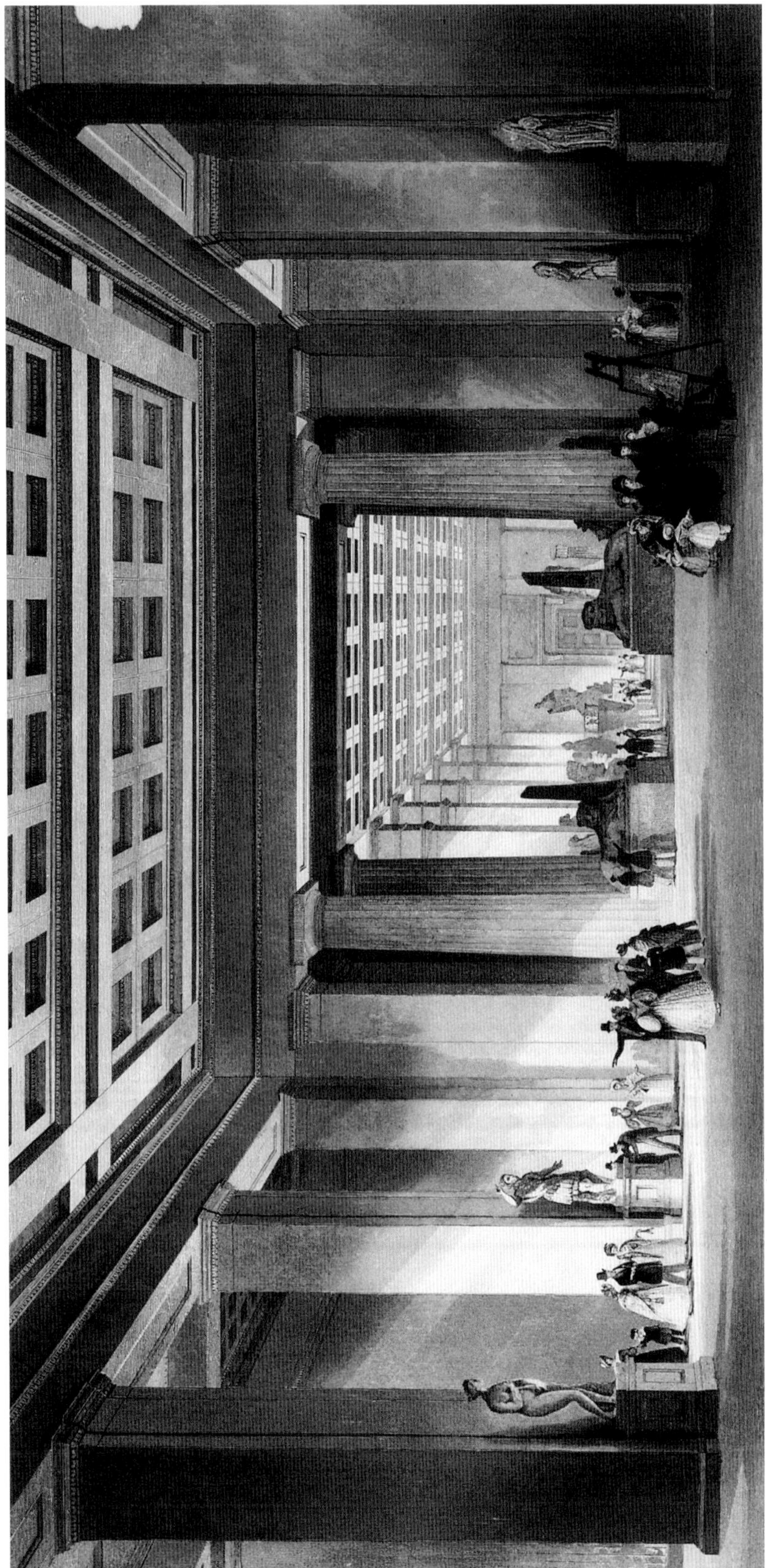

5.23. *(facing)* The Egyptian sculpture gallery, featuring the north division and the central saloon. Engraving by Robert Sands from a drawing by Thomas Allom. Published by W. H. J. Carter in *Stationers Almanack*, 1836. British Museum, Department of Prints and Drawings, no. 1865.5.20.491.

behind them and with the repeated vertical lines of the gallery. This addition of two symmetrically matched objects created a powerful effect, with the composition of the gallery now giving the visitor a sense that they were looking at a framed picture. Furthermore, with the lions flanking the entrance, an impressive introduction to the antiquities of Egypt had been created, an introduction that endowed the rest of the sculptures in the gallery with a raised profile. Finally, much larger pedestals were created to enhance the presence of the two colossal heads in the center of the room. Many other sculptures, previously without pedestals, were also raised so as to enhance the perception of height.

That the architectural features of the room provided a completely new context for the Egyptian sculptures can be gleaned from both the 1835 and 1836 images, however another illustration, published in 1840, shows more clearly how the new gallery functioned to elevate the status of the antiquities (fig. 5.24). Here we can see how the Egyptian collection no longer appears like a motley assortment of objects that has been crammed into an ill-suited environment, but rather as a cohesive assemblage of sculptures that has been well accommodated into its new surroundings. Not only do the towering colossal sculptures appear in better proportion with the height of the ceiling and the width of the gallery, but the large square pedestals, the strong lines of the pilasters, and the block-like nature of the ceiling decoration are more complimentary with the architectural qualities of the Egyptian sculptures than the softer features of the Townley Gallery. For instance, the ceiling decoration of the Townley Gallery was characterized by its large oval-shaped stucco decoration, and the columns framing the gallery were circular, both giving a more organic appearance than the hard lines characteristic of the Smirke Gallery. While the classical sculptures appeared dwarfed by the massive proportions of the new building, the Egyptian sculptures looked more at home in such spacious surroundings. Thus, although intended to reinforce Britain's connections with ancient Greece, Smirke's Grecian Revival–style designs inadvertently bestowed an important status on the civilization of ancient Egypt as well. More specifically, although ancient Egypt was excluded from the intimate connection that existed between the museum and the classical world, the architectural style of the new building provided a more austere and sophisticated setting for the Egyptian collection.[124]

The New Egyptian Room, 1837

Once the layout of the larger sculptures was completed in the Smirke Gallery, attention turned to how the smaller antiquities were to be displayed in the new Egyptian Room assigned to them on the upper floor of the museum. To this end, the trustees asked Smirke to present a plan, however the emphasis in his proposals appears to have been on the construction of display furniture as opposed to the way in which the collection

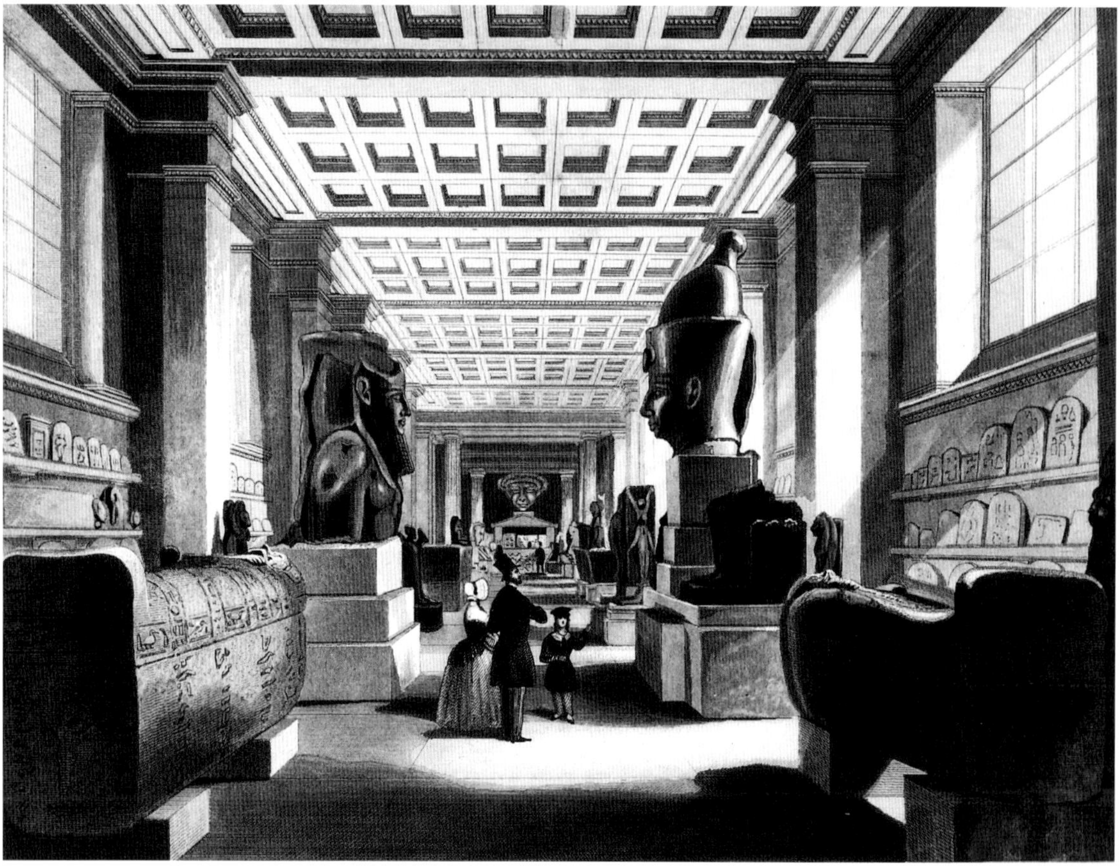

5.24. The Egyptian sculpture gallery. Engraving by William Radclyffe after B. Sly, c.1840. Published by J. Mead. British Museum, Department of Prints and Drawings, no. 1940.5.29.2 (23).

should be distributed.[125] Opened to the public in 1837, the new Egyptian Room showcased the vast numbers of everyday objects recently acquired from the collections of Sams and Salt, including furniture, jewelry, utensils, models, and small figurines.[126] While some of the hundreds of new papyri acquired were included in this room, most of these were displayed on the walls of the staircase leading from the sculpture gallery to the Egyptian Room.[127] An engraving of the new room from the *Penny Magazine* shows how the large new mummy cabinets, which occupied much of the floor space, would have commanded immediate attention (fig. 5.25). Appearing somewhat like a maze, the rows of mummy cabinets may have encouraged visitors to weave in and out around each one; however, there were still two straight paths by which visitors could quickly proceed through the room.

Lining the walls in the new Egyptian Room were tall, glass-fronted cabinets packed full of antiquities. Although grouped according to object type, the style of display for the Egyptian Room still adopted aesthetic principles. For instance, while the same classes of objects were presented together (e.g., furniture), some effort was devoted to placing the objects in visually interesting "microarrangements" within the cabinets (e.g., according to size). Rather than fewer, representative types of objects, all available specimens were crammed into the cabinets. Not only would the sheer volume of objects have created its own distinctive aesthetic effect, appearing somewhat like a treasure trove, the display would have also created a sense of visual overload, where it was difficult to distinguish anything in particular from the mass that lay before one. Indeed, after only three years after opening, overcrowding of the room was identified as a serious problem, and another room was designated for the presentation of the Egyptian collection.[128] Interestingly, however, even then the museum continued to display as much of the collection as was possible.

Finally, the displays in the Egyptian Room played a paradoxical role in defining ancient Egypt. On one hand, the vastly expanded collection with so many new types of objects conveyed a much enriched view of ancient Egypt, defining it as a society that was not as bizarre and peculiar as once thought. On the other hand, however, the sheer quantities of objects, all positioned in intimate proximity with each other, ensured that the Egyptian antiquities retained their status as awe-inspiring wonders. Thus, despite being placed together in an orderly manner, the arrangement as a whole was still reminiscent of a cabinet of curiosity.

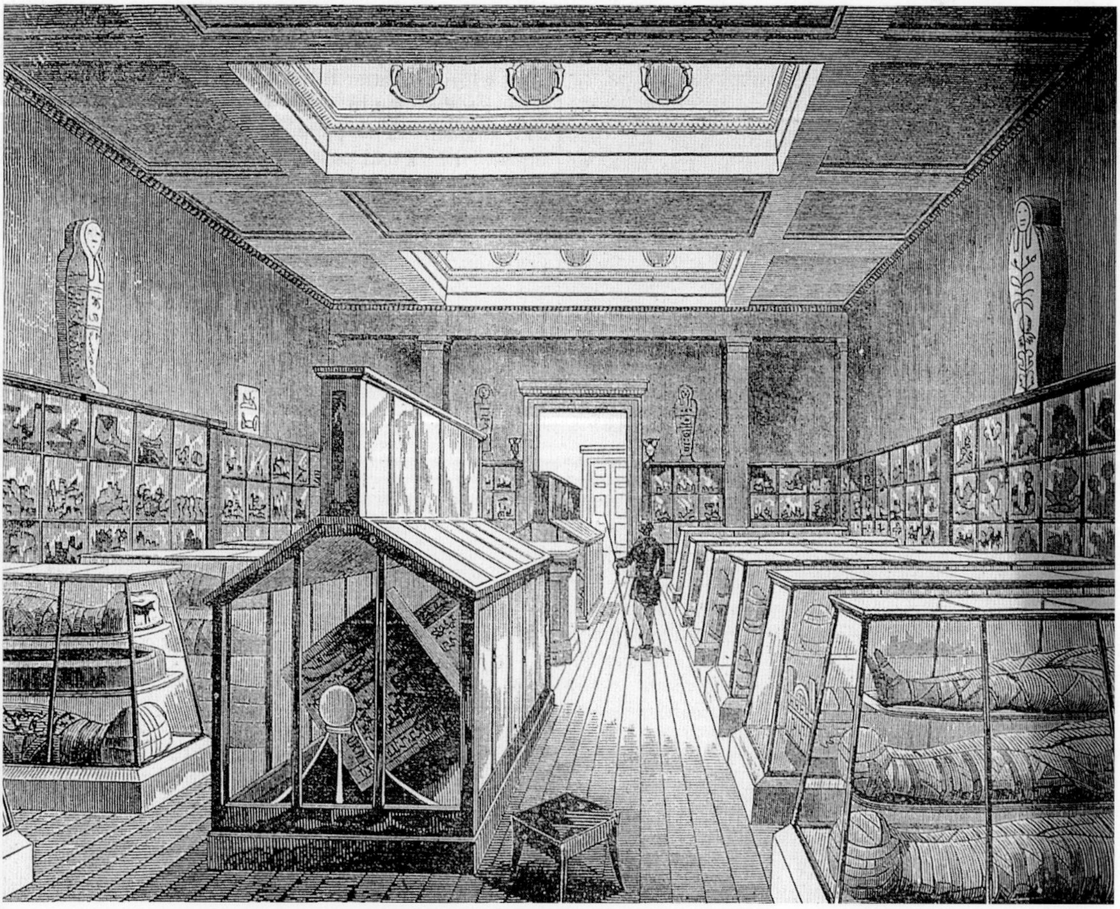

5.25. The new Egyptian Room, looking south. Engraving in the *Penny Magazine,* November 10, 1838: 436.

In considering the reception of the new Egyptian displays of 1834 and 1837, it is fundamental to acknowledge the proliferation of periodicals and educational literature in Britain around this time.[129] Stemming from a concern to disseminate knowledge more widely, these new, popular media provided new opportunities for the public to learn about the nation's great collections held in the museum. Of particular significance were the illustrated magazines and newspapers, such as the *Penny Magazine* and the *Illustrated London News*, which stimulated an interest in the museum with their regularly featured engravings of its galleries. This marked a significant contrast with the more learned journals who had previously reported on the galleries, such as the *Gentleman's Magazine*, the *Edinburgh Review*, and the *Quarterly Review*, as these had assumed some background knowledge and thus provided a supplement to the other written materials their readers may have consulted, rather than providing an introduction to the subject. Furthermore, the Egyptian antiquities gained a favored role in the illustrated magazines, with the editors being quick to capitalize on the mysterious and popular associations of ancient Egypt.[130] In addition to the appearance of the illustrated newspapers and magazines, the proliferation of popular guidebooks became an important means through which visitors gained access to the museum's collections. Indeed, a series of guidebooks on the museum published by the Society for the Diffusion of Useful Knowledge was initiated with a two-volume work on the Egyptian collection.[131] Such works, which sought to make knowledge on ancient Egypt more accessible to the general reader, played an important part in transforming the superficial reaction of awe and shock to a more insightful one in the reception of ancient Egypt. Finally, awareness of the museum's exhibits was increased by a much wider coverage in the explosion of London guidebooks.[132]

Also significant in assessing the reception of the 1834 and 1837 installations were the important developments that took place in widening access to the museum in the 1830s. Public holiday openings, initiated by the museum in 1837, signified the beginning of an extremely popular visiting tradition. That the museum sought to attract a wider audience is suggested by an article in the *Penny Magazine*, in which the appropriate mode of conduct for visitors is outlined for the neophyte. Not only does this set of instructions (including "Touch nothing," "Do not talk loud," and "Be not obtrusive') reinforce the notion that the galleries of a museum are a serious affair, but it also provides a fascinating insight into what the visitor was expected to know. For instance, under the rule "Be not obtrusive," the reader is informed, "You will see many things in the museum that you do not understand," and furthermore, "You must not expect to understand what you see all at once: you must go again and again if you wish to obtain

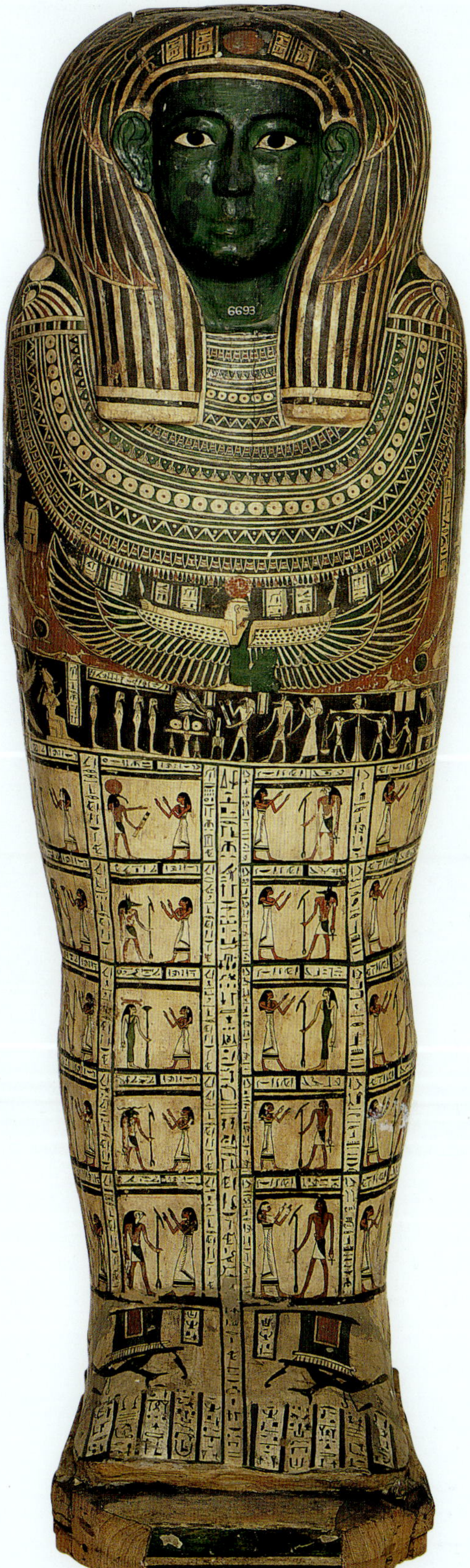

1. Coffin of Itineb (EA 6693) from Thebes, Ptolemaic. Donated to the British Museum in 1766 by King George III.

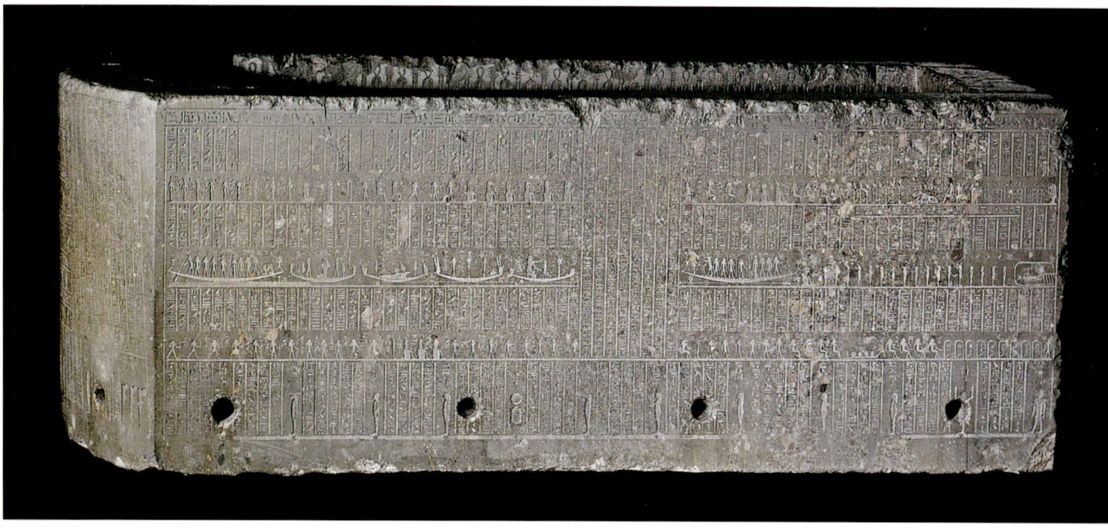

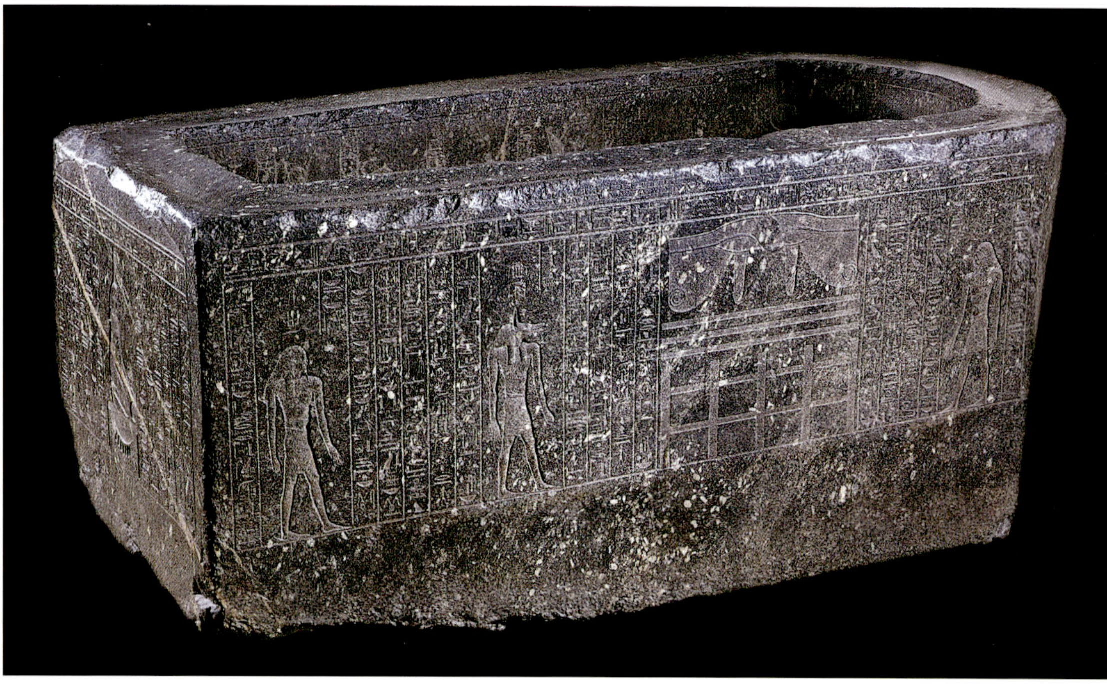

2. Sarcophagus of Nectanebo II (EA 10) from Alexandria, Thirtieth Dynasty. Acquired by the British Museum in 1802 as part of the British victory over the French in Egypt in 1801.

3. Sarcophagus of Hapmen (EA 23) found in Cairo, Twenty-sixth Dynasty or later. Acquired by the British Museum in 1802 as part of the British victory over the French in Egypt in 1801.

4. (*facing*) The Egyptian antiquities seized from the French displayed in the new Townley Gallery, 1810. Aquatint entitled "British Museum—New Building," in *The Repository of Arts, Literature, Commerce, Manufactures, Fashions, and Politics* (Anon. 1810, 3:16, plate 23).

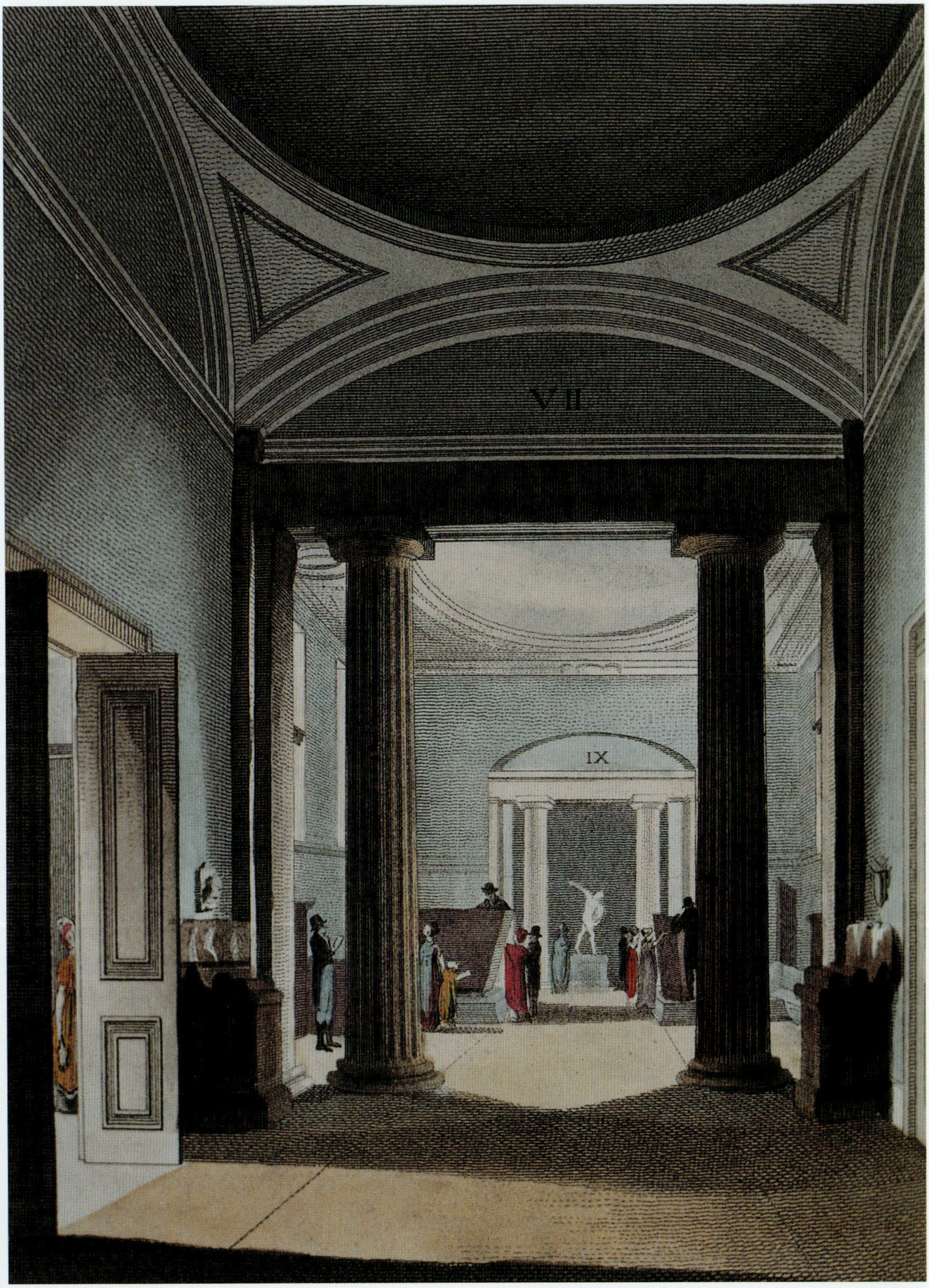
VII
IX

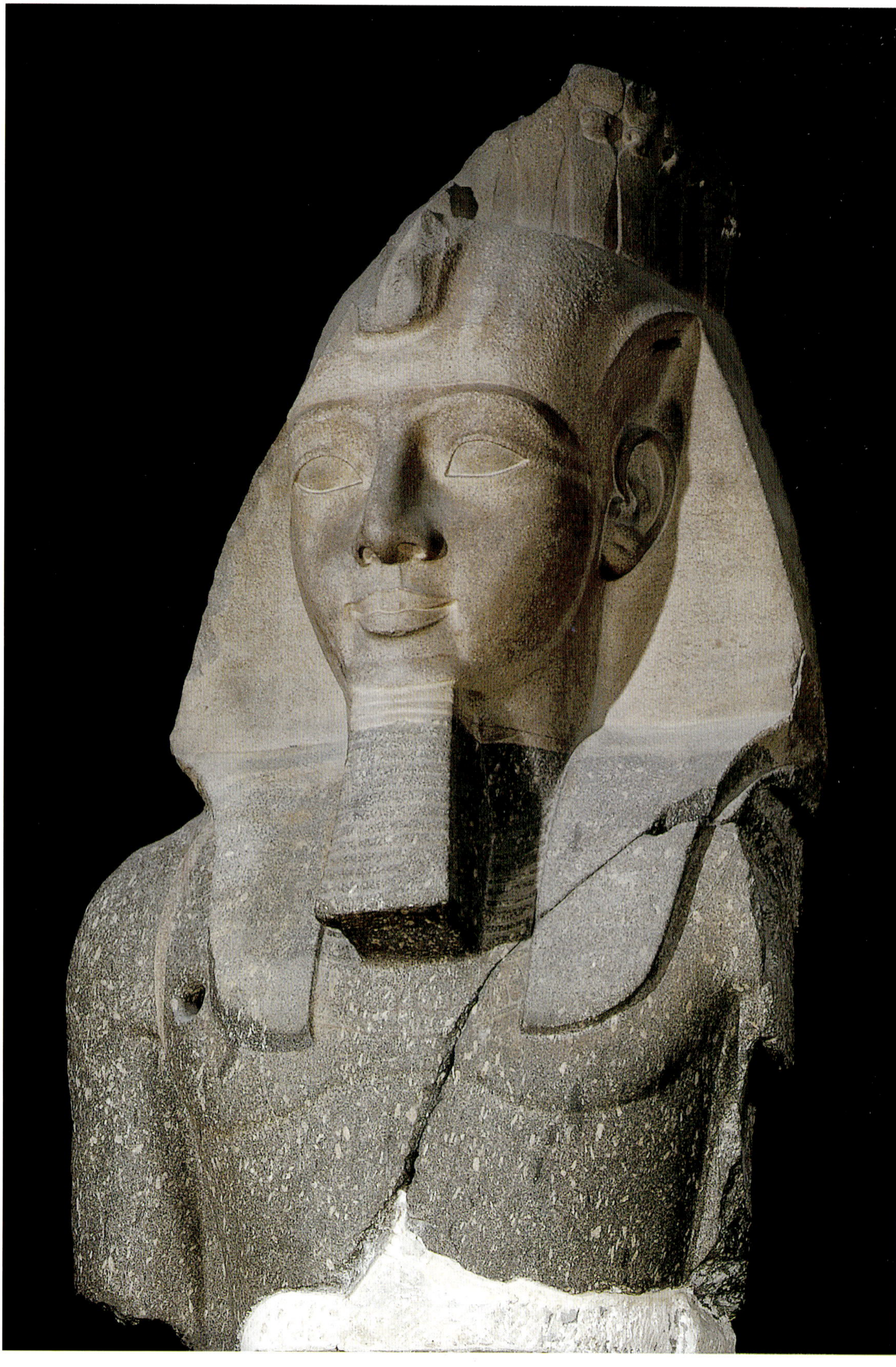

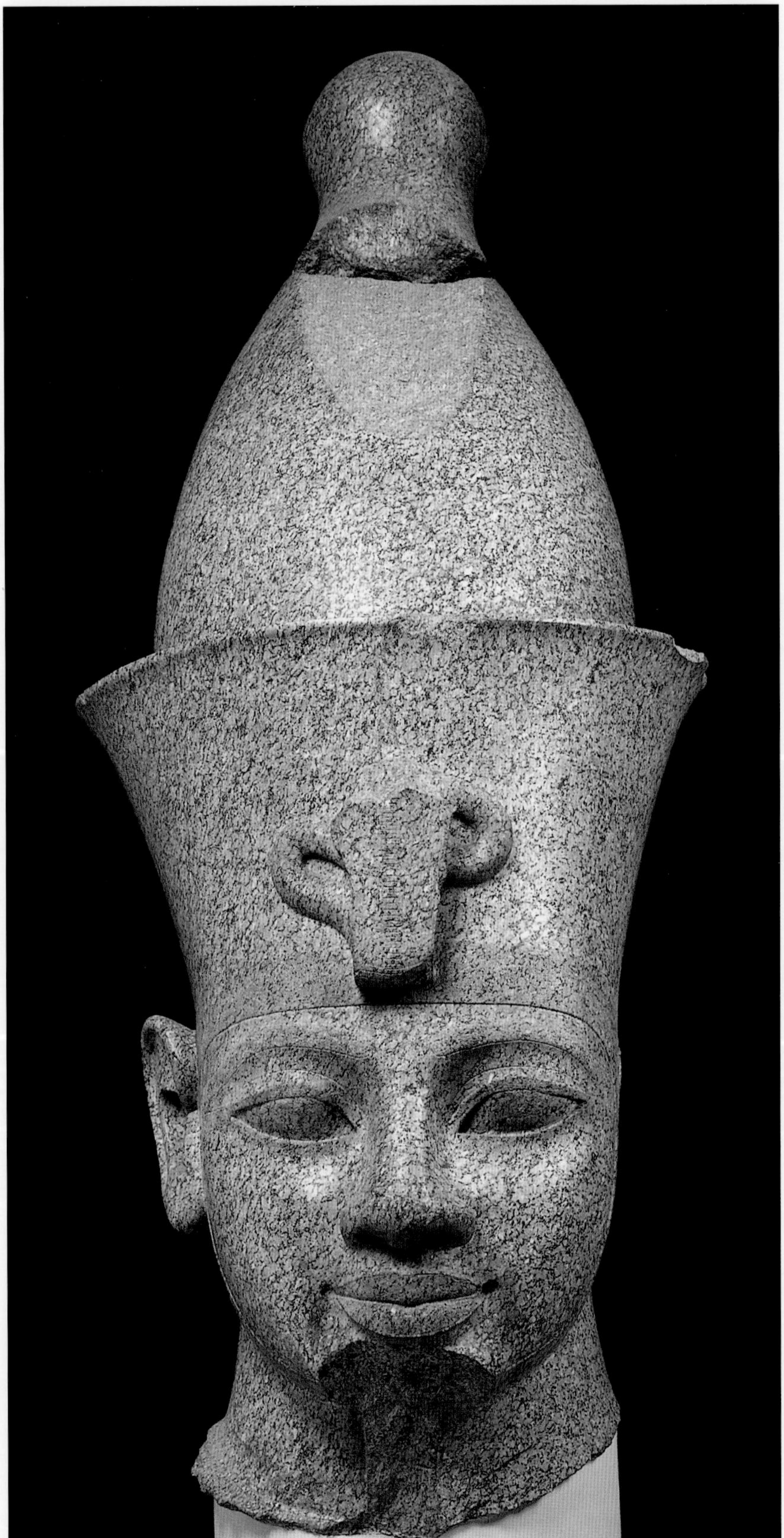

5. (*facing*) Colossal bust of Ramesses II (EA 19) from Thebes, Nineteenth Dynasty. Donated to the British Museum in 1818 by Henry Salt and Johann Ludwig Burckhardt.

6. Colossal head of Amenhotep III (EA 15) from Karnak, Thebes, Eighteenth Dynasty. Acquired by the British Museum in 1823 as part of the Henry Salt collection.

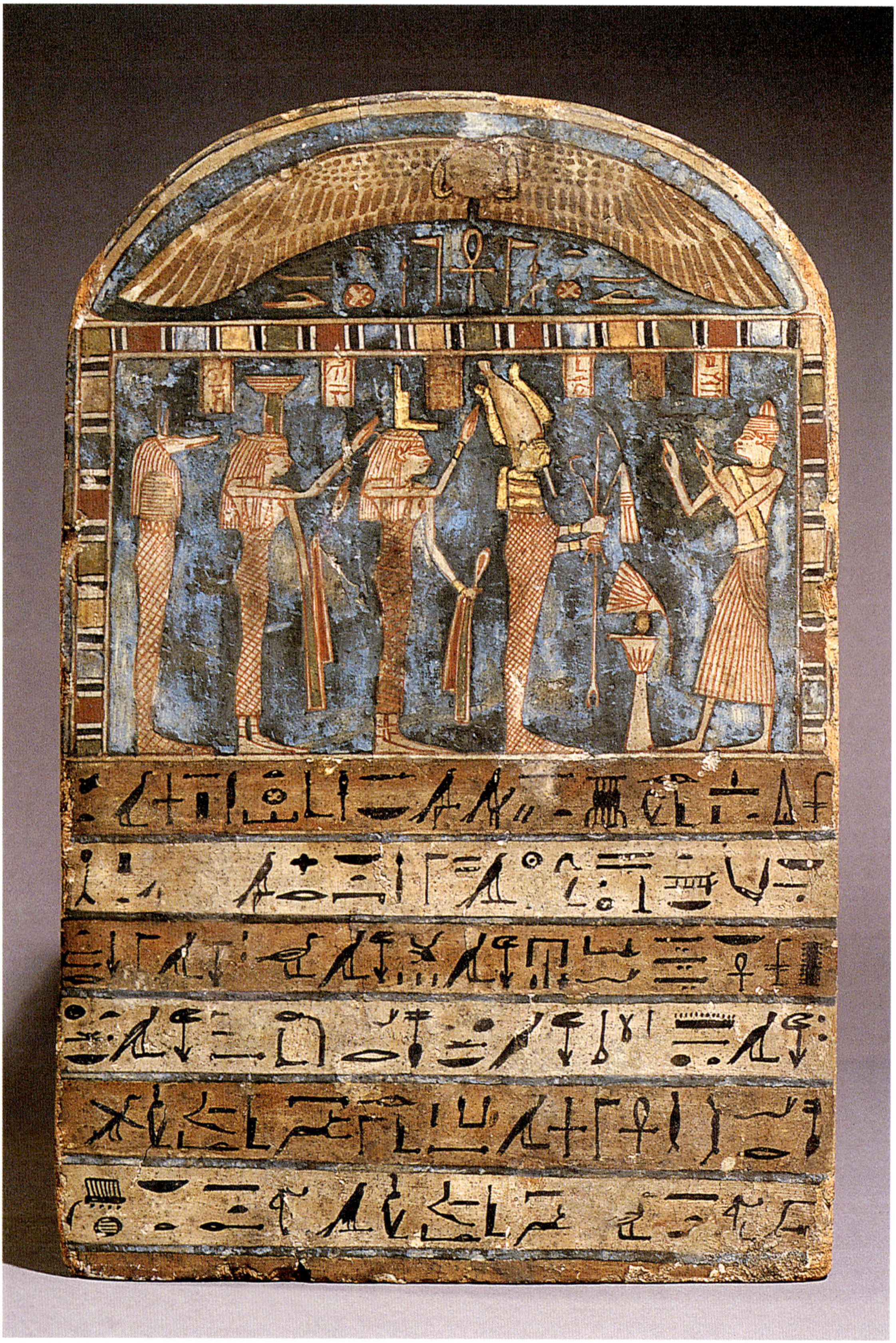

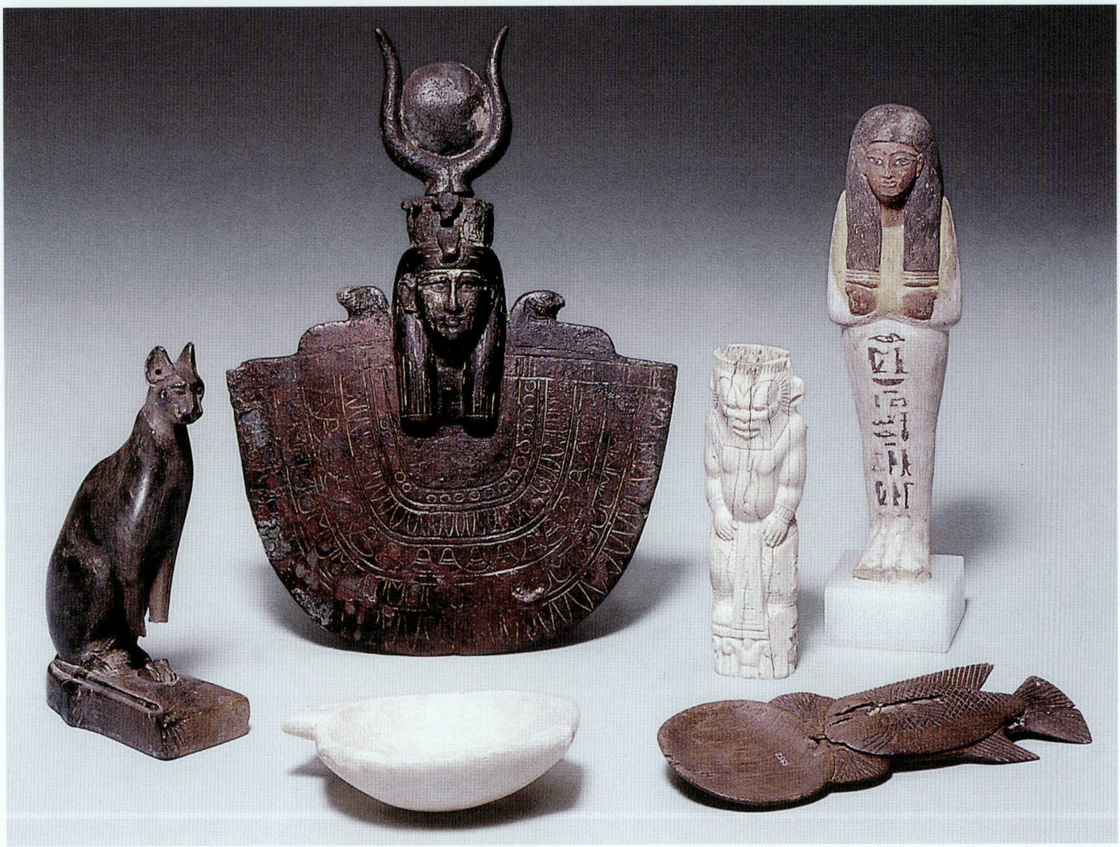

7. (*facing*) Stela of Panes (EA 8504) from Thebes, Twenty-sixth Dynasty. Acquired by the British Museum in 1823 as part of the Henry Salt collection.

8. Group of smaller antiquities collected by Salt and Belzoni, now in the British Museum, including a shabti for a woman named Iy-neferty, Nineteenth Dynasty; a wooden cosmetic spoon from Thebes (EA 5952), New Kingdom; and an ivory kohl tube in the form of Bes (EA 2571), New Kingdom.

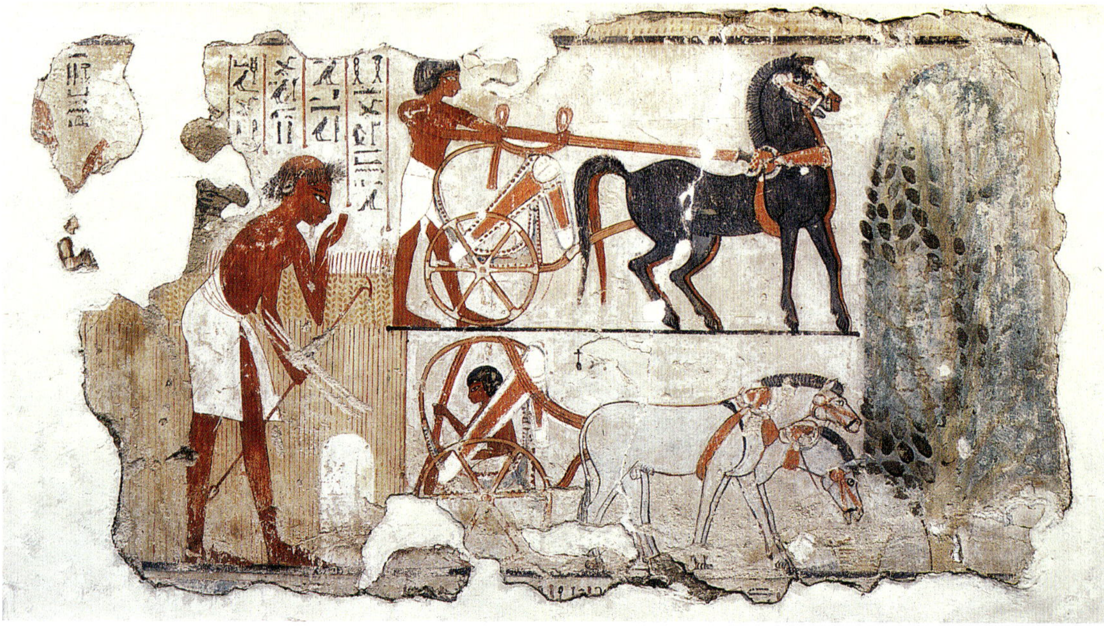

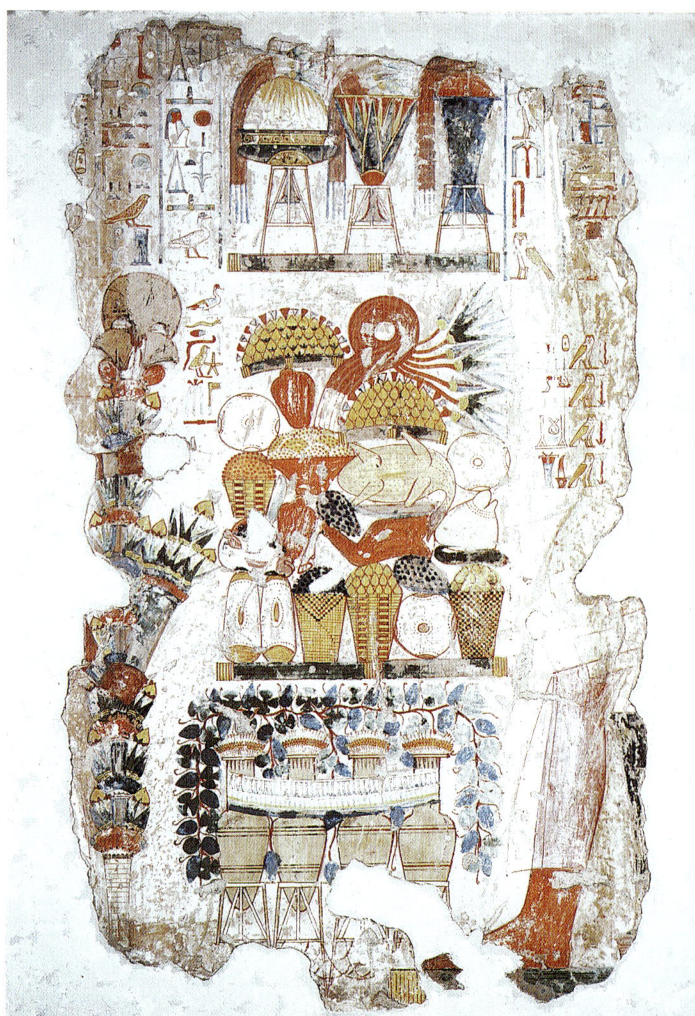

9a and 9b. Wall-painting fragments from the tomb of Nebamun (EA 37982 "Inspecting the fields," EA 37985 "Nebamun receives offerings from his son") from Thebes, Eighteenth Dynasty. Acquired by the British Museum in 1823 as part of the Henry Salt collection.

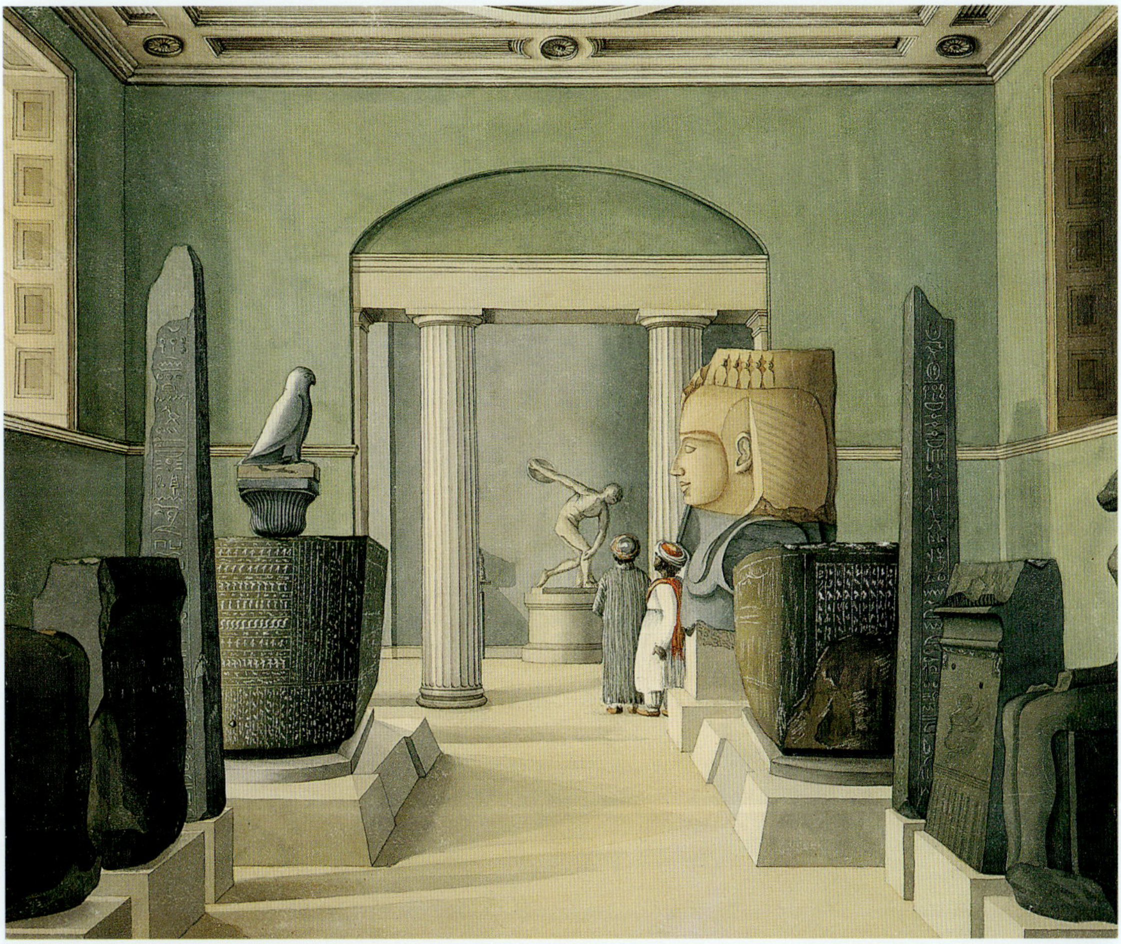

10. Egyptian sculptures displayed in the Townley Gallery. Anonymous watercolor entitled "A Room in the Sculpture Gallery of the British Museum. February 1820. From a sketch taken on the spot in September 1819." British Museum, Department of Prints and Drawings, no. 1881.11.12.137.

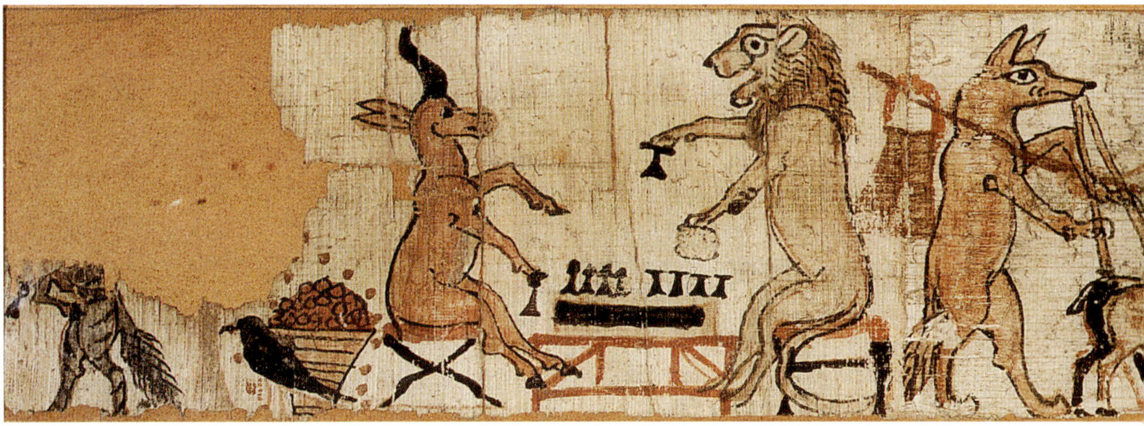

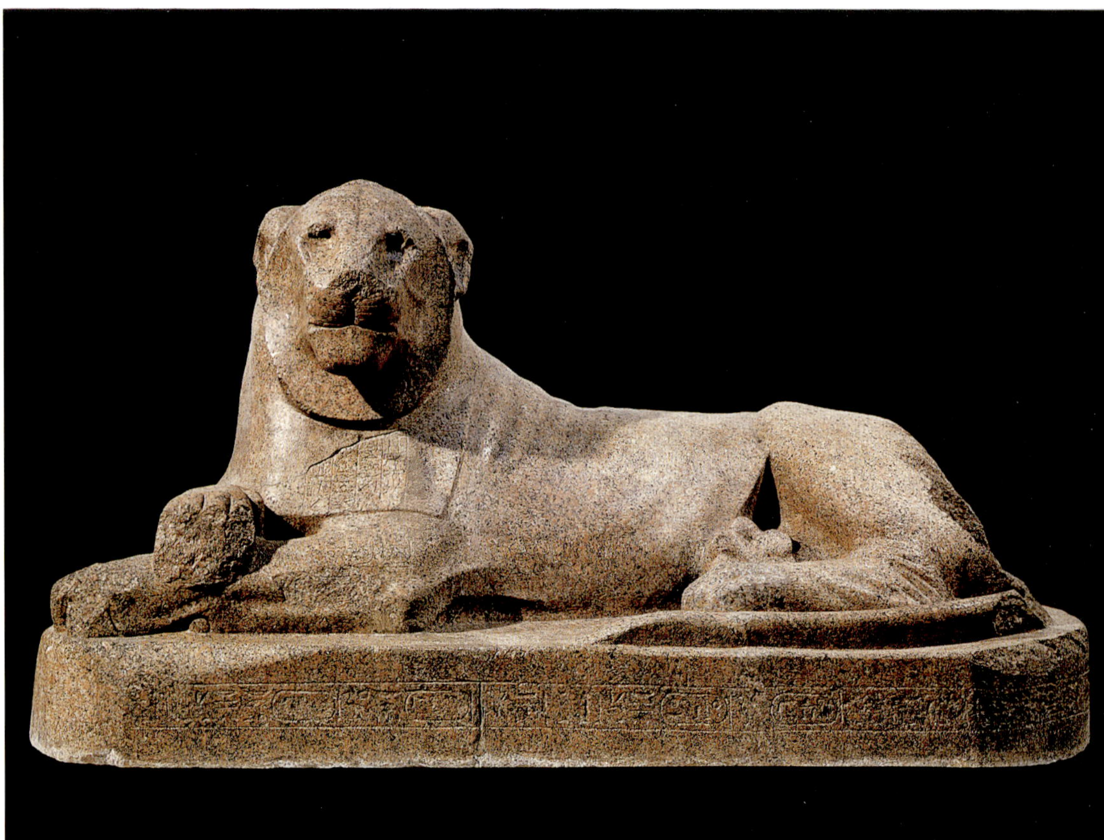

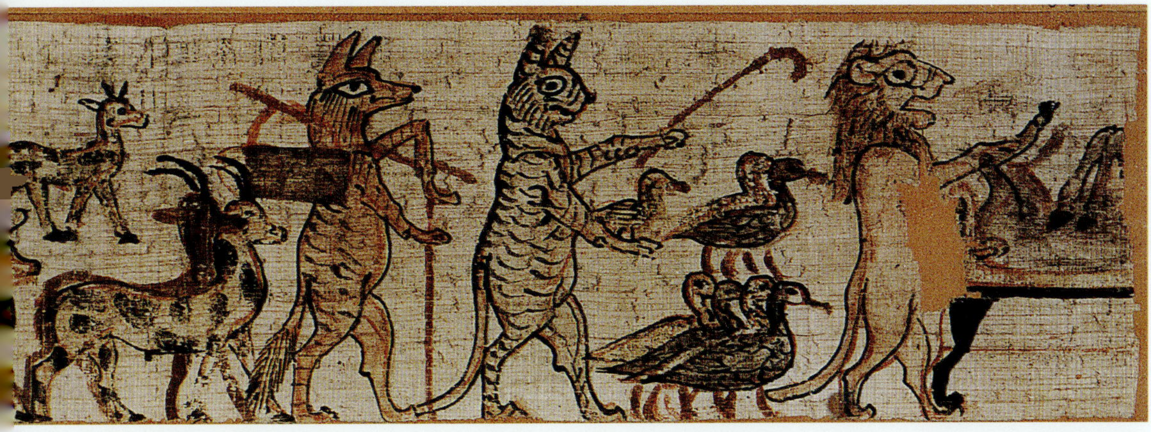

11. (*facing*) Lion statue (EA 2) from Gebel Barkal, originally set up in Soleb, Sudan, Eighteenth Dynasty. Donated to the British Museum in 1835 by Lord Prudhoe.

12. Scene from a satirical papyrus (EA 10016), possibly from Thebes, Late New Kingdom. Acquired by the British Museum from Joseph Sams in 1834.

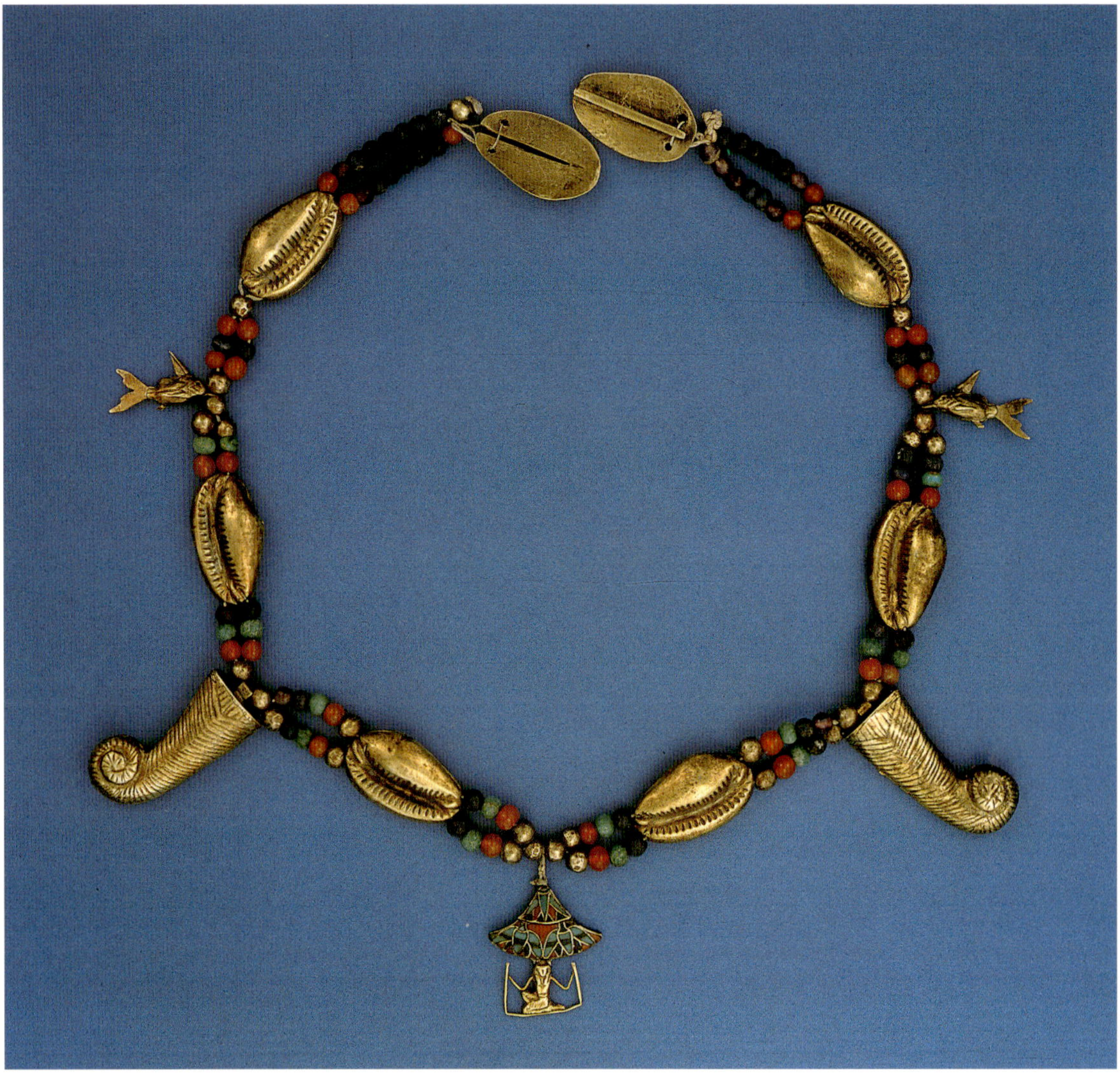

13. String of beads with amulets and semiprecious stones (EA 3077) said to be from Thebes, Middle Kingdom. Purchased by the British Museum in 1835 at the sale of Henry Salt's third collection.

real knowledge, beyond the gratification of passing curiosity."[133] Here we see how "proper" visitors to the museum are defined as those who seek to have more than their curiosity aroused—curiosity being characterized as a very superficial response to the objects in the museum.

The new displays of ancient Egyptian antiquities at the museum attracted a great deal of interest from the media. This interest not only reflected a continuing popular fascination with ancient Egypt, but signified how the discipline of Egyptology had become more formally established around this time.[134] While the publications resulting from Champollion and Rosellini's expedition to Egypt would have provided those with a scholarly interest in ancient Egypt with further understanding of Egyptian antiquities, the works of Wilkinson and Lane would have provided those with a more general interest in geography, travel, and anthropology with new insights into Egyptian antiquity and culture.[135] Indeed, by the time of the installations of 1834 and 1837, knowledge of ancient Egypt had significantly expanded in Britain due to the establishment of a national tradition of Egyptological scholarship by these scholars, although visitors may have been inspired by the stories of their travels in Egypt as much as by their findings. That Wilkinson's work was accorded a key role in promoting a wider understanding of ancient Egypt in Britain is attested to in a review from the *Gentleman's Magazine*, which also conveys the presence of things Egyptian in London at the time:

> Such treasures have been wafted from the rifled tombs to our country, that if we could revive a subject of old Rameses or Sesostris, draw him into life from his bituminous shell, and place him in one or two of the rooms of the British Museum, he would think himself at home, and miss little of the domestic comforts which he enjoyed in his Theban villa; while, in one adjoining vestibule, he might worship a whole synod of his granite divinities, and in another embrace the mummy of his own departed wife. In Mr. Till's cases he might gaze at his gods Apis and Anubis exposed for sale. In his morning's stroll he might behold Mr. Sotheby disposing by auction of an ichneumon or an ibis, his nation's revered, and consecrated animals; and in the evening he might, in the lecture-room in Albemarle Street, see Mr. Pettigrew unrolling the cotton bandages of a priest of Memphis, or the aromatic flavour of one of the queens of Egypt.[136]

In addition to the more scholarly productions on ancient Egypt, books that were aimed at a more general audience, such as Thomas Joseph Pettigrew's *History of Egyptian Mummies* (1834), may have also influenced the reception of the displays.

The museum's collection of Egyptian antiquities held a special place in the eyes of the public, whose interest in objects such as the bust of Ramesses II and the great sarcophagus of Nectanebo II continued. While the Swedish visitor Johan Peter Bager highlighted the sarcophagus, the bust of

Ramesses II was discussed at length in the *Penny Magazine*.[137] In this assessment of the bust, the writer is forgiving about the inferior quality of the piece compared to Greek art:

> Though there is a style of sculpture which we may properly call Egyptian as distinguished from and inferior to the Greek, and though this statue clearly belongs to this Egyptian style, it surpasses as a work of art most other statues from that country by a peculiar sweetness of expression and a finer outline of face. Though the eyebrows are hardly prominent enough for our taste, the nose somewhat too rounded, and the lips rather thick, it is impossible to deny that there is great beauty stamped on the countenance. Its profile, when viewed from various points, will probably show some new beauties to those only accustomed to look at it in front.[138]

The notion that it is the facial expression that makes the sculpture distinctive among Egyptian art is also maintained in a similar assessment from George Long's guidebook to the gallery:

> It is universally agreed that this is one of the finest specimens of Egyptian colossal sculpture now known to exist. . . . For so hard and unwieldy a mass to be wrought even into any resemblance to the human form, and polished to so high a degree, would itself be a labour worthy of admiration. But that the proportions of the parts should have been so well preserved, and that *beauty* should have been impressed on this colossal face, proves that at least some kinds of sculpture were once carried to a high degree of perfection in Egypt.[139]

That the Egyptian antiquities were popular with visitors is also indicated by the *Penny Magazine*'s series of reports on major objects displayed at the museum, including the obelisks of Nectanebo.[140]

The persisting appeal of the Egyptian antiquities reflected the fact that their qualities remained awe-inspiring. While visitors may have become more familiar with the distinctive artistic style of the sculptures, their colossal size would always create an impact. Museum staff recognized the monumentality of Egyptian objects as a key factor in their appeal to visitors as evidenced in their negotiations over the colossal statue of Ramesses II from Memphis, where the size of the sculpture was emphasized as an attribute that would make it popular among visitors.[141]

That the new architectural setting for the Egyptian sculpture collection had an impact on its appearance and status is suggested by comments on the new gallery. In *Pinnock's Guide to Knowledge*, for example, it was stated that "it is strictly Grecian in its form and embellishments, and breathes throughout a dignified simplicity, which although it may not be in strict accordance with the Egyptian sculptures, is, nevertheless, very far from producing an inharmonious combination."[142]

Although not necessarily in a style compatible with the qualities of the Egyptian antiquities, the Smirke Gallery was not seen as clashing or contrasting to the same extent that the Townley Gallery had. Approval of the architectural setting is also conveyed in the *Mirror*, where the writer admits that although "large sums" of public money had been used for this new addition, "we feel assured that the magnificence of the Saloon here represented, bespeaks the just appropriation of the national funds."[143] Significantly, while the architectural setting may have benefited the Egyptian antiquities, it was thought to be incompatible with the classical works. The German artist Johann David Passavant, for example, saw a regression from the earlier installations:

> On the tiptoe of expectation we entered the doors of the British Museum, and how deeply we were disappointed by the first *coup d'œil* of the interior, it is unnecessary to state. Those who remember the apartments which were first allotted to the collection of sculpture, will sufficiently understand and sympathize with my indignation at seeing those magnificent specimens of the purest antique, which had adorned the Parthenon, and glistened beneath the sunny skies of Greece, here crowded in a dirty, dark apartment, and loaded with the defiling accumulations of London soot and dust.[144]

Also characteristic of the reception of the Egyptian antiquities was a changing attitude in which the merits of the objects were more widely recognized. Indeed, reports in the media suggest that in some quarters a sense of respect for Egyptian antiquities was finally emerging. However, as with the seemingly positive evaluations of previous installations, there was always a qualifying remark or comment suggesting that the Egyptian antiquities were still perceived to be inferior to classical works. In the *Mirror*, for example, it was reported that "the noble relics of art assembled within these walls are indeed worthy of so palatial a depository. Of them it has been well observed that 'the colossal dimensions in which some figures are exhibited, the hardness of the materials employed, and the strange combinations of the human and animal form, all unite in exciting an intense desire to know in what country and in what age of the world, such marvellous specimens of human art were produced.' "[145] Here we can see how it is not so much beauty, grace, and elegance that are the criteria for valuing the Egyptian antiquities, but rather their size, material, and unusual subject matter. While earlier in the century these qualities had attracted scorn and repulsion, here they appear to be highlighted as virtues.

Furthermore, while for some the quality of purity was reserved for the Greek antiquities alone, others endeavored to see such an attribute in the Egyptian remains. In the *Literary Gazette* in 1839, for example, an article focusing on the acquisition of Anastasi's collections elaborates on the attributes of the stelae: "Some of the steles in bas-relief manifest a delicacy of execution and a purity of colouring which approach in their way the effects of Greek art; and no one, with any feeling for the progress of the arts, can regard these masterpieces, from which the early Greek sculptors avowedly took their ideas, till they far outstripped their instructors by the ideality of their unrivalled performances, without the most solemn emotions."[146]

Such reviews may have appeared glowing, but they still devalued Egyptian antiquities by qualifying their merits in terms of their connection to Greek art. In the *Pictorial Times*, for example, we are informed that "the Egyptian remains claim the first notice, on account of their extreme antiquity."[147] Thus it is age, rather than artistic style, that attracts comment. An important example of the contradictory nature of the praise that Egyptian antiquities received in the 1830s appears in Long's guidebook:

> The stranger who visits the Gallery of Sculpture, in the British Museum, cannot fail to be struck with the curious collection of objects in the room of Egyptian antiquities. Passing from the contemplation of the almost faultless representations of the human form in marble, the triumph of Grecian art, he comes to figures more remarkable, at first sight, for their singular forms and colossal size, than for their beauty. Though the contrast between what he has just left, and the new scene to which he is introduced, creates at first no pleasing impression, feelings of curiosity and admiration soon arise from a more careful examination of what is around him.[148]

That this introduction is presented as the justification for producing a major work on the subject of Egyptian antiquities reveals how they were still not valued on their own terms. We see, for instance, how the Egyptian antiquities are thought to provide a more instant and superficial gratification than those of the classical world. Furthermore, they do not offer a sustained sense of pleasure like the "faultless representation of the human form" produced by the Greeks. Observing that the first impression of the visitor, after having absorbed the pleasures of the classical antiquities, would be disappointment, Long reassures us that with time, the qualities of the Egyptian objects will become apparent. Despite this less than glowing introduction, Long's work was important because it sought to describe the antiquities in the context of their history, climate, and physical character. The justification for this focus was that descriptions of the objects would be "unintelligible" if they did not "connect them with the country from which they came, and the monuments of which they are but a part."[149] By contextualizing Egyptian antiquities in this way, Long provided an invaluable new resource for interpreting the museum's collections.

In the second volume of Long's work, a defence of Egyptian antiquities was presented in relation to Winckelmann's negative characterization of them: "It is generally assumed, that all Egyptian figures are stiff, ugly, and devoid of grace, which Winckelmann . . . attributes the general want of beauty in the nation. But the opinion of beauty differs so much among various families of the human race, that we must be careful before we come to hasty conclusions on this subject."[150] Long then proceeds to challenge Winckelmann's critique of the Egyptian representation of the human form, admitting that while it is "too angular and stiff," it is possible to find a few figures that are "placed in attitudes which are easy and grateful."[151] Overall, Long's evaluation adopts a forgiving tone with the Egyptian antiquities, trying desperately to see a glimmer of ability and achievement in them. However noble, this work still defines Egyptian antiquities in terms of how they compare to the classical works and, as such, they remain classified as the creations of the poorer cousins of the ancient world.

While there are many examples of those who evaluated the Egyptian antiquities in a more positive light, there are also many of those who continued to denounce them. An 1838 guidebook to the museum, for example, notes that the Egyptian gallery is "filled with works of art, which with respect to their general character are strongly contrasted with the productions of the artists of Greece and Rome. We have here statues and Bas-reliefs; but the former are distinguished chiefly for their colossal dimensions and formal attitudes, and the latter for laborious stiffness of execution, and the utter absence of taste or elegance in the designs."[152] Clearly offended by the lack of "taste" in the Egyptian style of art, this anonymous author also comments on the "monstrous compounds of forms of different kinds of beings, brutish or human."[153] A similar assessment of the sculpture gallery was offered by *Chambers's Edinburgh Journal* in 1839, which referred to the "many monstrous figures, half-human and half-bestial," which "are more calculated to astonish the eye than to enlighten the mind respecting the extraordinary nation from whom they proceeded."[154] The *Times* was similarly dismissive:

> The collection of antiquities in the great saloon of the British Museum, unconnected with the edifices of which they formed part, to the artist are comparatively useless. The monstrosities they represent can neither excite his emulation, nor improve his taste; while to the general visitor they are only regarded as matters of curiosity: he lingers around the mutilated blocks of granite, in vain endeavours to find the meaning of the strange and uncouth figures he sees so innumerably engraved upon them; on turning to the pages of the synopsis, he simply finds the names of Amenothoph, of Rameses, of Ilopth, of Shisask, or of Ptanenoph, and his curiosity remains unsatisfied.[155]

Aside from the observation that once taken out of their original context the antiquities are "useless" for the artist, this report denigrates Egyptian antiquities as curiosities that have no comprehensible meaning to the visitor.

Other indications of how the Egyptian antiquities were negatively received can be gleaned not so much from what was said about them, but rather from what was not said. In Henry Clarke's guidebook of 1843, for example, the classical antiquities are discussed in detail, with frequent glowing assessments, whereas the objects in the Egyptian collection are only very briefly listed, with no adjectives to embellish their status. In describing the Phigaleian Saloon, for instance, Clarke draws the visitor's attention to the "degree of refinement," the "fine qualities," the "delicately modeled" nature and the "remarkable" execution of the sculptures.[156] The Egyptian objects are by contrast, simply numbered with no additional description. When a new edition of the guidebook incorporated introductory paragraphs in order to present the various sculpture collections, this differential treatment became even more obvious. For example, the paragraph for the Lycian room opens with "These splendid Marbles," the one for the Phigaleian Saloon reads, "The beautiful marbles in this apartment," and the one for the Elgin Saloon states, "These splendid sculptures," whereas the introduction to the Egyptian Saloon reads, "The monuments in this room have been brought chiefly from Thebes."[157] Subsequent editions of Clarke's guide continued to endorse the disparity in the treatment of the Egyptian sculptures, such as the introduction of engravings for all the sculpture galleries except the Egyptian ones.

In the numerous articles on the Egyptian displays that appeared in the periodicals and illustrated press, much attention is devoted to discussing the new displays of smaller, everyday objects in the Egyptian Room. While in the guidebooks to the museum the colossal sculptures are still presented as the highlights of the collection, the types of objects featured in the Egyptian Room are elaborated upon much more fully than previously. For instance, the predominance of objects like the sarcophagi and the colossal heads in media reports is replaced with an appreciation of less "sensational" antiquities from Egypt. *Pinnock's Guide to Knowledge*, for example, highlights the "innumerable number of smaller articles of great antiquity and curiosity," and the *Times* praises the smaller items found in association with the mummies, including the jewelry, game pieces, models, basketry, woodwork, foodstuffs, bricks, clothes, furniture, and weapons.[158] Another such evaluation appears in the *Penny Magazine*, where it is noted that the large sculptures such as the obelisks, the sarcophagi, and the bust of Ramesses II had already been on display for some time, and that "it is only lately that the no less interesting articles of domestic life which have been found in the tombs and transmitted to this country have been arranged for public inspection."[159] The comment that these objects are "no less interesting" than the colossal works presented in the sculpture gallery suggests that visitors were equally fascinated with the remnants of everyday life in ancient Egypt. Indeed, there was something powerful and evocative about seeing a bed or stool once used in daily life, or a wig or necklace once worn to adorn the body. Part of this power lay in the inherent paradox that presented itself here, with the objects being seemingly familiar on one hand, yet extremely distant (both temporally and culturally) on the other.

That the new Egyptian Room was of great public interest can also be seen in a series of four reports published in *Chambers's Edinburgh Journal* in

1839.[160] Entitled "Walks in the British Museum," these reports began with the assertion that "no portion of the contents of this great national collection arrests the attention of visitors more forcibly than the relics of ancient Egypt."[161] While we are initially informed that the antiquity of these remains accords them this special status—"that objects of such extreme antiquity should still exist, and be actually shown in England, is one of the most interesting facts which could possibly be mentioned"—it was the sheer quantity and variety of objects that appear to have made a great impact:

> Until within the last few years, comparatively little has been done to explore the tombs and temples of Egypt; but this having now been effected on an extensive scale, the result has been the importation to England and other European countries of an immense variety of ancient objects of art, so that those curious in such things have an opportunity of forming almost as complete an idea of the state of Egyptian civilisation two or three thousand years ago, as they could that of any nation at the present day.[162]

The notion that the objects had the ability to communicate what life was like two or three thousand years ago seems to have greatly appealed to people at the time. Whereas prior to this the emphasis had been on the more sensational pieces, now we see a greater desire to get a sense of the everyday existence of the ancients. Indeed, in the *Chambers's Edinburgh Journal* the contents of the Egyptian Room are described at great length, contrasting with the very brief mention made of the sculpture gallery and the dismissive comment that here the objects were simply designed "to astonish the eye."[163] Clearly, this was not thought to be the case with the domestic antiquities of the same country, which were seen to possess a unique ability to capture people's hearts and minds.

Beginning with a description of the bricks in the Egyptian Room, the *Chambers's* account of the display then moves on to the various other classes of objects, including models, furniture, dressing-room and toilet items, shoes, kitchen utensils, food remains, carpentry tools, armor, musical instruments, weaving tools, children's toys, jewelry, writing implements, and basketry. Acknowledging that a significant omission in his account is the description of the figurines of deities, the sepulchral figures (shabtis), and the extensive collection of mummies, the writer reminds the reader that to include an account of them would conflict with the aim of the report, which has been: "to confine our descriptions chiefly to such articles as illustrated the condition of the domestic arts among this remarkable people, and thus to afford room for a comparison between the state of civilisation which the world had attained three thousand years ago, and that which it displays at the present hour. The result will be felt, we believe, to be much more favourable in many respects to antiquity, than could have been believed without such infallible testimonies as these relics present."[164]

While the use of Egyptian antiquities as a point of contrast to illustrate cultural accomplishments was certainly not new, the perspective this comparison afforded was completely different. Rather than primitive and culturally undeveloped, ancient Egyptians were now deemed to exhibit a level of civilization not too dissimilar from the present. Detailed accounts of the range of antiquities in the Egyptian collection such as those presented in the *Chambers's Edinburgh Journal* and in Long's guidebook did much to stimulate an interest and newfound respect for Egyptian antiquities.[165] In addition to making the point that ancient Egypt should be understood through many different objects other than mummies and colossal sculptures, such evaluations reflected how writers had become more informed about developments in Egyptology.[166] While Wilkinson's three volumes on *The Manners and Customs of the Ancient Egyptians* of 1837 did much to promote an awareness of the more ordinary remains of ancient life, Edward Lane's studies on the manners and customs of modern Egyptians stimulated further interest in the less spectacular aspects of Egypt.[167]

The fact that many other such reviews of the Egyptian Room appeared in the media further demonstrates the fascination with items of a more secular nature. In the *Pictorial Times*, for example, the writer focuses on the display of the "domestic antiquities of Egypt, including all the articles of the lady's toilet, even a most elaborately plaited wig, painter's palettes and brushes, carpenter's tools, etc., and a store of mummies, mummy-cases, and jewels, seals, necklaces, etc."[168] Even the critics who had been so dismissive of the "artworks" in the sculpture gallery showed a hint of appreciation for the objects displayed in the Egyptian Room. In Clarke's guidebook, for example, the Egyptian Room attracted a far more favorable view than the sculpture gallery: "The contents of this room . . . are extremely curious, and deserve a lengthened inspection from the visitor, as illustrating the most minute particulars of the domestic history of the ancient Egyptians."[169] Despite the appearance of more appreciative responses to the collections displayed in the new Egyptian Room, many visitors maintained a fascination with the mummies at the expense of all the other objects. For example, in an account of his visit to the museum, "Old Humphrey" highlights the Egyptian Rooms, exclaiming, "What a number of mummies and ornamented mummy cases are here! And yet this is London, and not Egypt."[170]

Finally, a very vivid idea of how the Egyptian collections were viewed and of the types of visitors they attracted is provided in a humorous account of a visit made to the museum by the antiquary Mr. Withers Grubbe from Brompton. Published in the *Illuminated Magazine* in 1843, this story tells of how Mr. Grubbe, a "walking catalogue" of the British Museum, got drunk at the docks one day and went to visit the museum in the hope that "its cool tranquillity would allay his cerebral excitement."[171] Entering the Egyptian gallery, "which was his usual lounge," Mr. Grubbe observed the caliber of visitors he encountered:

> There were, as usual, a great many people gaping about and asking foolish questions of the attendant; some mixing up the sphinx with the fossils they had seen, and asking if it ever was alive; others feeling rather afraid of going too near the mummies by themselves; and others lost in mental arguments as to whether the colossal fist of red granite was a thunderbolt or the hand of a petrified giant; together with a great many ill-conducted little boys, with no veneration for antiquities, who laughed at the different objects as they would have done at any of Mr. W. Bradwell's wondrous creations in a pantomime.[172]

As Mr. Grubbe pondered upon the objects in the gallery he became increasingly irritated by the other visitors around him, "whose inane remarks grated upon his learned ears," so he retreated to a remote corner behind the large sculptures, where he proceeded to fall asleep. When he awoke it was night and the gallery was deserted; light from the moon came through the windows falling upon the statues and "rendering them still more cold and ghastly." Locked in the building with "nothing but stony monsters," Mr. Grubbe then witnessed an amazing event—the sculptures came to life before his very eyes, starting with the giant beetle who stretched forth its feelers and opened its wings. No sooner had the bust of Ramesses II and the sphinx awakened, than there was a banging at the door. Soon the mummies from the upstairs gallery and the figures from the paintings and tablets joined them. All had come to worship the "greatest feature of the gallery—the mystic, awe-inspiring Memnon [Ramesses II]," who moved to the end of the room to receive his guests. Then commenced an "unearthly *gallopade*—a dreary carnival of the dead," which before long Mr. Grubbe joined in, "whirling round in the throng of deities, mummies, hieroglyphics, ibises, and anomalous creations." When all came to an end and Mr. Grubbe awoke the next morning, the gallery was as he initially remembered it, but he would never forget his privilege of being "admitted to the orgies of Memnon" and witnessing the "revelries and manners of the hitherto mysterious race."

Beyond being so entertaining, this article tells us something about the way the antiquities were perceived at the time and also who the main consumers of these antiquities were perceived to be. Mr. Grubbe is clearly a comedic figure and a source of some ridicule; however, he is also an antiquarian, and as such assumes a superior status to the lowly masses that gawk at the Egyptian antiquities. That the ignorance of these unenlightened visitors is emphasized reflects upon how the antiquities themselves were valued. Words like "cold and ghastly" and "stony monsters" demonstrate that the popular fascination with the Egyptian sculptures stemmed more from a ghoulish relish than any kind of aesthetic appreciation. The erotic connotations of Mr. Grubbe's adventures can also not be overlooked; the "orgies of Memnon" convey an Orientalist fantasy and emphasize a morally inferior, licentious version of ancient Egypt.

* * *

By the end of the 1830s, the Egyptian collection at the museum had grown very considerably. This period can be seen as the climax or high point in the formation of the collection, when intensified foreign activity in Egypt resulted in a significant expansion and diversification of objects displayed. Although the image of ancient Egypt as a mysterious civilization fixated on death and strange gods was still encouraged by the arrangements of the sculpture gallery, the presentation of the more familiar remnants of life in the Egyptian Room provided another dimension in the appreciation of ancient Egypt. It appears that when the Egyptian antiquities were not in the company of classical antiquities, or trying to compete with them as objects of art, they attracted praise and recognition as being worthy of study. Beyond emphasizing the monumental nature of Egyptian art, the displays now offered a glimpse into everyday life in the past. Thus, in addition to offering something exotic and curious, the Egyptian displays now offered something more familiar and accessible. With the new Egyptian Room, visitors were not only given the opportunity to appreciate the diversity of the Egyptian archaeological record, but were presented with an "alternative" Egypt that added a completely new dimension to this ancient culture. However this vision did not serve to replace previous visions; rather, it was added as another layer, so that in addition to seeing the colossal delights of Egypt visitors were encouraged to contemplate bricks, stools, food remains, and old shoes. Furthermore, the ancient works of Egypt were situated in a more flattering architectural setting than in the Townley Gallery, one that was more in proportion with their scale and which provided more generous accommodation for the vastly expanded collection. Finally, the new Egyptian installations of 1834 and 1837 appealed to visitors for a whole variety of reasons. Not only did they strike a chord with people because of their familiarity (e.g., the Egyptian Room and its household items), but because the appreciation of the objects did not require previous knowledge or training. Because Egyptology was not established to the same extent as Greek and Roman archaeology, these mysterious objects could be more freely understood and in a sense "owned" by commoners. Thus, the Egyptian galleries were not only of interest in terms of their content, but because they constituted a comfortable or less intimidating space than did the revered Greek and Roman galleries. Whereas the latter evoked a learned intellectual atmosphere, the Egyptian galleries were appropriated as a less serious place where people were free to express their awe and engage with the antiquities in less contrived way.

6 Historical Documents

THE EXTENDED SMIRKE GALLERIES, 1854–1880

By the middle of the nineteenth century the acquisition of antiquities at the British Museum had reached new heights. The arrival of several major new collections, particularly the Assyrian sculptures acquired in the late 1840s, ensured that the museum retained its status as a world leader in the discovery and definition of past cultures. From this period well into the late 1800s, a continued investment was made in acquiring antiquities, a key motivation for this being the rivalry between the museum and other national museums such as the Louvre. In this context, the presentation of ancient Egypt was transformed yet again—however this time it was not so much through the acquisition of more colossal sculptures or large collections of smaller objects, but rather through the first real effort to implement a collection management program for the Egyptian antiquities. This program resulted in the creation of a far more comprehensive collection, with the weaker components being strengthened and the stronger components further enriched. Before the mid-nineteenth century, little had been done to address the selective view of ancient Egypt that was conveyed in the displays, and with a new, much extended gallery opened in 1854, the opportunity came to present a more representative sample of Egyptian antiquities.

The new Egyptian gallery incorporated a revised system of presentation. More specifically, the sculpture collection was arranged chronologically, thus redefining the antiquities as historical documents as opposed to inferior works of art. This new method of structuring the presentation of the collection was made possible by the decipherment of hieroglyphs, and reflected how Egyptology had become internationally recognized as a scholarly discipline. Significantly, however, while the new arrangement of 1854 encouraged visitors to appreciate the archaeological significance of the antiquities for the first time, it continued to fulfill their expectations of witnessing a mysterious ancient society characterized by an obsession with death and the afterlife. Thus, although the value of Egyptian antiquities as a vital source of historical knowledge was established, the 1854 display functioned as yet another layer, as opposed to a replacement, in the complex representational schema for ancient Egypt.

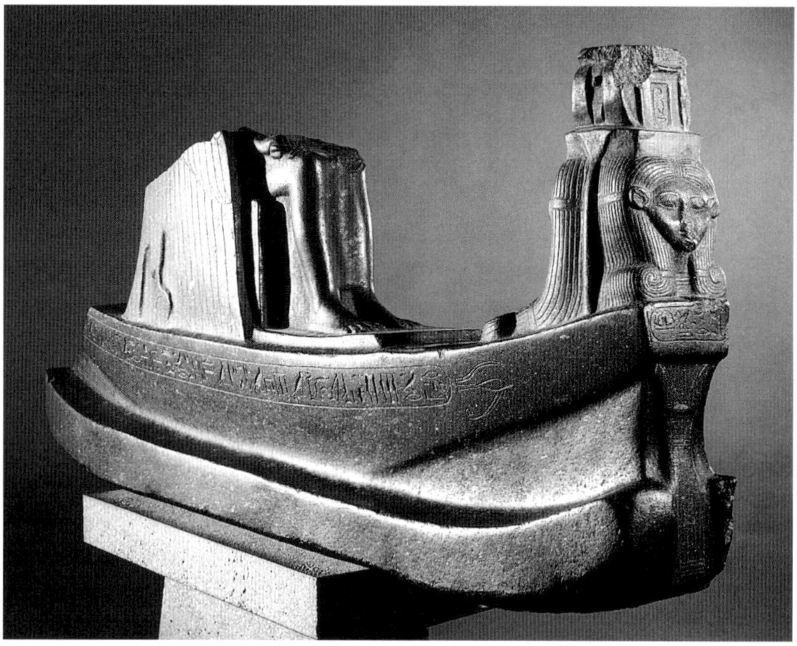

6.1

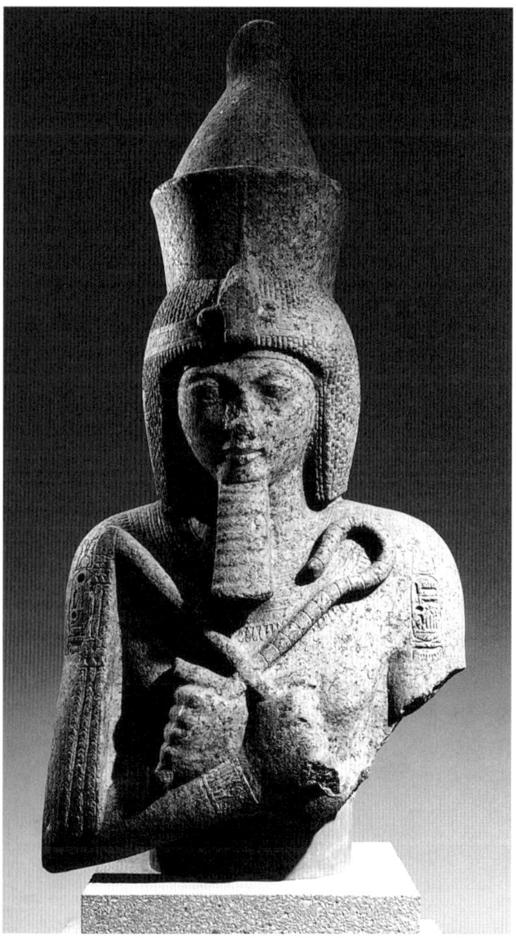

6.2

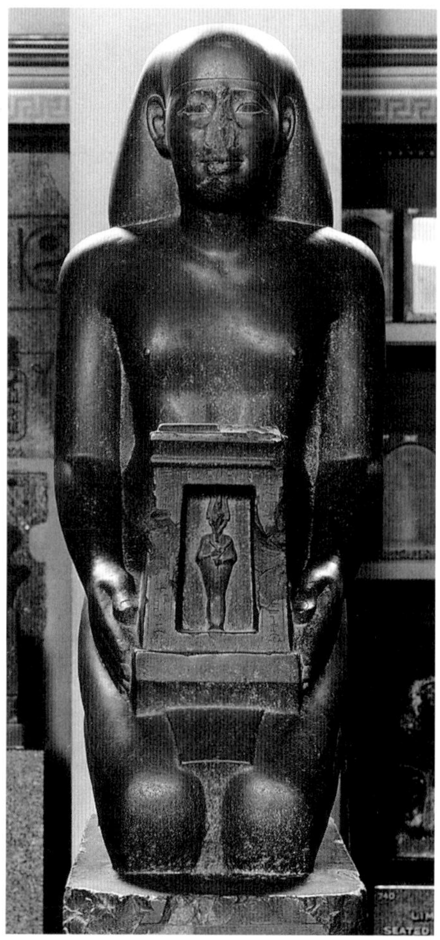

6.3

6.1. Sculpture of a boat with Queen Mutemwia (EA 43) from Karnak, Thebes. Means of acquisition unknown; however, in the collection by 1834.

6.2. Bust of a statue of Ramesses II (EA 67) from Elephantine Island, Aswan, Nineteenth Dynasty. Donated to the British Museum in 1840 by W. R. Hamilton.

6.3. Sculpture of Wahibre (EA 111) from near Lake Mareotis in the northwest Delta, Twenty-sixth Dynasty. Donated to the British Museum in 1844 by E. Fletcher.

ACQUISITION

With the arrival of the Assyrian antiquities from ancient Nineveh in the middle of the nineteenth century came the end of an era for the museum.[1] It was from this point that the grand collections obtained from exotic lands became increasingly rare, and offers of major collections by enterprising consuls, military officials, and collectors became much less frequent. While the museum was still offered collections of Egyptian antiquities for purchase, these were nothing like the great sculpture collections of Salt and the comprehensive collections of Sams. That the heady days of the 1820s and 1830s had passed is reflected in the minutes of the trustees meetings from the 1840s to 1880, which show a marked contrast to those from the earlier period. While the former provide pages and pages of detailed discussion on the extensive negotiations over the purchase of single objects and collections, the latter simply present short notices indicating whether an object or collection was purchased or declined. Notable exceptions include the continued communications over the removal of a colossal statue of Ramesses II at Memphis (see chapter 5), which never made it to the museum, and the negotiations regarding Cleopatra's Needle, which was initially offered to the museum in 1820, and which despite being "reoffered" in 1849 was eventually erected on the Thames Embankment in 1878.[2] Despite the lack of opportunities to purchase collections on the scale that had previously been the case, the museum began to purchase Egyptian antiquities from the many auctions and private sales being held in Britain and all over Europe, and several major works were thus incorporated into the 1854 installation.[3] These included the sculpture of the boat with Queen Mutemwia (fig. 6.1), the statue of Ramesses II from the Island of Elephantine (fig. 6.2), and the sculpture of Wahibre (fig. 6.3).[4] Important donations such as the bust of a Ptolemaic king, the Benha lion sculpture, and a statue of Khaemwaset were added to the display shortly after 1854.[5] In addition to these sculptures, thousands of smaller items were purchased in order to strengthen the representation of other object types in the Egyptian collection.[6]

The museum's changing approach to the acquisition of Egyptian antiquities was no doubt affected by the fact that the Egyptian authorities had become increasingly concerned with the loss of their antiquities to the museums of Europe. Evidence of this changing situation can be seen in the negotiations for the removal of the colossal statue of Ramesses II from Memphis, when in 1852 the British consul general reported to the trustees that removal would be extremely difficult as "the Pasha of Egypt had of late expressed his determination not to let any future collection of antiquities or individual specimens be removed from the country."[7] That the Egyptian government was not as tolerant of the export of antiquities as it previously had been was also made clear in 1873, when they refused permission for the collection of the Reverend Greville J. Chester to be sent to England.[8] Even so, foreign consuls in Egypt were becoming concerned with the way in which the ruling Turkish governors of Egypt were quarrying the ancient sites for building materials and thus destroying the remaining monuments of antiquity.[9] Furthermore, despite the establishment of a new rule to keep important antiquities in Egypt, there were instances where this was not adhered to. In 1855, for example, when the Archduke Maximilian of Austria visited Cairo and commented favorably on the antiquities he saw there, the Viceroy of Egypt, Khedive Said Pasha, gave him a collection of Egyptian antiquities. Despite such incidents, however, the creation of a National Antiquities Service in Egypt and the formation of a national collection of antiquities meant that European countries would no longer have the same access to major sculptural pieces for their museums.[10]

While the first half of the century was characterized by a more opportunistic and serendipitous approach to acquisition, the increasing awareness of the value of antiquities by foreign governments forced the museum to start developing a collection policy. From the mid- to late nineteenth century, for instance, the emphasis shifted to developing areas of the collection that were not well represented.[11] This was particularly so with the Egyptian antiquities, where a significant investment was made to fill in gaps in the collection.[12] The vast majority of items purchased under this system were smaller, cheaper ones, usually costing under £50. The trustees also became more selective in their purchases of Egyptian antiquities; certain classes of artifact, if already present in sufficient quantities in the collection, for instance, were generally not purchased.[13] Furthermore, on the rare occasions that substantial Egyptian collections came up for sale, the trustees showed little interest in obtaining them in their entirety. For example, in 1858 Dr. Henry Abbott's collection, which was priced at £10,000, was declined, and in 1871, the collection of Anthony Harris, priced at £15,000, was declined.[14]

As part of a more discerning approach to collection management, museum staff became more active in traveling to inspect collections overseas.[15] Related to this was the decision in 1863 by the subcommittee on antiquities to prepare instructions for British consuls abroad on how to acquire antiquities for the museum.[16] The acquisition of antiquities was further transformed when the keepers were finally allowed to take a more active role in recommending purchases. The Egyptian collection benefited enormously from this, with Birch being partially successful in getting the trustees to buy smaller Egyptian collections.[17] Furthermore, Hawkins and Birch were often given permission to attend sales of Egyptian antiquities, with the authority to make purchases.[18] Finally, the creation of new departments within the museum, such as the Egyptian and Assyrian Antiquities Department, meant that the collections began to be more extensively studied by specialist staff. Birch was extremely productive in this area, undertaking important work in cataloguing the collection, producing a detailed guide to the Egyptian rooms, and establishing a clearer idea of how the Egyptian collection should be developed.[19] Additionally, by persuading the trustees, via Hawkins, to have all the Egyptian papyri transferred from the Department of Manuscripts to the Department of Antiquities in 1839, Birch ensured that the range and importance of the Egyptian collection was greatly strengthened.[20] Furthermore, the series of important publications that he subsequently produced on Egyptian papyri were central in making acquisitions of Egyptian material more meaningful or desirable for the museum.[21]

Affecting the acquisition of the Egyptian antiquities in the museum from 1854 to 1880 were several major internal developments, not least of which was the major reorganization of the Antiquities Department. Begun in 1860, when the keeper for antiquities Edward Hawkins was nearing retirement, this process of restructuring reveals much about the different values attributed to the various classes of antiquities at the time. For instance, when the subcommittee for antiquities met to determine the future of the department they resolved that it should be divided into four new departments, including 1. Greek and Roman Antiquities, 2. Oriental Antiquities, 3. Coins and Medals, and 4. Ethnography and Medieval Antiquities.[22] While the trustees concurred with the first three departments, they suggested that the ethnographic and medieval antiquities be attached to one of these three as opposed to being assigned their own department.[23] It was thus decided that the Department of Oriental Antiquities should include the medieval, ethnographic, and British collections.[24] The Oriental Department, which primarily included the Egyptian antiquities, now represented a motley collection of subjects and lacked the focus and unity that the other departments had. The trustees clearly felt that none of the areas represented in this new department were important enough to have an independent status, and while this seems bizarre considering the extensive nature of the Egyptian collection and the substantial amount of space dedicated to its exhibition, it reflects the trustees' persisting attitude that Egyptian antiquities were not of equal importance to the classical ones. It was not long, however, before the museum authorities recognized that the new departmental structure for Oriental antiquities was completely inadequate to manage the diverse set of collections it encompassed. Thus, in 1866 the Oriental Antiquities Department was subdivided into two new departments—the British and Medieval Antiquities and Ethnography Department, and the Egyptian and Assyrian Antiquities Department. The new head of the latter was Samuel Birch, whose appointment marked the beginnings of a more focused policy of collection development for the Egyptian antiquities.

In addition to major organizational changes, the museum underwent another series of parliamentary investigations between 1850 and 1860, which tell us much about attitudes to Egyptian antiquities. Among the issues addressed in these inquiries was the nature of the position of antiquities keeper, the qualifications of antiquities staff, the procedure for purchasing collections, and the accommodation for the collections.[25] In the inquiry of 1850, for instance, Hawkins was asked to describe the duties of his post.[26] His response that the job of the curator was to "keep the antiquities and coins and ethnographical collections in order, and to look out for acquisitions which may be advisable for the museum," reflects how he envisaged a more active role in collection development for keepers, rather than one of simply considering offers made to the museum.[27] This attitude was particularly important for the continuing growth and systemization of the Egyptian collection, which had initially come to the museum through offers made by enterprising collectors such as Henry Salt and Joseph Sams (see chapters 4 and 5). Another subject of great interest to the commissioners of the inquiry was the issue of staff qualifications, upon which Hawkins explained that the requisite training was provided once employed in the museum.[28] Recognizing that staff were taken on without any prior training, he was at pains to emphasize that a good selection procedure existed: "The principle upon which we have gone into the Department of Antiquities has been, to get young men who are well educated, and of good character and attainments, and to educate them for the specific purposes of the department after they come here, but we have not thought it necessary to look out for persons who are already antiquaries; and if we had been so disposed, until very lately the study of archaeology has been so little attended to in the country that we could not have found them."[29]

At the time of Hawkins's comments there was no established career path or formal training for antiquities specialists. That there was not a pool of university-trained archaeologists the museum could readily call upon for employment reveals that the people who would have been responsible for curating the museum's collections acquired their skills through an apprenticeship-like system. This fact helps us understand why collection development was not informed by scholarly principles and disciplinary ideas. Although there were a growing number of researchers with a special interest in Egyptian antiquity in Britain, they were not involved in making decisions about the management and development of the Egyptian collection. It was the staff generated within the museum environment that determined how the collection was to be enlarged and presented, and these individuals tended to be recruited because of their educational backgrounds in classics. Because the Egyptian collection was overseen in this way it tended to be understood in terms of its relationship to other collections of which much more was known, for example, the Greek and Roman collections. This essentially meant that people whose primary interest was in classical antiquities managed the Egyptian antiquities. It was not until 1892 that the first university position in Egyptology was created, the Edwards Professor of Egyptian Archaeology and Philology at the University College London, which was awarded to Flinders Petrie.

On the subject of how purchases were made by the museum, the 1850 inquiry reveals that the keeper of antiquities was given little role or authority in the process, and that because all purchases had to be approved by the trustees, there were often delays resulting in the loss of collections.[30] Although Taylor Combe first raised the issue of keepers recommending the purchase of objects in 1810, and Frederic Madden raised the issue of purchasing objects without first obtaining permission from the trustees in 1849, Hawkins persisted with the idea that keepers be given a role in making acquisitions.[31] Although his pleas to achieve this were rejected at the time, six years later when he raised the idea again, it was finally agreed that keepers could spend up to £100 each year on acquisitions.[32]

Finally, the museum's more systematic approach to acquisition coincided with a time when scholarship on ancient Egypt was entering a new phase. For instance, it was around this time that the largest work on ancient Egypt yet produced appeared. Karl Richard Lepsius's *Denkmäler aus Aegypten und Aethiopien* (Discoveries in Egypt and Ethiopia) of 1849–1859 was based on the major expedition he led in Egypt from 1842 to 1845 to record monuments.[33] More significant perhaps was the appearance of major syntheses on the subject, and key here was Christian Bunsen's five-volume work *Aegyptens Stelle in der Weltgeschichte* (Egypt's Place in Universal History) of 1845.[34] Together with other general works on ancient Egypt, this study signified how much the field had grown. Notable British works included Samuel Sharpe's *History of Egypt* of 1846, John Kendrick's *Ancient Egypt under the Pharaohs* of 1850, and Reginald Stuart Poole's *Horae Aegptiacae* of 1851. This new trend of publishing general summary works did much to advance the appreciation of ancient Egypt and can be seen as culminating in the appearance of John Gardner Wilkinson's *A Popular Account of the Ancient Egyptians* in 1854. As the first attempt to provide an account of ancient Egyptian society for a wider reading audience, this important work signified the coming-of-age of the discipline. Although the trustees were not necessarily aware of or interested in this upsurge of work on Egypt, they were less quick to dismiss Egyptian antiquities with the claim that little substantial material existed to testify to their merits.

DISPLAY

The wealth of museum documentation on the 1854 installation reveals that issues of display had finally been accorded the importance they deserved. Until now, very little was written on how collections were to be structured and how objects were to be distributed within this schema. Indeed, matters of exhibition were treated with an unspoken commonsense approach where it was not thought necessary to elucidate upon the principles and strategies of display. For the first time we see a concern for the details of object placement and how this should serve scholarly agendas. The articulation of this approach was prompted with the completion of the Smirke Building in 1851, when Antiquities Department keepers were

6.4. *(facing)* Plan of the completed extensions to the museum, featuring the new west wing devoted to the antiquities galleries. At this stage the Egyptian gallery is still designated as occupying only the northern section of the main antiquities gallery. Lithograph produced by the museum in 1852. British Museum, Central Archives.

given the chance to rearrange the sculpture collections into a more coherent "system" in a series of new galleries on the west side of the museum.[35] Thus, the museum made the decision to arrange the collection according to a chronological sequence. Issues of display had become of much greater interest to museum keepers as the collections for which they were responsible had grown and diversified. Conscious of the importance of assigning order and structure, keepers now begun to determine an appropriate exhibition strategy. This marked a significant break with tradition in that outside experts had previously been given the responsibility of determining object layout. Now, however, when experts such as Sydney Smirke and Richard Westmacott submitted their ideas to the trustees, the trustees began to consult Hawkins.[36]

The new involvement of keepers in display is also evidenced in Charles Newton's (the keeper for classical antiquities) job description for antiquities keepers, where the role of the exhibition is accorded great significance: "It is not sufficient that Antiquities should be acquired, they must be arranged in an intelligent manner so as to convey the highest amount of instruction to the Archaeologist, the artist and the public generally."[37] What exactly Newton means by "an intelligent manner" is difficult to ascertain; however, it seems likely that it refers to placing objects in a chronological arrangement. Chronology, or the determination of the successive historic episodes that led to the rise and fall of ancient cultures, was the driving force of archaeological research at this time. In conveying the latest knowledge on chronological sequence keepers sought to make the antiquities galleries didactic in an archaeological sense as opposed to an aesthetic one. However, the idea of displaying objects so that they provided "instruction" on academic, aesthetic, and public levels reflected how the museum had not abandoned its aims to be visual pleasing and entertaining. Thus, rather than subsuming the previous modes of presentation, the new "intelligent" mode was combined with the established aesthetic one.

The complete rearrangement of the Egyptian sculpture gallery was planned when the whole suite of new antiquities galleries was nearing completion. Major changes to the arrangement of the Egyptian antiquities were proposed by Hawkins, who suggested that they should occupy an additional two galleries, these being the south division of the west wing and the central saloon (see fig. 6.4). With this plan, the space devoted to Egyptian antiquities was more than doubled in size, as the "south division" alone was equal in size to its current gallery.[38]

Before the Egyptian antiquities were rearranged into their newly allocated space, much effort was devoted to incorporating the recently arrived Assyrian collection, which necessarily made a significant impact on the way the Egyptian antiquities were arranged. For instance, when in 1850 Hawkins suggested that the new gallery built alongside the Egyptian gallery should be devoted to displaying the Assyrian antiquities, he

PAPER—BRITISH MUSEUM.

PLAN OF THE GROUND FLOOR OF THE BRITISH MUSEUM.

PLAN, (N.)

Corrected up to January 1st 1852.

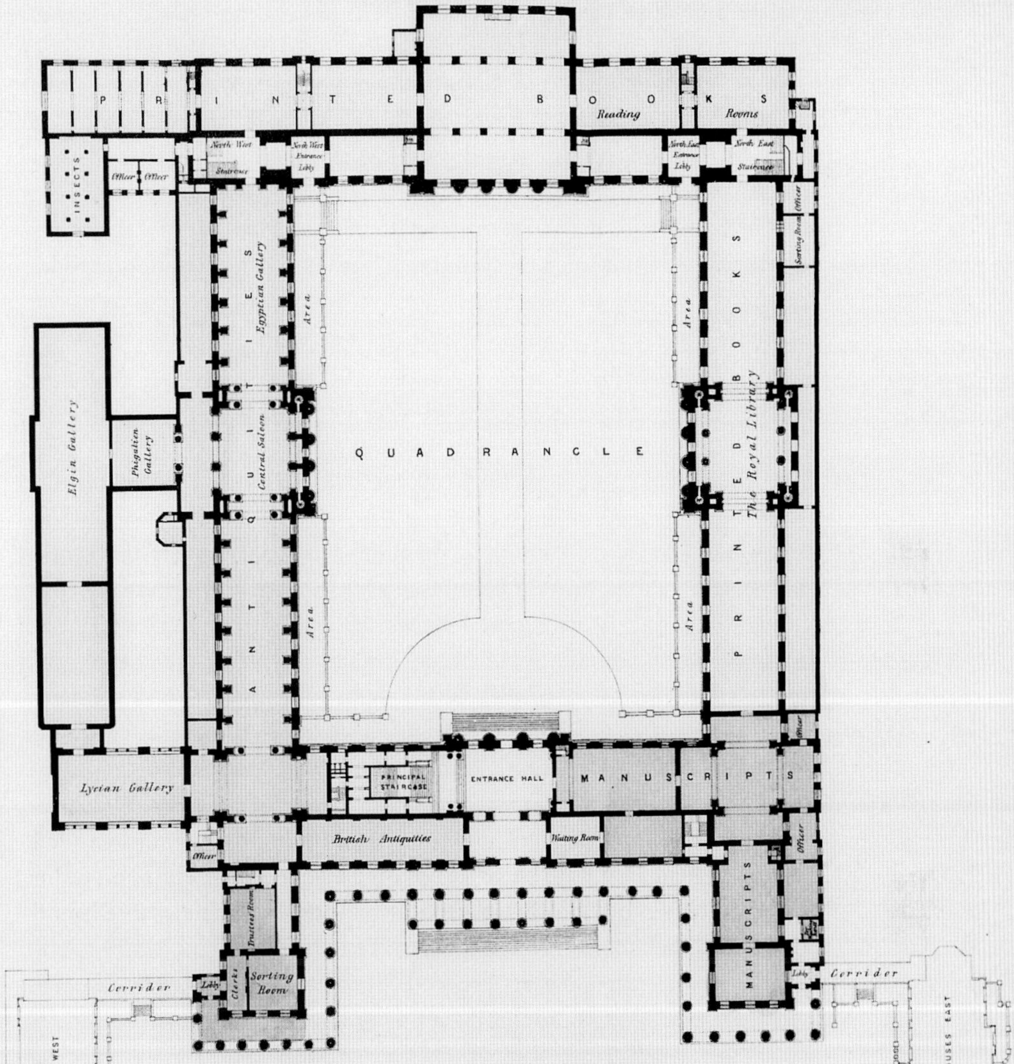

THE SECRETARY'S DEPARTMENT is defined by a Purple Tint
„ MANUSCRIPT DEPARTMENT „ Green „
„ PRINTED BOOK „ Yellow „
„ READING ROOMS „ Orange „

THE DEPARTMENT OF MINERALOGY is defined by a Brown Tint
„ „ ZOOLOGY „ Blue „
„ „ BOTANY „ Red „
„ „ ANTIQUITIES „ Pink „

SCALE

Day & Son, Lithrs to The Queen.

Henry Hansard, Printer.

No 557. Ordered, by The House of Commons to be Printed, 30th June, 1852.

justified this idea on the basis that it would ensure that the Egyptian and Assyrian monuments would occupy "one continuous line," and thus reinforce the "systematic and chronological arrangement" adopted for the presentation of all antique sculpture.[39] The plan would thus ensure that visitors experienced the Egyptian and Assyrian sculptures as related bodies of work, their colossal block-like character providing a distinct contrast to the classical antiquities. Furthermore, with this arrangement a set of three parallel lines was created through which visitors would pass in succession—Egyptian, Assyrian, Greco-Roman—the idea of course, being to convey a sense of historical development. A year later in 1851, Hawkins reiterated the importance of chronological arrangement, stating that the larger Assyrian objects would be placed in the central saloon next to the Egyptian sculptures and thus result in a more "chronological and scientific arrangement."[40]

From the end of 1851 to the end of 1852, Hawkins and his colleague Edmund Oldfield, who was assistant in the Department of Antiquities, provided detailed plans on how the Egyptian sculptures would be arranged.[41] While chronological arrangement was the focus, Hawkins reassured the trustees that "as much attention as possible" would be paid to "preserve a somewhat symmetrical and picturesque arrangement."[42] In proceeding to outline where specific objects should be placed, Oldfield elaborated upon the principle on which the new proposed arrangement was based, stating that he assumed the trustees "would wish to procure the best arrangement in all respects which our present knowledge and resources are able to command."[43] Following this premise, Oldfield sorted the entire collection chronologically, qualifying that it was possible to carry out this arrangement "without injury, but even with advantage, to the ornamental effect of the galleries."[44] The main changes included in his proposal were (1) that the main chronological divisions correspond with the architectural divisions of the gallery, (2) that the "most characteristic monuments" of each period be placed in a front row which will enable them to be "at once before the eye," (3) that the architecture of the gallery be emphasized by placing a single object in front of each pilaster and creating another row of objects in between them, (4) that a set of isolated objects be placed in the central avenue, none of which obstruct the view, and (5) that the colossal head of Amenhotep III and bust of Ramesses II be placed in entirely new positions apart from each other. Some discussion was devoted to the last suggestion, with Oldfield explaining how the separation of the two, which had until now been situated facing each other, had certain benefits. Describing them as an "imperfect match" due to their difference of form and treatment, Oldfield noted how it was not possible to view them properly with the short distance between them. A more serious concern, he argued, was their unsymmetrical outline, which interfered with the architecture of the northern door and which, seen from a distance, "impairs the architectural beauty of the view."[45] The idea of moving the colossal head of Amenhotep III to the middle of the central avenue so that it faced the visitors as they entered the gallery, and lowering it so that it would stand clear of the perpendicular lines of the door, would not only solve the problems of its previous situation, but would also have the advantage of forming an "object of interest all along the galleries." Corresponding with this, the colossal bust of Ramesses II would be moved to the center of the gallery, gaining "dignity by its isolation" and appearing double the size due to being twice as near the eye.[46] Another benefit would be that in facing the entrance to the Elgin gallery situated opposite it, it would "form a landmark in that direction."[47]

Although supportive of Oldfield's suggestions, Hawkins did not concur with his plan to move the two colossal heads. Reminding the trustees of the difficulties previously encountered with their removal, Hawkins argued that "there is not much objection in a few very large objects standing somewhat out of strict chronological order, for they [are] always conspicuous and are well impressed on the mind and memory."[48] His objections are important because they convey the idea that iconic objects, such as Ramesses II, could be understood in their own terms and did not need to be part of an explanatory system in order to be properly appreciated.

Also accorded some discussion in Oldfield's plan was the issue of lighting, where he argued that the light provided by the windows is "more advantageous with Egyptian sculptures than with any other, from their bearing so frequently inscriptions at the back and sides, whilst the unartistic treatment of the human form renders the absence of shadow of less importance."[49] Furthermore, the earliest Egyptian remains, which were defined as being "generally devoid of beauty," were designated for the northern vestibule, which suffered from being very dark.[50] While the argument that the inferior artistic quality of the Egyptian objects rendered the poor lighting conditions acceptable was familiar, the notion that sidelighting was beneficial because it enabled inscriptions on the back to be seen was new. Although it is true that inscriptions on the backs of sculptures would be rendered more legible if lit from the sides, this justification appears to be more of an ad hoc rationalization than a genuine argument concerning the type and quality of light appropriate for Egyptian antiquities.

Oldfield's plans for the dispersal of the objects in the Egyptian gallery were referred to a subcommittee, who agreed to the proposed arrangement except for the colossal bust of Ramesses II, which they suggested be moved to the west side of the central saloon.[51] In 1853 the objects began their move into the new, greatly expanded gallery according to Oldfield's chronological scheme (fig. 6.5). Thus ended Westmacott's reign over the presentation of the Egyptian antiquities and the prevalence of the aesthetic mode of display. With Oldfield's new vision, Egyptian antiquities were finally recognized to have archaeological or historical meaning; a revised introduction for the museum's *Synopsis* explained the rationale behind this new definition of ancient Egypt:

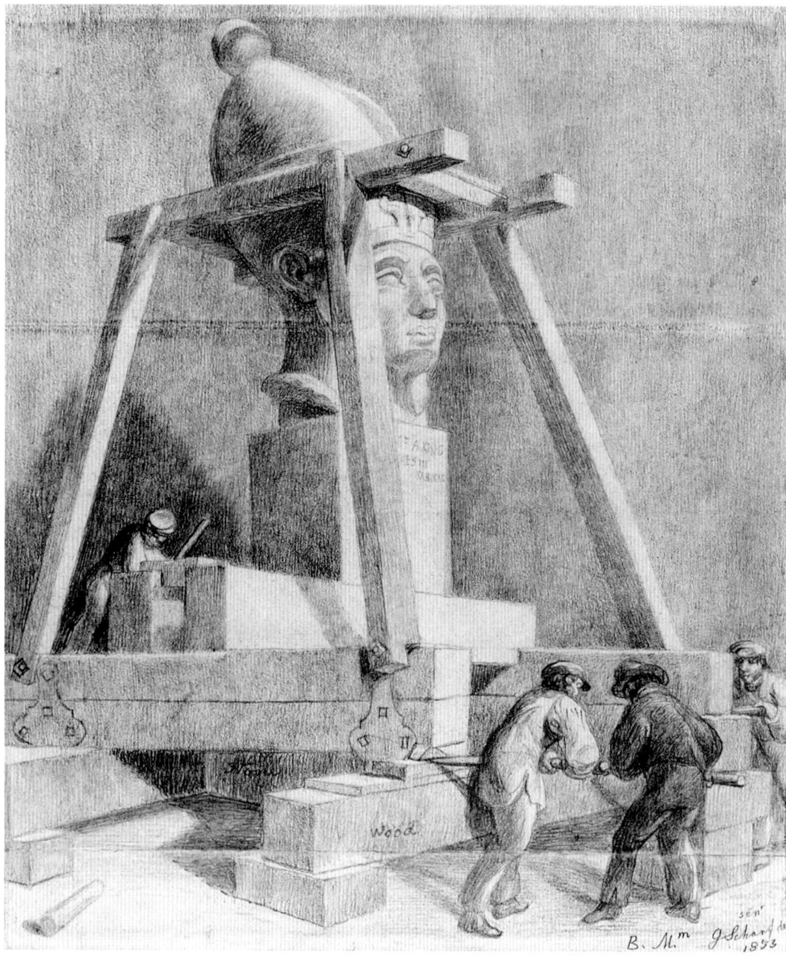

6.5. Moving the colossal head of Amenhotep III into the Egyptian sculpture gallery. Drawing by George Scharf, 1853. British Museum, Department of Prints and Drawings, no. 1862.6.14.625.

> The collection has, until very recently, been confined to the Northern Gallery and Vestibule, a space too limited to admit either of classification or advantageous display. The monuments, however, are now being rearranged, and placed in chronological order, from North to South, the dynastic divisions of Manetho forming the historical basis of the system. In the Vestibule will be preserved the remains of the early period; in the Northern Gallery those of the eighteenth dynasty; in the Central Saloon the monuments of Ramesses II; and in the Southern Gallery those posterior to that Empire. The three principal series in the collection of Antiquities, the Egyptian, Assyrian, and Greek, will thus, when the contemplated arrangements are complete, be exhibited in three parallel lines; whilst a fourth or transverse line, running along the Southern extremity of the others, will be appropriated to Roman remains.[52]

The emphasis here was on the ability of the new installation to address or solve the chaos of previous displays. Through chronological arrangement, ancient Egypt would be presented as a more three-dimensional culture, having its own distinctive phases of development.[53] Thus, when the new display was completed in 1854, an evolutionary perspective on ancient Egypt was finally endorsed and conveyed by the museum. The historical sequence began in the northern vestibule with the remains from the Fourth to Thirteenth Dynasties (Old and Middle Kingdoms), and continued into the northern gallery where the objects from the Eighteenth Dynasty (New Kingdom) were placed. In the central saloon were the remains from the Nineteenth Dynasty (New Kingdom), and in the southern section were included the objects from the Nineteenth and Twentieth Dynasties (New Kingdom), the Twenty-second (Third Intermediate period), the Twenty-sixth, Twenty-eighth, Thirtieth (late period), and the Ptolemaic and Roman periods. However, because visitors approached this sequence from the southern section, they effectively began with the most recent remains and worked their way back to the oldest material. One could argue that this was a confusing way of introducing the concept of chronology to visitors, however the objects in the northern section were considered the finest in the collection and thus offered a sense of having reached a climax in the walk through the long gallery.

The parliamentary investigations held around the mid-nineteenth century on issues relating to the museum are important to consider here because they reveal the growing tensions that existed between the aesthetic approach and the historical or archaeological approach to presenting the museum's collections.[54] For example, in the inquiry held on the Royal National Gallery in 1853, key museum figures were questioned as to whether part of the museum's collections should be moved to a museum of art, which gave them the opportunity to express their views as to whether the collections were primarily of aesthetic or historic value. While Westmacott suggested that the museum's sculpture collections, excluding the Egyptian and Assyrian works, should be joined with the national collection of pictures, the keeper of Greek and Roman antiquities, Charles Newton, argued that the sculpture collections must be kept together so as to maintain a comparative framework for understanding them.[55] With these perspectives we can see how Egyptian antiquities were designated as outside the realm of art, and that their value lay in their service role in the presentation of the classical remains. Despite these affirmations of the lowly status of Egyptian art, however, Oldfield challenged the prevalence of the aesthetic approach to display, asserting that it was the historical role of the antiquities that was of foremost importance.[56] This signified an important departure for the museum, as Oldfield played such a key role in determining the distribution of the Egyptian objects in the 1854 installation.

Space

The size of the new Egyptian gallery played a critical role in defining the Egyptian antiquities and in according them with a more respectable presence in the museum. At 380 feet in length and 41 feet in width, the size of the new gallery constituted a massive space that was nearly three times as big as the previous Egyptian gallery. In addition to this, the designation of two new rooms (the central saloon and the southern section; see fig. 6.4) for the presentation of the Egyptian collection suggested that this ancient culture had at last received some recognition from within the museum. The southern section of the wing was initially intended to accommodate other antiquities, but the crowded conditions in the existing Egyptian gallery forced the trustees to allow the collection to expand into the southern section. The new, less crowded display gave the collection a sense of clarity that it had not previously enjoyed. The increased height of the ceilings was also important, as it was much better suited to the colossal size of the sculptures. Indeed, an engraving of the new Egyptian gallery from the *Illustrated London News* emphasizes the sense of space created by the high ceiling and assigns the objects an "authentic" feeling, more in unison with their architectural setting (fig. 6.6). Significantly, while the scale of the room may have worked well for the Egyptian collection, it was not thought to be appropriate for the classical sculptures. The art critic Gustav Waagen, for example, was not impressed with the lofty size of the new galleries, which he thought dwarfed the classical antiquities.[57] The architect James Fergusson reiterated this point, stating that the size of the new Smirke Galleries was completely wrong for the classical sculptures, which appeared dominated by the high ceilings.[58]

Structure

The reorganization of the collection on a chronological basis not only stemmed from the fact that Egyptology had established a basic sequence of dates that allowed for a temporal distribution of the collection, but also reflected how the museum's keepers were finally given the authority to determine the arrangement of the Egyptian collection. As discussed earlier, keepers like Hawkins had sought to contribute to decisions about the organization of the collections, but it was outsiders like Westmacott who were entrusted with this power. Also worth noting in this context was the museum's avoidance of the new modes of display that were being developed at the time in Britain. Of key importance was the representation of ancient Egypt at the Sydenham Crystal Palace of 1854, which took the form of a large-scale architectural reconstruction of Egyptian monuments. This sumptuous and impressive display was characterized by its use of color and sense of design and offered a complete contrast to the somber vision presented by the museum (figs. 6.7–6.8).[59] Like the other architectural courts featuring ancient and historical cultures, this vision of ancient Egypt appealed to visitors in a way that was profoundly different from viewing relics in an austere museum setting.[60] Intended to transport visitors back in time, the architectural reconstructions constituted a new

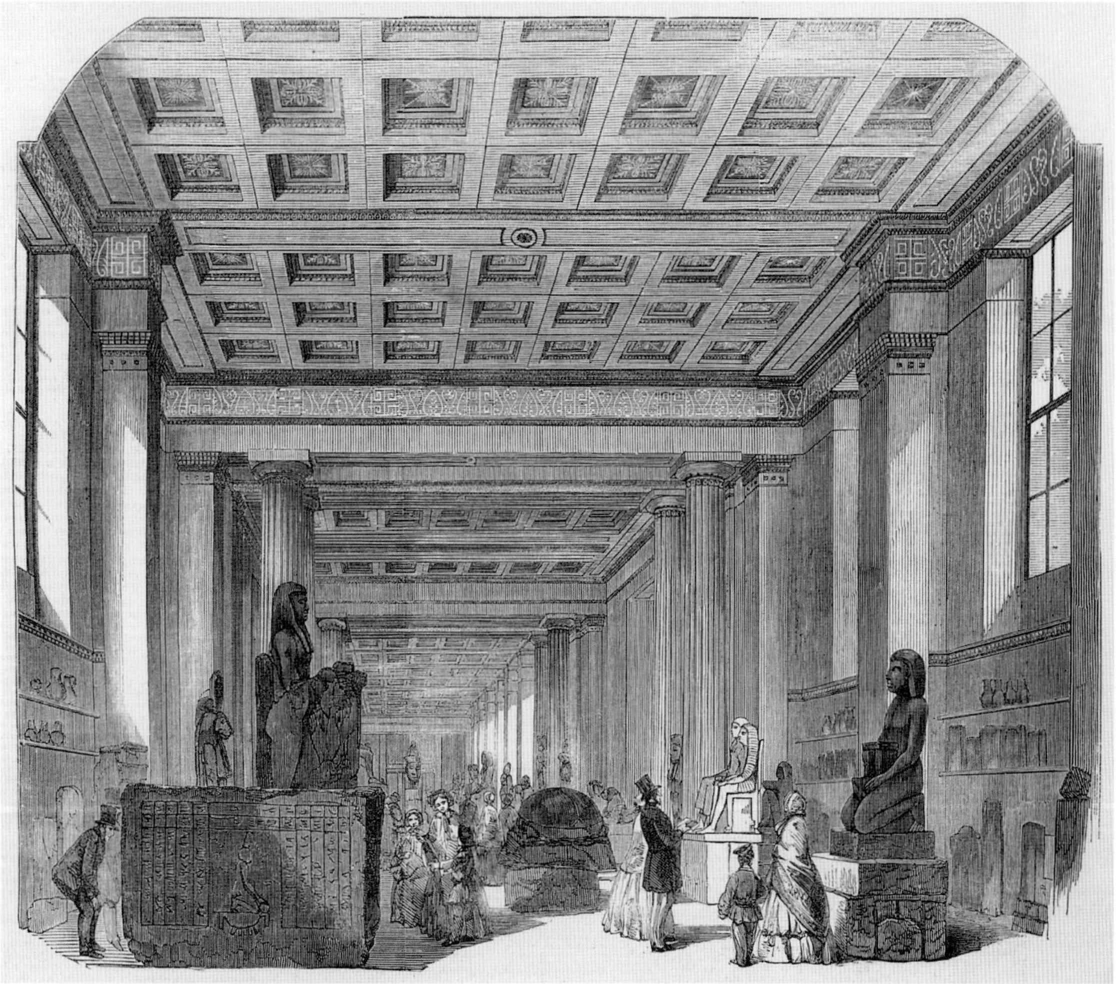

6.6. The Egyptian sculpture gallery. Engraving in *Illustrated London News*, April 15, 1854, 344.

genre of display that provided people with a sense that they were experiencing the past. More significantly, in the Egyptian Court, Egyptian monuments were characterized not as dark and gloomy, but as brightly and extensively decorated structures. Interestingly, although the museum was involved in the construction of this Egyptian exhibition at Sydenham, it was reluctant to indulge in such lavish representations itself.[61]

Beyond Sydenham, a more contextual style of presenting Egyptian antiquities had also been adopted by several museums, including the Vatican's Gregorian Egyptian Museum, which featured a mock-Egyptian entrance to the gallery and murals on the walls with pyramids and palm trees.[62] This exhibition style was further developed by the Neues Museum in Berlin in the 1850s, when the curator Karl Richard Lepsius designed a major new exhibit featuring a reconstructed Egyptian court scene with colorful murals. This strategy was not simply aimed at presenting a picturesque environment, but was designed to endorse the educational objectives

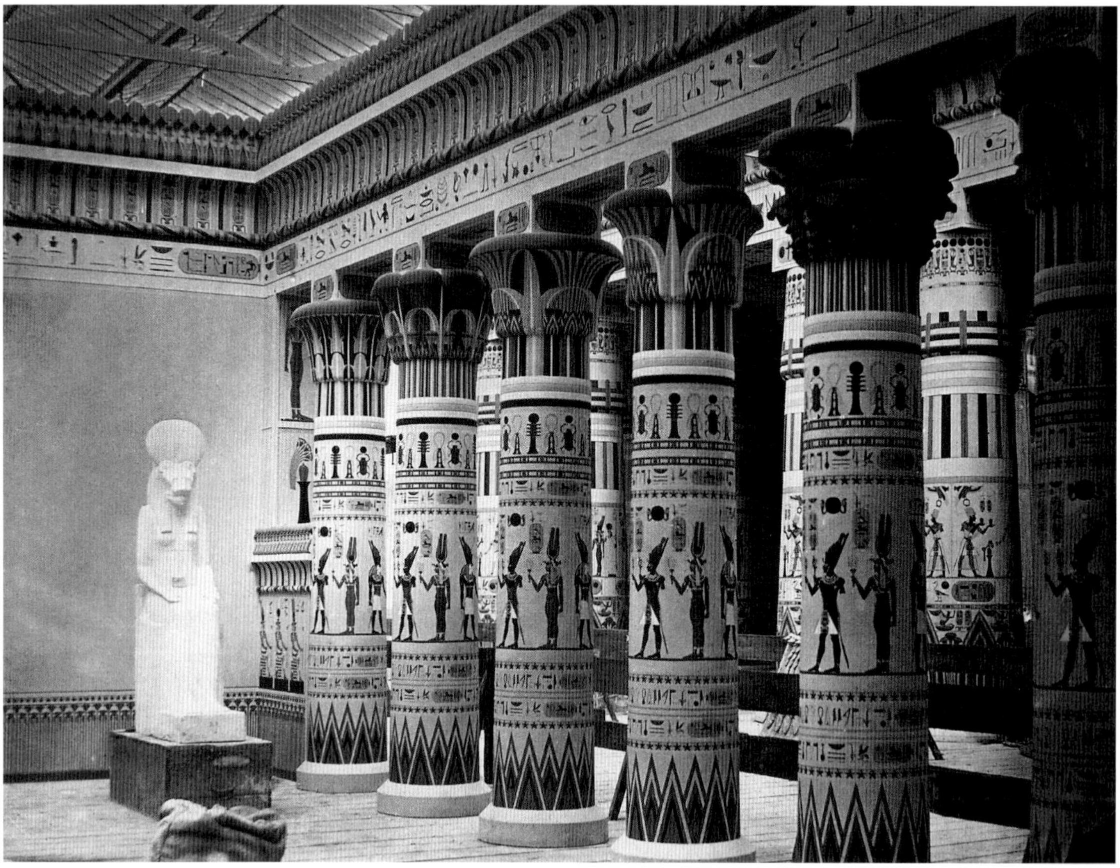

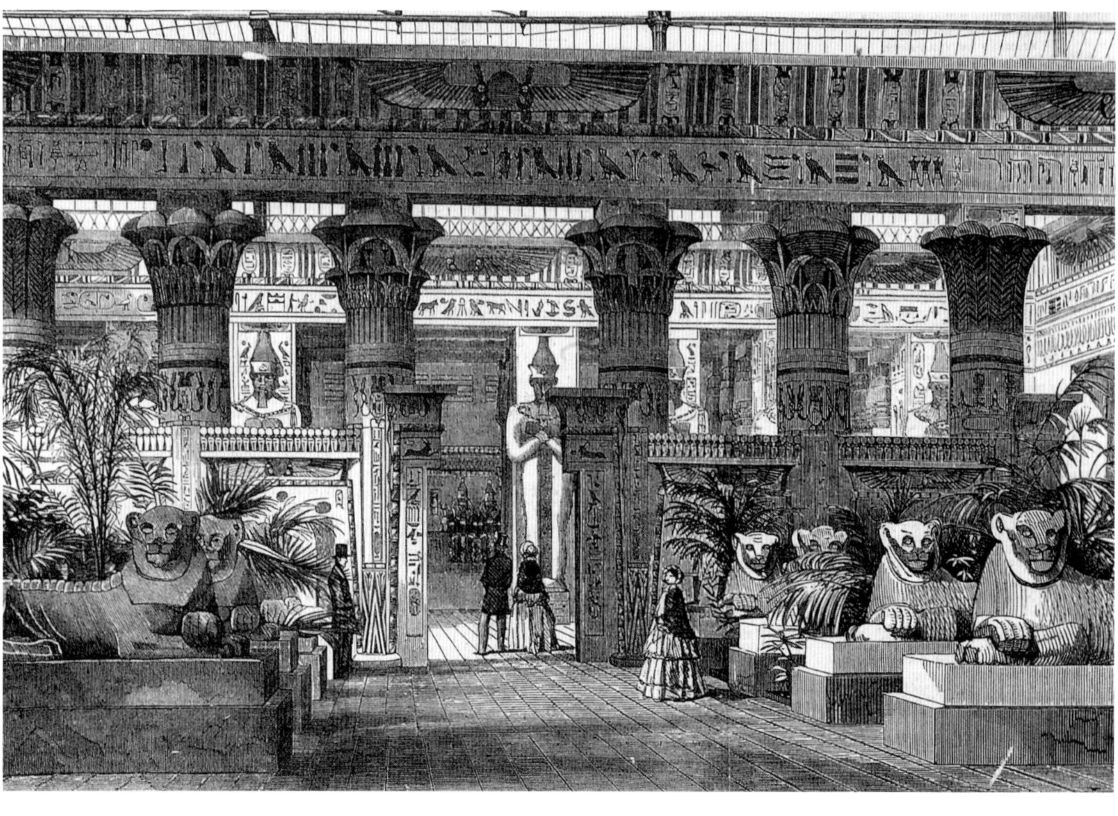

6.7. *(facing, above)* The Egyptian Court at the Crystal Palace, Sydenham. In P. H. Delamotte, *Photographic Views of the Progress of the Crystal Palace, Sydenham*, 1855, plate 68.

6.8. *(facing, below)* The Egyptian Court at the Crystal Palace, Sydenham. "Entrance to the Egyptian court from the nave, by the Avenue of Lions." Engraving in *Illustrated London News*, August 5, 1854, 112.

of the museum, where the displays served to convey the historical contexts of the objects. Didactic in its focus, this approach demonstrated that the collections were no longer seen as aesthetic curiosities but as "scientifically informative cultural relics."[63] Significantly, however, Lepsius's contextualization of the antiquities in this manner met with some criticism, and the Neues Museum reverted back to the more traditional mode of presenting the Egyptian collection.[64] Thus, the British Museum was not alone in resisting the augmentation of displays with picturesque interpretive enhancements.

Distribution

The new exhibition strategy adopted for the presentation of the Egyptian collection essentially involved distributing the objects according to a system of lines parallel to the walls. While a sense of this system can be gleaned from an engraving of the installation (fig. 6.6), a series of early museum photographs convey the new arrangement much more clearly (figs. 6.9–6.16).[65] Here we can see how a new row of objects, including the Rosetta Stone, colossal beetle, colossal fist, and ram's head, along with some display cases, was introduced in the center of the gallery. Relatively low in height, these objects and cases did not obstruct the visitor's view of the other objects in the gallery. Indeed, not only did this central row serve to break up the large, empty space in the center of the gallery, but it also provided a contrast to the height and vertical orientation of the many figurative sculptures lined up in the room. More significantly, it encouraged visitors to walk around objects and experience them in more three-dimensional terms. Flanking the central row of objects was an inner or front row of sculptures, which were situated on higher pedestals and placed directly in front of the pilasters. These were the "most characteristic monuments" of each period highlighted in Oldfield's plan, which were placed in these pronounced positions so as to be "at once before the eye." This row was arranged symmetrically so that a counterpart on the other side of the gallery matched each object. Furthermore, it was given a sense of structure by the positioning of the tallest objects in the center of the southern and northern sections. Behind this front row was another row of sculptures, which stood in between the pilasters. These objects included the smaller, less iconic sculptures, which were obstructed from view when entering the gallery. Behind this row was the shelving system on the walls, where stelae and other smaller objects were presented. This mode of arranging all the objects in a series of hard lines was very formal and almost military in nature. Although the rows facilitated a view of the entire length of the gallery, they also conveyed a rigidity that was reinforced by the long vertical lines of the pilasters.

One of the most significant changes to the new arrangement was the separation of the colossal sculptures of Ramesses II and Amenhotep III.

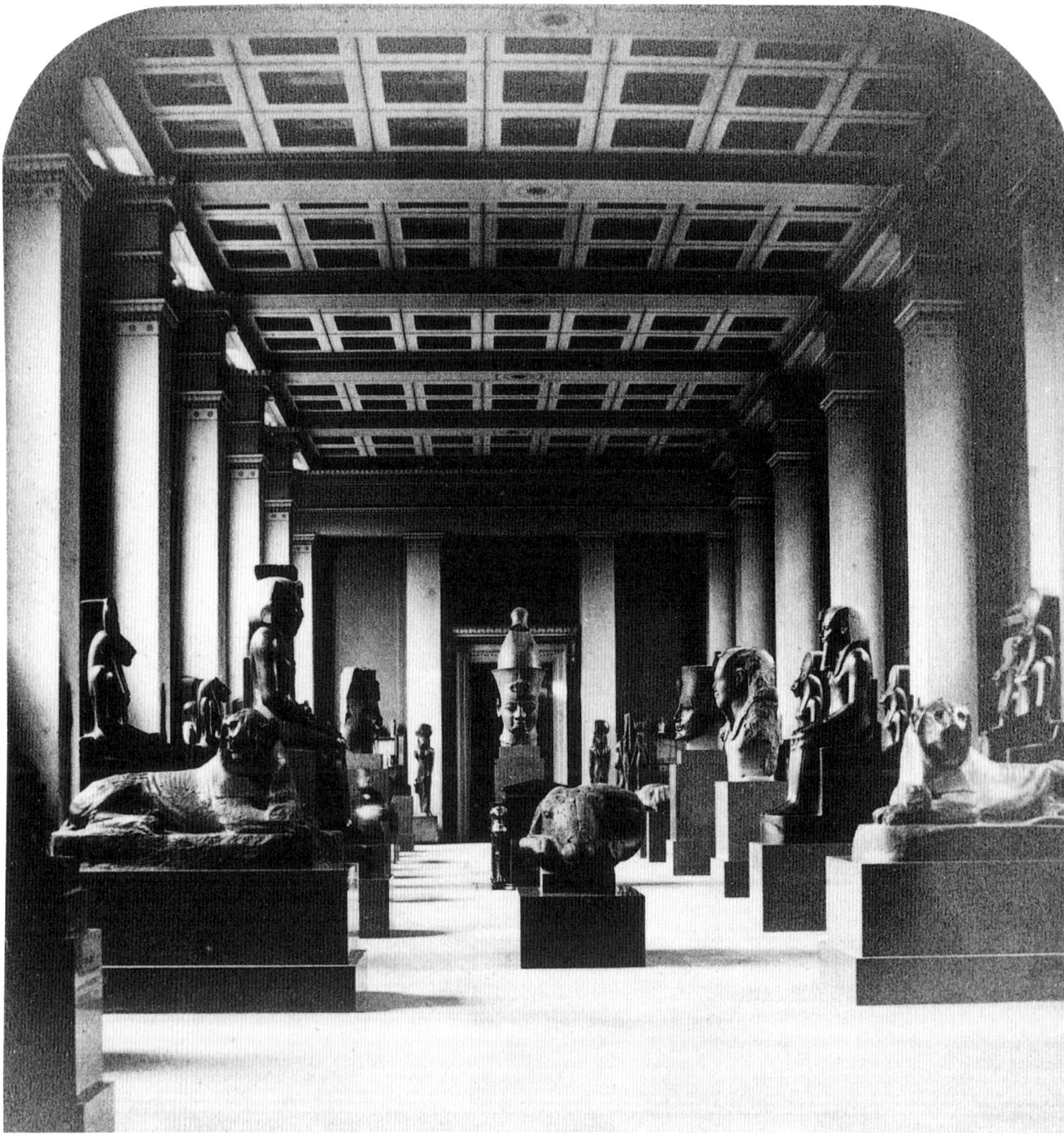

6.9. The northern section of the Egyptian sculpture gallery. Photograph by Roger Fenton, in the *Stereoscopic Magazine* 1 (1858). British Museum, Central Archives, no. CA 999.

Described by Oldfield as an "imperfect match," these two objects had been paired until now because of their similar size rather than any similarity in style of representation. While this matching had solved the problem of providing a symmetrical accompaniment for the colossal bust of Ramesses II a few years after its arrival in 1818, the result of placing the sculptures facing each other was that there was not enough space to view them from the front. Thus, Ramesses II was moved to the center of the gallery to stand alone once again. As Oldfield had asserted, the great work would appear even larger because it was now closer to the visitor than when it was placed at the end of the gallery. However, there were problems

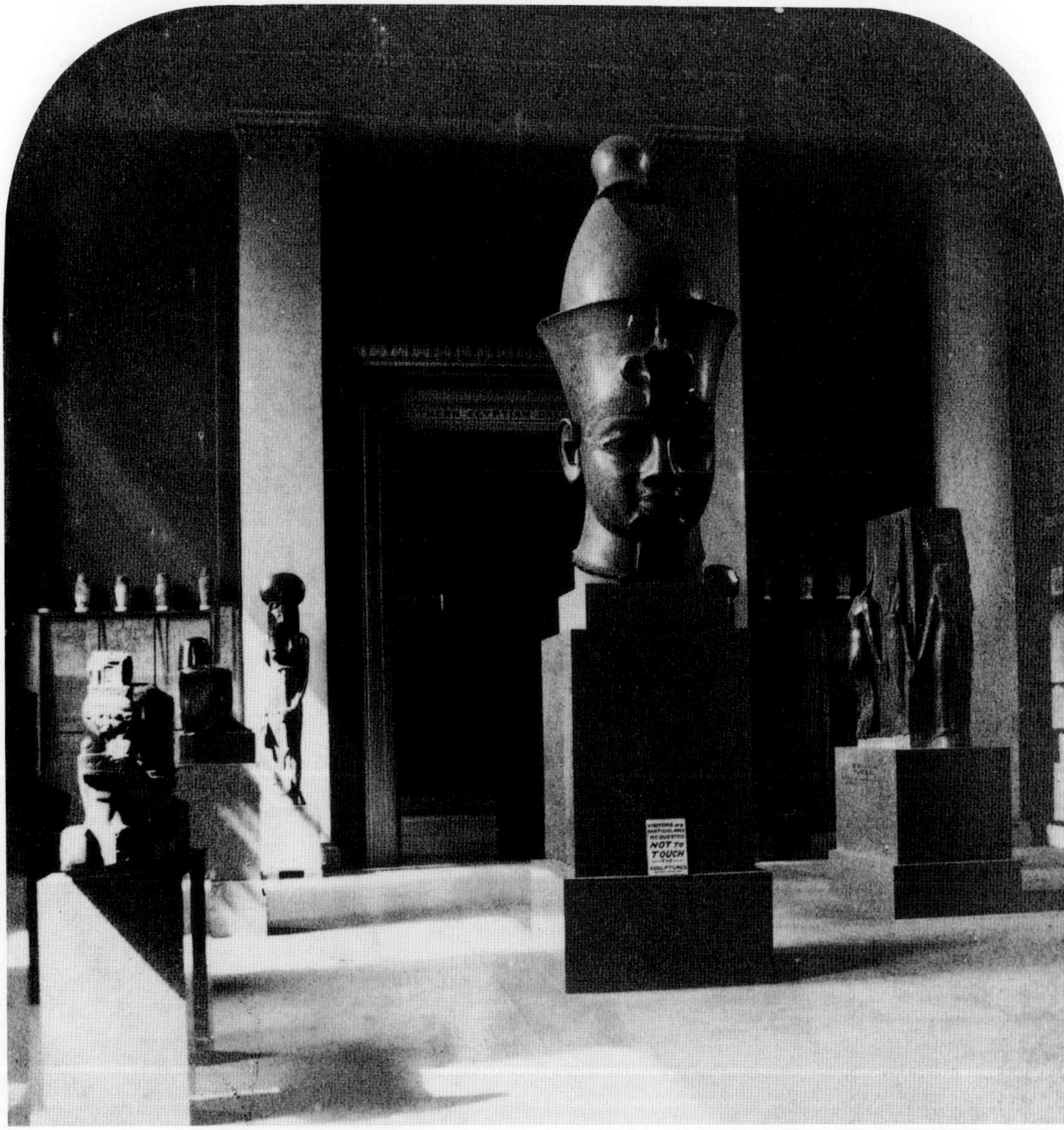

6.10. The colossal head of Amenhotep III in the northern section of the Egyptian sculpture gallery. Photograph by Roger Fenton, in the *Stereoscopic Magazine* 1, (1858). British Museum, Central Archives, no. CA 1011.

with this positioning, as the central saloon was very dark and the features of the sculpture could not be fully appreciated (see fig. 6.16). This problem was raised in 1857 when the subcommittee for antiquities requested that the bust of Ramesses II be moved; however, when the cost of carrying out this recommendation was presented to the trustees, they rejected it.[66]

Just as the two lion sculptures had been positioned so as to create an impressive entrance to the gallery in 1835, the colossal head of Amenhotep III in front of the doorway at the northern end of the gallery served as a striking exit point or closing statement on the Egyptian collection. With these two terminal points, the Egyptian collection seemed more self-contained

6.11. The Egyptian sculpture gallery. Northern section looking south, with colossal fist in foreground. The cast of the head of Ramesses II is second from the right. Photograph by Stephen Thompson, in Thompson (1872), plate 202.

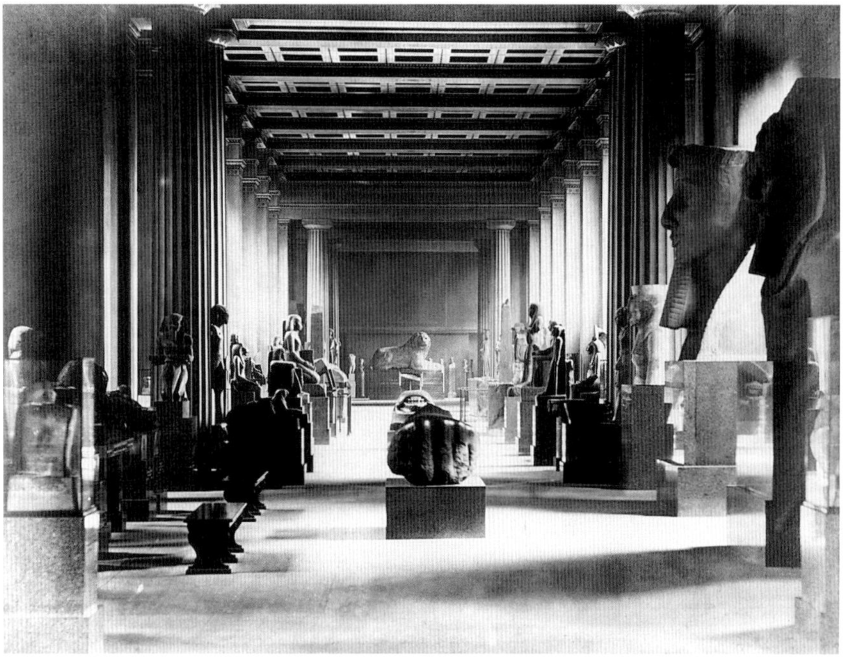

6.12. The Egyptian sculpture gallery. Southern section looking north, with Rosetta Stone in foreground. Photograph by Frederick York, 1875. The Frederick York Album, British Museum, Central Archives.

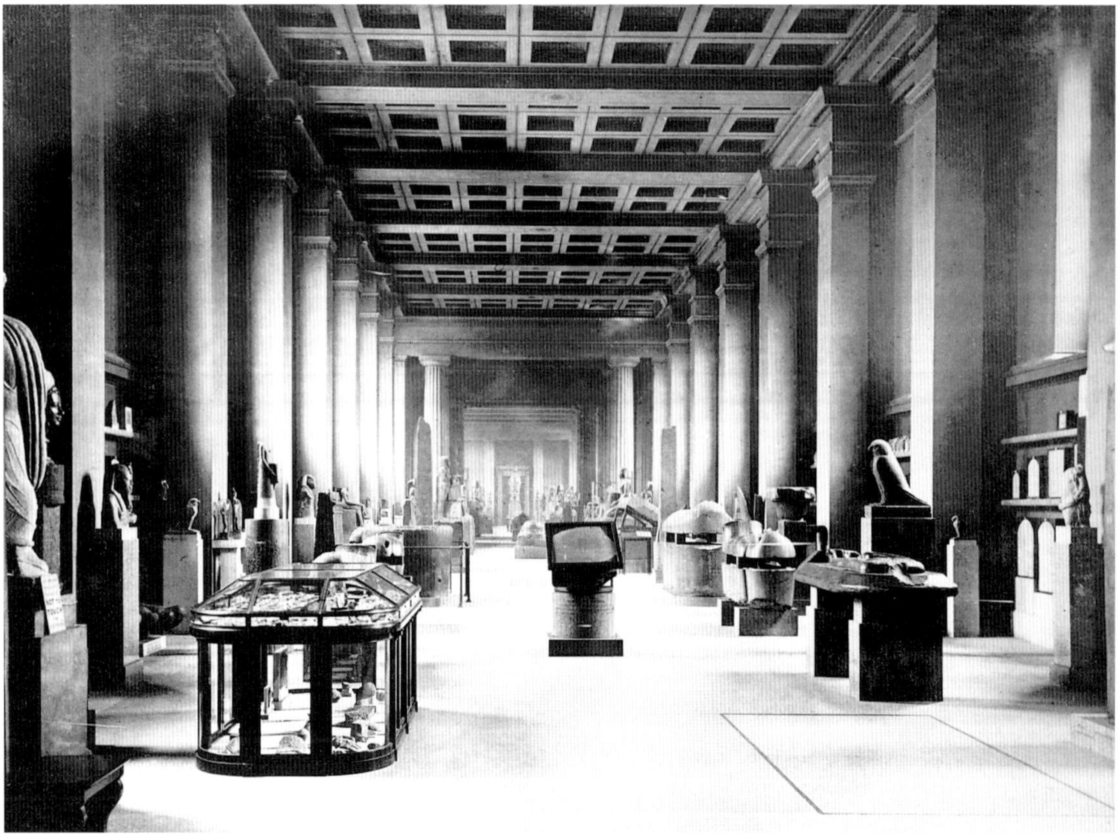

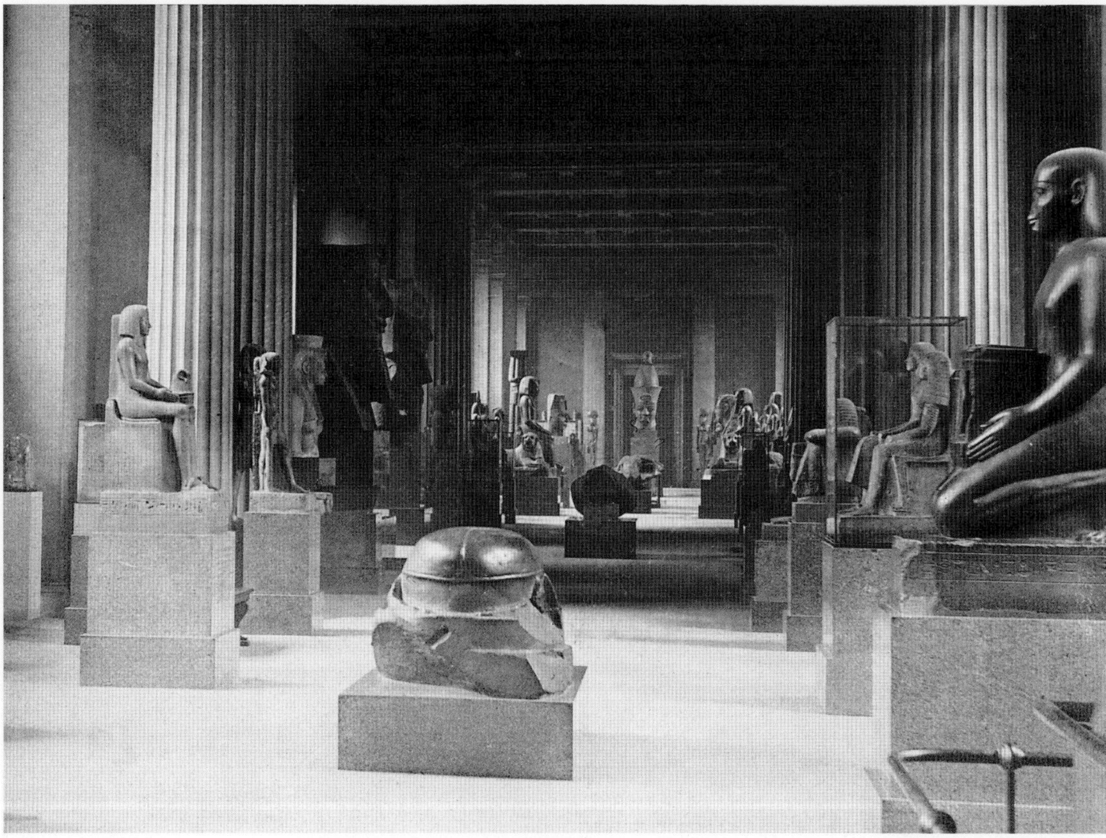

6.13. The Egyptian sculpture gallery. Southern section looking north, with colossal beetle in foreground. Photograph by Frederick York, 1875. The Frederick York Album, British Museum, Central Archives.

6.14. The Egyptian sculpture gallery. Southern section looking north, with colossal fist in foreground. Photograph by Frederick York, 1875. The Frederick York Album, British Museum, Central Archives.

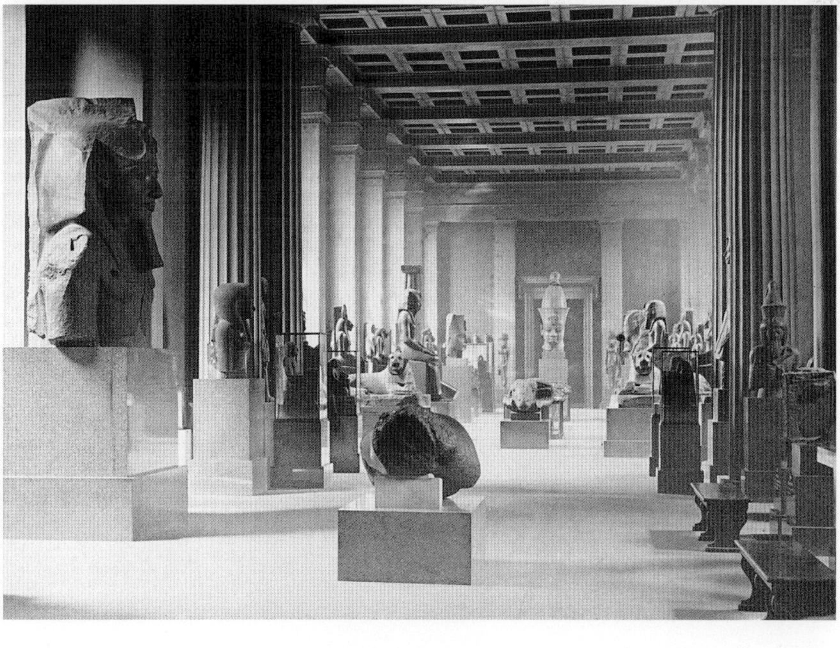

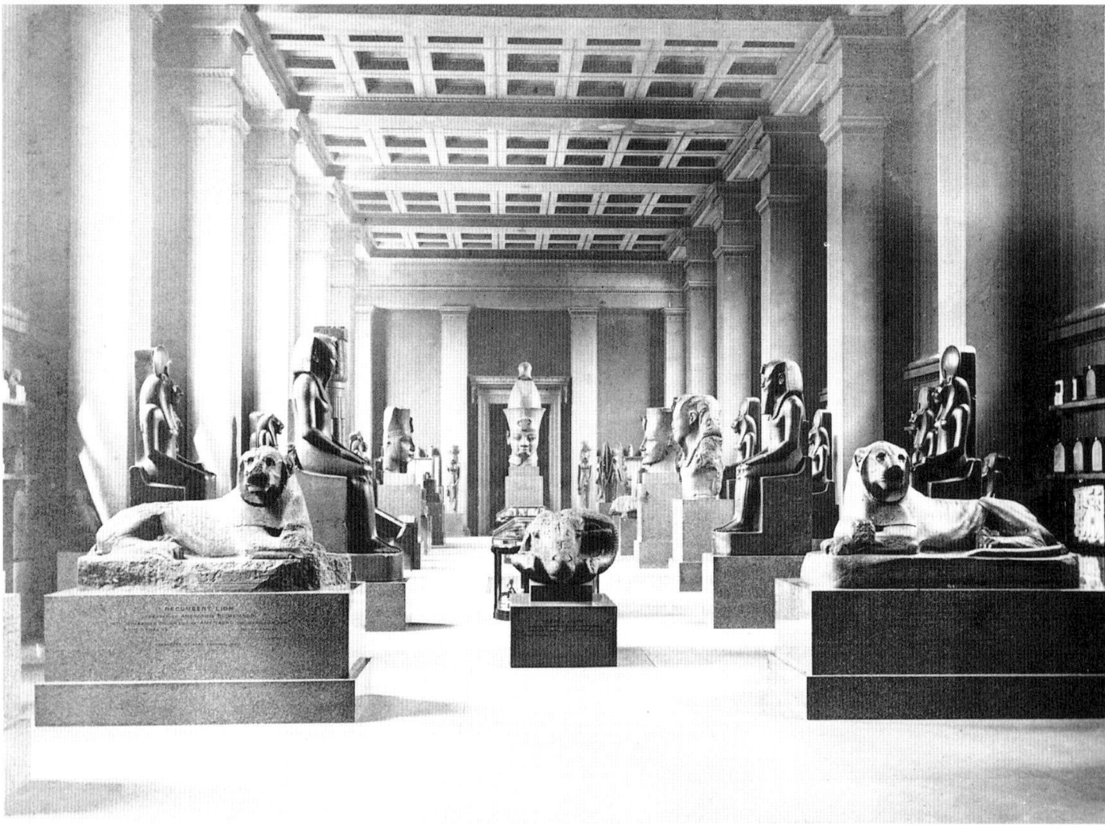
RECUMBENT LION

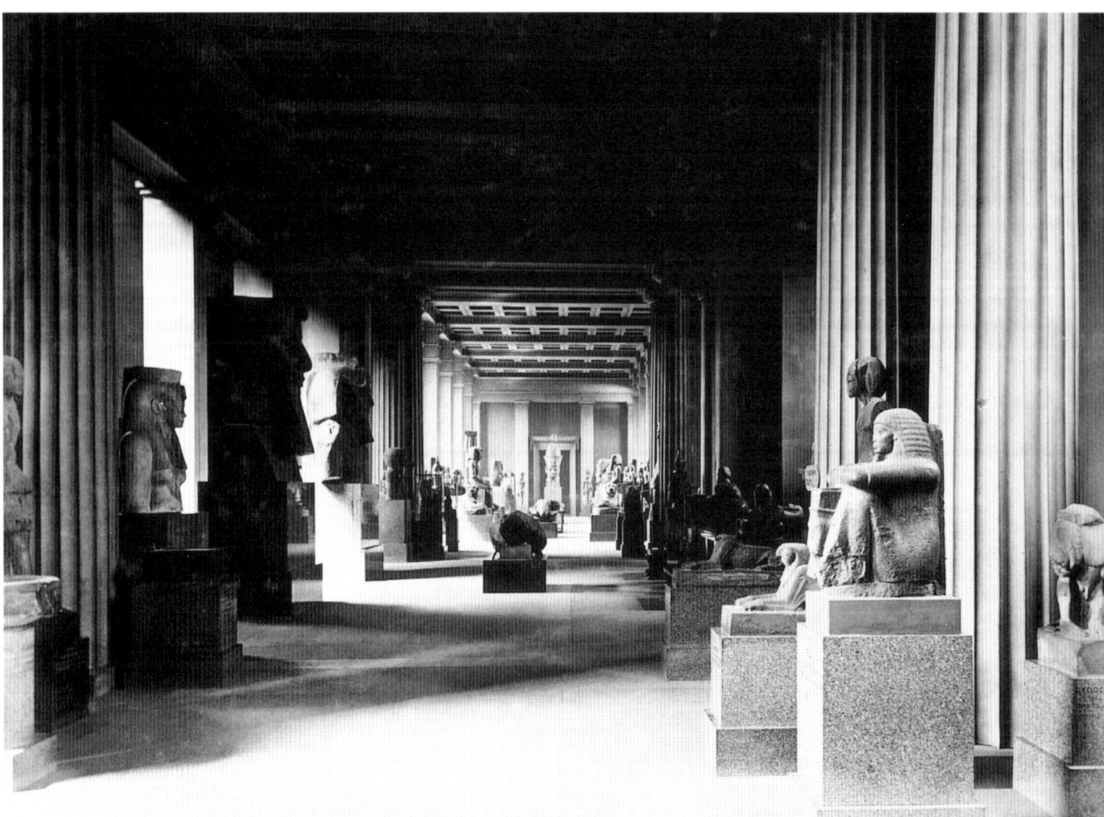

6.15. *(facing, above)* The Egyptian sculpture gallery. Northern section looking north, with ram's head in foreground. Photograph by Frederick York, 1875. The Frederick York Album, British Museum, Central Archives.

6.16. *(facing, below)* The Egyptian sculpture gallery. Southern section looking north, showing shadows cast over the room. Photograph by Frederick York, 1875. The Frederick York Album, British Museum, Central Archives.

and independent. Furthermore, visitors would now have an impressive Egyptian sculpture constantly in their vision as they viewed the gallery, as opposed to an empty doorway or a classical sculpture. Significantly, the positioning of the colossal Greek lion from Knidos as the point of interest from the other end of the gallery made a marked change from the way the Discobolus had been used to fill this function in the Townley Gallery (fig. 6.11). Unlike the Discobolus, the Knidos lion was also a colossal sculpture and thus did not appear too dissimilar from the Egyptian sculptures.

The overall visual effect of the new arrangement can clearly be seen in figure 6.15, which shows how much attention was devoted to the composition of the installation and in making it appear well balanced. The lions, for instance, function as a baseline, whereas the colossal head of Amenhotep III at the end of the gallery appears as the high point of the "picture." While the new position of Amenhotep III may have created an impact on visitors, however, appraisal of the object was compromised by the effects of cross lighting on the sculpture (fig. 6.10). Acknowledging this to be a problem, Oldfield later suggested that the colossal head be moved to a position where it would be "more advantageously seen than in its present position, where it stands in front of a doorway, and exposed to a cross light," but the implementation of this suggestion was also rejected.[67]

Although the arrangement of the sculptures was chronologically determined, aesthetic microarrangements were featured within this wider scheme. In the northern section, for example, the statues of Sekhmet were arranged in an alternative repeating symmetry behind the larger sculptures in front of the pilasters. They were also symmetrically placed on either side of the head of Amenhotep III as if to frame it (fig. 6.15). Other patterned effects can be identified in the distribution of smaller items, such as jars and small figurines on the shelves. Together with the layout of the sculptures, these reveal how the compositional arrangement of the gallery has been created to be pleasing to the eye.

Not long after the gallery was opened, Hawkins and Oldfield outlined suggestions for the rearrangement of the sculptures.[68] These recommendations were made in the context of wider discussions about a general overcrowding crisis in the museum, which prompted Hawkins and Oldfield to single out major problems with the Egyptian gallery. Among the flaws was the presentation of the collection from the most recent to oldest times, the separation of colossal antiquities from the smaller ones, the bad lighting conditions, and overcrowding. In order to solve these problems, they argued that the earliest remains should be moved to the southern section of the gallery so that the visitor would be able to encounter them first, and that the contents of the upper Egyptian rooms be moved downstairs to join the sculptures.[69] This latter suggestion was significant as it would have dismantled the false division that had been created within the Egyptian antiquities, whereby the larger sculptures were presented in a context that defined them as art, and the smaller objects were presented in a context that defined them as curiosities. By placing them together, the status of Egyptian antiquities as archaeological objects would have been more forcefully asserted. Despite the wisdom of these suggestions, the plans of Hawkins and Oldfield were not taken up, and the agreed resolution for the space crisis, reached in 1861, was to move the natural history collections of the museum to another site.[70] Although this decision allowed for some extensions to the Egyptian gallery, the layout of the sculpture collection and the divisions between the sculptures and smaller antiquities was retained.[71]

Architecture and Design

The style of the architecture of the new gallery was significant in attributing the Egyptian antiquities with a new meaning. Smirke's new Greek revival building evoked a sense of grandeur that rubbed off on the Egyptian collection in a way that the Townley Gallery had not. With its rows of pilasters, elaborate ceiling, and massive Doric columns giving the room a temple-like atmosphere, this large building associated the Egyptian antiquities with art and taste.[72] Although featured in the context of a Greek temple, as opposed to an Egyptian one, at least the Egyptian antiquities gained some sense of being related to a larger monumental building. Thus, although the gallery was not designed to convey or do justice to the architectural context of the Egyptian antiquities, it suited the qualities of the Egyptian sculptures better than those of the classical ones.

With its sunken square coffers brightly painted in Grecian designs and with a decorative frieze framing them, the decorated ceiling was central to the impressive appearance of the Egyptian gallery.[73] Furthermore, the decorative molding in red and gold that was used around the ceiling panels and under the windows would have provided a sense of color and life that contrasted with the dark stone sculptures in the Egyptian collection. Interestingly, some critics felt that the Egyptian antiquities did not merit being embellished in this way: "It is difficult to understand why antae and paneling should have been lavished as they have been on the Egyptian saloon, where the character of the antiquities did not require it, and entirely omitted among sculpture, which were designed and executed expressly to form integral parts of an architectural decoration."[74] Here the architect James Fergusson was referring to the lack of such decorative features in the Elgin gallery, which he argued needed "architectural assistance" more than any other set of sculptures in the museum.[75] While he surely realized that Egyptian sculpture was also created as part of an architectural system, he appears to resent the investment made in decorating the Egyptian gallery and fails to recognize that to have it denied any kind of architectural accompaniment would only serve to sever it further from its original context.

The dark red walls with an upper section in a sage-green color also presented the Egyptian objects in a more favorable way than had the previous gray or stone-colored walls.[76] The museum's new polychromatic color scheme for the galleries was important not only because it was archaeologically inspired, but because it was the first such example in a public building.[77] Originally lighter colors had been used in the antiquities galleries because of the lack of lighting, but darker wall colors were now seen to provide a better background for the sculptures, as they offered a contrast to them. It was the construction of the new Smirke Galleries that provided an opportunity for the museum to revisit the issue of wall coloring, which had since become a hotly debated topic among the keepers, architects, designers, and trustees. Because the antique sculptures in the museum had become much darker and dirtier as a result of pollution, it was increasingly felt that a darker color needed to be used. It was thus the problem of dirt that led to the introduction of the darker red color in the antiquities galleries.[78] For instance, when the trustees conducted their visitation of the galleries in 1851, they commented on the dirty appearance of the Egyptian sculptures, and suggestions were subsequently made to have darker walls.[79] However, this decision was controversial because the use of a darker color was not thought to be suitable for classical sculptures.[80] To resolve the issue, experiments were undertaken with different colors being applied to the walls, but there was still no agreement as to what the "proper" color was, and thus Sydney Smirke was given the final decision.[81] Smirke proposed a darker color for the gallery walls because the previous lighter color had given the Egyptian gallery the appearance of being cold, unfinished, and dirty.[82] This challenged Westmacott's suggestion that a light color be used because it counteracted with the darkness of London's atmosphere. However, Smirke's view was strongly supported by Hawkins, who argued that the sculptures should appear relatively light against a dark wall color. Critiquing Westmacott's use of drawing rooms in private houses as a guide, Hawkins stated that the "general impression sought to be conveyed in a drawing room, that of gaiety and festive brilliance is the reverse of what good taste would prescribe in the halls of a Museum." Furthermore, he argued that while in private houses "sculpture may be made subservient to decoration, in the galleries of a museum the decoration should be subservient to the sculptures."[83] This is an important declaration because it conveys how displays were intended to be didactic and thus understated when it came to decorative effects. Hawkins sought to strengthen his case by claiming that statuary could be properly appreciated only if its outlines were made distinct, and that this could not be achieved if the color of the walls were similar to that of the objects:

> But most of all clearness and sharpness of light and shadow are indispensable to artistic effect. For this purpose every care should be taken to keep the light direct and single and exclude all secondary or reflective light. Walls, floors and pedestals should all subserve to this end. If the contrary system be adopted, the reflected rays scattered over the room reach the

> sculptures in various and discordant directions, forcible shadows disappear and with them the effect of forcible light, the forms seem to lose their roundness, and vagueness takes the place of decision.[84]

To conclude his case, Hawkins noted how European museums used darker colored walls to exhibit their classical sculptures. All these points appear to have resulted in painting the walls red; however, agreement among the trustees was certainly not unanimous, with six supporting the motion and four opposing it.[85]

Despite the vastly improved display conditions for the Egyptian collection, the problems with lighting persisted. With the only source of light being the side windows, the objects were often hidden in darkness or obscured by the effects of cross lighting. Depending on borrowed light from the other galleries, the central section was particularly dark (fig. 6.16).[86] Although Hawkins advocated top-lighting, the trustees appear to have been satisfied with the same lighting conditions traditionally adopted for the Egyptian works, as they felt that appreciation of the Egyptian objects did not require the assistance of good lighting.[87] Elaborating on this perspective, the architect Fergusson provided strong views on the subject:

> The light is sufficient, and sufficiently diffused, and for Egyptian sculpture it is of very little consequence how or in what direction the light falls. The artists on the banks of the Nile never aimed at Aesthetic beauty of form, so that the sculptural products of their art scarcely depend more on their shadows than architectural members do. It would have of course have been preferable if the light had been stead on the colossal busts, and not on their backs in the morning, and their faces in the evening.[88]

That the poor lighting conditions were considered acceptable by the museum authorities is also evidenced in the parliamentary inquiry on the National Gallery of 1853, where it was reported that cross lighting was justified on the basis of the nature of the objects.[89] Furthermore, in 1857 the trustees declined to purchase the reflectors Smirke suggested be installed in the Egyptian gallery to address some of the lighting problems.[90]

Interpretive Aids

Several innovations in the museum's provision of interpretive aids reveal increasing concern about presenting the collections. Paramount here was the concern for providing more adequate labeling that would improve the understanding of objects in the Egyptian collection. In 1850, for example, the museum reported that "labels and names have been very extensively attached to objects in the Collection, which have made them more interesting and instructive."[91] In 1857 the museum was pushed to further their efforts in labeling, and in its annual report to government noted how explanatory titles had been painted on the granite pedestals in the Egyptian galleries.[92] Here it was noted how the subcommittee for antiquities was informed by the principal librarian that the House of Commons wanted to know to what extent institutions such as the museum had followed their rule of "attaching to objects of art a brief account of such objects for the information of the public."[93] Despite the museum's efforts, the media remained critical of the lack of labeling.[94] Also significant was the increasing involvement of museum staff in producing guidebooks to the collections, the main examples being William Vaux's *Handbook to the Antiquities in the British Museum* of 1851, and Thomas Nichols's *A Handy-book of the British Museum* of 1870.[95] These guidebooks provided far more contextual information on the collections than was provided in the *Synopses*, offering a balanced combination of fact and interpretation.

The Egyptian Rooms

The Egyptian Rooms located upstairs in the museum did not undergo the same amount of change as did the Egyptian sculpture gallery. Indeed, an engraving published in 1847 reveals that not much had changed since the 1837 rearrangement (fig. 6.17), this being essentially the same engraving that appeared in the *Penny Magazine* in 1838 (fig. 5.25), aside from the inclusion of more figures and a painted frieze on the wall. We know from the museum's *Returns of Accounts* to Parliament that regular rearrangements were made in these rooms in order to "incorporate acquisitions," to "improve their general classification," and to provide "an improved display of these antiquities."[96] However, from this documentation it appears that objects were simply slotted into the existing framework. Amid the many such reports of minor alterations made to the rooms, one worth highlighting mentions that the painting of the second Egyptian Room has been done in an "ornamental" fashion.[97] While the Egyptian Room had been transformed with the addition of a painted plaster frieze cast of the temple walls of Beit el-Wali in 1843, this was the closest that the museum got to enlivening the Egyptian displays with decorative effects.[98]

Despite the adoption of a chronological approach for the presentation of the sculptures, the displays in the two Egyptian Rooms were still arranged according to object type and subject. More specifically, the antiquities were initially grouped together according to class of object and then within this broad categorization subject divisions were created. For example, the different gods were assembled in their own subgroups. From visitor guides we know that in the upper row of the cases funerary figurines of the "wooden and stone figures from tombs and temples" were presented; in the second row were figurines of the "bronze and silver votive figures found under pavements or in walls"; in the third row were the smallest figures or "amulets in gold and faience, which were used in private

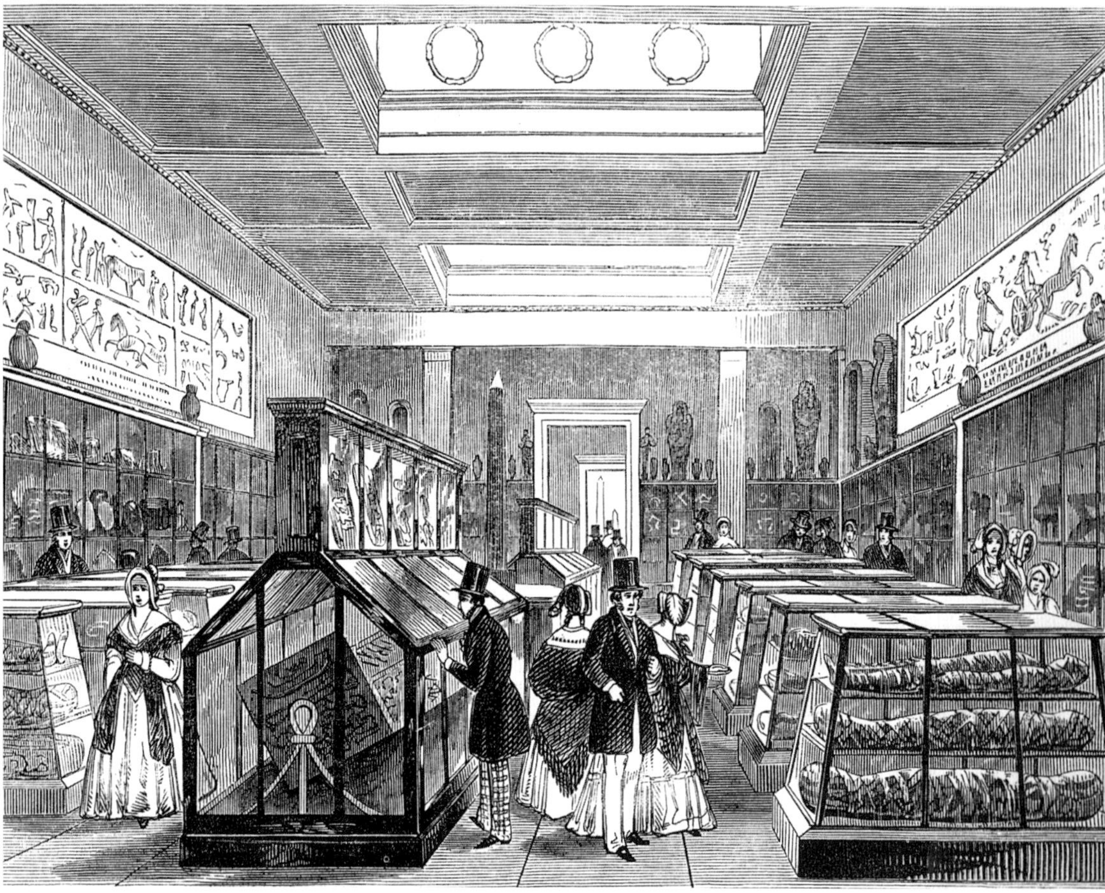

6.17. Mummies and other antiquities displayed in the Egyptian Room. Engraving in *Illustrated London News*, February 13, 1847, 108.

worship or placed with mummies"; and in the lowest row were the largest objects.[99] The smaller items were placed in the second and third levels of the shelves because this was the best vantage point to view them from, and presumably the larger items, which were heavier, were situated on the lower shelf so as not to overburden the unit. Within this overall scheme, the objects were then distributed in an aesthetic manner, which typically involved creating "microarrangements" in which the objects were presented in ascending order according to size (figs. 6.18–6.19). This had a striking visual effect when the hundreds of tiny amulets were lined up in rows as if in military formation. Other visual patterns were created by dividing the objects on one shelf into two sections, with the figures of each section facing each other.

The great quantities of objects packed into the cases reveal how the museum's collection of smaller Egyptian antiquities had continued to expand since the acquisition of Salt's and Sams's collections.[100] Continuing the established practice of including as many items as would physically fit in a display case, the keepers still avoided selecting representative samples of object types and placing less distinctive objects in storage. Whether this

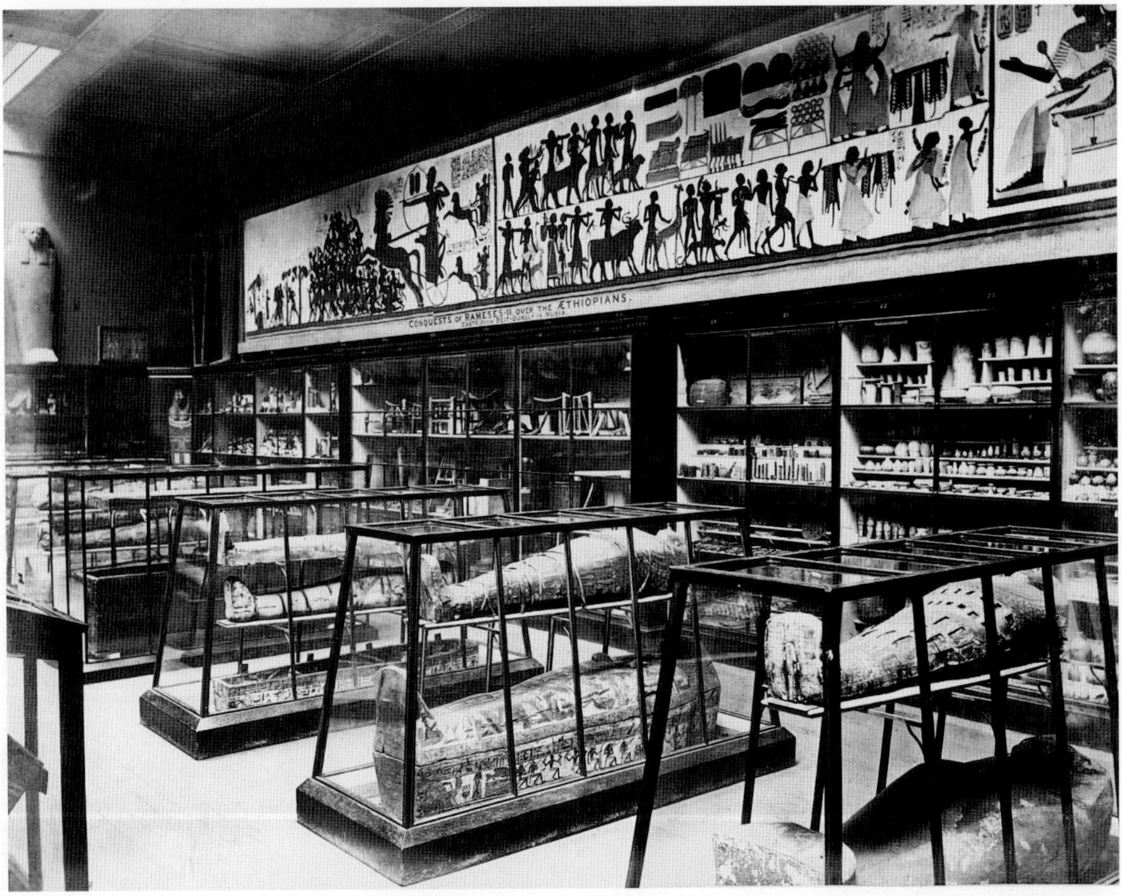

6.18. The Egyptian Room. First room. Photograph by Frederick York, 1875. The Frederick York Album, British Museum, Central Archives.

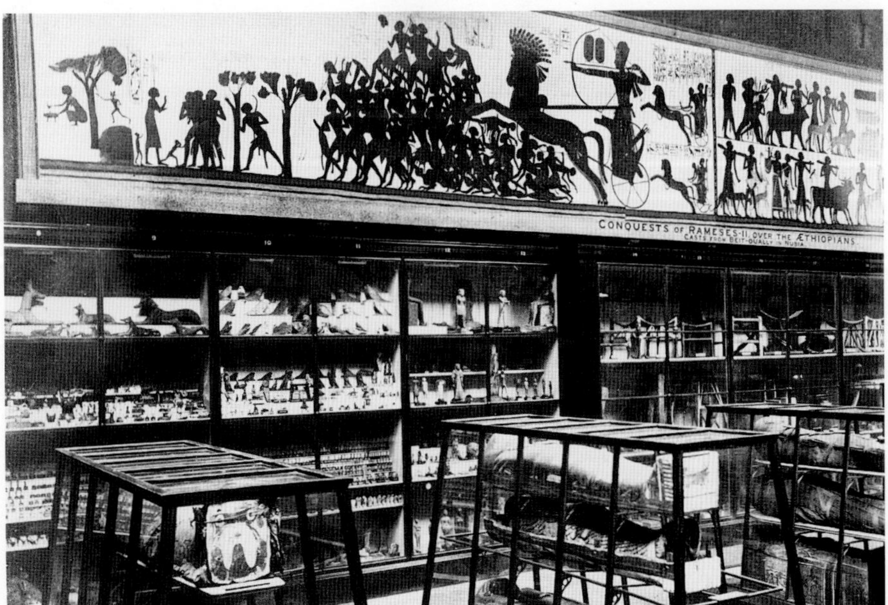

6.19. The Egyptian Room. First room. Photograph by Frederick York, 1875. The Frederick York Album, British Museum, Central Archives.

strategy was designed simply to impress or was based on the more didactic intention of demonstrating artifact variability is difficult to determine, as there was so little reflection on the motivation behind object placement. What we do know, however, is that the cramming approach adopted in these rooms was identified as a problem in guidebooks.[101] Although the display cases were neatly arranged and conveyed a sense of classificatory order, their crowding and the lack of any explanatory text would have rendered them little more than curiosity cabinets, with most of their appeal deriving from the accumulation of many unusual objects together. Furthermore, the decision to put as much as possible on display meant that the cabinets adopted a storage kind of display style, and while this approach was useful for reference, it rendered the collection confusing and overwhelming to those wishing to gain a basic idea of Egyptian history. Finally, the galleries themselves no doubt felt crowded, as most of the floor space was taken up with display cases featuring mummies. While this arrangement may have been satisfactory for a limited number of visitors, it would have been claustrophobic for those who visited on the much busier days such as weekends and public holidays. Although the concept of "visitor flow" was clearly not considered important at this time, the trustees and museum staff knew the Egyptian Rooms were one of the most popular attractions for visitors and thus may have considered strategies for reducing crowding in the room.

RECEPTION

In addition to the scholarly works available in the mid-nineteenth century on ancient Egypt, and particularly the work of Wilkinson, a proliferation of visual representations of ancient Egypt provided people with a greater sense of the context in which its ancient monuments were created. Key British examples included the lithographs of David Roberts (1796–1864), which were published in the immensely popular *The Holy Land, Syria, Idumea, Arabia, Egypt, and Nubia* of 1842–1849, and the photographs of Francis Frith (1822–1898), published in his enormously successful *Egypt and Palestine Photographed and Described* of 1858–60.[102] While the lithographs of Roberts encouraged a romantic response to the ancient sites of Egypt, the photographs of Frith enhanced the image of this ancient land as the home of monumental wonders, providing a vivid sense of the vast desert landscapes these ancient relics were once situated in.[103] Furthermore, with photography, people felt that they were witnessing a sense of reality not previously experienced with other representations of ancient Egypt.[104]

In addition to the lithographs and photographs, another important visual genre developed at the time was the panorama, and in 1849 the first feature-length British-made panoramic river trip—the *Panorama of the Nile*—was opened in London.[105] More than all of these types of representations, however, the architectural reconstructions of ancient Egypt created for the Crystal Palace at Sydenham in 1854 provided the strongest visual impression of this ancient society (figs. 6.7–6.8).[106] Created as part of a series of modeled historic courts, the Egyptian Court was arguably the most spectacular of this series, incorporating a model of the temple of Abu Simbel and the façade and hall of Karnak, a reconstruction of the tomb of Beni Hassan, and the portico of Philae.[107] A vast Egyptian Avenue lined with sphinxes and culminating with casts of the colossal sculptures from Abu Simbel made ancient Egypt a major highlight of this international exposition.

Beyond the array of visual representations of ancient Egypt then available, there were popular representations in literature and theater. An example of the former was Théophile Gautier's novel *The Romance of a Mummy*, published in 1856, and of the latter, the staging of the Egyptian drama *Nitocris*, opened in London in 1855. A review of this drama effectively conveys the qualities that ancient Egypt had come to represent in the mid-nineteenth century:

> Altogether, the appointments of this new drama, illustrating the life of what may be termed the most popular nation of the ancient world, are its great attraction. Thus the tutelary deities of the land, the sacred vessels of the temple, and all the symbols of the national idolatry, combined with bodies of soldiery, vestals, priests, and sovereign equipages, figure in great profusion. Again, the scenic effects are very striking: the colossal architecture, the grandeur and sublimity of the sculpture, and the mystic character of the hieroglyphics and decorations, materially assist in producing the very effective *ensemble.*[108]

Thus, the popularity of ancient Egypt was reinforced by the "scenic effects" it afforded, including the colossal nature of the architecture, the grandeur of the sculpture, and the mysterious nature of the artistic decoration.

Representations of ancient Egypt moved into a completely new dimension in 1867, when at the Paris International Exposition, the distant Egyptian past and the present were firmly aligned. There, a reconstructed Egyptian temple and Egyptian bazaar were featured alongside other model villages inhabited by different cultural groups from around the world.[109] While the recreation of an ancient building as the setting in which antiquities were displayed was not a new idea, what was significant about this exhibit was its juxtaposition with the reconstructed Egyptian bazaar. This atmospheric bazaar, with its cafés, crafts shops, donkeys, and modern Egyptian attendants, was a highlight of the Paris Exposition, providing visitors with an extraordinary vision of Egypt. By presenting ancient and modern Egypt in such a close relationship to each other, the exhibition reaffirmed the notion of a timeless culture in a tangible and everlasting way.[110] Knowledge of ancient Egypt was also becoming more widespread in association with the growth of the tourist industry in Egypt.[111]

A fast-growing body of British tourists had begun to see the monuments in context, and their travel accounts and diaries reveal how people were better appreciating the relationship of the antiquities to the landscapes and geography of Egypt.

Of particular significance for the reception of the Egyptian antiquities was the acquisition of the Assyrian antiquities, which began to arrive at the museum in 1847. With its colossal human-headed bulls and series of architectural slabs, the Assyrian collection constituted a major coup for the museum, reaffirming its place as a world leader in the presentation of ancient sculpture. More significantly, when it was displayed in the museum in 1853, the Assyrian installation introduced people to another ancient style of art that was interpreted as exotic and primitive.[112] Thus, visitors were now given the opportunity to see a variety of different styles of archaic art, and Egypt was no longer as isolated in terms of providing an understanding of the "primitive" origins of Greek and Roman art.

Finally, from the mid-nineteenth century the museum was increasingly attacked for being a show house for treasures as opposed to a useful educational resource, a perception that came to influence how the antiquities were received. Criticizing the museum for its failure to adopt the new approaches pioneered by other national museums, the government and media highlighted its failure to assume educational responsibilities. The pressure to change had started with the Parliamentary Enquiry on National Monuments and Works of Art of 1841, which argued that national collections like those of the British Museum should become more accessible to the public. Furthermore, the museum by that time had local competition in the form of the South Kensington Museum (later the Victoria and Albert Museum), which was characterized by its concern for education.[113] Indeed, the director Henry Cole publicly criticized the manner in which the British Museum presented its collections, where objects were "crowded in cases which are not dust-tight and sluttishly neglected."[114] Reports in the media backed up these appraisals of the British Museum, a particularly negative account appearing in 1859 in *Building News*, where the museum was criticized as being "too cramfull because their managers could not resist an ostentatious display of accumulated treasures," and for housing "mere curiosities, intended to be only stared at instead of being studied."[115]

Although the rearrangement of the Egyptian collection according to chronological principles constituted a major breakthrough in the museum's definition of ancient Egypt, the vast majority of reviewers of the gallery did not comment on the new method of display. An important exception was the art critic Gustav Waagen, who observed that the new chronological arrangement of the Egyptian gallery united the "highest instruction with the greatest enjoyment."[116] Despite the efforts to assign the Egyptian works with a new sense of credibility, however, they were still primarily understood in terms of their difference to the classical remains, perpetuating a negative assessment of the ancient Egyptians' artistic abilities. Furthermore, when the Egyptian sculptures were praised, it was usually because of their awe-inspiring effect rather than their archaeological significance. Nonetheless, some important changes did occur in the reception of Egyptian antiquities, revealing that a more nuanced perspective on the significance of these remains had finally emerged. This change reflects the availability of more scholarship on the subject, including the pioneering efforts of the museum's first Egyptologist, Samuel Birch.

Ever-Popular Curiosities

That the Egyptian collection remained one of the most popular attractions of the museum is suggested by a number of media reports offering positive evaluations of the new arrangement. A report in the *Illustrated London News*, for example, remarked: "The alterations which have taken place in this wing of the museum render it truly interesting. The various objects which some time since were crowded within the limits of which the large lions presented by Lord Prudhoe were the boundary, are now pleasingly displayed, ample space being allowed for the visitor to walk around them." This report also comments on the creation of an uninterrupted view of the entire length of the gallery and remarks on the colossal heads of Ramesses II in the central saloon, which "form striking objects as the visitor passes between them into the Phygalian Saloon." Finally, attention is drawn to the decoration of the gallery where the ceiling, the red colors of the walls, and the gilded molding under the windows are said to create a "whole effect" that is "very pleasing."[117] The Egyptian display also received much acclaim in John Weale's guidebook of 1854, where a section on the museum devotes more space to describing the Egyptian antiquities than any other collection displayed there.[118] While his account of the museum's attractions begins with high praise for the Greek and Roman antiquities, it quickly turns to the objects drawing the greatest number of visitors:

> A grand central saloon and several other rooms are devoted to remains of Greek and Roman art. Among these are forms of exquisite beauty, grace, and truth, which afford to modern sculptors and artists most valuable objects for study. But perhaps the most popular part of the gallery of antiquities, to the great masses of visitors who crowd the museum on holiday occasions, is that which contains the colossal sculptures of Egypt. These huge relics of an extraordinary people cannot fail to impress the beholder with wonder and curiosity. He longs to see the body to which that huge fist belonged, or the Sphinx which bore that immense but finely wrought ram's head. The swarthy heroes of the Nile seem to look down on him with a calm sense of superiority; and as he views their colossal proportions, and looks around on ancient stone coffins, also of colossal size, he can hardly persuade himself but that there were giants in those days, and that these

> were the works of their hands. He might even go on to fancy that the insect world of Egypt presented the same exaggerated proportions, for here we find a beetle in dark granite of such a size that a man cannot sit comfortably astride upon its back.[119]

Despite the fact that this is a more positive appraisal than many others, using the rarely selected word "fine" to describe the colossal ram's head, the Egyptian antiquities are valued not so much for learning or as "valuable objects for study" like the Greek and Roman works, but rather, for the curiosity and wonder they incite in visitors. That size is the main source of this curiosity is reflected by the use of "colossal" three times, together with "huge," "swarthy," "giants" and "exaggerated proportions." Furthermore, the fact that the word "colossal" was always used in the context of being a curious and awesome characteristic meant that it assumed a somewhat negative status. This was reinforced by the fact that colossal size was a physical characteristic and not a "higher" attribute such as the portrayal of emotion, which was deemed to be distinctive to Greek art. Also important here is the way in which the Egyptian remains are discussed in terms of the types of visitors they attract. For instance, it is the Egyptian antiquities which are sought after by the "holiday crowds"—that is, the less educated people taking advantage of the public holiday openings. Here in this guidebook, then, it is suggested that the Egyptian objects tend to attract visitors who are easily "satisfied" by awesome and wondrous curiosities such as giant beetles and massive figured stones. Unlike the more learned aesthetes, whose interest in antiquities would be better served by visiting the Greek and Roman galleries, the holiday visitor was hungry to see the exotic and bizarre, and for them the Egyptian collection served as the equivalent of a London sideshow or street spectacle. Finally, Weale's review asserts that the real appeal of the Egyptian collections is the mummies.[120] Together with the colossal sculptures, it was these iconic symbols of death that guaranteed the Egyptian antiquities a prime place in the museum.

That the mummies had continued to function as a major drawcard of the museum since its opening in 1759 is also indicated in a report on the Egyptian Room in the *Illustrated London News*, where it was observed, "But here, as everywhere, last of all comes death; and the floor of the room is mostly occupied with plate-glass cases of mummies, and various emblems of the painted pageantry to which mortals have fondly clung in all ages of the world. Here are coffins, sepulchral cones, and other ornaments, scaraboei [*sic*], amulets, &c. The casts illustrate the heroic life of Egypt, just as the contents of the cases illustrate the social life. This room has usually crowds of visitors; and, when we remember that Egypt was the cradle of civilisation, we shall not be surprised at its relics being so popular."[121]

While the writer suggests that the Egyptian Rooms were popular because they represented the cradle of civilization, it was the presence of dead bodies that really accounted for their popularity. This fact is reinforced in William Jerrold's guidebook, where it is reported that the visitor is usually "riveted at once upon the human remains."[122] Even with the enlargement and diversification of the Egyptian collection, and indeed the other antiquities collections, the Egyptian mummies retained their unrivaled status as the most popular antiquities in the museum.

Close behind the mummies in popularity was the colossal bust of Ramesses II, which had also not lost any of its magic and impact on visitors. In William Vaux's 1851 guidebook, for example, it is described as: "the most celebrated monument of Egyptian art in any European collection, whether we consider its history, its colossal proportions, or the style of its sculpture. . . . This statue deserves to take the first rank among the works of Egyptian art. . . . The countenance has an expression of great beauty, and the whole colossal form is pervaded by that calm majesty so characteristic of Egyptian sculpture."[123]

While much of the appeal of the Egyptian antiquities lay in their colossal size and unique artistic style, it also grew out of a fascination with the complex maneuvers that were involved in transporting such colossal works from North Africa to Britain. In Jerrold's guidebook, this notion is conveyed in a summation of the typical visitor experience, where it is noted that after entering the "great and wonderful Egyptian Saloon" the visitor would linger "for hours over ancient Egyptian tombstones; before colossal sarcophagi; thinking of the tough work Belzoni must have had of it with the young Memnon; endeavoring to realise the approach to the ancient Egyptian temples through rows of colossal and majestic sphinxes."[124]

That the Egyptian antiquities remained so popular and appealed to a wider audience than the other collections of antiquities reflects how they were still essentially seen as curiosities. Most visitors would have been unaware of the developments in scholarly thought relating to ancient Egypt, and would thus have still perceived the objects as a source of amusement and general interest rather than as serious documents of scientific importance. Their status as objects that were suitable for quick and easy consumption is reinforced by an illustration published in the *Illustrated Weekly News* in 1862, where a crowd of less "refined" people are featured in the gallery.[125] This popularity of the Egyptian antiquities was maintained well into the latter part of the nineteenth century. Indeed, in 1881 the Egyptian Rooms were opened daily due to public pressure to "view the mummies and other sepulchral antiquities on the two days when the rooms are closed."[126]

A Growing Appreciation

By the 1850s, accounts of the Egyptian antiquities in museum guidebooks had become much less severe in their assessments of these objects. Not only did the descriptions of the collection became far more detailed, but the language for describing the objects became far less pejorative. Key examples here include David Masson's guide of 1850, Vaux's of 1851, and Timbs's of 1855, with the publication of Sharpe's guide in 1862 signifying the emergence of a new type of guide that refrained from making any value judgments of the objects at all. Art critics were also notably less critical in their assessments of the Egyptian antiquities, but they still struggled to define what the positive attributes of these objects were. For instance, Gustav Waagen commented upon the effect of seeing the collection laid out in its new accommodation: "When I stood between the two lines in which the principal colossal monuments are ranged in the lofty hall . . . I felt in full force that elevated and solemn impression which these gigantic objects inspire."[127]

Thus, once again, it was the colossal size of the objects that engendered a sense of admiration for Egyptian antiquities. However, Waagen went beyond this, seeking to articulate what was special and distinctive about the Egyptian style. In describing the two lion sculptures, he refers to the "architectonic" nature of Egyptian representation: "The action is true to nature, and yet at the same time admirably corresponds with the severe rectilinear, architectonic style of Egyptian art. All the principal proportions are correct; the forms very much simplified, according to a certain rule; at the same time, with a fine feeling for what is most characteristic in nature, everything is retained which expresses the grandeur of the lion."[128] We can see here how it is the tendency toward naturalistic representation that is thought to be the greatest quality of the sculptures. Thus the lions warrant consideration as objects of art because the typically "severe" attributes of Egyptian sculpture are less apparent. In assessing the rest of the collection, Waagen further clarifies the nature of Egyptian sculpture, this time singling out technique and execution. For example, in referring to the qualities exhibited by certain pieces, Waagen highlights the "extraordinary sharpness and finish" of the workmanship, a "great nicety of workmanship," a "most admirable execution," and "admirable workmanship."[129] Unlike the classical sculptures, the Egyptian ones did not appear to have any deeper or moral effect.

Continued Denouncements

Despite an increasing awareness of the historical significance of the Egyptian antiquities, they were still presented in a negative and dismissive way in guidebooks, in personal accounts, in generalist books on ancient Egypt, and in the media. The ideas expressed in guidebooks would have been particularly influential, as visitors were more likely to read them than scholarly texts. In Masson's guidebook, for example, it is considered "remarkable" that in the body of Egyptian sculpture "no real change of style was introduced, no novelty of method." He argues that while there was occasionally "boldness" in the representation of animals, when it came to the human form, artists were "rigidly confined within a narrow circle of conventional rules, and were obliged to display their talent rather in correctness and finish than in conception."[130] The result of this was a "sameness of expression," a "want of freedom," and a "monotonous and expressionless" sculpture.[131] Once again, we see the view that Egyptian art was lacking when compared to classical sculpture, with Masson describing how Egyptian statues "never rose free-limbed and buoyant like the products of the Greek chisel. . . . A stiff figure, rock-bound, and enduring for ages—such was the Egyptian idea of a statue."[132]

Other guidebooks illustrated that although some progress had been made in the way the Egyptian antiquities were evaluated, the judgmental tendencies that were so unrestrained in earlier assessments still existed. For example, having called for a more contextually based evaluation of Egyptian sculpture, Thomas Nichols embarked on a rather patronizing explanation for its distinctiveness: "The Sphinx face is remarkable for its strangely mingled expression. Power, gentleness, reserve, thought, have all been traced in it. Was it not also the ideal of the *African* type? As Madonnas were glorified likenesses of Italian women, as the Greek gods were idealised Greeks, and a Dutch painter's Madonna is Dutch in type, so the poor lentil-eating African sculptures seem to have expressed in this one countenance all the possibilities of their strong and patient race."[133] Like many before him, Nichols resorted to an aesthetic judgment; however, added to this was the notion that ancient Egyptian society was culturally inferior:

> If there be any true analogy between the childhood of an individual and that of the world, does it not seem to receive apt illustration from the character of Egyptian architecture? It is (it appears to us) child-like in its realistic and minute representation of what is familiar; child-like also in its ideal of imaginative art, namely in its *invention* of *impossibilities*—griffin, sphinxes, and so on—which it works out into detail with the sober make-believe of a child. Is not the Egyptian love of vastness for its own sake also a note of the world's magnificent childhood. No idea fastens more powerfully on a child's imagination than that of size or bigness.[134]

This notion that the ancient Egyptians represented an infantile phase in the development of humanity was simply another way of articulating the progressivist perspective on ancient history, but it had the effect of being more patronizing than did other such evolutionary accounts.

That a negative attitude toward the Egyptian remains persisted is also evidenced in the way that the guidebooks to the museum were structured and illustrated. For example, in Vaux's handbook to the antiquities galleries, the descriptions of the objects are less pejorative, but the notion that Egyptian antiquities were inferior is clearly conveyed. In structuring the book in terms of the importance of the collections, Vaux states that "it has been thought best to begin with the Greek collection, as that directly tending to form and elevate the Public Taste."[135] Thus the section on Egyptian antiquities, which comes later, is implied to be less important. Furthermore, while the explicitly negative appraisals of Egyptian antiquities may have become less frequent in guidebooks, the differential space devoted to describing the museum's antiquities collections and the use of more elaborate language to describe some collections and not others, remained a key way of defining the Egyptian antiquities. In Augustus Hare's guidebook, for example, the Greek, Roman, and Assyrian collections are introduced with lively explanations of their discovery and lengthy quotations from the specialists involved in interpreting them.[136] Tacked on at the end is a very brief mention of the Egyptian gallery, noting a few of the objects that are typically mentioned in other guides.[137]

In personal accounts of visits to the museum, we still find vivid responses to the "monstrosity" of Egyptian art. The American novelist Nathaniel Hawthorne, who visited in 1855, provides a classic example:

> We passed, too, through Assyrian saloons and Egyptian saloons,—all full of monstrosities and horrible ugliness, especially the Egyptian and all the innumerable relics that I saw of them in these saloons and among the mummies, instead of bringing me closer to them, removed me farther and farther; there being no common ground of sympathy between them and us. Their gigantic statues are certainly very curious. I saw a hand and arm up to the shoulder fifteen feet in length, and made of some stone that seemed harder and heavier than granite, not having lost its polish in all the rough usage that it has undergone. There was a fist on a still larger scale, almost as big as a hogshead. Hideous, blubber-lipped faces of giants, and human shapes, with beasts' heads on them. The Egyptian controverted Nature in all things, only using it as a groundwork to depict the unnatural upon.[138]

Here we see the familiar sentiments so oft expressed of Egyptian antiquities. While the language is more extreme than in other reviews, the basic formula for evaluating the objects remains the same. Typically, the colossal size and curious nature of the objects are designated as the only qualities of merit, whereas the non-Western features of the sculptures and the way in which they combine human and animal forms are highlighted as their negative characteristics. It is interesting to note that Hawthorne softened in his views on ancient Egypt after subsequent visits to the museum: "I strolled through the lower rooms with a good degree of interest, looking at the antique sculptures, some of which were doubtless grand and beautiful in their day. . . . The Egyptian remains are, on the whole, the more satisfactory; for, though inconceivably ugly they are at least miracles of size and ponderosity."[139]

Another visit enabled him to further qualify the uniqueness of Egyptian antiquities: "They consist of things that would be very ugly and contemptible if they were not so immensely magnified; but it is impossible not to acknowledge a certain grandeur, resulting from the scale on which those strange old sculptors wrought. . . . There is a beetle, wrought out of immensely hard black stone, as big as a hogshead. It is satisfactory to see a thing so big and heavy. Then there are huge stone sarcophagi. . . . I positively like these coffins, they are so faithfully made, and so black and stern, —and polished to such a nicety.[140] It appears that although Hawthorne initially found the Egyptian antiquities to be repugnant and "inconceivably" ugly, by his third encounter with them he had begun to see something more becoming in them. Adopting an almost endearing tone, Hawthorne now refers to the "satisfactory" feeling they produced in him and confesses to "positively liking" the monstrosities he once so reviled.

Generalist books on ancient Egypt provided yet another source of negative attitudes on Egyptian antiquities. In George Wathen's *Arts, Antiquities, and Chronology of Ancient Egypt*, for example, we can see how the antiquities were perceived through a racist lens: "In Greece we see art rapidly advancing from infancy to unrivalled excellence: in Egypt it continued stationary or retrograded during long ages of peace, opulence and domestic refinement. This difference must no doubt be primarily attributed to the different constitution of the national mind."[141] Elaborating on the restrictive nature of Egyptian sculpture, Wathen continues: "The expression is grave, tranquil, and generally benign, the features are fixed, the limbs rigid, the joints rectangular and not articulated, flesh swollen, feet broad and flat, hands stiff and stretched, fingers and toes elongated and not divided—the whole figure motionless as a mummy."[142] Despite the important advances that had been made in understanding Egyptian antiquities by the mid-nineteenth century, it is clear that some authors remained loyal to the views so forcefully expressed a century earlier.

Finally, denouncement of Egyptian antiquities also continued to appear in media reports, and although not specifically commenting on the museum's new installation, an *Illustrated London News* report on the Egyptian displays at the Crystal Palace in Sydenham is important as it provides an idea of how Egyptian antiquities tended to be described by journalists at the time. Referring to the display of the colossal figures from Abu Simbel, the reporter asserts:

> We must take exception to the precise terms in which those giant sitting figures are characterised by Mr. Samuel Phillips in his official "Guide." They give us, no doubt, "an adequate idea of" something which distinguishes "*the monuments of ancient Egyptian art*"; and we will even grant that they give us an adequate idea of their "stupendous magnitude." But there we halt; we cannot go on to expatiate about their "passive grandeur." We should much regret the absence of those figures from the Exhibition. They are in themselves a chronicle and suggestive type of something which has passed away, and which was not notable under the sun. But "grand" we cannot call them in the virtual and practical import of that epithet, as it

> is at present understood amongst us. Grand they are in a literal sense; for "grand" is an anglicised Gallic word, meaning large, if taken according to that rule; and the magnitude of these prodigious statues ensures them so abundant a share of attention, that anybody who has but once sauntered through this maze of treasures and marvels will easily distinguish and always remember those huge masses, whatever else he may forget. All Egyptian sculpture and architecture were noticeable alike for massiveness and grotesqueness. But the massive and the grotesque united are not enough to constitute "the grand." There must be some high, if not imperishable, idea and sentiment conveyed by the vast blocks; such as the grief, or the courage, or the self-devotion, or the sense of majesty, or the instinct of love, which are, in their turns, shed over the glyphic production of Greece and other lands. Failing these impressions, there must be either exquisite proportion and physical beauty, or exquisite imitation. Neither of these classes of interest is attached to the abnormal and idol-like figures in the garden side of the Nave, sixty five feet in height.[143]

Once again, it appears that the primary attribute for which the sculptures were valued was their massive size. Furthermore, the writer is at pains to qualify why the Egyptian remains do not deserve to be associated with the word "grand," as in order to properly compare to the classical works the Egyptians needed to impart into their "vast blocks" the high ideas of Grecian art, including its "exquisite proportion," "physical beauty," and "exquisite imitation."

Contradictory Evaluations

One of the most characteristic features of the reports and descriptions of the new Egyptian displays at the museum is their contradictory nature. While writers would attest to the qualities of Egyptian art in one sentence, they would inadvertently denounce them in another. For example, they describe Egypt as the cradle of civilization in one paragraph, and then criticize its lack of cultural attainments on the next page. That the reception of the Egyptian displays was so contradictory in nature attests to the persisting love/hate mode of engaging with Egyptian antiquities. A good example of this can be found in the guidebook by William Jerrold, where the Egyptian remains are prominently featured. Here the Egyptian Room is described as "always an attractive part of the museum to the majority of visitors," and a comparison is made between ancient Egypt and modern Europe in order to demonstrate the achievements of this ancient civilization.[144] For instance, the Egyptian objects are described as the remains of an "advanced civilization" who lived when the people of Europe were in a "state of barbarism"; and further, "Here are graceful household vessels, compared with the art of which the willow pattern of the nineteenth century is a barbarism, and fabrics of which modern Manchester would not be ashamed."[145] He also compares the sculptures to contemporary British crafts, referring in particular to the sarcophagi, where the "proudest undertaker of modern times must look humbly" upon them, deploring the "decline of his business as an art."[146] However, no sooner having testified to the advanced qualities of the Egyptian objects, Jerrold then proceeds to denigrate them. Starting with the mummy cases, which are described as "huge and gaudily painted coffins" that have a "somewhat ghastly effect," he then turns to the sculpture galleries, where he shifts his comparisons from British crafts to classical art.[147] The massive bust of Ramesses II gets the following assessment: "Certainly, when we recall the time, realise fully the antiquity and the social state in which this great work was performed, we may see the sculptor's dawning soul in the majestic repose of this head. The lines are hard and stiff—have not the flow of the Parthenon decorations; but here is nothing mean or poor,—all large, solid, and carved with the force of a giant."[148]

Although the writer seemingly praises such sculptures, suggesting that their creators must have possessed great strength, his assessment of their aesthetic qualities is essentially negative. Offering a marked contrast to the "flow" of the Parthenon sculptures, the Egyptian sculptures remain "hard" and "stiff." This perceived contrast between Greek movement and Egyptian stasis in art embodied the attitude toward the cultural dynamism of these ancient cultures.[149] The lion sculptures are also described as possessing an "angular stiffness," thus endorsing the view that the lack of movement in the Egyptian sculptures represented inferior artistic skill.[150] Finally, although positive words like "great," "wonderful," and "graceful" are used to describe the Egyptian antiquities, these are promptly negated by words such as "gaudily," "ghastly," "hard," and "stiff."

Another good example of how appraisals of the Egyptian displays were contradictory can be seen in W. Fletcher's guidebook, where the objects are initially described in glowing terms: "In contemplating the fragments of Egyptian workmanship, we cannot but be impressed with a degree of awe and wonder at the greatness and grandeur of their works, of which the remains of this apartment give but an imperfect idea. Their physical power, the untiring energy, and the unceasing perseverance, necessary to form such stupendous Pyramids, carve such enormous figures, and yet often impart to them such beauty of form, and execute them with such accuracy and spirit is truly astonishing."[151]

Not only it is unusual to see the obelisks acquired in 1802 singled out above the colossal bust of Ramesses II and the head of Amenhotep III, but it is strange to see them described as possessing a "beautiful simplicity . . . undisfigured as they are by any irregularity, and ornamented with figures of great accuracy and outline."[152] Despite all this praise, however, it is once again to the classical sculptures that the visitor is directed, for while the

Egyptian antiquities can impress with their size, it is the Greek objects that have real substance. Arguing for the supreme authority of Greek sculpture, Fletcher reflects on the contents of the Elgin gallery, which

> contains those highly finished and pure works of the Grecian Sculptors, which all our most celebrated artists have united in pronouncing as the finest to be seen in this or any other country; and of the greatest importance, not only as tending to improve the public taste, but as an enduring and an unrivalled national school of art. Although this collection may be looked upon as the most valuable to the artist, it might not be the most interesting to the public. Such is its fragmentary nature, and such is the elevated character which these remnants are sufficiently perfect to show, that to enjoy them thoroughly, it is not only necessary that the individual should possess a taste for sculpture, but also of *feeling* for the grand in art, and for that purified simplicity, which are often united in the works of the Greeks. This feeling may be excited if not created, by frequently and attentively viewing them: it is by purifying and elevating the national taste, as well as by holding up a high and enduring standard of excellence to our artists, that they will honour the nation which possesses them, and repay the people who bought them.[153]

Here the visitor is told that while the Grecian sculptures may initially be difficult to interpret (because certain "qualifications" are required in order to truly appreciate them), they should persist with learning such skills. This conviction was also expressed by Nathaniel Hawthorne, who having failed to see the value of the fragments of classical sculpture in initial visits, ultimately concluded that there was an "excellence in ancient sculpture, which has yet a potency to educate and refine the minds of those who look at it carelessly and casually as I do."[154] Unlike this, the Egyptian sculptures were thought to offer a more two-dimensional or superficial form of satisfaction—they could not escape their identity as curiosities. The reason why so many accounts of ancient Egypt retained such a condemning attitude stems from the history of its representation. Early representations had established a vogue for using colorful language to describe ancient Egypt and it was clearly considered acceptable to continue doing so.

Historical Documents

Perhaps most significant in the reception of the new Egyptian displays was a more pronounced recognition of the historical significance of Egyptian antiquities. This recognition not only stemmed from the new chronological layout of the gallery, but reflected the availability of many more interpretive aids on ancient Egypt; particularly guidebooks and books of general synthesis. A good example of the newly appreciative attitude toward Egyptian antiquities was W. I. Bicknell's guidebook, where it was asserted that "though of a very different character from the finished sculptures of the

Greeks, and of a much earlier period, [Egyptian antiquities] are notwithstanding of immense importance in the history of art, pouring an astonishing flood of light upon the history of a singularly interesting people."[155] The value of the Egyptian antiquities in informing people about life in the past is also emphasized above their status as trophies of war:

> They form a collection of which an Englishman, under any circumstances, may justly boast; but without wishing to encourage any unworthy feelings towards our neighbours, and allies, the French, we cannot but remember that these very *remains* were purchased by the blood of many of our poor fellows, who perished in that memorable struggle, the result of which has so much changed the general appearance of Europe. They are, however, chiefly valuable, not because the trophies of victory, but from the important illustrations which they furnish of ages long since passed away.[156]

Bicknell's appraisal is significant because it suggests that the history of ancient Egypt has finally been designated as a subject worthy of study. More significantly, it reveals how the ancient material of Egypt has been assigned an important role in investigating this subject.

Corresponding with the recognition of the historical significance of the Egyptian antiquities was the challenge to the distinction between the objects displayed in the sculpture gallery, which tended to be judged as works of art, and the smaller antiquities in the Egyptian Rooms, which were defined as having ethnographic value. Some authors recognized that the problem with separating the smaller antiquities from the larger sculptures was that it prevented the sculptures from being valued for the historical information they embodied. Masson commented on how this distinction had the effect of devaluing the ethnographic or historical significance of the sculptures:

> This classification is by no means accurate. Although, for instance, there is an evident distinction between those mere antiquities, such as lamps, axeheads, or articles of furniture, which only illustrate the manners and customs of the ancients, and those works of art, such as statues and paintings, which illustrate the tendencies of their minds when making a high effort through their individual men of genius, yet in point of fact it is impossible to draw the line of separation, or to say which articles in any collection of antiquities are mere curiosities, and which are works of art. Strictly considered, also, works of art possess the same ethnographical value—that is, the same power of admitting us to a view of the life of the people that produced them—as mere curiosities.[157]

Thus, by separating the sculpture and "mere antiquities," the ethnographic value of the art is neglected. Another account in the *Illustrated London News* reiterates how the separation of sculptures and smaller antiquities had consequences for the understanding of ancient Egypt: "Egyptian deities, sacred animals, statues, household furniture, and other large objects;

besides vases, lamps, bowls, cups, agricultural implements, boxes, baskets, spoons, and bricks, tools, musical instruments, playthings, &c.: in short, a variety of most interesting illustrations of the industrial arts and domestic life of the Egyptian—all especially attractive, and so devoid of the mysticism usually attached to the antiquities of Egypt, as to render this Room one of the most frequented in the museum."[158] Here we can see how the everyday objects in the Egyptian Rooms were considered to be important because they were "devoid of the mysticism" typically associated with ancient Egypt.

Indicative of the growing recognition of Egyptian antiquities as historical documents was the fact that authors began to recognize the need to know something of the context in which the antiquities were produced in order to evaluate them properly. In Vaux's guidebook, for example, the reader is encouraged to learn something about Egyptian geography and culture: "It seems, indeed, hardly possible thoroughly to appreciate the remains of ancient art without some knowledge of the peculiarities of the lands which they once adorned and illustrated. Thus a knowledge of the religious creed of a nation or a race, the language they spoke, the ordinary life they led, are almost essential requisites in tracing out the course of their artistic history."[159] Nichols's guidebook also sought to situate the Egyptian antiquities in a historical context. Although Nichols initially advocates the moral and aesthetic role of the museum's antiquities collections—"not only does the intelligent study of these collections suggest and stimulate inventions, it also develops and enlightens taste, or the sense of the beautiful and befitting"—he then proceeds to make a strong case for recognizing the archaeological potential of Egyptian art.[160] This is achieved by informing the reader in some detail about the geography, history, religious traditions, and social context of Egypt. While Long had attempted to do this in his guide of 1832–1836, Nichols's was much more successfully pitched at a popular level. Furthermore, like others before him, Nichols justified the qualities of Egyptian sculpture by emphasizing its function as part of an architectural system: "It would, therefore, be unfair, in looking at the Egyptian remains, to judge these sculptures—which were really *parts* of a large design—as if they had been intended, like our own, separately to impress the mind. We should rather try to imagine for ourselves the noble porticoes to which they belonged, the temples which they guarded, and thus to understand something of their grandeur, and even sublimity, when in such positions."[161]

Making a significant departure from previous guidebooks, Nichols then avoids focusing on the sculptures, and rather, devotes a substantial amount of discussion to the stelae in the main galleries, the paintings and casts on the staircase, and the smaller items in the upper Egyptian Rooms. This account, which gives a much clearer sense of the diversity of objects in the collection, firmly treats Egyptian antiquities as historical documents as opposed to defining them in terms of the traditional dichotomy of works of art and curiosities. Furthermore, when the artistic development of particular specimens is referred to, it is done with reference to periods of Egyptian sculpture and not in comparison with Greek art.[162] Finally, the Egyptian sculptures that are usually ignored at the expense of the great colossal works finally get some attention in this guidebook. The statue of Ankhwa (fig. 5.8), for example, is described as having "one of the most agreeable profiles to be seen in any early Egyptian collection."[163] For all of these reasons Nichol's guidebook hails a true breakthrough in the reception of Egyptian antiquities, relinquishing them for the first time from their long-held role as a foil to Greek art.

* * *

The 1854 installation constituted a climax in the presentation of ancient Egypt in the museum. The vastly expanded exhibition space, the striking architecture of the gallery, and the elaborate decoration of the new accommodation all worked together to transform the status of the Egyptian antiquities, conferring upon them a sense of independence and grandeur that they had not previously enjoyed. However, despite the new emphasis on chronology, the 1854 installation still maintained some allegiance to the exhibition strategy that was established by the museum at its inception. Here objects were distributed in aesthetic arrangements that were designed to create an overall picturesque effect. Furthermore, even though the reception of the Egyptian antiquities indicates that they were finally recognized as having a historical dimension of their own without reference to Greek antiquities, the reviews of the 1854 installation still reveal a tendency to cast them as curiosities.

This study ends with the formal establishment of the discipline of Egyptology in British universities in the latter part of the century, which was directly associated with the formation of the Egypt Exploration Fund (later Society) in 1882, and the important work carried out at the museum by the keeper Ernest A. T. Wallis Budge, who joined the museum in 1883.[164] The appointment of Flinders Petrie at University College London in 1892, the Egypt Exploration Society's program of excavating sites, and Budge's work in collection development together formed the beginnings of Egyptology's professionalization and institutionalization. In addition to these developments in Britain, and similar ones in Europe, the Americans now entered the scene, competing for the purchase of significant objects and collections and establishing their own excavation programs.[165] It was at this point, around 1880, that the distinction between the academic study of ancient Egypt and its popular representation entered a completely new dimension. From this point on ancient Egypt asserted its identity in new ways; however, the legacy of the early exhibitions continued to live on.

Conclusion: Something for Everyone

THE BRITISH MUSEUM AND ITS CREATION OF ANCIENT EGYPT

From 1759 to 1880, the acquisition, display, and reception of Egyptian antiquities in the British Museum functioned to define ancient Egypt in distinctive ways. More specifically, through a series of five major installations created to present its Egyptian collections, the museum actively constructed a set of distinct identities for ancient Egypt. These identities were manufactured via a complicated representational process that centered around the ability of displays to tell compelling stories about the past. Intimately connected with this were the circumstances relating to the way in which the Egyptian collections were acquired and the manner in which the Egyptian displays were received by museum visitors. An examination of these three factors reveals that the exhibition of ancient Egypt was not simply a by-product of academic thought on this culture, but rather, that the museological representations made an active contribution toward defining it.

Throughout this study, the intention has not been to suggest a progression toward the recognition of ancient Egypt for its "true worth." Far from this, the aim has been to show that the different manifestations of ancient Egypt constructed by the British Museum have persisted and continue to survive alongside each other. Indeed, the real "magic" of ancient Egypt lies in its ability to tolerate these alternative identities. Furthermore, the different identities of ancient Egypt were not simply tailored to suit different audiences—serving as curiosities for the uneducated, for example, or as historical documents for scholars. Testimony to the representational potential of Egyptian antiquities was their ability to remain multidimensional for all audiences. In this sense they could satisfy the dual needs of those visitors wishing to be intellectually satisfied yet emotionally stimulated at the same time. Prior to elaborating upon how the museum manufactured this comprehensive representational scheme for ancient Egypt, I shall summarize the general patterns of acquisition, display, and reception identified in the study.

ACQUISITION

The acquisition of the Egyptian collection contributed to the construction of knowledge in that what was displayed conveyed definitive ideas about ancient Egypt. In order to understand the rationale behind the presence of particular objects in the displays, it is necessary to consider what kinds of collections were acquired, the methods by which these were acquired, the types of objects that were acquired, who was responsible for acquiring them, and how all of these factors related to current scholarship on the subject. Generally, the Egyptian collections initially acquired by the museum constituted a very limited sample of what was available at the time; however, the Egyptian collection grew at an exponential rate, arguably becoming the most important collection of Egyptian antiquities outside Egypt.

In considering the kinds of Egyptian collections that were acquired by the museum, it is possible to see a shift from the arrival of small, haphazard collections and miscellaneous objects (e.g., Sloane's collection, and the donations of the Lethieullier family and King George III), to the acquisition of large, specialized collections and significant single items (e.g., Salt's, Sams's, and Anastasi's collections, the donations of Lord Prudhoe's lions and Lord Elgin's colossal beetle). Punctuating this transition was the arrival of the somewhat systematic collection seized from the French.

For the period covered in this study, the Egyptian collection was essentially acquired through accident and special purchases. From the museum's foundation in the mid-eighteenth century to the late nineteenth century Egyptian objects were not actively sought after, and the collection grew more through the acceptance of what was offered than through a dedicated collecting strategy. The lack of an acquisitions policy for Egyptian antiquities was not a problem for the museum, however, as it was given and offered such outstanding collections by the king, the aristocracy, the military, and several enterprising collectors. The fact that the museum came to possess such an important collection of Egyptian antiquities so early in the nineteenth century reflects how it acted more as a reluctant recipient of important donations and bargain offers than as an institution intent on creating an impressive Egyptian collection.

With the select committee of 1836, the museum was encouraged to develop its collections by enlisting the services of British officials working overseas; however, no such policy was formally adopted and the collections continued to be acquired through a reactive system of accepting objects and collections that were offered for sale. This situation began to change when the staff of the Antiquities Department took more initiative in recommending acquisitions. It was around this time—the mid-nineteenth century—that keepers, notably Edward Hawkins, pushed for more involvement in the purchasing of objects and collections. In addition to this, staff began to travel to Europe to buy objects and collections, resulting in a more comprehensive and diverse collection that addressed the gaps and biases of the earlier collections. While Hawkins contributed here, it was Samuel Birch who significantly improved the approach to acquisition by building up the more poorly represented areas of the collection. Indeed, it is with Birch that we see the concept of collection development established for Egyptian antiquities for the first time. In summarizing the methods according to which the acquisitions were made, we can essentially say that they began with donations, then changed to limited purchasing of collections offered, and then finally developed into a more systematic and selective purchasing of objects from auctions.

In addressing the question of what types of Egyptian objects the museum selected for purchase and why, it is important to note that the basis for selection was what was available on the collectors' market, so the types of objects acquired reflected the interests of the enterprising collectors of the day. These interests typically revolved around collecting what was perceived to be saleable or desirable on the antiquities market, and thus tended to result in the accumulation of objects seen to have display potential, such as statues, mummies, and smaller "trinkets." Because little was known about Egypt, it was difficult to determine what was scientifically or historically significant. In this respect, it was not unreasonable for collectors to focus on objects that had a known currency; these were typically the curiosities that European collectors wished to include in their cabinets. There were of course collectors who were more systematic in their approach to collecting, such as Salt, who attempted to obtain representative samples of the range of material unearthed from sites. Furthermore, is important to note that what was available to purchase in Egypt was also a determining factor. Before 1820 domestic or daily-life objects were largely unavailable, and thus collectors were merely collecting whatever they could get their hands on. Finally, it is difficult to determine the extent to which the museum chose particular object types above others and how this may have shaped the nature of the Egyptian collection. In the early days it appears that collections were purchased in their entirety; later, when collections started to be purchased at auction, an increasingly discriminatory approach was adopted. Although the criteria for judging whether objects were worthy of purchase were rarely clearly stated, the possession of aesthetic qualities appears to have been a primary attribute. This fitted in with the museum's general interest in selecting what they perceived to be impressive works of art and rare pieces. By the mid-nineteenth century, this approach to object selection began to change and keepers became more interested in bolstering components of the collection that were weak.

An examination of the museum's Egyptian collection makes it clear that the types of items possessed communicated particular ideas about ancient Egypt. Amulets, scarabs, mummies, and figures of animal gods from the 1759 installation conveyed an image of ancient Egypt as a source of "wondrous curiosities"; the sarcophagi and large statues of animal gods from the 1808 installation suggested that ancient Egyptians were creators of "colossal monstrosities"; the figures of rulers and wall paintings in the 1823 installation defined Egyptian art as "monumental masterpieces"; the shoes, bricks, and toiletries of the 1837 display rendered Egypt as a repository of "accessible oddities"; and, finally, the augmentation and combinations of all of these types of objects in the 1854 installation ensured that Egyptian antiquities were perceived as "historical documents."

When it came to making the decisions about whether objects and collections should be purchased or not, it was the trustees who held the ultimate authority. However, from the mid-nineteenth century, the trustees became more dependent on the advice of Egyptologists, and the keepers assumed more power in determining whether collections on offer should be acquired. It is significant that it was the trustees who initially had all the control over acquisitions, given that so few were interested in Egyptian antiquities. While some had traveled to Egypt and thus had a basic awareness of Egyptian monuments, most of the trustees had educational backgrounds in classics, and thus it is not surprising that they were far more interested in classical antiquities and in developing this component of the museum's collections. Furthermore, the early antiquities keepers had little experience or training in the study of antiquities and even less knowledge of ancient Egypt, and thus they were unlikely to promote the acquisition of Egyptian antiquities. More significantly perhaps, the trustees were leading establishment figures who represented the major military, political, religious, and scholarly institutions of the country. Consequently, the museum was a conservative establishment and the trustees did not see themselves as risk-takers when it came to the presentation of cultural relics.

Central to making decisions about acquisition was the contribution of those invited to make evaluations of the Egyptian objects offered for sale. The background of the various individuals who were called upon to assess such materials was initially very diverse, including those who had traveled to Egypt, those who had general expertise in antiquities, those who were well known collectors and those who had written works on Egypt. That a wide range of credentials was accepted when considering the worth of Egyptian antiquities can be seen in the list of "experts" testifying to the value of Sams's collection (see chapter 5). As Egyptology became more established, however, experts, including those working as museum staff, were increasingly used to provide assessments for the trustees (for example, John Gardner Wilkinson and Samuel Birch).

Finally, while the growth of the museum's Egyptian collection can generally be seen as corresponding to the growth of Egyptology as a discipline, it is important to emphasize that the acquisitions were not motivated by the development of the subject, but rather by a desire to have a collection unrivaled by its European competitors seeking to assert their authority in establishing public collections of antiquities.

DISPLAY

In examining how the museum's displays of Egyptian antiquities constructed knowledge about ancient Egypt, it became apparent that the space dedicated to the presentation of the collection, the location of the collection in the museum, the way it was structured, its distribution or spatial layout, the architecture and design of the gallery, and the aids used to facilitate interpretation all played a part.

It is clear that the museum never really considered the Egyptian collection a priority when it came to assigning the objects' accommodation. Over the 120 years covered in this study it appears that the Egyptian collections were usually an afterthought when it came to allocating space. Initially featured in small rooms and spread over all sorts of locations, the collection was completely transformed with the construction of a purpose-built gallery (the Townley Gallery). With the final installations (the Smirke Galleries), the space grew substantially and provided the Egyptian antiquities with a far more sympathetic sense of scale. The location of the collection ensured that the Egyptian antiquities came to be understood via a comparative mode of evaluating ancient art. By juxtaposing Egyptian antiquities with those from the classical world and presenting the collections in a similar manner, an instant lesson could be learned. For instance, the qualities of Greek art that distinguished it above the rest of ancient art could be made most apparent through a comparison with Egyptian objects. This mode of viewing relegated chronology and historical context to an insignificant role; and because aesthetic qualities were most valued, the potential of Egyptian antiquities as a vital source of historical information was denied.

The organization of the Egyptian collection was a subject upon which little reflection was made. Although James Empson attempted to outline a plan for the distribution of the museum's collections when it was first established in 1759, a strategy for arranging the Egyptian antiquities was not articulated until the mid-nineteenth century, when the museum was determining how to relocate the Egyptian sculptures into their new accommodation (i.e., Oldfield's plan of 1852). Until then, the Egyptian collection was distributed according to the mode of display adopted for the classical sculptures, which was essentially aesthetic. Here objects were coordinated with the architectural features and decoration of the room, being disposed in situations that were thought to be visually pleasing. This mode of presentation, which was derived from the arrangement of antique sculptures in the major art collections of Europe, reduced the Egyptian sculptures to nothing other than inferior works of art. Since the aim of the museum was to showcase fine examples of beauty and artistic skill, as opposed to conveying information about historical or archaeological significance, the Egyptian displays were instantly relegated to secondary importance.

The fact that this mode of presentation left the Egyptian objects so uncontextualized eventually became an issue of concern for the antiquities staff, who called for the arrangements to be based on knowledge about ancient Egyptian chronology, rather than on its artistic merits (e.g., Hawkins's and Oldfield's proposals for the 1854 installation). Structuring the collection on a temporal basis had not been possible until the mid-nineteenth century because little was known about the archeological significance of the material and the sequence in which it was created. However, other methods of contextualizing the collection, which had been adopted in Europe, were avoided. Indeed, the attempt to convey the context of Egyptian antiquities via architectural reconstructions and Egyptian-inspired wall decoration, which had been pioneered in Italian museums and then taken up in French and German museums and British exhibitions, did not influence the museum, because such tactics appear to have been considered inappropriate for a national institution. Finally, while the museum did improve its explanation of context via the more comprehensive guidebooks, it was reluctant to contextualize the antiquities through a different style of arrangement. In summary, of the alternative ways in which the collection could have been structured—aesthetically-based, subject- or thematically based, chronologically or historically based, and collection-based—it was the first that predominated. Even when a more chronologically based display strategy was introduced in the last major installation of 1854, the aesthetic exhibition style was still central. Thus, while the keepers fought for the historical significance of the collections, they did not dismiss the value of the antiquities in shaping the public's conception of taste.

When it came to the distribution of the Egyptian antiquities in the gallery of the museum, it is important to note that there was a clear division of labor that affected the style of presentation adopted. The museum's antiquities staff were assigned the responsibility of cataloguing the collections and were deliberately excluded from making decisions on displays. The notion that display was an interpretive process, requiring specialist historical or archaeological knowledge, was initially not endorsed by the trustees. Seeing display as an "artistic" endeavor, they delegated the task to experts on sculpture and architecture. Although the architect Robert Smirke assumed a major role in creating the exhibitionary setting for the Egyptian antiquities in the early nineteenth century, it was the sculptor and president of the Royal Academy, Richard Westmacott, who was primarily responsible. As a firm advocate of the aesthetic approach to display, Westmacott replicated the kinds of picturesque arrangements of sculptures featured in princely mansions and collectors' homes. With the acceptance of Hawkins's and Oldfield's plans for a chronological arrangement of the Egyptian antiquities, Westmacott's long reign finally came to an end, and the antiquities specialists assumed a new responsibility for arranging the objects.

The arrangement of the museum's collection of Egyptian antiquities remained remarkably consistent in its style from the mid-eighteenth century to the mid-nineteenth century. By creating aesthetic arrangements centered on symmetry and balance, the museum sought to achieve a notion of harmony and compositional coherence in what was perceived to be a haphazard ensemble of objects, thus making the best out of a little understood set of antiquities. Lining the sculptures up in rows against the walls reinforced a sense of rigidity and stiffness commonly associated with the Egyptian works and made the gallery appear alienating and oppressive. Of course, the nature of the Egyptian sculptures presented a major challenge in terms of museological arrangement. Not only was their colossal size an issue, but their dark color and block-like quality made them difficult to present in the conventional manner. Furthermore, despite the fact that they provided such a strong contrast to the classical sculptures, no alternative mode for displaying the Egyptian objects appears to have been considered. Thus, by arranging the Egyptian sculptures according to the same system as the classical works, the museum did not do justice to their distinctive qualities, instead making them appear awkward and uneasy. While this situation began to be addressed as the collection grew and a greater variety of Egyptian objects were acquired by the museum, it was the new architectural settings created for the collection in 1834 and 1854 that gave the Egyptian objects an identity apart from that of the classical collections.

The status and identity of the Egyptian collection was significantly affected by the architecture and décor of the rooms in which the objects were accommodated. Initially housed in various rooms of the mansion of Montagu House, the Egyptian antiquities appeared very much at odds with the ornate architectural style and decorative scheme of the building, strongly reinforcing their role as curiosities. When the opportunity came to create a purpose-built gallery for the sculptures seized from the French, the unique architectural and artistic style of the objects was not taken into account and they were forced into a setting appropriate for classical antiquities. The result was that the qualities of the collection clashed with the style of the gallery, and, once again, the strangeness or "monstrosity" of the Egyptian works was emphasized. When featured in the spacious galleries created by Smirke, the collection finally assumed a far more prominent and respectable status than it had in the much smaller Townley Gallery. Furthermore, the Greek Revival features of the Smirke Galleries (e.g., the pilasters and coffered roof) and the colorful new decorative elements created a much enlivened setting in which the Egyptian antiquities could finally be appreciated as majestic monuments of antiquity.

The lighting and coloring of the walls of the Egyptian sculpture galleries also served to define the collection in particular ways. While great pains were made to ensure that the classical antiquities were properly lit, the Egyptian sculptures suffered from bad lighting conditions that, significantly, were not considered inappropriate for their appreciation. Not only were they poorly lit from side windows, but the source of light had a confusing effect, making some of the objects difficult to see properly. Cross lights obscured certain parts of individual sculptures, and overexposed other parts with strong direct light. As for wall color, the gallery was simply painted the same color as the classical antiquities galleries, without consideration for the nature of the Egyptian sculptures. Thus the walls were a light stone color, which created a somber, cold, and lifeless atmosphere. The need to find a more appropriate color for the walls of the Egyptian gallery was finally addressed with the 1854 installation, where it was determined that a darker color was preferable to a light one. With the introduction of a darker red color, a greater contrast between the walls and the antiquities was created, and thus the profile and features of the sculptures were able to stand out more clearly.

Finally, the provision of aids to explain the collection, such as labels, guidebooks, and guides, served to reinforce the image of ancient Egypt presented by the museum. For some time, a minimal investment was made in labeling, and when labels were more comprehensively produced, they provided only the most basic description of the object. Slow in producing guidebooks, the museum initially relied on guides to present the collections to visitors. When deficiencies in the descriptions of the Egyptian collections were identified, the Antiquities Department created official guidebooks, but these offered the bare minimum of information, often highlighting the circumstances in which the collection came to be in the museum above the significance of the objects themselves. Commercial guidebooks quickly became the main resource for making sense of the collections, but these were highly variable in quality and often distinguished by their disdain for the Egyptian collections. It was not until the 1850s that a quality product appeared in the form of guidebooks that described the collection in relation to Egyptian history.

RECEPTION

The reception of the museum's installations of Egyptian antiquities, as conveyed in diaries and correspondence, in newspapers and illustrated magazines, in guidebooks and in depictions of visitors in the galleries, reveals that they attracted a great deal of attention. Indeed, from the first installation of 1759 to the last major installation of 1854, reviews of the museum rarely fail to mention the Egyptian collections. Overall, the reception of the Egyptian antiquities in the museum can be characterized as bipolar, in that visitors either loved or hated them; rarely, if ever, was an attitude of indifference expressed toward this set of material culture. Egyptian antiquities were appropriated as the "light relief" of the ancient world, and at the same time they were used as an invaluable didactic aid. The inclusion of the Egyptian antiquities in a museum primarily devoted to collecting and displaying classical antiquities, and more particularly by an establishment that was focused on exhibiting the finest works of ancient artists, had great implications for how the Egyptian remains were received. Within this framework, visitors were encouraged to make judgments on Egyptian antiquities and to assess them as less competent works of art when compared to the sculptures of the classical world. This is very much reflected in the published accounts of the day, where rather than trying to understand or explain the "strange" qualities of the Egyptian antiquities, writers routinely dismissed them as grotesque aberrations. Furthermore, when a glimmer of appreciation was apparent, the criteria for which the Egyptian antiquities were valued (e.g., their colossal size), reveals that they remained defined within the domain of curiosities and that they were never really accorded equal status as objects of art.

Although several major studies on the monuments of Egypt had been published by the beginning of the nineteenth century, when the first three installations of 1759, 1808, and 1823 were created, Egyptology did not yet exist as a recognized discipline. Thus, until the middle of the century the conceptual basis upon which the sculptures were evaluated was derived from classical studies and theories of art history. More specifically, the primary intellectual framework according to which the Egyptian antiquities were presented was Winckelmann's progressivist scheme for the history of art. Within this scheme, the Egyptian objects were appreciated through a comparison with ancient Greek art and not recognized in their own terms. The result of this was that Egyptian sculpture was perceived as an affront to the principles according to which Greek art was produced.

Beyond their role in illustrating the achievements of classical art, the Egyptian objects were essentially appreciated in very two-dimensional terms. For instance, beyond the observation that the prevalence of funerary items represented Egypt as a culture haunted by an obsession with death, the Egyptian objects were enjoyed as curiosities that stimulated the basic emotional responses of wonder and awe. In this way, they functioned as a source of amusement rather than of serious contemplation and thus served to satisfy the desire within visitors to be entertained by the unusual or strange. So while classical art satisfied the tastes of the learned and enlightened, Egyptian art was designated to serve popular interest—it was the poor-man's domain of antiquity. More specifically, while educated visitors would evaluate (and thus denounce) the Egyptian collection according to the notion that Greek art was the pinnacle which all art sought to emulate, the uneducated visitors were not restrained by this way of thinking and thus could more readily appreciate the uniqueness of the objects. In this sense, the nonelite were liberated in their approach to Egyptian antiquities and were quick to appropriate them because they were not intellectually owned in the same way as were the classical antiquities. That nonexperts were able to speak with such confidence about the Egyptian objects reveals the widely held belief that anyone was qualified to pass judgment on them. Unlike the assessment of the Greek and Roman objects, which required some knowledge of the subject and an appreciation of the artistic accomplishments they represented, the evaluation of the Egyptian antiquities did not appear to require such knowledge.

Although the Egyptian objects continued to be perceived as curiosities well into the mid-nineteenth century, they were increasingly appreciated for their distinctiveness. Moreover, the Egyptian antiquities began to be valued for qualities other than their aesthetic attributes. This can be seen with the Egyptian Room installation of 1837, when ancient Egypt was seen to offer something important to the understanding of life in ancient times. A climax was reached in the installation of 1854, at a time when more authors were expressing an interest in understanding the context in which the Egyptian antiquities had been produced. Significantly, however, a continuing distinction was made between the sculptures and works of a more domestic nature. While the former continued to be understood in comparison to the Greek and Roman antiquities, thus retaining their status as curiosities, the latter were appreciated in an ethnographic sense as objects that informed one about daily life. The crucial difference was that the Egyptian objects were not thought to provide information or inspiration on the higher mental achievements of humanity.

Until the mid-nineteenth century many of the assessments of the museum's Egyptian collection were highly judgmental, demonstrating how people felt confident in critiquing the Egyptian objects. The language used to describe the displays, particularly the commonly used words "grotesque" and "monstrous," revealed a strong sense of disdain toward these antiquities. While the word "grotesque" was ostensibly used to describe the objects that combined human and animal forms, it was also used to convey the aberrant status of the objects. Even so, a love-hate relationship appeared to exist between visitors and the Egyptian antiquities. While they may have described them as grotesque aberrations, people were drawn to their curious aspects. While many descriptions convey a sense of disgust and horror, others convey delight in encountering Egyptian antiquities for the first time.

CREATING ANCIENT EGYPT

Based on a scanty and eclectic array of objects that had been collected in a rather serendipitous fashion, the museum's first display of Egyptian antiquities was not intended to explain ancient Egypt or indeed, provide any statement on this ancient culture. Regardless, the museum's arrangement served to define ancient Egypt as a source of "wondrous curiosities." It was as a consequence of this that ancient Egypt became much maligned, since curiosities were distinctly perceived as objects that provided shallow gratification rather than functioning as a source for learning and study. What's more, they were objects that attracted visitors' attention because they aroused basic human emotions, such as a fascination for the strange and bizarre. The Egyptian objects inspired awe and wonder not because they possessed "important" qualities like the accurate representation of nature or the ability to capture a (Western) sense of beauty, but rather, because they portrayed unusual subjects and provided an intimate glimpse into ancient funerary rituals. For example, the mummies, amulets, shabtis, and figurines of animal gods served to define ancient Egyptian culture as one that engaged in bizarre religious and mortuary practices, and thus ancient Egypt was cast as an aberrant civilization suitable for ghoulish relish rather than as an exemplary culture demanding serious contemplation. Accordingly, the reception of Egyptian antiquities did not require the same kind of contemplation and insight that the classical antiquities required; they could be read promptly, easily, and without any prior knowledge. Furthermore, while aesthetic familiarity typically facilitated the reading of ancient art, this was not the case with the Egyptian remains. Rather, an interpretative filter was created by the museum, which made Egyptian art more legible for the less educated visitor. Thus, curiosity was a form of escapism that did not demand anything from the viewer—no special knowledge was required and no elaborate response to the antiquities was expected. Finally, the museum's initial installation on ancient Egypt was highly significant simply on account of being the first or original representation of ancient Egypt in an internationally significant public museum. Once established, this vision of ancient Egypt would be difficult to dilute or replace.

When the museum transformed itself from a vast collection of curiosities to a repository of fine antiquities collections at the beginning of the early nineteenth century, the Egyptian collection maintained its status as a source of the unusual and bizarre. However, Egyptian antiquities came to assume another identity as "colossal monstrosities": awkward because of their size, peculiar because of their unique artistic style, and monstrous because of their subject matter. The major collection of sculptures acquired in 1802 came to the museum through accident rather than as a sought-after and desired acquisition, and when transported to England and placed within the confines of the museum's new Townley Gallery, these colossal sculptures appeared like a strange intrusion in the nation's great repository of taste. Harmonious with the bright and vast desert landscapes of Egypt, the colossal sculptures looked decidedly peculiar when crammed into a dark London gallery fitted up in an architectural style more compatible with classical works. Not only were they a stark contrast to the "beautiful" examples of classical sculpture so attentively laid out in the museum's antiquities galleries, but by being forced to conform to the same display conventions established for the presentation of the classical sculptures, they were rendered somber, gloomy, and lifeless. Cast in the role of throwing the artistic achievements of classical civilization into relief, the Egyptian sculptures became an integral part of the museum's grand narrative or story of the history of art. By defining ancient Egypt in terms of its relationship to the art of ancient Greece, the museum relegated it to being a heuristic device; however, there was a paradox here in that on one hand Egyptian art was accorded a place in the evolutionary scheme for Western art, and on the other it was defined as alien and different from Western art. Thus, ancient Egypt was simultaneously appropriated as Western and dismissed as exotic. Finally, the reception of the 1808 installation suggests that visitors were greatly influenced by the image of ancient Egypt created by the displays. Celebrated as trophies of war, the Egyptian antiquities assumed an important role as political symbols, yet they were also seen as monstrous and aberrant and of little use beyond their function as entertainment.

That the Egyptian antiquities maintained their uncertain and somewhat liminal status on the fringes of what were considered respectable antiquities was evidenced by the fact that the museum's trustees were highly indifferent about purchasing the substantial collection of sculptural works offered in 1818 by Henry Salt. Displayed in the Townley Gallery in 1823, where they were incorporated into the 1808 installation, the objects from Salt's collection appeared even more exotic than ever. However, with the museum's new installation, a number of objects achieved recognition as works of art, and thus the Egyptian antiquities assumed a new incarnation as "monumental masterpieces." The acquisition of the colossal bust of Ramesses II was central to this fundamental transition in thinking, being an object that was much celebrated before its arrival in Britain. Despite the creation of this new representational layer, in which Egyptian antiquities were acknowledged to share some of the higher attributes of classical antiquities, the Egyptian collection was still not thought to be worthy of serious contemplation, and its previous definitions as wondrous curiosities and colossal monstrosities prevailed. Although some interest did exist in understanding the historical and archaeological significance of Egyptian antiquities, visitors to the museum appeared to value them more for their popular reputation and their educational role in elucidating the history of classical civilization.

With the opening of the new Smirke Sculpture Gallery in 1834 and the new Egyptian Room in 1837, the museum's collection of Egyptian antiquities finally achieved a more comprehensive and less curious appearance. The excavation of tombs in Egypt provided an array of new object types not previously available on the collectors' market, leading to the formation of the first specialist Egyptian collections. With their acquisition of such collections (e.g., those of Salt, Sams, and Anastasi), the museum facilitated the creation of a new identity for Egyptian objects as "accessible oddities." While the sculptures were still defined as curiosities and monstrosities because they were presented according to the comparative aesthetic framework set up for the presentation of the classical antiquities, the smaller items displayed in the Egyptian Room attracted widespread interest because of their familiarity as functional objects. The extensive range of domestic artifacts displayed in the new Egyptian Room was deemed to provide a unique glimpse into the Egyptian households of 3,000 years ago, and as such offered yet another interpretive dimension to the construct that was ancient Egypt. Visitors could form an image of ancient Egyptians as people not too different from themselves, and while these distant ancestors may have worshiped strange animal-like gods and carried out peculiar funerary practices, they were now seen as people who crafted practical utensils for the kitchen, built interesting furniture for their homes, and made innovative toys for their children. In contrast with the image of Egypt as a home of colossal monuments of unknown kings, the museum had created an image of Egypt that was intimate and accessible.

Significantly, however, the objects were presented in a different gallery, separated from the large works displayed downstairs in the sculpture galleries. Thus, the potential of Egyptian antiquities to be something other than curious and colossal was limited to a particular set of objects. Nonetheless, the style of display in the Egyptian Room had a dizzying effect on visitors, since the cramming of hundreds of items into cases served to emphasize their quality as awe-inspiring trinkets. Finally, the reception of the installations of 1834 and 1837 demonstrates how visitors were greatly influenced by the setting in which the Egyptian antiquities were presented. The new Greek Revival–style gallery in which the sculptures were laid out provided them with a much more appropriate scale, and accordingly, visitors responded more positively toward them. Complementing this was a vibrant enthusiasm expressed for the vast array of domestic items presented in the Egyptian Room.

The last major installation of Egyptian antiquities, which was opened in 1854, was not prompted by the acquisition of another substantial collection. Rather it reflected a steady accumulation of objects that had been more selectively purchased from auctions and offers of sales. By the mid-nineteenth century, the circumstances in which Egyptian antiquities were being acquired by the museum had drastically changed. The heyday of snatching up monumental sculptures from the entrepreneurial collectors of the first half of the century had passed, and now it was up to museum staff to take some initiative in maintaining the superb Egyptian collection that they had gained with so little effort and at virtually no cost. The last major installation analyzed in the study was the central turning point in the museum's creation of ancient Egypt, offering a vision of Egyptian antiquities that suggested they had finally been recognized as important historical documents. By displaying the collection chronologically, the museum assigned the Egyptian antiquities with a new status as objects worthy of intellectual contemplation. The greatly expanded space, central location, and elaborate setting also contributed to defining the Egyptian works as serious contenders in the antiquities realm. Despite this, however, the exhibition of 1854 was inherently a conservative one, retaining the aesthetic emphasis created at the beginning of the century and denying the Egyptian antiquities a sense of context that was distinctive to them. Finally, the reception of the installation reveals how, rather than being perceived as a two-dimensional culture, defined solely in terms of its attitudes to death and unusual artistic style, the Egyptian antiquities finally acquired their own terms of reference. Situated within a basic temporal framework, where some consideration was made of wider cultural practices and Egypt's own artistic evolution, the Egyptian antiquities no longer appeared as isolated curios.

* * *

Ancient Egypt enjoyed great popularity for what it represented rather than for what it ever actually was. Indeed, part of Egypt's appeal in terms of popular representation was the extent to which it could be appropriated for other agendas. Absorbing a multiplicity of meanings that were readily manipulated to suit museum priorities, ancient Egypt played a particularly significant role as a comparative yardstick for measuring the attainments of ancient Greece. Ancient Egyptian antiquities possessed this flexible quality because they were not intellectually owned in the way that Greek and Roman ones were—there being no recognized tradition of scholarship associated with ancient Egypt beyond the biblical one. Despite this malleability, it would be unfair to characterize Egyptian antiquities as sponges that simply took on the meanings assigned to them. These were also objects that possessed a unique ability to assert their own meanings—meanings that some struggled to articulate within the limited theoretical resources available to them.

Similarly, beyond simply revealing contemporary attitudes to Egyptian art, the installations at the museum articulated their own distinctive arguments about the significance of such objects. The power of the visual rhetoric of the displays was such that it ensured they had a lasting impact, creating an enduring image of ancient Egypt. Indeed, the acquisition, display, and reception of Egyptian antiquities at the museum worked together to create ideas of ancient Egypt that were so convincing they still survive to this day. Central to the success of these constructions was that the museum created an ancient culture that effectively had something for everyone. Defined as wondrous curiosities, colossal monstrosities, monumental masterpieces, accessible oddities, and historical documents, Egyptian antiquities satisfied the interests of many different interest groups. In addition to this, ancient Egypt combined a suite of contrasting qualities, such as formal statues of great personages, intimate encounters with dead people, and glimpses into everyday life. The power of Egyptian antiquities to satisfy different needs was fueled by the fact that even though new representations were established in association with the expansion of the collection and the creation of new gallery spaces to house it, the old images—or initial representations—were never truly abandoned. In this sense, the Egyptian antiquities had the capacity to be all things to all people; they could be awe-inspiring, entertaining, or informative, and yet at the same time they could be odd, inferior, and grotesque. Furthermore, ancient Egypt assumed a special role as an ancient culture that could be easily digested or consumed by those who did not possess the prerequisite knowledge to appreciate the works of classical antiquity. Unlike Greece and Rome, ancient Egypt was the province of the people, and museum visitors enjoyed a right of access to it that they had not felt permitted to enjoy with other ancient civilizations. More specifically, ancient Egypt did not simply function as an ideal opposite for the mighty empires of Greece and Rome, but rather, emerged as an accessible alternative for those who felt intimidated or excluded by the intellectualism associated with classical art.

From the British Museum's opening in 1759, its exhibitions of ancient Egypt made a significant contribution to shaping understandings of this ancient culture for international audiences. The powerful role that the museum assumed in constructing ancient Egypt came more as a result of accident and opportunity than it did the result of any dedicated interest in presenting ancient Egypt. Indeed, the first set of Egyptian objects to be displayed in the museum's galleries, and which played such a profound role in defining Egyptian antiquities as "wondrous curiosities," came to the museum as a somewhat insignificant part of a much wider collection of antiquities, and very little thought was put into its distribution. Similarly, the second major collection of Egyptian antiquities, which sealed their fate as "colossal monstrosities," came as war booty, rather than as a desired acquisition, and attention to its arrangement was neglected at the expense of the classical antiquities. The timing was fortuitous: by acquiring such a substantial collection of Egyptian sculptures so early in the nineteenth century, and some time before other national museums established their own Egyptological installations, the British Museum effectively created an "original" representation of ancient Egypt. The fact that ancient Egypt was of such little interest to the museum and that so little investment was made in its presentation did not mean that this interpretation had little significance or impact. To the contrary, once this had been produced, it was destined to be reproduced by others.

The museum's representation of ancient Egypt can be considered in the context of the arguments that have been made about Orientalism and antiquities. Here, the displays can be seen as serving a wider political agenda of constructing the East in terms of its opposition to the West. Egyptian antiquities were appropriated as a tool for evaluating the achievements of Western society, and in this sense they were a useful way of making sense of the present. While the use of ancient Egypt as a heuristic contrast to ancient Greece broadly corresponds with the theoretical perspective of Orientalism, the museum's representation of ancient Egypt can also be seen as constituting an Orientalist stereotyping of this culture as a symbol of alterity or as a vehicle for self-representation. For instance, Orientalist thinking constituted an effective or easy way of coming to terms with a body of ancient relics that had arrived unsolicited on the museum's doorstep. While Europeans had become increasingly familiar with visual representations of ancient Egypt since the early modern period, these had been filtered through a normalizing lens, presented according to the conventions of Western art. This same kind of mediation was not possible with the antiquities and objects from Egypt, which had their own distinctive physical presence. Thus, the "real thing" was not so malleable, and provided a confronting experience for British audiences. Furthermore, although Egyptianizing décor had been utilized to facilitate the consumption of ancient Egyptian material culture in Italy, France, Germany, and Britain itself, the British Museum refrained from easing the interpretive process in a way that recognized the objects' distinctive qualities. Rather, the Egyptian objects were quickly appropriated to serve another purpose, and for the museum they were more useful to the wider agenda of eulogizing ancient Greece if they were left unexplained and difficult to read.

The way that objects were placed when presented for viewing had an enormous impact on the meanings that were bestowed upon them. While designed to have a visual effect and thus please the viewer, displays were also intended to inform and impart messages. Seeing objects in comparative contexts was critical to receiving such messages, and thus seeing the installation as a whole and in relation to other installations was far more important than the presentation of the individual specimens in the collection. As the early modern displays were intended to instruct visitors about biological diversity, the displays of antiquities at the British Museum were designed to impart knowledge about the great civilizations of the ancient world. Without the intellectual framework of archaeology to guide the presentation of the antiquities, the museum avoided constructing a narrative or sequence that would inform visitors about the existence of distinctive cultural histories in antiquity, and rather, the displays were arranged so as to educate visitors about the rise of Western art. Thus it was in terms of an ascending trajectory of achievement in artistic expression that the antiquities came to be understood. Accordingly, the exhibition of all the collections of antique sculptures was presented as part of a wider dialogue in which ancient Egypt was reduced to being understood in terms the rise of the classical world. The notion that variation in artistic forms should be accounted for against a wider historical and social context took some time to assert itself, and by the time it did, the progressivist understandings had already been very firmly rooted.

Through its various manifestations of ancient Egypt, the museum made this ancient civilization "everybody's domain." Presented as a poor cousin to Greece and Rome rather than a distinctive cultural event in the history of humanity, ancient Egypt was characterized as not possessing any of the scholarly barriers that safeguarded the interpretation of classical art. Thus with its displays, the museum created ancient Egypt as the most consumable of all ancient cultures, conveying a sense that it was unpretentious, escapist, and easily digestible. When the museum finally recognized the significance of Egyptian antiquities it was too late to significantly change the representations that were already so powerfully entrenched in their displays. In this way, the museum created a powerful conception of ancient Egypt before a more scientific or archaeological understanding of Egyptian antiquity was formally established; and thus when research projects and scholarly works on ancient Egypt started to proliferate in the late nineteenth century, it was impossible to eradicate the images already created by the museum. The power of the museum's early exhibitions on ancient Egypt is evidenced by the fact that their legacy is maintained in current representations, and if it seems natural that we continue to express awe at the wondrous curiosities, colossal monstrosities, monumental masterpieces, and accessible oddities, this is because we are expected to—the representations have instructed us to do so.

Appendix

PERIOD DATES AND DYNASTIES

For a detailed listing of the kings of Egypt and of the dates of each dynasty see Baines and Malek (2000: 36–37).

Early Dynastic Period, c.2950–2575 BCE (Dynasties 1–3)
Old Kingdom, c.2575–2150 BCE (Dynasties 4–8)
First Intermediate Period c.2125–1975 BCE (Dynasties 9–11)
Middle Kingdom, c.1975–1640 BCE (Dynasties 11–14)
Second Intermediate Period, c.1630–1520 BCE (Dynasties 15–17)
New Kingdom, c.1539–1075 BCE (Dynasties 18–20)
Third Intermediate Period, c.1075–715 BCE (Dynasties 21–24)
Late Period, c.715–332 BCE (Dynasties 25–30)
Greco-Roman Period, c.332 BCE–395 CE

Notes

ABBREVIATIONS

MGMT = Minutes of the General Meeting of Trustees
MSCT = Minutes of the Standing Committee of Trustees
MSCA = Minutes of the Sub-Committee for Antiquities
OP = Original Papers
OR = Officers' Reports
BMDAES = British Museum, Department of Ancient Egypt and Sudan

INTRODUCTION

1. Hutton (1785: 110–115).

2. In museum studies the work of Hooper-Greenhill (1992, 1995, 2000) has been important; in sociology Macdonald (1998, 2002) has pioneered the field; in the history of science it is the work of Findlen (1994, 1998, 2000) that has best demonstrated the potential of the subject, and in archaeology the work of Merriman (1999) is central.

3. There is a growing number of works in museology that address how visitors contribute to the meaning of the displays they "consume." Typically classified as "visitor studies," the investigations of how audiences bring their own perspectives to exhibitions have evolved significantly beyond the earlier studies that focused on observing visitor behavior. It is now agreed that interviews with visitors provide a much richer and more detailed sense of how visitors play a role in meaning making (e.g., Macdonald 2002: chap. 8).

4. Wider theoretical ideas about reception as articulated by art historians were also considered. Here researchers have become increasingly interested in how audiences receive images, texts, and objects, and have moved away from questions of authorial intentionality (or production) to questions about reception (or consumption) (Bermingham 1997: 15). More recently, Bohrer (2003) has provided a useful summary of reception theory in the first chapter of his study on the nineteenth-century representation of ancient Assyria, arguing that it constitutes a complicated process whereby meaning is actively produced by the viewer.

5. It is in the research on the display of non-Western cultures that we have seen the greatest amount of discussion on the power of exhibitions to create meaning, particularly on the subject of race and cultural difference. Examples include Karp and Lavine (1991), Ames (1992), Karp, Kreamer and Lavine (1992), Coombes (1994), Kaplan (1995), Simpson (1996), Henderson and Kaeppler (1997), Lidchi (1997), Kirshenblatt-Gimblett (1998), Maxwell (1999), and McLoughlin (1999).

6. On museums and the emergence of disciplines, see, for example, Findlen (1994, 1998), Dias (1998), Bennett (1995), and Zimmerman (2001).

7. Two examples of the ethnographic approach in museum studies include Roberts (1997) and Macdonald (2002). As Macdonald (2002: 8) asserts, this type of ethnographic approach provides a "fuller account of the nature and complexities of production: of the disjunctions, disagreements and 'surprise outcomes' involved in cultural production."

8. Examples of works that have reflected on the communicative power of museum displays include Vergo (1990), Kavanagh (1991), Sherman and Rogoff (1994), Dean (1997), Moore (1997), Roberts (1997), Caulton (1998), Hein (1998), Crane (2000), and Asma (2001). The work of Hooper-Greenhill (1992, 1995, 2000) and Macdonald (1998, 2002; Macdonald and Fyfe 1996) has been especially important here.

9. At the time of this research, the Department of Egypt and Sudan did not have a separate archives section. Access to material has now been greatly improved with Dr. Patricia Usick's creation of an Archives Room.

10. A number of important studies on representation focus on palaeontological imagery, where it has been shown how dinosaur iconography has had a deeply formative influence on thinking about prehistoric times. Rudwick (1992) has produced the main study on this topic, but other historians of science, particularly Gould (1989, 1993), have written on the power of illustration in palaeontology.

11. The work of Sam Smiles (1993), Frederick Bohrer (2003), and Tim Mitchell (1988) are leading examples.

12. The primary works in this emerging field are Day (1997), Wyke (1997), Moser (1998), Finn (2004), Hines (2004), Phillips (2004), Kulik (2005), and Smiles and Moser (2005). For a list of articles on archaeological representation, see Moser (forthcoming).

13. For example, in his analysis of the representation of prehistoric animals in film, Greg Mitman (1993) accounts for the scientific community's neglect of popular culture in this kind of diffusionist model of knowledge creation. A recent study that challenges the separation of popular culture and science is Mitchell's (1998: 55) study of dinosaur imagery, where it is argued that "the dinosaur image is not, then, *simply* a popularization of scientific understanding, a mere vehicle for reporting and representing scientific knowledge," but rather, is "a key element in the process of scientific thinking and discovery as such." I have made a similar argument in relation to the illustrations of our early ancestors, where it is demonstrated that such pictures constituted theories about human evolution (Moser 1998).

14. On material culture studies, I have found the work of Kingery (1996), Pearce (1997), and Miller (1998) most useful. On museums and the representation of cultural difference, the books by Karp and Lavine (1991), Ames (1992), Coombes (1994), Simpson (1996), Henderson and Kaeppler (1997), Maxwell (1999), and McLoughlin (1999) were very helpful.

15. For example, see Mirzoeff (1998: 232), who argues that "the visual culture of colonialism had a significant role to play in both explaining and defining the colonial order"; and also Coombes (1994).

16. See, for example, Bazin (1967), Holst (1967), Scheicher (1979), Impey and MacGregor (1985), Pomian (1990), Kenseth (1991a), Bredekamp (1995), Goldthwaite (1993), Brown (1995), and Pearce (1999).

17. A major exception is Bohrer's (2003) detailed analysis of the reception of ancient Assyria in the nineteenth century. Bohrer's insights on the relationship between the archaeological remains that were exhibited in the galleries of the British Museum and artistic representations inspired by them are important because they reveal that although images were constructed in accordance with archaeological knowledge, they also functioned to satisfy the different needs of museum visitors.

18. Beard and Henderson (2001: 8–9), for instance, have argued that the history of museums and their strategies for display, of aesthetics and art theory, of archaeological discovery and academic scholarship, have "helped to determine how we see and understand the art of the ancient world." In their study of the art of Greece and Rome, they seek to strip the revered

objects of antiquity of their purity, recontextualizing them within the history of presentation and interpretation.

19. See Caygill (1992), Jenkins (1992), and Wilson (2002). In his *Museums of Influence*, Hudson (1987: 22) stated that the British Museum warranted recognition for its collections of antiquities.

20. The fact that the Egyptian objects acquired in the earlier years of the museum remain among its most celebrated objects is indicated in contemporary surveys of the museum's Egyptian collection. For example, see Francis (1971).

21. James and Davies (1996: 7), Russmann (2001: 9), Wilson (2001: 13). Wilson served as director of the museum from 1977 to 1991.

22. On the history of the Egyptian collections at the Louvre, see Duncan (1995), Porterfield (1998), and Ziegler (1990); at the Museum of Turin, see Curto (1976) and Ridley (1998); and at the Neues Museum in Berlin, see Wildung (1999).

23. While Jenkins's (1992) history of the sculpture galleries of this institution is the main work on the subject, the publications of James (1981, 2001) and Bierbrier (1988, 1993, 1999) on the history of the Egyptian collections at the museum are also very useful.

24. As Rice and MacDonald (2003: 1) argue in their volume on the consumption of Egypt, "No other ancient society evokes so many responses, at so many levels, as Ancient Egypt." Meskell (2004: chap. 7) has also elaborated on ancient Egypt's enduring appeal, arguing that it continues to exude a powerful aura in the present. This auratic appeal, she argues, stems from the distance of ancient Egypt in temporal and spatial terms, its perceived cultural difference, and its ever prevailing mysteriousness.

25. On the European consumption of ancient Egypt in the classical, medieval, and Renaissance periods, see Curl (1994), Dannenfeldt (1959), and Curran (2003, 2004, forthcoming). Recent research by El Daly (2005) has demonstrated the Arabic interest in the ancient past from the seventh to the sixteenth centuries.

26. General accounts of the seventeenth- and eighteenth-century interest in representing ancient Egypt can be found in Greener (1966), Clayton (1982), Whitehouse (1992, 1995), Iversen (1993 [1961]), James (1997), David (2000), Starkey and Starkey (2001), Siliotti (1998), and Wolff (2003).

27. On the emergence of an Egyptian style in art and architecture, see Honour (1955); Pevsner and Lang (1956), Johnson (1966), Wittkower (1975), Carrot (1978), Conner (1983), Humbert (1989), Curl (1994), and Humbert et al. (1994).

28. On the impact of Napoleon's campaign, see Moore (2002). As Humbert (1994: 25) has argued, "Egyptomania moulds itself effortlessly to the art of the day and remains relatively unaffected by new archaeological findings or developments in Egyptology, unlike the ancient cultures of China, Japan, India or Greece and Rome, which have not been as laden with messages."

29. On the representation of ancient Egypt in nineteenth-century photography, see Armstrong (1998), Evans (2000), and Nickel (2004); in nineteenth-century writing, see Montserrat (2000a) and Barrell (1991); in nineteenth-century filmmaking, see Lant (1992); and in the nineteenth-century British press, see Warner (1994). There has even been a trend in creating exhibitions on Egyptomania. For example, see exhibition catalogues by Conner (1983), Brier (1992), Humbert et al. (1994), Evans (2000), and Montserrat (2000b). Furthermore, a number of art historians have also begun to reappraise the representation of ancient Egypt in light of research in postcolonial studies. Armstrong (1998), for instance, discusses how the photographs that Francis Frith took of the monuments in the mid-nineteenth century endorsed social Darwinism by making constant comparisons between the people of Egypt and the great nations of Europe. She also demonstrates how the emphasis on monuments as natural wonders, and the treatment of people in the photographs as accessories rather than potential creators of such objects, ensured that ancient Egyptian antiquities became naturalized and completely divorced

from the people of modern Egypt. Finally, while earlier studies on the fashion of using Egyptian motifs in late eighteenth and early nineteenth-century design tended to avoid situating this practice in a wider social and political context, more recent studies have shown how the use of Egyptian style was a specific strategy designed to reinforce the power and control of the aristocracy (e.g., Moore 2002).

30. See Hornung (2001) on the appropriation of ancient Egypt by esoteric movements.

31. For example, David (2000) has attributed the opinions and beliefs of Egyptologists as having a place in the understanding of the subject. Notable exceptions, however, include the research on the colonial construction of Egypt undertaken by Mitchell (1988), Reid's (2001) work on the impact of the Western construction of ancient Egypt upon Egyptians, and Montserrat's (2000a) analysis of the European appropriation of Akhenaton. While both Mitchell and Reid have demonstrated how the nineteenth-century idea of Egypt was constructed not just in Oriental studies and colonial administrations, but in the many ways Europe began to represent the world, including museums, worlds fairs, architecture, schooling, tourism, fashion, and the commodification of everyday life, Montserrat examines the continuing dialogue that exists between past and present manifestations of ancient Egypt as seen in the range of Amarna-inspired modern cultural artifacts. Of particular interest is his detailed account of the way Akhenaton was consumed by fiction writers in the early twentieth century, as it demonstrates the specific ways in which the West has "internalized ancient Egypt and made it its own" (Montserrat 2000a: 10).

32. The recent series of publications on the representation of Egypt, based on a conference at the University College London, suggest that this trend is beginning to change (e.g., Macdonald and Rice 2003; Ucko and Champion 2003). Furthermore, researchers like Hassan (1998), Roth (1998), Meskell (1998, 2003, 2004), and Montserrat (2000a) have shown the potential of theoretically informed analyses of the representation of ancient Egypt.

33. Even today the sculpture collection is still recognized as the "most striking element" of the museum's Egyptian collection (Wilson 2001: 59).

34. This phase was characterized by the introduction of more systematic methods of excavation and new approaches to the treatment of sites. The first chair in Egyptology was created at University College London in 1892, with the pioneering archaeologist Flinders Petrie taking this post. See Wortham (1971) on the emergence of a community of British scholars dedicated to advancing the field of Egyptology.

35. On the history of the Egypt Exploration Fund, later Society, see James (1982).

36. On the contribution of the Metropolitan, see Howe (1913, 1946) and Tomkins (1970).

37. Under its first director, Auguste Mariette, the Egyptian Antiquities Service demanded that all new discoveries be submitted to them and export licenses were required for the removal of objects. For a history of the Cairo Museum, see Tiradritti (1999), and for a detailed account of the formation of both the museum and the Antiquities Service, see Reid (2001: chap. 3).

38. See, for example, the work of Lawrence Alma-Tadema and Edwin Long.

CHAPTER ONE

1. This phrase is taken from the frontispiece of the catalogue for Francesco Calceolari's collection in Verona, 1622.

2. Accounts of these early collections can be found in Murray (2000 [1904]), Schlosser (1978 [1908]), Taylor (1948), Bazin (1967), Holst (1967), Balsiger (1970), Scheicher (1979), Rheims (1981), Lugli (1983, 1997), Impey and MacGregor (1985), Schnapper (1988), Pomian (1990), Kenseth (1991a), Olmi (1992), Bredekamp (1995), Goldthwaite (1993), Findlen (1994), Grote (1994), Pearce (1995), Brown (1995), Daston and Park (1998), Swann (2001), and Mauries (2002).

3. On the connection between the proliferation of collections and the rise of consumerism, see Belk (1995). On the rise of consumerism and the desire for objects, see Mukerji (1983), Brewer and Porter (1993), Jardine (1996), and Bermingham and Brewer (1997).

4. Mullaney (1983) discusses the connection between collecting and the court masques and royal entries.

5. While Kemp (1985: 17) describes these creations as "cultural migrators," Daston and Park (1998: 296) describe them as "heuristics for imagining how nature and art might in theoretical and practical ways be bridged."

6. As Pomian (1990: 64) has noted, there was a taming of curiosity as a result of the formation of scholarly communities.

7. As Bedini (1986: 258) suggests, Italy's lead in collecting objects reflected the role that its missionaries played in bringing back items from their travels. On the central role of Italy in establishing encyclopedic collections, see Pomian (1990), Olmi (1985, 1992, 1993), Laurencich Minelli (1985), and Findlen (1994, 1998, 2000).

8. Daston and Park (1998: 74).

9. On the origins of the taste for "the marvelous," see Kenseth (1991b).

10. On the link between collecting and the rise of natural history and natural philosophy, see Olmi (1992), Findlen (1994), and Daston and Park (1998); on the role of collecting in the establishment of art history, see Bazin (1967), Holst (1967), Goldthwaite (1993), Haskell (1993), and Brown (1995); on the relationship between collecting and the beginnings of anthropology, see Shelton (1994), and Bassani (2000).

11. As Grafton and Jardine (1986: 220) have shown, collections were used to demonstrate one's moral and intellectual caliber and thus one's ability to contribute to the community. Related to this is the significance of collecting for self-fashioning, a concept articulated by researchers in their discussions of how individuals related to material things in the sixteenth and seventeenth centuries (e.g., see Tribby 1992; Swann 2001). Here it has been shown that collections were a central part of identity formation in early modern Europe and that they must be seen in the context of the aspiring courtiers who were promoting themselves. For instance, Tribby (1992: 140) refers to the significance of collections as a "mode of comportment" or an extension of the body; he also argues that the courtier's body itself became a vehicle of social meaning and thus it was not just the collection that was on display but the individual as well. Daston and Park (1998: 158) reinforce this point, stating that collections were aimed to "transfer the emotion of wonder from the objects themselves to their erudite and discriminating owner."

12. On the rise of humanist scholarship, see Grafton and Jardine (1986).

13. Schulz (1990) emphasizes the importance of Pliny's work in the history of scientific collections.

14. As Daston and Park (1998: 273) have observed, the princely "wonder cabinets" were not created to generate an inquiring response, but rather one of awe.

15. Olmi (1993: 254).

16. The work of Olmi (1985, 1992, 1993) and Findlen (1994) has been central in documenting this process.

17. As Pomian (1990: 50) notes, the aim of the illustrations was not so much to create a faithful portrait of a particular room on a particular date but rather to convey the very essence of such a room. The illustrations also functioned as a form of advertising, reflecting how collectors were opening their displays up to a wider audience. As Findlen (1998: 117) argues, these images revealed the trend toward openness, sociability, and publicity.

18. The focus here is on the illustrations of the displays as opposed to descriptions of the contents of the collections, so the contributions of important early scientific collectors, particularly Ulisse Aldrovandi (1522–1605) are not discussed because there are no remaining representations of their "museums." Olmi (1978, 1985), Findlen (1994), and Daston and Park (1998) have outlined Aldrovandi's central role in the establishment of the encyclopedic collections.

19. See Accordi (1981) on the geological component of Imperato's collection and his contribution to this nascent field.

20. Kenseth (1991a: 235).

21. *Artificialia* represented fire in the sense that they were often made through the process of burning, e.g., pottery.

22. Findlen (2000) discusses how early collections were created in the home as part of a study and that they were then transformed into museums.

23. Kenseth (1991a: 234) notes that this display stood in contrast to many other collections of the time because there were so few items of *artificialia.*

24. On the subject of the gestures of the figures, Findlen (1994: 117) refers to two civil gestures that mark the action of the museum: the arm of Imperato's son Francesco, which directs the gaze of the visitors, and the hand of the middle gentleman that registers his response to seeing such marvels.

25. As Wittlin (1970: 60) has observed, there were displays that represented monologues and those that represented dialogues. While the former refers to the "storeroom" style of presentation, where the collectors selected pieces from storage and placed them on view in their living quarters, the latter was the "study style," where objects stood in closed ranks on shelves.

26. Crocodiles are known to have been hung in medieval churches, and the practice of hanging other large creatures such as sharks in royal collections has also been documented (e.g., the collection of the Archduke Ferdinand II at Ambras Castle.) For illustrations of such displays, see Scheicher (1985), and Daston and Park (1998).

27. This point has also been made by Balsiger (1970: 515) about Besler's display.

28. Such rooms were typically included in the palaces of the royalty for the entertainment of the princes and their friends. A major example was Francesco I de' Medici's *studiolo* in the Palazzo Vecchio in Florence, c.1570–1575. Liebenwein (1977) provides an account of the development of this particular room type.

29. This illustration is featured in the second of two catalogues of the collection. The first catalogue was compiled by the physician Giovanni Battista Olivi in 1584. The second one was produced after Calceolari had died and his nephew had added to the collection.

30. Calceolari was known to have excelled in preparing prescriptions, and his collection was highly regarded as a medical collection (Accordi 1977: 21).

31. While the emphasis on symmetry in this illustration may be more a convention of the representation than a reflection of reality, it can be assumed that a sense of symmetry was a distinguishing feature of the collection.

32. For example, the placement of the puffer fish in a similar position in both displays is striking.

33. In Kenseth (1991a: 238) it is suggested that Calceolari's collection may have been partly modeled after Imperato's.

34. Accordi (1977: 39).

35. The illustration of an Egyptian stela with hieroglyphs appears to be the only antiquity amid the many other illustrations of zoological and geological specimens (Ceruto and Chiocco 1622: 292). Stelae are stone or wooden slabs that were used in a funerary context or set up in temples to commemorate events or to make proclamations.

36. In Kenseth (1991a: 237) it is noted that Francesco the Younger added arms, armor, lighting devices, statuary, Egyptian artifacts, and ancient inscriptions to the collection.

37. The text which is placed above the image reads "Spectator ocvlos inserito calceolari mvsaei admiranda contemplator et volvp animo tvo facito."

38. This manner of arrangement has been described as "alternating microsymmetry" (see n. 39 below) by Laurencich Minelli (1985), who also identifies it in other collections of the time. Examining the inventories of collectors such as Antonio Giganti (1535–1598) in Bologna, Laurencich Minelli defines the display model of *theatrum naturae*, where every space was filled, where no distinction was made between *naturalia* and *artificialia*, and where the objective was to convey a sense of symmetry.

39. Laurencich Minelli (1985: 19) defines these as an "alternating microsymmetry," where

similar items were not displayed alongside each other, but rather were alternated with different kinds of objects; and a "repeating macrosymmetry," where groups of objects were arranged thematically, usually those from a similar category.

40. Worm had begun to form his collection in his house around 1620.

41. Whether this was an artificial device used to introduce the catalogue and was not a real feature of the museum is not clear.

42. Besler's research on botany was based on his role as superintendent of the bishop of Eichstätt's garden in Bavaria (Kenseth 1991a: 236).

43. It is not possible to determine whether these items were placed on the floor for the sake of the picture, or whether they were a permanent part of the display; however it seems likely that the best specimens were given a prime position in the picture even if they were usually situated elsewhere in the room.

44. A geode is a rock with a cavity that is lined with crystals or other mineral matter.

45. The presence of such material in Worm's collection reflected how increasing travel in the seventeenth century had enabled early scientists to more readily obtain ethnographic materials, particularly those from South America, Asia, and Africa.

46. Besler's catalogue is dominated by the large and beautifully engraved pictures of virtually all the specimens featured in the display.

47. Worm's catalogue is structured according to sections on minerals, vegetables, animals, and ethnographic and archaeological material. The latter section was testimony to his classificatory work on antiquities and pioneering role in the development of Nordic archaeology. For example, in 1643 Worm published the major work on Danish antiquities *Danicorum Monumentorum Libri Sex*. Furthermore, histories of archaeology have highlighted Worm's role in the emergence of prehistoric archaeology as a discipline (e.g., Schnapp 1996: 160–165).

48. For a detailed discussion of Worm's museum, see Schepelern (1985, 1990), who has matched the objects held in the collection with those featured in the engraving.

49. However, that some sense of aesthetic arrangement was adopted can be seen in Worm's display, where the spears, implements, and large lizards featured on the wall are laid out in contrasting horizontal and vertical patterns.

50. Building upon his father's collection, Settala established a museum of great fame that was characterized by its substantial size and unique contents (Aimi et al. 1985: 26). These qualities are identifiable in the illustration, which represents only one of the four rooms that comprised Settala's collection.

51. For example, Olmi (1985: 13–15) has argued that displays like Settala's and Cospi's were not centers of research and that they represented a retrogression when compared to those of the sixteenth-century naturalists. Similarly, Schlosser (1978 [1908]: 204–207) defines Settala's and Cospi's collections as curiosity cabinets rather than reference collections. That Cospi's collection functioned more as a symbol of the courtier's status than as a vehicle for professional study is suggested by the absence of stored and labeled specimens like those in Besler's and Worm's displays.

52. Aimi et al. (1985: 27) state that there are a large number of items on display that are not in accordance with the catalogue, and thus it "should be regarded as a stylized arrangement rather than a realistic disposition of the objects." However, while there are no labels to assist with identifying the contents on display, we are still able to obtain a basic idea of how the collection was laid out.

53. Kenseth (1991a: 240).

54. The illustration reveals Cospi's interest in ethnographic materials and archaeological objects, particularly Egyptian, Etruscan, and Roman artifacts. Featured among the illustrations in the catalogue are a garment from Greenland, South American objects, Greco-Roman figurines, and Egyptian shabtis.

55. As Findlen (1994: 119) notes, with his gesture Cospi "invites other patricians to achieve

what he already has accomplished; mastery of nature, appreciation of culture, social prestige, and potential immortality." Tribby (1992: 155) argues that this stylized stance reflects the order Cospi imposed on the objects.

56. Here it is possible to see what Pearce (1995: 109) has identified as a shift from the notion of representing the cosmos to representing repeated patterns as reflected in material culture.

57. The collection was formed in 1651. As Accordi (1976: 113) notes, Kircher's museum was one of the most famous in the world at this time.

58. As miniature representations of the obelisks that Kircher helped restore in Rome for various popes and cardinals, these objects featured in detail in the catalogue of the collection, where there are ten large, detailed folio engravings of them. Findlen (1998: 86) sees the obelisks as embodying Kircher's success in decoding Egyptian hieroglyphs.

59. Quiccheberg was the administrator of the ducal art collections in Munich, and his work was based on his knowledge of the collection of his patron, the Duke Albrecht V of Bavaria. For a brief discussion of the rationale behind his plan, see Kenseth (1991a: 84–85).

60. Wittlin (1970: 64).

61. Mullaney (1983: 86), for example, states that "no system determines the organization of the objects on display or separates one variety of the marvellous from another"; in Kenseth (1991a: 235), Imperato's installation is described as disorderly and "confused" as a result of lack of exhibition space; and Swann (2001: 29) describes the arrangements depicted in seventeenth-century engravings as "hodgepodge."

62. As Pomian (1990: 49) notes, the displays reveal the "desire to miniaturize the constituent parts of the world in such a way as to allow the eye to take them all in at the same time, without losing any of their most intimate features."

63. As Schulz (1994: 186) has commented, the collections of the 1600s were not "indiscriminate medleys born of a purely encyclopaedic zeal for collecting, or out of mere pleasure in oddities of a passion for representation. They were formed according to values based upon the scientific knowledge of the time."

CHAPTER TWO

1. Details of Sir Hans Sloane and his collection can be found in Wilson (2002: 11–21); see also MacGregor (1994a).

2. On the history of the foundation of the British Museum, see Edwards (1870), Crook (1972), De Beer (1953), Miller (1973), Caygill (1992, 2003), Caygill and Date (1999), and Wilson (2002). Although never published, Sir Edward Maunde Thompson's history of the museum offers useful insights into matters of finance and management not covered in other works (BL Add. MS 52292).

3. As general meetings of the trustees were held only four times a year, the main business of the museum was conducted at the meetings of the Standing Committee of Trustees, which included three principal trustees, a trustee appointed by the Crown, and sixteen other trustees appointed annually. Subcommittees, which included up to nine trustees, were appointed by the Standing Committee to deal with specific issues. For a list of the trustees, see Wilson (2002: 21, note 64).

4. Access to the museum required a ticket, which could be collected from the museum porter. Once details had been provided, including name and address, the ticket was submitted to the principal librarian for approval. After picking up the ticket, visitors were entitled to visit the museum in parties of five. These visits were controlled by a guide (one of the museum's officers) who kept them limited to two hours. *Statues and Rules Relating to the Inspection and Use of the British Museum* 1759: 9.

5. Cash (1992) has discussed the restricted nature of public access to the collections from 1753 to 1836. Government criticism of how the museum treated its visitors can be found in the

papers of the select committee enquiries of the nineteenth century; the media reports on public access can be found in many of the leading papers of the day. See chapter 5.

6. Reported in the list of Sloane's collection given to his executors in 1753. Reproduced in MacGregor (1994a: 29).

7. A document listing the Egyptian items from the Sloane collection includes the following categories of artifact: "Figures of Metal," "Scarabei," "Periaptae," "Ingravings," "Single Figures of Terra Cotta," "Two or more figures," "Bustos and heads of Clay or Terracotta," "Basso Relievos," "Ægyptian figures of Earth or Stone," "Models of Mummies," and "Urns." BMDAES, "The catalogue of Ægyptian Antiquitys from Sloane." This list reveals that the largest category of objects was the metal figures at forty-seven in total, with thirty-seven shabtis, fifteen scarabs, and sixteen terracotta figures following this. These figures may not be entirely accurate, as it is possible that not all the items on this list are from the Sloane collection. For instance, the "from Sloane" part of the title of the document is in different writing, suggesting that it may have been added later. It is thus possible that the list represents the first attempt to produce a catalogue of the Egyptian antiquities. Further details on the Egyptian items in Sloane's collection and where he obtained them from can be found in Bierbrier (1993) and MacGregor (1994b).

8. On the antiquities acquired from Gualtieri's collection, see Fileri (2002). Jenkins (1994: 167) notes that the Sloane collection of antiquities was small until the 1730s, when he acquired the "dross" of Cardinal Gualtieri's collection from Rome and other items from the Roman dealer Abbé Sterbini. Sloane acquired antiquities from Kemp's collection at a sale of 1721. Sandys traveled to Egypt in 1611, returning home with a number of antiquities, as did the Earl of Sandwich, who went there in 1736. MacGregor (1994b: 177) suggests that the mummy in Sloane's collection may have been acquired as part of the collection of John Kemp. On the major antiquities collectors and dealers in Britain in the eighteenth century, see Scott (2003: chap. 2).

9. Lethieullier made this donation in his will of July 23, 1755. Here he stated that "I give to the Public Museum at Mountagu House my Egyptian Mummy, with everything thereunto appertaining; with the rest of my Egyptian antiquities." MGMT, February 20, 1756: 83. This mummy and the other items left to the museum are listed in a museum document from 1756; included on the list are "the skull of a mummy," "two feet and a hand, seemingly of a mummy," "two scarabei, a ring, two small horses heads," an "earthen urn," and five "small brass images." BMDAES, "The Bequest of Colonel William Lethieullier . . . 1756." The inner coffin of Lethieullier's mummy is that of Irtyru from Memphis, Twenty-sixth Dynasty (EA 6695). One of the brass images was the figure of Osiris featured on the left in figure 2.5.

10. A museum document reports that the mummy was found "in its coffin amongst the antient catacombs, about three leagues from Cairo, in the year 1721." BMDAES, "The Bequest of Colonel William Lethieullier . . . 1756." Lethieullier acquired this mummy at a time when travel to Egypt was rare; that his trip was unusual is indicated by the fact that it was reported upon in the British press (Black 1999: 72). Gordon's 1737 discussion of the Lethieullier mummy was published in the context of his investigations into the hieroglyphics on a series of mummy cases. The essay was accompanied by twenty-five plates featuring other notable mummies in Europe; the Lethieullier mummies are featured in plates 11 and 12.

11. MGMT, February 20, 1756: 83–84; *Gentleman's Magazine* 1756 (26): 145.

12. In 1756 Pitt Lethieullier donated a "mummy in its original sycamore coffin with the hieroglyphical paintings placed over its breast and leggs [*sic*], and the masque for covering of the face"; an antique bronze Aelurus on a pedestal; a bronze Harpocrates on a pedestal; a bronze ox head representing Osiris; and "other of the icunculae as belonged to Mr. Pitt Lethieullier." These were said to be mixed with a number of William Lethieullier's objects, including an ancient marble term and an ancient marble bust; both which were brought from Egypt by the colonel. MSCT, February 27, 1756: 67–68. In 1758 Smart Lethieullier (an antiquary and trustee) donated "a small box made of the same sycamore as the Egyptian coffins" and two figures.

BMDAES, "The Bequest of Colonel William Lethieullier . . ." 1756. A more detailed discussion of the Lethieullier donations to the museum can be found in Bierbrier (1988).

13. The Egyptian Society was founded in 1741 and became defunct in 1743. Founding members included John Montagu, Earl of Sandwich, Charles Perry, Richard Pococke, and Frederick Norden, all who had traveled in Egypt. See Dawson (1937) for a brief history and account of the society.

14. The inventory numbers for these are: the slabs, EA 22, EA 20; the limestone relief (which depicts the ritual slaying and dismemberment of four oxen), EA 430; the sphinx, EA 115; the mummy, EA 6696; the coffin, EA 6693; the figure of Pa-sr, EA 510.

15. The sculpture is a statue of the priest Henat (EA 134).

16. Quirke (1997) has identified the majority of these objects, noting how the collection was unusual compared to other collections featuring Egyptian antiquities because it was primarily restricted to scarabs. Hamilton was the British ambassador in Naples and his collection was purchased for £8,410. See Jenkins and Sloan (1996) for a description of this collection.

17. The stelae are numbered EA 36255, EA 60961.

18. See Wilson (2002: 45–48) on the significance of Hamilton's collection for the development of the museum.

19. The first obelisk was transported to Rome in 10 BC. With regard to the other antiquities that were collected by the Romans, Ziegler (1994: 18) notes that the works from the Late Period were most popular, with those from the Old Kingdom and Middle Kingdom being less sought after. Furthermore, among representations of the gods, animals were preferred, especially falcons and monkeys. That Late Period sculptures were popular reflects the fact that they were more easily acquired than objects from earlier periods; i.e., they were often lying exposed in sites and did not need to be excavated, as did objects from earlier periods. On the Romans' interest in acquiring ancient Egyptian monuments, see Rouellet (1972), and Pantazzi (1994: 38), who refers to the construction of an Egyptian pavilion constructed by Hadrian or Aurelian, where a number of Egyptian statues were displayed.

20. *Mummia* was a powder or the bitumen used for embalming the mummy. On the history of mummy consumption, see Aufrère (1990) and Pringle (2001).

21. Johann Georg Herwart van Hohenburg published the first major collection of Egyptian antiquities in 1607–1611, and, soon after, Egyptian antiquities started to appear in the European collections of Nicolas-Claude Fabri de Peiresc, Lodovico Settala and Athanasius Kircher. Van Hohenburg's work *Thesaurus Hieroglyphicorum* is characterized by its reproductions of inscriptions on monuments. While Settala acquired his Egyptian antiquities in Italy, the French antiquarian Nicolas-Claude Fabri de Peiresc (1580–1637) sent an agent, the Franciscan friar Theophilus Minutus, to Egypt around 1630 to collect antiquities for his museum at Aix-en-Provence. It was Minutus who obtained the two mummies that went to Kircher's collection. On Peiresc's interest in ancient Egypt, see Aufrère (1990).

22. A major example was the Villa of Cardinal Alessandro Albani in Rome, created around 1750–1760 (see Pantazzi 1994: 39).

23. Curran (2004) has demonstrated how the monuments in various locations around Rome took on a papal and Medicean meaning. More specifically, the sphinx and Egyptian lion were adopted by Pope Leo X (1513–1521) as Egyptianizing variations on his leonine emblem.

24. For instance, an Egyptian sarcophagus was included in the catalogue of Paul Petau, *Antiquariae supellectilis portiuncula*, 1612; numerous shabtis and figurines were included in Legati's catalogue of Ferdinando Cospi's collection, 1677; and detailed illustrations of obelisks were featured in Athanasius Kircher's catalogue of 1678. Kircher's more detailed work on obelisks appeared in his four volumes of *Oedipus Aegyptiacus* of 1652–1654.

25. The Egyptian objects in the University of Leiden collection included shabtis, a canopic jar, mummy cases, and a mummy, all which were donated by David le Leu de Wilhem in 1619 (MacGregor 1994b: 174). See also Schupbach (2001 [1985]: 232–233).

26. As MacGregor (1994b: 177) remarks, Sloane's "marked degree of bulk-buying seems accurately to reflect the unfocused and undiscriminating character of Sloane's Egyptology interests, suggesting little more than a conscious attempt to boost an underdeveloped facet of an otherwise well-rounded collection." James (1981: 4) also comments on Sloane's lack of strategy in acquiring Egyptian pieces.

27. Scott (2003: 38, 36).

28. Gordon was a member of the Egyptian Society who illustrated the Egyptian objects in the possession of twelve British collectors, including Hans Sloane, William Lethieullier, and Richard Mead. His illustrations of objects held in these collections can be found in the British Library edition of his 1737 work (shelfmark 146.1.2). The Sackler edition (Oxford), and the British Museum edition (Department of Ancient Egypt and Sudan) provide figures of the mummies held in various collections.

29. For example, George Sandys (1615: 133) brought back a number of antiquities that were incorporated into the collection of John Tradescant (and then later in the Ashmolean Museum), and Richard Pococke (1743: plate 76) gave a number of antiquities to the Duke of Richmond.

30. According to Kenseth (1991b: 40–53), items that were wondrous and marvelous had one of eight characteristics—they were novel/rare, foreign/exotic, strange/bizarre, unusually large/small, demonstrated supreme technical skill, exhibited vividness and verisimilitude, were transcendent and sublime, or were surprising/unexpected. In the matter of size, it was the miniature characteristics of some of the figurines that collectors found appealing.

31. Curran (2003: 126).

32. Peiresc's mummies were obtained by his agent in Egypt (see Aufrère 1990); the mummy in Leiden was obtained from David le Leu de Wilhem in 1619 and donated to the university in 1620 (MacGregor 1994b: 174).

33. The appearance of antiquities in early modern collections occurred in association with a number of developments, including the rise of humanist scholarship, the excavation of sites in Italy, the emergence of the earth sciences, and travel to Africa and the Middle East. Archaeological objects were particularly desirable if they were connected to a historical event or story. Crane (2000: 72) emphasizes the importance of stories in the history of collecting, showing how the desirability of objects reflected their link with a known or accepted story.

34. Montfauçon (1719–1724); Caylus (1752–1757). Caylus is recognized as the first major antiquarian to accord Egyptian antiquities a place in the development of art (Iversen 1993 [1961]: 106).

35. See Olmi (1993: 244–247), who discusses the affinities between the methodological approaches of scholars interested in the history of humanity and those interested in the history of nature.

36. For example, Aldrovandi in his *Musaeum metallicum* of 1648 classed stone points with *glossopetrae* or tongue stones, which were sharks' teeth.

37. Rudwick (1972) has documented the interpretation of fossils in the early modern period.

38. On the presence of ethnographic items in early collections, see Pomian (1990: 36), Shelton (1994), and Bassani (2000). The majority of ethnographic items in Renaissance collections were a result of travel in Africa, the Americas, and Asia. Such items were collected because of their ability to signify what was invisible to most Europeans—exotic lands and strange peoples. The hunger for acquiring unique, strange, and marvelous items was increasingly satisfied by exploration of the New World, and later the Pacific.

39. Quirke (1997: 260) has noted the omission of objects like shabti boxes and texts (on papyri and linen), raising the issue of what this tells us about the collecting practices of the time.

40. In his account of antiquities collecting in eighteenth-century Britain, Scott (2003: vi) excludes consideration of Egyptian objects because the British collectors of the time "bought their scarabs and mummies as mere curios."

41. "A Plan for the General Distribution of Sir Hans Sloane's Collection." OP, August 29, 1756. As an executor of Sloane's will, Empson was responsible for communicating Sloane's wishes on the future arrangement of his collection to the trustees. In 1758 Empson was appointed as head of the museum's Department of Natural and Artificial Productions.

42. Ibid., 40.

43. Ibid., January 14, 1757: 51.

44. Linnaeus was the Swedish botanist who is widely known as the father of taxonomy.

45. "A Plan for the General Distribution of Sir Hans Sloane's Collection." OP, August 29, 1756: 40.

46. Ibid., 46.

47. "We must add, that, as these Curiosities will not cover the Inside of the Shelves in the Manner as Books so, it may not be improper, in Order to set them off the better, to have the Inside of the Repositories and the Shelves painted with a whitish or any other light color." Ibid.

48. Hamilton was very active in museum affairs, serving as a trustee from 1783 until 1803. His ideas on the importance of light are conveyed in the museum's *Original Papers* of 1772: "Sir William Hamilton having examined with Dr. Maty the room which he thought the properest for the reception of his collection of antiquities, desired that the Saloon, and the Southroom adjoining to it, which I call the Antechamber, might be appropriated for that use; the first being made to contain the tables, and the other the presses required for the reception of the several parts of his collection. The want of a sufficient light for the inspection of several pieces, determined Sir William's choice with respect to the antechamber, as the sides of the Saloon were judged by him too dark for that purpose, and would become so much more by the tables that are to stand in it." Regarding Hamilton's ideas on furniture: "Five tables are intended to be placed round about the Saloon, and one in the middle, in the position and of the dimensions marked in the plan delivered in by Mr. Keene. They are to be of Mahogany, but without any carving or useless ornament. It is necessary that they should be covered with glass frames, made as light as possible, in order that the things contained in them may be seen on all sides, and to the greatest advantage. The presses in the Antechamber are likewise proposed to be made of mahogany, with glass doors." OP, April 9, 1772: 275–276.

49. "Proposal for the Establishment of the British Museum," n.d., Papers Relating to the British Museum, 1753–1760: 82–85, BM Add. MS 4449, f.82.

50. Ibid.

51. Ibid., 89–92, f.89.

52. "Proposal for the Removal of the Sloanian Books and the Natural and Artificial Curiosities, the Cottonian Library, Mr. Edwards's Books, And the Harleian Manuscripts, And for Assigning the Rooms proper for the present Collections and where Each Collection may be Ranged and placed . . . ," n.d, Papers Relating to the British Museum 1753–1760: 86–88, BM Add. MS 4449, f.86.

53. It is difficult to ascertain how the Egyptian antiquities were originally arranged in the museum, as there are no illustrations of what the displays looked like from this early period. Although the verbal descriptions in early guidebooks and museum documents vary, a basic idea of how the objects were presented can be inferred from these sources. Of these, the article entitled "Description of the British Museum, with a General Account of the Collection, the Manner of Seeing It, the Contents of Each Room, and the Order in Which They Are Shewn.," from the *Imperial Magazine* 1760: 689–695, is most useful because it provides an accompanying plan.

54. Thomson (1767: 6). These "pieces of greenish marble" were the stelae sent from Egypt by Wortley Montagu, including the slab of Nectanebo (EA 22) and the slab of Psamtek (EA 20). The "mausoleum of Cleopatra" appears to be the site of the ancient museum in Alexandria. In 1778 it was ordered that the two "Egyptian Basaltine Inscriptions" be moved into the base story of the museum, but in 1780 it was ordered that they be moved to the platform before the main door of the museum. MSCT, April 10, 1778: 1611; November 24, 1780: 1744.

55. Wendeborn (1791: 318). These were probably the coffins donated by the Earl of Bute via Edward Wortley Montagu.

56. Ibid. Also displayed in the hall were three large bustoes "seemingly designed to express Cheerfulness and Abundance," "several curious pebbles, flints, and two ancient heads," two fragments of granite columns, and a "great number and variety of ancient epitaphs and inscriptions in Latin, Greek, and other languages." Anon. (n.d. [c.1760]: 5).

57. These were thought to be those of two adults, a child of seven or eight, and an infant (Thomson 1767: 12).

58. Powlett (1761: 6).

59. BMDAES, "The Bequest of Colonel William Lethieullier . . . ," 1756.

60. This suggestion is made in the Reverend Weeden Butler's play about the museum, where the character named Index refers to the mummy case and states, "Pray Dr. G_d turn it round," and then the character Elizala refers Dr. G_d to the spring handle. British Library Add. MS 27276, f.11–12.

61. Powlett (1761: 8). Anon. (n.d. [c.1760]: 12) states that these idols were placed in a row above the head.

62. Powlett (1761: 9). The "models of mummies" were probably shabtis. Anon. (n.d. [c.1760]: 12) provides a slightly different account, stating that the "urn was laid in a wooden case, next to the coffins of the deceased. The urn's case is in the opposite corner, over the coffin, and next by are the models of the mummies, which were likewise placed by the coffin."

63. In 1794 the trustees permitted the physician John Frederick Blumenbach to open the three small mummies then existing in the museum's collection (one from Sloane's collection and two that were acquired in 1772 as part of Hamilton's collection). Upon opening Sloane's miniature mummy—11 $\frac{6}{10}$ inches in length—Blumenbach (1794: 180) reported that "although when viewed externally nothing appeared suspicious in this little mummy, I found, however, on examining the successive integuments, that the outward ones had some traces of our common *lint paper*, with which it seemed to have been *restored*, and afterwards painted over."

64. A description of the contents of this room provided by the museum reports that quadrupeds, birds, their eggs and nests, insects and their nests and eggs, dried fishes, vipers and serpents, crustacea or crabs, and shells were displayed. OP, August 29, 1756: 44.

65. Powlett (1761: 11); the reference to the sea fan and feather is from Anon. (n.d. [c.1760]: 13), and the reference to the jay comes from Harrison (1775: 395).

66. In addition to the Sloane antiquities, this room included the collections donated by Thomas Hollis and the Lethieullier family. OP, August 29, 1756: 44. Thomas Hollis donated a substantial collection of Roman antiquities to the museum in 1757. MGMT, March 19, 1757: 158–159.

67. Chamberlain (1770: 343). The "ceramic figures" were glazed composition or faience.

68. Powlett (1761: 20); Thomson (1767: 21).

69. Harrison (1775: 396); the reference to the stone lion and sphinx come from Thomson (1767: 21). Harrison's guide appears to be copied from Powlett's description, but has some other details added. The bas-relief is probably EA 22 and suggests that this may have been moved from its original place under the colonnade of the museum to the first exhibition room. The "oblong-pieces of enamelled earth" were djed pillars, later described as Nilometers.

70. Sarrett (1803–1804: 172).

71. Chamberlain (1770: 345).

72. Malcolm (1803: 520). Another account reports that over one of the mummies was displayed a model of Laocoön and his sons, and over the other a model of a Chinese junk. Feltham (1808: 188).

73. Malcolm (1803: 515). The contents of a third case are described, containing "small Egyptian jars, with the heads of dogs, females, the ibis &c. of earthen-ware and stone, with several brazen urns and vessels." See also Feltham (1808: 188), who reports that one stand is filled with

Egyptian remains "among which are numerous small representations of mummies," while two other stands, a larger case, and the other presses are filled with classical remains.

74. Feltham (1808: 189).

75. On the presence of classical material in early collections, see Vickers (2001 [1985]), Jenkins (1992), and Haskell (1993).

76. As Vickers (2001 [1985]: 315) has noted, the archaeological objects were eventually studied as scientifically as the shells, tomahawks, and other unusual items included in the collections. The major works of Bernard de Montfauçon (1719–1724) and the Comte de Caylus (1752–1757) were central here. On British antiquarianism and its moves toward more systematic inquiry, see Sweet (2003).

77. Winckelmann (1764).

78. The interiors of the museum were highlighted by foreign visitors to London and in early museum guidebooks. For example, the French writer Peter John Grosely talked more of the building and its interiors than about the collections themselves: "Montague-house deserves to be taken particular notice of. By its extent, the variety of parts in which it is laid out, the magnificence of its ornaments, and its agreeable situation, it appears to be rather a royal palace, than the house of a private nobleman. . . . The Museum, independent of what it contains, is of itself capable of exciting the curiosity of strangers: it is of all the houses in London the largest, the completest, and the most magnificent." (Grosely 1772, 1:42, 2:23). For examples of glowing reviews of the museum's interiors in guidebooks, see Powlett (1761: 11), and Harrison (1775: 395). The famous ceiling paintings were created by the artists Charles de la Fosse, Jacques Rousseau and Jean-Baptiste Monnoyer. See Caygill and Date (1999: 10–11).

79. The lack of a clear function for curiosities is briefly alluded to by Benedict (2001: 3) in her study of literary representatives of "the curious" in early modern inquiry: "[Curiosities are] objects without a clear use. They are ornaments selected because they look too strange to be ornamental; broken tools or implements immobilized in cabinets so that they can never be used; coins in cases or framed paper money that serve as icons outside economic circulation: things that have no function but to be looked at."

80. In the representation of Ferdinando Cospi's display (fig. 1.6), at least thirteen small funerary statuettes can be seen dispersed among other items in the collection.

81. The presence of Egyptian sculptures in Renaissance collections is documented by Curran (forthcoming).

82. For discussion on the entrance procedure, see Caygill (1992) and Cash (1992). On eighteenth-century views of the admissions procedure, see Bayne-Powell (1951: 69), who reports that "Englishmen complained of the difficulties they met with on trying to visit the British Museum."

83. *Statues and Rules Relating to the Inspection and Use of the British Museum* (1759: 5–6).

84. "A Plan for the General Distribution of Sir Hans Sloane's Collection," OP, August 29, 1756: 40.

85. Although a few natural history museums were established around this time, there were no other public museums with such collections of antiquities. Major natural history museums included the Leverian Museum and Dr. William Hunter's Museum.

86. Anon. (1774: xxi).

87. "A Plan for the General Distribution of Sir Hans Sloane's Collection." OP, January 14, 1757: 52–53.

88. In this brief sketch of how Western interest in ancient Egypt grew it is not my intention to suggest that there was a consistent progressive trend; fascination for ancient Egypt was sporadic and had its own undulating patterns.

89. Key here was the work of Herodotus, Diodorus Siculus, Strabo, Plutarch, and Pliny the Elder. On the classical writings on Egypt see Greener (1966: 9–20), Siliotti (1998: 16–23), and David (2000: 51–58).

90. While these pilgrims endeavored to find the sites associated with Moses and Joseph, Jesus, Saint Mark, and Saint Antony, they also referred to the Pyramids and ancient monuments encountered as part of their travels. An important example was *Evagortium in Terram Sanctam* written by Dominican Friar Felix Fabri of Ulm, Germany, in 1483. For a more detailed discussion of interest in ancient Egypt in medieval times, see Iversen (1993 [1961]: chap. 3), Greener (1966: 21–33), Siliotti (1998: 24–25), David (2000: 58–61), and Wolff (2003).

91. See Dannenfeldt (1959) and more recently, David (2000: 62–70) and Curran (2003, 2004, forthcoming) for discussion on the Renaissance interest in Egypt. Also relevant is Whitehouse's (1992) discussion of the graphic documentation of Egypt in the sixteenth and seventeenth centuries. For an account of the reerection of obelisks in Rome in the sixteenth century, see Clayton (1982: 8–9, 11–12).

92. Notable examples include Pellegrino Bruccardo, Marco Grimani, and André Thévet, all who produced images of the Pyramids, obelisks, mummies, and the sphinx in their accounts.

93. This reflected the fact that more travel to Egypt had resulted from Europe's increasing control of the trade routes of the Mediterranean. On eighteenth-century travelers to Egypt and their published works, see Greener (1966: 70–81) and Siliotti (1998: 37–79).

94. Such initiatives involved royalty commissioning scholars to carry out such expeditions; the major example being the king of Denmark, Christian VI, who sent Frederick Ludwig Norden to Egypt on such a mission in 1737. Another example of royalty commissioning the recording of antiquities was the French regent Philippe d'Orléans, who sent Father Claude Sicard to Egypt in 1707. Sicard is credited with the rediscovery of Thebes in 1718.

95. This was signified by important publications such as Richard Pococke's *A Description of the East and some other Countries* of 1743–1745, and the founding in 1741 in London of the Egyptian Society, which became defunct in 1743.

96. The first British artist to work in Egypt was Richard Dalton, who traveled there in 1749. Following him was Luigi Mayer, who was appointed by the British ambassador in Constantinople, Sir Robert Ainslie, to produce drawings of Egypt and Turkey.

97. Notable were individuals such as Pietro della Valle, who traveled to Cairo in 1615 and conducted exploratory excavations at Saqqara; John Greaves (1602–1652), who went to Egypt in 1639 to conduct the first survey of the Pyramids of Giza; and Jean de Thevenot, who published an illustrated account of his travels in 1664. Pietro della Valle (1586–1652) is known for bringing back two mummies from Egypt, which went into the collection of Cardinal Flavio Chigi; the results of Greaves's survey were published in the work *Pyramidographia* of 1646; and the title of Thevenot's account was *Voyage au Levant*. See Greener (1966: 46–57) for a useful account of the seventeenth-century European works on Egypt.

98. Pococke's and Norden's studies remained the key resources on Egypt for travelers and artists until Denon's *Voyage dans la Basse et la Haute Egypt* was published in 1802. Historians of Egyptology have credited Norden with making the "first attempt to introduce elements of style into an evaluation of Egyptian archaeological material" (Iversen 1993 [1961]: 109), and with producing a "landmark in Egyptian studies, providing a scale not before encountered" (Whitehouse 1995: 18).

99. The representation of ancient Egypt in the visual arts became increasingly common from the 1750s as part of the neoclassical movement. Notable examples of such representations include William Hogarth's painting *Moses Brought to Pharaoh's Daughter*, Johann Dinglinger's *Apis altar* created in 1731 for King Saxony, and Giovanni Battista Piranesi's interior for the Caffè degli Inglesi, designed in the 1760s. See Curl (1994).

100. Notable examples of the representation of ancient Egypt here include the tragedies of John Sturmy (*Sesostris, or Royalty in Disguise* 1728), Edward Young (*Busiris, King of Egypt* 1730) and Charles Marsh (*Amasis, King of Egypt* 1737), the operas of Jean Philippe Rameau (*The Birth of Osiris* 1751), Mozart (*The Magic Flute* 1791), and Jean Terrasson's novel *Séthos I* (1731).

101. For instance, James (2001: 49) has argued that there was "little to nourish the interest

of the generally educated person, and the few Egyptian objects in the British Museum scarcely represented a strong attraction for the general public."

102. Anon. (n.d. [c.1760]: 12–13).

103. Powlett (1761: 6–9).

104. Thomson (1767: 6–19). These were the slab of Nectanebo I (EA 22) and the slab of Psamtek (EA 20). While the slabs may have attracted the attention of such early visitors, James (1998: 13) has observed that "interesting and important though the intercolumnar slabs are to Egyptologists today, and fine though their royal representations of Psammetichus and Nectanebo are, they did not, apparently, greatly please the king, who passed them on, perhaps unseen, to the British Museum."

105. Rymsdyk and Rymsdyk (1778: 33).

106. The authors themselves stated that their aim was to present a variety of the "picturesque, curious, and scarce" objects in the museum (Rymsdyk and Rymsdyk 1778: iii).

107. Anon. (1761: 31); *Imperial Magazine*, December 1761: 660–662.

108. Letter to Mrs. A. Berkeley, Berkeley Papers 3, Correspondence 1710–1776, BM Add. MS 39, 311, f.83.

109. Butler (1767), BL Add. MS 27, 276 f.11–12; Coltman (1895 [1780]: 81–82); Moritz (1965 [1782]: 59); La Roche (1933 [1786]: 110); Wendeborn (1791: 318).

110. Quirke (1997: 255) observes that complete mummies were rare because people were superstitious about transporting dead bodies on their ships. Besides the museum, owners of mummies included Robert Hubert, John Kemp, and Dr. Mead, all of London, and all members of the Royal Society of London. As the early historian of museums David Murray (2000 [1904]: 50–51) claimed, when a mummy was obtained for a museum "it formed a prominent object in the collection, and became the subject of elaborate description."

111. Powlett (1761: 19).

112. Ibid., 18.

113. Karamzin (1957 [1790]: 308). Other Egyptian antiquities are mentioned in the account of Wendeborn (1791: 318–319).

114. Thomson (1767: 21, 28).

115. BL Add. 27, 276 f.11–12.

116. Woodward (1786). In discussing the Israelites' stay in Egypt and the influence of this country upon Moses, he outlines in detail the religious and cultural practices of the ancient Egyptians. This article was published posthumously, as Woodward died in 1728.

117. Ibid., 238, 256. Woodward's evaluation of ancient Egyptian religion offers numerous other colorful quotations: "It will not be very much beside the present subject, to take notice how universally fond the Egyptians were and addicted in all ages to charms, magic, sorcery, divination, and other like vain arts" (p. 253); "In consequence of this ignorance of God, and that senseless devotion to the most absurd idols that ever appeared, they were possessed with a turn of mind the most stupid and depraved; and were the most corrupt and dissolute in their manners that could well be" (p. 264).

118. Ibid., 218

119. Ibid., 231–233.

120. See Potts (1994) on the significance of Winckelmann's ideas for understanding the art of the ancient world.

121. Winckelmann 1881 [1764]: 172, 173–174.

122. On eighteenth-century aesthetic theory, see Ashfield and Bolla (1996) and Dickie (1996).

123. For example, in 1739 Norden wrote in a letter to the Baron de Stosch, "Let them talk to me no more of Rome; let Greece be silent. What magnificence! What mechanics! What other nation ever had the courage to undertake work so surprising!" (Norden 1757, 2:xxiii).

124. Piranesi (1769). Piranesi was famous for his Egyptian inspired designs, including his in-

teriors for the English coffee house in Rome—the Caffè degli Inglesi, and his elaborate drawings for chimney pieces in the Egyptian style (see Wilton-Ely 1993). In addition to presenting 13 such designs in his *Diverse Manners of ornamenting chimneys* . . . of 1769, Piranesi included an introductory essay in which he challenged the existing bias against Egyptian art. Piranesi argued that it was unjust to judge Egyptian art without a consideration of the architectural context in which it originally featured.

125. Piranesi (1769: 14).

126. Ibid.

127. One notable exception from this period was the theologian and philosopher of history, Johann Gottfried Herder (1744–1803). Herder was also critical of Winckelmann's views, arguing that art should not be evaluated by the values of another culture (see Haskell 1993: 224–226).

128. Criticism of Piranesi's Egyptian designs were made by the painter Thomas Jones, who in 1776 described the English Coffee House in Rome as a "filthy vaulted room the walls of which were painted with sphinxes, obelisks and pyramids from capricious designs of Piranesi, and fitter to adorn the inside of an Egyptian sepulchre, than a room of social conversation." (Ford 1946–1948: 54). On Piranesi's pioneering role in establishing an Egyptian taste in design see Wilton-Ely's entry in Wilton and Bignamini (1996: 116), which argues that "well before the mature nineteenth-century Egyptian Revival had been fueled by the experiences and publications of Napoleon's campaigns on the Nile, Piranesi's work was the first comprehensive attempt to create a novel contemporary interior in this taste."

129. On the way in which Egypt came to be viewed as the "profound source of all esoteric lore," see Hornung's (2001: 3) history of the esoteric tradition associated with ancient Egypt. On how the "popularity of Egypt became a veritable Egyptomania" in classical times, see Kákosy (1995: 11).

130. Entick (1766: 427).

131. Letter from John Coltman to his brother Sam; Coltman (1895 [1780]: 81–82).

132. Faujas de Saint-Fond (1907 [1797]: 86).

133. Ibid., 88.

134. Ibid., 88–90.

135. Ibid., 88.

136. Campbell (1947 [1775]: 71–72). Despite this he was pleased most by the ruins of Herculaneum, the "magnitude of the crocodile (20 feet) and the horn (5 feet at least) growing out of the nose of the unicorn fish."

137. Over thirty years after the museum opened, the German author Gebhardt Wendeborn (1791: 316) complained about the need for a catalogue and the labeling of artifacts: "I know not that any complete, or satisfactory catalogue, of the curiosities of the British Museum has been published; but it were to be wished, that the public might soon be in possession of one, and that the denominations of the curiosities might be affixed to them in legible characters."

138. British Library Add. MS 4449 f.123.

139. Hutton (1818 [1785]: 110–115).

140. Grosely (1772, 2:25).

141. Moritz (1924 [1782]: 68–69). Prior to this he stated that "So quickly was I conducted through this museum, however, that I saw merely the rooms, glass cases and book repositories: not the true British Museum" (Moritz 1965 [1782]: 59).

142. The book he was using was Wendeborn's (1791). Moritz (1965 [1782]: 59).

143. Kielmansegge (1902 [1762]: 101). This comment is made in the context of discussing Kielmansegge's visit to the Ashmolean Museum in 1761, but is a general reference to guides he encountered in English places of interest. For his account of the British Museum see pp. 170–173.

144. Ibid., 100.

CHAPTER THREE

1. For detailed discussions of this expedition, see Beacour et al. (1990) and Russell (2001).

2. France's interest in the antiquities of Egypt was further evidenced by their establishment of the Institut d'Egypte in Cairo in 1798. The French, however, were not alone in recognizing the need to document the archaeological relics of Egypt, as in 1792 the British ambassador in Constantinople, Sir Robert Ainslie, employed Luigi Mayer to undertake a detailed pictorial record of the antiquities, landscapes, and people of Egypt.

3. This was article 16 of the Treaty of Alexandria.

4. Hutchinson rejected this request on the advice of the diplomat and antiquarian William Richard Hamilton, who was aware of the significance of the antiquities and thus encouraged the military to persist in getting them. For details of the negotiations that took place between General Menou of the French army and Hutchinson, and the debates over whether the collections constituted public property or were owned by individuals, see Beacour et al. (1990: 132), Solé and Valbelle (2001: chap. 5), and Parkinson (2005: 24–32).

5. This set of sculptures does not include all the antiquities collected by the French, as many were retained as personal possessions. An original catalogue of the antiquities collected by the French in Egypt was drawn up by F. Fourier, the secretary to the French Institute, BL Add. MS 46839. Colonel Turner then produced a new list in English entitled "An Account of Pieces of Ancient Sculptures Taken by the British Forces under the Command of Lt. General Lord Hutchinson, in Egypt from the French Army in Alexandria and Sent to England in the Charge of Colonel Turner, 1801 September." This list is held in BMDAES. Turner was then given leave to have drawings made of some of the seized antiquities, which are held together with his list of the objects; MSCT, August 6, 1802: 2225. The inventory numbers of the known items on Turner's list are: 1. An Egyptian Sarcophagus (EA 10, sarcophagus of Nectanebo II from Alexandria;); 2. D'o (EA 23, sarcophagus of Hapmen from Cairo); 3. D'o (EA 86, sarcophagus of Hentra from Menouf); 4. A colossal fist (EA 9, from Memphis); 5. Five fragments of Statues with Lion's Heads (EA 37, 57, 68, 880, statues of Sekhmet from Thebes); 6. A mutilated figure kneeling; 8. A stone with three inscriptions (EA 24, Rosetta Stone); 9. Four statues with Lion's Heads, as large as life (including EA 88, Sekhmet statue); 10. Two small fragments of statues with lions heads (two fragments of Sekhmet); 11. A small figure kneeling (EA 137, statue of the scribe Amenmose); 12. Five fragments of statues with lions heads (Sekhmet); 13. A fragment of a sarcophagus (EA 66, sarcophagus of Pairkap); 14. Two obelisks (EA 523, 524, of Nectanebo II from Cairo); 15. A colossal ram's head (EA 14, from Thebes); 16. A statue of a woman sitting (EA 81, statue of Roy); 17. A fragment of a statue with a lions head (Sekhmet). Also included but not mentioned on the list was a statue of Ramesses II (EA 104). More specific discussion of the list can be found in Fiechter (1997) and Bierbrier (1999).

6. A compilation of detailed drawings of the Egyptian antiquities seized from the French was produced by William Alexander (1805–1807), who was assistant to Taylor Combe in the Department of Antiquities. The original location of the sarcophagus of Nectanebo II is uncertain, but after the time of Alexander the Great in 332 it was moved to Alexandria and used as a public bath. When it arrived in London it was thought to have been the tomb of Alexander the Great. The sarcophagus of Hapmen was originally discovered by the French, and then used in the mosque of Ibn Tulun in Cairo as a bath. It was commonly referred to as the "Lover's Fountain." The two basalt obelisks were originally found in Cairo, where they were taken possession of by the French, one having been used as the door sill of a mosque in the castle of Cairo.

7. James (1981: 6).

8. The list of the thirty-nine objects in the Egyptian Sculpture gallery as reported in the *Synopsis* of 1808 was: "1. sarcophagus green breccia, of Nectanebo II [EA 10]; 2. sarcophagus black granite, of Hapmen [EA 23]; 3. statue of Isis—presented in 1767 by the Earl of Bute [EA 510]; 4. fragment of Egyptian deity; 5. a sphinx—presented in 1767 by the Earl of Bute [EA 115]; 6.

capital of an Egyptian column—presented in 1805 by Earl Spencer; 7. an Egyptian monument with two female figures standing side by side—from Sloane collection; 8. a figure of Isis sitting on the ground; 9. a figure kneeling on a plinth [?EA 25]; 10. statue of Egyptian deity in chair; 11. similar to 10; 12. fragment of porphyry column; 13. coffin; 14. fragment of porphyry column; 15. part of frieze of Egyptian temple—presented by His Majesty [EA 20 or 22]; 16. an Egyptian obelisk [EA 523 or 524]; 17. part of frieze of Egyptian temple—presented by His Majesty [EA 20 or 22]; 18. figure with beard, short apron and "terrific aspect'–from Charles Townley collection [EA 47973]; 19. head of a sphinx—from Charles Townley collection; 20. figure kneeling and supporting with his hands a kind of altar—presented by Matthew Duane; 21–22. fragments of an Egyptian Deity similar to no. 10; 23. the Rosetta Stone [EA 24]; 24. colossal head of ram [EA 14]; 25. obelisk [EA 523 or 524]; 26. colossal fist [EA 9]; 27. colossal fist of smaller size than 26–presented by Earl Spencer 1805; 28. fragment covered with hieroglyphics—presented by Earl Spencer 1805; 29. fragment of large sarcophagus; 30. fragment found at foot of Pompey's pillar; 31. bas relief—presented in 1767 by the Earl of Bute [?EA 430]; 32. fragment of porphyry column; 33–34. statues of Egyptian deities similar to no. 10; 35. mutilated kneeling figure—presented by Earl Spencer 1805; 36. a votive column—presented by Dr. Nancroft, Jun.; 37. a colossal hawk—presented by Mr. T. Philipe [EA 1420]; 38. a fragment of an Egyptian deity similar to no. 10; 39. a small mutilated figure kneeling."

9. George John Spencer, second Earl of Spencer (1758–1834), was a politician and famous book collector; Charles Townley (1737–1805) was a well-known collector of antiquities, and T. Philipe was an auctioneer.

10. *Synopsis* (1808: 92). Thomas Hollis (1729–1774) was a political propagandist who was a member of the Society of Arts and fellow of the Royal Society.

11. Ibid.

12. For example, in his appraisal of Napoleon's scientific expedition Greener (1966: 1) states that "never before, and perhaps never since, has a description of a foreign land been made so completely, so accurately and so fast, or under such difficulty, as that which these men made." More recently, Dykstra (1998: 137) has commented that "the ideas and images of an Egypt so thoroughly and authoritatively 'described' here would shape European thinking about Egypt for generations"; and David (2000: 89) has argued that the commission "had a profound effect upon Europe's knowledge of the ancient civilization of Egypt, and this marked the beginning of scientific awareness of the monuments and artefacts."

13. Discovered on July 19, 1799, the Rosetta Stone is the ancient decree in Greek, hieroglyphic, and demotic script that is dated to 196 BC and written in honor of King Ptolemy V Epiphanes. See below on the publications associated with the expedition.

14. Vivant Denon (1747–1825) was a diplomat and artist who became closely associated with the project and who went on to have a distinguished career in Egyptology in France. *Description de l'Egypte* included 900 folio engravings of the monuments, antiquities, topographic views, and customs of modern Egyptians. Five volumes were dedicated to antiquities, with a total of 601 engravings.

15. Although many other illustrations of the monuments and antiquities of Egypt had been seen in Europe, the engravings in the French publications were special because they were characterized by a sense of realism not previously seen before. Furthermore, although Denon's work was criticized in Britain for not making any important additions to the state of knowledge on Egyptian monuments, it was acclaimed for its "many beautiful engravings." *Edinburgh Review* 1803 (1): 332. As Jacobs (1995: 42) has argued, Denon "appreciated the Egyptian monuments independent of any classical context, and was accordingly more rigorous in his recording of them."

16. *Synopsis* (1808: xii).

17. Ibid., xxvi–vii.

18. MSCT, August 6, 1802: 2226.

19. MSCT, December 18, 1802: 2228. Saunders had previous experience in designing antiquities galleries. See "George Saunders," *Oxford Dictionary of National Biography*, by F. M. O'Donoghue, rev. by R. Bowdler, at http: www.oxforddnb.com/view/article/24695.

20. MSCT, April 30, 1803: 2232.

21. The trustees resolved that a committee be formed to take directions from the Chancellor of the Exchequer on accomplishing the plan. Included in this committee were The Speaker of the House of Commons, Sir Joseph Banks, Sir George Cornewall, Mr. Townley, Mr. Sloane and Mr. Annesley later the Earl of Mountnorris. MSCT, June 30, 1804: 2247.

22. MGMT, May 14, 1803: 962–966; July 14, 1804: 970.

23. These are outlined in Cook (1977: 56–59).

24. An account of the contents of the smaller room is provided in the *Synopsis*, which identifies three items—"An Egyptian Mummy, with its coffin" (presented by the king), "Another Egyptian mummy with its coffin" (presented by Lethieullier) and "A manuscript taken from a mummy" (presented by W. Hamilton), and then provides a general description of the other items in the room: "The smaller articles contained in this room, which are too numerous to be each separately described in a succinct account like the present, consist of mummies of the Ibis and other sacred animals; of idols in wood, stone, porcelain, and bronze; of vases, the lids of which are severally adorned with a head of Isis, a hawk, a wolf, or a baboon; of fragments of statues; of sistrums, amulets, and a great variety of other monuments of art, which serve to illustrate the religious worship of the ancient Egyptians." *Synopsis* (1808: 92). Another account of the contents of the smaller Egyptian gallery is presented in the *Repository of Arts, Literature, Commerce, Manufactures, Fashions, and Politics*: "In one of the coffins is a conical vessel of baked clay, inclosing an embalmed ibis. Opposite the entrance to this room, against the wall, is a frame containing the bones of another embalmed ibis. Underneath it is a manuscript taken from a mummy; it is written on papyrus in the Egyptian language. Near it are the fragments of another manuscript of the same kind; and on the right of the door is a frame containing an Egyptian painting, taken from the breast of a mummy" (Anon. 1810: 259).

25. In 1803 the makeup of the committee had changed; with Thomas Astle replacing William Hamilton, who had died in April. Astle was an archivist who had been engaged by the museum to work on the manuscript collections from 1761.

26. OP, May 14, 1803: 768–770; see also MSCT, May 14, 1803: 962–966.

27. Saunders's "Design for the West Wing" is in OP, May 14, 1803: 768, drawings 9 and 10. See also plan of principal story (Cook 1977: fig. 40), which clearly shows two sarcophagi positioned in the center of the room in a symmetrical arrangement. See Caygill and Date (1999: 17) on the building plans for the Townley Gallery.

28. Tresham (1750/51–1814) was primarily known for his history paintings; Westmacott (1775–1856) was a leading authority on art in Britain, who was famous for his neoclassical style.

29. Westmacott (1808: 48–49).

30. As Cook (1977: 61) has noted, "While shape and size are the dominant factors in the arrangement, the placing of terminal heads on square pedestals and the choice of portraits of real people for the brackets suggest that thought was also given to the subject matter."

31. This has been described as the first such historical reconstruction in the modern period, and along with the development of an Egyptian iconography of design, it appears to have inspired many other examples of "Egyptian Rooms." Pantazzi (1994: 39).

32. As McClellan (1994: 107–108) argues, "The former aimed to concentrate the beholder's attention first and foremost on pictorial qualities within the frame, whereas the latter encouraged appreciation of a given painting in terms of its place in a diachronic, national sequence."

33. McClellan's (1994) study of the history of the Louvre outlines the discussions and tensions in determining the appropriate mode of display for the art and antiquities collections. He

documents how the "comparative mode of pictorial display" that was created to present the paintings in the Luxembourg Gallery from 1750 to 1779 was rejected in favor of a more chronological and scientific arrangement when it became the Louvre in 1793 (McClellan 1994: 42). More specifically, the latter involved grouping the artists according to their affiliation with famous masters, who were then arranged in order of birth or historical succession (138).

34. McClellan (1994: 107–108) demonstrates how the Louvre's first displays reverted back to an "eclectic" display that would facilitate stylistic comparison.

35. However, when the drawings gallery was opened in 1797, the chronological mode of arrangement was once again abandoned in favor of an aesthetic one (ibid., 129). Similarly, when the completed Grand Gallery was opened in 1801, "Once again it seems decorative demands compromised the goal of historical demonstration" (ibid., 140).

36. The stelae were probably those sent from Egypt by Edward Wortley Montagu and which had previously been displayed in the great hall of the museum.

37. The focus on the symmetrical arrangement of the Townley sculptures mirrored the way they had been positioned in Townley's house at Westminster. See Cook (1977: 44).

38. Charles Townley acquired this statue from excavations in Rome. It is an ancient copy in marble of the bronze statue by Myron.

39. OP, May 14, 1803: 768–770.

40. The highly elaborate arrangements of the classical antiquities can be seen in Combe's illustrated catalogues of 1810.

41. For instance, in 1808 Combe reported that "Mr. Combe has altered the arrangement of the antiquities in the Egyptian Room" (OR, June 11, 1808: 122), and in the following year he reported that he had "completed arrangement of the mummies and other Egyptian antiquities in Room VIII of the New Building" (OR, February 11, 1809: 167).

42. Here Westmacott was referring to decisions made by himself and Tresham. MSCT, April 9, 1808: 2376.

43. On the role of antique sculpture in architectural decoration, see Scott (2003: 49), who emphasizes the decorative aspects of collecting in eighteenth-century Britain.

44. The appropriate display style for antiquities was elaborated upon by people like Winckelmann, who determined that in order to best appreciate the qualities of antique sculpture it was necessary to have the objects sufficiently spaced so that they could be viewed from different angles. He also raised the importance of lighting.

45. Thomas Hope's (1769–1831) collection in London offers a major example of this.

46. Ackermann 1808–1809: (1)101.

47. In commenting on the decoration of the house and the work of the three painters, Ackermann (1808–1809: (1)102) comments that "the union of these discordant styles produces a kind of garish splendour, which, with the heavy carved and gilt furniture of that day, must have had a large proportion of cumbrous magnificence."

48. Prior to Winckelmann's emphasis on lighting as critical for the proper appreciation of objects, the German scholar Caspar Neickel argued that galleries should have good lighting so that the objects "may be presented with the greatest clarity and without a dazzling glare." Neickel (1727), as cited in Taylor (1948: 133).

49. As Jenkins (1992: 110) has observed, side lighting was considered appropriate for the Egyptian sculptures because they could tolerate the "confusion of crossing side-lights which were undesirable for pure outlines of classical works."

50. An exception was made with the first rotunda, which was papered. MSCT, August 1, 1807: 2333–2336; August 8, 1807: 2336–2343. It was Saunders who initially recommended that distemper be used to save money.

51. Architectural thought on the appropriate use of color in early nineteenth-century interiors is outlined by Bristow (1996).

52. For example, in representations of Townley's collection as displayed in his home in

Westminster, we see bright blue walls and columns painted red in imitation of porphyry (see Sloan and Burnett 2004: 176, figs. 162, 163).

53. See Cook (1977: 59–60) for an account of the decision to color the walls in distemper.

54. Hope (1971 [1807]: 26).

55. OP, July 12, 1805: 784. In part 3, on the Department of Natural History, Antiquities, and Artificial Curiosities, it was stated that "1. Inscriptions are wanting upon the cases in some of the Rooms. 2. There are no printed catalogues for any branch of this department."

56. Ibid., 785.

57. With a training in classics, Combe (1774–1826) developed an interest in classical antiquities, particularly coins. He served as keeper of the department until 1826. MGMT, February 28, 1807: 1008. According to Wilson (2002: 60), it was the death of the underlibrarian of natural and artificial production, Edward Gray, in 1806 that prompted the creation of this new department.

58. The list of works to be undertaken by the new department included: "1. A Manual or inventory for the Gallery of Antiquities, when placed in the New Building. 2. Cataloguing the Egyptian Antiquities. 3. Correcting the catalogue of Sir Wm. Sloane, supposed to be very inaccurate." MGMT, February 28, 1807: 1013.

59. OP, February 18, 1808: 865.

60. *Synopsis* (1808: xii–xxvii).

61. The main early example of this was the presentation of the Egyptian antiquities in the Cesi collection in the 1550s, including three lion statues, two sphinxes, a statue of Sekhmet, a sculpture of a crocodile, and a Thoth ape. These were displayed amid the other antique sculptures in the collection, with the lions and sphinxes assuming important positions at various entrance and axis points (see Curran forthcoming: chap. 9). Other major examples include the installation of a set of four statues in the Capitoline Museum around 1715–1720. Statues of Queen Tuya (wife of Seti I and mother of Ramesses II) and of Arsinoe (wife of Ptolemy II Philadelphus) were positioned between the columns of the portico of the Palazzo Nuovo, and statues of Ptolemy II Philadelphus and of an unidentified princess were set in the portico of the Palazzo dei Conservatori (see Pantazzi 1994: 38). A later example was the Vatican's installation of two Egyptian Telamons from Hadrian's Villa in Tivoli in the entrance of the Pio-Clementino Museum in 1779–1782. Here the Egyptian statues were used as decorations of a portal that led to the famous rotunda and other rooms with classical statuary (see Pietrangeli 1993: 83, fig. 66).

62. Discovered at Hadrian's Villa at Tivoli, these objects were installed under the order of Pope Benedict XIV, who was the first to give official papal sanction to the inclusion of Egyptian objects.

63. Mackenzie's (1995: 51) argument about the differences between French and British Orientalism are relevant here. He argues that the British never "indulged in the grandiose gestures" of the French artists, and that with the exception of David Roberts, their "approach was generally more pragmatic and low key."

64. Porterfield (1998: 91).

65. MGMT, February 28, 1807: 10009. The new rules on visiting were also recorded in the *Annual Return to the House of Commons*, no. 10: "Report of the Sub-Committee 11th April 1807 Respecting Regulations for Admission to the Gallery of Antiquities." OP, April 23, 1807: 854–855.

66. While the *Description de l'Egypte* was the official publication relating to the expedition, Denon's book was more influential because it was cheaper and smaller in size.

67. That Denon's book was widely read is suggested by a review in the *Edinburgh Review*, which comments on its "extensive circulation" (1803 [1]: 330).

68. Zoëga (1797); Quatremère de Quincy (1803); Hamilton (1809). Not to be confused with the collector Sir William Hamilton, William Richard Hamilton was an antiquarian and diplomat who served as undersecretary at the Foreign Office and established a connection with Egypt when, as secretary to Lord Elgin, he was sent to Egypt to help facilitate the French

evacuation and conduct a study of the country. Hamilton later became a trustee of the museum, serving from 1838 to 1858.

69. On the sarcophagus, see Clarke (1805); on the Rosetta Stone, see Hamilton (1809).

70. On the passion for Egyptian motifs in architecture and the arts, see Humbert et al. (1994). The kinds of motifs that found favor were pyramids, obelisks, sphinxes, palm-leaf capitals, lotus flowers, and winged scarabs. On the neoclassical movement in late eighteenth- and early nineteenth-century art and its appropriation of archaeological motifs, see Irwin (1997).

71. An illustration of this room was published in Hope's *Household Furniture and Interior Decoration* (1971 [1807]: plate 8).

72. See Bland (1998) and Saglia (2002: 322) on the Wedgwood Egyptian range.

73. In 1800 the comic opera *The Egyptian Festival* was held in Drury Lane (see Saglia [2002: 320] and Werner [2003]), and in 1801 the lantern show "Phantasmagoria," in which ancient Egypt was featured, ran in London. This was based on the "Fantasmagorie" of 1799 that appeared in Europe; see Lant (1992). In 1802 the show *Aegyptiana*, based on the images of Denon's book with an "intermixture of recitations" was performed at the Lyceum (Feltham 1802: 190).

74. As Bierbrier (1999: 113) has also observed, "the arrival of these Egyptian pieces in London was of major importance in the development of interest in Egyptian antiquities, as monumental sculpture had never before been seen by the British public except for the intrepid few who had gone to Egypt or seen surviving objects in Rome."

75. The sarcophagus is 274.4 cm long, 119.4 cm high, and 139.7 cm wide.

76. *Edinburgh Review* 1811 (18): 443.

77. Feltham (1802: 186).

78. *Times*, August 10, 1802: 3.

79. Ibid.

80. Malcolm (1803: 531).

81. Sarrett (1803–1804: 173, 179).

82. Feltham (1808: 186–187).

83. Anon. (1810: 230).

84. Ibid.

85. *Gentleman's Magazine* 1810 (80): 209.

86. *Edinburgh Review* 1803 (1): 341.

87. Hope (1971 [1807]: 36).

88. See above, chapter 2.

89. Simond (1815: 83–84).

90. *Edinburgh Review* 1811 (18): 435–436.

91. Ibid., 436.

92. *Edinburgh Review* 1806 (7): 481.

93. *Times*, July 8, 1805: 3. International visitors were also still complaining about the lack of time assigned to visits; the American Benjamin Silliman (1810: 297) said of his visit in 1805, "It is really distressing to be surrounded by a host of things which are full of information, and then to be hurried away from them just as one is beginning to single out particular objects."

94. Simond (1815: 84). A footnote added later states, "I am informed that a great improvement took place soon after we were there, and that the museum is now shewn much more conveniently."

95. *Times*, July 8, 1805: 3.

CHAPTER FOUR

1. The Phigaleian marbles were from the Temple of Apollo at Bassae, in Phigalia, Arcadia; the Elgin marbles were from the Parthenon in Athens. For details of the museum's acquisition of these antique sculptures, see Jenkins (1992).

2. Previously, Britain had placed representatives in temporary visiting positions.

3. The Germans also played a role, but they did not enjoy the same success as the French and the British. Under the German crown agent, Freiherr von Minutoli, a collection of antiquities was made between 1820 and 1822, however the shipment sank before reaching Europe (see Wildung 1999: 3).

4. The French had made an even earlier start than this, with their consul Benoit de Maillet shipping a collection of antiquities to France in 1735. Drovetti was the consul general for France in Egypt 1810–1815 and 1820–1829. He amassed three major collections, the first which was rejected by the king of France and subsequently purchased for 400,000 lire by the king of Sardinia in 1824 for the museum in Turin; the second was purchased for 150,000 francs by King Charles X of France in 1827 for the Louvre, and the third was purchased for 30,000 francs by the Berlin Museum in 1836. Ridley's (1998: 67–112) biography of the consul provides some fascinating insights into the communications between Drovetti and Salt and Belzoni, challenging the widely held assumption that relations between the competing collectors were always bad.

5. Salt also made use of other agents, namely the Genoese naval captain Giovanni Battista Caviglia (1770–1845), who excavated at Giza on behalf of Salt in 1816, and the Greek collector Giovanni d'Athanasi (1798–1854), who worked in Thebes from 1817 to 1827. In 1819 Caviglia presented several antiquities to the museum obtained as a result of his work at the Pyramids and the great sphinx, including a sphinx, horns of an altar, a small hawk, some tablets, and a fragment of the plaited beard from the great sphinx (EA 58). For a detailed account of Salt's consular work and his collecting in Egypt, see Manley and Rée (2001).

6. Letter from Salt to the Earl of Mountnorris, December 28, 1816 (Halls 1834: 472).

7. Ibid.

8. Ibid. At this time Salt was collecting on behalf of the earl; for an account of this relationship, see Manley and Rée (2001: 154–171).

9. Letter from Salt to Richards, June 1, 1823 (Halls 1834: 366). Sir Joseph Banks was a natural historian (botanist) and explorer who became president of the Royal Society in 1778.

10. Inventory number EA 19, originally called "Younger Memnon." For an account of the adventures Belzoni and Salt experienced in trying to remove this head, see France (1991: 27–57).

11. Among these was the British traveler and collector William John Bankes (1786–1855), who had traveled in Egypt from 1815 to 1819. On his attempt to remove the sculpture, see Usick (2002: 51).

12. For example, in 1817 Drovetti arranged for the Bey in charge to forbid the English from accumulating more antiquities, because the French "could not find or buy a single article in consequence of the English, who laid their hands on everything"; Belzoni (2001 [1820a]: 181).

13. Ibid., 109. The bust had initially been observed by the traveler Norden to be lying face downward, and although Belzoni does not suggest who must have turned it upward, (and indeed, separated the bust from its body by an explosion), it is likely to have been the French.

14. Ibid., 154.

15. Salt's biographer Halls (1834: 296) was not impressed with this lack of gratitude and remarked upon "this princely gift, which probably, had it been disposed to any of the great powers of Europe, would have secured to the owners many thousand pounds."

16. OR, January 9, 1819: 1168.

17. Indeed, Belzoni's account of his exploits was so popular that it was rewritten for younger readers in 1821. Irby and Mangles (1985 [1823]: 137–147) were commanders in the Royal Navy, who in their travels in Egypt spent some time with Belzoni; they offer a highly readable account of the nature of collecting in Egypt around this time, documenting how all kinds of "wheeling and dealing" was undertaken in order to secure choice objects.

18. Inventory numbers EA 15 and 55. The sculpture of Amenhotep III was originally thought to be that of Thutmose III and was believed to have come from the temple of Amen-Re.

However, the torso was later found at the Temple of Mut at Karnak, where the head is now thought to have been originally located.

19. Inventory number EA 12. The sculpture is featured in *Description de l'Egypte*, vol. 3 of *Antiquités*, plate 31. It is also included in the frontispiece, which features the main monuments and antiquities recorded by the French. Russell (2001: 232) reports that the "French Commission were so impressed by the arresting beauty of this piece they tried, in vain, to have it moved to the Nile for transportation to Paris. They ruefully observed: 'If we had been able to transport it, we would possess in Europe, one of the most perfect productions of Egyptian sculpture.'" As a sign of his triumph Belzoni inscribed his name on the top surface of this sculpture.

20. Inventory number EA 61. James and Davies (1996: 31) report that the style of the facial features suggested that the statue was made for Thutmose III or Amenhotep II, however, the names of two Ramesside kings are inscribed on the body—Ramesses II and Merneptah. They conclude that the original Tuthmoside inscription was either never made or was erased.

21. Dated to the reign of Amenhotep III, over six hundred of these statues were originally set up by the king in Thebes.

22. A list of all the antiquities forwarded to the British Museum by Salt can be found in BMDAES, "Early Papers (Salt and Sams Collections)," 141–155, 158–182. Another list by Salt can be found in BMDAES, "Salt and Sloane Collections."

23. Furthermore, this series of paintings from Nebamun's tomb is distinguished by great skill in composition, drawing, and use of color. See Manniche (1988: 136–57).

24. The sarcophagus and lid of Ramesses III ended up in the Louvre and the Fitzwilliam Museum (Cambridge) respectively; the alabaster sarcophagus went to the John Soane Museum in London.

25. Letter from Salt to Hamilton, June 10, 1818 (Halls 1834: 299–300).

26. Ibid.

27. Halls (1834: 301–302).

28. A copy of the letter from Salt to Banks can be found in OP, May 28, 1822: 1734. A few months later Hamilton admitted that he had had a role to play in this unfortunate incident, stating, "I ought certainly to have suppressed the catalogue, as it was priced." Letter from Hamilton to the Earl of Mountnorris, September 30, 1819 (Halls 1834: 313).

29. The letter from Salt to Banks, dated November 16, 1818, was read at the general meeting of February 13, 1819. MSCT, February 13, 1819: 2719.

30. MGMT, February 13, 1819: 1169; Letter from Banks to Salt, February 14, 1819 (Halls 1834: 303–304).

31. Letter from Hamilton to Salt, February 16, 1819 (Halls 1834: 305).

32. The Elgin marbles were bought in 1816, and the Phigaleian in 1814.

33. The collection was later purchased by Friedrich Wilhelm IV of Prussia for the Berlin Museum. The initial asking price made to the French in 1826 was 400,000 francs, but Passalacqua accepted the much-reduced price of 100,000 francs from the Prussian ruler.

34. Letter from Yorke to Banks, November 5, 1819 (Halls 1834: 317–318). Yorke (later the fourth Earl of Hardwicke) had a special interest in Egyptian antiquities, evidenced by the work he coauthored with William Martin Leake in 1826, *Remarks on Some Egyptian Monuments in England.*

35. Letter from Hamilton to Banks, November 9, 1819 (Halls 1834: 319).

36. Letter from Banks to the Earl of Mountnorris, November 11, 1819 (Halls 1834: 320).

37. "Mr. Charles Long reported that the Sub-Committee (consisting of himself, the Earl of Aberdeen, and Mr. Banks) appointed at the general meeting of Feb. 20th 1820 communicated at the time with the Admiralty respecting the collection of antiquities made in Egypt by Mr. Salt and Mr. Belzoni, but they understand that no steps have as yet been undertaken respecting them." MSCT, January 13, 1821: 2772–2773; February 10, 1821: 2775; OP, February 10, 1821: 1626–1627; MSCT, November 10, 1821: 2796.

38. OP, May 10, 1822: 1733–1734.

39. OP, May 12, 1822: 1793; September 5, 1822: 1781; December 31, 1822: 1795; January 8, 1823: 1803–1804; MSCT, January 11, 1823: 2832; OP, January 27, 1823: 1811; April 2, 1824: 1890; MSCT, April 10, 1824: 2871.

40. Letter from Salt to Richards, May 26, 1822 (Halls 1834: 323). His confidence rested on his claim that Drovetti had offered him $10,000 for the alabaster sarcophagus alone, and his belief that he could get twice what he asked for the whole collection in France.

41. Letter from Richards to Planta. OP, January 8, 1823: 1803–1804.

42. Drovetti made the offer on behalf of the French, and Baron Minutoli made the offer on behalf of the Prussian government. Ibid. As these offers did not include the cost of removing and transporting the sarcophagus to England, Salt hoped to double them.

43. Ibid.

44. Memorandum of Richards regarding meeting at British Museum, February 13, 1823 (Halls 1834: 353).

45. Letter from Richards to Salt, February 18, 1823 (Halls 1834: 355–356).

46. Letter from Richards to Salt, February 22, 1823 (Halls 1834: 355).

47. Letter from Salt to Richards, June 1, 1823 (Halls 1834: 366).

48. MSCT, June 14, 1823: 2483.

49. By this time Belzoni's partnership with Salt had ended and a settlement was made between them. Evidence for this exists in the form of an agreement between Salt and Belzoni signed at the consulate house in Cairo. Here it was stated, "Whereas it appears that some erroneous ideas had been entertained by Signor Giovanni Battista Belzoni, with respect to the objects collected under the auspices and at the expense of Henry Salt, Esquire in Upper Egypt, as being intended for the British Museum; and whereas it has since been satisfactorily explained to Signor Belzoni that such ideas were altogether founded on a mistake, it has been agreed and determined, between the above parties in a friendly manner, to terminate, and they do hereby terminate, all differences between them by the present agreement." OP, April 20, 1818: 1489–1491. For a more detailed account of the negotiations between Salt and Belzoni, see France (1991: 58–80) and Manley and Rée (2001: 82–99).

50. Letter from Belzoni to Trustees. OP, September 10, 1821: 1681–1682. Emphasizing his contribution to the museum's antiquities collection, Belzoni hoped that his request "might perhaps be considered not unfavourably by the enlightened and liberal institution to which I am addressing myself or toward an individual who has been mainly instrumental in enlarging the National Collection of antiquities placed in your charges." On the trustees' rejection of this request, see MSCT, May 11, 1822: 1196.

51. Letter from John Soane to G. B. Tyndale. OP, April 1, 1824: 1878. This misunderstanding was prompted by the fact that in January of that year the trustees had resolved to reconsider their decision regarding the sarcophagus "should it not be taken away from the museum by Mr. Richards before that time." MSCT, January 24, 1824: 2861.

52. Memorandum of Richards regarding meeting at British Museum, February 14, 1824 (Halls 1834: 372).

53. Ibid.; OP, April 2, 1824: 1890.

54. Soane paid £2,000 for the sarcophagus. On rejection of the sarcophagus, see MGMT, February 8, 1823: 1202; on confirmation of trustees' rejection, see MSCT, April 10, 1824: 2871; for confirmation of Richards's sale to Soane, see letter from Bingham Richards to Joseph Planta, OP, April 17, 1824: 1893. Other factors may have also played a role in this rejection. As Wilson (2002: 352, note 121) has pointed out, when the trustees refused to purchase the alabaster sarcophagus, they had just accepted the gift of the Royal Library, and thus "it may well be that the thought of such a purchase, at a time when the Trustees would have to go to Parliament to request money for a new building, seemed impolitic."

55. Salt's biographer, Halls (1834: 297, 381), did not conceal his disgust over the way the

British consul was treated, stating that Salt "did not contemplate that he could be a loser from the undertaking, much less that he would be exposed to unsparing censure for his well-meant endeavour," and that "his risk, his activity, perseverance, and judgement in assembling it, all passed wholly unrewarded." Wilson (2002: 75) has also remarked that "the Trustees, quite disgracefully, were growing cool towards Salt and his antiquities, feeling that in terms of art they were neither as good, nor as inspiring, as the classical sculpture that had taken London by storm." Salt himself also remarked on how "shabbily" he had been treated. Letter from Salt to Hamilton, October 4, 1824 (Halls 1834: 238).

56. George Annesley had visited Egypt and the Near East in 1802, and Salt was employed as his secretary and artist during his travels in India and the Red Sea in 1805; see Annesley (1809). Upon his return to England, the earl served on the committee that planned the new Townley building to house the Egyptian antiquities. MSCT, June 30, 1804: 2247.

57. Obtained between 1819 and 1824, this collection included the highly valued bottom half of the Ramesses III sarcophagus. As Greener (1966: 128) has observed, it is "ironical that a large and important part of the antiquities collected by Salt, who worked for Britain, was bought by the French government; while one of the great collections made by Drovetti, who worked for the French, is the principal part of the great collection at Turin."

58. Ridley (1998: 260) makes the same observation regarding Drovetti's motivation for collecting, stating that it was a "legitimate and customary method of recouping expenses and providing for retirement."

59. Letter from Salt to Richards, May 2, 1824 (Halls 1834: 375).

60. MGMT, May 14, 1818: 2691. Taylor Combe subsequently reported that the statue was inserted into the existing line of objects. OR, February 13, 1819: 1180.

61. The sculpture of a Horus falcon (EA 1420) was donated by the auctioneer T. Philipe in 1805.

62. Other identifiable sculptures in the picture include the sarcophagi and obelisks from the 1802 collection, and what appears to be the statue of Bes (EA 47973) acquired as part of the Townley collection in 1805.

63. The Salle d'Isis at the Louvre is described by Porterfield (1998: 91) as "centring on a Roman imperial colossal statue of Isis, amid an ensemble of two dozen objects relating to Egypt: ancient Roman, Egyptianizing, and even eighteenth-century Egyptoid objects."

64. Built by William Bullock and opened in 1821, the Egyptian Hall in London was inspired by the great temple of Hathor at Dendera. A prestigious location for mounting an exhibition, as Altick (1978: 235) describes, it was the "center of the miscellaneous-exhibition branch of the trade for almost a century."

65. Belzoni's antiquities included two statues of Sekhmet, two mummies, and other objects. Detailed descriptions of Belzoni's displays can be found in Pearce (2000a, b).

66. Before Belzoni's exhibit, the Egyptian Hall had featured a display with mounted exotic animals in a reconstructed habitat diorama. For a description and illustration of this *Pantherion* display, see Wonders (1993: 30–31).

67. The six models included the portico of the temple of Isis at Philae, the ruins of the temple at Erments, the temple of Ramesses II at Abu Simbel, a section of the passages and chambers of the pyramid of Chephren, a model of Chephren's pyramid, and a model of the origins of arches.

68. *New Monthly Magazine,* December 1, 1821: 113. Other reports in the media that spoke highly of the new strategies of exhibition included the *Times* (April 30, 1821: 3), who commented on the "skilful arrangement" of the display.

69. The popularity of Belzoni's book is evidenced by the fact that a second edition was printed in the following year.

70. For example, Belzoni's transportation of the bust of Ramesses II to England and his other exploits in Egypt were reported in the *Quarterly Review* 1818 (18): 368–370; 1818 (19): 190–192.

71. These individuals were not only interested in ancient Egypt because of the exotic appeal of the objects but because of Egypt's allegorical role in representing mystery, death and eternal life. On how ancient Egypt captured the imagination of poets and artists, see Conner (1983: 75–82) and Leask (2002: chap. 3). Here we learn that John Keats was inspired by the displays in the museum, writing seven poems in 1818 on the subject of ancient Egypt. In 1819 Keats visited the museum and subsequently wrote of "a Sphinx there of a great giant size, and most voluptuous Egyptian expression" (this was probably the bust of Ramesses II). Similarly, Shelley's sonnet "Ozymandias" of 1818 is said to have been inspired by the imminent arrival of Ramesses II, and Byron referred to the sarcophagus of Nectanebo in "The Age of Bronze" of 1823. Finally, in 1825 Haydon met Belzoni and "assiduously examined" the sarcophagus of Seti I and the Egyptian antiquities in the British Museum (Conner 1983: 79).

72. *Gentleman's Magazine* 1822 (92): 351.

73. Ibid., 351–352. The word "beautiful" had been used earlier to describe the sarcophagi seized from the French (Sarrett 1803–1804: 179; Feltham 1808: 186–187).

74. Hamilton (1809: 177). Hamilton's knowledge of ancient sculpture was developed in association with his role in the purchase of the Elgin marbles, and as James (1997: 60) has observed, "Hamilton's eye was distinctly in advance of most other educated eyes at that time, and . . . he demonstrated a judgement free from prejudice and remarkably confident." Burckhardt's quote is cited in Manley and Rée (2001: 92).

75. Egyptologists have remarked on the impact of this sculpture and its role in according Egyptian antiquities with aesthetic potential. For example, Quirke and Spencer (1992: 126) argue that it "transformed the debate among the scholarly and wider public on the merits of Egyptian as opposed to Greek art."

76. *Annals of the Fine Arts* 1819 (10): 494–498; (11): 589; De Quincy (1889: 41n). Of the smile, de Quincy remarked, "It is co-extensive with all time and all space, an Aeonian smile of gracious love and Panlike mystery, the most diffusive and pathetically divine that the hand of man has created."

77. On stories of the journey of the sculpture to England, see the *Quarterly Review* 1818 (18): 368. As France (1991: 66) has noted, these stories "delighted a readership that enjoyed a waspish treatment of French claims to scholarship in Egypt."

78. *Quarterly Review* 1818 (18): 368.

79. Irby and Mangles 1985 [1823]: 79. Like others, however, Irby and Mangles could not restrain themselves from noting the "imperfections" of Egyptian sculpture: "The necks are short, out of all proportion, and the ears are placed considerably too high, a defect very common among the Egyptian figures; the bodies also seem to lean rather too much forward for the natural position of a sitting figure" (ibid.).

80. *New Monthly Magazine*, December 1, 1821: 617.

81. *Annals of the Fine Arts* 1820 (13): 183.

82. Peter Patmore was a writer and journalist who later became editor of the *New Monthly Magazine*.

83. Patmore (1826: 3–4).

84. Ibid., 27.

85. Ibid., 28.

86. Ibid., 30.

87. Ibid., 30. In her brief analysis of guidebooks to the museum, Grewal (1996: 111) singles out Patmore's comparison of Egyptian antiquities to nightmares, citing this as evidence of the way in which these ancient remains were treated as erotic and sexual objects—"Limited to the realm of nightmares, they become part of the unclaimed, 'unspeakable' domain of aberrant sexuality."

88. Patmore 1826: 32.

89. Ibid.

90. Ibid., 33.

91. Ibid., 35.

92. Ibid., 48.

93. Social historians have emphasized its role in fostering an interest in Egypt. Altick (1978: 245), for example, comments that "it was a dramatic exhibition which did much to spread interest in ancient Egypt and in archaeology at large among the general public."

94. *New Monthly Magazine*, December 1, 1821: 615–616.

95. Ibid., 617.

96. For example, reacting to a criticism of Belzoni's efforts made by the French Institute in Egypt, the *Quarterly Review* (1818 [19]: 195) claimed that "the government of France was at no one period more jealous of the power of England, than the members of the French Institute are at this moment of her progress in the sciences and the arts." For further criticisms of the French in the context of discussing Belzoni's work in Egypt see *Quarterly Review* 1820 (23): 94–96.

97. Pückler-Muskau 1987 [1826–1829]: 32.

98. Wheaton 1830: 149.

99. Literary Gazette, March 9, 1822: 153–154.

100. Ibid., 153.

101. Ibid., 154.

102. Ibid., 153.

103. Ibid., 154.

104. Ibid., 153.

CHAPTER FIVE

1. The collections in Florence and Turin went on display in 1824; the Louvre collection was opened in 1827; and the Gregorian Egyptian Museum in the Vatican was opened in 1838–1839.

2. On August 15, 1835, Pasha Muhammad Ali issued an ordinance to curb the excesses of the antiquities trade, which prohibited the exportation of "carved stones and objects." In the same year a site in Cairo was designated for the conservation and display of antiquities; however, this project did not begin in earnest until the 1850s. On the 1835 ordinance, see Reid (2001: chap. 3); on the history of the Cairo Museum, see Tiradritti (1999).

3. *Report of the Select Committee Appointed to Inquire into the Condition, Management, and Affairs of the British Museum* (1835). The inquiry was proposed to the House of Commons by Mr. Benjamin Hawes, MP for Lambeth. The main sections of the report were listed as I. Management, Income, and Expenditure of the Museum. II. Collections in the Museum. III. Accommodation of the Public. IV. Suggestions for Improvements. V. Foreign Literary Institutions and Libraries.

4. *Report from the Select Committee Appointed to Inquire into the Condition, Management, and Affairs of the British Museum* (1835) 7 (1): 115–116, para. 1497–1520. Ellis was appointed principal librarian in 1827.

5. Ibid., para. 1499. Julius Michael Millingen (1800–1878) was a physician and archaeologist with an interest in classical archaeology.

6. Ibid.

7. Ibid., para. 1511.

8. Ibid., para. 1515.

9. Obtained between 1819 and 1824, this collection of over 4,000 objects was sold to the king of France (for the Louvre) for £10,000.

10. *Report from the Select Committee Appointed in the Following Seasons to Consider the Same Subject* (1836 [10]:1, appendix 1): "Heads of Inquiry Relative to the Improvement of the British Museum—III, Department of Antiquities," sec. 9:55.

11. Ibid., sec. 10:56–57.

12. Letter from Forshall to Hawkins, April 15, 1836, in Correspondence of the Department of Ancient Near East, vol. 6, 1882.

13. OP [c. May] 1818: 1451.

14. The rapid growth of the collection around this time is evidenced in the museum's *Synopsis*, where the 74 significant Egyptian antiquities listed in 1827 had grown to 181 in 1835.

15. The trustees did not buy all of Salt's collection, but rather obtained a large portion of it at auction. Furthermore, Salt's "third collection" was not an inventoried collection designed for sale as a unit; it essentially included all the material in his possession at the time of his death.

16. Objects from Barker's collection were purchased at auction in 1833, Burton's in 1836, and d'Athanasi's in 1837 (see catalogues in the Department of Ancient Egypt and Sudan). Wilkinson donated part of his collection to the museum in 1834. MSCT, January 11, 1834: 3721. A list of the objects is held at BMDAES archives, "Catalogue of Egyptian Antiquities Presented to the British Museum by John Gardner Wilkinson, 1834." John Barker was the consul general in Egypt after Salt.

17. The Abydos King list (EA 117) is a tablet listing the Egyptian kings that was from the temple of Ramesses II at Abydos and dates to c.1270 BCE. It was purchased at the sale of the collection of Jean François Mimaut, the French consul general in Egypt from 1829 to 1837. The lions (EA 1 and 2) donated by Prudhoe were acquired from a journey to the Sudan in 1828. They were intended to be a pair, made under Amenhotep III for his temple at Soleb in Nubia. Left unfinished, they were completed by Tutankhamun, and then taken to Soleb by his successor, King Ay. The Meroitic ruler, Amanislo then moved them to Gebel Barkal in the third century BC. The sarcophagus of Ankhnesneferibra (EA 32) was purchased from a sale in Paris. The colossal beetle (EA 74) donated by Lord Elgin was found in Constantinople.

18. The statue of a sphinx did arrive in England but was burnt in a fire at the Plymouth dockyard sometime between 1840 and 1842. This object was originally offered to the museum by the politician John Bowring in 1838, Bowring having visited Egypt in 1837. MSCT, December 1, 1838: 4911. In 1839 the Admiralty informed the trustees that the sphinx had been taken from Alexandria to Malta and that it would be sent to England by the first ship of war coming home. MSCT, September 21, 1839: 5170–5171. Having been successfully transported from Malta to England, its arrival was never reported to the Lords Commissioners. After the fire, the loss of the statue was reported to the trustees in 1842. MSCT, May 21, 1842: 5922. Fragments of a colossal granite statue of Sarapis were offered by the collector Anthony Harris via Edward Lane in 1839. The trustees agreed to pay £150 for the transport of these fragments. MSCT, February 2, 1839: 4977–4978. See also MSCT, February 23, 1839: 5003, where it is reported that the Foreign Office had written to the trustees confirming Patrick Campbell's (consul general in Egypt) role in facilitating transport of the remains. However, delays in arranging transport were caused by the bursting of the banks of the Canal of Alexandria and the building of a new one, and the matter became more complicated when Harris reported that in digging around the statue of Sarapis another statue appearing to be that of Isis had been found, and that this could also be removed for double the price (i.e., £300). MSCT, May 24, 1839: 5080; October 12, 1839: 5199–5200. The trustees agreed to this, but were then informed by Harris that this statue was too massive for removal. MSCT, November 2, 1839: 5214; August 8, 1840: 5449–5450. The acquisition of the statue of Sarapis finally fell through after its removal was impeded by rising waters in the canal. Furthermore, the statue was found not to be of Sarapis. MSCT, January 14, 1843: 6114.

19. These were refused because Hawkins stated that he "could not recommend the purchase." MSCT, September 25, 1841: 5696. See Parkinson (2003).

20. That such objects were becoming more widely available reflected the fact that the intact tombs of Thebes had been excavated in the 1820s.

21. Samuel Birch became assistant keeper of the Department of Oriental Antiquities in 1844 and in 1861 became keeper, serving in this post until 1885.

22. For example, Hawkins encouraged the trustees to purchase the sarcophagus of Ankhnesneferibra (EA 32), which he defined as "extremely desirable" in 1835. MGMT, February 14, 1835: 1477. This object was brought to France by the French officers who were employed in transporting the obelisk that now stands in the Place de la Concorde in Paris. Hawkins was a numismatist and botanist who joined the museum in 1825. A fellow of the Society of Antiquaries, the Linnaean Society, and the Royal Society, Hawkins became keeper of antiquities in 1826 when the previous keeper Taylor Combe died. He served in this post until 1860.

23. Note Hawkins' efforts in facilitating the purchase of the Sams, Salt, and d'Athanasi collections below. The smaller collections that Hawkins recommended for purchase are too numerous to list here; however, examples are reported in MSCT, May 9, 1835: 3984; August 1, 1835: 4041–4043; March 12, 1836: 4219; July 23, 1836: 4332–4333; July 11, 1840: 5425; November 28, 1840: 5515; April 23, 1842: 5884; December 10, 1842: 6081. Many other small collections and objects were offered but refused, for example, the collection of a Mr. Campanari. MSCT, December 11, 1841: 5764–5765.

24. For example, the sarcophagus of Ankhnesneferibra was purchased from a sale in Paris.

25. Asserting the historical significance of the colossal statue of Ramesses II, Wilkinson stated the likelihood that it was one referred to by Herodotus and Diodorus as being made by Sesostris; he also emphasized "its great beauty, the face being in the same graceful style as the Colossi of Aboosimbel, and the Head in the museum." The "Head in the museum" was the bust of Ramesses II (EA 19), which arrived in 1818. MSCT, November 21, 1835: 4119–4120. Despite continued negotiations over the statue of Ramesses II in the 1850s, it never made it to the museum (see chapter 6, note 2, below). On the sarcophagus of Ankhnesneferibra, Wilkinson stated that it was in a good state of preservation and that "he should be very glad to see so interesting a sarcophagus in the museum"; Letter from Wilkinson to Hawkins dated March 12, 1835, and cited in MSCT, April 11, 1835: 3903–3904. On Lane's promotion of the statue of Sarapis, see MSCT, February 2, 1839: 4977–4978.

26. The Duke of Hamilton (Alexander Douglas) served as a trustee from 1834 to 1853. The trustees received his appraisal of the sarcophagus via the Archbishop of Canterbury, who conveyed how "His Grace spoke highly of its remits both as a beautifully worked and well-preserved relic of ancient Egyptian art, and as a curious monument in the history of Egypt." MGMT, July 9, 1836: 1512. The duke's comments on the uniqueness, excellent workmanship, and good preservation of the object were also emphasized in a letter to the trustees. MSCT, July 23, 1836: 4332–4333. The story of how the sarcophagus came to be in the museum is quite complicated, as in order to facilitate its speedy purchase, the duke paid for it in advance, expecting to be reimbursed when the funds from Treasury were finally transferred to the museum's accounts. However, it appears that the duke mistakenly purchased a different sarcophagus, one made of green basalt. MSCT, November 12, 1836: 4377–9. Based on Hawkins's assessment that the sarcophagus of Ankhnesneferibra was of "far greater interest" than the one of green basalt, the trustees informed the Duke of Hamilton that the money they had claimed from Treasury was for this particular sarcophagus, and that they felt precluded for applying for money for any other purpose. Recognizing his mistake, the Duke willingly paid the trustees for the green basalt sarcophagus, and negotiations for the original sarcophagus were then resumed by Hawkins, who arranged for the payment of 16,000 francs to its proprietors. MSCT, November 12, 1836: 4377–4379; December 10, 1836: 4402–4405; January 21, 1837: 4426–4427. The sarcophagus of Ankhnesneferibra finally arrived at the museum early in 1837.

27. Letter from d'Athanasi to the trustees, July 11. MSCT, August 1, 1835: 4041–4043. D'Athanasi was the Arabic and Turkish interpreter for the British consul, but soon became involved in Salt's collecting activities. From 1819 to 1824 he formed a collection that was sold to the French government in 1826. From 1824 to 1827 he was instrumental in forming Salt's third collection. Inspired by the spate of museum purchases of consular collections in Europe,

d'Athanasi was seeking to follow in the footsteps of Salt, who had once been his employer. He informed the trustees that the experience he had gained from this employment ensured that he was "competent to put the British Museum in a condition to rival the Royal Collection at Paris," and requested £1,500 a year for five years for providing this service. While Hawkins supported this offer, describing d'Athanasi as the "most skilful and best informed excavator at present existing," the trustees refused to enter into any such agreement, stating that such ventures could only be undertaken under the sanction of government. Ibid.

28. A catalogue of the antiquities purchased by Sams can be found in the British Museum Early Papers, Salt and Sams Collections: 2–136.

29. Sams emphasized the comprehensive nature of his collection when later pleading with the trustees to reconsider their reduced offer. "It may perhaps be said, how is it these collections are so remarkable? I wd [would] reply that, tho' I had a Firman expressly from the Pasha to excavate where I pleased, and tho' I used the greatest perseverance (even to much injury of health) that I was capable of, as well in searching out, as in purchasing, yet the collections wd. not have been thus rich, but that, having recommendations by letter to persons of eminence and learning, who had resided in Egypt about 20, and one in Upper Egypt, even 23 years, I induced them, by the offers I made, and by the kindness that existed between us, to cede me collections, they had been long amassing. That, my stores may, in truth, be said to be a collection of collections." OP, January 23, 1834: n.p.

30. A captain in the Royal Artillery, Leake traveled widely in Greece and published on its topography and antiquities. He also accompanied William Richard Hamilton on his travels in Egypt at the beginning of the century, and collaborated with Charles Philip Yorke on the publication of *Remarks on Some Egyptian Monuments in England* of 1826. His oral testimony on the collection was reported at the MGMT, April 20, 1833: 3583–3584.

31. Letter from the Earl of Mountnorris to the Trustees. MGMT, April 20, 1833: 3583–3584.

32. Ibid.

33. OP, April 20, 1833: n.p.

34. *Gentleman's Magazine* 1833 (103): 312–315.

35. Ibid., 315.

36. Ibid.

37. MGMT, May 11, 1833: 3595–3596.

38. Letter from Sams to the Trustees. OP, June 29, 1833: n.p.

39. A list of the rare objects referred to was attached. Letter from Sams to the Trustees. OP, June 29, 1833: n.p.

40. Letter from Sams to Trustees. OP, July 11, 1833: n.p.

41. Sams suggested to the secretary Josiah Forshall that he distribute this article to the other trustees who were making a decision on his collection. Ibid.

42. MSCT, July 13, 1833: 3638–3639.

43. Ibid., 3656; Letter from Sams to Forshall. OP, July 15, 1833: n.p. Sams repeated his offer in another letter written the following day, once again stating that "so much does he desire his extensive and rare collections to remain in England, and become the nation's property, that tho' felt a sacrifice, he reduces the price further, to the sum named." OP, July 16, 1833: n.p.

44. After writing *Remarks on Some Egyptian Monuments in England,* Yorke and Leake were considered authorities on the subject.

45. Letter from Yorke to the Trustees. OP, July 17, 1833: n.p.

46. Letter from Leake to Forshall. OP, July 30, 1833: n.p.

47. MSCT, November 9, 1833: 3684.

48. Ibid.

49. OP, January 11, 1834: n.p. Another copy of this testimonial with slightly different wording can be found in BMDAES, "Salt and Sloane Collections. . . ."

50. The other names were listed as the Earl of Mountnorris, C. Yorke, W. M. Leake, J. J. Halls (John James Halls, a painter and the biographer of Salt), Robert Richardson (a physician who traveled in Egypt 1816–1818), Frances Douce (antiquary and collector), B. Nichols (John Boyer Nichols, painter and antiquary), John Britton (antiquary and topographer), Isaac Cullimore (Egyptologist), T. J. Pettigrew (Thomas Joseph Pettigrew, surgeon and antiquary), J. Davidson (James Davidson, antiquary and bibliographer), Fras. Graham Moon (Sir Francis Graham Moon, printer seller and publisher), and George Offer. There was also a note at the bottom of the document from Halls stating that "at the request of the Lord Chancellor, about a year ago, I visited Mr. Sams's Collection, and stated to his Lordship, in writing, my *high* opinions of its merits—I conceive it well worth 4000." OP, January 11, 1834: n.p. On the other copy of this testimonial in BMDAES, "Salt and Sloane Collections . . . ," several other names are mentioned, including Bexley, Trowbridge, Rae Wilson, S. Briggs, Donnelly, Lane, Williams, Lee.

51. Letter from Sams to Trustees. OP, January 23, 1834: n.p. Here Sams stated that although he desired that the collection "be placed in our national repository for general benefit," several other governments had shown an interest in purchasing it at the original price of £4,000, particularly Russia.

52. Ibid. Yorke is described as an "author of a work on Egyptian antiquities"; Leake as an "author of a work on Egyptian antiquities and many other important works, [who] has travelled much in Egypt"; Francis Douce as having "much knowledge of Egyptian antiquities and [who is the] author of various valuable works"; the Earl of Mountnorris as having "travelled much in Egypt, [and who has an] acquaintance with Salt who was his secretary"; T. J. Pettigrew as having "written on Egyptian antiquities"; John Davison as having "travelled much in Egypt"; John Britton as the "author of many important works and [who has] knowledge of the subject"; Colonel Fox as having "examined the collections and [who] studies subjects of antiquity"; I. Cullimore as the "author of various learned and important papers on Egypt"; and finally, John Halls as having a "connection with late consul general Salt of Egypt, [a] large knowledge on the subject, [and who was] asked by Lord Chancellor to report on the collections with a view to purchase for the nation."

53. Ibid. See also MSCT, February 18, 1834: 3730.

54. See letters from Sams to Forshall, OP, February 3, 1834: n.p. February 4, 1834: n.p. February 20, 1834: n.p. April 24, 1834: n.p. April 30, 1834: n.p.

55. OP, February 20, 1834: n.p.

56. OP, April 30, 1834: n.p. see also April 24, 1834: n.p.

57. OP, April 30, 1834: n.p.

58. MSCT, May 10, 1834: 3804–3805.

59. This third collection came to England late in 1834; Giovanni d'Athanasi was central in its formation and was responsible for presenting it to the auctioneers. He provided a detailed list of the items in the collection as an appendix to his book of 1836: 153–261.

60. The inventory numbers for these are: statue of Viceroy Paser, EA 1376 (which was indicated as the property of Belzoni in the 1835 sale catalogue); statue of Ankhwa (formerly thought to be Bedjmes), EA 171; and statue of Ramesses II, EA 96. Other important pieces included the two wooden figures of a king from the tomb of Ramesses I or Seti I.

61. Waagen himself had viewed Salt's collection at Sotheby's (Waagen 1838).

62. MSCT, May 27, 1835: 3991.

63. Lord Ashburton was Alexander Baring (1773–1848), the merchant and banker. MSCT, June 4, 1835: 3993.

64. Ibid.; MSCT, June 13, 1835: 3997–3998. John Davidson (1797–1836) was a physician and traveler with a special interest in Egyptology and mummification. The Reverend George Tomlinson (1801–1863) had some publications relating to Egyptology (see Bierbrier 1995: 417).

65. Ibid.

66. Ibid.

67. On the contribution of Petrie to the emergence of "scientific" archaeology, see Drower (1995).

68. MSCT, July 11, 1835: 4012–4015. Salt received a total of £7,168 18s. 6d. for the whole collection.

69. Anastasi served as the Swedish consul general at Alexandria from 1828 to 1857. Like Salt and other European consuls, he employed agents and formed several major collections with the intention of selling them. Before selling this collection to the British Museum he sold one to the Dutch government in 1828. His offer to the museum came in the form of a letter from Wilkinson to the trustees. MSCT, April 16, 1836: 4252–4253. A list of the antiquities in his collection is in BMDAES, "Collection of Anastasi."

70. These were the sarcophagus of Sasobek, EA 17, the sarcophagus of Pahemnetjer, EA 18, and the statue of an unnamed man and woman, EA 36.

71. Letter from Wilkinson to the Trustees. MSCT, April 16, 1836: 4252–4253.

72. Ibid.

73. MSCT, May 26, 1838: 4771–4772.

74. MSCT, February 23, 1839: 5003–5006.

75. Lepsius was an international authority on Egypt; in 1832 he worked on the Egyptian collections at the Musée Charles X, and he became professor of Egyptology at the University of Berlin shortly before leading the Prussian expedition of 1842–1845.

76. MSCT, February 23, 1839: 5003–5006.

77. Sallier wanted 9,000 francs for this collection, and offered to include with it a basalt figure. MSCT, March 20, 1939: 5025–5027. Sallier had many key papyri, some of which Champollion had examined.

78. They stipulated that the collection was to be delivered to the British consul at Leghorn and that it should be packed and shipped under the direction of Messrs. Hahner and Gebhardt, the gentlemen who Lepsius recommended, and who packed a similar collection for the museum in Berlin. MSCT, February 23, 1839: 5003–5006.

79. The trustees also rejected Bunsen's and Lepsius's requests that funds be paid in advance, informing them that no money would be released until the antiquities arrived in the museum. MSCT, March 20, 1939: 5025–5027; December 7, 1839: 5242–5243.

80. MSCT, November 21, 1835: 4119–4120.

81. MSCT, September 20, 1836: 4361.

82. MSCT, October 8, 1836: 4363–4364.

83. Letter from Wilkinson to the Trustees. MSCT, September 20, 1836: 4361.

84. MSCT, October 8, 1836: 4363–4364.

85. Ibid.

86. MSCT, November 12, 1836: 4377–4379.

87. MSCT, December 10, 1836: 4402–4405.

88. MSCT, January 21, 1837: 4428.

89. MSCT, February 11, 1837: 4457–4458.

90. Ibid.

91. MGMT, March 11, 1837: 1518–1519.

92. This offer was made by the civil engineer John Perring, who had been responsible for constructing the railroad from the Mokuttum Mountains to Cairo; his offer was contingent upon the provision of a firman from the Pasha who would organize the necessary implements. MSCT, May 26, 1838: 4771–4772.

93. This time his words were that there was not "anything interesting about the statue below the drapery round the body." Ibid.

94. MSCT, June 9, 1838: 4784–4785.

95. Ibid.

96. MSCT, June 23, 1838: 4798.

97. MGMT, July 14, 1838: 1614–5.

98. Ibid. The decision that a new building was required was based on Smirke's opinion that his plan would have to be adapted in order to create such a place. MGMT, July 28, 1838: 4837.

99. MSCT, October 10, 1846: 7026.

100. MSCT, November 14, 1846: 7065–7066.

101. In June the consul general Charles Murray suggested sawing off the head, and then a month later Hawkins further stated that he had "consulted Mr. Bothwick one of the engineers engaged in the construction of the great railway between Alexandria and Cairo who would shortly return to Egypt, and would take an opportunity of examining the statue, and would report upon its state and cost of removal." MSCT, June 2, 1852: 8427; July 10, 1852: 8448.

102. It was Charles Murray who informed the trustees of the new difficulties in securing this statue. MSCT, January 22, 1853: 8513; MGMT, February 12, 1853: 2144–2145.

103. This time the trustees were prompted by letters from the painter and collector Henry Wallis and the Egyptologist Peter le Page Renouf, reminding them that, as a gift, this statue was the property of the English nation. MSCT, May 14, 1887: 17600–17601. Treasury rejected the request on the basis of the "adverse opinion expressed by Sir Evelyn Baring." MSCT, June 11, 1887: 17619; July 9, 1887: 17651.

104. MSCT, February 12, 1887: 17529–17531.

105. On the significance of Wilkinson's work for the foundation of Egyptology in Britain, see Thompson (1992).

106. The latter work is widely recognized as important because rather than focusing on sites, it adopted a more thematic approach and sought to describe the everyday life of ancient Egypt. Thompson (1992: 156) notes how it presented ancient Egyptians as "real people" for the first time, and David (2000: 97) describes it as the "most comprehensive description of Egyptian civilization, concentrating on daily life, religion and culture rather than political history and chronology." Other major British publications that helped establish the foundations of Egyptology more securely included Edward Lane's *Account of the Manners and Customs of the Modern Egyptians* of 1836 and Thomas Joseph Pettigrew's *Encyclopaedia Aegyptica* of 1842.

107. For a general discussion of the work of these travelers and artists, see Clayton (1982) and James (1997).

108. Champollion and Rosellini had other motives beyond surveying the sites. Appointed as the curator of the Louvre's Egyptian collection in 1826, Champollion was eager to expand the collection, whereas Rosellini aimed to expand that of the Egyptian Museum in Turin. The two main publications produced as a result of this expedition were Rosellini's *I monumenti dell'Egitto e della Nubia* (1832–1844), and Champollion and Rosellini's *Monuments de l'Egypte et de la Nubie d'après les dessins exécutés sur les lieux, sous la direction de Champollion le jeune* (1835–1847).

109. This breakthrough is most typically associated with the publication of Champollion's *Lettre à M. Dacier* in 1822 and his *Précis du système hiéroglyphique* in 1824. See Parkinson (1999).

110. In 1821 the trustees decided to request a new building to accommodate their rapidly expanding collections, and in 1823 plans for the new building program began. MSCT, January 11, 1823: 2832.

111. Plans to create shelving for the Townley Gallery had been proposed in 1824 by Richard Westmacott, i.e., to "form a Frieze or Belt around the room about 6 feet from the floor and 3–0 [feet] in width similar to the Elgin Room. I should by this mode be able to dispose of at least 150 objects." OP, February 13, 1824: 1868. It was then resolved that "Mr. Bankes, Mr. Knight, Sir Charles Long and Mr. Tyndale" form a subcommittee to confer with and give directions to Mr. Westmacott on this subject. MSCT, February 14, 1824: 2863. By 1827 these changes had been made; primarily featured on the new shelving system were the objects from Salt's collection,

especially the stelae and smaller figures. *Synopsis* (1827: 120). Although this provided some relief, a need for more room was apparent by 1830.

112. MSCA, June 14, 1828: 14.

113. MSCT, July 13, 1833: 3647; Letter from Westmacott to Officer of Woods and Forests regarding estimates for removal of Egyptian antiquities into the new building. OP, August 17, 1833: n.p. In 1834 correspondence from the Board of Ordnance reports on the tackle ordered for the transport of the Egyptian sculptures. MSCT, May 10, 1834: 3808–3809.

114. MSCT, June 14, 1834: 3820; July 12, 1834: 3853.

115. Figures 5.17–5.19 and 5.21 were produced by the artist E. W. Cooke. One can see a striking similarity between Cooke's recording of this event and his depiction of the demolition of old London Bridge, where there is an emphasis on pulleys, chains, ropes, and other equipment associated with the removal of large objects. See Smiles (2000: 143).

116. Completed in 1830, the arrangement of the sculpture collection of Ludwig of Bavaria in the new Glyptothek museum was designed by the architect Leo von Klenze and the sculptor J. M. von Wagner. See Potts (1980).

117. Despite the appreciation for ancient Egypt that had been expressed in the work of Denon and the *Description de l'Egypte*, France had not pursued the creation of an Egyptian collection until now, having refused Drovetti's collection in 1823. After 1824, however, the Louvre's acquisition policy changed and several major Egyptian collections were purchased. These were displayed in four of the nine rooms of the Musée d'Egypte, which was part of the new Musée Charles X. The ceiling paintings included the "Study and the Genius of the Arts Revealing Ancient Egypt," "Egypt saved by Moses," and the "Expedition to Egypt in 1798 under the Orders of Bonaparte." See Porterfield (1998), and Peltre (2000: 24).

118. Porterfield (1998: 84) outlines how ancient Egypt was appropriated for political gain, with the ceiling paintings being created to "legitimize the regime through the presentation of a reactionary historicism, to reinforce a sense of national identity based on French scientific exploits in Egypt and to promote its reactionary foreign policy in Europe and its imperial foreign policy vis à vis the Orient." See also Chaudonneret (1991: 498), who discusses the "pedagogical intent" of the painted decorations.

119. On the Vatican's Egyptian Museum, see Pietrangeli (1993: 186–187).

120. Westmacott's proposal for the new arrangement was prepared as a model for approval by the trustees. OP, October 11, 1833: n.p.; MSCT, October 12, 1833: 3680.

121. OR, July 11, 1833: 3400. MSCT, October 12, 1833: 3680.

122. On the incorporation of Anastasi's collection, see MSCT, November 16, 1839: 5232; February 15, 1840: 5311.

123. *Pinnock's Guide to Knowledge*, September 19, 1835: 331.

124. A report in the *Illustrated News* claimed that the Greek design characterized the principal contents of the museum (December 6, 1845: 358).

125. MGMT, July 12, 1834: 1467–1468. For example, discussion centered on the construction of special glass display cases for the presentation of the mummies, which allowed for several to be displayed together and viewed from all angles. MSCT, March 14, 1835: 3943–3944.

126. MSCT, October 14, 1837: 4580; November 11, 1837: 4598.

127. While Long (1836: 271) refers to a nine-foot-long papyrus displayed in the Egyptian Room, Sharpe (1862: 139) provides details on the "Papyri in Frames on the Staircase." That papyri and paintings are so rarely mentioned in guides to the museum's collections probably reflects the fact that they were displayed on the staircase and that this was not recognized as a gallery space.

128. *Returns of Accounts* (1844: 8).

129. Altick's (1957) classic study on the rise of periodicals during this period remains the most comprehensive treatment of the subject. In a detailed study on the coverage of archaeology in

British nineteenth-century periodicals, Phillips (2004) has shown how the antiquities collections of the museum were a favored subject for reporting.

130. The *Penny Magazine,* in particular, devoted many articles to Egyptian antiquities.

131. Long (1832 and 1836).

132. Examples of London guidebooks offering a basic description of the museum include Cruchley (1831), Whittock (1836), and Mogg (1838).

133. *Penny Magazine*, April 17, 1832: 13–14.

134. The success of Jane Webb Loundon's novel *The Mummy—A Tale of the 22nd Century* (1827) signified the continuing popular fascination with ancient Egypt.

135. Champollion and Rosellini (1835–1847), Rosellini (1832–1844), Wilkinson (1835, 1837), and Lane (1836).

136. *Gentleman's Magazine* 1842: 235.

137. Bager (2001 [1840]: 105) comments that among the Egyptian items "is a remarkable sarcophagus, which it is said, once held the body of Alexander the Great."

138. *Penny Magazine*, May 26, 1832: 77.

139. Long (1832: 253). Long was a classicist who had a special interest in the dissemination of knowledge and geography.

140. *Penny Magazine*, May 26, 1832: 76–77; June 2, 1832: 92.

141. MGMT, March 11, 1837: 1518–1519.

142. *Pinnock's Guide to Knowledge*, September 19, 1835: 331.

143. *Mirror*, September 16, 1837: 178. This article was accompanied with an engraving based on the 1836 illustration from the *Stationers Almanack* (fig. 5.23).

144. Passavant (1978 [1836]: 15).

145. *Mirror*, September 16, 1837: 178. The source for this quote is Long (1832: 5).

146. *Literary Gazette*, November 30, 1839: 762–763.

147. *Pictorial Times*, March 25, 1843: 25.

148. Long (1832): 4–5.

149. Ibid., 5.

150. Long (1836): 1.

151. Ibid., 2.

152. Anon. (1838): 271.

153. Ibid., 272.

154. *Chambers's Edinburgh Journal* 1839 (8): 91.

155. *Times*, November 22, 1839: 2.

156. Clarke (1843: n.p.).

157. Clarke (1847: 2, 4, 6, 8, 14).

158. *Pinnock's Guide to Knowledge*, September 14, 1833: 510–11; *Times*, February 5, 1838: 5.

159. *The Penny Magazine*, November 10, 1838: 436–438. Accompanying the article is the engraving of the new Egyptian Room referred to above.

160. *Chambers's Edinburgh Journal* 1839 (8): 90–92, 125–126, 178–179, 276.

161. Ibid., 90.

162. Ibid.

163. Ibid., 91.

164. Ibid., 276.

165. Another important example was Arundale and Bonomi's guidebook of 1842.

166. In the *Chambers's Edinburgh Journal* (1839 [8]: 276), for example, references are made to the "magnificent work of the learned Italian professor, Rosellini, as well as the excellent production of Mr. Wilkinson."

167. As David (2000: 98) has commented, Wilkinson's work appealed to a popular readership, his publications defining ancient Egypt for the first time in terms of social class, architecture,

furniture, arts and crafts, religion, and daily activities. Lane was a pioneer of Arabic studies in Europe, and his *An Account of the Manners and Customs of the Modern Egyptians* (1836) remains of great interest today.

168. *Pictorial Times*, March 25, 1843: 25.

169. Clarke (1847: 19).

170. Mogridge (1843: 252).

171. *Illuminated Magazine* 1843 (1): 33.

172. Ibid.

CHAPTER SIX

1. The monumental sculptures came from the mounds of Nimrud (ancient Kalhu), Khorsabad (ancient Dur-Sharrukin), and Kuyunjik.

2. Interest in acquiring the sculpture of Ramesses II had initially been expressed in 1835 (see chapter 5). In 1852 Hawkins received a proposal from the British consul general in Egypt, Charles Murray, who suggested that sections of a colossal statue of Sesostris be sawn off and sent to England. Although Hawkins suggested that the time was favorable for undertaking such a project, as English engineers who could supervise the operation were present in Egypt, the trustees were reluctant to support the idea and no decision was made. MSCT, June 12, 1852: 8427–8428. In 1853 William Richard Hamilton conveyed to the trustees a communication he had received from a Mr. Leonard Horner regarding a statue of Ramesses II and some other colossal statues that had been recently discovered at Memphis. MSCT, January 22, 1853: 8513. The trustees requested that the consul Charles Murray be consulted upon the subject, and he duly clarified that they were connected with the colossal limestone statue of Ramesses II that had been described by Joseph Bonomi in the *Transactions of the Royal Society of Literature*, and that they had previously been offered to the British Museum. MGMT, February 12, 1853: 2144–2145. Cleopatra's Needle attracted interest from the trustees around this time, who felt it "would prove an object of great public interest both on account of its antiquity and its association with the military glory of the country." MSCT, October 9, 1852: 8467. However, they later changed their minds, reporting to government that "owing to the nearly obliterated state of the hieroglyphics, the removal of this obelisk to England would not afford an adequate requital for the large expense which such removal would render necessary." MSCT, May 4, 1867: 11226. Thus in 1875 it was the travel writer James Alexander (1803–1885) who arranged for removal of the obelisk to London. A detailed account of how the obelisk eventually came to London can be found in Iversen (1972).

3. Listings of the items acquired during this period were reported in the *Returns of Accounts* until 1858, when there were too many to continue recording them. The items recorded until then include a lid of a sarcophagus of the Ptolemaic period, a tablet, and a wooden figure of Pasht acquired in 1853; fragments of statues bearing the name of Aakh-en-aten from Tel-el-Amarna, a bronze figure of Horus, a wooden sepulchral coffin, and a scarab with the name Ramesses III acquired in 1854; a statue of King An, sixteen Egyptian and Coptic sepulchral tablets, and a complete mummy cloth acquired in 1855; two large bronze hawks acquired in 1856; a wooden sepulchral figure of Seti I, a papyrus from Greco-Roman Egypt, and a portrait of a female from a mummy case acquired in 1857.

4. The sculpture of Mutemwia's boat (EA 43) was purchased from Somerset Lowry-Corry c.1835; the statue of Ramesses II (EA 67) was donated in 1840 by William Richard Hamilton; and the statue of Wahibre (EA 111) was donated in 1844 by the merchant Edward Fletcher (having stood in his premises in Ironmonger Lane in London since around 1790).

5. The bust of a Ptolemaic king (EA 941) came in 1854, having been given to Queen Victoria by the consul general Charles Murray; the Benha lion sculpture (EA 857) was donated by Charles Murray in 1856. MSCT, May 10, 1856: 8999; and the statue of Khaemwaset, described

in the minutes as Shaemuab (EA 947), was donated by Samuel Sharpe in 1866. MSCT, November 10, 1866: 11107. When the trustees refused to buy this statue at auction, Sharpe purchased it and promptly donated it to the museum.

6. These acquisitions are too numerous to list; however, an idea of what kinds of things entered the collection during this period can be found in the *Synopses*.

7. MGMT, February 12, 1853: 2144–2145.

8. This collection was left in the care of the British consul in Alexandria, who asked the museum to contact the Foreign Office to arrange transport for the collection. MSCT, June 14, 1873: 12726; December 13, 1873: 12872.

9. The US consul at Cairo, George Gliddon was most vocal about this problem. He warned that if antiquaries did not work toward preserving the monuments "in a very few years travellers may save themselves the trouble of a journey beyond the precincts of the British and the Continental museums." He also added that in destroying the monuments for building materials, when the Turkish-Egyptian governor "has a choice between a sculptured or an unsculptured Monument or Tomb, . . . he invariably chooses those which are *painted and sculptured*, because, by so doing, he *knows* that he hurts the feelings of the European, and renders nugatory a journey of some thousand miles to view an ancient pillar, or to copy a hieroglyphic legend" (Gliddon 1841: 4, 43).

10. Efforts to establish the National Antiquities Service began in the 1830s. In 1858 an attempt to establish the first Egyptian museum, known as the Bulaq Museum, was made; however, it was not until in 1863 that the Cairo Museum was opened. See Reid (2001) for a detailed account of the emergence of these institutions.

11. A good example of a major antiquities collection that the museum did acquire during this period was that of the Duc de Blacas. This French nobleman and his son created a vast collection, which the museum obtained a special Treasury grant to purchase in 1866 for £48,000. Among the Egyptian items included were a number of papyri. Another earlier exception included the Earl of Belmore's collection, which was purchased in 1843 and which included sculptures, stelae, papyri, and smaller items.

12. For example, in 1857 selected objects were purchased from the sale of Anastasi's collection, and in 1867 the keeper Samuel Birch got approval to spend £1,000 at the sale of Robert Hay's collection. After Birch's request was initially declined, the Sub-Committee of Finance resolved that £1,000 be included in the following year's estimates for this collection. These funds were spent on papyri and smaller objects. MSCT, July 13, 1867: 11281–11282; Minutes of the Sub-Committee of Finance, November 30, 1867: 1458–1459; MSCT, December 7, 1867: 11363.

13. For example, in 1859 a sarcophagus and the front of a sarcophagus offered by a Mr. Moore and the Earl of Bessborough, respectively, were declined. MSCT, July 9, 1859: 9617; August 6, 1859: 9648.

14. The trustees did agree to the purchase of some items from Harris's collection, particularly the papyri. Harris (1790–1869) was a British merchant and commissariat official in Alexandria. In 1869 Birch had emphasized the importance of this collection and suggested to the trustees that Stuart Poole (assistant keeper in the Department of Antiquities) examine it. MSCT, December 11, 1869: 11762. On the trustees' rejection of the collection, see MSCT, December 9, 1871: 12312. In the following year, Harris's daughter offered part of the collection for £5,000, which they also declined. MSCT, March 9, 1872: 12374. Birch challenged this decision, recommending that a special grant be obtained for the purchase of the collection, and singling out the hieratic papyrus of the reign of Ramesses III that was included in it. MSCT, April 13, 1872: 12407. The trustees then agreed to the purchase of the papyrus for £2,000. MSCT, October 12, 1872: 12530. In 1874 the remainder of the Harris collection was offered for £1, 700, and the trustees reluctantly agreed to purchase it. For the offer of sale, see MSCT, June 13, 1874: 13029; on the terms of purchase, the trustees asked permission from Treasury to include the

amount in the estimates for the next financial year. MSCT, November 14, 1874: 13124–13125. Treasury did not object to this, but requested that it be taken from the general budget for purchases. MSCT, December 12, 1874: 13135–13136.

15. Hawkins encouraged his assistant Samuel Birch to engage in such trips. A good example of this was the trip that Birch took to Europe in 1846 to inspect antiquities for sale. These included a collection offered by Messrs. Hahner and Gebhardt, an alabaster sarcophagus offered by Signor D. Campanari, and some vases and other objects in Rome. MSCT, September 5, 1846: 6987–6988. James (1981: 21) has argued that during the years of Birch's keepership "very few positive steps were taken to enlarge the collections. Nevertheless, there was a steady flow through benefactions and the activities of the Reverend Greville Chester."

16. MSCA, June 5, 1863: 1315; MSCT, June 13, 1963: 10354–10355.

17. By 1855 Birch was contributing to the process of recommending collections for purchase. MSCT, October 13, 1855: 8896. Examples where Hawkins and then later Birch had their recommendations approved include MSCT, October 13, 1855: 8896; June 8, 1861: 9980; June 8, 1867: 11259; January 25, 1867: 11393; April 26, 1873: 12679; April 24, 1875: 13245. Although the trustees generally approved the purchases recommended by Hawkins and Birch, they did on occasions decline them. For example, the purchase of seventeen Egyptian tablets offered by Mr. Cahill of Wandsworth for £114 was declined in 1858 (MSCT, April 17, 1858: 9387–9388); the collection of Mr. H. De Montout was declined in 1863 (MSCT, January 10, 1863: 10263; March 14, 1863: 10299); and a statue offered by Sotheby's for £325 was declined in 1866 (MSCT, August 4, 1866: 11062).

18. For example, in 1858 Hawkins was allowed to spend £60 at a sale of Egyptian antiquities at Messrs. Stevens (MSCT, May 22, 1858: 9408); in 1866 Birch was given permission to spend £60 at the sale of Yuppa Bey (MSCT, November 10, 1866: 11105); in 1867 Birch was authorized to spend £50 on the collection offered by Mr. Feuardent (MSCT, January 12, 1867: 11141); in 1867 Birch was allowed to spend £118.9.0 at the sale of H. A. Raife's collection in Paris (MSCT, March 9, 1867: 11189); in 1878 Birch was authorized to spend £100 at the sale of Mr. Allemant (MSCT, May 4, 1878: 14292); and in 1880 Birch was allowed to spend £110 at the sale of Mr. S. Hull (MSCT, May 8, 1880: 15112).

19. MSCT, October 11, 1873: 12839.

20. MSCT, December 1839: 5254.

21. E.g., Birch (1841–1844).

22. MSCA, July 5, 1860: 1159–1160.

23. MSCT, November 10, 1860: 9843. An alternative suggestion was to put ethnography and medieval antiquities in a separate department with British Antiquities, but this motion was not supported. MSCT, December 8, 1860: 9852.

24. MSCT, January 26, 1861: 9890; February 2, 1861: 9896.

25. The first two commissions were ordered on June 17, 1847, and May 5, 1848, respectively. The aim was to inquire into the organization of departments, with a "view of ascertaining in what manner that National Institution may be made most effective for the advancement of Literature, Science, and the Arts." *Report of the Select Committee on the Constitution and Government of the British Museum* (1850 [24]: iii). The successive inquiries were published as the following reports: *Communications made by the Architect and Officers* (1852 [28]:201); *Communications made by the Architect and Officers* (1857–1858 [33]: 373); *A Copy of All Communications* (1859 [14]: 51); *Report from the Select Committee* (1860).

26. *Report from the Select Committee* (1850 [24]: 163/3155).

27. Ibid.

28. Ibid., 163/3230.

29. Ibid., 170/3328.

30. Ibid., 159/8066.

31. OR, July 14, 1910: 311; MSCT, November 9, 1850: 8101.

32. MSCT, April 5, 1856: 8960.

33. In Lepsius's expedition over 15,000 antiquities and casts were taken back to Berlin. It was translated into English in 1852 by K. R. H. Mackenzie (London: S. I. Bentley).

34. The translation of this work into English by Charles Cottrell and Samuel Birch in 1848–1867 (London: Longmans, Green and Co.) ensured that it became a primary source for the interpretation of ancient Egyptian history and archaeology.

35. That the antiquities collections gained a great deal from the building program is reflected in a report from the antiquities subcommittee in 1851, who noted with the "greatest satisfaction" that the north side gallery would be given to the Department of Antiquities instead of the Department of Prints and Drawings. MSCA, December 17, 1851: 521. Featured were a new gallery containing the Lycian marbles (opened in 1847), the Xanthian Room (opened in 1848), the Nineveh Room (opened in 1853), and two additional Elgin Marbles galleries (opened in 1852 and 1868). The *Illustrated London News* published an engraving of the new Xanthian room in 1848 (January 15: 15), and of the new Nineveh Room in 1853 (March 26: 225). See Jenkins (1992) for an account of these new sculpture galleries.

36. For example, when in 1852 the architect Sydney Smirke offered his own suggestions as to how the ancient sculptures should be arranged, the trustees turned to Hawkins for comment. MSCT, June 19, 1852: 8432. Sydney Smirke was Robert Smirke's younger brother, who took over the task of completing the new west wing in 1846.

37. Letter from Newton to A. Panizzi, November 9, 1856 (BL Add. MS 36717, ff.612–620); as reproduced in Wilson (2002: 147–149).

38. Similarly, the plan of 1835–1836 (fig. 5.20) states that this southern section is reserved for "miscellaneous antiquities."

39. Hawkins also suggested that the Elgin, Lycian, and intermediate gallery then in course of erection be appropriated for Greek sculptures and that these would be approached through the British and Roman monuments, thus providing "as near an approach to a systematic and chronological arrangement" as the nature of the museum buildings would allow. MSCT, January 11, 1850: 8135–8136.

40. MSCT, April 12, 1851: 8192.

41. Appointed as an assistant in the Department of Antiquities in 1848, Oldfield quickly assumed a key role in matters of arrangement, devoting much of his time to producing plans for the distribution of the sculpture collections in the new Smirke Building. For the Assyrian gallery, see MSCT, September 20, 1851: 8294; and October 11, 1851: 8309. For the Greek and Egyptian sculptures, see OR, November 9, 1852: 17110/33; MSCT, November 13, 1852: 8477. The most specific plan for the arrangement of the Egyptian antiquities was written by Oldfield on November 25, 1852, and presented to the trustees by Hawkins the following day. OR, November 26, 1852: 17141/341–17144/344. The "Table of References in the Plan" is in OP, November 26, 1852.

42. OR, November 9, 1852: 17110/33.

43. OR, November 25, 1852: 17141/341.

44. Ibid., 17141/341–17142/342.

45. Ibid., 17143/343.

46. Ibid., 17143/343.

47. Ibid., 17143/343.

48. Ibid., 17141/341.

49. Ibid., 17143/343.

50. Ibid., 17144/344.

51. The members of this committee were the Earl of Aberdeen, the Right Honorable Sir David Dundas, and William Richard Hamilton. MSCT, November 27, 1852: 8484. The committee also recommended that the cast of Ramesses II over the north door be moved to this location. MSCA, December 2, 1852: 546–547.

52. *Synopsis* (1853: 137).

53. See *Returns of Accounts* (1853: 12), where it is reported that "Egyptian sculpture is being expanded into the Center and South Principal Gallery, in which and in the North Principal Gallery they will be arranged in chronological order."

54. *Communications Made by the Architect and Officers* (1852 [28]: 201); *Report from the Select Committee on the Management of the National Gallery* (1853 [35]); *Communications Made by the Architect and Officers* (1857–1858 [33]: 373); *A Copy of All Communications Made by the Officers and Architect* (1859 [14]: 51).

55. *Report from the Select Committee on the Management of the National Gallery* (1853 [35]: 9051). Jenkins (1992: 198–205) provides a useful summary of Newton's contribution at the inquiries.

56. *Report from the Select Committee on the Management of the National Gallery* (1853 [35]: 8284).

57. More specifically, Waagen (1854: 39) commented that "the new buildings, the interiors of which have been finished since my first visit in 1835, were less satisfactory to me. Much as might be separately urged against the suite of little rooms in which the Townley marbles were first placed, I cannot agree that any change for the better has been made. The small rooms, by their more correct proportion with the size of the sculptures, produced a far more favorable effect, while the sculptures were incomparably better lighted than in the present large and lofty hall in which they are now in great measure lost."

58. Fergusson (1849: 23).

59. The emphasis on color and design not only reflected a concern with conveying ancient Egypt's rich system of pictorial representation, but was a result of the passion for polychromy shown by chief architect and designer of the courts, Owen Jones.

60. Much of the literature on world's fairs has highlighted the significance of the displays of ancient and ethnographic cultures (e.g., Allwood 1977; Rydell 1985; Coombes 1994; Bennett 1995; Auerbach 1999; Maxwell 1999; Hoffenberg 2001; Hobhouse 2002; Piggott 2004).

61. Their main contribution was to supply molds of Egyptian sculptures. The lions in the avenue at the entrance to the Egyptian Court were cast from the museum's Prudhoe lions, and the columns in the temple were cast from the papyrus column in the museum. Correspondence of Department of the Ancient Near East (1852: 413). Furthermore, Birch contributed to a companion guide on the exhibition collections (Wilkinson and Birch 1857).

62. See figures 153 and 154 in Pietrangeli (1993).

63. Gaehtgens (1996: 61).

64. On the alterations made to the Neues gallery, Wildung (1999: 3) has commented, "The combined effect of the pseudo-Egyptian architecture and the garish murals was to overshadow and overwhelm completely the original pieces on display. It was an experimental style, which was soon abandoned in favour of less disastrous approaches."

65. While the latter group of photographs were taken some time after the 1854 installation was completed, they nevertheless remain a good source for gaining an understanding of the arrangement style.

66. The subcommittee suggested that the bust be moved to the east side of the gallery opposite the door, and also that it be lowered two feet. MSCA, February 21, 1857: 951–952; MSCT, February 28, 1857: 9158–9159.

67. Report submitted by Oldfield to the trustees in 1858, and then subsequently to Parliament in 1860, on a new arrangement for the Greek and Roman galleries. Appendix to the Minutes of Evidence from the *Report from the Select Committee on the British Museum* (1860).

68. With the continuing growth of the antiquities collections, the galleries fast became overcrowded again and were unable to accommodate the arrival of new collections. As early as 1855 Smirke warned the trustees that the "demand for more room in the Antiquities Department will be brought seriously before them and that probably at no distant period." MSCT, July 7, 1855: 8864–8865; Minutes of the Sub-Committee for Buildings, February 16, 1856: 904. In addressing how an increased provision for accommodating antiquities might be provided, several solutions

were proposed, including the construction of a columbarium and the erection of a new wing for antiquities. MSCT, July 7, 1855: 8864–8865; Oldfield 1858–1860, as cited in Edwards (1969 [1870]: 724). By 1860 the problem of accommodating the museum's collections had reached a crisis point, and decisions had to be made about whether some collections should be removed. Hawkins had reported on this situation to the select committee, stating that "a great many of our collections are in a state of entire confusion" because of the need for space. *Report of the Select Committee on the Constitution and Government of the British Museum* (1850: 159/8131).

69. Published in Appendix to the Minutes of Evidence of the *Report from the Select Committee on the British Museum* (1860 [16]: 173).

70. The suggestions that were subsequently made for the proper provision of space for the collections led to the decision by Treasury that the mineralogical, geological, palaeontological, and natural history collections should be removed from the museum. MSCT, October 27, 1860: 9832–9834; MSCA, January 21, 1862: 1232–1248.

71. MSCA, January 21, 1862: 1245, 1247–1248.

72. For example, the gallery is reminiscent of Thomas Hope's (1769–1831) spectacular picture gallery.

73. A watercolor from 1847 shows the details and color of the designs, which were executed by Leonard Collman and Mr. Davis. British Museum, Department of Prints and Drawings 1902-1-29-1. This has been reproduced in Jenkins (1992, plate 3).

74. Fergusson (1849: 21).

75. Ibid.

76. *The Builder* 1851 (9) (419): 99, reported that the "upper part of the walls is coloured sage green, with panels formed by red lines, and the lower part (the podium) is to be coloured dark red, as a background for the sculptures."

77. See Bristow (1996: 182) on the impact of archaeological knowledge on the use of color in interiors. The deep red color, for example, was inspired by the walls of ancient Roman villas uncovered at Herculaneum and Pompeii.

78. Smirke argued that "had the sculpture been clean and more nearly of the natural color of marble, a lighter background would have sufficiently relieved them, but their dingy hue renders a deep-toned background unavoidable. The upper part, however, of the walls against which no sculpture can be placed should be painted in lighter tints, more in unison with the ceiling." OP, November 29, 1850: n.p. Hawkins also argued that because of the dirty appearance of the sculptures the walls should be a "dark rich color." OR, February 21, 1851: n.p.

79. MGMT, May 24, 1851: 2122.

80. When, in 1850, Smirke informed the trustees that the Egyptian gallery was ready for painting, Hawkins asked to be involved in making a determination on the subject, but the trustees were more eager to consult Westmacott and Smirke, who had been involved with previous decisions of this kind. MSCT, January 9, 1947: 7137; August 15, 1850: 8060.

81. On determining what the "proper" color might be, the trustees resolved that Westmacott and Smirke, under the view of Sir Charles Lock Eastlake (painter and president of the Royal Academy), were to paint the gallery "according to their judgement," and that they should place statues in the gallery "as an experiment for the decision of the Trustees." MSCT, March 8, 1851: 8173; February 22, 1851: 8163.

82. OP, April 9, 1859.

83. OR, May 5, 1859: 424.

84. Ibid., 425.

85. MSCT, June 25, 1859: 9607.

86. In 1858 this section had become much darker as a result of the construction of the reading room in the inner courtyard.

87. Hawkins argued that top-lighting was preferable for the antiquities galleries because lighting from side windows alone would require a larger space between buildings. OR, July 7,

1858: 5354/44. Furthermore, "galleries with windows on both sides, such as our Egyptian, expose every statue in a detached position to a variety of cross lights destructive to artistic effect." Ibid., 5353/43–5354/44.

88. Fergusson (1849: 20).

89. *Report from the Select Committee on the Management of the National Gallery* (1853 [35]: appendix 8,n. 39).

90. MSCT, July 11, 1857: 9242.

91. *Returns of Accounts* (1850: 10).

92. *Returns of Accounts* (1857: 12).

93. MSCA, February 21, 1857: 951–952.

94. *Edinburgh Review* 1866 (251): 69.

95. William Vaux was an assistant in the Department of Antiquities; Thomas Nichols was a senior assistant in the principal librarian's office.

96. *Returns of Accounts* (1861: 13; 1862: 13). Reports from over a five-year period, 1864–1869, provide a good example of the kind of work that was undertaken: in 1864 two new cases for the exhibition of wooden coffins were placed in the second Egyptian room and several of the wall cases were rearranged and refitted for a better display of their contents; in 1865 a statue in the northern vestibule of the Egyptian galleries had a glass case placed over it for better protection; in 1866 arrangements of the first Egyptian room were modified so as to admit the incorporation of recent acquisitions; in 1868 six compartments in the northern Egyptian gallery were fitted up and glazed for the reception of objects and some cases in the second Egyptian room were provisionally rearranged for the display of objects acquired from the Blacas collection; and in 1869 recesses in the northern Egyptian gallery were fitted up for objects, which were then mounted on pedestals, covered with glass cases, and arranged.

97. *Returns of Accounts* (1859: 12). It is difficult to identify any such decoration in the early photographs that were taken of the gallery.

98. This cast was made by Robert Hay and Joseph Bonomi. MSCT, September 25, 1841: 5696; December 11, 1841: 5764; *Returns of Accounts* (1843: 8).

99. Nichols (1870: 112).

100. That the Egyptian objects here were very numerous is reflected in the guidebooks. For example, in Masson (1850), thirty-three pages are devoted to the antiquities in the Egyptian Room.

101. Masson (1850: 21), for example, reports that in the antiquities rooms "the articles are so multifarious, being arranged more according to their size than their nature."

102. Roberts's work constituted the most comprehensive series of views of the sites of the Near East yet published (see Guiterman 1986). Frith's photographic work on Egypt had a particularly significant impact in reaching wider audiences in Britain (see Armstrong 1998 and Nickel 2004).

103. Other notable examples of the early photographic work in Egypt included Maxime Du Camp's *Egypte, Nubie, Palestine, et Syrie: Dessins photographiques recueillis pendant les années 1849, 1850 et 1851*, published in 1852; and Félix Teynard's *Egypte et Nubie* of 1858.

104. Nickel (2004: 74) comments on the potency of this photography of Egypt, arguing that it appealed "directly to the sense of sight, effectively transporting the viewer—seemingly without artistic mediation or rational effort—to an actual place and moment in time."

105. This show opened at the Egyptian Hall on July 16, 1850. A report on *Panorama of the Nile* appeared in the *Illustrated London News* March 30, 1850: 220–221. The museum became involved with the promotion of this exhibition when Joseph Bonomi, who contributed to its production, requested that attendants in the Egyptian Rooms give out tickets to "intelligent visitors." Letter from Bonomi to Birch, August 21, 1850, British Museum, Correspondence of the Department of the Ancient Near East, 410.

106. On the creation of the Egyptian Court at Sydenham, see Owen and Bonomi (1854). See Piggott (2004: chaps. 3 and 4) for a recent evaluation of the Egyptian and other courts.

107. The other historic courts included the Byzantine, Roman, Medieval, Renaissance, Italian, Assyrian, Greek, and Alhambra courts.

108. *Illustrated London News*, October 20, 1855: 485.

109. Displayed in the Egyptian temple were sculptures lent from the Bulaq Museum in Cairo and reproductions of other pieces; the walls were decorated with paintings and hieroglyphics in the style of the Old Kingdom. The Egyptian exhibits were associated with the other "Oriental" buildings recreated for this World's Fair, including a Tunisian barbershop and camel stable, and Turkish baths and a mosque. For more detailed descriptions of the Egyptian temple and bazaar at the Paris Exposition of 1867, see Norton (1974: 7); McCabe (1876: 60–62, 147–148); Greenhalgh (1991: chap. 4); Humbert et al. (1994: catalogue entries 214, 215); Auerbach (1999: 201).

110. Commentators on the fairs noted the way in which they blended ancient and modern civilizations (e.g., McCabe 1876: 148).

111. See Reid (2001: chap. 2) on the impact of the steamboats on tourism.

112. On the reception of the Assyrian antiquities at the British Museum, see Bohrer (2003).

113. Historians of the Victoria and Albert Museum have defined it as making a "pioneering attempt at vocational education" (Burton 1999: 13, 98).

114. *Edinburgh Review* 1866 (251): 69. Entries in Cole's dairy provide further negative comments on the British Museum: in 1863 he described it as "dirty and neglected," and in 1870 he noted that it had "bad-lighting," that dirt was "destroying the Egyptian Mummies," and there was "imperfect labelling." Cited in Burton (1999: 98).

115. *Building News*, April 1, 1859: 306.

116. Waagen (1857: 1) stated that since the publication of his 1838 book, "the arrangement of the sculpture in the British Museum has been greatly improved. The Egyptian and Assyrian monuments have, in the first place, been disposed in that chronological succession which alone best unites the highest instruction with the greatest enjoyment."

117. *Illustrated London News*, April 15, 1854: 343.

118. Weale was a publisher who wrote several books on architecture.

119. Weale 1854: 558.

120. Ibid.

121. *Illustrated London News*, February 13, 1847: 108.

122. Jerrold (1852: 84). Jerrold was a journalist and writer.

123. Vaux (1851: 297, 300). Similarly, in Timbs's (1855: 521) guide the "celebrated" head of Ramesses II is highlighted as one of the main attractions of the museum, being described as "first-class Egyptian art."

124. Jerrold (1852: 228).

125. *Illustrated Weekly News*, August 16, 1862.

126. MSCT, June 11, 1881: 15635.

127. Waagen 1854: 40.

128. Ibid.

129. Ibid., 41, 42, 42, 43.

130. Masson 1850: 272.

131. Ibid., 273.

132. Ibid., 286.

133. Nichols (1870: 33–34).

134. Ibid., 34.

135. Vaux (1851: iii).

136. Hare (1878: 166–178). While thirteen pages are devoted to the Greek, Roman, and Assyrian remains, only one is assigned to the Egyptian collection.

137. Ibid., 179. These objects include the Rosetta Stone, the two large sarcophagi acquired in 1802, the colossal bust of Ramesses II, the Prudhoe lions, and the colossal head of Amenhotep III.

138. Hawthorne (1870: 376).

139. Ibid., 403.

140. Ibid., 437–438.

141. Wathen 1843: 238.

142. Ibid., 240.

143. *Illustrated London News*, July 22, 1854: 70.

144. Jerrold (1852: 84).

145. Ibid., 84, 123.

146. Ibid., 137, 128.

147. Ibid., 84.

148. Ibid., 142–143.

149. Wathen's (1843: 238) quote—see above—also suggests this connection.

150. Jerrold (1852: 150).

151. Fletcher (c.1850: 40).

152. Ibid.

153. Ibid., 42–43.

154. Hawthorne (1870: 431). This quote is associated with a visit to the museum in 1857.

155. Bicknell (1847: 312).

156. Ibid.

157. Masson (1850: 20).

158. *Illustrated London News*, February 13, 1847: 108.

159. Vaux (1851: 289).

160. Nichols (1870: 12). Nichols was a senior assistant in the principal librarian's office at the museum.

161. Ibid., 33.

162. For example, when discussing the architectural slab featuring Psamtek (EA 20), Nichols (1870: 100) writes, "We may refer to this slab for illustrations of the fine artistic feeling which sprang up at the Renaissance, and was peculiar to this, the *third period* of Egyptian sculpture."

163. Ibid., 41.

164. On the history of the Egypt Exploration Fund, later Society, see James (1982). The first chair in Egyptology was created for the pioneering archaeologist Flinders Petrie at University College London in 1892. See Wortham (1971) on the emergence of a community of British scholars dedicated to advancing the field of Egyptology.

165. The key players here were the Metropolitan Museum of Art, the Museum of Fine Art in Boston, and the Art Institute of Chicago. On the contribution of the Metropolitan, see Howe (1913, 1946) and Tomkins (1970).

Works Cited

Primary Sources

CENTRAL ARCHIVES, BRITISH MUSEUM

(Public Records Office class number is listed in brackets.)

Minutes of the General Meeting of Trustees. 1753–1963 [CE 1].
Minutes of the Standing Committee of Trustees. 1754–1963 [CE 3].
Original Papers. 1743–1946 [CE 4].
Officers' Reports to the Trustees. 1805–1869 [CE 5].
Minutes of the Sub-Committees of the Trustees. 1828–1963 [CE 7].
Indexes to minutes of meetings. 1754–1939 [26].
Letter books (from the Director's/Principal Librarian's office). 1829–1946 [CE 27].
Books of Presents (Benefactions book). 1756–1960 [CE 30].
Plans and Drawings of the British Museum. 1725– [CE 48].
Reports of the Sub-Committees of the Trustees. 1805–1809 [CE 53].
Illustrations of the British Museum. (2 vols.) [CE 115/1 and 2].
British Museum Cuttings and Extracts. (The Ellis scrapbooks); up to 1862 [CE115/3].
Roger Fenton's stereoscopic views of the galleries. 1858–1862 (2 vols.).
The Frederick York album of photographs. 1875 (2 vols.).

CENTRAL LIBRARY, BRITISH MUSEUM

Returns of Accounts, Estimates etc. to Parliament/Annual Returns. 1817–1881.
Synopsis of the Contents of the British Museum (annual). 1808–1856. Became British Museum *Guidebooks* in 1859.
Statues and Rules Relating to the Inspection and Use of the British Museum, 1759.

DEPARTMENT OF PRINTS AND DRAWINGS, BRITISH MUSEUM

The George Scharf collection of illustrations.
Illustrations of the British Museum.

DEPARTMENT OF ANCIENT EGYPT AND SUDAN, BRITISH MUSEUM

"The catalogue of Aegyptian Antiquitys [*sic*] from Sloane." N.d. 5 folio pages. (Note: The "from Sloane" part of the title appears to have been added later on.)

"The Bequest of Colonel William Lethieullier, left by his Will, dated July 23, 1755." Dated February 23, 1756.

"An Account of Pieces of Ancient Sculptures, Taken from the British Forces under the Command of Lt. General Lord Hutchinson, in Egypt from thé French Army in Alexandria, and Sent to England in the Charge of Colonel Turner, 1801 September." This document includes sketches of the antiquities, and appears in the folder "Early British Museum Register Pages, Department of Egyptian antiquities."

"Salt and Sloane Collections." N.d. Catalogue of Egyptian antiquities and various museum correspondence.

"Early Papers." N.d. Documents and correspondence, including some relating to the collections of Henry Salt, Joseph Sams, and Giovanni Anastasi.

"Catalogue: Anastasi Collection." 1839. A catalogue of the 2nd Anastasi collection purchased by the British Museum.

"Department of Antiquities, Anastasi Collection." 1857. A catalogue of the 3rd Anastasi collection auctioned in Paris.

DEPARTMENT OF GREEK AND ROMAN ANTIQUITIES, BRITISH MUSEUM

Letters on Antiquities. 1757–1834.

DEPARTMENT OF THE ANCIENT NEAR EAST, BRITISH MUSEUM

Correspondence. 1826–1860.

DEPARTMENT OF MANUSCRIPTS, BRITISH LIBRARY

An Essay towards Illustrating the History, Chronology, and Mythology of the Ancient Egyptians. By Alexander Gordon. 1741. BL Add. MS 8834.

Papers Relating the Foundation and Establishment of the British Museum. 1753–1760. BL Add. MS 4449.

Letter from Miss Catherine Talbot to Mrs. Anne Berkeley, describing her visit to the British Museum in 1756. Berkeley Papers, BL Add. MS 39311, f.82.

Museum: Pleasing Recollection; or, A Walk through the British Museum: An Interlude of Two Acts. By the Reverend Weeden Butler. 1767. BL Add. MS 27276.

List of Confiscated Antiquities by Joseph Fourier. 1801. BL Add. MS 46839, ff.12–13b.

Letter from Charles Newton to A. Panizzi. November 9, 1856, in Correspondence of Sir A. Panizzi, vol. 4. BL Add. MS 36717, ff.612–620.

History of the British Museum, by Sir Edward Maunde Thompson. N.d. [c.1900]. BL Add. MS 52292.

UNPUBLISHED WORKS IN THE DEPARTMENT OF PRINTED BOOKS, BRITISH LIBRARY

A Collection of Views, Cuttings from Newspapers and Magazines, Etc., Illustrating the History of the British Museum, Made by Sir Frederick Madden. 1775–1870. 4 vols.

PARLIAMENTARY PAPERS, REPORTS OF COMMISSIONS—HOUSE OF COMMONS

Report from the Select Committee Appointed to Inquire into the Condition, Management, and Affairs of the British Museum. 1835 (7): 1.

Report from the Select Committee Appointed in the Following Seasons to Consider the Same Subject. 1836 (10): 1.

Report from the Select Committee on Arts and Their Connexion with Manufactures. 1836 (9): 1.

Report from the Select Committee on the Constitution and Government of the British Museum. 1850 (24).

Communications made by the Architect and Officers of the British Museum to the Trustees Respecting the Enlargement of the Building of That Institution; and Communications between the Trustees and the Treasury upon the Same Subject, Subsequent to the Period when the Commissioners upon the Constitution and Management of the British Museum Presented Their Report to Her Majesty. 1852 (28): 201.

Report from the Select Committee on the Management of the National Gallery; also to Consider How Collective Monuments of Antiquity etc. Possessed by the Nation May Be Preserved, Judiciously Augmented, and Advantageously Exhibited to the Public. 1853 (35).

Communications Made by the Architect and Officers of the British Museum to the Trustees, and between the Trustees and the Treasury. 1857–1858 (33): 373.

A Copy of All Communications Made by the Officers and Architect of the British Museum and the Trustees Respecting the Want of Space for Exhibiting the Collections in That Institution, as Well as Respecting the Enlargement of the Buildings. 1859 (14): 51.

Report from the Select Committee on the British Museum. 1860 (16): 173.

PERIODICALS AND ILLUSTRATED MAGAZINES

Annals of the Fine Arts

1819 (10): 494–498. "Arrival of a Colossal Head Said to Be of Memnon; Some Shafts of Columns, Capitals, and Other Sculptures, from Africa, at the British Museum."

1819 (11): 589. Conclusion of Article Above.

1820 (13): 178–215. "A Brief View of the Fine Arts among Various Nations of Antiquity; From Millin and Other Authorities."

Chambers's Edinburgh Journal

1839 (8): 90–92. "Walks in the British Museum: Room of Egyptian Antiquities."

1839 (8): 125–126. "Walks in the British Museum: Room of Egyptian Antiquities; Second Article."

1839 (8): 178–179. "Walks in the British Museum: Egyptian Room; Third Notice."

1839 (8): 276. "Walks in the British Museum: Egyptian Room; Fourth Article."

Edinburgh Review

1803 (1): 330–345. Review of Vivant Denon's *Voyage dans la Basse et la Haute Egypte.*

1806 (7): 480–502. Review of Edward Daniel Clark's *The Tomb of Alexander.*

1811 (18): 435–447. Review of William Hamilton's *Aegyptiaca.*

Gentleman's Magazine

1802 (72): 726–727. [Editor's note on the arrival of objects taken by the French.]

1810 (80): 209, plate 1. The New Gallery at the British Museum.

1822 (92): 351–352. "Egyptian Antiquities in the British Museum."

1832 (102): 65–66. "Antiquarian Researches."

1833 (103): 312–315. "Egyptian Antiquities."

1842 (117): 235–246. Review of *Manners and Customs of the Ancient Egyptians* by Sir J. G. Wilkinson.

Illustrated London News

1845 (March 29): 202. "Easter Monday at the British Museum."
1845 (October 11): 237. "The British Museum."
1845 (December 6): 357–358. "The New British Museum."
1847 (February 13): 108. "The British Museum."
1854 (April 15): 343. "The British Museum: The Great Egyptian Gallery."
1854 (July 22): 70, 72. "The Crystal Palace at Sydenham."

Illustrated Weekly News

1862 (August 16): 716. "'London Town': Country Visitors in the Egyptian Ante-room, British Museum."

Imperial Magazine

1760: 689–695. "Description of the British Museum, with a General Account of the Collection, the Manner of Seeing It, the Contents of Each Room, and the Order in Which They Are Shewn."
1761: 660–662. "A Pamphlet, Entitled, The General Contents of the British Museum, with Remarks, &c. Has Lately Appeared . . ."

Literary Gazette

1822 (March 9): 152–154. "Sketches of Society: The Tomb, By Lady Blessington."
1839 (November 30): 762–763. "Egyptian Papyri: British Museum."

New Monthly Magazine

1821 (December 1): 615–617. "Belzoni's Egyptian Tomb Re-opened, with Additions."

Penny Magazine

1832 (April 7): 13–14. "The British Museum."
1832 (May 26): 76–77. "The British Museum: No. 2."
1832 (June 2): 92. "The British Museum: No. 3."
1832 (June 23): 113–114. "Thebes."
1834 (February 15): 61–63. "The Obelisk of Luxor."
1834 (February 22): 66–67. "The Obelisk of Luxor."
1836 (March 11): 106–107. "Mummies."
1836 (June 12): 237–238. "Arts of Ancient Egypt: Glass and Porcelain."
1838 (March 3): 81–82. "The Luxor Obelisk, in the Place Louis XVI, Paris."
1838 (November 10): 436–438. "New Egyptian Room, British Museum."

Pictorial Times

1843 (March 25): 25.

Pinnock's Guide to Knowledge

1833 (September 14): 570–571.
1835 (September 19): front page, 331.

Quarterly Review

1817 (10): 391–424. "Observations Relating to Some of the Antiquities of Egypt, from the Papers of the Late Mr. Davison."

1818 (17): 230–262. "Belzoni's Discoveries in Egypt and Nubia."

1818 (18): 335–379. Review of *Narrative of an Expedition to Explore the River Zaire.*

1818 (19): 178–204. Review of *Travels in Egypt, Nubia, Holy Land, Mount Libanon, and Cyprus in the Year 1814.*

1820 (23): 83–96. Review of *Voyage dans le Levant en 1817 et 1818.*

1821 (24): 139–169. Review of *Narrative of the Operations and Recent Discoveries within the Pyramids, Temples, Tombs, and Excavations in Egypt and Nubia.*

The Builder

1850 (8) (385): 295.

1851 (9) (419): 99.

The Illuminated Magazine

1843 (1): 31–35. "Mr. Grubbe's Night with Memnon."

The Mirror

1837 (September 16): 177–178. "The British Museum: The Egyptian Saloon."

The Times

1802 (August 10): 3. "Egyptian Relics Presented to British Museum."

1805 (June 8): 3. "Mr. Townley's Collection."

1805 (July 8): 3. Letter on Purchasing Mr. Townley's Collection.

1805 (August 24): 2. "Egyptian Antiquities in the British Museum."

1821 (April 30): 3. "Belzoni's (Mr.) Exhibition of his Egyptian Monument."

1838 (February 5): 5. "British Museum."

1839 (November 22): 2. "British Museum and Its Antiquities."

GUIDEBOOKS TO THE BRITISH MUSEUM; REVIEWS OF THE BRITISH MUSEUM

Anon. N.d. [c.1760]. "A View of the British Museum; or, a Regular Account Relating to What Is Most Remarkable and Curious to Be Seen There . . ." London.

Anon. 1810. "Account of the New Gallery of the British Museum." In *The Repository of Arts, Literature, Commerce, Manufactures, Fashions, and Politics* 3:16, 255–261. London: R. Ackermann.

Anon. 1838. *A Visit to the British Museum: Containing a Familiar Description of Every Object of Interest in the Various Departments of That Establishment.* London: Chapman Hall.

Clarke, H. G. 1843. *The British Museum; A Hand-book Guide for Visiters* [*sic*]. London: H. G. Clarke and Co.

———. 1847. *The British Museum; A Hand-book Guide for Visitors.* Rev. ed. London: H. G. Clarke and Co.

Fergusson, J. 1849. *Observations on the British Museum, National Gallery, and National Record Office, with Suggestions for Their Improvement.* London: John Weale.

Jerrold, W. B. 1852. *How to See the British Museum in Four Visits.* London: Bradbury and Evans.
Long, G. 1832 and 1836. *The British Museum: Egyptian Antiquities.* 2 vols. (Vol. 1, 1832; vol. 2, 1836.) London: Charles Knight.
Mason, W. 1847. *A Guide to the British Museum; Fully Descriptive of All the Most Interesting Natural Curiosities, Wors [sic] of Art, Greek and Roman Sculptures, Egyptian Antiquities, and Other Objects, Worthy of the Attention of Visitors in General.* London: Published by the Editor.
Masson, D. M. 1850. *The British Museum, Historical and Descriptive.* Edinburgh: William and Robert Chambers.
Mogridge, G. 1843. *Old Humphrey's Walks in London and Its Neighbourhood.* London: Religious Tract Society.
Nichols, T. 1870. *A Handy-book of the British Museum, for Every-day Readers.* London: Cassell, Petter, and Galpin.
[Patmore, P]. 1826. *A Guide to the Beauties of the British Museum, Being a Critical and Descriptive Account of the Principal Works of Art Contained in the Gallery of Antiquities of the Above National Collection.* London: Thomas and George Underwood.
Powlett, E. 1761. *The General Contents of the British Museum: With Remarks; Serving as a Directory in Viewing That Noble Cabinet.* London: R and J. Dodsley.
Rymsdyk, J., and A. Rymsdyk. 1778. *Museum Britannicum, Being an Exhibition of a Great Variety of Antiquities and Natural Curiosities, Belonging to That Noble and Magnificent Cabinet, the British Museum.* London: Printed for the authors by I. Moore.
Sharpe, S. 1862. *Egyptian Antiquities in the British Museum.* London: John Russell Smith.
Thomson, A. 1767. *Letters on the British Museum.* London: Printed for J. Dodsley.
Thompson, S. 1872. *British Museum: Egyptian Antiquities Photographed by Stephen Thompson.* 2 vols. London: W. A. Mansell and Co.
Vaux, W. S. W. 1851. *Handbook to the Antiquities in the British Museum: Being a Description of the Remains of Greek, Assyrian, Egyptian, and Etruscan Art Preserved There.* London: John Murray.
Westmacott, R. 1808. "Account of the Arrangement of the Collections of Antique Sculpture Lately Placed in the British Museum." In *Academic Correspondence, 1803: A Summary Report of the Transactions of the Royal Academy of London.* London: Prince Hoare for Royal Academy of London.
Yorke, C. P., and W. M. Leake. 1827. *Principal Egyptian Monuments in the British Museum.* London.

GUIDEBOOKS TO LONDON; VISITORS' ACCOUNTS OF LONDON

Ackermann, R. 1808–1809. *The Microcosm of London; or, London in Miniature.* 3 vols. London: Ackermann.
Anon. 1761. *London and Its Environs Described: Containing an Account of Whatever Is Most Remarkable for Grandeur, Elegance, Curiosity, or Use, in the City and in the Country Twenty Miles Round It.* London: Printed for R. and J. Dodsley.
Anon. 1774. *The Ambulator; or the Stranger's Companion in a Tour Round London; within the Circuit of Twenty-five Miles . . .* London: Printed for J. Bew.
Bager, J. P. 2001 [1840]. *Impressions of London from the Late Summer of 1840.* Transcr. Hans Ersgård, ed. Lars Hansen, trans. Mark Wells, res. Viveka Hansen. London: IK Foundation.
Bicknell, W. I. 1847. *Illustrated London, or a Series of Views in the British Metropolis and Its Vicinity.* London: E. T. Brain and Co.
Campbell, T. 1947 [1775]. *Dr. Campbell's Diary of a Visit to England in 1775.* Edited by James L. Clifford. Cambridge: Cambridge University Press.
Chamberlain, H. 1770. *A New and Compleat History and Survey of the Cities of London and Westminster, the Borough of Southwark, and Parts Adjacent.* London: J. Cooke.

Coltman, J. 1895 [1780]. Letter from Jonathan Coltman to Sam Coltman. In C. Hutton, *Catherine Hutton and Her Friends*, 81–82. Birmingham: Cornish Brothers.

Cruchley, G. F. 1831. *Cruchley's Picture of London, or, Visitor's Assistant.* London: G. F. Cruchley.

Entick, J. 1766. *A New and Accurate History and Survey of London, Westminster, Southwark, and Places Adjacent, etc.* 4 vols. London: Edward and Charles Dilly.

Faujas de Saint-Fond, B. 1907 [1797]. *A Journey through England and Scotland to the Hebrides in 1784.* 2 vols. Rev. ed. Glasgow: Hugh Hopkins.

Feltham, J. F. 1802. *The Picture of London for 1802; Being a Correct Guide to All the Curiosities, Amusements, Exhibitions, Public Establishments, and Remarkable Objects, in and near London.* London: R. Phillips.

———. 1808. *The Picture of London for 1808; Being a Correct Guide to All the Curiosities, Amusements, Exhibitions, Public Establishments, and Remarkable Objects, in and near London.* 9th ed. London: R. Phillips.

Fletcher, W. c.1850. *A Guide to the British Museum.* London.

Grosely, P. J. 1772. *A Tour to London; or, New Observations on England and Its Inhabitants.* 2 vols. Translated from the French by Thomas Nugent. London: Locyer Davis.

Hare, A. 1878. *Walks in London.* 2 vols. London: Daldy, Isbister and Co.

Harrison, W. 1775. *A New and Universal History, Description, and Survey of the Cities of London and Westminster, the Borough of Southwark, and Their Adjacent Parts.* London: J. Cooke.

Hawthorne, N. 1870. *Passages from the English Note-books of Nathaniel Hawthorne.* London: Strahan and Co.

Hutton, W. 1818. [1785]. *A Journey from Birmingham to London Comprising a Description of the Most Interesting Objects of Curiosity to a Visitor of the Metropolis.* London: Pearson and Rollason.

Karamzin, N. M. 1957 [1790]. *Letters of a Russian Traveler 1789–1790.* Trans. F. Jonas. New York: Columbia University Press.

Kielmansegge, F. 1902 [1762]. *Diary of a Journey to England in the Years 1761–1762.* Trans. Countess Kielmansegg [*sic*]. London: Longmans, Green and Co.

La Roche, M. S. von. 1933 [1786]. *Sophie in London, 1786: Being the Diary of Sophie v. la Roche.* Translated from the German by Clare Williams. London: Jonathan Cape.

Leigh, S. 1818. *Leigh's New Picture of London.* London: Printed for the Author.

Malcolm, J. P. 1803. *Londinium Redivivum; or, an Antient History and Modern description of London.* 4 vols. London: Printed by J. Nichols.

Mogg, E. 1838. *Mogg's New Picture of London; or, Strangers' Guide to the British Metropolis.* London: E. Mogg.

Moritz, C. P. 1924 [1795]. *Travels of Carl Philip Moritz in England in 1782.* A reprint of the English translation of 1795, with an introduction by P. E. Matheson. London: Humphrey Milford.

———. 1965 [1782]. *Journeys of a German in England in 1782.* Translated and edited by R. Nettel. London: Jonathan Cape.

Passavant, J. D. 1978 [1836]. *Tour of a German Artist in England.* 2 vols. Translated from the German by Elizabeth Rigby. East Ardsley, Wakefield: EP Publishing.

Pückler-Muskau, H. 1987 [1826–1829]. *Puckler's Progress: The Adventures of Prince Pückler-Muskau in England, Wales and Ireland as Told in Letters to His Former Wife, 1826–9.* Trans. Flora Brennan. London: Collins.

Sarrett, H. J. 1803–1804. *Tegg and Castleman's New Picture of London for 1803–4, or, a Guide through This Immense Metropolis.* London: Printed for the authors.

Silliman, B. 1810. *A Journal of Travels in England, Holland, and Scotland, and of Two Passages over the Atlantic, in the Years 1805 and 1806.* 2 vols. New York: Ezra Sargeant.

Simond, L. 1815. *Journal of a Tour and Residence in Great Britain, During the Years 1810 and 1811, by a French Traveller.* 2 vols. Edinburgh: A. Constable and Co.

Timbs, J. 1855. *Curiosities of London: Exhibiting the Most Rare and Remarkable Objects of Interest in the Metropolis.* 8 vols. London: Bogue.

Waagen, G. F. 1838. *Works of Art and Artists in England.* 3 vols. London: John Murray.

———. 1854. *Treasures of Art in Great Britain.* 3 vols. London: John Murray.

———. 1857. *Galleries and Cabinets of Art in Great Britain.* London: John Murray.

Weale, J., ed. 1854. *The Pictorial Handbook of London.* 8 vols. London: H. G. Bohn.

Wendeborn, G. F. A. 1791. *A View of England towards the Close of the Eighteenth Century.* 2 vols. London: G. G. J. and J. Robinson.

Wheaton, N. S. 1830. *A Journal of a Residence during Several Months in London . . . in the Years 1823 and 1824.* Hartford, CT: H. and F. J. Huntington.

Whittock, N. 1836. *The Modern Picture of London, Westminster, and the Metropolitan Boroughs.* London.

References

Accordi, B. 1976. "Contributions to the History of Geological Sciences: Illustrators of the Kircher Museum Naturalistic Collections." *Geologica Roma* 15: 113–126.

———. 1977. "Contributions to the History of Geological Sciences: The Musaeum Calceolarium (XVIth century) of Verona Illustrated in 1622 by Ceruti and Chiocco." *Geologica Romana* 16: 21–54.

———. 1981. "Ferrante Imperato (Napoli 1550–1625) e il suo contributo alla storia della geologia." *Geologica Romana* 20: 43–56.

Aimi, A., V. de Michele, and A. Morandotti. 1985. "Towards a History of Collecting in Milan in the Late Renaissance and Baroque Periods." In O. Impey and A. MacGregor, eds., *The Origins of Museums*, 24–28. Oxford: Clarendon Press.

Alexander, W. 1805–7. *Egyptian Monuments from the Collection Formed by the National Institute under the Direction of Bonaparte . . . Now Deposited in the British Museum.* London: Longman, Hurst, Rees, and Orme.

Allwood, J. 1977. *The Great Exhibitions.* London: Studio Vista.

Altick, R. D. 1957. *The English Common Reader.* Chicago: University of Chicago Press.

———. 1978. *The Shows of London.* Cambridge, MA: Belknap Press.

Ames, M. 1992. *Cannibal Tours and Glass Boxes: The Anthropology of Museums.* 2nd ed. Vancouver: University of British Columbia Press.

Annesley, G. (Viscount Valentia, Earl of Mountnorris). 1809. *Voyages and Travels to India, Ceylon, Red Sea, Abyssinia, and Egypt in the Years 1802–6.* London.

Armstrong, C. 1998. *Scenes in a Library: Reading the Photograph in the Book, 1843–1875.* Cambridge, MA: MIT Press.

Arundale, F., and J. Bonomi. 1842. *Gallery of Antiquities Selected from the British Museum.* London: J. Weale.

Ashfield, A., and P. de Bolla, eds. 1996. *The Sublime: A Reader in British Eighteenth-century Aesthetic Theory.* Cambridge: Cambridge University Press.

Asma, S. T. 2001. *Stuffed Animals and Pickled Heads: The Culture and Evolution of Natural History Museums.* Oxford: Oxford University Press.

d'Athanasi, G. 1836. *A Brief Account of the Researches and Discoveries in Upper Egypt, Made under the Direction of Henry Salt Esq.* London: John Hearne.

Auerbach, J. A. 1999. *The Great Exhibition of 1851: A Nation on Display.* London: Yale University Press.

Aufrère, S. 1990. *La momie et la tempête: Nicolas-Claude Fabri de Peiresc et la "curiosité égyptienne" en Provence au début du XVIIe siècle.* Avignon: Barthélemy.

Baines, J., and J. Malek. 2000. *Cultural Atlas of Ancient Egypt.* New York: Checkmark Books.

Balsiger, B. J. 1970. "The Kunst–und Wunderkammern: A Catalogue Raisonné of Collecting in Germany, France, and England, 1565–1750." PhD diss., University of Pittsburgh.

Barrell, J. 1991. "Death on the Nile: Fantasy and the Literature of Tourism, 1840–60." *Essays in Criticism* 41 (2): 97–127. Reprinted in 2000 in C. Hall, ed., *Cultures of Empire: A Reader*, 187–206. Manchester: Manchester University Press.

Bassani, E. 2000. *African Art and Artefacts in European Collections, 1400–1800*, ed. M. McLeod. London: British Museum Press.

Bayne-Powell, R. 1951. *Travellers in Eighteenth-century England*. London: John Murray.

Bazin, G. 1967. *The Museum Age*. Trans. Jane van Nuis Cahill. Brussels: Desoer.

Beacour, F., Y. Laissus, and C. Orgogozo. 1990. *The Discovery of Egypt*. Trans. Bambi Ballard. Paris: Flammarion.

Beard, M., and J. Henderson. 2001. *Classical Art: From Greece to Rome*. Oxford: Oxford University Press.

Bedini, S. A. 1986. "Citadels of Learning: The Museum Kircheriano and Other Seventeenth-century Italian Science Collections." In M. Casciato, M. G. Ianniello, and M. Vitale, eds., *Enciclopedismo in Roma barocca*, 249–267. Venice: Marsilio Editori.

Belk, R. W. 1995. *Collecting in a Consumer Society*. London: Routledge.

Belzoni, G. B. 1820a. *Narrative of the Operations and Recent Discoveries within the Pyramids, Temples, Tombs, and Excavations in Egypt and Nubia*. London: John Murray.

———. 1820b. *Forty-four Plates Illustrative of the Researches and Operations of Belzoni in Egypt and Nubia*. London: John Murray.

———. 2001 [1820]. *Belzoni's Travels: Narrative of the Operations and Recent Discoveries in Egypt and Nubia*. Edited by A. Siliotti. London: British Museum Press.

Benedict, B. M. 2001. *Curiosity: A Cultural History of Early Modern Inquiry*. Chicago: University of Chicago Press.

Bennett, T. 1995. *The Birth of the Museum*. London: Routledge.

Bermingham, A. 1997. Introduction." In A. Bermingham and J. Brewer, eds., *The Consumption of Culture 1600–1800: Image, Object, Text*, 1–20. London: Routledge.

Bermingham, A., and J. Brewer, eds. 1997. *The Consumption of Culture 1600–1800: Image, Object, Text*. London: Routledge.

Besler, B. 1616. *Fasciculus rariorum et aspectu dignorum varii generis quae collegit et suis impensis aeri ad vivum incidi curavit atque evulgavit*. Nuremberg.

Bierbrier, M. L. 1988. "The Lethieullier Family and the British Museum." In J. Baines and I. E. S. Edwards, eds., *Pyramid Studies and Other Essays Presented to I. E. S. Edwards*, 220–228. London: Egypt Exploration Society. Occasional Publications 7.

———. 1993. "The Sloane Collection of Egyptian Antiquities." In L. Limme and J. Strybol, eds., *Aegyptus Museis Rediviva: Miscellanea in Honorem Hermanni De Meulenaere*, 15–33. Brussels: Musées Royaux d'Art et d'Histoire.

———. 1995. *Who Was Who in Egyptology*. 3rd rev. ed. London: Egypt Exploration Society.

———. 1999. "The Acquisition by the British Museum of Antiquities Discovered during the French Invasion of Egypt." In W. V. Davies, ed., *Studies in Egyptian Antiquities: A Tribute to T. G. H James*, 111–113. London: British Museum Occasional Papers 123.

Birch, S. 1841–1844. *Select Papyri in the Hieratic Character from the Collections of the British Museum*. London: W. Nicol.

Black, J. 1999. *The British Abroad: The Grand Tour in the Eighteenth Century*. London: Sandpiper Books.

Bland, A. 1998. "Egyptian Influence on Wedgwood Design, 1769–1978." Master's diss., Victoria and Albert Museum, Royal College of Art.

Blumenbach, J. F. 1794. "Observations on Some Egyptian Mummies Opened in London." *Philosophical Transactions of the Royal Society of London* 84: 177–195.

Bohrer, F. N. 2003. *Orientalism and Visual Culture: Imagining Mesopotamia in Nineteenth-century Europe.* New York: Cambridge University Press.

Bredekamp, H. 1995. *The Lure of Antiquity and the Cult of the Machine: The Kunstkammer and the Evolution of Nature, Art, and Technology.* Translated from the German by Allison Brown. Princeton: Marcus Wiener.

Brewer, J., and R. Porter, eds. 1993. *Consumption and the World of Goods.* London: Routledge.

Brier, B. 1992. *Egyptomania.* Exhibition catalogue. Brookville, NY: Hillwood Art Museum.

Bristow, I. C. 1996. *Architectural Colour in British Interiors, 1615–1840.* New Haven, CT: Yale University Press.

Brown, J. 1995. *Kings and Connoisseurs: Collecting Art in Seventeenth Century Europe.* Princeton, NJ: Princeton University Press.

Bruce, J. 1790. *Travels to Discover the Source of the Nile in the Years 1768, 1769, 1770, 1771, 1772, and 1773.* 5 vols. Edinburgh: J. Ruthuen.

Bunsen, C. C. J. 1848–1867. *Egypt's Place in Universal History.* 5 vols. Translated from the German by Charles H. Cottrell. London: Longmans.

Burton, A. 1999. *Vision and Accident: The Story of the Victoria and Albert Museum.* London: V&A publications.

Carrot, R. G. 1978. *The Egyptian Revival: Its Sources, Monuments, and Meaning 1808–1858.* Berkeley: University of California Press.

Cash, D. 1992. *Access to Museum Culture: The British Museum from 1753 to 1836.* PhD diss., University of Cambridge. British Museum Occasional Papers no. 133.

Caulton, T. 1998. *Hands on Exhibitions: Managing Interactive Museums and Science Centres.* London: Routledge.

Caygill, M. L. 1992. *The Story of the British Museum.* 2nd ed. London: British Museum Press.

———. 2003. "From Private Collection to Public Museum: The Sloane Collection at Chelsea and the British Museum in Montagu House." In R. G. W. Anderson, M. L. Caygill, A. G. MacGregor, and L. Syson, eds., *Enlightening the British: Knowledge, Discovery, and the Museum in the Eighteenth Century,* 18–25. London: British Museum Press.

Caygill, M. L., and C. Date. 1999. *Building the British Museum.* London: British Museum.

Caylus, A.-C.-P. Tubières, comte de. 1752–1757. *Recueil d'antiquités égyptiennes, étrusqnes, grecques, romaines et gauloises.* 7 vols. Paris: Chez Desaint and Saillant.

Ceruto, B., and A. Chiocco. 1622. *Musaeum Francesco Calceolari.* Verona: Apud Angelum Tamum.

Champollion, J.-F. 1814. *L'Egypte sous les pharaons, ou Recherches sur la géographie, la religion, la langue, les écritures et l'histoire de l'égypte avant l'invasion de Cambyse.* Paris: Bure Frères.

———. 1822. *Lettre à M. Dacier: relative a l'alphabet des hiéroglyphes phonétiques employés par les Egyptiens pour inscrire sur leurs monuments les titres, les noms et les surnoms des souverains grecs et romains.* Paris: F. Didot.

———. 1824. *Précis du système hiéroglyphique des anciens egyptiens.* 2 vols. Paris: Treuttel and Würtz.

Champollion J.-F., and I. Rossellini. 1835–1847. *Monuments de l'Egypte et de la Nubie d'après les dessins exécutés sur les lieux, sous la direction de Champollion le jeune.* 4 vols. Paris.

Chaudonneret, M.-C. 1991. "Historicism and 'Heritage' in the Louvre, 1820–40: From the Musée Charles X to the Galerie d'Apollon." *Art History* 14 (4): 488–520.

Clarke, E. D. 1805. *The Tomb of Alexander: A Dissertation on the Sarcophagus Brought from Alexandria and Now in the British Museum.* Cambridge: Cambridge University Press.

Clayton, P. A. 1982. *The Rediscovery of Ancient Egypt: Artists and Travellers in the 19th Century.* London: Thames and Hudson.

Combe, T. 1810. *A Description of the Collection of Ancient Marbles in the British Museum.* London: British Museum.

———. 1810. *A Description of the Collection of Ancient Terracottas in the British Museum.* London: British Museum.

Conner, P., ed. 1983. *The Inspiration of Egypt: The Influence on British Artists, Travelers and Designers, 1700–1900.* Brighton: Brighton Burrough Council.

Cook, B. 1977. "The Townley Marbles in Westminster and Bloomsbury." In *Collectors and Collections.* British Museum Yearbook 2:34–78. London: British Museum Publications.

Coombes, A. 1994. *Reinventing Africa: Museums, Material Culture, and Popular Imagination in Late Victorian and Edwardian England.* New Haven, CT: Yale University Press.

Crane, S. A., ed. 2000. *Museums and Memory.* Stanford: Stanford University Press.

Crook, J. M. 1972. *The British Museum: A Case-study in Architectural Politics.* London: Penguin/Allen Lane.

Curl, J. S. 1994. *Egyptomania, the Egyptian Revival: A Recurring Theme in the History of Taste.* 2nd ed. Manchester: Manchester University Press.

Curran, B. 2003. "The Renaissance Afterlife of Ancient Egypt (1400–1650)." In P. J. Ucko and T. Champion, eds., *The Wisdom of Egypt: Changing Visions through the Ages,* 101–131. London: UCL Press.

———. 2004. "The Sphinx in the City: Egyptian Memories and Urban Spaces in Renaissance Rome–and Viterbo." In S. J. Campbell and S. J. Milner, eds., *Artistic Exchange and Cultural Translation in the Italian Renaissance City,* 294–326. Cambridge: Cambridge University Press.

———. Forthcoming. *The Egyptian Renaissance: The Afterlife of Ancient Egypt in Early Modern Italy.* Chicago: University of Chicago Press.

Curto, S. 1976. *Storia del Museo Egizio di Torino.* Turin: Centro Studi Piemontesi.

Daly, O. El. 2005. *Egyptology: The Missing Millennium: Ancient Egypt in Medieval Arabic Writings.* London: UCL Press.

Dannenfeldt, K. 1959. "Egypt and Egyptian Antiquity in the Renaissance." *Studies in the Renaissance* 6: 7–27.

Daston, L. J., and K. Park. 1998. *Wonders and the Order of Nature, 1150–1750.* New York: Zone Books.

David, R. 2000. *The Experience of Ancient Egypt.* London: Routledge.

Dawson, W. R. 1937. "The First Egyptian Society." *Journal of Egyptian Archaeology* 23: 259–260.

Day, D. H. 1997. *A Treasure Hard to Attain: Images of Archaeology in Popular Film.* London: Scarecrow Press.

Dean, D. 1997. *Museum Exhibition.* London: Routledge.

De Beer, G. R. 1953. *Sir Hans Sloane and the British Museum.* London: Oxford University Press.

Delamotte, P. H. 1855. *Photographic Views of the Progress of the Crystal Palace, Sydenham, Taken during the Progess of the Works.* 2 vols. London: Photographic Institution.

Denon, D. V. 1802. *Voyage dans la Basse et la Haute Egypte.* Paris: P. Didot l'Ainé.

———. 1803. *Travels in Upper and Lower Egypt.* Trans. A. Aiken. London.

De Quincey, T. 1889. *The Collected Writings of Thomas De Quincey.* Edited by David Masson. Edinburgh: Adam and Charles Black.

Description de l'Egypte ou recueil des observations et des Recherches qui ont été faites en Egypte, pendant l'expédition de l'armée française. 1809–1828. 21 vols. Paris: Imprimerie Imperiale/Royale.

Dias, N. 1998. "The Visibility of Difference: Nineteenth-century French Anthropological Collections." In S. Macdonald, ed., *The Politics of Display: Museums, Science, Culture,* 36–52. London: Routledge.

Dickie, G. 1996. *The Century of Taste: The Philosophical Odyssey of Taste in the Eighteenth Century.* New York: Oxford University Press.

Drower, M. S. 1995. *Flinders Petrie: A Life in Archaeology.* 2nd ed. Madison: University of Wisconsin Press.

Du Camp, M. 1852. *Egypte, Nubie, Palestine et Syrie: Dessins photographiques recueillis pendant les années 1849, 1850 et 1851, accompagnés d'un texte explicatif.* Paris: Gide et Baudry.

Duncan, C. 1995. *Civilising Rituals: Inside Art Museums.* London: Routledge.

Dykstra, D. 1998. "The French Occupation of Egypt, 1798–1801." In M. W. Daly, ed., *The Cambridge History of Egypt,* 2:113–138. New York: Cambridge University Press.

Edwards, E. 1870. *Lives of the Founders of the British Museum.* London: Trübner and Co.

Evans, E. A. 2000. *Scholars, Scoundrels, and the Sphinx: A Photographic and Archaeological Adventure up the Nile.* Knoxville: Frank H. McClung Museum, University of Tennessee.

Fergusson, J. 1849. *Observations on the British Museum, National Gallery, and National Record Office, with Suggestions for Their Improvement.* London: John Weale.

Fiechter, J.-J. 1997. "La pierre de Rosette et les autres antiquités égyptiennes prises par les anglais en 1801." *Revue d'égyptologie* 48: 283–289.

Fileri, A. 2002. "Le collezioni del Cardinale Filippo Antonion Gualtieri 'Principe amantissimo delle scienze e d'ogni sorte di erudizione.'" *Storia dell'arte* 102: 31–44.

Findlen, P. 1994. *Possessing Nature: Museums, Collecting, and Scientific Culture in Early Modern Italy.* Berkeley: University of California Press.

———. 1998. "Possessing the Past: The Material World of the Italian Renaissance." *American Historical Review* 103 (1): 83–114.

———. 2000. "A Site of Encounter: The Emergence of the Science Museum." In L. Guzzetti, ed., *Science and Power: The Historical Foundations of Research Policies in Europe,* 47–62. Luxemburg: Office for Official Publications of the European Communities.

Finn, C. 2004. *Past Poetic: Archaeology in the Poetry of W. B. Yeats and Seamus Heaney.* London: Duckworth.

Ford, B., ed. 1946–1948. "The Memoirs of Thomas Jones." *Walpole Society* 32.

France, P. 1991. *The Rape of Egypt: How the Europeans Stripped Egypt of Its Heritage.* London: Barrie and Jenkins.

Francis, F., ed. 1971. *Treasures of the British Museum.* London: Thames and Hudson.

Frith, F. 1858–1860. *Egypt and Palestine Photographed and Described.* 2 vols. London: James Virtue.

Gaehtgens, T. W. 1996. "The Museum Island in Berlin." In G. Wright, ed., *The Formation of National Collections of Art and Archaeology,* 53–77. Washington, DC: National Gallery of Art.

Gliddon, G. R. 1841. *An Appeal to the Antiquaries of Europe on the Destruction of the Monuments of Egypt.* London: J. Madden.

Goldthwaite, R. A. 1993. *Wealth and the Demand for Art in Italy 1300–1600.* Baltimore: Johns Hopkins University Press.

Gordon, A. 1737. *An Essay towards Explaining the Ancient Hieroglyphical Figures on the Coffin of the Ancient Mummy Belonging to Captain William Lethieullier.* London.

Gould, S. J. 1989. *Wonderful Life: The Burgess Shale and the Nature of History.* London: Penguin.

———. 1993. "Preface: Reconstructing (and Deconstructing) the Past." In S. J. Gould, ed., *The Book of Life,* 6–21. New York: W. W. Norton.

Grafton, A., and L. Jardine. 1986. *From Humanism to the Humanities: Education and the Liberal Arts in Fifteenth and Sixteenth Century Europe.* London: Duckworth.

Greener, L. 1966. *The Discovery of Egypt.* London: Cassell.

Greenhalgh, P. 1991. *Ephemeral Vistas: The Expositions Universelles, Great Exhibitions, and World's Fairs, 1851–1939.* Manchester: Manchester University Press.

Grewal, I. 1996. *Home and Harem: Nation, Gender, Empire, and the Cultures of Travel.* Durham: Duke University Press.

Grote, A., ed. 1994. *Macrocosmos in Microcosmo: Die welt in der Stube: Zur Geschichte des Sammelns, 1450–1800.* Opladen: Leske and Budrich.

Guiterman, H. 1986. *David Roberts R.A., 1796–1864.* London: Privately printed.

Halls, J. J. 1834. *The Life and Correspondence of Henry Salt, Esq., . . . FRS.* 2 vols. London: Richard Bentley.

Hamilton, W. R. 1809. *Remarks on Several Parts of Turkey, Part 1: Ægyptiaca; or, Some Account of the Antient [sic] and Modern State of Egypt, as Obtained in the Years 1801, 1802.* London: Payne.

Hassan, F. A. 1998. "Memorabilia: Archaeological Materiality and National Identity in Egypt." In L. Meskell, ed., *Archaeology under Fire: Nationalism, Politics and Heritage in the Eastern Mediterranean and Middle East,* 200–216. London: Routledge.

Haskell, F. 1993. *History and Its Images: Art and the Interpretation of the Past.* New Haven, CT: Yale University Press.

Hein, G. 1998. *Learning in the Museum.* London: Routledge.

Henderson, A., and A. Kaeppler, eds. 1997. *Exhibiting Dilemmas: Issues of Representation at the Smithsonian.* Washington, DC: Smithsonian Institution Press.

Hines, J. 2004. *Voices in the Past: English Literature and Archaeology.* Cambridge: D. S. Brewer.

Hobhouse, H. 2002. *The Crystal Palace and the Great Exhibition.* London: Athlone Press.

Hoffenberg, P. H. 2001. *An Empire on Display: English, Indian, and Australian Exhibitions from the Crystal Palace to the Great War.* Berkeley: University of California Press.

Holst, N. van. 1967. *Creators, Collectors, and Connoisseurs: The Anatomy of Public Taste from Antiquity to the Present Day.* London: Thames and Hudson.

Honour, H. 1955. "The Egyptian Taste." *Connoisseur* 135: 242–246.

Hooper-Greenhill, E. 1992. *Museums and the Shaping of Knowledge.* London: Routledge.

———. 1995. *Museum, Media, Message.* London: Routledge.

———. 2000. *Museums and the Interpretation of Visual Culture.* London: Routledge.

Hope, T. 1971 [1807]. *Household Furniture and Interior Decoration.* New York: Dover Publications.

Hornung, E. 2001. *The Secret Lore of Egypt: Its Impact upon the West.* Ithaca: Cornell University Press.

Howe, W. E. 1913. *A History of the Metropolitan Museum of Art.* Vol. 1. New York: Metropolitan Museum of Art.

———. 1946. *A History of the Metropolitan Museum of Art.* Vol. 2, *1905–1941.* New York: Metropolitan Museum of Art.

Hudson, K. 1987. *Museums of Influence.* Cambridge: Cambridge University Press.

Humbert, J.-M. 1989. *L'égyptomanie dans l'art occidental.* Courbevoie, Paris: ACR.

———. 1994. "Egyptomania: A Current Concept from the Renaissance to Postmodernism." In J.-M. Humbert, M. Pantazzi, and C. Ziegler, eds., *Egyptomania: Egypt in Western Art, 1730–1930,* 21–25. Catalogue of exhibition held in Paris, Ottawa, and Vienna. Paris and Ottawa: Musée du Louvre and National Gallery of Canada.

Humbert, J.-M., M. Pantazzi, and C. Ziegler. 1994. *Egyptomania: Egypt in Western Art, 1730–1930.* Catalogue of exhibition held in Paris, Ottawa, and Vienna. Paris and Ottawa: Musée du Louvre and National Gallery of Canada.

Imperato, F. 1599. *Dell'historia naturale, libri xxviii.* Naples: Costantino Vitale.

Impey, O., and A. MacGregor, eds. 1985. *The Origins of Museums.* Oxford: Clarendon Press.

Irby, C. L., and J. Mangles. 1985 [1823]. *Travels in Egypt and Nubia, Syria and Asia Minor during the Years 1817 and 1818.* London: Darf.

Irwin, D. 1997. *Neoclassicism.* London: Phaidon.

Iversen, E. 1993 [1961]. *The Myth of Egypt and Its Hieroglyphs in European Tradition.* 2nd ed. Princeton: Princeton University.

———. 1972. *Obelisks in Exile.* 2 vols. Copenhagen: Gad.

Jacobs, M. 1995. *The Painted Voyage.* London: British Museum Press.

James, T. G. H. 1981. *The British Museum and Ancient Egypt.* London: British Museum Press.

———. 1982. *Excavating in Egypt: The Egypt Exploration Society, 1882–1982.* London: Thomas Garnet Henry.

———, ed. 1997. *Egypt Revealed: Artist-Travellers in an Antique Land.* London: Folio Society.

———. 1998. *Ancient Egypt: The Land and Its Legacy.* London: Guild Publishing.

———. 2001. "The Formation and Growth of the Egyptian Collection of the British Museum." In E. R. Russman, ed., *Eternal Egypt: Masterworks of Ancient Art from the British Museum*, 46–63. London: British Museum Press in association with the American Federation of Arts.

James, T. G. H., and W. V. Davies. 1996. *Egyptian Sculpture*. 6th ed. London: British Museum Press.

Jardine, L. 1996. *Worldly Goods: A New History of the Renaissance*. London: Macmillan.

Jenkins, I. 1992. *Archaeologists and Aesthetes: The Sculpture and Galleries of the British Museum in the Nineteenth Century*. London: British Museum Press.

———. 1994. "Classical Antiquities: Sloane's Repository of Time." In A. MacGregor, ed., *Sir Hans Sloane: Collector, Scientist, Antiquary*, 167–173. London: British Museum Press.

Jenkins, I., and K. Sloan. 1996. *Vases and Volcanoes: Sir William Hamilton and His Collection*. London: British Museum.

Johnson, J. S. 1966. "Egyptian Revival in the Decorative Arts." *Antiques* 90: 420, 428.

Jones, O., and J. Bonomi. 1854. *Description of the Egyptian Court Erected in the Crystal Palace*. London: Crystal Palace Library, Bradbury and Evans.

Kákosy, L. 1995. "Egypt in Ancient Greek and Roman Thought." In J. Sasson, ed., *Civilisations of the Ancient Near East*, 1:3–14. New York: Charles Scribner's Sons.

Kaplan, F. E. S. 1995. *Museums and the Making of "Ourselves."* Leicester: Leicester University Press.

Karp, I., and S. D. Lavine, eds. 1991. *Exhibiting Cultures: The Poetics and Politics of Museum Display*. Washington, DC: Smithsonian Institution Press.

Karp, I., C. M. Kreamer, and S. D. Lavine, eds. 1992. *Museums and Communities: The Politics of Public Culture*. Washington, DC: Smithsonian Institution Press.

Kavanagh, G., ed. 1991. *Museum Languages*. Leicester: Leicester University Press.

Kemp, M. 1985. "'Wrought by No Artist's Hand': The Natural, Artificial, and Exotic in Some Artefacts from the Sixteenth Century." In C. Farago, ed., *Reframing the Renaissance: Visual Culture in Europe and Latin America, 1450–1650*, 177–196. New Haven, CT: Yale University Press.

Kendrick, J. 1950. *Ancient Egypt under the Pharoahs*. London: B. Fellowes.

Kenseth, J., ed. 1991a. *Age of the Marvelous*. Hanover, NH: Hood Museum of Art, Dartmouth College.

———. 1991b. "The Age of the Marvelous: An Introduction." In J. Kenseth, ed., *Age of the Marvelous*, 25–59. Hanover, NH: Hood Museum of Art, Dartmouth College.

Kingery, W. D., ed. 1996. *Learning from Things: Method and Theory of Material Culture Studies*. Washington, DC: Smithsonian Institution Press.

Kircher, A. 1655. *Oedipi Aegyptiaci: Oedipus Aegyptiacus; Hoc est, universalis hieroglyphicae veterum doctrinae temporum iniuria abolitae instauration, etc.* Rome: V. Mascardi.

———. 1678. *Romani Collegii Societatis Jesu Musaeum Celeberrimum*. Amsterdam: Janssonio-Waesbergiana.

Kirshenblatt-Gimblett, B. 1998. *Destination Culture: Tourism, Museums, and Heritage*. Berkeley: University of California Press.

Kulik, K. 2005. "Mediating Archaeology: The Relationship between Archaeology, the Media, and the Public in Britain (1996–2002)." PhD diss., Department of Archaeology, University of Southampton.

Lane, E. 1836. *An Account of the Manners and Customs of the Modern Egyptians: Written in Egypt during the Years 1833, –34, and –35, Partly from Notes Made during a Former Visit to That Country in the Years 1825, –26, –27, and –28*. 2 vols. London: Charles Knight.

Lant, A. 1992. "The Curse of the Pharaoh, or How Cinema Contracted Egyptomania." *October* 59: 86–112.

Laurencich Minelli, L. 1985. "Museography and Ethnological Collections in Bologna during the Sixteenth and Seventeenth Centuries." In O. Impey and A. MacGregor, eds., *The Origins of Museums*, 17–23. Oxford: Clarendon Press.

Leask, N. 2002. *Curiosity and the Aesthetics of Travel Writing, 1770–1840*. Oxford: Oxford University Press.

Legati, L. 1677. *Museo Cospiano Annesso a quello del famoso Ulisse Aldrovandi e donato alla sua Patria dell'illustrissimo Signor Ferdinando Cospi*. Bologna: Giacomo Monti.

Liebenwein, W. 1977. *Studiolo: Die Entstehung eines Raumtyps und seine Entwicklung bis um 1600*. Berlin: Gebr. Mann.

Lepsius, K. R. 1849–1859. *Denkmäler aus Aegypten und Aethiopien*. Berlin: Niclaische Buchhandlung.

Lidchi, H. 1997. "The Poetics and the Politics of Exhibiting Other Cultures." In S. Hall, ed., *Representation: Cultural Representations and Signifying Practices*, 151–208. London: Sage.

Lugli, A. 1983. *Naturalia et Mirabilia: Il collezionismo enciclopedico nelle wunderkammern d'Europa*. Milan: Gabriele Mazzotta.

———. 1997. *Wunderkammer: La stanza della mervaviglia*. Turin: Allemandi.

McCabe, J. D. 1876. *The Illustrated History of the Centennial Exhibition Held in Commemoration of the One Hundredth Anniversary of American Independence*. Toronto: J. B. Magurn.

McClellan, A. 1994. *Inventing the Louvre: Art, Politics, and the Origins of the Modern Museum in Eighteenth-century Paris*. Cambridge: Cambridge University Press.

MacDonald, S[ally], and M. Rice, eds. 2003. *Consuming Ancient Egypt*. London: UCL Press.

Macdonald, S[haron]. 1998. "Exhibitions of Power and Powers of Exhibition: An Introduction to the Politics of Display." In S. Macdonald, ed., *The Politics of Display: Museums, Science, Culture*, 1–24. London: Routledge.

———. 2002. *Behind the Scenes at the Science Museum*. Oxford: Berg.

Macdonald, S[haron], and G. Fyfe. 1996. *Theorizing Museums*. Oxford: Blackwell.

MacGregor, A. 1985. "The Cabinet of Curiosities in Seventeenth Century Britain." In O. Impey and A. MacGregor, eds., *The Origins of Museums*, 147–158. Oxford: Clarendon Press.

———. 1994a. "The Life, Character, and Career of Sir Hans Sloane." In A. MacGregor, ed., *Sir Hans Sloane: Collector, Scientist, Antiquary: Founding Father of the British Museum*, 11–44. London: British Museum in association with Alistair McAlpine.

———. 1994b. "Egyptian Antiquities." In A. MacGregor, ed., *Sir Hans Sloane: Collector, Scientist, Antiquary: Founding Father of the British Museum*, 174–179. London: British Museum in association with Alistair McAlpine.

MacKenzie, J. M. 1995. *Orientalism: History, Theory, and the Arts*. Manchester: Manchester University Press.

McLoughlin, M. 1999. *Museums and the Representation of Native Canadians: Negotiating the Borders of Culture*. London: Routledge.

Manley, D., and P. Rée. 2001. *Henry Salt: Artist, Traveller, Diplomat, Egyptologist*. London: Libri.

Manniche, L. 1988. *Lost Tombs: A Study of Certain Eighteenth Dynasty Monuments in the Theban Necropolis*. London: KPI.

Mauries, P. 2002. *Cabinets of Curiosities*. London: Thames and Hudson.

Maxwell, A. 1999. *Colonial Photography and Exhibitions*. London: Routledge.

Merriman, N., ed. 1999*: Making Early Histories in Museums*. London: Leicester University Press.

Meskell, L. 1998. "Consuming Bodies: Cultural Fantasies of Ancient Egypt." *Body and Society* 4 (1): 63–76.

———. 2003. "Pharaonic Legacies: Postcolonialism, Heritage, and Hyperreality." In S. Kane, ed., *The Politics of Archaeology and Identity in a Global Context*, 149–171. AIA Monographs/Cotsen Institute Los Angeles.

———. 2004. *Object Worlds in Ancient Egypt: Material Biographies Past and Present*. Oxford: Berg.

Miller, D., ed. 1998. *Material Culture: Why Some Things Matter.* Chicago: University of Chicago Press.

Miller, E. J. 1973. *That Noble Cabinet: A History of the British Museum.* London: Deutsch.

Mirzoeff, N., ed. 1998. *The Visual Culture Reader.* London: Routledge.

Mitchell, T. 1988. *Colonising Egypt.* Cambridge: Cambridge University Press.

Mitchell, W. J. T. 1998. *The Last Dinosaur Book.* Chicago: University of Chicago Press.

Mitman, G. 1993. "Cinematic Nature: Hollywood Technology, Popular Culture, and the American Museum of Natural History." *Isis* 84: 637–661.

Montfauçon, B. de. 1719–1724. *l'antiquité expliquée et représentée en figures.* Paris: Chez F. Delaulne et al.

Montserrat, D. 2000a. *Akhenaten: History, Fantasy, and Ancient Egypt.* London: Routledge.

———. 2000b. *Ancient Egypt: Digging for Dreams.* Traveling exhibition featured in London and Glasgow. Catalogue published by Glasgow City Council, Culture and Leisure Services.

Moore, A. H. 2002. "Voyage: Dominique-Vivant Denon and the Transference of Images of Egypt." *Art History* 25 (4): 531–549.

Moore, K. 1997. *Museums and Popular Culture.* London: Cassell.

Moser, S. 1998. *Ancestral Images: The Iconography of Human Origins.* Ithaca: Cornell.

———. 1999. "The Dilemma of Didactic Displays: Habitat Dioramas, Life-groups, and Reconstructions of the Past." In N. Merriman, ed., *Making Early Histories in Museums,* 65–116. London: Cassell/Leicester University Press.

———. 2001. "Archaeological Representation: The Visual Conventions for Constructing Knowledge about the Past." In I. Hodder, ed., *Archaeological Theory Today,* 262–283. Cambridge: Polity Press.

———. Forthcoming. "Archaeological Representation: The Consumption and Creation of the Past." In B. Cunliffe, C. Gosden, and R. Joyce, eds., *The Oxford Handbook of Archaeology.* Oxford: Oxford University Press.

Mukerji, C. 1983. *From Graven Images: Patterns of Modern Materialism.* New York: Columbia University Press.

Mullaney, S. 1983. "Strange Things, Gross Terms, Curious Customs: The Rehearsal of Cultures in the Late Renaissance." *Representations* 3: 40–67.

Murray, D. 2000 [1904]. *Museums: Their History and Their Use.* 3 vols. Edited by P. Findlen. Staten Island, NY: Pober Publishing.

Musée du Louvre. 1996. *L'Egyptomanie à l'épreuve de l'archéologie.* Paris: Louvre.

Neickel, C. F. (and J. Kanold). 1727. *Museographia, oder Anleitung zum rechten Begriff und nüzlicher Anlegung der Museorum, oder Raritäten-Kammern.* Leipzig.

Nickel, D. R. 2004. *Francis Frith in Egypt and Palestine: A Victorian Photographer Abroad.* Princeton: Princeton University Press.

Norden, F. L. 1757. *Travels to Egypt and Nubia.* 2 vols. Trans. and enl. by P. Templeman. London: L. Davis and C. Reymers.

Norton, F. H. 1974. *A Facsimile of Frank Leslie's Illustrated Historical Register of the Centennial Exhibition, 1876.* New York: Paddington Press.

Olmi, G. 1978. *Ulisse Aldrovandi: Science e natura nel secondo cinquecento.* Trent: Università di Trento.

———. 1985. "Science-Honour-Metaphor: Italian Cabinets of the Sixteenth and Seventeenth Centuries." In O. Impey and A. MacGregor, eds., *The Origins of Museums,* 5–16. Oxford: Clarendon Press.

———. 1992. *L'inventario del mondo: Catalogazione della natura e luoghi del sapere nella prima età moderna.* Bologna: Società editrice il Mulio. Annali dell'Istituto Storico Italo-Germanico, Monografia 17.

———. 1993. "From the Marvellous to the Commonplace: Notes on Natural History Museums (16th–18th Centuries)." In R. G. Mazzolini, ed., *Non-verbal Communication in Science Prior to 1900*, 235–278. Florence: Olschki.

Pantazzi, M. 1994. "Italy and the Grand Tour." In J.-M. Humbert, M. Pantazzi, and C. Ziegler, eds., *Egyptomania: Egypt in Western Art, 1730–1930*, 38–45. Exhibition catalogue Paris: Musée du Louvre and National Gallery of Canada.

Parkinson, R. B. 1999. *Cracking Codes: The Rosetta Stone and Decipherment.* London: British Museum Press.

———. 2003. "The Missing Beginning of 'The Dialogue of a Man and His Ba': P. Amherst III and the History of the 'Berlin Library.'" *ZÄS* 130: 120–133.

———. 2005. *The Rosetta Stone.* London: British Museum Press.

Pearce, S. 1995. *On Collecting: An Investigation into Collecting in the European Tradition.* London: Routledge.

———, ed. 1997. *Experiencing Material Culture in the Western World.* London: Leicester University Press.

———, ed. 1999. *Museums and Their Development.* 8 vols. London: Routledge/Thoemmes Press.

———. 2000a. "Belzoni's Collecting and the Egyptian Taste." In A. Yarrington, ed., *The Lustrous Trade: Material Culture and the History of Sculpture in England and Italy c1700–1830*, 193–211. Leicester: Leicester University Press.

———. 2000b. "Giovanni Battista Belzoni's Exhibition of the Reconstructed Tomb of Pharaoh Seti I in 1821." *Journal of the History of Collections* 12 (1): 109–125.

Peltre, C. 1998. *Orientalism in Art.* Translated from the French by John Goodman. New York: Abbeville Press.

Pettigrew, T. J. 1834. *History of Egyptian Mummies.* London: Longman.

———. 1842. *Encyclopaedia Aegyptiaca; or Dictionary of Egyptian Antiquities.* London: Whitaker and Co.

Pevsner, N., and S. Lang. 1956. "The Egyptian Revival." *Architectural Review* 119: 242–254.

Phillips, J. 2004. "The Past and the Public: Archaeology in the Periodical Press in Nineteenth Century Britain." PhD diss., Department of Archaeology, University of Southampton.

Pietrangeli, C. 1993. *The Vatican Museums: Five Centuries of History.* Rome: Edizioni Quasar Biblioteca Apostolica Vaticana.

Piggott, J. R. 2004. *Palace of the People: The Crystal Palace at Sydenham 1854–1936.* London: Hurst and Co.

Piranesi, G. B. 1769. *Divers Ways of Ornamenting Chimneypieces and All Other Parts of Houses Taken from Egyptian, Etruscan, and Grecian Architecture with an Apologia in Defense of Egyptian and Tuscan Architecture.* Rome.

Pococke, R. 1743–1745. *A Description of the East and Some Other Countries.* 2 vols. London: W. Boyer.

Pomian, K. 1990. *Collectors and Curiosities: Paris and Venice, 1500–1800.* Trans. Elizabeth Wiles-Portier. Cambridge: Cambridge University Press.

Poole, R. S. 1851. *Horae Aegyptiacae; or, The Chronology of Ancient Egypt Discovered from Astronomical and Hieroglyphic Records upon Its Monuments.* London: John Murray.

Porterfield, T. 1998. *The Allure of Empire: Art in the Service of French Imperialism, 1798–1836.* Princeton, NJ: Princeton University Press.

Potts, A. D. 1980. "Die Skulpturenaufstellung in der Glyptothek." In K. Vierneisel and G. Leinz, eds., *Glyptothek München 1830–1980*, 258–283. Munich: Glyptothek München.

———. 1994. *Flesh and the Ideal: Winckelmann and the Origins of Art History.* New Haven, CT: Yale University Press.

Pringle, H. 2001. *The Mummy Congress: Science, Obsession, and the Everlasting Dead.* London: Fourth Estate.

Quatremère de Quincy, A. C. 1803. *De l'architecture egyptienne, considérée dans son origine, ses principes et son goût, et comparée sous les mêmes rapports à l'architecture greque.* Paris: Barrois l'aine et fils.

Quiccheberg, S. 1565. *Inscriptiones vel tituli theatri amplissimi.* Munich: Adam Berg.

Quirke, S. 1997. "Modern Mummies and Ancient Scarabs: The Egyptian Collection of Sir William Hamilton." *Journal of the History of Collections* 9 (2): 253–262.

Quirke, S., and J. Spencer, eds. 1992. *The British Museum Book of Ancient Egypt.* London: British Museum Press.

Reid, D. M. 2001. *Whose Pharaohs? Museums, Archaeology, and Egyptian National Identity, from Napoleon to World War I.* Berkeley: University of California Press.

Rheims, M. 1981. *Les collectionneurs: De la curiosité, de la beauté, du gout, de la mode et de la spéculation.* Paris: Editions Ramsay.

Rice, M., and S. MacDonald, eds. 2003. "Introduction: Tea with a Mummy; The Consumer's View of Egypt's Immemorial Appeal." In S. MacDonald and M. Rice, eds., *Consuming Ancient Egypt*, 1–22. London: UCL Press.

Ridley, R. T. 1998. *Napoleon's Proconsul in Egypt: The Life and Times of Bernardino Drovetti.* London: Rubicon Press.

Roberts, D. R. A. 1842–1849. *The Holy Land, Syria, Idumea, Arabia, Egypt, and Nubia.* 2 vols. London: F. G. Moon.

Roberts, L. 1997. *From Knowledge to Narrative: Educators and the Changing Museum.* Washington, DC: Smithsonian Institution Press.

Rosellini, I. 1832–1844. *I monumenti dell'Egitto e della Nubia.* Pisa.

Roth, A. M. 1998. "Ancient Egypt in America: Claiming the Riches." In L. Meskell, ed., *Archaeology under Fire: Nationalism, Politics and Heritage in the Eastern Mediterranean and Middle East*, 217–229. London: Routledge.

Rouellet, A. 1972. *The Egyptian and Egyptianizing Monuments of Imperial Rome.* Leiden: E. J. Brill.

Rudwick, M. J. 1972. *The Meaning of Fossils: Episodes in the History of Palaeontology.* London: Macdonald and Co.

———. 1992. *Scenes from Deep Time: Early Pictorial Representations of the Prehistoric World.* Chicago: University of Chicago Press.

Russell, T. M., ed. 2001. *The Napoleonic Survey of Egypt.* 2 vols. Aldershot: Ashgate.

Russman, E. R. 2001. "Eternal Egypt: Masterworks of Ancient Art from the British Museum." *Minerva* 12 (3): 9–16.

Rydell, R. W. 1985. *All the World's a Fair: Visions of Empire at American International Expositions, 1876–1916.* Chicago: University of Chicago Press.

Saglia, D. 2002. "Consuming Egypt: Appropriation and the Cultural Modalities of Romantic Luxury." *Nineteenth-century Contexts* 24 (3): 317–332.

Sandys, G. 1615. *A Relation of a Journey Begun An. Dom. 1610, in Foure Books.* London: Printed for W. Barret.

Scheicher, E. 1979. *Die Kunst- und Wunderkammern der Habsburger.* Vienna: Molden Edition.

———. 1985. "The Collection of Archduke Ferdinand II at Schloss Ambras: Its Purpose, Composition, and Evolution." In O. Impey and A. MacGregor, eds., *The Origins of Museums*, 29–38. Oxford: Clarendon Press.

Schepelern, H. D. 1985. "Natural Philosophers and Princely Collectors: Worm, Paludanus, and the Gottorp and Copenhagen Collections." In O. Impey and A. MacGregor, eds., *The Origins of Museums*, 121–127. Oxford: Clarendon Press.

———. 1990. "The Museum Wormianum Reconstructed: A Note on the Illustration of 1655." *Journal of the History of Collections* 2 (1): 81–85.

Schlosser, J. von. 1978 [1908]. *Die Kunst und Wunderkammern der Spätrenaissance.* 2nd ed. Würzburg: Braunschweig Klinkhardt and Biermann.

Schnapp, A. 1996. *The Discovery of the Past.* Trans. Ian Kinnes and Gillian Varndell. London: British Museum Press.

Schnapper, A. 1988. *Le géant, la licorne, et la tulipe: Collections et collectionneurs dans la France du XVIIe siècle.* Paris: Flammarion.

Schulz, E. 1990. "Notes on the History of Collecting and of Museums." *Journal of the History of Collections* 2 (2): 205–218.

Schupbach, W. 2001 [1985]. "Some Cabinets of Curiosities in European Academic Institutions." In O. Impey and A. MacGregor, eds., *The Origins of Museums*, 231–243. London: House of Stratus.

Scott, J. 2003. *The Pleasures of Antiquity: British Collections of Greece and Rome.* New Haven, CT: Yale University Press.

Sharpe, S. 1846. *The History of Egypt: From the Earliest Times Till the Conquest by Arabs, A.D. 640.* London: E. Moxon.

Shelton, A. A. 1994. "Cabinets of Transgression: Renaissance Collections and the Incorporation of the New World." In N. J. Elsner and R. Cardinal, eds., *The Cultures of Collecting*, 177–291. London: Reaktion Books.

Sherman, D. J., and I. Rogoff, eds. 1994. *Museum Culture.* London: Routledge.

Siliotti, A. 1998. *The Discovery of Ancient Egypt.* New Jersey: Chartwell Books.

Simpson, M. 1996. *Making Representations: Museums in the Post-colonial Era.* London: Routledge.

Sloan, K., with A. Burnett, eds. 2004. *Enlightenment: Discovering the World in the Eighteenth Century.* London: British Museum Press.

Smiles, S. 1993. *The Image of Antiquity.* New Haven, CT: Yale.

———. 2000. *Eye Witness: Artists and Visual Documentation in Britain, 1770–1830.* Aldershot: Ashgate.

Smiles, S., and S. Moser, eds. 2005. *Envisioning the Past: Archaeology and the Image.* Oxford: Blackwell.

Solé, R., and D. Valbelle. 2001. *The Rosetta Stone.* Trans. S. Randall. London: Profile Books.

Starkey, P., and J. Starkey, eds. 2001. *Travellers in Egypt.* London: Tauris Parke.

Swann, M. 2001. *Curiosities and Texts: The Culture of Collecting in Early Modern England.* Philadelphia: University of Pennsylvania Press.

Sweet, R. 2003. *Antiquaries: The Discovery of the Past in Eighteenth-century Britain.* London: Hambledon and London.

Taylor, F. H. 1948. *The Taste of Angels: A History of Collecting from Rameses to Napoleon.* London: Hamish Hamilton.

Terzago, P. M. 1664. *Musaeum Septalianum Manfredi Septalae patritii Mediolanensis industrioso labore constructum.* Tortona: Elisei Violae.

Terzago, P. M., and P. M. Scarabelli. 1677. *Museo ò galeria adunata dal sapere, e dallo studio del Sig. Canonico Manfredo Settala.* Tortona.

Teynard, F. 1858. *Egypte et Nubie: Sites et monuments les plus intéressants pour l'étude de l'art et de l'histoire.* 2 vols. Paris: Goupil et cie.

Thompson, J. 1992. *Sir Gardner Wilkinson and His Circle.* Austin: University of Texas Press.

Thompson, S. 1872. *British Museum: Egyptian Antiquities Photographed by Stephen Thompson.* 2 vols. London: W. A. Mansell and Co.

Tiradritti, F. 1999. "The History of the Egyptian Museum." In F. Tiradritti, ed., *The Cairo Museum: Masterpieces of Egyptian Art*, 12–23. London: Thames and Hudson.

Tomkins, C. 1970. *Merchants and Masterpieces: The Story of the Metropolitan Museum of Art.* New York: Dutton.

Tribby, J. 1992. "Body/building: Living the Museum Life in Early Modern Europe." *Rhetorica* 10: 139–163.

Turner, H. 1810. "Letter to the Society of Antiquaries on the Rosetta Stone." *Archaeologia* 16: 212–214.

Ucko, P. J., and T. Champion, eds. 2003. *The Wisdom of Egypt: Changing Visions through the Ages.* London: UCL Press.

Usick, P. 2002. *Adventures in Egypt and Nubia: The Travels of William John Bankes (1786–1855)*. London: British Museum Press.

Vergo, P., ed. 1990. *The New Museology*. London: Reaktion Books.

Vertue, G. 1724. *Cadaver balsamo conditum: Simul cum loculo ferali ἀνθρωποειδῆ Picturâ hieroglyphicâ pulcherrime insignito: Ex vetustis Ægypti Sepulchretis sublatum Londinum attulit D Guil: Lethieullier*. London: Society of Antiquaries.

Vickers, M. 2001 [1985]. "Greek and Roman Antiquities in the Seventeenth Century." In O. Impey and A. MacGregor, eds., *The Origins of Museums*, 309–318. London: House of Stratus.

Vyse, H. W. H. 1840. *Operations Carried out at the Pyramids of Gizeh in 1837 with an Account of a Voyage to Upper Egypt, Etc.* London.

Warner, N., ed. 1994. *An Egyptian Panorama: Reports from the 19th Century British Press*. Cairo: Zeitouna.

Wathen, G. H. 1843. *Arts, Antiquities, and Chronology of Ancient Egypt: From Observations in 1839*. London: Longman, Brown, Green, and Longmans.

Werner, A. 2003. "Egypt in London: Public and Private Displays in the 19th Century Metropolis." In J.-M. Humbert and C. A. Price, eds., *Imphotep Today: Egyptianising Architecture*, 75–104. London: UCL Press.

Whitehouse, H. 1992. "Towards a Kind of Egyptology: The Graphic Documentation of Ancient Egypt, 1587–1666." In E. Cropper, G. Perini, and F. Solinas, eds., *Documentary Culture: Florence and Rome from Grand Duke Ferdinand I to Pope Alexander VII*, 63–79. Bologna: Villa Spelman Colloquia 3.

———. 1995. "Egypt in European Thought." In J. M. Sasson, ed., *Civilisations of the Ancient Near East*, 1:15–31. New York: Charles Scribner's Sons.

Wildung, D. 1999. *Egyptian Art in Berlin: Masterpieces in the Bodemuseum and in Charlottenberg*. Mainz: Verlag Philipp von Zabern.

Wilkinson, J. G. 1835. *Topography of Thebes and General View of Egypt*. London: John Murray.

———. 1837. *The Manners and Customs of the Ancient Egyptians*. 3 vols. London: John Murray.

———. 1854. *A Popular Account of the Ancient Egyptians*. 2 vols. London: J. Murray.

Wilkinson, J. G., and S. Birch. 1857. *The Egyptians in the Time of the Pharaohs: Being a Companion to the Crystal Palace Egyptian Collections: To Which Is Added an Introduction to the Study of the Egyptian Hieroglyphs by S. Birch*. London: Bradbury and Evans.

Wilson, D. M., ed. 2001. *The Collections of the British Museum*. London: British Museum Press.

———. 2002. *The British Museum: A History*. London: British Museum Press.

Wilton, A., and I. Bignamini, eds. 1996. *Grand Tour: The Lure of Italy in the Eighteenth Century*. London: Tate Gallery.

Wilton-Ely, J. 1993. *Piranesi as Architect and Designer*. New York: Pierpont Morgan Library.

Winckelmann, J. J. 1881 [1764]. *The History of Ancient Art*. Translated from the German by G. H. Lodge, 1881. 2 vols. London: Sampson Low, Marston, Searle, and Kivington.

Wittkower, R. 1975. "Piranesi and Eighteenth-century Egyptomania." In R. Wittkower, *Studies in the Italian Baroque*, 259–273. London: Thames and Hudson.

Wittlin, A. S. 1970. *Museums: In Search of a Usable Future*. Cambridge, MA: MIT Press.

Wolff, A. 2003. *How Many Miles to Babylon? European Travels and Adventures in Egypt, 1300–1640*. Liverpool: Liverpool University Press.

Wonders, K. 1993. *Habitat Dioramas: Illusions of Wilderness in Museums of Natural History*. Uppsala: Acta Universitatis Upsaliensis.

Woodward, J. 1786. "Of the Wisdom of the Antient Egyptians; a Discourse Concerning Their Arts, Their Science, and Their Learning: Their Laws, Their Government, and Their Religion. With Occasional Reflections upon the State of Learning among the Jews; and Some Other Nations." *Archaeologia* 4: 212–310.

Worm, O. 1655. *Museum Wormianum seu historia rerum rariorum.* Leiden: Lugduni Batavorum. Iohannem Elsevirium.

Wortham, J. D. 1971. *British Egyptology.* Newton Abbot: David and Charles.

Wyke, M. 1997. *Projecting the Past: Ancient Rome, Cinema, and History.* New York: Routledge.

Yorke, C., and W. Leake. 1826. *Remarks on Some Egyptian Monuments in England.* [London: A. J. Valpy].

Ziegler, C., with the collaboration of C. Barbotin and M.-H. Rutschowscaya. 1990. *The Louvre: Egyptian Antiquities.* Paris: Scala.

———. 1994. "From One Egyptomania to Another: The Legacy of Roman Antiquity." In J. M. Humbert, M. Pantazzi, and C. Ziegler, eds., *Egyptomania: Egypt in Western Art, 1730–1930,* 15–20. Catalogue of exhibition held in Paris, Ottawa, and Vienna. Paris and Ottawa: Musée du Louvre and National Gallery of Canada.

Zimmerman, A. 2001. *Anthropology and Anti-humanism in Imperial Germany.* Chicago: University of Chicago Press.

Zoëga, G. 1797. *De origine et usu obeliscorum Rome.* Rome: Typis Lazzarinii Typographi Cameralis.

Figure Credits

Photos by permission of The Bodleian Library, University of Oxford: 1.1 (frontispiece from Lister E.1), figures 1.2 (frontispiece from Ashm.1695), 1.3 (title page from Lister D.52a), 1.4 (frontispiece from B.5.9.Art), 1.6 (frontispiece from C.1.12.Art Seld), 1.7 (frontispiece from Fol. Delta 742), 2.3–2.5 (Tab. XIII, XIV, and XXIX from G.A. Lond. b.27).

Photos by permission of The British Library, London: figures 1.5 (957.d.35), 2.2 (146.i.2), 2.6 (3.Tab.24, pl. 31, 32), 5.22 (C.55.i.1), 6.7 (Tab.442.a.5).

Photos © copyright The Trustees of the British Museum: figures 2.1, 2.7–2.10, 3.1–5.5, 5.7–5.21, 5.23–5.24, 6.1–6.5, 6.9–6.10, 6.12–6.19; plates 1–3, 5–13.

Photos courtesy of Hartley Library, Southampton University: figures 6.8, plate 4.

Figures by Alex Jones: 2.11, 3.9.

Photo courtesy of Sackler Library, Oxford: figure 6.11.

Photos by Andy Vowles: figures 5.6, 5.25, 6.6, 6.8, 6.17.

Index